Colonel W. N. Nicholson, C.M.G., D.S.O., Colonel, The Suffolk Regiment, 1939-47 (Author).

THE SUFFOLK REGIMENT

1928 to 1946

BY

COLONEL W. N. NICHOLSON, C.M.G., D.S.O.

COLONEL THE SUFFOLK REGIMENT

1939-1947

PUBLISHED BY THE EAST ANGLIAN MAGAZINE LTD., IPSWICH.

DEDICATION

Dedicated to the Memory of the
Officers, Warrant, Non-commissioned
Officers and Men,
The Suffolk Regiment,
Who in the War 1939-1945 gave their
lives for their Country.

All profits from the Sales of this History are being given to the Suffolk Regiment Old Comrades Association, an Association that was formed in 1907 for the welfare of discharged soldiers who had served in the Regiment.

PREFACE.

The British Army that was everywhere victorious in the later stages of the World War, 1939-1945, was probably the finest army in our history. Efficiency and tenacity were its outstanding qualities as great in degree as the fortitude of the front line men in the Great War, 1914-1918. No arm won greater renown than the British Infantry, among whom Battalions of the Suffolk Regiment took a worthy place.

Victory depends on the courage and efficiency of the man in the ranks, on the leadership of the Section and the Platoon, on the skill with which all portions of the modern Battalion are set in motion and co-operate, and above all on the quality of the Battalion Commander.

A Regimental history tells of many Battalions and space does not permit of more than a very brief account of the actions of a Battalion, a Company or a Platoon; while the telling depends largely on eye-witnesses from those units. No Regimental History can include but a fraction of those countless miniature battles which make up the microscopic but sparkling facets in the grand mosaic of our nation at war.

Throughout the long history of our Regiment there has been constant change; in organisation, in training, in personnel. But loyalty to the Regiment has remained constant. Now at the end of this World War a re-grouping of infantry has been made. The Royal Norfolk, Suffolk, Bedfordshire and Hertfordshire, Essex and Northamptonshire Regiments have been collected into an East Anglian Group. This will enlarge our loyalties, but will in no way lessen our devotion to all that stands for The Suffolk Regiment.

The writing of this History has been made easy by the willing help of many contributors. I should specially like to mention: K. C. Menneer, R. De Quincey, A. H. Dodson, S. Hemingway, and the Editor, the *11th Suffolk Home Guard*, who permitted extracts from the Battalion Souvenir.

My thanks are also due to Captain J. G. A. Beckett and Major K. S. Few for their account in Chapter 7 of the Cambridgeshire Regiment. This is necessarily brief; but a full History of this most gallant Regiment is being compiled.

Brigadier E. H. W. Backhouse, Colonel, the Suffolk Regiment assisted me with most valuable criticisms and suggestions. Major Vernon Pereira, the Editor *The Suffolk Regiment Gazette*, has been responsible for the illustrations and has given me the greatest help at all times. I am most grateful to them and to Lieut.-Colonel R. E. Goodwin who served with them on the History Committee. Also to Sgt. Mercer who produced the maps from my rough sketches.

W.N.N.

NORNEY ROUGH,
EASHING.

CONTENTS

CHAPTER I.

SUFFOLK.

CHAPTER II.

FIRST BATTALION. SEPT., 1939—JAN., 1945.

CHAPTER III.

FIRST BATTALION. JUNE, 1943—JULY, 1944.

CHAPTER IV.

FIRST BATTALION.

CHAPTER V.

SECOND BATTALION.

CHAPTER VI.

4TH AND 5TH BATTALIONS.

CHAPTER VII.

THE CAMBRIDGESHIRE REGIMENT.

CHAPTER VIII.

THE SEVENTH BATTALION AND 142ND REGIMENT, R.A.C.

CHAPTER IX.

SECOND LINE BATTALIONS.

CHAPTER X.

THE HOME GUARD, THE ARMY CADETS, THE A.T.S.

APPENDICES.

SKETCH MAPS.

ILLUSTRATIONS.

THE HISTORY OF THE SUFFOLK REGIMENT

CHAPTER I.

SUFFOLK

Bury St. Edmunds—The Freedom of the Borough—Ipswich—Cambridge and the Isle of Ely—The Suffolk Regiment—Regimental Re-unions—Changes in Training—The Years 1929-1939—2nd Battalion receives New Colours—The 250th Anniversary—September 3rd, 1939, The Depot—Training at the Depot—The Soldier.

THAT broad, undistinguished, mile long Risbygate Road that links Gibraltar Barracks with the centre of Bury St. Edmunds is an abiding memory to the thousands of Suffolk recruits who have tramped its length, temporarily free from the restrictions of barrack life, out to sample the amenities of the town.

From the other lovelier side many a young officer of the Regiment pays his first visit to this county town; he has come from Colchester, where so often a Suffolk Battalion is garrisoned. The young officer's first fleeting visit to the ancient borough is likely to be as firmly fixed in his memory as the effect of the oft repeated walk is on the rank and file.

Suitably enough the two routes meet on Angel Hill, the heart and centre of the borough. On this broad expanse where Abbeygate Street emerges and where the great gateway of the Abbey dominates its surroundings there have been memorable occasions when a Regular Battalion of the Suffolk Regiment has paraded in the presence of the Mayor and Burgesses.

I know of no approach to an ancient town that is so full of its history as the road which threads its way past the little houses of Sparhawk, takes a sharp turn at the old precincts of the Abbey, falls silent under the shadow of St. Mary's Church, and then finally sweeps past the West doors of the two great Churches to end on Angel Hill.

No one building throughout this route takes precedence over another; the smallest cottage is as complete and satisfying in its place as the walls and ruins of the ancient Abbey; each helps to build the goodly picture of the past.

For us, in the Suffolk Regiment, St. Mary's Church is of prime interest; the memorials of the Regiment are here. The Rood Screen is to the fallen in the South African War. There is a magnificent Alabaster Cenotaph under the Colours of the Service Battalions "To the glorious memory of 360 Officers and 6,513 Warrant Officers, N.C.O.s and Men" who fell in the Great War. Seventeen Battalions and the Depot of the Suffolk Regiment are included in the illuminated Roll of Honour placed in front of the Cenotaph. The Regimental Chapel is in the North East corner ; this was decorated and furnished in 1935 to commemorate the 250th Anniversary of the Regiment.

They say the ceiling of the nave of this great church is the finest example of open timber work in existence. It is called the Angel Roof. A few pennies will flood light the projecting life size Angels, twenty-two of which range along its complete length. Angel faces Angel, no two pairs alike.

But there are seldom any sightseers to spend their pennies viewing the roof of St. Mary's, or walking the old streets outside. Bury St. Edmunds is not in a tourist country. It is well for us that Suffolk is still a land of country towns and villages where men are born and live and die; where old traditions and customs have changed but little ; a land that has so much of the past to bring to its county Regiment, and in the bringing has ensured that the Suffolk Regiment to-day is Suffolk.

But while for the Regiment the heart and centre of Suffolk is Bury St. Edmunds, its Depot town, it draws its strength not from Suffolk alone, but from all the land inhabited by the "South-Folk"—Suffolk, Cambridge and the Isle of Ely.

The 12th Foot, before it became the Suffolk Regiment, had but little connection with East Anglia. After it had been raised by the Duke of Norfolk in Ipswich it spent most of its service abroad ; not until the Siege of Gibraltar was there any official connection with the county, and the relation was not established until the depot was built in Bury St. Edmunds in the last quarter of the 19th century. The 12th Foot was a Regiment with a great tradition—proudly bearing the Battle Honours of Minden, Dettingen, Gibraltar, and fully conscious of the immortal glory of the Birkenhead: but it had no particular territorial interest.

All know how great a Regimental tradition can be. It is a quality peculiar to our army, and has made British Infantry practically unbeatable. This tradition was reformed and strengthened when Infantry Regiments of the Line were given a territorial home, and their depots established in their county towns. By the time of the South African War the 12th Foot had become "Suffolk" not only in name but in fact; from then on to the present day the character of the Regiment has been greatly influenced by the East Anglian character of the men from Suffolk, Cambridgeshire and the Isle of Ely.

Few, if any, of the Regiments of the Line have been so intimately connected with their recruiting area as the Suffolk Regiment. At the time of the South African War, and for many years after, approximately ninety per cent. were county men. "Jack Frost," poor pay, lack of employment may have accounted for a proportion in the early days ; but with the stabilisation of recruiting a strong family spirit grew, young men joining because their fathers, their uncles and their cousins had been in the Regiment.

Tradition, custom, habit all change very slowly. Battle Honours were the hall marks of the courage, fortitude and spirit of the old Regiment. Loyalty, unselfishness and a cheerful disregard of real hardship were the qualities common to all good soldiers. On to this temper was grafted the individual characteristics of the men of East Anglia—and the graft had taken.

Photo—H. I. Jarman.

The Suffolk Regiment Chapel.

From this time onward the Regiment had a two-fold history; one that began with the formation of the Duke of Norfolk's Regiment in 1685, the other that went right back to the invasion of Britain in the Fifth Century.

This East Anglian birthright might have passed unnoticed had it not been for the two great wars of 1914 and 1939. In the Great War of 1914 all the military elements of the nation were engulfed:—Regular, Territorial and New Army ; there were twenty-three Battalions bearing the name and wearing the badges of the Suffolk Regiment. In the world war of 1939, the depot at Bury St. Edmunds was the core and centre of the expansion of the Regiment into front line Battalions, Training and Holding Battalions, Young and Old Soldier Battalions, Category Battalions, and in one case a Tank Unit.

But whereas in the South African War the First Battalion was made up of county men, in the "Great War" of 1914 not more than half the strength of the twenty-three Battalions came from the Regiment's recruiting areas; while in the "World War" of 1939, the proportion of East Anglians sometimes dropped to not more than ten per cent.

Yet in this last "World War" the spirit of the Suffolk Battalions of the Suffolk Regiment was never more truly "Suffolk."

The 75 years since the Depot had been established in Bury St. Edmunds had seen the complete incorporation of East Anglian thought and character. In 1939 a good number of the officers were county men, a large proportion of the Warrant Officers and N.C.O.s came from its towns and villages; it was the Officers, Warrant Officers and N.C.O.s that ensured the continuation of the "Suffolk" tradition. An account of the Suffolk Regiment in the War, 1939-1945 would not be complete if it did not begin with East Anglia.

There is no area of England that has a more distinctive history than East Anglia, or has retained its individuality so fully down to present days. In the early days of the Anglo-Saxon and Danish invasions this conservatism was due to the Eastern Counties being cut off from the rest of the country by the Wash, the fens and by long stretches of forest. This great area fell into the two big divisions under the North Folk and the South Folk. Although originally one people the North Folk and the South Folk developed distinctions in manner and speech. It is said that once in Egypt when a Norfolk Battalion was passing its sister Suffolk Unit, the former imitated the "Suffolk Whine" as a friendly gibe.

The "North Folk" and the "South Folk" were men of sturdy independence. They were essentially a free people; kinsmen fighting side by side in battle in defence of their honour and their rights. They made their own laws, and woe betide the "foreigners" who offended their sense of justice. An eye for an eye was the payment.

The Danish invasions forced the North Folk and the South Folk, farming peacefully, to seek protection from Thegns ; from being freeholders of land, knowing no superiors, they gradually sank to tenants bound to do service to their lords in return for protection ; although they never became feudal as elsewhere in England.

During the Ninth Century East Anglia became the Kingdom of Guthram the Dane, the great opponent of Alfred the Great ; but by the time of the

"Conquest" by the Normans, the Danes had been absorbed by the North Folk and the South Folk of East Anglia. All were English when William the Conqueror fought Hereward the Wake and the men of the Fens in what was then the almost impregnable Isle of Ely.

From the Norman Conquest to comparatively recent years, East Anglia was the most thickly populated part of England. Gradually the fens were drained, forests cleared and communications with the rest of England were improved. It was an agricultural land; but under the Tudor Kings and Queens a flourishing wool trade grew up with the Low Countries across the "Flemish Sea." This trade in raw wool and worsted goods was a domestic industry affecting not only the towns but the life of every village.

We can see proofs of the wealth of the past in the great churches and the fine houses in every town and village; but what is sometimes forgotten is that the English history of those days was stamped with the character of the men of these counties. East Anglia had big interests over seas; public opinion throughout its length and breadth, in town and village, was keenly interested and freely expressed on all national and international questions.

This strong public opinion, with its Puritanical tendency, came to a head when the Stuarts succeeded the Tudors. Emigration to America was one of the outcomes, an emigration that was fostered by the Stuart Kings who were by no means sorry to see the departure of such stubborn opponents of their policy.

Boston, in Lincolnshire, is historically connected with the Pilgrim Fathers, who sailed in the "Mayflower" in 1620; but the bulk of the men and women who followed these pioneers came from East Anglia. As was written about them at the time, "They desired only the best. Men driven forth from their fatherland not by earthly want, not by greed for gold, not by lust for adventure; but by the fear of God and zeal for a Godly worship."

This exodus was due to the early religious persecution in Charles the First's reign. Later, when Civil War broke out, no part of England was more solidly on the side of the Parliament than the Eastern Counties. The "Association of the Eastern Counties" at Cambridge, which had been formed in the zenith of the wool trade, was a chief centre of opposition to the rule of Charles the First. From this Association came Oliver Cromwell's Ironsides and later the New Model Army—the Model for the Regiments of the Restoration, and so the model for our own.

The Suffolk Regiment has every right to-day to claim as part of its ancient history the battles of Cromwell's men. Those same great fighting qualities have always been latent in East Anglia.

But the 12th Foot, prior to its becoming the Suffolk Regiment, was nobody's particular concern. Minden and Gibraltar brought the Regiment great renown throughout all England. When those and other campaigns were won the men were discharged, penniless; many became either beggars or highwaymen; while their fellow countrymen dubbed their comrades who were still serving "brutal and licentious." This divorce from the country they served only ended when the Regiment's depot was established at Risbygate in Bury St. Edmunds.

Then, during the years that followed, there grew between the Regiment and the county not only a friendship, but a sense of kinship. The county realised that the Regiment belonged to their land.

Photo—"East Anglian Daily Times."

PRESENTATION OF THE FREEDOM OF THE BOROUGH OF BURY ST. EDMUNDS TO THE SUFFOLK REGIMENT, MINDEN DAY 1944.

COLONEL W. N. NICHOLSON, C.M.G., D.S.O., COLONEL THE SUFFOLK REGIMENT, ADDRESSING THE LARGE GATHERING AFTER RECEIVING THE SCROLL.

Left to right—THE MARQUESS OF BRISTOL, THE EARL OF STRADBROKE (LORD LIEUTENANT OF SUFFOLK), HIS WORSHIP THE MAYOR (ALDERMAN E. L. D. LAKE), COLONEL W. N. NICHOLSON, LT.-COLONEL H. R. GADD, THE RECORDER (MR. GERALD HOWARD), MR. THOMAS WILSON (TOWN CLERK).

THE FREEDOM OF THE BOROUGH.

A seal was set on this intimate relation when the Mayor and Corporation offered the Honorary Freedom of the Borough of Bury St. Edmunds to the Suffolk Regiment in the following correspondence:—

Borough Offices,
Bury St. Edmunds.
16th June, 1944.

Dear Sir,

I am instructed by the Corporation of this Borough to write to you, as Colonel of the Suffolk Regiment, and say that they would like to confer upon the County Regiment the Honorary Freedom of this Borough, as a mark of their appreciation of the services of the Regiment, its close association with this Borough, and the kindly co-operation of all ranks with the inhabitants of the Borough over a long period of time.

May I suggest that it would be suitable for this ceremony to be performed on Minden Day, the 1st August next ?

I should be glad if I might hear from you whether the Regiment would accept the Honorary Freedom of this Borough, and if so, whether you agree that the 1st August would be a suitable day for the ceremony.

Yours faithfully,
THOMAS WILSON,
Town Clerk.

Colonel W. N. Nicholson, C.M.G., D.S.O.

Norney Rough,
Eashing.
27th June, 1944.

Dear Sir,

Will you please express to the Corporation of the Borough of Bury St. Edmunds the very great appreciation felt by the Suffolk Regiment at their proposal to present to the Regiment the Honorary Freedom of the Borough ; a high Honour which they will very gladly accept.

Minden Day, August 1st, will be a most appropriate date.

Yours faithfully,
W. N. NICHOLSON,
Colonel, The Suffolk Regiment.

To the Town Clerk,
Bury St. Edmunds.

Before the actual ceremony His Worship the Mayor, Alderman E. L. D. Lake, held a reception in the Mayor's Parlour for the Officers of the Regiment. Some sixty past and present Officers with their wives attended, most of whom had not met for the last five years owing to the difficulties of travelling during war time. At the close of this reception the guests proceeded to the Abbey Grounds.

Here, at the Mustow Street end of the Gardens, the Council Table had been set. Behind, on the mound, was seated a large and distinguished gathering of town and county folk. Beyond was ranked a parade representing all units of the Suffolk Regiment, with Minden Roses in their caps. Great numbers of the general public with representatives of all war organisations encircled the scene, enhanced by the lovely trees and the grey ruins which have witnessed so much during the centuries.

The Mayor's procession came from the new municipal buildings across Angel Square and entered at the Great Gate. The Mayor, wearing his robes and chain of office, was preceded by the Mace and Sword Bearers, and was accompanied by the Marquess of Bristol, High Steward of the Borough, and by Lord Stradbroke, the Lord Lieutenant of the County. The procession included members of the Council, Mr. Gerald Howard the Recorder, the Town Clerk, the Clerk of the Peace and other officials. On arrival, the Civic Party was greeted with Purcell's "Trumpet Voluntary."

A Guard of Honour and a party of other ranks representing all Battalions of the Regiment, headed by the First Battalion Band, marched through the Great Gate and formed up opposite the Council. Colonel W. N. Nicholson, Colonel, The Suffolk Regiment, inspected the Guard of Honour and took his seat at the Council Table.

After a prayer by the Provost, the Very Rev. J. L. White, the Mayor's Chaplain, the resolution of the Council was read by the Town Clerk as follows:—

> "That this Council having regard to the eminent and valuable services rendered to the Borough by the Suffolk Regiment (12th Foot) and as a mark of appreciation of the many gallant acts and noble exploits performed by it from the date of its formation in the year 1685 up to the present time, of the close and friendly relations which have at all times existed between all Battalions of the Regiment and the inhabitants of the Borough and also of the ready help given to them by all members of the Regiment in general and in particular by those members who have from time to time been stationed at the Regimental Depot, Gibraltar Barracks, the home of the Regiment, do hereby, in pursuance of Section 259 of the Local Government Act, 1933, and in recognition of the aforesaid services, confer upon the Suffolk Regiment the Honorary Freedom of the Borough of Bury St. Edmunds and do hereby admit the Regiment to be an Honorary Freeman of the said Borough accordingly."

The Mayor, proposing the resolution, said this was a great day in the history of the Borough, and he hoped also for the officers and men of the Regiment, in which he had served as a humble Territorial member. His Worship reviewed the history of the Regiment, which, he said, would always carry with it memories of great deeds loyally and dutifully performed. He spoke of the heroic deeds at Dettingen, Minden, Gibraltar, Seringapatam, leading on through the Great War to the present conflict, with its tragedy of Singapore; records which would enhance the reputation of the Regiment when its history came to be told.

> "It is not only because of its gallant record that we wish to honour them to-day; but because of the close and cordial relations which have always existed between the Regiment and its Depot town of Bury St. Edmunds."

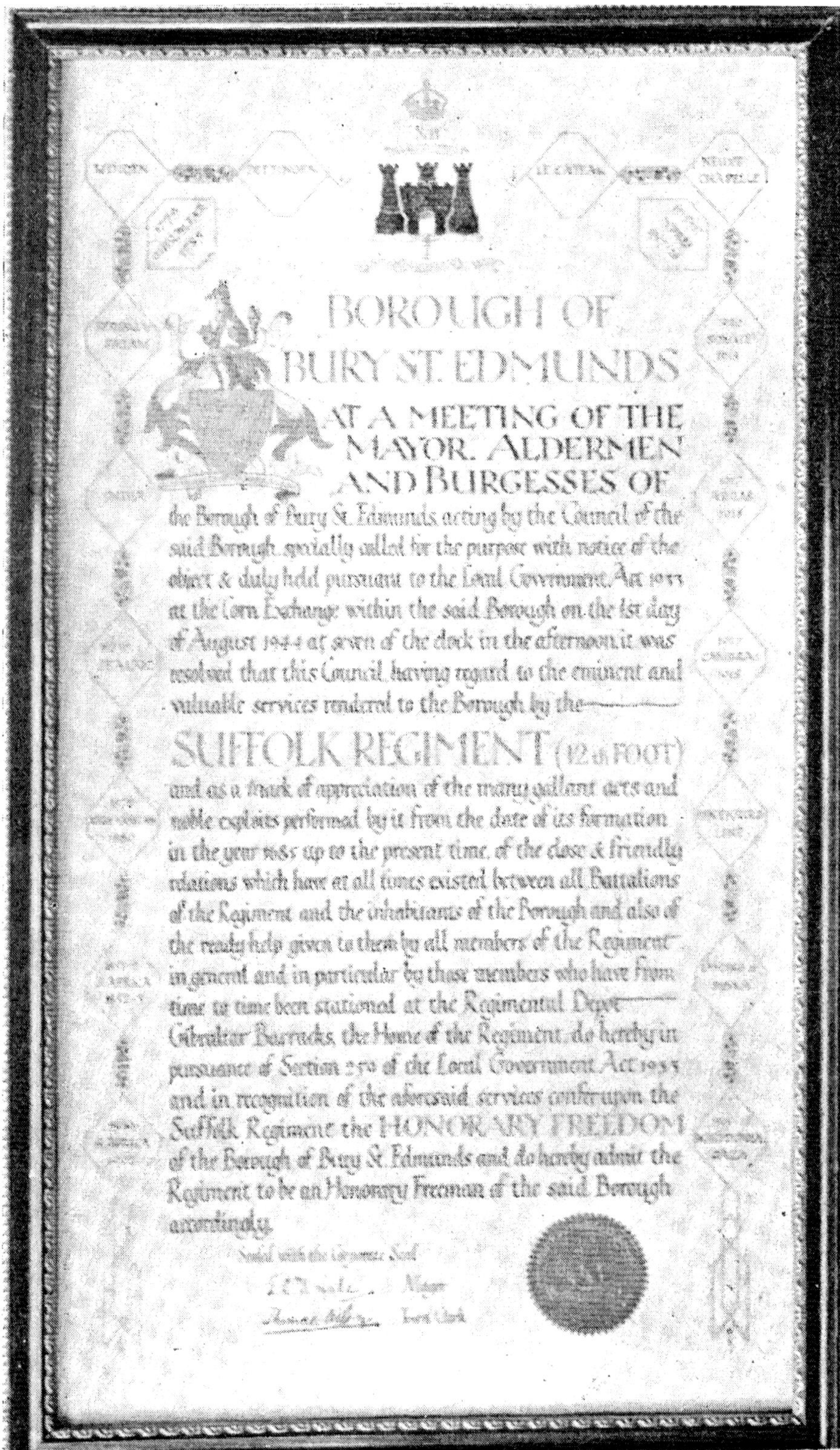
BOROUGH OF
BURY ST. EDMUNDS
AT A MEETING OF THE
MAYOR, ALDERMEN
AND BURGESSES OF
the Borough of Bury St. Edmunds acting by the Council of the said Borough specially called for the purpose with notice of the object & duly held pursuant to the Local Government Act 1933 at the Corn Exchange within the said Borough on the 1st day of August 1944 at seven of the clock in the afternoon it was resolved that this Council having regard to the eminent and valuable services rendered to the Borough by the
SUFFOLK REGIMENT (12th FOOT)
and as a mark of appreciation of the many gallant acts and noble exploits performed by it from the date of its formation in the year 1685 up to the present time, of the close & friendly relations which have at all times existed between all Battalions of the Regiment and the inhabitants of the Borough and also of the ready help given to them by all members of the Regiment in general and in particular by those members who have from time to time been stationed at the Regimental Depot Gibraltar Barracks, the Home of the Regiment, do hereby in pursuance of Section 259 of the Local Government Act 1933 and in recognition of the aforesaid services confer upon the Suffolk Regiment the HONORARY FREEDOM of the Borough of Bury St. Edmunds and do hereby admit the Regiment to be an Honorary Freeman of the said Borough accordingly.
Sealed with the Corporate Seal
Mayor
Town Clerk

Photo—H. I. Jarman.

THE SCROLL DEPICTING THE RESOLUTION OF THE MAYOR, ALDERMEN AND BURGESSES OF THE BOROUGH OF BURY ST. EDMUNDS, CONFERRING THE HONORARY FREEDOM OF THE BOROUGH ON THE SUFFOLK REGIMENT.

He paid tribute to the soldierly bearing and the splendid behaviour of the men stationed there during the five years of war and to the help given not only to pre-service units but to the borough as a whole, and concluded:—

> "As I said when I addressed the Regiment in 1927, so long as Suffolk is Suffolk there will always be Suffolk men and Suffolk women, yes, and Suffolk boys and girls too, who will be ready, willing, anxious and proud to serve their King, Country and Empire. Furthermore, I hope that the ceremony of to-day will give some satisfaction to the officers and men fighting in so many different parts of the world."

The resolution was unanimously carried, and Colonel Nicholson signed the roll of freemen.

The Recorder, Mr. Gerald Howard, presented the illuminated scroll to the Colonel, the Suffolk Regiment. Mr. Howard said:—

> "There is no town that bears upon its face a clearer imprint of the history of England than Bury St. Edmunds. There is no Regiment more remembered for the highest traditions of our British Infantry than the Suffolk Regiment. It is fitting that one should honour the other."

He referred to Magna Carta and the fact that the very word "Freedom" seemed to have a special significance on this historic spot. Paying another tribute to the Regiment, he recalled that there had been no more gallant fighters than the men from the English countryside who filled the ranks of our county Regiments of the line, among whom none took precedence over the men of Suffolk.

> "Suffolk men, your ancestors, your fathers, brothers and sweethearts—they have fought; they are fighting in Europe, Asia and on the Pacific to-day. They have seen, and are seeing, many strange and wondrous things; but the picture all of them carry in their hearts is the picture of a little bit of Suffolk that they know best as their home."

The Colonel, The Suffolk Regiment, in accepting the scroll on behalf of the officers and all ranks of the Suffolk Regiment, spoke of the high honour accorded to the Regiment and the fitting occasion chosen for its presentation, when two great Wars and an intervening truce had engendered a sense of realities, a knowledge that the soldier and the civilian were indivisible.

> "The soldier of Minden and Gibraltar was, as he is to-day, a man of infinite courage, a staunch companion, a carefree individual; he has remained fundamentally the same throughout the two and a half centuries of the life of the Suffolk Regiment—his qualities far outweighing his faults. What he was, that he still is to-day; maybe a thought too carefree in a world that has become too full of care.
>
> "You, to-day, Mr. Mayor, instead of spurning the soldier as in the past, have conferred upon the Suffolk Regiment the Honorary Freedom of the Borough of Bury St. Edmunds. You have, at the same time, issued a challenge to us. Happy to be outside politics; untrammelled by higher finance; our own lawyers, and rather proud of the fact; you have reminded us that there are also civic responsibilities—great in peace, invaluable in war. The thousand years' history of this ancient borough, the qualities and deeds of its citizens;

the unselfish service of its Mayors and Councillors, and your own great personal example all help to remind us that we too have our share with you, in peace as well as in war."

The session of the Council having closed, Lord Stradbroke, the Lord Lieutenant, offered to the Regiment the hearty congratulations of all the people of Suffolk on an honour rightly given by a borough which at all times was only too anxious to do everything for all connected with the regulars and the auxiliaries. The reputation of the Regiment stood very high everywhere, said Lord Stradbroke; and added that on such an occasion they could not help thinking of the misfortunes that happened to the 4th and 5th Battalions at an early stage in the war.

The guests who were present on this historic occasion included:—

The Mayoress, Lady Bristol, Lady Stradbroke, the Bishop of St. Edmundsbury and Ipswich and Mrs. Brook, Lord and Lady Erskine, Sir George and Lady Branson, Major E. M. Keatinge, M.P., and Mrs. Keatinge, Mr. and Mrs. H. C. Drayton, Major Durham Matthews (High Sheriff), Captain H. R. King (Chairman, West Suffolk County Council), the Bishop of Dunwich and Mrs. Maxwell-Gumbleton, Air Marshal Sir Patrick and Lady Playfair, Colonel Blest, Col. Grant, Col. Castle and Col. Douglas (U.S. Forces), the Deputy Mayoress, Mrs. Gerald Howard, His Honour Judge Alfred Hildesley, K.C., and Mrs. Hildesley, and Sergt. Saunders, V.C., and Mrs. Saunders.

The Suffolk Regiment were represented by:—

Major B. W. J. Amphlett, Brigadier D. V. M. Balders, O.B.E., M.C., Lieut.-Colonel I. R. B. Bond, M.C., Lieut.-Colonel W. M. Campbell, D.S.O., M.C., Colonel A. M. Cutbill, M.C., Major and Mrs. B. G. F. Drew, Lieut.-Colonel H. R. Gadd, D.S.O., M.C., Captain and Mrs. F. W. Garrard, Lieut.-Colonel and Mrs. R. E. Goodwin, Major and Mrs. G. T. E. Grey, Major-General R. Gurney, C.B., Major-General, Mrs. and Miss Harter, Colonel H. R. Hooper, O.B.E., M.C., T.D., the Rev., Mrs. and Miss Lummis, Major and Mrs. R. Q. March, Colonel W. N. Nicholson, C.M.G., D.S.O., Major N. B. Oakes, Lieut.-Colonel and Mrs. C. D. Parry Crooke, Major and Mrs. F. V. C. Pereira, Lieut.-Colonel E. C. Rands, T.D., Lieut.-Colonel F. T. D. Wilson, O.B.E., Lieut.-Colonel H. D. Wise, M.C., Lieut.-Colonel, Mrs. and Miss Yates, Major G. S. Cubitt, Colonel F. L. Tempest, O.B.E., M.C., Captain J. Hearn, Major D. W. McCaffrey, Major M. G. Eliot, Captain W. N. Breach, Mrs. Backhouse, Mrs. Monier Williams, Mrs. Rice and Mrs. D. G. Lawrence.

IPSWICH.

Bury St. Edmunds, as the Depot home of the Regiment, stands foremost in the affections of the majority; but tribute must also be paid to Ipswich and Cambridge—those two great towns that furnish so many Suffolk recruits. Ipswich is a larger and more prosperous Borough than Bury St Edmunds, its industries far outstripping the agricultural interests of the latter; but there is a notable resemblance in their history. The East Anglian characteristics are as marked in one as in the other.

Their histories have kept step. The Danes who killed the Saxon King Edmund, landed in the Orwell. The first Charter granted to Ipswich came from King John, in the early days of his reign ; while later, under the same King, the Barons assembled in the abbey at Bury St. Edmunds and travelled thence to Runnymede with their Magna Carta. The great woollen trade with the Low Countries affected both boroughs ; though its loss was a greater blow to Ipswich.

Outwardly different in appearance, on closer view they are alike. The throngs in the streets of Ipswich, the modern industrial buildings, the huge advertisements, conceal but do not obliterate the records of its history. Every one of its narrow streets in the centre of the town has houses of a bygone time, some most beautiful, proving the wealth and importance of its burgesses. By no means the oldest is the "Ancient House" of the Sparrowes, the fame of which has spread far beyond the bounds of the Borough. Ipswich has not the great Abbey churches of Bury St. Edmunds ; but the Church of St. Mary-le-Tower, where the Colours of the 4th Battalion were nobly displayed throughout the war, can vie with the latter.

There may be rivalry between East Suffolk and West Suffolk, a larger and more glorified edition of the spirit that is so common in England where every man and every village skirmishes with his neighbour. It is a rivalry that in no way extends to the Regiment, which is equally sure of the great history of the East as of the West. There can be a justifiable pride in the difference between the two sides of the county, that in the West having a character and loveliness peculiar in itself, while in the East there stretches a coast line that has seen much history and produced many fine sailors. What is there more beautiful in England than the magnificent estuaries, the finest of all being along the Orwell to Ipswich.

The difference between the two sides of the county may perhaps be likened to the difference between the busy tidal Orwell and the comparatively sluggish Gipping, which meet in Ipswich, the latter giving its name to the capital. Suffolk men may seem to some more like the Gipping—slow of thought, chary of speech, immovable in their views ; difficult to convert when once their minds are made up. These are great Suffolk qualities. While on the other hand the tidal Orwell gives an equally good picture of Suffolk character in its ebb and flow. What great town in England was harder hit by the loss of its staple industry than Ipswich when the wool trade failed ? How many a town in England in like case has shrunk to nothing ? The grit and industry that have wrested a living from the cultivation of poor agricultural land, furnishing a lesson to the rest of England, is equally manifest in the place Ipswich takes to-day, notwithstanding this disaster in the days of the Stuarts.

It has been said by a Suffolk man of the East Anglian:—

"If it wasn't for hope, the heart 'ud die."

The history of Suffolk is written in the every day life of its villages and country towns ; in its small farms, in its individual men and women. It is a history of freedom, of independence of thought and action. It is manifest in every country place; and it is true equally of this town.

If Bury St. Edmunds can claim the Regiment as peculiarly its own in recent years, Ipswich can claim the past. We may not be able to include the battle of Crecy as one of our battle honours ; but we can recall that Edward III. assembled his great fleet at the mouth of the Orwell, before defeating the French Fleet at Sluys and so preparing the way for the campaign that ended in Crecy. It was at Ipswich in 1757 that the Regimental H.Q. and five companies of the 12th Foot were garrisoned. Here with the rest of the Battalion they were inspected. The report reading: "a very good Regiment, well disciplined, well appointed, and fit for service." In 1759 they left Ipswich for the campaign that ended at Minden, and they must have had many a man from Ipswich in their ranks.

CAMBRIDGE AND THE ISLE OF ELY.

Equidistant from Bury St. Edmunds lies Cambridge ; Cambridge needs no description. There are some Regiments in the British Army that have double names. There are some men who feel that Cambridge and Cambridgeshire are apt to be forgotten in the one title "Suffolk." To a great degree this feeling must have been dissipated by the "Cambridgeshire Regiment"—a Territorial unit in peace time ; but emphatically a war unit during the 1914-1918 and 1939-1945 wars.

No Regiment had a finer record than that gained by the 1st Cambridgeshires in 1914-1918 ; their Regimental history of that campaign is an epic. Their two Battalions were engulfed at Singapore in 1942 ; a Regimental tragedy.

But at all times Cambridge men flow into the Suffolk Regiment, and to the men of the Suffolk Regiment, Cambridge and Cambridgeshire are integral parts of the Regiment.

The Isle of Ely has its own history, separate and distinct from the history of England. A history that rarely impinged on the world outside, save in that one great moment when Hereward the Wake made it his Island of Refuge and successfully defied the "Conqueror." That is a story as popular and as widely known as the feats of Richard Coeur de Lion, or the exploits of Robin Hood.

The geographical conformation of the Isle of Ely made this last stand possible, and it was the fenland character of the land that has influenced the fenmen through the centuries down to the present days. Their isolation provided the other incidents:—the quarrel with Cromwell over the draining of the fens ; the rising at Littleport. Their stubbornness in resisting the draining of the Fens can be compared with the same inflexible quality of the Dutch in their wars, save that the former lasted some centuries longer.

The Littleport rebellion is a token of the Fen men's love of liberty, and his determination to fight for it. The Isle of Ely is—or was—an archipelago of scattered islands in a sea of marshland ; the largest island being that on which Ely with its great Cathedral stands. North of this is an islet holding the village of Littleport. Here in the year 1816 none were harder hit by the injustice of the "Enclosure Act." Moreover the draining of the fens, after fruitless attempts since 1480, was at last in process of accomplishment thus bringing to an end the abundance of fish and wild fowl with which the peasantry had been able to eke out their wages of nine shillings a week.

The men of Littleport rose in arms—and small blame to them. They marched on Ely with their guns, pistols and scythes; but, this is what makes the affair so notable, they marched behind a wagon on which they had mounted four punt guns used for wild fowl shooting, with barrels eight feet long and each charged with no less than a pound of gun-powder. This "armoured vehicle" cleared the way of all opposition.

Having done themselves a thought too well in the matter of refreshment in Ely, they retired in good order to Littleport on the arrival of the military; still covered by their "A.F.V." Five were hanged by the Bishop for this escapade.

This abuse of power by the Bishop of Ely ended the long arbitrary reign which had begun under the Princes of the Iceni when this great tribe of Early Britons were driven out of East Anglia into the fens in the fifth and sixth centuries, and had continued under the Abbesses and Abbots of the Abbey Church and Abbey of Ely.

THE SUFFOLK REGIMENT.

It is half a century since the soldier was deemed a vagabond; but save during the First World War he has never yet received his proper place in the nation, such as the sailor rightly occupies. The soldier, officer or man, is never believed to take his profession seriously. There have been apologists who say that the pay does not offer sufficient inducements. But notwithstanding a chorus of disapprobation every critic agrees that British Infantry has been supremely good in war.

British infantry could not have proved themselves supremely good in all our wars, however great their courage, if their efficiency was at fault. The supremacy of British infantry has been due to a quality peculiarly their own—a Regimental Tradition—that has been built up during long years of peace and war, growing deeper and stronger with each succeeding generation.

It was sufficient in the time of Marlborough that the soldier could handle his arms, that the officer could manoeuvre his men; only a few needed to be soldiers of distinction. Wellington and Napoleon controlled the whole battlefield; a unit commander rarely, if ever, had to do more than he was told. With passing years close columns and squares became the "thin red line" and by the time of the South African war was an extended formation.

At every stage a higher degree of leadership and initiative was required, first of the officer, then of the officer and the non-commissioned officer, and in this last world war, of every infantry soldier. It has not been higher pay or coercion, but pride in their Regiment that has kept efficiency in pace with needs.

This Regimental worth can be traced in the history of the officers and men. Until a century ago a large proportion of the officers were wealthy men making the army a temporary profession; in later generations, no longer wealthy, they were the sons of their soldier fathers, already soldiers when given their first commission.

So it was with the other ranks; the Regiment had become their home. Its pre-eminence was their ambition. The Warrant and Non-Commissioned Officers with the passing years grew into leaders, instead of mere drill instructors. The private soldiers became specialists.

The glitter and the gold of a full dress parade catches the eye of the spectator; the discipline, spit and polish they see there are still the solid basis of victory ; but on this rock-like foundation have been continuously built the leadership and all the skilled technical training that is essential to the infantry soldier. This is the compound that makes up a Regimental Tradition, a Regiment's inheritance, the spirit of its history.

Cromwell's Ironsides were imbued with religious fervour in a war that affected their religion ; the early French revolutionary armies fought for liberty ; hate of the Germans must have been an overpowering incentive to the victorious Russian Armies. Such motives as these make the well trained army practically invincible. A great Regimental tradition is of the same nature and equally effective. The last two great wars so widely different in almost every particular had this one Regimental bond in common.

There were twenty-three Battalions of the Suffolk Regiment between the years 1914 and 1918, fifteen of whom were engaged in active operations. Some were Territorial, some were New Army Units, some were specially raised for specific duties. During the four years of war the Regular Battalions were always unmistakably the "Regular" Battalions, notwithstanding the distribution of regular officers and men to all Battalions. The Territorial and Service Battalions were "Suffolk" by birth, "Regimental" by adoption.

There were but five front line Battalions of the Suffolk Regiment and two of the Cambridgeshire during the World War of 1939-45 ; and four of them, the 4th and 5th Suffolk and the 1st and 2nd Cambridgeshire, were made prisoners by the Japanese in Singapore in 1942 before they had seen any service ; another, the 7th Battalion, became the 142nd Regiment, R.A.C., though until disbanded in Italy in 1945 it retained its Suffolk individuality. The Suffolk Regiment in addition to these, comprised Holding Battalions, Category Battalions, Young and Old Soldier Battalions ; officers and men being graded in accordance to their fitness.

Notwithstanding the great expansion in both World Wars, Regimental Tradition retained its full force. Its influence was paramount. The Battalions no matter from what source they drew their men remained in every respect "Suffolk."

Arthur Bryant, the Historian, has written of the deeds of the British Army in this second World War in unforgettable fashion:—

"The most neglected and least considered of all our pre-war Services was the Army. A popular cartoonist of genius had made the figure of Colonel Blimp, the professional Army officer, the prototype of all that was stupid, blindly conservative and useless. Yet it was the profession which Blimp was supposed to typify that in the hour of our direst need produced such men as Wavell, Dill, Brooke, Alexander, Montgomery, Paget, Gort, Slim, Auchinleck, Lindsell, Freyberg, the two Morgans, Dempsey, Maitland-Wilson, O'Connor, Cunningham, Stopford, Adam and Wingate ; all of them in their different ways leaders of outstanding greatness of intellect of character and at least three of them among the greatest military commanders of all time.

"And, as anyone who saw the Army at war knows, there were officers commanding brigades and battalions every whit as remarkable as those to whom seniority and the fortune of war had given the command of armies. The astonishing thing is that this wealth of talent sprang out of the soil of an Army which in time of peace was starved of almost everything it needed.

Most of our military leaders, after their formative experience as company and platoon commanders in the last war, had to practise their trade in exercises in which flags and paper markers did service as tanks and guns, and single privates as battalions.

"Perhaps the very obstacles against which they had to contend made them the greater men. One thing is certain: that, like their naval brethren, they drew their strength from the greatness of a tradition that, though forgotten by the country, had been zealously preserved and fostered in their little disciplined communities. The Regiment—that sacred and abiding thing—was the parent of all our victories, from the deathless defence of Calais in 1940 to the great battle on the Dutch-German border that broke the back of the Reichwehr in 1945."

In the above, Arthur Bryant refers to the quality of the officers and to the difficulties under which they trained during this interval between the two great wars.

The First World War greatly enlarged the horizon of the Regiment. For the first time in its history the full importance of the Territorial Battalions was appreciated, that they, with the Regular Battalions, formed one family. This had a marked influence on the quality of the leaders in the Second World War.

Although but little was done to modernise the army in this interval between the two wars, the Regimental officer had become a professional soldier, and was thinking for himself. The standard of efficiency of the officers in the Regiment had never been higher; the seniors had served, many with distinction, in the First World War.

There was a time, after the South African War, when an officer, the first after an interval of eight years to pass into Camberley, was asked: "Why do you want to go? What's wrong with the Regiment?" In the years between 1919 and 1939 there was seldom a Staff College Course that did not include at least one Suffolk officer; on one occasion no fewer than three officers were at Camberley together. Needless to say the quality of all the officers of the Regiment was automatically raised and the effect of this on the whole Regiment was far reaching.

When war came there was an immense demand on trained and qualified Regular Regimental Officers; during the five years that followed, a Battalion of the Suffolk Regiment rarely had more than two Regular Officers serving with it.

The great majority of the men who filled the vacant places, and a large proportion were from Suffolk, were "called up," served through the ranks, graduated in officers' training units and were granted Emergency Commissions. They proved themselves fine leaders, as will be seen in the chapters that follow; and this was due in no small degree to the standard set in peace by serving Regimental Officers.

REGIMENTAL RE-UNIONS.

War with all its tragedies has one great redeeming attribute—comradeship. Danger, hardship, captivity shared brings out all that is finest in man. Leaders are known, soldierly virtues are unmistakeable. How great this bond of comradeship is could be judged by the numberless "Re-unions" held throughout the county by the Service Battalion of the First World War and by those great Territorial units—the 4th Suffolk and the 1st Cambridgeshire Regiment. It was these "Re-unions," this torch that was passed down the years, that was of such inestimable value to the men who became the leaders in the Second World War. For the measure between officers and other ranks was changing; the Battalion and Company Commanders of the past were being merged with the Platoon and Section leaders, down to the private soldier and his individual initiative.

No account of the Regiment between the years 1919 and 1939 could be complete without reference to the 4th Suffolk and the 1st Cambridgeshire Regiment at Ipswich and Cambridge. No Territorial units in the country did more than these two to bridge the gap in those most difficult years and to maintain enthusiasm and efficiency when all around were decrying militarism.

The 4th Battalion had a succession of three enthusiastic commanding officers: Colonel E. P. Clarke, Colonel H. R. Hooper and Lieut.-Colonel E. C. Rands. Colonel Hooper for six years devoted his whole-hearted energy to the welfare of the Battalion perhaps at as critical a time as the Territorial Army has ever known. He set an example of enthusiasm, covering thousands of miles to speak on the good work being carried out by the Territorials.

The 1st Cambridgeshire Regiment has a Regimental tradition that has always inspired it to the finest deeds. A great history in the last war which it fully lived up to during the peace.

But while these Battalions justified every hope, the value of the "Re-unions" of Service units of the last war was of inestimable consequence. The 5th, 7th, 9th, 11th, 12th and Cyclist Battalions were meeting and discussing old times. Officers and men were not merely foregathering at their weekly rendezvous; they were coming from long distances at costs they could with difficulty afford to meet their old friends who had proved themselves men and leaders. Over all these Re-unions was the Spirit and the Tradition of the Suffolk Regiment, a common bond.

In May, 1931, three hundred and twenty old comrades of the 5th Battalion met for their fourth re-union dinner coming from all parts of the country including London and Colchester. Among the speakers, the Mayor of Bury St. Edmunds said: "I want to remind you that there is still a sense of obligation and service to the younger men coming along." Another speaker echoed this: "Every man in the room is a recruiting agent."

At the Fourth Re-union dinner of the 9th Battalion in 1932, Colonel De la Pryme, proposing the Suffolk Regiment, said that the previous day they assembled in cities, town and villages to salute fallen comrades. That night they met to renew old friendships, and to revive happy memories. One of the most cherished memories they had was that when the great adventure came they went out and were in the Suffolk Regiment. In those swamps in Belgium, North Flanders, and on the Somme, they fought side by side with the regular battalions, wore their uniform, shared their hardships and fought the same battles. Any success they might have had in those days was largely due to the immense admiration and pride they had for the Suffolk Regiment."

Photos—G. L. Lambert, F.R.P.S., A. Inst. B.P., Bury St. Edmunds.

REUNIONS. OLD COMRADES RETURNING FROM CHURCH PARADE AT ST. MARY'S CHURCH, BURY ST. EDMUNDS.

Over eight hundred officers and men of the Regiment past and present, assembled on Sunday, August 5th, 1932 to take part in a Church parade; a great many coming from such distances as Wisbech, Cambridge, Ely, Woodbridge, Southwold and Felixstowe, and representing all Battalions, past and present, of the Regiment. The oldest members and the disabled were taken by coach to St. Mary's Church which was filled to the utmost capacity.

A suggestion that war was inevitable was contained in the sermon preached by the Rev. G. C. Danvers, M.C., Vicar of Aldeburgh, and chaplain to the 2nd Battalion of the Suffolk Regiment in France during the Great War.

"There are some people," he said, "who to-day would decry war and say, 'Let us away with the Army, the Navy and all the rest of it.' You know, as long as there are men in this world there will be war, because nations which believe in God must stand up for what is right, and true, and just, and if you have no other means with which to convince your fellows, you must do it with the crude instruments of shot and shell. No one wants to go to war; but every decent man wants what is right, and true, and just, and he wants those things because he believes in God. You will find that even war, with all its evils, brings out the greatest things which man has in him—that spirit of self-sacrifice which will make him lay down his life for the cause."

Mr. Danvers based his sermon on the text: "It is good for us to be here" (St. Matthew's Gospel, chap. 17, verse 4). He pointed out that he was a Suffolk man, born near Martlesham "Red Lion," about which they had all heard, and he could say without any desire to please that he looked back on those days he had spent with the Suffolk Regiment as being the greatest he had ever lived. He thought they would agree with him that they were sometimes happy days, sometimes sad days, and sometimes terrible days. If there was anything which could be said in honour of the Suffolk Regiment it was that Suffolk characteristic of being able under any circumstances and all circumstances, to stand firm and carry out orders, even unto the very last. When they went back to ordinary life they should remember that although they were dressed in civilian clothes they had not ceased to serve God, King or country. "They still have a claim upon your services," concluded the preacher. "You can still stand firm, although you do not do it with your rifle or your bayonet. You can still stand up for what is right, and true, and just. There is work for every soldier of God until the end of his life."

The service was conducted by the Rev. W. M. Lummis, M.C., at the time Vicar of Kesgrave, Ipswich, late Captain in the Regiment, assisted by the Vicar (the Rev. J. H. Sandford), then officiating chaplain to the Depot.

CHANGES IN TRAINING.

Arthur Bryant refers to the lack of opportunities in training for modern war. It is of interest to compare the training of the 1st Battalion in 1930 with their training in 1940, in peace and in war.

Early in 1930 the First Battalion went from Colchester to Blackdown and joined the 6th Infantry Brigade, one of the two Experimental Brigades in the Army. Here the Battalion had to carry out trials in the carriage and handling of mechanically drawn machine guns and anti-tank guns.

Lieut.-Colonel D. V. M. Balders, Commanding the First Battalion, writing at the time says:—"At present all our organisation and practical handling is purely experimental and each year, and I may say each month, brings forth new ideas and new problems, which have to be faced and grappled with.

The only parts of the Battalions of the 6th Infantry Brigade which are mechanised are the Machine Gun Coys. and the Anti-Tank Platoons.

The Machine Gun Coy. is kept up to full peace strength, and the strength of Rifle Coys., in these days of shortage of recruits, has in consequence to suffer. The M.G. Coy. is organised on the normal lines, i.e., a Major or Captain Commanding Coy., a 2nd in command and 3 platoons each commanded by a subaltern, the 4th platoon which comes into being on mobilisation is in peace time only a skeleton platoon represented by flags during training in the field. Each platoon has 4 machine guns and is subdivided into two sections of 2 guns each, so that in war a M.G. Coy. has a total of 16 machine guns. In the experimental organisation that we are carrying out, one platoon is horse drawn, the other two platoons are mechanised.

The machine guns of the mechanised platoons are carried on petrol driven tractors or carriers called "Carden Loyds." Each Carden Loyd carrier takes one complete machine gun and tripod and two men, of whom one is the driver and the other the No. 1 of the gun; attached to each tractor is a trailer which carries 4 men, the remainder of the gun team. The Platoon Commander travels in a Carden Loyd tractor without a trailer. A maximum speed of 25 miles an hour can be obtained on the road, with trailer attached, across country 6 miles an hour with trailer and 8 miles an hour without trailer.

At present we are experimenting with one mechanised platoon working without trailers. The gun is mounted on the Carden Loyd and is fired from the vehicle by No. 1, who sits beside the driver. The gun is not allowed to be fired whilst the vehicle is on the move. Last year this platoon was called the "Infighting Platoon"; but this name is not considered to be appropriate. I shall refer to this platoon as the "Light Machine Gun Platoon." It is enough to say that some form of mobile machine gun is required to keep really close up with the forward infantry to protect them and help them forward. It is felt that this "Light Machine Gun Platoon" may be the answer, as it can move over rough ground rapidly, is a comparatively small target, and can come into action rapidly without wasting time or having to take the gun off the vehicle.

With the coming of the tank into modern warfare, Battalions should have some means of protection against a tank attack and for protection against armoured cars. A gun capable of knocking out a tank must have a fairly heavy projectile, and therefore the gun itself and carriage must be fairly large; the difficulty of transport of such a gun is therefore apparent and the answer is a mechanical vehicle.

The Anti-Tank Platoon in a Battalion consists of 1 Subaltern, 1 Sergeant, 4 Corporals and 12 Privates, with 4 Anti-Tank Guns. Each anti-tank gun is drawn by a Carden Loyd tractor to which is attached a trailer, the Carden Loyd and trailer being of exactly the same pattern as those of the M.G. Coy.

At present some Battalions are experimenting with a .5 Vickers M.G., whilst others have the .8 Oerlikon gun. The 1st Suffolk has the .8 Oerlikon. It is mounted on a carriage with tracks—gun, less mounting, weighs 140 lbs. The bullet is armour-piercing and weighs about 1 lb.; loading is by means of a magazine which holds 15 rounds. Rate of fire 80 rounds per minute approximate. 60 rounds of ammunition per gun are at present carried in the trailers. The gun carriage has to be detached from the trailer in order to come into action. The gun has a low position on carriages for travelling and is raised up on the carriage for firing. It is capable of moving over rough ground across country, and the Carden Loyd trailer and gun has a maximum speed of 15 miles per hour on the road with an average of 10 miles an hour and 6 miles per hour across country."

The First Battalion was engaged in these experiments during the years 1930-31-32, the Machine Gun Company being under the Command of Capt. F. V. C. Pereira. The experiments ended in 1932. Lieut.-Colonel D. V. M. Balders writing later says:—

"In 1932 the M.G. Coy. became the 'Support Coy.,' with 3 mechanised platoons of Vickers guns and one platoon of 3-inch mortars, also mechanised. This year the experiment was tried of giving to each platoon a six-wheeled lorry, which could tow the four trailers of the Carden Loyds, so that any platoon could go forward as real forward guns, the gun firing from the vehicle. This method of using platoons without trailers was called 'Armoured Action.' This year's training was the most interesting of all, and we learned many valuable lessons. The value of the 3-inch mortar as an Infantry Battalion weapon was very strongly brought out, as also the immense value of an Austin Seven car for the use of O.C. Support Company and the Battalion Commander.

During these three years, the M.G. Company worked with great keenness and energy, and won for the Battalion great praise from higher authority in all their work."

In 1932, owing to financial stringency the 6th Brigade reverted to its normal organization and the Battalion to its horse drawn vehicles.

How slow peace time* progress is under severe financial restrictions can be gauged when it is remembered that six years later this same Battalion on mobilization for war was still without its anti-tank guns. How fast war time efficiency becomes when there is no limit to expense can be appreciated by comparing the organisation of an Infantry Battalion, such as the First Battalion, after Dunkirk. The training and organisation of the Battalion in the Aldershot Experimental Brigade fell very far short of the standard required of the Battalion preparing for "D" Day.

* The fault was not all on the side of the Economists. In the first world war British Infantry suffered a complete eclipse. In the second world war it re-emerged as the most important arm on the battlefield.

In the past our Infantry has been world famous; Crecy, Minden, Waterloo and many other battles had proved their superiority over all opponents; but in the first world war they had been used only as cannon fodder, man-material to winkle out an enemy after his fortifications had been pulverised by the heaviest possible artillery fire. It was a tactical use of infantry that ensured stalemate.

P.B.I., "Poor Bloody Infantry," was the term of supreme compassion that these men earned. Never in the history of the British Army had the courage, the fortitude, the endurance of the British infantry soldier been so sorely tested by such vile usage, or stood the test more nobly.

No one would dare refer to the front line British Infantry of the second world war as "Poor Bloody Infantry." Yet at the outset of this second war it would have seemed that their task in battle was even more formidable than their predecessors. They started scarcely better trained and equipped than in 1914, and they were driven back fighting a series of rear-guard actions to Dunkirk in many ways comparable to the retreat to the Marne. But when the retreat ended it was in our own fortress island where re-organisation and training could be carried out uninterruptedly.

Equipment came slowly ; but magnificent use was made of the time before these infantry were once again face to face with the enemy. The primary truth had been finally accepted that if infantry were to advance victoriously they must do so covered by their own fire power, and manoeuvred by their own officers and N.C.O.s.

In the trench warfare of 1914-1918, fire-power had been built up outside the infantry unit, the attack was planned and launched far behind the front line. Costly failure succeeded costly failure as a result of such tactics. But during the re-organisation after Dunkirk, infantry were taught and learnt that it was on their own fire power and their own leadership that success depended.

Not that infantry needed less outside help in this Second World War—they needed more. They depended in the greatest degree on the close co-operative support of tanks, they called for and received artillery support at all stages of their advance, command of the air was all important. But the battle was fought and won by the forward Infantry Commander—sometimes even a Platoon or Section Commander. The free play of subordinate infantry leadership was as much the reason of the triumphant quality of our infantry in 1945, as the repression of initiative from 1914 to 1918 had been the cause of its failure to achieve success.

Mention during the First World War was rarely made of a smaller unit than a Company or a lower rank than a Company Commander; but in the Second World War, the section of seven men, the Bren gun group of three, the 2″ Submortar section, above all the leader of each of these small units had a vital role when the Company was in action; while behind them any sub-section of the Carrier, the Anti-tank or 3″ Mortar platoons might tip the scale between success and failure by seizing the initiative at the crucial moment. Whereas in 1918 the Company Commander was all important, in 1945 there were more Company Commanders in the Company than Henry Bolingbrokes at Bosworth Field.

British infantry had a long and arduous task in reaching these heights. They had the mortification during the early years of the war of seeing many of their best leaders leave for other corps which seemed to offer greater scope for adventure. Months lengthened into years, orders for embarkation came and were cancelled—there was every excuse for staleness or boredom. Yet all ranks persevered, and they reaped the full reward. When victory finally came they received their just tribute; no troops in the world so good as British infantry. No more "P.B.I.," thank you,—Never again, it is to be hoped.

The First Battalion that landed in Normandy in June 1945 had no resemblance to the First Battalion at the end of the First World War; and little to the First Battalion under Lieut.-Colonel Balders in the 6th Experimental Brigade from 1930 to 1932. It was no longer a rigid formation; but an aggregate of many sub-units mutually dependent. The horses had gone; their place doubled and trebled by motor vehicles.

The First Battalion in June, 1945 had four Rifle Companies, the spearhead of its attack, the core of its defence. Each of these Companies had three platoons and each of these platoons with its subsection of 3, 2" mortars, and its three sections of ten men, (each section including a Bren gun detachment of three) was a formidable fighting unit.

In the fluid actions that were fought in Normandy and through France to Germany a platoon, when led with initiative and imagination by its subordinate commanders, was capable of infiltration into an enemy's position and holding its own against counter attack. A Company with its three platoons could sustain a considerable action.

Meanwhile the Battalion Commander in addition to these four Rifle Companies had as part of his front line strength a support Company consisting of Carrier platoon, Anti-tank platoon, 3" Mortar platoon and Assault Pioneer platoon—a powerful aid to his forward Rifle Companies.

This Support Company was an off-shoot from the Headquarters Company, which included Signallers, Transport, Stretcher Bearers. The Support Company was the natural corollary to a Battalion organized to fight itself forward and to hold what it had gained. All its four platoons were essentially fighting units, a portion at least of whom were employed from the outset of the action in support of the forward Rifle Companies.

The Carrier platoon consisted of four sections, each section having three part-armoured motor trucks carrying a Corporal, two men and a Driver. The Fire power of each of these sections was three Bren guns, a 2" Mortar and a Piat in addition to the rifle power of men not otherwise employed. It was an essentially mobile unit to be employed in close support of the leading riflemen during the last stages of an attack, or to cover their flanks. But skill had to be exercised in coming into action for the unit was employed dismounted.

The 3 inch Mortar Platoon had six detachments each of a Commander, three men and a driver in a motor truck. The Mortar fired a ten pound bomb at an extreme range of 2,750 yards with a minimum range of 250 yards. The mortars could be used singly or as a Battery.

The anti-Tank platoon was subdivided into three sections each of two six pounder anti-tank guns with a carrier to tow each gun. The gun team was made up of a Sergeant and four men with a driver of the carrier. The gun had a range of 800 yards at a moving target. It was a heavy weapon and in action had to be man-handled into position.

The Assault Pioneer platoon was composed of two Assault sections and a Pioneer section. Each of the former had a Corporal, two men and a driver; their main role was to deal with mines and obstacles, while the Pioneer section could be called upon to construct minor bridges and obstacles. But the role of all these three Sections fell largely on the Rifle Companies, whose personnel, in addition to their many other duties, were trained in mine clearance.

Battalion Headquarters consisted of Headquarters, Signal platoon, and Administrative platoon, a considerable rifle power which could be used if necessary, and was fully used on many occasions. Among its sub-units was a Sniper section of 8 men under a Sergeant. Its largest sub-unit was the Signal platoon of 30 other ranks, which could be split into four parties of a size to suit requirements.

A study of the Infantry Battalion organisation shows what a powerful and flexible weapon was at the disposal of the Battalion Commander. Above all it emphasizes the vital importance of leadership right down to the most subordinate commander. Battle fronts in Europe were of great extent. Although the defensive power of modern fire was even greater than in 1914 it had to be widely dispersed. There was always scope for an attacker who was prepared to press his attack home. But, however good the Commander's preparation and plan might be, success would not be achieved without the full co-operation of every subordinate leader.

The Battalion Commander who directed a Company on to an objective and arranged the necessary support from the Carrier, Anti-tank and 3 inch Mortar platoons was dependent on the Company Commander's dispositions of his rifle platoons. While the latter in turn trusted to the character and knowledge of these platoon Commanders and on the courage and initiative of the leaders of the Rifle sections, the Bren guns and the 2 inch Mortars; the success or failure in co-operation of any one of these junior N.C.O.s might easily turn the scale.

The campaigns of 1914/1918 and 1939/1945 had in common the supreme importance of the Battalion Commander. During the trench warfare in France in the first World War his personality was the focal point. A fine Battalion Commander would carry his Battalion forward against terrible odds; but if he was killed its value might quickly fall. In the second World War the greatness of a Battalion was once again the reflection of its Commander. But during months of training he had the opportunity of selecting and stamping his likeness on every leader who commanded. If he were killed, the pattern still remained.

THE YEARS 1929—1939.

As can be seen in the interval between the two World Wars British infantry had lagged behind in modern military science; but both Regular Battalions of the Suffolk Regiment and indeed the 4th Suffolk and 1st Cambridgeshires kept up the high standard of markmanship for which they have always had renown. The First Battalion had a particularly successful year in the A.R.A. results in 1932. The Second Battalion did equally well in India in 1933. No small measure of the credit won by the Regiment was due to a succession of fine rifle shots who served in one or other Battalion.

Perhaps the most outstanding of all these was Capt. A. G. Rumbelow, M.B.E., who won the Revolver Thirty Cup (A.R.A.) in 1927, 1931, 1933; the Revolver Gold Medal in 1927 and the Revolver Challenge Cup in 1927. With the rifle he shot in the Regular Army Eight in 1927 and 1929. He represented England in the Mackinnon in 1930. Another exceptionally good marksman and instructor was Major E. M. Ransford.

In all respects both Regular Battalions maintained their high standards as can be judged by the following inspection reports.

> "The march past was very good. I have had first class reports of your unit from various Commanders. It was a very good parade and the turn-out was excellent. I am sure that if you are ever called upon to do anything serious you will live up to the traditions of your excellent Regiment."

These remarks were made by H. E. Field Marshal Sir Philip Chetwode, Bart., G.C.B., K.C.M.G., D.S.O., Commander-in-Chief of The Army in India, following the Inspection of The Second Battalion at Madras on 31st December, 1934. In a letter to the G.O.C., Madras District, regarding the Inspection, he said:

> "I inspected The Suffolk Regiment under Colonel Stubbs, and they gave me the impression of being well up to the very best standard of County Regiments in every way. They gave me a feeling of great confidence."

The First Battalion was also congratulated. Major-General H. C. Jackson, C.B., C.M.G., D.S.O., Commanding the 2nd Division, on bidding the Battalion goodbye at Blackdown on 20th January 1935 said:

> "Everything you have done has been done well."

Lt.-Colonel C. C. R. Murphy continued the history of the Suffolk Regiment down to 1928. The peace which his last pages heralded, the great reward for the sacrifices of the war he had recorded, proved but a disastrous truce. He closed his volume with the First Battalion at Colchester, the Second Battalion at Shanghai.

The command of the First Battalion changed in June, 1929. Lt.-Colonel W. N. Nicholson, C.M.G., D.S.O., being appointed A.Q.M.G. Northern India after two and a half years in command. He was succeeded by Lt.-Colonel D. V. M. Balders, O.B.E., M.C., who had been Adjutant of the First Battalion in 1914. Lt.-Colonel Balders came from a soldier family, every male member since the time of his great-great-grandfather (who retired in 1803) having served in the Army; save two who were sailors. They numbered twenty-five. One of Lt.-Colonel Balders' ancestors, Lt. Peter Campbell, served in the 12th Foot at Minden and commanded the Battalion at the close of the battle.

In February 1930 the First Battalion moved from Colchester to Alma Barracks, Blackdown, forming part of the 6th Infantry Brigade under Brigadier A. Wavell (later Field Marshal Lord Wavell).

In January 1932 Lt.-Colonel W. M. Campbell, D.S.O., M.C., completed his four years in Command of the 2nd Battalion and was succeeded by Lt.-Colonel G. C. Stubbs, D.S.O. Lt.-Colonel Stubbs had been Adjutant of the 2nd Battalion in 1909 and later distinguished himself in the First World War where he commanded the 2nd Battalion and later the 121st Infantry

Brigade. Lt.-Colonel Stubbs was one of the best Regimental officers the Regiment has had; a man of sound commonsense, direct and outspoken in manner, generous and most hospitable.

Lt.-Colonel D. V. M. Balders, O.B.E., M.C., completed his four years in command of the 1st Battalion on 4th June, 1933, and was succeeded by Lt.-Colonel A. M. Cutbill, M.C., who had been Adjutant of the 2nd Battalion when it proceeded to France in the First World War. Very few officers in the Regiment have served so continuously with Battalions of the Regiment as Lt.-Colonel Cutbill. Shortly after completing his command, Lt.-Colonel D. V. M. Balders was promoted to command an East Anglian Territorial Brigade.

SECOND BATTALION RECEIVES NEW COLOURS.

In November, 1933, the 2nd Battalion moved from Trimulgherry to Fort St. George, Madras. While here, on 16th March, 1935 the Battalion was presented with new colours by H.E. the Governor of Madras, Lord Erskine, G.C.I.E.

The Battalion was paraded in Fort St. George and marched to Government House. For the purpose of the parade, the Battalion was organised as follows:—

Commanding Officer: Lt.-Colonel G. C. Stubbs, D.S.O.
Adjutant: Captain F. A. Milnes.
Senior Majors: Major H. R. Gadd, D.S.O., M.C. and Major D. R. A. Eley, D.S.O.
Regimental Sergeant Major: R.S.M. J. Chalk, M.M.
Band Master: B.M. J. Longstaff.
Drum Major: D.M. S. Gray.
Escort for the Colours: Capt. J. W. Josselyn, 2/Lt. D. G. Lawrence, 24 Files of "B" Company.
Officers to carry the Colours: Lieut. A. J. D. Turner and Lieut. P. A. Morcombe.
No. 2 Company: Capt. A. A. Johnson, M.C., Lt. J. W. Trelawny, 24 Files of "C" Company.
No. 3 Company: Capt. H. C. Carrigan, 2/Lt. R. M. Marsh, 24 Files of "A" Company.
No. 4 Company: Capt. J. S. D. Lloyd, Lt. R. E. B. Moriarty, 24 Files of "D" (S) Company.

On the arrival of the Governor on the parade ground, the old Colours were trooped. The band and drums marched across the parade in slow time to the march, "Gold and Silver," and back in quick time to "The Duchess," the old Regimental March of the Battalion. No. 1 Company, the Colour escort, marched out to "The Grenadiers," and took over the old Colours from the Sergeant of the Colour party and double sentries, who were in position on the left of the parade. The Colours were then trooped through the ranks of the Battalion. On reaching the right of the Line the old Colours proceeded, in slow time, down the front of the Battalion, to the left of the line, followed by the Escort and Band playing "Auld Lang Syne." They were then cased and left in rear of the Battalion in charge of two Company Sergeant Majors.

PRESENTATION OF NEW COLOURS TO 2ND BATTALION BY HIS EXCELLENCY, THE GOVERNOR OF MADRAS, 1935.

Back Row—Capt. A. R. C. Southby (A.D.C.) Indian Pln. Commander, Lt. R. E. B. Moriarty, Lt. J. W. Trelawny, Lt. N. S. Holmes, Lt. K. J. K. Pye, Lt. (Q.M.) J. Hill, Lt. R. E. Goodwin (A.D.C.)
Centre Row—Capts. H. C. Carrigan, J. W. Josselyn, 2nd Lts. R. M. Marsh, D. G. Lawrence, Lts. A. J. D. Turner, P. A. Morcombe, Lt. N. M. Barnardiston, 2nd Lt. P. W. G. Papillon, Capt. A. A. Johnson, M.C.
Front Row—Bt. Major V. C. Russell, D.S.O., M.C., Major F. V. C. Periera, Capt. F. A. Milnes (Adjutant), Lt. Col. G. C. Stubbs, D.S.O. (C.O.), H.E. The Lord Erskine, G.I.C.E., Majors H. R. Gadd, D.S.O., M.C., D. R. A. Eley, D.S.O., E. G. Fraser, Capt. J. S. D. Lloyd.

The Battalion then formed three sides of a square. The drums were piled in the centre and the New Colours laid against them. They were blessed by the Lord Bishop of Madras, and were then presented to the Governor: the King's Colour, assisted by the Senior Major, to the Senior Subaltern on parade; the Regimental Colour, assisted by the second Senior Major, to the second Senior Subaltern on parade.

Having presented the Colours, the Governor said:

> "I have very great pleasure in presenting these Colours to the officers, non-commissioned officers and men of the 2nd Battalion the Suffolk Regiment, more especially as I am myself so closely connected with your county and have there spent so many happy years. Since the late Colours were presented by Her Royal Highness the Duchess of Connaught in 1879, the Battalion has nobly borne its part in many engagements, and the battle honours enshrined on them show that the 12th Regiment has even added to the laurels that it won so long ago at Minden and Fontenoy, and many another action famous in history. We all hope that a prolonged period of peace is before us; but should the Regiment be called upon again to take the field for the King and country, I am sure that its deeds will be worthy of so glorious a past. I am indeed proud of having had the great honour of performing this ceremony."

Lieut.-Colonel G. C. Stubbs, D.S.O., Commanding the Battalion, replied:—

> "Your Excellency, on behalf of the officers, non-commissioned officers and men of the Battalion under my command, I thank you for the honour you have conferred upon us in presenting new Colours to the Regiment this morning. We are especially glad to receive them from your hands owing to your close connection with our County of Suffolk. To-day will long be remembered in the Regiment, and I can assure you that should necessity arise, all ranks of the Regiment will uphold all that these Colours stand for—Honour, Loyalty, Duty to the King."

The new Colours were saluted by the Battalion and were marched into position to the National Anthem. The Battalion then marched past in column in slow time to the Regimental Slow March and in close column in quick time to "The Duchess." The old Colours, cased, were carried in the rear of the Battalion. The Battalion having re-formed, line "advanced in review order."

THE 250TH ANNIVERSARY.

The 250th Anniversary of the formation of the Regiment in 1935 was celebrated by both 1st and 2nd Battalions with a Troop of the Regimental Colour. The programme for the celebration in Suffolk at Bury St. Edmunds comprised:—

Friday, 21st June—South African Veterans' dinner in the Town Hall, attended by nearly a hundred who had fought in South Africa with the Regiment.

Saturday, 22nd June—The naming of a new L.N.E. Railway locomotive "The Suffolk Regiment" took place first at Ipswich and subsequently at

Bury St. Edmunds. The engine driver, E. N. Brown, had been a sergeant in the 4th Battalion and the fireman, W. H. Mortimer, a private in the 2nd and 7th Battalions.

The Annual Sergeants' Dinner Club dined in the Athenaeum, Bury St. Edmunds. The attendance numbered approximately a hundred, the oldest member being Ex-Q.M.S. "Billy" Woods, of 80 years. The guests included three Chelsea pensioners of the Regiment.

Sunday, 23rd June.—The Regimental Chapel in St. Mary's Church, Bury St. Edmunds was dedicated. The Service was conducted by the Lord Bishop of the Diocese, the Rt. Rev. Dr. W. G. Whittingham, who was accompanied by the Bishop of Dunwich and the Archdeacon of Sudbury, the Rev. Dr. E. H. Thorold, C.B., C.B.E., Chaplain General to the Forces, with the Assistant Chaplain General, Eastern Command, the Vicar of St. Mary's and the Rev. G. Elliott Lee (Methodist).

The Lord Lieutenant of Suffolk and Lady Stradbroke with the Colonel, the Suffolk Regiment, Major General Sir John Ponsonby, K.C.B., C.M.G., D.S.O. formed the first procession, the National Anthem being played as the Lord Lieutenant entered the Church. A short voluntary was then played whilst the procession of clergy and choir came to the Chapel from the West end by the Main Aisle.

At the conclusion of this Service a Drumhead Service was held in the Abbey Gardens. During this Service the old Colours of the 2nd Battalion, which had been carried since 1879, were handed over to the Vicar of St. Mary's for safe keeping. The parade then formed up in the Abbey Grounds and marched past the Lord Lieutenant at the Corn Exchange in three detachments. The Colonel of the Regiment led. The first detachment included all past and present members of the Regular Battalions. The second detachment under Brigadier General S. E. Massy Lloyd, C.B.E., had representatives of the 3rd, 4th and 5th Battalions. The third detachment, under Major General R. M. Luckock, C.B., C.M.G., D.S.O., included past and present members of the Cambridgeshire Regiment with ex-members of the Service Battalions. At the Saluting Base the Lord Lieutenant was accompanied by the High Sheriff and Lady Magnay, the Mayor of Bury St. Edmunds and the Town Clerk.

During the rest of the week, cricket and tennis matches were played, and on Saturday, 29th June, an Old Comrades' Association Re-union was held at the Portman Road Ground at Ipswich, which was attended by between three and four thousand. Lt.-Colonel H. R. Hooper, M.C., Commanding the 4th Battalion, had arranged a parade of Guard Mounting of the time of Minden, with soldiers dressed in the uniform of that period. This re-union was attended by Sir John Ganzoni, M.P. and the Mayor and Mayoress of Ipswich (Mr. G. A. and Miss Ida Mallett).

The Suffolk Regimental Chapel which was dedicated during this 250th Anniversary, had been entirely re-furnished by past and present members of the Regiment, assisted by the people of Suffolk. This included the oak panelling and the wrought iron gates. The architect was Mr. J. N. Comper. The woodwork was carried out by Mr. Harvey G. Frost, who served with the 9th Battalion.

The wrought iron gates at the west end of the Chapel are a memorial to Colonel Frank Pretty, T.D., who commanded the 4th Battalion, 1920-1923.

The silver candlesticks on the Altar a memorial to Lt.-Colonel A. S. Peebles, D.S.O.; the Credence Table is a memory of Brigadier General C. R. Townley and Major E. C. Doughty; the Altar rails in memory of Major G. H. Walford and his brother; the priest's chair in memory of Colonel J. E. Harris; and the prayer-desk commemorates his son, Captain P. G. Harris. The Bible is in memory of Major E. P. Prest. The floral wreath on the altar front is an exact copy of the wreath of flowers embroidered on the old Stabilis Colour carried by the Regiment at the Battle of Seringapatam in 1799.

The Regiment had been allied to the Auckland Regiment (Countess of Ranfurly's Own) of the Dominion of New Zealand since 1913.

On 16th December, 1930 His Majesty the King graciously approved an alliance between the 12th Battalion, Australian Infantry and the Suffolk Regiment.

Haile Hall,
Beckermet,
Cumberland.
March 31st, 1931.

Dear Colonel Sampson,

As Colonel of the Suffolk Regiment, I write on behalf of the Regiment to express our gratification at the alliance of the 12th Battalion (The Launceston Regiment) Australian Military Forces and the Suffolk Regiment (12th Foot), official notice of which appeared in Army Orders dated 31st January, 1931.

It is hoped that if any Officers, N.C.O.s or men of the Launceston Regiment are either in England or India at any time they will visit the 1st Battalion and 2nd Battalion or the Depot, Suffolk Regiment, at Bury St. Edmunds, Suffolk.

I need hardly say that any such visits would be very much appreciated by us and help to cement our alliance.

Wishing you and the Regiment all luck and prosperity.

Yours sincerely,
JOHN PONSONBY, Major General.
Colonel, The Suffolk Regiment.

COMMONWEALTH OF AUSTRALIA.

The Senate,
Canberra, F.T.C.,
Australia.
June 16th, 1931.

Dear Sir,

Please accept the very best thanks of all ranks of the 12th Bn. (The Launceston Regiment) Australian Infantry for copies of the Suffolk Regimental Gazette, and especially for the very kindly references to ourselves in the March—April, 1931, issue. The announcement that H.M. the King has been graciously pleased to approve of the alliance between the Old Twelfth Foot and ourselves was received by all ranks with the greatest pleasure and satisfaction. We feel it is a very great honour indeed, to be linked with our kinsmen of the Motherland serving in such a famous and historic Regiment as The Suffolk.

This letter is being written from the Federal Capital and the address may puzzle you—the reason is that though the writer is a citizen soldier and C.O. The Launceston Regiment, he is also one of Tasmania's Senators in the Commonwealth Parliament. The Headquarters of the Battalion are in the old Barracks, Launceston, Tasmania, the self same building which was occupied by a portion of the Old Twelfth, when the Regiment formed part of the garrison of Van Dieman's Land in the fifties of last century.

We would much appreciate it if you would be so good as to add on the cover of your journal, after 12th Battalion, the words "The Launceston Regiment"—such has been our title since formation in 1878—and also after Launceston, add Tasmania. We are islanders, and though all good Australians, do like to keep our identity. It has been said, and rightly, I think, that Tasmania resembles the Old Land more than any other part of the Empire, most of our place names are derived from England, and our city is named after Launceston, that very charming and ancient town in Cornwall, and like it is on the Tamar, in the county of Cornwall, Tasmania.

In conclusion, please accept our very best thanks for copies of the Gazette, wishing you all the luck we would wish ourselves.

Yours sincerely,

BURFORD SAMPSON, Lieut.-Colonel,

C.O. 12th Bn. (The Launceston Regiment)
Australian Infantry.

Since this correspondence a visit of representatives of the Australian Battalion has been made to the Depot, and the Regiment has had news of its activities through the medium of the Regimental Gazette.

Early in 1935 the First Battalion moved from Alma Barracks, Blackdown to Crownhill, Plymouth, to form part of the 8th Infantry Brigade of the 3rd Division, a formation with which it was to earn great renown in the not too distant future.

A year later, in 1936, the Second Battalion moved from Madras to Mhow. In the previous August the Command of the Battalion had changed. Lieut.-Colonel Guy Stubbs, D.S.O., being promoted A.Q.M.G., Malta, his place being filled by Lieut.-Colonel H. R. Gadd, D.S.O., M.C.

1938 saw the completion of Command of Lieut.-Colonel H. R. Gadd, D.S.O., M.C., who was succeeded by Lieut.-Colonel D. R. A. Eley, D.S.O.

On the 4th June, 1937, Lieut.-Colonel A. M. Cutbill, M.C. completed his three years' Command of the First Battalion. Lieut.-Colonel R. Gurney was appointed in his stead; but only held the Command for a few months before being posted to the Staff. Lieut.-Colonel Gurney was to have a distinguished career at the War Office, the revised rates for the pay of officers and other ranks in 1945 being chiefly his work. Lieut.-Colonel R. Gurney was succeeded by Lieut.-Colonel E. H. W. Backhouse.

In November, 1937 the First Battalion had left Plymouth for Malta in H.T. "Dunera" and was quartered at Floriana and St. George Barracks; a short tour which ended in June, 1939 when the Battalion returned to

Plymouth. While here the Command once again changed—Lieut.-Colonel E. G. Fraser succeeding Lieut.-Colonel E. H. W. Backhouse, who was promoted to the 64th Infantry Brigade.

The Establishment of the Depot at Bury St. Edmunds in 1878 had done more than mould a County Regiment, it led, slowly it is true, to a blending of all the Regiment's interests and activities. Rivalries between the two Regular Battalions scarcely existed and have long since completely disappeared; the idea of the Depot as a place of leisure was negatived by the time of the South African War. Then in the years that followed, plans for the improved welfare of the Regiment gradually developed.

An Old Comrades' Association was formed in 1908, the first President being Colonel C. R. Townley, with Captain and Adjutant F. T. D. Wilson as Hon. Secretary. During the twenty years of peace after 1918, much had been done by this Association under the Presidency of Lieut.-Colonel C. D. Parry Crooke, C.M.G., to assist all cases of distress. Speaking at a big re-union in 1937, attended by some two thousand old soldiers, their wives and families, Lieut.-Colonel Parry Crooke said: "During the last five years the 'O.C.A.' has helped no less than 1,500 cases at an outlay of about £2,700."

Much was also done, thanks to the energy of Lieut.-Colonel M. S. Chase, to find employment in civil life for the men who had served with the Battalions of The Regiment during the war.

A Regimental Museum was opened in Gibraltar Barracks, Bury St. Edmunds early in 1935. Here was displayed a considerable collection of articles of uniform dating from 1800 and representing the badges, head-dress and uniforms worn by officers and men of the 12th Foot, the Cambridgeshire Regiment, the West Suffolk and Cambridgeshire Militia, the Suffolk Volunteer Battalions as well as the Suffolk Regiment. The majority of the exhibits had been collected by Colonel E. Montagu, C.B.E., and Major E. C. Doughty, D.S.O., respectively and presented by them to the Officers' Mess, the Depot.

The Suffolk Regiment Association was formed in 1930 to foster *Esprit de Corps* and to control and co-ordinate through Regimental Committees the funds and activities of the many Regimental Organisations that had grown up. Through this Committee, recommendations on points of policy of Regimental interest could be made to the Colonel of the Regiment. The Regimental Gazette, the Regimental Cottage Homes, and from 1935 the Chapel and the Museum, were included in this Association. In due course, the Regimental Golfing Society, the Officers' Benevolent Fund, the Officers' Dinner Club and the Old Comrades' Association came under their auspices.

The Committee at the present time, 1946, consists of:—President: The Colonel of the Regiment, six Vice-Presidents; the Officers Commanding all Unit Members of the Association (or their Representatives); the Regimental Sergeant Majors of the 1st and 2nd Battalions and the Depot; with the Officer i/c Depot Administration Details as Hon. Secretary and Treasurer.

Tentative changes in the discipline of the Army at home were also taking place. The following was published in the Regimental Gazette at the end of 1929:—

"The coming of mechanization, the development of education and the changed type of soldier have called for a new and more intelligent kind of discipline and with this in view a number of changes have been made in the disciplinary regulations of the Army at home.

The first change relaxes some of the limitations on the soldier's freedom during his off-duty hours. On Friday, Saturday and Sunday evenings, soldiers are to be allowed to stay out of barracks up to midnight without the formality of obtaining a pass.

The next important modification is that a soldier granted leave of absence will not be required to state where he is going unless his leave is for more than twenty-four hours; notification of his destination is not necessary to enable him to procure a ticket at reduced price.

These changes have been introduced as an experiment and if the soldier plays up to them, as we feel sure he will, no doubt further privileges will be granted; on the other hand, of course, if this experiment does not prove a success, we must expect a re-introduction of the old restrictions.

Another important change in the administration of the Army recognises that the modern non-commissioned officer is better educated and more capable than his predecessor. N.C.O.s must now expect at least to command a platoon in the field.

Commanding Officers are to be allowed to use their discretion in placing an armed or unarmed party of twenty men or more in charge of an N.C.O. instead of calling upon an Officer in order to comply with the regulations.

Further, on various Boards which are periodically assembled, Warrant and Senior Non-Commissioned Officers are now to be allowed to sit; and lastly, Officers in charge of Regimental funds may delegate details of administration to selected Warrant or N.C.O.s.

All this must be for the good, because not only will it give the Non-Commissioned Officer a greater interest in his profession, but it will also leave the Officers free for the more important task of training and for study, and it probably will help to attract keen and intelligent men into the Army."

In February, 1939, Major General Sir John Ponsonby, K.C.B., C.M.G., D.S.O., completed his time as Colonel, the Suffolk Regiment and was succeeded by Colonel W. N. Nicholson, C.M.G., D.S.O.

A farewell dinner was held in his honour at Gibraltar Barracks, Bury St. Edmunds. Those present were:—Colonel W. N. Nicholson, C.M.G., D.S.O., the new Colonel of the Regiment; Lieut.-Colonel F. T. D. Wilson, O.B.E., Colonel A. M. Cutbill, M.C., Lieut.-Colonel R. G. Coles, Lieut.-Colonel Parry Crooke, C.M.G., Major E. E. Pearson and Lieut.-Colonel M. S. Chase, Major Pereira, Major F. V. Oborne, Captain R. E. B. Moriarty, Captain R. E. Goodwin and Major B. G. F. Drew.

Colonel Nicholson proposed the health of the Colonel of the Regiment, and said that to give a record of Sir John's achievements as a soldier would not be sufficient. Both in peace and in war he had shown that his ability and courage were second to none; but his services to the Regiment went much deeper than that. He was a man of conspicuous personality, and his wide experience and wisdom had ever been at their service. He left them on attaining the age-limit; but a man's age could not be judged by the number of years he had lived. Sir John would never be old, for he would always have the heart of a young man. That quality of youth had endeared him to all ranks and all ages, and had enabled him to exert a paramount influence during his fourteen years as Colonel. The traditions of a regiment were built up by the outstanding characters of the men who had served, and to the long and glorious history of the Suffolk Regiment Sir John had made a great contribution.

SEPTEMBER 3RD, 1939. THE DEPOT.

War was declared on September 3rd, 1939.

The Depot of the Suffolk Regiment at Gibraltar Barracks, Bury St. Edmunds at once became a Training Unit. Lieut.-Colonel H. Read Gadd, D.S.O., M.C., assumed Command on September 5th, giving up the Command of the 2nd Battalion, Cambridgeshire Regiment. He had Major I. Owen as Second in Command and Major Vernon Pereira as Administrative Officer. The organization of the new Training Unit was a Headquarters Company, one Infantry Company, one Recruit Company and one Specialist Company, the personnel being made up from that existing at the Depot supplemented by picked instructors from the First Battalion Suffolk Regiment.

It was understood that in six months a second Training Unit would be formed, but long before this time had elapsed the order was issued for its formation and the title of the Regimental Depot was altered to Suffolk Regiment Infantry Training Centre.

Lieut.-Colonel Gadd thus found himself with a formation consisting of a Headquarters Company, two Recruit Companies, two Infantry Companies and a greatly enlarged Specialist Company; but with only the trained instructors of the original Unit. The necessary additional instructors were supposed to come from the Territorial Army, but this Territorial Army had been called up, was busy duplicating itself and in no state to provide or to give the help which it so badly needed for itself.

There was nothing unusual about this in the past history of the British Army. Every war in which a quick expansion of strength has been required has presented similar problems to the unfortunate Depot Commander. The Suffolk Regiment was lucky to have available an officer of such ability, and Gadd was equally lucky in being very largely left to his own devices by the Authorities, who in the first press of a crisis of this nature are far more likely to do harm than good by interference and instructions.

When mobilization has been ordered, a campaign will not wait to allow a methodical organization of raw material. The experiences of 1914 were repeated in 1939; there was everything to do, and no one trained to do it. Additional so-called instructors did arrive, but they were little better than raw material, many of them were N.C.O.s who had but recently been promoted from privates, and such key men as drivers could hardly have obtained a civilian driving licence.

It was impossible to get a raw war time organization going with such teachers. Every man sent to the Infantry Training Centre was therefore utilized only in the capacity for which he proved best suited, and a general hunt was made of all sources from which instructors could be found; those who proved fitting being immediately taken on the Strength. But this would not have been successful had not all ranks done their utmost to fit themselves for their new jobs, and had not the Officer in Charge Records proved most sympathetic to the sometimes unorthodox methods of impounding suitable men.

Accommodation was one of the immediate problems. During 1938 and 1939 ten huts had been approved for Gibraltar Barracks to accommodate the increase of Militia recruits expected under the Belisha Scheme. Not all these huts had been completed by the outbreak of war. Even if they had been they would have been hopelessly insufficient; for the new Infantry Training Centre speedily required accommodation for 1,500 men and there was a prospect of this reaching 2,000; a total which was actually exceeded at peak periods.

Existing accommodation was quite inadequate. The original proposal was that any overflow from Gibraltar Barracks should be billeted in the western area of Bury St. Edmunds. But the difficulty of training men to be soldiers when scattered in billets was obviously so great that it was decided to ignore the proposed plan and instead to find empty suitable buildings throughout the town; such buildings to be big enough for the recruits to live a barrack room life. By Christmas, 1939 nearly 1,000 men were accommodated in comparatively large houses within one and a half miles of Gibraltar Barracks; central cookhouses and dining rooms were organized and thus practically the whole of Bury St. Edmunds played its part in becoming the Greater Gibraltar Barracks.

It was even reported that "Lord Haw Haw" in his broadcasts from Germany, foretelling the awful future that awaited England, had remarked on the obvious logical consequences that would follow if drilling continued in the Churchyards in Bury St. Edmunds. "Lord Haw Haw" always sought to impress his listeners by a supposed intimate knowledge of wartime conditions in England; but no one in Bury St. Edmunds will remember any Churchyard becoming a drill ground.

As has always proved true, the inhabitants of Bury took the greatest personal interest in the military tide that flooded the town; they helped to their utmost to make things easy for the Infantry Training H.Q. and comfortable for the men. Many Clubs and Reading Rooms were opened by the citizens; the largest of them all, the Athenaeum, with a most efficient and hard-working band of ladies, under the leadership of Miss Lake, gave a more than generous welcome which will never be forgotten by the Regiment or by the countless men of all arms and nationalities that filled it every day throughout the war.

Before the war a site for a hutted camp had been earmarked on the Newmarket Road between Sexton's Farm and the aerodrome. The site was ideal in relation to Gibraltar Barracks, but the question of its drainage had been overlooked. The town sewers were beyond reach in the further valley, and the R.E. demanded that a fresh site should be selected. Fortunately the urgency of the war finally over-rode this objection and it was decided to instal electric pumps to empty the cesspools into the town sewers. But the question of drainage had delayed a start and the buildings of West Lines, as the new camp was temporarily called, did not begin until March, 1940.

The lay-out of the camp was on the elaborate scale that marked most war-time projects, with the most modern Cookhouses and Dining Halls and a full proportion of Company Offices and Lecture Halls. No time was wasted once the camp was approved and a portion of it was ready to accommodate men by November, 1940, a year after the war had started; although the whole camp was not handed over until well into 1941. When all the billets in the town had been given up, training and general efficiency benefited considerably.

TRAINING AT THE DEPOT.

In the early months of the war there was no syllabus of training, no detailed instructions, beyond the inference that could be drawn from the Establishment of Recruit, Infantry and Specialist Companies. The training was left in the hands of the Officer Commanding the Infantry Training Centre. There was however a time allowance: 8 weeks for recruit training, a further 8 weeks for the Infantry Company training if a soldier was to be a Rifleman, or a rather longer period if he was to become a Specialist.

The subjects taught in the Specialist Company were driving I.C., signalling, 3 inch mortar and carrier training. But owing to the lack of equipment it was well into 1941 before all these forms of training were a going concern. An old car was bought at an early date out of the Regimental Institute Funds to train the drivers; this had to last for many months until eleven old cars arrived from Colchester after a precarious journey. It was many months before a 30 cwt. truck could be obtained. The Officer Training Corps of a local school produced the signalling equipment. Wooden mortars and other expedients enabled a start to be made in most other of the Specialist subjects.

Training in the Recruit Companies was comparatively straightforward; every foot of hard surface in and about Barracks was occupied by squads struggling with the simplicities of the new drill. An excellent standard was reached; this branch gave little trouble.

It was a different matter with the Infantry Companies. Company instructors were very scarce, the best were with Field Force units who were loath to give them up. Tactics were changing, weapons were in short supply. Moreover, from July, 1940, onwards the Infantry Training Centre had a considerable defence role which fell to the lot of the Infantry Companies and of necessity interfered with their training. At one time all men of over eight weeks' training had to "stand to" daily at 0300 hours. To fit this in with normal rest hours Infantry Companies started their training at 0500 hours and finished at 1300 hours.

Range accommodation was another great difficulty. The Range was at Thetford, 14 miles away. Since there was no M.T. available in the early months of the war, billets in Thetford had to be found. Later in the war the Barton Mills range was enlarged and used. A Mortar Range was also made here.

The standard of training was tested at a passing out drill parade for recruits, and a final test scheme for Infantry Companies. This latter took many forms; but besides testing the soldier's tactical training, special attention was paid to the individual self-reliance and endurance of each man. In due time detailed War Office Syllabus were issued, based on the experience of war conditions.

It may seem that in this account of the conditions at the Depot during the early months too much has been made of the difficulties and too little said of the success attained. The standard of training was high and this was due to the enthusiasm of everyone concerned and the spirit in which they overcame the difficulties. Establishment, accommodation, equipment, stores, had all been worked out for a unit of a particular size to do a particular job. Anything outside these dimensions naturally tended to throw everything out of gear.

But in arriving at a right solution of all problems nothing was so essential as the instructional staff. It had to expand to the requisite strength and yet be of the best quality. The demands made on it not only for the training of the doubled establishment, but also from outside, were increasing. In 1940 within the space of six weeks, the entire W.O. and N.C.O. Staff of two and a half Battalions had to be found from the "sources at your disposal" and "without interfering with the efficiency of your unit." Thus were the 7th and 8th Battalions the Suffolk Regiment staffed; followed in a few weeks by a further demand to find half the W.O.s and N.C.O.s for the 13th Sherwood Foresters. Moreover, every Battalion Commander looked to the Infantry Training Centre for the highest possible standard of drafts of all ranks. Few realized, save in theory, that the heart of a Regiment must be its Depot; that the very best of officers and instructors must be there to "train the young idea."

The Regiment was fortunate during these war years to have Lieut.-Colonel H. R. Gadd in Command. He had an intimate knowledge not only of the requirements of his own Command; but of the needs of all the other units of the Regiment. All went to him for assistance, and he never failed them. There was a ceaseless change of officers under his command, a constant urge among them to get into front line units; in consequence the Depot became a "one man show." During the five years Gadd commanded he rarely allowed himself a day off—when he did it was to indulge in an occasional Newmarket race meeting.

The Command of the I.T.C. was more than a whole-time occupation for one man, but Gadd's responsibilities at first were not bounded by the organisation and training of this unit. No account of the Infantry Training Centre would be complete without a reference to the defence role allotted to it when the invasion of this country appeared imminent. The I.T.C. Commanding Officer was given command of an area which roughly corresponded to West Suffolk and included several aerodromes and many areas in every respect suitable for the landing of an enemy airborne force. The force at his disposal for its defence was mainly from his own men of over eight weeks' training; but transitory units quartered in the area came under his command periodically. Later in the war, Bury St. Edmunds became a "Nodal Point" with Lieut.-Colonel H. R. Gadd as its Commander.

One of the most obvious landing grounds for an enemy force was the well known Lime Kiln Gallops at Newmarket; an ideal place for gliders.

Superior authority directed that this area should be trenched, and dotted its "i" and crossed its "t" by stating that an excavator would shortly be made available for this military precaution. Gadd broke the alarming news to the Clerk of the Course. The future of Newmarket as a training centre was at stake. The Senior Steward was called down from the North of England and the Jockey Club expressed the considered opinion that since England had not been invaded for a thousand years why should she be invaded now.

Fortunately this was one of the rare occasions when the universal shortage of equipment was a positive blessing. The officer in charge of the excavator was spoken to on the telephone and it was found that his instrument of destruction was booked for at least a year. The Newmarket gallops continued to be the training centre for racing, as vital to the Nation as any other training centre. Higher authority were placated with tree trunks laid across the gallops.

In due course a local Command was formed and was responsible for all such matters dealing with the defence of the locality, the Infantry Training Centre being relieved of all responsibility.

A re-organisation of Infantry Training Centres was made in July, 1942. Many depots throughout the country were given up; Regimental Depots were amalgamated. In September, 1941 the Bedfordshire and Hertfordshire Regimental I.T.C. arrived from Kempston Barracks, Bedford, to form No. 3 I.T.C. with our existing I.T.C., Lt.-Colonel H. R. Gadd continuing in Command of this combined I.T.C.

At first separate Companies of the two Regiments were maintained, but eventually the two Regiments trained as one unit, an arrangement that in no way stultified the pride that each had in its Regimental name and traditions. The best of good feeling united all ranks of both Regiments, not only under Lt.-Colonel H. R. Gadd, D.S.O., M.C., but under his very efficient successor, Lt.-Colonel G. A. Anstee, M.C., the Bedfordshire and Hertfordshire Regiment.

In the long course of a Regiment's History, occasional enduring friendships, and sometimes enmities, are found with other Regiments. Often the reasons for these ties have long been forgotten, though the link still holds. The seed of a lasting friendship between The Suffolk and The Bedfordshire and Hertfordshire Regiments was planted at Bury St. Edmunds during these war years, due in large measure to the wise leadership of Lt.-Colonel G. A. Anstee.

THE SOLDIER.

There were two fine representatives of the best Suffolk soldiers in the Quartermaster, Capt. F. W. Garrard, who came to the Depot from the First Battalion after Dunkirk, and the Regimental Sergeant Major, J. Chalk, M.M., who served there throughout the war. The 80,000 men who during the course of the war joined the Army at Bury St. Edmunds, graduated in the elements of soldiering, and passed thence to units and formations, all learnt something of what makes the British Army from these two men.

Mention in this chapter has been made of the Regimental Officers during the twenty years' peace and the potential reserve for war. The chapter can conclude with a note on the men who filled the Depot from the day of mobilization.

How did Churchill's Army in the raw state compare with Kitchener's? Lt.-Colonel H. R. Gadd, D.S.O., M.C., who had first hand experience of both Armies and is well qualified to express an opinion gives the palm to Churchill's Army. He considers the "Volunteers" who came forward in such numbers at the outset of the war in 1914 contained a larger proportion of men who failed to make good than the "Conscripts" of 1939.

The concensus of opinion in this country is in favour of the volunteer to the pressed man—for any employment; the general feeling being that the paid man does no more than he must, while the volunteer does all that he can. In any case the above opinion is a tribute to the quality of the men of 1939, who represented a fair cross section of national life.

No fair comparison of Churchill's Army with Kitchener's could be made after the recruits had joined and been trained. There was no doubt the former were far superior in every particular. Gadd commenting on the Churchill Army recruits says: "The 'minuses' were largely outnumbered by the 'averages' and the 'pluses' and so not only rarely showed up, but were actually carried along to better things. They hardly ever scrimshanked, in fact they felt shame when their physical disabilities prevented their doing what others had accomplished."

Two factors helped to make Churchill's Army the undoubted superior to Kitchener's. One was Battle Training, in which must be included a vastly improved physical training; the other was the introduction of Personnel Selection.

In Battle training every man was subjected to a graduated course of battle fighting. At first there were only noises and squibs; but those soon gave way to near misses from bullets and heavy explosive charges—and the bullets did not always miss. This training was carried out with the appropriate degree of fatigue, dirt and squalor, which would have been appropriate to the battle field. Every man knew what to expect, and better still, what his reactions would be in the real thing; what he must do to master them.

The Personnel Selection System played its part in another way. The recruit was given a series of intelligence tests followed by an interview with a Personnel Selection Officer—"Crystal Gazers" as they were called by the soldiery. On the results it was decided how a man could best be employed in the Army. Both the American and the German Army had long since adopted this system with good results. But apart from the advantage to the Army, the psychological effect on the recruit was great. He felt that a personal interest was being taken in him and that his personal value was such that it must not be misapplied. The result was a happier, more enthusiastic, soldier.

But there was one outstanding weakness. Other Corps demanded special qualifications for their intake; what was left went to the infantry. After the demand for possible infantry officers had been deducted, few outstanding men remained for future infantry N.C.O.s.

At the Depot the recruit joins a great soldier family to which he will belong not only during the years he serves with the Colours, but for the rest of his life. The training at the Depot will be common to the rest of the Army, but the Regimental Badge on the recruit's buttons is his own

OFFICERS, 1ST BATTALION, AUGUST, 1939. *Photo—Gale & Polden.*

Back Row—2nd Lt. W. J. Calder, 2nd Lt. E. T. Lummis, Lt. R. de Z. Manser, 2nd Lt. F. A. V. Roberts, Lt. W. D. Gordon, Lt. J. W. Tyndale.
Centre Row—Capt. E. A. Pickard Cambridge, Capt. S. D. G. Robertson, Lt. C. A. Boycott, Lt. R. P. Newcomb, Lt. P. S. W. Dean, 2nd Lt. R. J. Hildesley, Capt. E. H. Gregory Capt. K J. K. Pye.
Front Row—Lt. and Q.M. F. W. Garrard, Capt. F. A. Milnes, Lt. Col. V. C. Russell, D.S.O., M.C., Capt. W. A. Heal (Adjutant), Lt. Col. E. H. W. Backhouse (C.O.), Col. W. N. Nicholson, C.M.G., D.S.O. (Colonel, the Suffolk Regiment), Major E. G. Fraser, Major A. A. Johnson, M.C., Major R. H. Maxwell, Capt. R. N. Charrington, Capt. R. E. Goodwin.

inheritance ; he is taught the stories of the battle honours on the Colours and when he joins one or other Battalion he has his own personal pride in his Regiment.

Field Marshal Lord Wavell writes:—"However good and well trained a man may be as an individual, he is not a good soldier till he has become absorbed with the corporate life of his unit and has been entirely imbued with its traditions.

"I think it is arguable that soldiers oftener fight well because they have a good leader than because they have a good cause. I am sure they fight best of all when they are part of a good unit and feel it.

"I have never believed in the formation of Commandos picked from a number of units. I believe that a complete living unit, taken and trained for the special work required, with the elimination, if necessary, of the weaker men, would produce better results."

This belief was amply borne out by the two units that made the backbone of Wingate's "Phantom Army" in Burma. We also in the Suffolk Regiment have an example in the 7th Battalion Suffolk Regiment that became the 142nd Regiment R.A.C. Their renown was due in a great degree to their Suffolk Traditions.

Yet in the war that has ended the Regimental System, though in theory approved by the Authorities, in practice was not possible.

Never before has the Regimental system been so undermined or made so difficult to work; yet it emerged as the one unalterable rock in a sea of change. The Regimental system flourished and held firm because all ranks approved it. Their loyalties were unshaken, the older soldiers to their Regiment, the younger to their Battalion.

The difficulty of conforming to a peacetime organisation, far too limited in scope to deal with a world war ; the formation of innumerable and unforeseen units to cope with new situations ; the control of armies in many theatres throughout the world—are all big excuses. But the fact remains that infantry is supreme in battle and the supremacy of British infantry is due to its Regimental system.

CHAPTER TWO.

FIRST BATTALION.

SEPT. 1939 — JAN. 1945.

The first months of the War—The German Offensive—Allied Advance into BELGIUM—Allied retreat from BELGIUM—From the SCHELDT to DUNKIRK—DUNKIRK—Moves in England and Scotland—Training—The Soldier—The Battalion—The Battalion Commander.

THE FIRST MONTHS OF WAR.

The First Battalion, the Suffolk Regiment, returned to England from MALTA in July 1939. It landed at SOUTHAMPTON and was stationed at DEVONPORT where two months later Lt.-Colonel E. H. W. Backhouse handed over the command to Lt.-Colonel E. G. Fraser on August 27th.

As the months passed it became increasingly clear that our Statesmen would be unable to avert war and on the 1st September orders to mobilize were received. A week later the Battalion moved to the 3rd Divisional Concentration area at AXMINSTER where it formed part of the 8th Infantry Brigade in the 3rd Division—a formation it was to remain with throughout the war. Major-General Montgomery, later to become Field Marshal Sir Bernard Montgomery, commanded the Division, "the Iron Division", one of the finest formations in the British Army. Among the infantry Battalions of the Division, the First Suffolk proved itself second to none.

On mobilization a large proportion of the men were Reservists, and there was an air of a family re-union. September was well spent in shaking down, and included some strenuous training. General Montgomery carried out the first of those hard and realistic exercises which, regardless of weather, were to tune the army up to a high pitch of training. During September, His Majesty the King visited the Battalion.

The Battalion remained at AXMINSTER until 1st October, a valuable breathing space, for it enabled the officers, many of them from the reserve, to get to know their men, while the reservists who had joined could brush up their training. The Signal Platoon for example had but nine men and received fifteen reservists. But the time was all too short to do more than shake down into a workable unit; many of the men had never seen a Bren gun or an anti-tank rifle, while the Anti-tank platoon only came into existence on Mobilization. Fortunately there were to be many months available for training in France.

During the first week in October the Battalion embarked on the s.s. "Bruges" at SOUTHAMPTON and landed at CHERBOURG; the M.T. going from PLYMOUTH to BREST.

At CHERBOURG was first felt that air of unreality that was to hang over the Expeditionary Force until the Germans struck on May 10th, 1940. There were few signs of war, and the Battalion moved peacefully by rail to the

HIS MAJESTY VISITS 1ST BATTALION, 1939.

Left to right—CPL. W. F. JENNER, ——————— ————, R.S.M. H. R. COTTON, HIS MAJESTY KING GEORGE VI., LT.-COLONEL E. G. FRASER, COMMANDING 1ST BATTALION.

A GROUP OF WARRANT OFFICERS AND SERGEANTS, 1ST BATTALION, B.E.F., 1940.

Left to Right—Sgt. Fitzpatrick, C.S.M. Pearson, Sgt. Wade, Sgt. Wilding, B/Sgt. Upson, C/Sgt. Mawby, Sgt. Ellis, C.S.M. Attmore, Sgt. Ward, R.S.M. Cotton, Sgt. Bacon, Sgt. Blowers, P.S.M. Baker, Fitter Sgt. Squires (R.A.O.C.), D/Major Wilson, Sgt. Leigh, P.S.M. Gant, Sgt. Gooderham, P.S.M. Daley, Sgt. Isaacson.

Concentration area of the Second Army Corps, ST. OUEN, about one hundred miles south-west of PARIS. Thence on the 12th October it moved forward to take over a sector of the French frontier defences on the R. SAAR in the LILLE area; Battalion H.Q. being at PERONNE with one Company forward.

While in this area the Battalion was visited by His Majesty the King; and later by the Commander-in-Chief, Lord Gort.

In January, 1940, the 8th Brigade took over a Battalion sector of the French Army outposts to the MAGINOT Line, in the neighbourhood of HALSTROFF, about 25 miles North-East of METZ.

The cold was intense, and the country snowbound. The positions consisted of very inadequate sandbag posts and occasional trenches; but the frost made any improvement impossible. There was some half-hearted shelling, and some active patrolling, under Lieut. Eliot, the Battalion Patrol Officer.

But, again, an air of unreality. Those who visited the great MAGINOT forts were impressed with the feats of engineering and ingenuity; but conceptions of depth and of treating the Great Line as a basis for manoeuvre seemed to be lacking. All the French troops wore a badge; "Ils ne passeront pas". Some British troops accepted it as a souvenir; others postponed acceptance.

Nevertheless, experience was gained. Men felt the eeriness of a deserted countryside. They learned the sounds of shells, the effects of airbursts, the tenseness of patrolling, and first reactions to an occasional German patrol or snipers. Above all—how to live in the open in the snow, and how to march by night on ice-covered roads.

Apart from the period spent on the SAAR front in January, the Battalion remained in and around BOUVINES until May. Although strenuous exercises were held periodically, units were mainly employed, day in, day out, in constructing what came to be known as the "Gort Line". When the Force eventually fell back on this line, after its advance to the RIVER DYLE in May, 1940, the situation had so deteriorated that only a matter of hours was spent there, before a further withdrawal.

It was a period of great monotony, relieved by seven days leave to England, expeditions to LILLE and the kindness of the French people on whom troops were billeted.

During daylight, most men—jerkined and muffled—dug, splashed, sand-bagged and revetted. No. 1 Platoon at last drained its trenches; No. 2 promptly flooded as a result. Spy scares abounded, as did spies. Farmers explained that in France, rabbits were game, not vermin; difficult this for the Suffolk men to live up to. Madame gave a party for the men in her billet, Monsieur pleaded against a change round of billets; No. 3 Platoon were his garçons. Marianne, aged 6, was spoiled. Yes, they hoped to put in a hot water system; but better wait and see if the Bosches came—a frequent and ominous theme, this. Field of Fire or no Field of Fire, the tree must NOT be cut down; the Bosche had cut down too many trees in the last war. To-morrow's leave train cancelled. To-day's mail late. Hot baths at the nearest coalmine—20 miles in the rain. Gracie Fields, the singer, in LILLE.

But, chiefly, MUD—and RAIN. All the factors present to undermine morale. But, to the eternal credit of the soldier, morale did not lower; discipline did not deteriorate.

Roll of Officers Serving with the First Battalion.
31st December, 1939.

Bn. Headquarters

Lt.-Colonel E. G. FRASER	...	Commanding Officer
Major A. A. JOHNSON, M.C.	...	Second in Command
Capt. W. A. HEAL ...	...	Adjutant
Lt. J. S. H. SMITHERMAN	...	Intelligence Officer
Lt. & QM. F. W. GARRARD	...	Quartermaster.
Rev. P. W. CATO ...	...	Chaplain
Lt. E. A. SPARKS ...	...	Medical Officer
H. R. COTTON ...	...	R.S.M.

H. Q. Company.

Major F. A. MILNES ...	...	Commanding Company
Capt. W. D. GORDON ...	...	M.T.O.
Lt. E. G. W. BROWNE ...	...	Signal Officer
Lt. R. P. NEWCOMB ...	...	Carrier Platoon

"A" Company.

Major J. W. JOSSELYN ...	...	Commanding Company
Lt. D. J. ARGENT		
Lt. R. T. BARTON		

"B" Company.

Bvt. Major E. A. PICKARD CAMBRIDGE		Commanding Company
Capt. K. C. MENNEER		
2/Lt. F. A. V. ROBERTS		

"C" Company.

Major R. H. MAXWELL ...	...	Commanding Company
Lt. G. N. R. STAYTON		
2/Lt. M. G. ELIOT ...	...	Fighting Patrol

"D" Company.

Major L. J. BAKER, M.C.	...	Commanding Company
Capt. R. W. BURKIS		
2/Lt. L. G. OSGERBY		

1st Reinforcements.

Lt. A. J. A. LACY
Lt. A. S. D. DIGBY

Among the above Roll of Officers were six destined to command Battalions of the Suffolk Regiment during the War:—Johnson, Milnes, Josselyn, Maxwell, Baker and Menneer.

It had been a wet autumn, a very cold winter, a mild spring. Writing within two months of arrival one soldier passes the censor with:—

"Having arrived somewhere in France and seen some other places in France, we are now at a place in France. It is a very muddy place, and "C" Company's part of it is particularly muddy. We have begun, however, rather to like our mud, and we take a reasonable pride in showing round our mud those who live further behind. It is real mud—not mere earth

A GROUP OF OFFICERS, 1ST BATTALION, B.E.F. *Crown copyright reserved.*

Left to Right—French Interpreter, Lt. G. N. R. Stayton, Lt. E. G. W. Browne, Lt. R. P. Newcomb, Lt. W. D. Gordon, Lt. A. J. A. Lacy, Capt. and Adjutant W. A. Heal, Capt. (Qr. Mr.) F. W. Garrard, Major L. J. Baker, M.C., Lt. Col. E. G. Fraser (C.O.)

and water; it sticks to one's shovel, works its way into our systems, and provides both the strong men and the wags of the Company with plenty of material to sling.

The great majority of our Company are Reservists, and they have not lost their touch for digging, marching and cheerfulness, under conditions which might well try lesser men.

Wherever we have been, the French people have been extraordinarily kind to us, and we are very grateful."

Another wrote:—

"By this time all the troops should be able to go back into 'civi street' as qualified navvies, owing to the fact that we have already dug up half of France. The spirits of the Platoon are kept high by the humorous remarks and entertainments given by Dyre. Very pointed sometimes."

Within two months of arriving in France the main topic was leave home to England.

Christmas 1939 was celebrated by all ranks in time honoured fashion, the intense cold being at least partially tempered by the much appreciated "comforts" from the organisations sponsored by the Lord Lieutenant of Suffolk and Mayor of BURY ST. EDMUNDS.

A letter from "B" Company says:—

"Greetings! everywhere to everyone. The sun is shining, Spring is in the air, Sam has a glamour overcoat, and I have just heard there is a rum issue, so you see it isn't such a bad war after all.

We welcome heartily all those young lads that have recently joined us. It is certain they will agree it is not a bad life when once they have settled in. Especially do we welcome the new officers, and trust their stay with us will be one of length and very pleasant.

Life here is much the same as it has been all along. Our billets are good and now the spring flowers are on show it gives us the feeling we are in our own country. The people here are very friendly and obliging. Most of the Company have had their first leave and it has proved a good tonic. Congratulations to those that entered into marital bliss and took unto themselves a wife whilst on leave". Many of them did.

No doubt the High Command had not been idle as the winter months passed. But it was the Germans who struck.

THE GERMAN OFFENSIVE.

The plan and execution of this tremendous attack is so well known that it will not be necessary to do more than recount its main outlines and then detail the share the First Battalion took.

It was a skilful plan carried through with German resolution and thoroughness. There were many after the Great War of 1914/1918 who believed that when the next totalitarian war came the blow would be unheralded, a bolt from the blue. It happened now against BELGIUM and HOLLAND. There may be arguments in favour of such action when countries stake their future existence on aggression. But there can be no argument in favour of the brutality and treachery that accompanied the German assault on the practically defenceless LOW COUNTRIES. Fifth Columnists in HOLLAND had been bribed to sow dissension, while the great cities were terrorised by bombing. All was over in HOLLAND within five days.

But this sudden and complete defeat of HOLLAND was only incidental to the main German plan of campaign. It did no more than divert attention from the point that had been chosen for the decisive attack.

According to Plan "D" that had been made to meet an invasion the Allied forces pushed forward their left wing to join up with the Belgian Army under King Leopold, which stood along the MEUSE and the ALBERT Canal. But as the Allies arrived the Belgians were being forced back; LIEGE had been isolated; NAMUR was invested and the Germans were sweeping on to BRUSSELS.

Meanwhile the main German blow was being delivered on the stretch of the River MEUSE that runs South from NAMUR towards the Western end of the MAGINOT Line. This attack was overwhelmingly successful. The Allied Command had not believed that the difficult ARDENNES country would be chosen as a line of attack. Indifferently trained and badly led troops were entrusted with the defence of this Sector. River bridges were captured intact, the enemy coming forward with innumerable tanks, supported by swarms of dive-bombing aeroplanes and followed by a great force of motorized infantry units.

On May 19th General Weygand took over supreme command from General Gamelin; but the battle was already lost. The Germans had reached the River OISE; they were in BRUSSELS. The bulge became a rent and the enemy mechanized forces swept like a scythe round the open flank into the rear of the Northern armies. The French centre hurriedly attempted to rally on the line of the Rivers AISNE and SOMME. At first it was hoped that they could counter-attack from here; but events proved that the magnificent "elan" for which the French had once been world famous, no longer existed.

There was worse to come for the British Expeditionary Force, for on May 28th King Leopold ordered the capitulation of his army. BOULOGNE and CALAIS were already in German hands. The Northern road to DUNKIRK, the last port, was open to the enemy's advance.

The Germans were now confident that with overwhelming force by land and air the annihilation of the British Army was assured. But from all available ports in England came every boat that could steam or sail; and this invincible armada, so typically British, carried back to England the vast majority of their comrades.

THE ALLIED ADVANCE INTO BELGIUM.

During these events the horizon of the First Suffolk was bounded by the marches, the counter-marches and the battles of the 8th Infantry Brigade. Officers and men at such a time may hear rumours, but know nothing; save what immediately affects them.

There was great enemy air activity over HOLLAND, BELGIUM and NORTHERN FRANCE on May 10th, the day Germany invaded HOLLAND. Plan "D" which had been made in anticipation of this enemy move was at once put into operation. The First Battalion was ordered to move by Mechanical Transport on Sunday afternoon, May 12th, to the neighbourhood of LOUVAIN.

WOLUWE ST. ETIENNE was reached by 0400 hours on the 13th May. The Battalion bivouacked here. The marks of the invasion were already visible. ALOST had been heavily bombed, and to avoid possible loss the 8th

Infantry Brigade moved by bye-roads South of the town. Mechanised units of the Belgian army who had already been in action told tales of heavy bombardments. Refugees streaming back to Brussels were passed; while the civilians in the town looked very depressed. It began to dawn on our men that the Germans must have made a considerable advance and could not be far away. Later on in the day they watched with horror German planes swoop down and machine gun the defenceless refugees, and this at a time when there were no troops or military vehicles of any kind on the road.

The advance was continued on the night 13th/14th May in pitch black darkness; the main BRUSSELS-LOUVAIN road was avoided on account of bombing and low flying attacks, but the side roads were not easy to locate. At one point the leading Company took a wrong turning up a sunken lane; the platoon 15-cwts. blocked the narrow track and it took an hour to reach the head of the Company and get it back on to the road again. At another point a Battalion of Belgian infantry withdrawing was met. This unit was headed by a line of men with fixed bayonets at the "On guard." It was on account of these delays that the tail of the Battalion did not get under cover in EIKEN BOSCH before daylight.

The 8th Infantry Brigade was now in Divisional Reserve behind LOUVAIN and the Battalion took up positions in the EIKEN BOSCH Wood. In the distance stood the spire of LOUVAIN Cathedral. But though the country seemed utterly peaceful there was not a soul to be seen working on the well kept fields; cattle had been turned loose and were roaming about in the wheat and arley. The wood occupied by the Battalion was full of Lilies of the Valley.

Yet far away could be heard the rumble of war; and reports came back that the Belgian Army was being hard pressed. Enemy planes came over and bombed the LOUVAIN-BRUSSELS Road; then shelling in the immediate neighbourhood commenced.

The 3rd Divisional Artillery were located near woods in the vicinity and the enemy were evidently searching for them. All were very "Gas minded" at this time; several men put on their respirators, detecting the unusual smell of bursting shells.

Heavy shelling in the South was heard throughout that night, and positions were manned on account of enemy pressure in that direction. By the morning of May 15th much digging had been done on this line, wire had been put up, Anti-tank guns were in position. With daylight enemy planes came over and our line was shelled. More trenches were dug, some to confuse enemy observers.

For the first time the usefulness of trenches was appreciated, and before long Battalion H.Q.s and H.Q. Company folk who had not considered trench digging as one of their duties, were hard at it with pick and shovel. The lesson "on arrival get underground" had been learnt. Men also learnt to judge from the sound of an approaching shell whether to take cover or not.

The cannonade continued throughout the night of May 14th/15th over on the right front. The enemy attacked here. He was pushed back. All next day the work went on and confidence grew; everyone believed that within two or three days the Battalion would be in a strong position.

And then the first rumours circulated that all was not well with our allies. The Brigade was to move. It was at first presumed that this would be forward. But news came that the 3rd French Army had given way in the ARDENNES and that the allied line must be straightened. The Brigade must fall back behind BRUSSELS.

THE ALLIED RETREAT FROM BELGIUM.

At 0100 on the 17th May the retirement commenced; necessitated by the retreat of the Belgian army on the left as well as by the enemy break through in front of the French in the Sedan area.

The First Battalion covered this withdrawal of the 3rd Division from an intermediate position at ETERRE BEEK; the remainder of the 8th Infantry Brigade retiring through the First Suffolk position. The only difficulties were the darkness of the night and the poor maps. Owing to short notice no daylight "recce" had been possible.

This was the first quick operational move carried out by the Battalion. All vehicles, and therefore baggage, were ordered to a rear rendezvous at an early hour, only 15-cwt. trucks being allowed up to the Battalion position. More than half the HQ mess gear, so carefully selected during training, was left behind!

The retirement continued through BRUSSELS, the Battalion halting on the West side of the city. Here a halt was made in some public gardens. It was a hot sunny day; the streets were full of civilians and it was plain they could not understand why the army was moving in a Westerly direction. But they were very generous with their gifts of all kinds from biscuits and cigarettes to bottles of wine. Except that some streets were covered with broken shop-window glass, where neighbouring bridges had been demolished, there was no suggestion that the enemy would be into the town that night.

At BRUSSELS the Battalion enbussed at 2100 hours and moved to LEEWE BRUSSE on the River DENDRE, arriving at 0200 hours on the 18th May. By 0800 hours a position on the river bank had been occupied.

Here, for the first time, the Battalion came into actual contact with the enemy. The latter made no attempt to cross the river; but early on the morning of 18th May their snipers were on the far bank. As in the EIKEN BOSCH shelling had quickly overcome the reluctance on the part of the men to dig, so snipers on the DENDRE gave our men their first lesson in not moving about carelessly in forward positions. Unfortunately, this lesson was not fully mastered until the Battalion occupied the River SCHELDT position.

On the early morning of the 19th May a further short withdrawal to a railway line 300 yards in rear was ordered.

This railway siding at LEEWE BRUSSE contained considerable quantities of military stores—trucks loaded with aeroplane engines and parts, three or four full petrol tanks. Orders were received that no destruction by burning was to be done lest an intention of withdrawing from the river should be disclosed; but the Pioneer Platoon under Sgt. Major Gant, succeeded in emptying the petrol tanks. The gutters and ditches by the roadside literally ran with petrol.

The original orders were to get away from the river DENDRE whilst it was still dark. The Divisional Commander, Major-General Montgomery, was anxious to move the Battalion during the night, as he anticipated a difficult situation by daylight; but in actual fact the Battalion had to hold the river until 0900 hours on the 19th May, and did so with light automatics only. At this hour the withdrawal continued, the river SCHELDT being reached by 1900 hours on the 19th May and a position occupied on the river by 0600 hours on the 20th May.

This retirement proved very hot and dusty. For a considerable time two enemy reconnaissance planes flew overhead directing artillery fire, until eventually shot down by our Hurricanes. There was a fifteen mile march before the lorries were reached; the men marched well and kept together, passing small parties of other units on the road; but they were very tired. The Battalion crossed the SCHELDT at OUDENARDE and then turned South concentrating near PECQ about 1900. That night, May 19th/20th, the Battalion took over a line from a unit of the 1st Division with two companies up, the right resting on PECQ (exclusive).

The transition of the countryside from Peace to War was unforgettable. The day on which the Battalion arrived on the River SCHELDT the local inhabitants had no idea war would be upon them so soon; they were carrying on with their normal daily tasks, the farmers in the fields, the women shopping and hanging out the washing, the shops doing their normal trade, the roads thronged with civilian motor-cars, cycles, horses and carts.

Early next morning all had warning and began to evacuate; later on in the day the traffic on the road changed from civilian to military vehicles of all sorts, a large number carrying troops to their new positions, with just one civilian car here and there. By midnight, all troops had been deposited. Next morning the whole district was uncannily quiet; no sound but the lowing of unattended cattle, the barking of dogs, and the singing of birds. The only people to be seen were soldiers digging: these gradually disappeared as their trenches deepened; and then all was still save an occasional officer or orderly visiting Companies. The following day enemy shelling commenced and soon the town of PECQ, some 300 or 400 yards from the SCHELDT, began to suffer. The Church spire was hit, the cross-roads grew choked with debris, houses near road junctions had gaping holes, windows broke, fires started up here and there, some burning fiercely, other belching black smoke; now and then petrol tanks caught fire and exploded.

During the withdrawal from the River DENDRE Major J. W. Josselyn Commanding "A" Company had been wounded. At the end of this account of the retreat will be found a letter from his Company Sgt. Major, G. E. Clarke, who gives the story of "A" Company during the actions that followed.

It was in the early morning of May 20th that Lt.-Col. E. G. Fraser commanding the Battalion was wounded and subsequently died. He had been forward with Capt. J. W. Trelawny, Commanding "B" Company, to reconnoitre the platoon positions, one of which, taken over in the dark, was found to be very exposed. Coming back from a front line section he was hit twice by a sniper. At 0600 he was back at his Battalion H.Q. in his car where he met Major F. A. Milnes. Fraser had been wounded in the head and leg and was concious. But he gave Milnes a clear picture of the situation before he was evacuated. He died on the way back to England. Major F. A. Milnes assumed Command of the Battalion.

The Valley of the SCHELDT where the Battalion was now in position was commanded on its western side by an escarpment some 80 feet high. The river itself ran close to the bank, except on the right of the Battalion sector where it made a loop, which at its farthest point was about ¾ mile from the escarpment. On this loop was a rectangular copse, 50 yards wide and 100 yards long, running out towards the river. The other side of the river was flat with plenty of cover for upwards of a mile; then the ground rose to a wooded summit with a tower overlooking the whole valley.

The Battalion had to stop the enemy crossing the SCHELDT and the line held by the forward Companies was along the escarpment. This gave them the advantage of overlooking any advance in strength towards the river; but a disadvantage against snipers. The enemy did not attempt to force a crossing but his snipers and sniping anti-tank guns caused many casualties, as did a very heavy barrage on the forward trenches. The enemy also fired hundreds of small Anti-tank shells at houses, probably believing that these had been fortified and that an ordinary bullet would not be able to penetrate.

The three days May 20th to May 23rd on the SCHELDT taught the Battalion what good observers the Germans were, and continued their lesson on the dangers of moving about a position in daylight. At our forward point of the river bulge were situated two posts manned by a section in narrow slit trenches. For several periods during the first day they were heavily mortared. The Company Commander expected to find casualties in the section when they were relieved at night; but not a man had been hit. A further lesson in the art of digging. But elsewhere enemy snipers took advantage of any movement they saw.

A temporary withdrawal by a unit on the right of our line threatened the Battalion position; fortunately the reserve Company positions were good; the Battalion right flank was better covered by fire than the actual river line.

While holding this line of the River SCHELDT a Battalion "Farming" organisation was working well; where possible, one man was detailed to milk the cows, whose udders, owing to their being in "full milk," were soon streaming, another to collect the eggs, another to water and feed the cattle and poultry. The Battalion butcher was employed to kill a pig, steer or calf; this variety in messing was much appreciated.

While the First Battalion is holding the line of the River SCHELDT from May 20th to May 23rd it will be as well to outline the situation which developed and was to end so dramatically at DUNKIRK.

"Plan D"—the counter stroke that was to turn the tables on the German invasion of Holland and Belgium, was foredoomed to failure. The French were no longer the great military nation that had once dominated Europe. The Belgians were no match for the Germans. At no stage before the capitulation of these two countries did their armies show any sign of being able to hold, let alone counter-attack the victorious advances of the enemy. An Allied defeat was inevitable from the moment "Plan D" was put into operation.

But the British army, confident in itself, was unaware of the weakness of its allies. They constantly believed that the successive lines they fell back to would be stabilized and that at the right moment they and their allies would advance and drive the Germans back. There was never any defeatism in the ranks of the British Army.

"Plan D" had been put into effect on May 10th. On May 14th Lord Gort reports serious news from the River MEUSE. By May 16th there was no longer any doubt that the Plan had failed. As we have seen orders for the withdrawal to the SCHELDT were issued; the British Army holding in succession the lines of the Rivers Senne and Dendre, and establishing itself by the night of 18th/19th May on the River Scheldt.

During this retirement the 'Bulge' over the Meuse had become a break-through opposite the French in the neighbourhood of the Forest of Mormal. On May 18th the Germans were at Amiens. On May 20th elements of their army had reached Abbeville and the break between the Allied Armies in the North and South was complete. The British Army had lost its bases—supplies for the future had to be improvised through the Channel ports.

On May 21st Lord Gort, the British Commander-in-Chief, made an attempt to cut the German corridor that separated the Allies in the North from the French armies in the South. A most gallant attempt; but there was only half-hearted co-operation from the French and the result was failure. The Northern armies became dependent on the ports of Zeebrugge, Ostend, Nieuport, Dunkirk, Calais, Boulogne. But that night, on May 21st, it was decided that the Belgian army must fall back on the line of the Yser and therefore Zeebrugge, Ostend, and Nieuport were cut out. On May 21st Boulogne was under fire; on May 23rd Calais was isolated.

Dunkirk alone remained for the provisioning or the evacuation of the Armies.

On May 23rd the British Army was placed on half rations; while petrol and ammunition had to be most carefully husbanded.

The perimeter on the River Scheldt held by the Northern Armies to cover their lines to the Channel Ports stretched some 125 miles; but on the night 26th/27th May it was decided to shorten this by withdrawing to the line of the River Lys and thereby save some 50 miles. This day, May 26th, the Belgians were heavily attacked and defeated; they capitulated and the gap caused on the left flank had to be hastily filled by the British.

On Sunday, May 26th, the evacuation of the fighting forces from Dunkirk began. The rearguard being embarked on June 1st.

There have been many notable re-embarkations of British Armies from foreign shores in face of overwhelming enemy forces; but here as never before in the History of England have the difficulties been so great or success so improbable. Sir John Moore in his retreat to Corunna had a safe harbour and a large fleet to fall back on. Now a shrinking shallow sandy shore, a long wooden mole at Dunkirk, no preliminary preparations, an undefeated and greatly superior enemy on land and in the air all weighed heavily against escape.

The Harbour of Dunkirk and the beaches need describing. Dunkirk harbour was completely wrecked by bombing. Nothing was available save the East Mole, and that had been and continued to be hit many times. This East Mole was a narrow pile plankway only wide enough for three men to walk abreast. It was not constructed for ships to berth alongside and it was exceedingly difficult for them to do so. Even when during the evacuation they had berthed, it was no easy matter for the men on the Mole to board the ship, and very difficult indeed to embark the large quantity of wounded who lay waiting on stretchers. Yet it is estimated that nearly 200,000 men marched along this plank way to safety. No praise is too high for the ships of small tonnage, and above all for our destroyers, who continued throughout the re-embarkation to lie alongside this Mole.

Along the DUNKIRK beach lay the little villages of MALO LES BAINS, BRAY DUNES, LA PANNE and COXYDE. The coast was low and flat, with a wide beach and a shallow foreshore that ran out for half a mile at low tide to a wide deep water channel that ran parallel to the coast. Beyond this channel lay more shallows—so that craft approaching the shore could not come direct but had to sail up the deep channel parallel to the coast thus greatly increasing their danger. The East Mole and the deep channel could take the comparatively bigger ships; but the beaches depended on the "Little ships."

By May 28th the "Little ship" flotillas were collecting at Home and were proceeding on their way to the rescue. In every river basin, in every port the little ships gathered and were made seaworthy after their long winter rest. From the river Estuaries and Ports they sailed to the DUNKIRK coast working either in the deep channel or between the channel and the shore. Meanwhile fresh flotillas of "Little Ships" were constantly moving up and down the coast to take the place of casualties—motor boats, pleasure boats, beach boats, life boats, barges, launches, lighters; every kind of boat.

May 28th was foggy with a minor gale blowing. May 29th the weather improved. On May 30th it was estimated that only 80,000 British troops remained within this shrunken perimeter. This day the weather was at its best, poor visibility, a calm sea. The whole beach was now lined with thousands of men, some of them up to their knees or waists in the water, waiting to be taken off. There was a high wind and a rough sea on May 31st. The Germans were close; the beaches were under shell fire. It has been said that of the many thousand craft that carried out the re-embarkation scarcely one escaped damage. On June 1st the rearguard embarked complete.

FROM THE SCHELDT TO DUNKIRK.

The position on the River SCHELDT was held from May 20th until 0300 hours on the 23rd May when the First Suffolk was retired to WATRELOS on the Belgian-French frontier.

There was nothing difficult about this withdrawal; but it was the first time the Battalion had broken off an engagement while in close contact with the enemy. It was therefore an anxious time until the covering carrier platoon had withdrawn over an intermediate canal and the bridge had been blown.

The new position was part of the line made by the French in 1937. There was an anti-tank ditch and a few pill boxes; but trenches had to be dug. Houses were at once sandbagged and once again all thought they would stand and fight. By this time the Battalion had mastered the technique of withdrawal. Reserves and Riflemen vacating their positions over a period of two or three hours, the Bren guns of forward platoons remaining to hold the line till the appointed time and then being brought back by M.T. covered by the Carrier Platoon Brens. But full tribute must be paid to the Sappers for the thoroughness of the demolitions which made these withdrawals so safe.

It was once again understood that the withdrawal had ended and that the enemy would be finally held on this frontier line. To emphasise this and to establish our supremacy on this new front before the enemy had time to build up his strength, an attack was ordered.

All three Battalions of the 8th Brigade took part in the operation which was directed to make good the line of the railway a mile to the front. "D" Company led, with "A" Company following to mop up and to ensure their safe withdrawal. The Carrier Platoon of the Battalion moved out to cover the right flank of the leading Company. Artillery support was only to be called for in an emergency and on the authority of the Division.

The First Suffolk on the right, and the R. Berks in the centre, came up against very considerable opposition and did not reach the railway. The East Yorks on the left met little opposition and reached their objective successfully.

"D" and "A" Companies of the Battalion crossed the open ground to their front; but when they got amongst the trees and in the village which lay between them and their objective, came under heavy mortar and close range automatic fire. From commanding ground on the right flank the enemy brought very heavy MMG fire on to the front from which the attack started and on to the open ground in rear of the attacking Companies. Artillery support to assist in the withdrawal of the Companies was asked for; but was not forthcoming. The Companies were not able to get back until darkness had come.

There may have been every justification for an operation of this nature; but from the accounts of those in the Battalion who took part it was badly "laid on" and the Battalion suffered severely in consequence. Captains R. W. Burkis, R. de Z. Manser and 2nd-Lt. L. G. Osgerby were wounded and missing. Captain D. J. Argent, 2nd-Lts. Taylor and McLaren were wounded and there were 69 Other Rank casualties. The Carrier Platoon suffered badly, four vehicles being lost. Officers and men of the Battalion, when they were finally evacuated to England, always spoke of this action with bitter regret; at no time throughout the retreat had they any doubt about their man to man superiority to the Germans; but here they felt lives were needlessly wasted.

At a Brigade Conference about midday 26th May it was made known that the B.E.F. was to be withdrawn to the coast and an attempt would be made to re-embark for the United Kingdom. Advance parties were ordered to be withdrawn forthwith. This was completely unexpected, and there was a deep sense of depression felt by those who listened to this order.

The Battalion was ordered to withdraw in its own M.T. Priorities of loading were: the men with their personal weapons and ammunition; unit weapons and equipment; important baggage. All the rest was to be jettisoned. There was, of course, only room for a small quantity of unit equipment and later Lt.-Col. F. A. Milnes greatly regretted that he didn't select signal equipment even at the expense of weapons.

At 2100 hours on the 27th May the Battalion withdrew as ordered to the line of L'YSER and took over this front from the 2nd Middlesex by 0600 hours on the 28th May.

The withdrawal to and occupation of the L'YSER was uneventful.

Except on one position, the Battalion had not been much affected by refugees, as was the case further behind the lines. At each new position the advance party found a certain number of the inhabitants had already departed. Those left were at once told that it was not advisable for them to stay as the position might become dangerous; they invariably replied that there could be no danger and they did not intend to move. But the arrival of the Battalion, the preparation of the ground for fighting, soon made up the minds of most, who left forthwith; the few remaining hastily departing as soon as enemy shells dropped in the vicinity.

At one place where the H.Q. Mess had just arrived one old lady was sitting with her small packages ready to leave. She was asked:—"Where are you going, Madame?" and her reply was, "I do not know, monsieur. A farm-cart is coming for me at 10 p.m.; we are taking enough food for three days; we have bedding with us; the men know the way as far as ROUBAI—and after that we must take our chance."

The usual scene at a country village was a farm-waggon being loaded with bedding and blankets, the women and children climbing on the top, and a farm hand leading the horses as the pathetic little assembly moved slowly off down the road. The Suffolk soldier looked after them and thought, "What will happen to them?" "How far will they get?" "Will their food last?"—and then "To hell with —— Boche!"

May 29th was a bad day. The position on L'YSER was quite strong provided the flanks held. Late in the morning the enemy put in a determined attack and succeeded in crossing the river on the right front of the Brigade. The R. Berks who were holding the right were pushed back; "B" company, the right forward company of the First Suffolk, withdrew in face of intense mortar and small arms fire, stragglers from "B" Company eventually taking up a position by advanced Battalion H.Q. The centre, "C" Company, had also been forced to withdraw to its left rear. "D" Company in reserve was ordered to counter attack; this was countermanded and this Company took up a position on the left of "B" Company with two carriers and odd men of the Battalion H.Q. to assist. Meanwhile "A" Company on the left had been forced to fall back and with "C" Company had joined the 2nd E. Yorks, the left Battalion of the Brigade.

During this fighting the enemy in front of the Battalion tried unsuccessfully to put an assault bridge across the river; as fast as one party of German sappers had been put out of action, fresh men took their places. A soldier speaking of this action said "We could not but admire the courage of the German sappers; but the German infantry did not appear so good. We experienced no difficulty in holding them."

Before this fighting had reached its height, the Second in Command, Major L. J. Baker, M.C. had gone back to "recce" the next position; while the Officer Commanding, Lt.-Col. F. A. Milnes, was at the Brigade H.Q. receiving orders for withdrawal; Brigade Headquarters was being shelled and the Brigade Commander had to run from one slit trench to another to give his orders to each Battalion Commander.

It was during this conference that information came in to say the enemy had crossed the River YSER on the R. Berks front.

When Lt.-Col. F. A. Milnes returned to his H.Q. he found the position serious. The Battalion had to hold on for at least another six hours. The enemy were through the right flank; the two forward platoons of "B" Company had been over-run. A section of the Second Middlesex MG's had withdrawn in accordance with their orders, but unknown to Milnes, from a house on the right flank, level with "B" Company's Headquarters.

The enemy could be seen from Battalion H.Q. well across the River on the right flank and were getting dangerously into the right rear. A defensive flank was at once formed extending from "C" Company, Centre forward Company, on the River YSER, through "D" in reserve, to which Company the remainder of "B" had withdrawn, thence through Battalion H.Q. to a farm in the rear occupied by "B Echelon". Fortunately on this line the Battalion was able to stay until it was time to go, though under persistent shelling and MMG fire.

It was here that the absence of Sig. Equipment was felt. It was difficult to get the orders for withdrawal to Company Commanders, or to get from them a clear picture of the changing situation.

From this line of the River YSER the Battalion was ordered back to the FURNES CANAL. At about 1830 hours on May 29th the Battalion began thinning out, until at 2030 hours only Bren gunners were left. Then these withdrew and embussed at rear Battalion H.Q. At this time the enemy was about 600 yards from our rear troops; but was disinclined to advance. The first part of the route of the retirement was heavily shelled and there were a number of casualties. One of the bridges on the road to FURNES was blown, it was said, by a shell hitting the charge set ready for blowing when we had all passed. Fortunately a Pontoon Bridge had been built alongside by the Div. R.Es. in case of such an emergency. There was a considerable block in the column; vehicles were three deep and nose to tail for two miles before the bridge. Many casualties to men and vehicles occurred here, the enemy artillery fire being extremely accurate; but had he known the state of affairs the losses would have been even heavier.

The Battalion had pulled out gradually that night 29th/30th May. Each Company, as it withdrew a truck load of men, sent it off to a rendezvous to the North of FURNES. The night was pitch dark and the road, especially through FURNES, was difficult to find. Nevertheless, when Lt.-Col F. A. Milnes reached the rendezvous at about 0300 hours he found his Second-in-Command Major L. J. Baker with practically all the Battalion.

The casualties for the day were:- 2nd Lt. F. A. V. Roberts killed, Lt. G. O. McIntosh (Medical Officer), 2nd Lts. M. G. Eliot and P. H. Almack wounded, with approximately 200 Other Ranks.

During the early hours of the 30th May the Battalion reached the FURNES CANAL, which ran inland from NIEUPORT and S.W. through the outskirts of FURNES. Here they were ordered to take over from a Battalion of the 4th Division. This proved a somewhat difficult operation for the ground was intersected with deep water ruts and the Officer in Command had not had time to see the whole of his front. Fortunately a brick kiln with a tall chimney stood in the centre of the Sector, and as it grew light orders for the occupation of the ground were based on this landmark. A quick reorganisation of Companies had to be made before moving off. This was done by combining "A" and "C" Companies under Captain K. C. Menneer to hold the canal on the left and "B" and "D" Companies under Capt. Anthony Lacy on the right; H.Q. Company, including all cooks and drivers, was in reserve.

The guides provided by the Battalion in occupation of the line did not know their way about; but the factory chimney came to the rescue;

by full daylight the Companies were on the canal and the relieved Companies were on their way to NIEUPORT.

During the day the Battalion was reinforced by one of the Divisional R.E. Field Companies under Major Henniker. Another Field Company under Major Drayson went to the R. Berks on the Battalion right. Henniker's Field Company was placed in reserve on the left of H.Q. Company. It was evident that the attenuated forward Companies lining the built up bank of the canal could not prevent a crossing if a determined attempt, well supported by Artillery and Mortar fire, was made. But from the reserve line, which occupied a good position, any enemy crossing could be stopped from advancing beyond the canal.

During the 30th May only light artillery fire was experienced; but by the early morning of the 31st May the whole Battalion front was subjected to heavy shelling. During the night the Battalion had been ordered to extend its front to the left to assist the 4th Division fighting in NIEUPORT. This extension resulted in a gap between the right and left companies and in this gap the enemy at 1100 hours succeeded in throwing a pontoon bridge and establishing a bridgehead. There was a temporary withdrawal on the right of the Battalion and a portion of the H.Q. Company in reserve, who had suffered from mortar fire, withdrew; but these were quickly rallied and collected by Major L. J. Baker and with every available man from Q.M. Staff, Signallers and others, the line was re-occupied and the enemy held.

During the remainder of the day, attempts were made to drive the enemy back over the canal. Though not successful he was pinned to his ground; but although his infantry did not attack he continued shelling with H.E. and mortars. Captain G. N. R. Stayton, Lieut. C. A. Boycott, and Lieut. A. S. D. Digby were wounded during this fighting.

It must be remembered that at this time almost all the Battalion M.T. had been discarded, ammunition replenishment was scarce, the only equipment left was that carried on the men.

By 1900 hours on the 31st May the fighting had died down and the front appeared to be stabilized. Orders were at this hour received to commence withdrawing to the beach at LA PANNE where boats were reported to be waiting to take off the troops.

DUNKIRK.

The plan for evacuation was as follows:- Canal to be held till 0200 hours 1st June. Thinning out to commence at 2000 hours 31st May. Companies to concentrate their men at a rendezvous behind Battalion H.Q. Here the half dozen trucks remaining were assembled to assist in the move back of the men to LA PANNE - those who could not be so transported being formed up to move back in parties of 20. At LA PANNE it was hoped to form the Battalion into bodies of 200, to hold them in the sand dunes until they could be embarked by the Divisional Embarkation Staff. Each man as he passed through Battalion H.Q. was to be given a tin of bully and a packet of biscuits.

All went smoothly, at about 0200 hours June 1st the last of the L.A.A. teams came through and a move was made at all speed to the beaches by

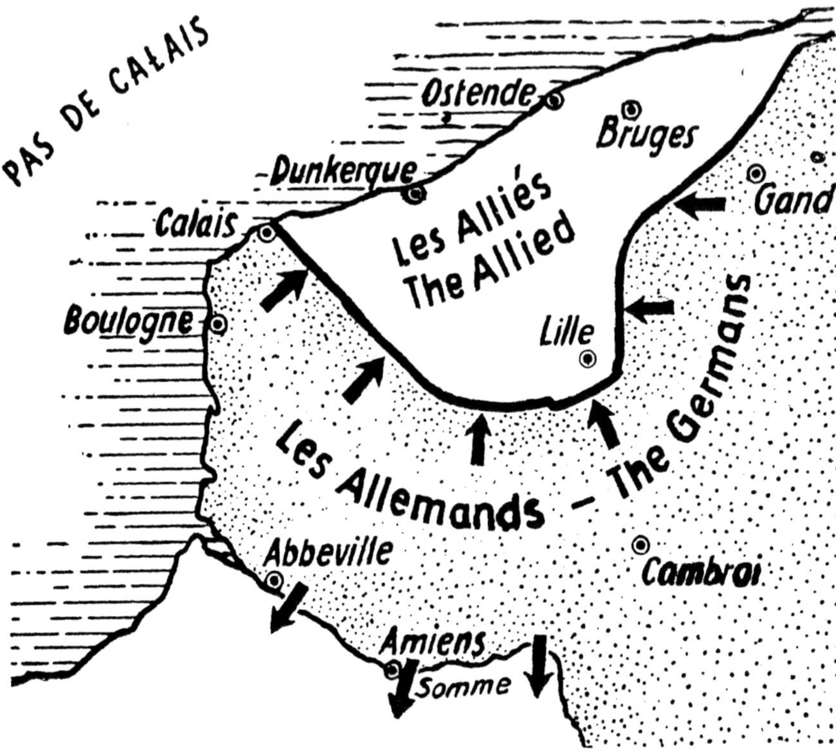

Camarades!

Telle est la situation!

En tout cas, la guerre est finie pour vous!

Vos chefs vont s'enfuir par avion.

A bas les armes!

British Soldiers!

Look at this map: it gives your true situation!

Your troops are entirely surrounded —

stop fighting!

Put down your arms!

A Leaflet dropped by The German Air Force in 1st Battalion area a few days prior to "Dunkirk."

Battalion Headquarters, the H.Q. Company and other companies having preceded them.

LA PANNE and the road to it were being systematically shelled. The town itself, full of abandoned vehicles, was burning fiercely. Ammunition lorries were exploding and it was a place to get through as quickly as possible.

At LA PANNE the Divisional Embarkation Staff had all been killed or wounded; but embarkation had been taking place and there was no difficulty in finding the embarkation point. The tide was out, and the water's edge some 500 yards from the dunes showed as a dark line. In the light just before dawn Lt.-Col. F. A. Milnes found thousands of men waiting quietly for boats.

Soon after it got light, enemy planes appeared and began to machine gun the beach and water's edge. They were met by terrific small arms fire from some 5,000 rifles. One of them was brought down into the sea, whether by rifle-fire or fire from the ships was difficult to say. Then several flights of enemy dive-bombers came over, and, although met by very heavy A.A. fire both from the shore and the ship's guns, succeeded in sinking or damaging a number of naval and merchant ships. Towards mid-day heavy bombers attacked the dock area at DUNKIRK. There were three destroyers taking men off in small boats from the shore, wounded mostly, and Lt. Col. F. A. Milnes noticed that there was no rush to overload the boats as they came in to the shore.

It was obvious that only a small fraction of the men could be got off before daylight. Milnes had been warned, but told not to include it in his orders, that embarkation at LA PANNE would cease at 0400 hours June 1st and that any remaining troops were to make their way to DUNKIRK. Bearing this in mind, as many men of the Battalion as possible were collected and set off along the sand dunes for DUNKIRK.

All were very tired and the march along the edge of the dunes seemed unending. However by keeping a slow pace and observing a ten minute halt every hour, the men kept well together.

At about 0800 hours a halt was made for an hour for breakfast, bully beef and biscuits and for some, hard-boiled eggs. Private Gent, the Commanding Officer's batman, producing a dozen out of the pack on his back.

While having breakfast this last remnant of the First Battalion had a grandstand view of a terrible though intensely exciting dive bombing attack on a destroyer. Four dive bombers circled overhead, then one after another peeled off to deliver their attack. The bombs could be seen leaving the aircraft, one large and four small. The destroyer below was taking violent avoiding action and the air was full of A A. shell bursts, every Pom-Pom which could be brought to bear was firing. Three of the aircraft missed their target, but scored close misses; the fourth hit the destroyer fair and square about the bridge. The ship took a list; but continued steaming in a small circle. Before our men had finally disappeared over the hills she was still afloat.

At about 1000 hours on 1st June this last party reached what they believed to be DUNKIRK; but Lt.-Col. F. A. Milnes going forward to enquire found it to be BRAY DUNES and that DUNKIRK was five miles further. Marching on they crossed the perimeter of the fortress of DUNKIRK and knew that they no longer need keep watching over their left shoulders for fear the enemy should be coming in to cut them off.

As they approached the outskirts of the town the beach was being shelled and a French Battalion which was lying up appeared to be suffering many casualties. As the party crossed the shelling ceased. Two of our sailors came along the front and said there was a ship lying at the mole, anxious to get some passengers and be off—the BEN MACREE. So, very thankfully, this last party of the First Battalion trooped on board, and sailed at about 1300 hours.

So the history of 1914 was repeated in 1939. The 2nd Suffolk in 1914 retiring from Mons was overwhelmed at LE CATEAU; the remnants, little more than a hundred men, retreating thence to the River MARNE, the 1st Suffolk in 1940 withdrawing but fighting hard on the SCHELDT, L'YSER and the FURNES CANAL until the remnants were evacuated from LA PANNE and DUNKIRK. Each of these retreats signified a great strategical victory by the enemy. In each he proved his undoubted superiority in his preparation for war, in the organisation and training which enabled his Commanders to sweep forward and to be in a position to gain decisive victory. In neither war did he gain that decisive victory, thanks to the courage and tenacity of our men. The British armies in 1914 and 1940 were rapidly driven back; but they were never routed. At the end of both retreats they were still undefeated.

In 1914, on the River MARNE; they turned joyfully to the offensive, and won a great victory. In 1940, the same fighting spirit prevailed. From the beaches of France they returned to the ports of England.

The railway stations through which the trains carried these men from the Kent ports were crowded with their fellow countrymen who welcomed the train loads as if a great victory had been won. Everywhere throughout the British Isles there was a feeling of the highest exaltation.

"If Hitler could see these men to-day, he'd know he never could win".

That was the thought uppermost in everyone that waved a hand. There were no doubters in this supreme moment.

History may well ask what possible justification existed for this optimism. Lt.-Col. F. A. Milnes, recounting the above events, speaks of lessons learned of German snipers and the carelessness of our men in walking about, of the neglect to dig. It is worthy of comment that when three years later the First Battalion landed on "D" Day in Normandy, as finely trained a Battalion as existed in the Army, they still ignored the sniper. Capt. Coppock writing of the men under his Command at this later period said: "Little was seen of the Germans in front of us. In fact, they don't go in for the habit, as we do, of strolling about casually in full view." But this great retreat brought out something far greater than these details; it proved once again that the British soldier will never accept defeat. To such victory must always eventually come.

The people of England, exulting in the escape of their men and acclaiming them as if they were victors, were not far from the truth. The record of the First Suffolk is a record to be proud of. They had a lot to learn, lessons that only war will ever teach the British soldier; they laughed and blamed themselves. They never belittled their enemy's courage or skill; but they never doubted for a moment their own superiority. Time after time they fortified lines, successfully held them, only to be withdrawn when success seemed assured. But they were never disheartened. They suffered very heavy casualties in all ranks; but invariably closed up and never lost their unit solidarity.

Throughout the retreat they exercised their fundamental sense of fun, and only grew indignant at any unfair play; their hatred of the German was always inflamed at the sight of helpless refugees. Truly the British soldier is a great fighting man, not to be beaten by anything that a man like Hitler can raise.

Sir Walter Scott wrote that to paint a picture of Battle you should 'get a great cloud effect as the first part of the process; and as the second paint here and there an arm or two, and here and there a leg and a body.' This record taken mainly from the personal accounts of the soldiers who took part in the Campaign aspires to no more. The following letter from C.S.M. G. E. Clarke, D.C.M. of "A" Company written after his return to England to his Company Commander, Major J. W. Josselyn, follows this rule of Sir Walter Scott's.

"Dear Sir,

"Following your casualty, Mr. Argent got us capably through some difficult withdrawals till the evening of Empire Day when we carried out a mad-brained scheme of attack, without supporting weapons, in which we lost two killed; Mr. Argent and Mr. Taylor and 14 others wounded. Mr. Argent had a nasty knee wound; but he was ever so cheerful about it and told us to get on with the job.

"Mr. Boycott took over and we had some very hurried moves and got a severe strafing with mortar fire on a canal. "B" and "C" Company Headquarters were in house which got shot up; but our H.Q. was in a trench where things were not so comfortable; but the trench saved us. After a short withdrawal we were ordered back. This trip was a bad one for me, Sir, having to cross several wide dykes. I was in a very fatigued state on reaching the rendezvous where we found the enemy already in possession; but we got out safely and made a damp but safe journey to a canal where we joined a composite Company of the Battalion.

"This new position seemed to get the same treatment from the enemy as the previous ones. Mr. Boycott got wounded in the foot; but managed to crawl back to R.A.P. first giving me instructions about our next move. We lost King, Steele and one other killed and several wounded. I got a message back to Battalion H.Q. saying I had no officers left, and what I had in mind to do and I had some difficulty in keeping some from getting panicky.

"Then Mr. Newcomb took over and he and I got the few that were left back the seven miles to the beaches at LA PANNE and from there one seemed to get into the sea and fend for oneself. I managed to make a boat with Mr. Newcombe and after being aboard two destroyers which were bombed and sunk, I reached DOVER.

"Of our original Company strength 57 have turned up and have just about reformed and re-equipped. The Orderly Room Sgt. has ascertained from me the Casualties; but I regret, Sir, that owing to the destruction of every Army Form by those behind us during our moves I am unable to give you any addresses of next of kin. Edwards has done something in regards to King as I understand he lives near his old folks.

"Well, Sir, I cannot say whether this letter will give you much information, but I have sat and thought for quite a while and I sincerely hope it will give you an insight of what we have been doing.

"There is just one other thing. The 'Pickup' was eventually scuttled following a straffing and the balance of the imprest account went with it, and there is Flatman here concocting a story as to its whereabouts for the benefit of the Command Paymaster."

Company Sgt. Major G. E. Clarke was awarded a most well deserved D.C.M. for his share during this retreat. His citation read:— "For continuous good conduct and coolness." It was a most popular award.

Space does not permit of mentioning the many who distinguished themselves in the retreat; but an exception must be made for Major L. Baker, M.C.

'Louis' Baker had served with special distinction in the Regiment during the war 1914/1918; but he was old for his place on the regimental list, and in 1937 had to retire when he reached the age limit for Captain, which was then 45. He was back again with the Regiment in 1939, and none was more welcome. Modesty personified, his character on Service was a tower of strength to all. Unassuming, diffident in manner, yet he impressed his very strong personality on all with whom he came in contact. He gave invaluable support to Lt.-Col. F. A. Milnes during this most difficult retreat, and proved an ideal Second in Command. Later he was to prove an equally great Commanding Officer when he was promoted to command the Fifth Suffolk, fated to be captured at Singapore.

MOVES IN ENGLAND AND SCOTLAND.

So the First Suffolk came home, and almost at once were concentrated at FROME in Somerset, moving from there on the 5th June to CUCKLINGTON; here the Battalion Headquarters worked in no more than two rooms and a cupboard, an inconvenience that did not unduly trouble them, at this time.

Many were the tales of how individual soldiers had been billeted up and down the peaceful countryside during the brief breathing space after they had been landed and transported inland. No one could say enough for the kindness with which they had been received by the civil population. Before rejoining in Somerset there was a forty-eight hours' leave—and in the opinion of all it was worth a pound a minute.

Then without further delay reorganization and re-equipment was pushed forward. Drafts of 150 Suffolk, 150 Essex and 50 Bedfordshire and Herts. arrived from Bury St. Edmunds and elsewhere; N.C.O.s were exchanged with the Territorial Battalions of the Regiment. Despite differences in age, service and experience the Battalion proceeded forthwith to shake down into a well knit and extremely happy unit. With their nucleus of veterans they considered they could march, shoot and dig with the best. They were intent on once again facing the Hun, and proving it.

But four long years were to elapse before this wish was gratified. Four years during which the role of the 3rd Division to which they belonged changed from an anxious defence to a most carefully prepared but hazardous overseas landing. On an average they shifted their Station every two months;

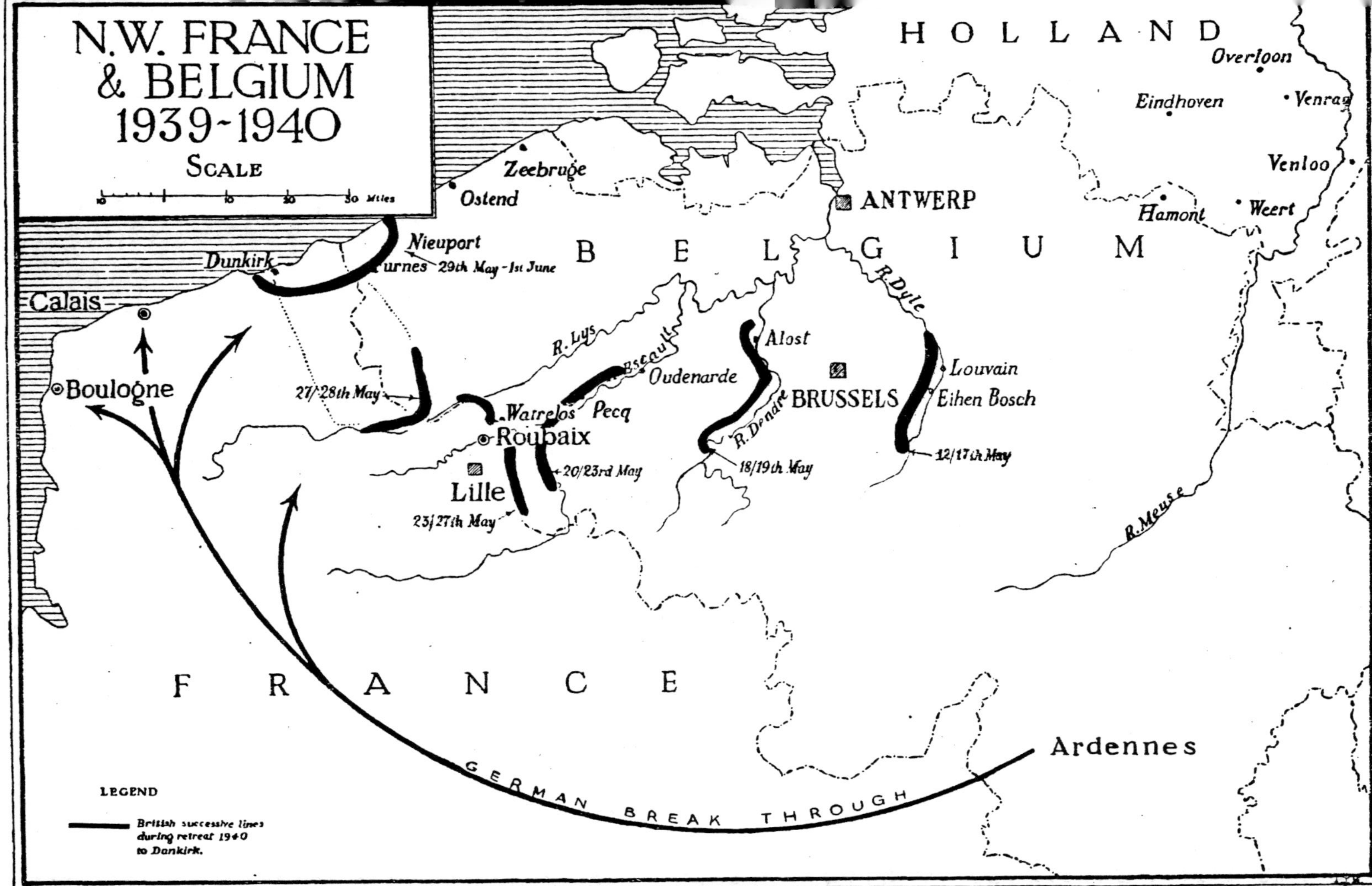
N.W. FRANCE
& BELGIUM
1939-1940
SCALE
10 0 10 20 30 Miles
HOLLAND
Overloon
Eindhoven
Venray
Venloo
Hamont
Weert
Zeebrugge
Ostend
ANTWERP
BELGIUM
Nieuport
Furnes 29th May - 1st June
Dunkirk
Calais
Boulogne
R. Dyle
Alost
Louvain
Eihen Bosch
BRUSSELS
R. Dendre
12/17th May
18/19th May
R. Lys
R. Escaut
Oudenarde
Pecq
Watrelos
Roubaix
Lille
27/28th May
20/23rd May
23/27th May
R. Meuse
FRANCE
Ardennes
GERMAN BREAK THROUGH
LEGEND
British successive lines during retreat 1940 to Dunkirk.

and throughout the four years there was a continual change of personnel, officers, N.C.O.s and men coming and going in a constant stream. And as year succeeded year the tempo of the training almost unconsciously increased.

In 1940 there seemed every probability that England would be invaded; there were many of sound judgment who believed an invasion could succeed if the enemy was prepared to sacrifice men in the overseas attempt. If the German established a bridgehead, however small the invading force might be, it would have been opposed by a phantom defender only. During the first few months no defensive army was in existence.

For many months long strips of the Southern Coast of England:—SWANAGE, WEYMOUTH and later FOLKESTONE, were among the localities entrusted to the First Suffolk for defence. Then, as the fighting value of other Home defence units increased, the Division was employed on more concentrated training.

An itinerary of the moves of the First Battalion during these four years at home is of interest. In June 1940 they moved from SOMERSET to SUSSEX to WOOLBEDING, WISPERS, STEDHAM and TROTTON. In August to WEST GRINSTEAD with a visit to the STANWAY area in GLOUCESTERSHIRE. September saw them at CHEDDAR, AXBRIDGE and WINSCOMBE. But in November 1940 they came south to WEYMOUTH moving from there to SWANAGE in June 1941. By this time the 3rd Division was once again a fine fighting formation, practised over long distances in Divisional operations. "Exercise BUMPER" saw the Battalion operating with the 3rd Division as far away as HOUGHTON REGIS, BEDFORD.

But in November 1941 the Battalion was once again on the move, this time to WELWYN Garden City which was by no means so popular a station as those left. In March 1942 the Battalion was housed at BEACONSFIELD, short of men on account of the many drafts despatched to other units, including the 4th and 5th Suffolk Battalions.

May 1942 saw the first journeys to Scotland which were to continue till "D" Day. During the next two years they visited INVERARY, CARRON BRIDGE, DUMFRIES, DORLAN and NAIRN for long and short periods. It was during these visits that they practised embarking and disembarking on an open coast.

In June 1942 the Battalion came South to MAIDENHEAD and then on to the ISLE of WIGHT, and December that year to FOLKESTONE. It was while the Battalion was at FOLKESTONE that it was equipped with its 6 pounder Anti-Tank guns. It was here, too, that it received an order to mobilize, later to be cancelled. For a time it was possible that the 3rd Division would be employed on the DIEPPE raid.

In 1943 the Battalion was for the most part in Scotland, with a visit to PEMBROKE DOCKS in order to gain experience in working with tank formations.

The last move of the First Battalion was from Scotland to HORNDEAN in Hampshire, preparatory to embarking for "D" Day.

As our own invasion day approached, Scotland became the pivot for land and sea exercises. The pattern was blurred by uncertainty throughout all the four long years. The probability of enemy invasion slowly faded; but later there was a possibility that the Division might be employed in the

Dieppe Raid or sent to North Africa. It was not till the end of 1943 that it was finally determined to use the Division for the "Second Front". Needless to say no hint of these plans and counter-plans were ever known to the rank and file.

TRAINING.

Such conditions impose a severe strain on all Company Commanders and particularly on the Commanding Officer. To be always "on your toes" for the unexpected, with no off period, save short individual leave periods, is apt to result in staleness among the rank and file. It can be said once and for all the Battalion came through this four year test magnificently. It gained and maintained the highest possible reputation with its Divisional and Brigade Commanders. Unconsciously to most the organization and training of the Battalion gradually changed. They came back from France completely confident in themselves; they could, they said, march and shoot and dig with the best. But within a year men in the ranks were writing to their friends:— "Nothing but schemes, every day. We had begun to think the days of marching were over; but no fear. That's all we seem to do now-a-days."

Another caps this with:—"Practice alone cannot make perfect, whereas practice and fitness can. Route marches and the notorious six mile run. Our rifle Company marched 35 miles in 17 hours and beat even that later on with 51 miles in 41 hours."

While another man refers to:—"The extra polish which makes the difference between the well trained and the expert; for in the battle that must come it is the experts who will win."

The requirements for victory were being absorbed.

I frequently visited the First Battalion during those four years of training. The old soldier who had served in Belgium and come back from DUNKIRK in some ways sensed and resented the new atmosphere. He felt that the praise that was being gained by this changing Battalion was a reflection on the Battalion as it had been. "You couldn't find a finer Battalion than we were," he would assert.

This was voiced in the deep regard the old soldiers had for Lt.-Col. F. A. Milnes. In due course he had vacated the Command; this is an extract from a letter describing a visit he paid:

"We have had a visit from Lt.-Col. F. A. Milnes. When the news of his arrival was known among us, there was great excitement, for it would be hard to express what a high place Col. Milnes holds in the affection of the Battalion. Those of us who served under him when he took command of the Battalion in Belgium, after Lt.-Col. E. G. Fraser had received the wound from which he later died, do not forget the calm and undaunted way he steered us through those hard days; and, perhaps most important of all, how, knowing so much more of the seriousness of the situation, which some might have thought hopeless, he radiated an atmosphere of such calm and matter-of-fact confidence, the benefit of which communicated itself to each one of us. He brought us back and at once threw himself into the task of reforming, expecting immediately to return to France. Events outstripped us, though, and we have not yet gone back; in these circumstances, the initial regret

"PRACTICE ALONE CANNOT MAKE PERFECT, WHEREAS PRACTICE AND FITNESS CAN."

felt when Col. Milnes left us can well be imagined. It was reflections of this sort that were in our minds when he visited us a few days back—and we felt more strongly than ever how much he would like to be with us again. This feeling was particularly apparent when Col. Milnes looked into the Sergeants' Mess, the vast majority of its members having served with him since the beginning of the war."

The standard of the marching, the digging, the shooting was rising. "Think of a number; then double it." That described the length of the marches. The doubled march could not be made without the highest possible physical efficiency. The old soldier had never been through so exacting a course of physical training as the young soldier experienced first at the depot and then in the ranks of his Battalion. Shooting was no longer confined to the rifle; the Battalion had its own batteries of all natures, the fire of all had to be co-ordinated on the point of attack. While digging, essential as ever, was now not a primary but a secondary factor; the slit trenches were wanted on the position that had been won, to consolidate it against the almost certain counter-attack. But before the position was won there must be an attack requiring the very best leadership, initiative, courage, not from some few individuals, but supreme in each man.

The constant change of locality may have helped training; but there were disadvantages in the increasing turnover of personnel. As one man wrote:—"Our officers come and go so quickly that we almost get 'tennis neck' watching them whiz to and fro on courses, transfers, duties with other units." While another platoon writes: "Four good men have gone to the Paratroops. We wish them 'Happy Landings'."

Here was a grave infantry disadvantage. The air force, special army formations like Paratroops and Commandos, inevitably attracted the more adventurous. Many of our best young officers served for a period with a Battalion, volunteered for service elsewhere, and disappeared. Infantry, the Queen of Battles, was being drained of many of her best.

Meanwhile incessant drafts were required for service overseas and with newly formed bodies. Landing operations called for many new organisations such as Beach landing parties. A proportion went to India where unfortunately they rarely reached the 2nd Suffolk; a proportion was lost due to normal wastage, or to courses. There was a contingent of 70 Suffolk men who fought together at the ANZIO beachhead, and who though they were absent never forgot that they were men of the Suffolk Regiment. It is safe to say that in every theatre of operations there were officers and men fighting who had served and been trained in the Suffolk Regiment.

"No victory can be won save by the quality of the Infantry." All were agreed on this great truth. Yet selection was given to every arm in the Service save only the Infantry, who took what was left.

It may well be that it was the Regimental Tradition, not only in the Suffolk Regiment, but in all other Regiments, that saved the situation. There was always throughout these four years a solid core of Suffolk soldiers in the First Suffolk; leavened by these the Battalion always belonged unmistakeably to the Suffolk Regiment, a mirror of all that the Regiment had been in the past.

THE SOLDIER.

It is many years since Battalions at home have seen much of their native land; in this war they travelled far and wide. I visited the Battalion in Somerset, at WEYMOUTH, SWANAGE, FOLKESTONE, NAIRN and near PORTSMOUTH. Sometimes they were under canvas, occasionally in huts; but generally in big empty houses, or requisitioned schools. There is no luxury in an empty house. As bare as a barrack room is a peace time expression to compare the comfort of home; but a barrack room is cosy compared with the great majority of the billets the Battalion occupied. Houses that have lost their owners, their fitments and their furniture, soon have mud-plastered floors and stairs, walls without paint or paper, ceilings with hanging strips of plaster; while it would seem that the more pretentious the mansion the more degrading are the kitchen premises.

Such were the temporary homes of the Battalion in their native land. Unless these billets are kept up to a barrack room standard then each unit leaves the mansion a little more battered than it was found, the mud surging up the drive to the unwashed steps, the weeds choking all shape out of the garden, the fences with yawning gaps; desolation everywhere. A tribute can be paid to the discipline and organisation of the First Battalion in that their billets always approximated to barrack room standards.

But even at their best the soldier wants to escape temporarily at least from his surroundings. His welfare becomes a most important factor. It is natural that leave, the opposite sex, the cinema, sports, should have an exceptional value.

No one worked harder for the social welfare of the Battalion than the padre, the Rev. P. W. Cato, who served with the First Suffolk from the first days of the war till the end of 1941. A letter from an Officer of the Battalion expresses the general feeling:

"During his time in the Battalion he had endeared himself to us all, officers and men alike. For his activities took him very much beyond administering to our spiritual needs; certainly his interpretation of that term covered a very wide field, including music and dancing to no small extent. There are many men in the Battalion who have reason to be grateful for his most human help and advice—not less so because so much of this personal help and comfort was carried out by him quite unknown to any other person. It can truly be said of him that he "went about doing good"—and so we wish him every success for the future and the happiness that he will derive from helping others."

Battalion life and also the stringent secrecy imposed on all ranks can be gleaned from these letters to the Suffolk Regimental Gazette:

"There is little of importance to record, not because little of importance has happened, but possibly because what has happened has been too important to record at all. Our activities must therefore remain something of an enigma. We have moved, of course; we always do. We cannot tell you where to or even where from; we never can. We aren't doing quite what we were a couple of months ago; but we can't tell you what it is. But don't think that all this secrecy is nothing but a cloak for idleness; we are doing something. We do, for instance, a few innocent things such as P.T. and W.T. at odd hours of the day. We are being educated; slowly, it is true, and a bit scrappily, that is unavoidable; but it is happening. We still play football and box; we were knocked out of the Boxing League, but are still in the running for the football cup. We are training for cross-country running."

The standard of training in January, 1943, is described by a soldier in No. 9 platoon of "A" Company; the platoon Commander for this excercise being Lance Corporal Garnham:

" 'A' Company was picked from the Battalion to enter a platoon for the Brigade physical efficiency contest, and, naturally enough, being the best company, we pulled it off with ease. Really, this was a very good show considering that we had had absolutely no practice at all for the competition. The morning was taken up by rope-climbing and jumping tests, with ¼-mile run to be done in 4 minutes, all in F.S.M.O. It was hard to convince the "Staff" that we didn't come from the jungles as we passed so easily. As the boys said, "It was a bit of cake." The afternoon saw the real test, with a 10-mile forced march in 2 hours. The greater majority did this test in well under the time, and three actually did it in 1½ hours, which must be very nearly a record. These three said they stopped for char on the way, but . . . Another record was put up when the boys found a tea shop."

All the letters to the Gazette express the same keenness and good temper, often under most trying circumstances.

"A week under canvas, surrounded by a sea of mud. Though we managed to get and remain soaking wet the whole time, yet everyone's spirits remained high."

While the Mortar Platoon welcomed Sgt. Sturgeon back from the battle school and hoped he'd teach them some new stuff. The writer says:

"I think I can say the platoon have enjoyed their stay. It hasn't been all play and you who think the mortars are "cushy" just ask the chaps who carried the bombs on the stunts. The easiest load, of course, is the D.C.'s consisting of wireless, satchel and aerial, telephone satchel and cable, aiming posts, rifle and Verey Light Pistol. The brass hats are now considering whether he should carry the carrier, so as to save the tracks!"

There was sport as well as training:—

"We moved our station, of course, but not before we had put up some good performances on the sports field—and all who contributed to them deserve to be congratulated—in particular, in Cross-country running. We had the pleasure of winning the Brigade contest and coming second in both Divisional and Corps runs, on both occasions being beaten by a Battalion of the Lincolnshire Regiment. In the Boxing-ring, some spirited fights were seen in an inter-Company competition, of which the winners, "A" Company, are to be congratulated. Later in the year teams of runners and footballers visited The Depot, and showed their rivals there a clean pair of heels over a difficult cross-country course and some twinkling foot-work on the football field. We were fortunate enough to win both contests. As a contrast to this athletic prowess, the existence of philosophers and sages was revealed at the sessions of the Battalion Brains Trust, at which lively and informative discussion took place on subjects both witty and learned."

But it was the women, the A.T.S. and the W.A.A.Fs and all the other conscripted and non-conscripted girls of the many neighbourhoods who occupied the spare time of the great majority. There were numberless marriages. "Leave continues uninterrupted and Privates Rice, Wade and

Groom all have taken full advantage of this to taste the fruits of matrimony". Congratulations of this nature showered down from every platoon after the end of every leave period.

To be followed later by "Private Thomas is now a Daddy. Lance Corporal Pattison is the proud father of "Enery", "Arfer", "William". Lance Corporal Willingham always said he would not get married as it was against his principles to make some girl happy and hundreds miserable. But he did! While Private Blundell said of his marriage that it was sudden 'But oh! Boy! It was worth it.'"

Then there were congratulations to Miss Maureen Bridger, aged 0, future Suffolk A.T.S. While Sid Peck could be heard telling Bob Pulford how his son was going to do his 21 years in the Army. To which came the reply: "What happens if it's a little girl, Sid?"

There was of course embarrassment when the Battalion returned unexpectedly to previous Stations, where on departure there had been promises "to be sure and write", which of course the Romeos had failed to do. Jealousy was occasionally awakened. "What has Private Case got that we haven't. Is it his curly head, or can it be his chocolate ration?" But it was "Jungle" in the Second Battalion who complained to a comrade that he "wrote to his girl so often that the postman eventually married her."

"We are all feeling sorry for young Chambers, he is having an awkward time with his harem, having written two letters to two different girls and putting them in the wrong envelopes, and did his regular girl tell him things!"

But lasting devotion of the many outweighed the fickleness of the few. As one soldier recorded:—

"Recently the Platoon had occasion to use a canteen of an unusual nature—chocolate, biscuits, cigarettes, soap, etc., were available in unlimited quantities, and all that was needed was the cash. Some days later the local Post Office was practically knocked down by a solid mass of "devoted" husbands and fiancees who had trekked down there with parcels for their loved ones, which equalled anything that a 'Magic Lamp' could have produced."

The Suffolk soldier has always had an exemplary character. Military offences were practically non-existent during the whole time the Battalion was in England. Absence was the only offence:

"The majority of the Platoon began the New Year in the best possible way with 10 days' leave. Many New Year resolutions were made; but so far only one has not been broken. Young Freddie Coe stated that he would not return to these hilly lands on time, and so far he has not."

The only break in the good temper that prevailed that I have been able to trace was recorded by one of the officers:—

"Our Catering Officer was camping on a quite delectable little peninsula of grass and trees during the course of an extended reconnaissance of the district. Unfortunately it was simple for waterfowl to come ashore and visit the tent, which was what the local swannery did with great pertinacity, especially at meal-times. Now a swan in a tent, still more entangled in a tent-rope, is both out of place and liable to be dangerous. One dinner-time exasperated beyond endurance by the inquisitive thrustfulness and acquisitive greed of a large swan, which was actually plucking him by the shorts, and tapping him on the knee with its beak to call attention to its own alleged

DIAGRAM of an INFANTRY BATTALION

EUROPEAN CAMPAIGN

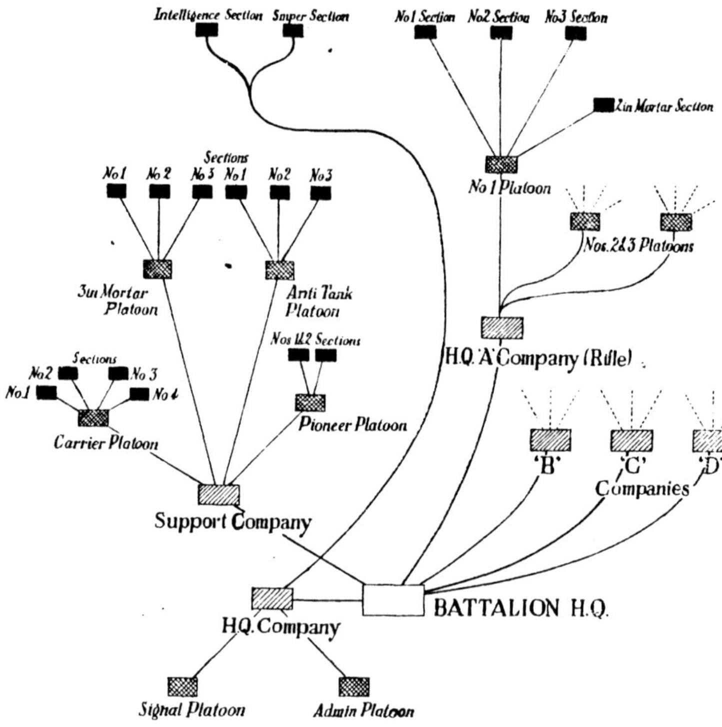

LEGEND

Rifle Company:- Each Platoon has one 2in Mortar
Each Section has one Bren Gun

Support Company:- Anti Tank Platoon - each Section has 2 Six Pounders
3in Mortar Platoon - each Section has 2 3in Mortars
Carrier Platoon - each Section has 3 Carriers, 3 L.M.Gs., & 1 2in Mortar all fired normally from dismounted positions.

The P.I.A.T.:- Fires a 2½ lb bomb at a range of approximately 100 yds at Armoured Fighting Vehicles, Pill Boxes, or similar targets. It is operated by one man. There are 23 P.I.A.Ts distributed throughout the Battalion.

The Bren:— There are 63 Bren L.M.G's. distributed throughout the Battalion.

hunger and emptiness, he jumped up, seized his camp chair, and presented it direct at the embattled plumage of the intruder. As the Hun is said to be incapable of facing up to cold steel, so the bird's martial entrails melted at the sight of four wooden legs and a canvas seat. The fact is reported and no pseudo-psychological explanation is offered: let it suffice that it is true. The bird appeared for carving on the table of the Officer's Mess!"

It was the exception rather than the rule that the Officers or the Sgts. managed to get a central mess. Billeting conditions generally necessitated company messes. But the great Regimental advantage of centralized Officers' and Sgts.' messes was always recognised and whenever possible arranged. Thus there were memorable times when in the Sgts.' Mess 'Euchre' was the order of the night, or after close collaboration with the Navy when Jack Tolley (R.Q.M.S.) could be heard telling how he had his "Hand on his Heart" in a loud tuneful voice, or Darkie Gilbert (C.S.M.) describing to a horrified audience what happened to "Little Nell" when she disobeyed her Dad.

One and all, from the most senior to the most junior, made friends everywhere. "They are the pleasantest, best behaved men we have ever had" was the invariable report of the many public-spirited committees who did their best to entertain the Battalion wherever they were located.

THE BATTALION.

I spent three days with the First Battalion in NAIRN in March 1944, and I quote from the notes I made.

"What impressed me most was their physical fitness. I had never seen a fitter Battalion. You could recognise this outstanding quality even when they were standing still on parade and before they gave some training demonstrations. There was a bitter N.E. wind, the snow came in skurries, it was freezing hard; the men were not wearing coats and obviously didn't need them; the sea off the coast was grey black with lines of white breakers—they had been in it up to their armpits on a landing exercise a few days previous and they were none the worse. The least observant of soldiers could not have failed to be greatly impressed by their radiant health and strength.

McCaffrey's company gave a demonstration of street fighting. This company, going through the Course at the Army School was reported as outstandingly good, perhaps the best in the army; but I was told was run close by the other companies of the Battalion. The war-time soldier of today is trained as a recruit to turn a somersault over a bench, to be agile on a 'horse', to cross a very stiff assault course in full kit. But severe though these progressive steps may be they are but an introduction to a flying leap, head foremost and fully armed, through a window into a room held by the enemy; to the fight from room to room with grenades and tommy guns, each man backing up his companion. Here not only physical fitness; but the concomitant quickness in leadership was apparent.

Street fighting is but one of the many matters that the present infantry soldier must master; the open country with its land mines, its concrete pill boxes, its booby traps, runs it close. This world war with the desert dust of Africa; winter mud of Flanders; the heat of a Burmese tropical sun; or the snow of midwinter in Italy, make up a test that none but the supremely fit can survive.

The officer is even more dependent on physical fitness than the men; for when exhaustion threatens to overcome the men the officer must still be up and doing. Hence the youth of the officer of the Battalion today. This is another outstanding difference between the Battalions of the past and the front line service Battalions of today. The Commanding Officer will have reached the retiring age at 40 if not earlier. Ten to twelve years will separate top from bottom. Physical strain has proved the deciding factor, overriding service experience. A man of forty or upwards may have greater judgment, particularly in this all arms infantry war where an infantry Commander must have a kaleidoscopic knowledge. The man of 45 might be best if the campaign ran in the gentler channel; but at the present extreme pressure it is the younger man who alone can stay the course.

Here in the First Battalion there are none but young officers. So often in the past where the C.O. has been about 50, his Majors 45 and Captains from 40 to 30, there has been a great gap between these ranks; a gap in age, in community of ideas and in knowledge and experience. A gap that even Mess life has failed to bridge, a gap that becomes a real stumbling block to the team spirit. But in the First Battalion youth is at the helm, and I never met a team better welded together, or better fitted to meet whatever may befall.

It is not often that the standard of the officers of a Battalion will be uniformly high so that all the Companies are well commanded; so often one weak man may spoil the whole; here the Battalion could not have done better than to have Papillon, Boycott, McCaffrey, Ryley, with Gough from the Lincolnshires as second in command; or to have them backed up with—Gordon, Hemingway, Morrison, Claxton, Sperling, Mayhew, to mention only a few of the many outstanding junior officers.

It would be a rash statement to say that this is perhaps the best Battalion we have ever had in the Regiment, unwise because great Battalions depend on great Commanders; but however great the Commander he is dependent on his team of officers and the quality of his N.C.O.s and men. I do not believe we have ever had a fitter or more efficient Battalion, or a happier and keener complement of officers than those under Dick Goodwin's Command.

Other Battalion Commanders in the past have had other problems, Montagu, probably the best Commander during my service, had a mixed team of officers, generally speaking the young were better than the old. His enthusiasm as much as his real ability made the Battalion one of the best in the Army. Frank Wilson had none but young officers, most of whom had begun soldiering in the 1914 war that had just ended. Under each of these Commanders the First Battalion made a name for itself, ranking above contemporaries. But these were peacetime conditions and they were never put to the test of war.

Good as the First Battalion undoubtedly was under these Commanders it was not, I believe, as good as I found it at NAIRN. The men were not so fit, not so eminently efficient, not so close knit a team, not so well led—and by leading I mean not by the Commanding Officer; but by the officers and the N.C.O.s.

To be reasonably fit and to shoot straight was the criterion of the average man in the ranks of Montagu's time. To have a general understanding of field duties; this was a great advance on the standard after the South African War when I remember the First Battalion forming square at the double with bayonets fixed ready to receive the Second in Command who represented Calvary charging.

Today the infantry soldier must be an expert in many methods of destruction. He has a battery of six heavy anti-tank guns to be hauled across obstacles and brought into immediate action; he has mortars and machine guns in "carriers" to be manoeuvred; he has a flame thrower; he must be an expert signaller in wireless, flag or lamp; he must be a mine detector; he has a motorized Column of some sixty vehicles, and the medical officer expects real knowledge from his stretcher bearers. He must moreover combine all these into an efficient whole, able to act without delay, and fight infantry fashion in all countries, through all climates, over all natures of ground.

In one respect there will always be a great difference between a peacetime and a wartime Regiment. The Regiment in peace recruits largely from its County area. In war the Hampshire born man may go to the Berkshire Depot for training, thence be drafted to a Buckinghamshire Holding Battalion and be sent from there to a Yorkshire Service Battalion where he may be moved to India or the Far East, to yet some other unit. What loyalties will he have? Probably to the Battalion with which he stays the longest, or finally remains.

How vital it is under these circumstances that the parent Regiment should have the strongest possible tradition to pass on to its Battalions. For the measure of a Regiment is the depth and steadfastness of its traditions, its unshakeable belief in itself. Its roots should go deep down into the past to stand all square to any tempest.

Here, in the First Battalion, was a glorious proof of this strength. By great good fortune about half the personnel of the Battalion came from Suffolk; but the other half were so strongly imbued with the Regiment that they might well have been born in East Anglia. Not of course that a wartime Battalion owes all to its upbringing. The men serving with the First Battalion came from all classes and occupations; they had far too much individual character to follow like sheep. The quality of every wartime Battalion is to a great degree what it makes itself.

History too often judges by results; it only records such Victories as Minden and Dettingen, and praises the Regiments which fought there. But it isn't only the victories that deserve the praise. It isn't only what we do, it is what we are capable of doing. It's the quality that matters. The First Suffolk was a very fine Battalion when it came back from DUNKIRK. The men had no doubt whatever that they were better than the Germans. Today it is an even finer Battalion"

THE BATTALION COMMANDERS.

During the four years since the outbreak of the war the First Battalion had had four Battalion Commanders. In war, no subordinate Commander is of such outstanding importance to the whole army. A Regimental History should therefore, as far as it is possible, portray these men.

Character, personality, knowledge are the essential qualifications; but the most important of these is character. General SMUTS declares that men of action live on the surface of things, they do not create. A Battalion Commander in battle lives "on the surface of things." Without hesitation to take responsibility and act, he must be a man of outstanding character. Lord MORAN has written that a man's character can be judged by the moral strength, the courage, with which he will take action on his knowledge, real or instinctive.

No two Battalion Commanders are identical; there is no standard gauge. The magnetism of one fine leader will be balanced by the 'common touch' of another, by the obstinacy of a third. But it must not be forgotten that as CROMWELL said "Men are led as much by the heart as by the head."

The First Battalion went to FRANCE under the Command of Lt.-Col. E. G. FRASER, who on May 20th was wounded while reconnoitring the Battalion position on the River SCHELDT and subsequently died.

Lt.-Col. FRASER, who had been seriously wounded in the First World War, commanded the Battalion during eight difficult months. He was a brave, wise, determined and popular C.O. Great force of example is needed in leading an un-blooded battalion into its first battles. Col. FRASER kept the morale of the Battalion high during the trying months of waiting, and, under his leadership, it went into battle with that high-hearted confidence and well knit morale from which it never looked back. He served the Regiment well.

He was succeeded by Lt.-Col. F. A. Milnes. A fine and just tribute has been paid to him in the letter quoted earlier in this Chapter. There are no better judges of a Commanding Officer than those who serve under him. A superior officer will often err in his assessment of his subordinates; the man who is commanded is in a position to know. I consider 'Tony' Milnes one of the outstanding Battalion Commanders in the Regimental history of the war. He inspired the affection and confidence of his men to an unusual degree. If there was a fault, too much depended on his personality and character; but there was an excuse, he had been the mainstay during the retreat to DUNKIRK, the main prop during the reorganization in England.

A 'one man show' is always a weakness. The test came when Lt.-Col. Victor Oborne succeeded Milnes in August 1942. It was a natural succession and nine times out of ten the new Battalion Commander would have proved successful. But he lacked one of the many qualifications of a Commanding officer—the necessary ruthlessness. A chief concomitant of success is the choice of subordinates and the removal of those who either fail or do not take their proper place in the team. A man of proved ability such as Milnes could enforce his own views on his subordinates. Lt.-Col. V. Oborne served with distinction elsewhere, as he well deserved to do. He was succeeded by Lt.-Col. R. E. Goodwin.

So often the misfortunes of one man paves the way for his successor. Under Lt.-Col. R. E. Goodwin the First Battalion became a magnificent team. But the better the team the more important it is that the leader shall be undoubtedly the best among them. No better choice as Battalion Commander could possibly have been made; under Goodwin the Battalion had the highest possible reputation, while his own stood out as a great Battalion Commander.

Comparisons are always difficult. I knew these two Battalion Commanders Milnes and Goodwin intimately. Milnes would preface his remarks with "Don't you think" and there was great determination behind what he had determined you ought to think. Goodwin was modesty personified; but he swept all forward on the high crest of his enthusiasm.

Throughout the war the Regiment was fortunate in all its Battalion Commanders. Greatly as some varied, all were enthusiastic Regimental officers. The Suffolk Regiment and the Suffolk soldier was always the background of their soldiering.

CHAPTER THREE.

FIRST BATTALION.

JUNE 1943—JULY 1944.

Training in Combined Operations—Move to the pre-invasion area—Preliminary "briefing"—The invasion plan—"D" Day—The advance from the beach—Assault of "HILLMAN" by "A" Company—The Bridgehead—CHATEAU DE LA LONDE—"B" Company in the attack—Consolidation.

TRAINING IN COMBINED OPERATIONS.

June 1940 witnessed DUNKIRK. In June 1943 the responsible officers knew that the 3rd Division was to be an assault Division and that the 8th Brigade in which the First Battalion had served throughout the War was to be the Assault Brigade.

Prior to this the Battalion at INVERARY had done two spells of training in Combined Operations, so that they already had a good grounding in the technique of assault landings.

Early in June 1943 the Battalion moved to DURLIN in the WESTERN HIGHLANDS for an intensive "toughening" course, including several assault landings, using live ammunition. Then the Commanding Officer Lt.-Col. R. E. Goodwin and all Company Commanders spent four days at the Divisional Battle School learning the technique of assaulting, and how to "open up" enemy concrete strong points surrounded by wire and mines.

In July each Company went to this Battle School for three days' practice in the Assault of a "strong point". "A" Company had been adjudged the best Company in the Brigade; but owing to an unforeseen move was unable to take part in the Divisional Competition.

In August the Battalion took part in Battalion "Group" training; the group consisting of the Battalion, an S.P. Battery, a Squadron of Churchill Tanks and a platoon of Machine Guns; with minor landing craft manned by an R.A.S.C. Motor Boat Company. During this training every type of weapon used live Ammunition and explosives against wire and other objectives. This training ended on a high note with an exceptionally realistic Exercise "MILLHOUSE".

In September and October there was a Divisional Exercise "SALMON" to practise the Division advancing on two roads, against a defended river crossing. This was a test of the endurance of the men.

Then the Battalion went down to PEMBROKE to carry out training with an Armoured Division. Here the Companies worked with the Squadron 13/18th Hussars with whom later in Normandy the Battalion was affiliated. This Squadron was organised into troops of 4 Tanks each, one tank in each troop carrying a 17 pounder.

In November the Battalion was back again in SCOTLAND and on this occasion married up with the Navy. The 3rd Division went to sea in Force

"S", embarking in L.S.I.—newly built American ships of about 7,000 tons, of special design, each carrying 18 L.C.A. The 8th Brigade, in Force "S3", was based on INVERGORDON, the L.S.I. being manned by Merchant Navy, with Marines as crew of the L.C.A. (See Appendix for Abbreviations).

In February and March at NAIRN there were two major full dress rehearsals for final tie up of craft allotment. The Battalion by now was very well trained and thoroughly conversant with assault landing procedure.

At NAIRN General Dempsey Commanding the Second Army visited the Battalion. General Montgomery had previously in January spoken to the Battalion on parade.

When Major Charles Boycott rejoined the battalion in November 1943, he was met with the remark "I suppose you know what we are on ?" Despite some scepticism right up to "D" Day, the majority of the battalion knew that they were on the job this time, and felt that it had been worth waiting for.

In this last period of training the Battalion had to build their own "beach obstacles". This involved many working parties, sometimes at night to take advantage of low water, and sometimes in rough cold weather with gusts of snow falling. They were building a breakwater and the scene has been described as most weird. Bulldozers charged up and down the sand and in and out of the surf collecting shingle; arc lights on the low cliff lit the main scene, the bulldozers with their great fore and aft lamps giving the effect of theatre spot lights gone mad.

Exercises at sea were held and one of them, "GRAB", provided the battalion with an unpleasant experience. In this operation the troops were lowered away in L.C.A.s from the davits of the L.S.I. for a 10 mile run-in to the land. Craft were to be lowered by night in two 'flights', so that the Battalion could touch down on the beach shortly after dawn. It was one of their first exercises with troops, and neither the Royal Marine L.C.A. crews, nor the crew of the L.S.I., had had much experience in lowering away; moreover unfortunately the sea was rough.

Boycott, who gives this account, was in the second flight and was able to watch the first get away. The L.S.I. was rolling heavily, and as the L.C.A.s were lowered they started to swing, crashing with all their 25 tons against the side of the ship. Two of the four L.C.A.s on the starboard side reached the water where they stayed pitching up and down. At one moment they were waterborne on the crest of a wave; the next they hung suspended once again from their davits above a deep trough. It was almost impossible for their crews to free the tackles. Eventually one of the two craft in the water was released and started to drift down the side of the ship; but at this moment a winchman decided to lower one of the remainder, still high up, and it fell with a frightful crash on to the drifting craft. It looked as if there would be heavy casualties in the lower craft; mercifully a deep wave trough freed the pair and all was well. None was hurt; but it was a tricky moment for all concerned..

Boycott's turn came next. The bashing of his L.C.A. against the side of the ship as it fell away was very unpleasant both for the occupants and the craft; the latter knocked a large hole in herself in the process, then continued to hit the water with a succession of heavy bumps until enough slack from the davits had been let out to counteract the rise and fall of the waves. With great efforts the Royal Marines got the tackles off, and, after they had narrowly avoided death from the swinging blocks, the L.C.A. moved away, to start forming up for the run-in to the beach. A minute or two later the coxswain shouted that the L.C.A. was sinking fast; seemingly only too true, as the stoker was up to his waist in water. This, as far as Boycott was concerned, ended the exercise. Several other craft had a similar fate to his; luckily there were no casualties to men. Exercise "GRAB", although a valuable experience, was not a pleasant one.

During this winter training there were a number of non-tactical questions to be considered and practised. One was the waterproofing of vehicles. A "drowned" vehicle was a nuisance on the beach, while its non-appearance at the right time and place might well prove disastrous to the sub-unit concerned, who depended on it for a bare minimum of essential stores.

'Personal' waterproofing was also very necessary—a watch, cigarettes, matches, all had to be kept dry. All kinds of ways were tried out, including the inside of steel helmets when worn. Another problem was dress. 'Winter' fashions were warm; but very wet when wet. 'Spring' fashions dried more easily. Since no spares could be carried, a balance had to be struck to cover a period of from four to five days. Usually socks could be changed about three hours after landing; by this time boots had become fairly dry. Luckily salt water is never so wet or so cold as fresh.

Each Company possessed five motor vehicles on which all the company and platoon stores, reserve ammunition and personal kits had to be stowed. Of these five, two were of great importance, the carrier and one 15 cwt. truck; these were to land on 'D' Day and D+1 respectively. None of the others would arrive before D+8. It will be seen, therefore, that the proper loading of the carrier and 15 cwt. truck was vital. Consideration of what should be carried had continued throughout the winter and the Company lists were prepared in great detail.

Rations were carried by each man for the first 48 hours after landing. During the early part of their training a "48 hour ration" was issued; but for the actual assault this was changed to two "24 hour rations". These were in waterproof packages specially designed for assault operations. They were in two sizes:- one to fit the big and the other to fit the small halves of the mess tin. Each ration contained biscuits, oatmeal blocks, tea, sugar and milk blocks, dehydrated meat blocks, chocolate, sweets, chewing gum, meat extract cubes, salt. In addition a "Tommy" cooker with stand and two tins of fuel, a waterproofed tin of 20 Players, with a rough edge for striking matches, and four vomit bags very stoutly constructed ! All this weighed just over 5 lbs. and made an appreciable extra weight for a man to carry.

The L.S.I.s, prefabricated and mass produced, were specially built in America. They were glorified transports in the British sense, every inch of space being available for troop accommodation; they epitomized the Englishman's idea of things American with their drinking water fountains and other shiny gadgets. They were, of course, specially designed to carry a large number of minor landing craft hoisted on their davits.

They were extremely well victualled. In the early days, the troops on Exercise ate the food that had been put on board in America for the ships' first commission. This was of real peace-time standard—white

Officers, 1st Battalion, March, 1944.

Back Row—Lts. G. N. Casson, R. Garnham, D. G. Lumb, P. W. Keville, F. M. B. Russell, T. J. F. Tooley, A. C. L. Sperling, V. A. Gorham, E. A. Tribe, M. L. Wilson, F. N. Matthews.
Centre Row—Lt. D. N. Garle, Capts. H. C. Elliott, H. G. Woodall (C.F.), J. S. Coppock, A. H. Claxton, K. G. Mayhew, P. W. Spurgin (Q.M.), W. H. Archdall, P. A. Robinson, (R.A.M.C.), Lt. S. Hemingway.
Front Row—Capt. W. N. Breach, Major C. A. Boycottt, Capt. H. K. Merriam (Adjutant), Lt. Col. R. E. Goodwin (C.O.), Col. W. N. Nicholson, C.M.G., D.S.O., Major J. G. M. B. Gough, Major P. W. G. Papillon, Major D. W. McCaffrey, Capt. R. G. Ryley.

bread, any amount of butter, sugar, etc. The troops' messing was on the cafeteria system—as each soldier arrived he was given a special 'eating' tray into each compartment of which was put the various bits and pieces of food for his meal. Besides the rations, the L.S.I.s had well stocked canteens where soldiers bought as much chocolate, sweets, tobacco and cigarettes, soap, as they could stagger ashore with. Many young women and children benefited greatly from these periodical "Exercises".

During Exercises the men were practised coming up from mess decks and manning craft. Getting over the side and into the craft when dressed in full assault order was not an easy job. It meant scrambling over a flat iron side rail; heavily nailed boots were very awkward, slipping as a man was poised over the gap between ship and craft. A small matter to a sailor; but for a soldier unversed in the sea behaviour of ships it could be very upsetting. Normally, during the first morning after embarkation in L.S.I., all the craft were lowered away and the whole L.C.A. flotilla manoeuvred round the harbour—partly to give the troops fresh air, and partly to give the Royal Marine crews experience in handling fully loaded craft. On a fine morning this was a pleasant outing;—there was usually a cruiser and some destroyers to look at in the harbour, besides sister L.S.I.s and all the other strange types of major and minor assault craft. On a rough morning it was not so pleasant.

The routine was breakfast at 4 a.m. to give time for the troop decks to be cleaned up before leaving. Then the various orders: over the loud hailer 'Make ready'. Dressing was a long and complicated business. All put on. 'Battle' make-up; a dark green non-vanishing cream which camouflaged their faces. Those already suffering from 'mal-de-mer' hardly needed this addition to their appearance. 'Officers join serials': when the officers left their own quarters and joined their men on their mess decks.

Towards the end of March 1944 the Battalion Commander was 'Briefed' as to the task the Battalion had to carry out. He, with the other C.O.s in the 3rd Division, was locked up in a large house in SCOTLAND for nearly a week. There they studied all available air photographs of the assault area, and considered their unit plans for carrying out their orders, working on a large scale model. These plans were then approved in outline by the Divisional Commander. After the C.O.s had dispersed, each elaborated his plan for future issue to his own unit. No detail of this conference was passed to the Company Commanders; except that, very secretly, each was given an objective for intensive training and this objective had a direct bearing on the final operations. Company Commanders were not allowed to explain to their men the reason of this training; but were allowed to say it was for the 'Second Front'. Even so, a good number of the rank and file thought it was a leg pull.

MOVE TO THE PRE-INVASION AREA. APRIL 1944 - MAY 30TH, 1944.

In April 1944 the Battalion, less first reinforcements to GRAVESEND, moved down to the assembly area at HORNDEAN near PORTSMOUTH.

While here all ranks wore equipment every day until 1300 hours, and every other day they had to be out of camp, either on a route march or field training. A final large scale Exercise "FABIUS" was held, with a landing in LITTLEHAMPTON area, chiefly to practise movement control and test the machinery for marshalling and embarkation; many snags arose and were rectified. During this time General Montgomery and Sir James Grigg, the Secretary of State for War, were with the Battalion for half an hour.

The pre-invasion assembly areas along the South Coast had been organised into three zones. "The Concentration Area" stretched back inland from a line seven to ten miles from the Coast; in this units occupied hutted camps or other semi-permanent buildings. South of this line came the "Marshalling transit Area"; here accommodation was for a stay of up to 48 hours. Lastly came the "Embarkation Areas", with no accommodation; troops occupied this area immediately prior to their Embarkation.

Arrangements had to be made for sealing the camps during the "briefing" in the Concentration Area. One of the first fatigues on the arrival of the Battalion was to build a barrier of barbed wire round the camp—movement in and out, except during briefing, was free.

Before the details of the Battalion's arrangements for embarkation and deployment on the hostile shore can be understood their role in the final assault must be explained. The First Suffolk was the reserve battalion of the assault brigade, the 8th Brigade, landing an hour after the first infantry of the two front line assault battalions had touched down. The 8th Brigade's task was to secure the selected beaches and then press forward to form a small beach-head for the subsequent landing of the remainder of the 3rd Division; which would penetrate inland, enlarging the beach-head to allow further formations to operate. Within the 8th Brigade objective the Battalion's tasks were; firstly, to be prepared to assist either of the two actual assaulting battalions if they failed to secure their section of beach and, secondly, their main task, to advance quickly inland and seize the 'apex' of the beach-head, which was certain high ground about 3,000 yards from the coast.

To carry out the above plan, two companies of each of the assault battalions of the brigade touched down at 'H' Hour. Their follow-up companies landed at H+30 minutes with tasks on or adjacent to the beach. The First Suffolk followed at H+60 minutes and hoped to find the beaches reasonably clear; at any rate of aimed small arms fire.

The Battalion was to be split into four main groups for the sea passage. Battalion H.Q. and two rifle companies on the L.S I. "BROADSWORD"; two rifle companies on the L S.I. "BATTLEAXE"; 'Stand-in' Battalion H.Q. and the "LOB" (Left out of Battle) personnel in a L.C.I.; mortars, carriers, anti-tank guns and vehicles, and a few others in L.C.T. All battalions in the brigade were similarly split, on the principle of not having too many eggs in one basket. The vehicles, of necessity, had to go in different craft from the infantry.

Detailed timings, the positions of the various units and vehicles in each ship and craft were set out in 'Landing Tables'. These were made out at Divisional H.Q.s. For a full scale "Exercise" the Divisional Landing Table had comprised over 1,000 foolscap pages ! From this clerical monstrosity the brigades made up their tables, and then in their turn the units made out theirs. It had been reckoned to take nearly a month to mount an Exercise in co-operation with the Navy.

Warrant Officers and Sergeants, 1st Battalion, March, 1944.

Back Row—Sgt. Goodchild, L/sgt. Hart, Sgts. Mouncer, Edwards, Couchman (A.C.C.), Callaby, Davis, Amiss, Lorrimer (R.E.M.E.), ———————.
3rd Row—Sgts. Copeman, Peck, Cook, Robinson, Gilbert, Owen, J. Lankester, Hastings, Barwood, Keeble, G. Lankester, Sgt. Instr. Weeks (A.P.T.C.), Sgt. Hewitt (R.E.M.E.).
2nd Row—Sgts. Chapman, Dell, Redding, Fenn, Killick, Gibbs, Moggridge, Filby, M.M., Chapman, Rawnsley (A.C.C.), Lishman, DeYong, Byrne.
Front Row—C.S.Ms. Hambling, Gant, Overman, R.Q.M.S. Tolley, Lt. Col. R. E. Goodwin, Col. Nicholson, R.S.M. Langran, C.S.M. Tyler, C/Sgt. Bray, C.Q.M.S.s Liles, Ablitt.

Battalions were split up into the above four main groups on moving from the "Concentration Area" into the "Marshalling Area". It was a form of "General Post"—each shipload being collected complete into one camp. The shipload then moved down to its ship via the "Embarkation Area"—the O.C. party carrying almost a shipload of nominal rolls and "bumph".

The local moves within the Marshalling Area and the final move down to the sea involved "Briefed" troops going out into the world where they would have an opportunity of giving away vital bits of information. Accordingly, when the time came for troops to march out, fully dressed in all their paraphernalia, there were security police keeping pace on either side; when embussed into T.C.V.s not even an officer was allowed to sit in front beside the unbriefed driver.

On arrival at the Dock Area there was a pause for checking the "ship-sheet"; while this was being done the soldier ate the chocolate and biscuits, provided from the Marshalling Area. Here he also got his cup of "char" without which no military manoeuvre or event should be started. They were then divided into craft serials—parties of about thirty, and marched, still shepherded by relays of security police, down to the quay.

During the last few weeks before "D" Day, besides 'Will' making and a drive on Army Savings, the Battalion got its own Welfare Scheme going. Every soldier's next-of-kin was to be "looked after" by the wife or mother of one of his officers. Names and addresses of all the next-of-kin were sent to each of the officer's wives or mothers, who wrote to the soldiers' next-of-kin. The scheme was designed to supplement any lack of news of officers or men after the invasion had started. This plan was welcomed by the next-of-kin and the troops, and did in fact work quite well, until the casualties in the battalion became so heavy that all lists got out of date. From the various letters that were exchanged, however, and the obvious pleasure that this extra contact gave, the scheme fully justified the trouble that had been taken.

PRELIMINARY "BRIEFING".

One evening after the Battalion had assembled in the concentration area Lt.-Col. R. E. Goodwin decided that the time had come to take his Company Commanders further into his confidence about the invasion plan, so that they might be planning on more exact lines. The vital importance of the most absolute secrecy was fully appreciated by everyone at this time and what was far more difficult, was practised. So, the Commanding Officer with his Company Commanders drove out one afternoon to the downs and there on the bleak side of a bare hill overlooking a valley he told them the Battalion's task and the exact role of each Company. But no place names were mentioned; none yet knew on what part of the coast the landing was to be made. After a few questions the diagram outlining the plan was burnt, the ashes were trodden into the hillside and the sun having by now set the party returned to camp colder but wiser men.

On the 15th May the Division had a visit from the Supreme Commander-in-Chief, General Eisenhower who spoke to 100 officers and men of the Battalion. They were much impressed by his personality.

On the 22nd May the Battalion lined the Havant Road when His Majesty the King paid the troops a visit. He spoke to several men of the Battalion.

During this period, the camp sealed but not briefed, money was changed. Francs ! One cat was out of the bag at any rate, although there was still a lurking suspicion in their minds that it might be a bluff and that at the last moment francs might be swopped for gulden. At about this time, too, they were issued with a little guide book on France. This contained phonetically arranged sentences to cope with every conceivable situation that might confront the British soldier whilst in foreign parts.

Towards the end of May the Company Commanders received an introductory briefing in the Brigade briefing centre. At this they saw for the first time a large scale model of their beach sector. This was topographically correct; but bearing false place names. They were given a rough outline of the Allied plan and heard the Brigade plan explained in some detail by the Brigade Major. They also listened to the plans of the two assaulting Battalions told in outline by officers from those two units.

Two days later the Commanding Officer held his own briefing for the Battalion. To this came all officers and N.C.O.s down to Platoon Sergeant. The Brigade model was used and a large scale wall enlargement was drawn by the Battalion Intelligence staff. There were also many photos, some of them much enlarged, showing beach obstacles, beach defences, landmarks and wave-top views of the run-in to the beach.

This briefing was thorough and lasted for nearly seven hours. The Commanding Officer explained the plan and the Intelligence Officer spoke on the topography of the beaches and hinterland and the state and strength of the enemy defences. After him the Adjutant gave a, by now, routine explanation of the familiar "landing tables". Representatives of the Navy and R.A.F. gave their listeners a most encouraging picture of the fire support and protection they were to get from them. This lasted for about two hours, and after a break the Commanding Officer gave out the Battalion Operation Order—Order No. 1 ! The action of every sub-unit was then gone into in great detail. Finally officers of the R.A., R.E. and R.A.C. detailed their tasks in support of the Battalion. Everything was extremely well done and added much to the feeling of confidence—as indeed it was meant to. Boycott, from whose account this is taken, said that at the end of the Briefing he felt almost sorry for the Germans, who were going "to have to put up with the hell of a lot at breakfast time one morning before long."

Officers on the "X" list who knew both real and bogus names had to take great care during any discussion with anyone not on the list. None of the "X" list in the Battalion were ever heard to give anything away; but a few days later, when studying air photos at another H.Q. a photographic interpreter referred to "CAEN" when he meant "POLAND". To know the secret at last was quite a shock to one hearer, who, however, kept a straight face and didn't let the speaker know what a brick he had dropped.

The selected beach assault areas were covered daily by photographic aircraft and the Battalion received the lastest information at frequent intervals. ROMMEL had inspected the West Wall about a month or six weeks before 'D' Day. During this inspection he had emphasised the importance of actual beach obstacles and the Battalion officers watched the results of his recommendations increase before their eyes.

In all the "Briefing" lasted for four days. After the Commanding Officer's briefing to Company Commanders the centre was allotted in turn to the various Companies. The troops were thus briefed on the model and had a chance of looking at all the photos and of asking all the questions they wanted. This they much appreciated. So often through force of circumstances the soldier has to carry out some hazardous operation without any idea of the reasons. This is always unsatisfactory, though generally unavoidable. It didn't happen on this supremely important occasion.

The foregoing has been taken from an admirable account written by one of the Company Commanders, Major Charles Boycott. Now it will be as well to describe the plan for the 'D' Day invasion in more detail. Lt. -Col. R. E. Goodwin, Commanding the First Battalion, has provided this.

THE INVASION PLAN.

The 3rd Division which included the 8th Brigade and First Suffolk was on the extreme Eastern flank of the seaborne assault and was to make a landing just West of the town of OUISTREHAM standing on the Western bank of the ORNE estuary. Further to the East the 6th Airborne Division was to land during the night of D-1/D on the high ground East of the River ORNE.

The 3rd Division was to land on "QUEEN" beach; a flat beach with a very gradual slope and a considerable stretch of sand to traverse at low water. To the East sand and mud had silted up considerably round the mouth of the R. ORNE and a landing there would have been extremely hazardous if not impossible. To the West lay a rocky reef, covered at high water. Immediately on the West bank of the estuary of the R. ORNE stood OUISTREHAM, and running away to the West from this fair sized town were two rows of seaside villas, which stretched along the sea front for three or four miles until merging with the seaside resorts of LUC-SUR-MER and LION-SUR-MER where there were a number of larger houses and hotels.

"QUEEN" beach was in front of the seaside villas. There were two lateral roads near the beach, one immediately overlooking the sea, the other about seventy five yards inland, on the other side of the houses. A number of short roads connected between the two laterals; these promised well for beach exits.

Inland from the beach the ground was low lying with small cultivated fields separated by biggish ditches, and a number of small orchards. There were also one or two woods and in all there was considerable cover to facilitate movement inland. The ground immediately inland from the second lateral was in most places soft, could be flooded, and was not considered safe for tanks, which would probably have to keep to the roads for the first three-quarters of a mile or so. The road which was to be the First Suffolk axis of advance was only eight feet wide. This proved an unfortunate complication.

The villages which concerned the Battalion were HERMANVILLE-SUR-MER about a mile and a half from the Western end of the beach "QUEENWHITE", and COLLEVILLE-SUR-ORNE, about two and a half miles inland from the eastern end of "QUEEN RED". Beyond COLLEVILLE the ground rose to a ridge and overlooked the beach. On the far side of this ridge the ground dropped away to a wooded valley where lay a small village PERRIERS-SUR-

LE-DAN. Six or seven miles inland from the ridge was the town of CAEN, an important centre of communication.

The River ORNE and the ORNE Canal ran parallel to each other almost dead straight from CAEN to the sea. About four miles from the mouth of the river, bridges crossed the river and canal respectively. The importance of capturing these bridges intact was vital; they were the only link between the main force and 6th Airborne Division.

On the beach, immediately affecting the Battalion, various obstacles had been placed, mostly during the month prior to the Invasion. These consisted of three types:—A ramp constructed of balks of timber; the ramps being about sixteen feet long rising to a height of about eight feet, with the lower end of the ramp facing seaward. Vertical posts about six to eight feet high. A 'Hedgehog' consisting of three steel or iron girders lashed together at the centre and played out to form a sort of single knife rest.

The ramps and posts had in most cases Teller mines or other explosive charges fastened to the top of them.

The obstacles were fully exposed at low water and about half covered at half tide.

Along the front there were various defended posts and localities—a fairly strong platoon locality was at the junction of "QUEEN RED" and "QUEEN WHITE" beaches. An enemy six gun coastal battery at OUISTREHAM could fire on all the beaches; another battery was sited about a mile and a half inland on the other side of the river. A heavy battery on the bulge EAST of HAVRE was a potential danger both to the beaches and to the big ships, as it could undoubtedly reach the lowering position. These three batteries were included in the pre-invasion tasks of the R.A.F.: they did their job when the time came, for the heavy battery did nothing and the others very little.

Inland there was a four gun 105 mm battery ("MORRIS") immediately to the West of COLLEVILLE-SUR-ORNE; this was surrounded by two belts of wire and protected by various automatic weapons. During the last two months prior to the Invasion the Germans had been setting these guns in heavy concrete casemates and by 'D' Day three were completed and the fourth under construction. This battery was to be attacked by the R.A.F. during the early hours of 'D' Day.

Six hundred yards South of this battery was the headquarters strong-point ("HILLMAN") of the Infantry Regiment responsible for the coast defence of this sector. This position was some five hundred yards by three hundred, surrounded by two belts of wire, the intervening space of forty yards being sown with mines. Inside was a network of trenches, concrete shelters and pillboxes.

During the last two or three weeks a number of new defence works had appeared in the area and one or two new batteries; while the latest information on the afternoon before 'D' Day reported mobile 88mm guns to have moved up to the South of HERMANVILLE-SUR-MER; also the 21 Panzer Division and another Panzer Division had come into the CAEN area.

During the preliminary Briefing stages all types of maps were available from ¼ inch to 1.2500, including 'Going' maps which showed the type of country, state of the ground, width of roads. Aerial photographs were in profusion; verticals, high obliques, low obliques, 'Blow-ups' of particular

By kind permission of the Air Ministry.

BEACH OBSTACLES, MINED AND UNDERWATER AT HIGH TIDE, ENCOUNTERED BY 1ST BATTALION ON "D" DAY.

positions, and "Wave-top height" photographs of the beach and sea front. These latter were of great value as they gave an accurate picture of the beach as would be seen from an L.C.A., and by studying them in conjunction with the obliques and verticals it was possible to fix as landmarks the particular beach houses where the Battalion would land.

In addition to the necessary maps, each officer and N.C.O., down to and including the section commander, had for the assault a beach folder of a set of aerial photographs, wave-top, oblique and vertical, pasted on to a sheet of thin cardboard which he could carry in his battle dress pocket.

Code names were substituted for the various localities in the Battalion area. They were:-

HERMANVILLE-SUR-MER	'MEXICO'
COLLEVILLE-SUR-ORNE	'BRAZIL'
4-gun 105 mm Bty	'MORRIS'
Regtl. H.Q. Strong Point... ...	'HILLMAN'
Bridges over R. ORNE	'RUGGER and CRICKET'

For the operation the 3rd Division included in its assault strength extra artillery, tanks, assault engineers and Commandos; the total numbers being not far off 40,000.

The assault on the one Infantry Brigade front thus gave great depth to the attack, though the narrow front resulted in a gap between the 3rd British and 3rd Canadian Infantry Division on the right. The 8th Infantry Brigade was the assault brigade, with 185th Infantry Brigade follow-up and 9th Infantry Brigade reserve.

The task of the 8th Brigade was to destroy the beach defences and establish a bridgehead to a depth of about three and a half miles, and to take over the defence of the bridges "RUGGER" and "CRICKET" from the 6th Airborne Division. One Battalion was to seize and consolidate on the PERRIERS-SUR-LE-DAN ridge to form a firm base for the forward movement of the other Infantry Brigades. The 185th Infantry Brigade was to land two hours after the 8th Infantry Brigade and to push forward with all speed with the object of capturing CAEN. One Battalion was to ride forward on the tanks of the STAFFORDSHIRE YEOMANRY who were in support of the 185th Brigade. The 9th Infantry Brigade was in reserve with orders to concentrate in the area of HERMANVILLE-SUR-MER: thereafter being at the Divisional Command's disposal.

Air support was on a vast scale. The combination of the Allied build-up and the steady wearing down of the enemy's production capacity had resulted in a relative strength of available aircraft of 10,500 Allied to 800 enemy. Air support for the 'Second Front' opened long before the actual Invasion with the bombing of aircraft factories, centres of communication such as railway yards, and finally targets more directly affecting the operation; coastal batteries, bridges over the Seine. The batteries in the landing zone were only bombed during the last two or three days, to maintain surprise as long as possible. To avoid large craters on the beach, which would greatly hinder the passage of vehicles across it, the R.A.F. were to drop no bombs heavier than 20-lbs on the beach area. During the operations a fighter cover of ten squadrons was to be maintained over the beaches. It required a total of fifty-five Squadrons to keep these in the air.

The 8th Infantry Brigade consisted of First Suffolk, 2nd E. Yorks and 1st S. Lan. with 13/18th Royal Hussars, 33rd and 76th Field Regiments R.A., A. Company, 2 M.M.G., No. 4 Commando, No. 41 R.M. Commando, 246th Field Company R.E. and 8th Field Ambulance as well as some other minor units. Under command for landing only was No. 6 S.S. Brigade under Brigadier Lord Lovat. Supporting arms were sub-allotted so that each Battalion had in support one Squadron 13/18th Hussar Field Batteries and one platoon M.M.G., with detachments of 246 Field Company R.E. and 8th Field Ambulance. In addition attached to each Battalion H.Q. was a F.O.B. (Forward Officer Bombardment) who controlled the fire of whatever warships had been allotted for the Battalion support. First Suffolk had one 6-inch cruiser, H.M.S. "DRAGON", and one Fleet destroyer, H.M.S. "KELVIN".

The brigade plan was to assault with two Battalions, S. Lan. R. right, and E. Yorks left, with First Suffolk in reserve. The two assault Battalions were to land at H-Hour, their tasks being:-

S. Lan. R. to land on "QUEEN WHITE" beach and destroy the beach defences with the two assault companies. The two reserve companies to push forward and capture HERMANVILLE-SUR-MER, the Battalion finally consolidating at the South end of that village.

E. Yorks to land on "QUEEN RED" beach and destroy the beach defences with the two assault companies, then with the reserve companies to destroy various enemy localities inland and slightly S.E. from the beach. At the same time the Battalion was to be prepared to send one company and a squadron of tanks to take over the defence of the bridges "RUGGER" and "CRICKET". Finally to consolidate the area of St. AUBIN D'ARQUENAY, a village to the East of COLLEVILLE-SUR-ORNE.

Reserve Companies and Battalion H.Q. of both assault Battalions to land at H plus 20.

The task of the reserve Battalion, First Suffolk, was to land at H plus 60 on "QUEEN WHITE" beach, assemble inland of the beach, advance and capture COLLEVILLE-SUR-ORNE, the battery "MORRIS", and the headquarters strongpoint "HILLMAN", finally consolidating on the PERRIERS-SUR-LE-DAN feature with the object of forming a firm base for further forward movement.

The Special Service Brigades and Commandos were landing between H plus 30 and H plus 75 with tasks briefly as follows:-

No. 41 R.M. Commando to exploit to the right—landing on "QUEEN WHITE" beach—and clear LUC-SUR-MER and LION-SUR-MER.

No. 4 Commando to land on "QUEEN RED" beach and exploit to the left with the object of clearing OUISTREHAM.

No. 6 Special Service Brigade, less No. 4 Commando, to land and move with all speed over the bridges "RUGGER" and "CRICKET" to the assistance of 6 Airborne Division taking over the defence of the bridges en route.

The task of the Battalion included the breaking open of two strongpoints "MORRIS" and "HILLMAN", and as previously stated the Battalion was trained for this type of operation, D Company being split up to provide "Breaching Platoons" for A, B and C Companies. This particular role for D Company had been practised during the previous ten months, and D Company Platoons always went to the same rifle companies, so that officers and men were accustomed to working together. The detachment

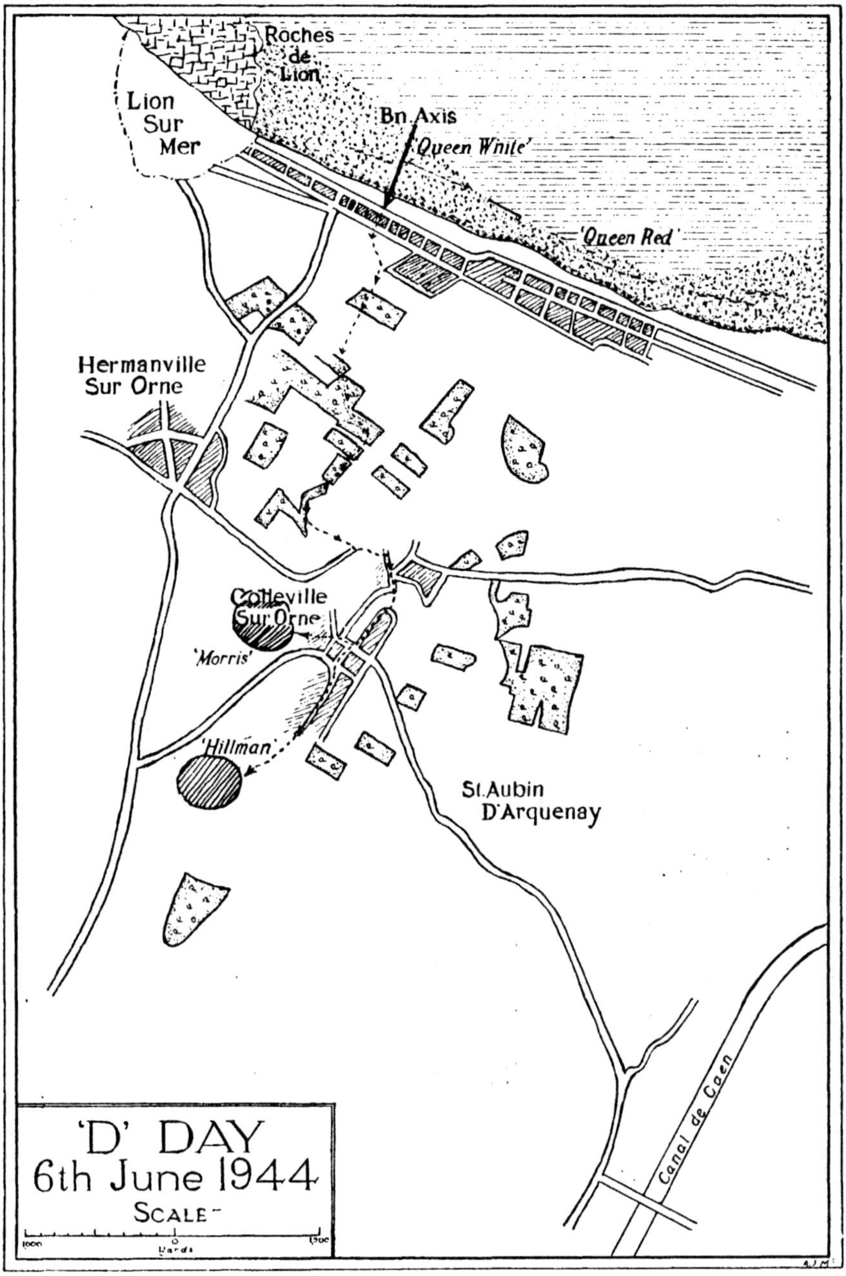
Roches de Lion
Lion Sur Mer
Bn. Axis
'Queen White'
'Queen Red'
Hermanville Sur Orne
Colleville Sur Orne
'Morris'
'Hillman'
St. Aubin D'Arquenay
Canal de Caen
'D' DAY
6th June 1944
SCALE
Yards

from 246th Field Company R.E., 1 officer and 26 Other Ranks, mine clearance teams, who had been with the Battalion for nearly a year, also worked with the same companies on each Exercise.

The Battalion had carried out a field firing exercise on the South Downs Training Area during the latter half of May, framed so that the roles of the Companies should approximate to their actual roles on the operation; breaching platoons, sappers and pioneers being attached to their actual companies.

The tasks of breaching "MORRIS" and "HILLMAN" were given to "B" and "A" Companies respectively.

The operation was to be carried out in five phases as follows:-

PHASE ONE. LANDING AND ASSEMBLY :-

The Battalion to land on "QUEEN WHITE" beach at H plus 60 and move independently by Companies to the Battalion Assembly area.

At the Assembly Area small packs and respirators were to be taken off and the 'O' Group was to meet the C.O. at a previously stated point.

When the Battalion was assembled with its tanks and other units 'D' Company (less the two breaching platoons to 'A' and 'B' Companies) would move through the orchards to a position from which they could observe and if required shoot on "MORRIS".

PHASE TWO. CAPTURE OF COLLEVILLE-SUR-ORNE :-

'C' Company, with one troop C Squadron 13/18th HUSSARS, would move through the orchards in a S.E. direction and clear the village from North to South. It might be necessary en route to deal with two pill-boxes if the E. Yorks or Commandos had not been there first. 'C' Company's first task in clearing the village was to give 'B' Company a clear run in the approach to their assault on "MORRIS", after which they would move forward to observe "HILLMAN" and assist 'A' Company by fire in their assault on that locality.

PHASE THREE. CAPTURE OF "MORRIS":-

'B' Company with one breaching platoon 'D' Company, to assault "MORRIS". The best approach was through the lower part of the village. When the O.C. 'B' Company was ready the previously prepared fire plan would be laid on. After its capture 'B' Company was to move forward and take up a position to assist by fire 'A' Company's assault.

PHASE FOUR. CAPTURE OF "HILLMAN" :-

'A' Company with one breaching platoon 'D' Company to assault "HILLMAN". The best approach was through the village and then, provided it was not covered by a M.G., up through a sunken track with high hedges on both sides, breaching the wire at the north-west corner of the position.

As for the assault on "MORRIS" there was a prepared fire plan when the O.C. 'A' Company was ready to assault.

After capture of the position the Company was to move to its consolidated area.

PHASE FIVE. CONSOLIDATION :-

Each company knew its approximate consolidation area and a plan of the Battalion area had been issued. The companies would be at the four corners of a square, grouped round "HILLMAN", with Battalion H.Q. in the area of the left rear company near the road which came south from COLLEVILLE.

The two forward Companies would be on the ridge and could shoot forward along it, while the two rear companies had a very good reserve slope position.

The 8th Brigade orders had stated that the Battalion was to send forward strong patrols to some woods about a mile and a half in front of the ridge, these patrols to wait until 185th Brigade had passed through. 'C' Company had been assigned to this task with a section of 3-inch mortars under command and a F.O.O. attached. However on the day 'C' Company did not have to carry out this mission as the 185th Brigade passed through before the Battalion had finished with "HILLMAN."

During the first part of the operation "C" Squadron 13/18 HUSSARS (less the troop with "C" Company) was to support the Battalion from the right flank and to assist in the prepared fire plans as stated below. During the assault on "HILLMAN" the troop with 'C' Company was to support the left while the remainder of the Squadron was to move forward on the right according to the enemy's anti-tank defence.

On consolidation the squadron was to move up the ridge and be prepared to deal with any enemy armoured counter attack, until the normal anti-tank defence had been established.

FIRE PLAN:—

Available: H.M.S. DRAGON (6-in. Cruiser).
H.M.S. KELVIN (Fleet Destroyer).
One battery 33 Field Regiment R.A.
One battery 76 Field Regiment R.A.
'C' Squadron 13/18 HUSSARS.
3-in. Mortar Platoon 1 SUFFOLK.

Major Waring, the commander of the battery from 76 Field Regiment, who co-ordinated the fire of the two batteries, and Captain Llewellyn, the F.O.B., who controlled the fire of the Warships were at Battalion H.Q., 'B' and 'C' Companies each had a F.O.O. from the batteries.

There was no set fire plan during the early part of the operation, shooting to be by opportunity and by observation, except that as soon as the F.O.B. had established communication with the ships he was to bring down fire on "HILLMAN."

For the assaults on "MORRIS" and "HILLMAN" set piece fire plans had been prepared: a 5 minutes H.E. followed by three minutes smoke. The tank Squadron was to fire by observation with special attention to filling up any windows in the smoke.

The advantage of this plan was that it was simple and every officer and man knew exactly how much fire and smoke to expect prior to the assault.

The fire plan was to be initiated in each case by a code word:—"SMASH" in the case of "MORRIS", and "GRAB" in the case of "HILLMAN". The Company Commander concerned reporting over the air:—"Ready for "SMASH" or "GRAB." The Commanding Officer allowing five or ten minutes for the message to get through to the guns, would give all stations on the net:—"SMASH" at . . . . hours."

When "SMASH" was finished the guns were to lift on to "HILLMAN" at a slow rate and when "GRAB" was finished a lift of three or four hundred yards beyond the locality. Fire could also always be brought down by observation as required.

The M.G. Platoon was not of much use in the set fire plans against concrete; but would be employed for opportunity shooting and to deal with any enemy break through towards the beaches, or infantry counter-attack.

COMMUNICATIONS:—

The normal Battalion 18-set net would be in operation. In addition rifle companies and Battalion H.Q. were on a 46-set net. Thus communications to companies were duplicated. Within companies there was a 38-set net, all platoons being equipped with these sets. Artillery and M.G. were on the Battalion 18-set net. Communication to Brigade was by 22-set duplicated by 46-set. Success signals fired from Verey pistols always duplicated wireless. A system of light signals for close work with the tanks was also devised.

"D" DAY.

MAY 30th — JUNE 6th.

On the 30th May marshalling commenced. This entailed breaking the battalion up into various ship and craft loads and moving to other camps where the various ship loads were being assembled.

During this period the troops were given plenty of E.N.S.A. Concerts, cinemas, and there were games grounds available; while all spare time was spent in additional "briefing", cleaning of ammunition and making up last minute deficiencies.

During this marshalling period there was only one (old) absentee, and no sick. There can be no better tribute to the morale of the Battalion.

On the 3rd June loading of L.S.I. began.

The march from Victoria Barracks to the Harbour Station was through streets that had been cleared and deserted, with military and civil police at frequent intervals on either side of the road. Thence in a paddle steamer to the L.S.I. lying anchored in the Solent. Here a practice with full equipment was carried out at 2330 to practise the men in finding their way in the dark from the troop decks to the landing craft.

The Battalion was distributed as follows:—

Half Bn. H.Q. "A" and "C" Companies	L.S.I. "Empire Broadsword."
"B" and "D" Companies	L.S.I. "Empire Battle Axe."
Half Bn. H.Q.	L.S.I. (L.) 228.
L.O.B.	L.S.I. 229.

Anti-Tank Platoons, Mortar Platoon, Carriers. Distributed out in 3 L.C.T.s.

All the above to be landed on Tide 1.

M.O.'s Truck, 1 Am. and 3 ton, L.S.T. with Q.M. to be landed on Tide 2.

June 4th. Code Signal at 0800. Suspension of loading. Weather bad and gale blowing up.

June 5th. L.C.T. Convoys moved down SOLENT. Signal from Admiral:

"Good Luck." "Drive on."

Final information was given to all concerned about enemy dispositions, defences, beach obstacles. Also information that beach obstacles had been considerably increased during the last few days and that the 21st Panzer Division had moved nearer to the beach area.

Men in very good heart; but rather quiet.

2045 hours. L.S.I. Convoy weighed anchor and moved slowly down SOLENT—Escort five destroyers.

Padre said one or two prayers over loud speaker. Much appreciated; nearly all troops on deck.

Several officers described the sea passage from England to Normandy on the memorable 'D' Day, June 5th.

Major Charles Boycott felt that it was just like another Exercise—only this time there was no return ticket to England. He found it hard to believe that the training was over and the great adventure about to start.

Captain J. S. Coppock who commanded the small party of 4 officers and 90 other ranks "Left Out of the Battle", incidentally on the Normandy shore, wrote:—

"As our party marched to the embarkation point at 0530 on June 3rd the "WRENS" leant out of the windows of their billets on the seafront and waved to us. On reaching the embarkation point we heard the operation was postponed, so we all marched back, hoping no one would see us.

Next day, the weather seemed worse and there were no "WRENS" to wave to us. Everyone this time was quiet, serious and determined. The sea was choppy and practically all the officers and men were sick. At breakfast next morning few had the courage to touch more than a cup of tea.

Charles Boycott gives this account of the passage:—

"SOUTHAMPTON WATER was a fine sight. Never before in its history can it have contained such a variety of ships or craft of such strange design. The various flotillas of landing and assault craft were moored in long lines with destroyers, a few cruisers and monitors amongst them. The weather had by now turned gloomy with a stiff breeze and white horses were kicking up all over the SOLENT. The "BROADSWORD" was moored furthest away from the quay and so we were able to see the whole vast array on our way out, and we remembered there were similar spectacles to be seen in other English harbours.

Everything was normal on board. The same ship's company that we knew so well were there to help us on board, and everything went according to plan. The troops were passed down to their messdecks without delay and went oft at once to get their first meal. The officers had theirs, and then a short conference was held to decide the next day's routine, for the operation had been postponed.

The day dragged somewhat! Several of the troops did, however, find some amusement in having their hair cut; the fashion spread round the ship of having the head practically shaved and then cutting out a large 'V' sign! All very well if one was to be away from England for a good long time, but if for any reason we returned early it might be embarrassing, women being as suspicious as they are!

The issue of maps presented an unexpected last minute problem. Each company got an enormous issue, and each man had to carry about five; an appreciable extra burden to all of us who had already worked out our carrying "economy."

Tuesday, June 5th we were at sea. Early next morning, true to routine the Merchant Navy provided us with egg and bacon for breakfast, coffee, white bread, marmalade and all the sugar and butter one could wish for to make a good foundation for the forthcoming frolic.

Outside it was getting light. A long double row of lighted buoys marked the swept channel stretching ahead; near at hand was the dim outline of other vessels, just astern was a destroyer. It struck me at the time that she was sailing mighty close to the line of buoys, and shortly after I had gone below I heard a dull explosion. She had struck a mine and sank almost immediately. She was "One of the two" lost on the whole operation —and our first sign of battle.

At 0610 came the order "Craft Serials Numbers . . . . 745 move Now". Up we went, I leading, along the decks and up the steep ladders to the top deck, and into the waiting craft. Whilst hanging from the davits I listened to the ship's mate giving forth. He was a Welshman and gave of his best, cheerfully and freely to all who crossed his path. Talking at such a stage was bad discipline, and, except for the mate and the hum of the winch engines, the ship was very quiet. I was anxious to be away, and to disassociate myself from this large target. We had expected to be under fire from shore batteries at this point, and I hoped we shouldn't tempt Providence too long.

At 0623, exactly to time, we were lowered away, and, as we were on the lee side, our R.M. crew were able to free the tackles quite early. It was a perfect lowering. As we moved away, to shouts of "Good luck" from the ship's crew, it got much rougher, but by then there was a lot to look at, and our little private troubles were forgotten. Like clock work the L.C.A. flotilla completed its forming up with the L.C.I. to the front of the flotilla to lead us in. There was much waving and ineffective shouting as she passed by on her way up.

So we started off at 0700. The line of homely L.S.I.s at their moorings receded as we moved in towards the land and they were soon lost to view in the poor visibility. By now 95% of the Battalion was all together again, it seemed like a conjuring trick, and in their correct position for deployment on the beach.

We had in all about an hour and forty minutes run-in to the beach. I had my field glasses and one of my two company snipers got out his telescope. With these, and what I could remember from the fire support programme, I was able to keep something of a running commentary on events.

We could hear shells, probably from the monitor "ROBERTS", passing over on our left flank. One of the troops remarked, "Cor, they sound like ruddy council houses". An expressive remark.

H Hour! 0720. We couldn't hear much as we were still a good five miles out, but my thoughts were with the assaulting troops. How was the beach? Were they catching it badly as they crossed that wide stretch of hard sand? Were the beach obstacles proving as difficult as expected? Had the Navy put them down in the right spot? We wanted to know the answers to these and a hundred other questions, not only for their sakes but for our own.

We passed several Allied ships of various kinds and saw the Brigade H.Q.s destroyer moving towards the beach at high speed. It was still too thick to pick out even a glimpse of the hostile coast.

At about 0800 we passed some returning L.C.A. of the first flight from our own L.S.I. Our crew shouted and semaphored for information as to "what it was like?" Some of the crew put their thumbs up, but others put them down. Apparently it wasn't all a picnic. We were too far away to see any damage to these returning craft.

Suddenly my coxswain said "You can see the craft on the beach now, Sir." You could indeed—a great long line of them silhouetted against the pall of smoke; through this bank of smoke no detail of the land could be seen. It was a sombre picture and I wondered what lay behind. Being the craft commander I had the use of a vizor in the front shield, out of which I could peer and watch the scene develop in front of me. I studied the photos in my hand. Looked up, and like a film getting in focus, the whole beach was clear. On a signal from the flotilla leader all the craft fanned out into line abreast; we seemed to rush at the beach; the details coming into ever sharper relief. There was the "Funny" house bang slap in front; I didn't notice the "Tower", but the house was enough. The land still couldn't be seen clearly, because of the mass of twisting, jerking wrecked craft, through which it seemed impossible to pick a path. I remember thinking we were going dangerously fast and must crash into the wrecks. In next to no time we were into the melee. The coxswain found a gap, did a sharp turn to starboard and the beach was fifty yards ahead. As we turned I saw a filthy yellow mine on a stake flash past on the port bow. Thank God we missed that. There was a grating on the keel and we were aground. "Down doors" and out I leapt, clean forgetting all the rules about stepping carefully to avoid headers. It had been a fine bit of seamanship by my coxswain and I hope and think I remembered to thank him.

I cannot remember how deep the water was—but we must have splashed through it for about twenty yards or so. As I got out of the craft I just missed falling over a corpse rocking face up in the surf; at the time I was convinced that he was a German—something about his uniform—but now I am not sure. This made me think about enemy fire; for the first time I noticed the waterspouts being kicked up by the bursting bombs and shells. I increased my pace sharply.

We were on the beach. A background of shattered, smoking seaside houses with naked slats in their roofs. The narrow stretch of sand covered with tanks and men. A pungent, burning and explosive sort of stink. Three wounded men sitting under the lee of a burned out tank—one of them with a cigarette. Just in front a flail tank struggling to get off the beach through a narrow exit. My craft load had all caught up with me by now, and I decided to move off right handed along the sea side of the beach houses.

Here I found the C.O. and two other Company Commanders. The C.O. was being "put into the picture" by the acting Commanding Officer of the Assault Battalion. He confirmed the position of our assembly.

At the back of the houses we struck an area which had been inundated by the enemy; the dry weather had, however, dried it out almost entirely. In a near-by ditch some soldiers of the Assaulting battalion said there were snipers ahead.

In a very short time we reached our position of assembly.

It was almost too good to be true. The whole thing had gone like clockwork; we were in the right place at the right time and at full strength. The troops were in good form, and none the worse for their experience on the beaches. They had been well trained mentally and physically—their training and discipline stood them in good stead.

It had been a great experience, something that none of us will ever forget. Superb organisation, long months of training and meticulous attention to detail, had all paid their dividend. There can be no higher praise of the organisation of a great and complicated undertaking than to say "It all seemed easy."

To borrow a sentence with which to conclude—"We were jerked from 100% peace to 100% war in a night. It appeared that we had taken the first strain; our share in Operation 'OVERLORD' was off to a flying start."

Not that everything went without a hitch. The L.C.I. that carried Major Gough, the Second in Command, and 150 men of the Battalion beached as it should; but its ramp, the only possible means of landing, jammed. Then the craft listed to an alarming angle and all men were moved to the other side to dress ship as far as possible. For twenty minutes the Navy toiled in vain—and the craft had to be backed from the shore and the men transferred to another boat. A very trying ordeal.

Some hours later the 'Q' side of the Battalion also had an unlucky break. The "tide three" boat carrying the R.Q.M.S., four C/Sgts., several M.T. drivers, vehicles and stores was sunk by lucky hits. Luckily all the members of the Battalion were saved and eventually rejoined; but for a time the quartermaster was understaffed and the difficulties of supplying men was greatly increased.

Dick Goodwin gives a brief account of the crossing and a more detailed picture of the subsequent attack by the First Suffolk in which they made good all their objectives.

He writes: "The voyage was uneventful. The Convoy carrying the Battalion was in the left hand lane but one, the warships for bombardment and counter battery work being in the left hand lane. Mine sweepers leading in all lanes. The lanes were marked by buoys. Sea rough, strongish wind.

The Lowering Position, seven miles from shore, was reached at 0525 and here the destroyer on the left hit a mine and folded up like a jack knife, a small portion of her stern remaining above water for a considerable time while two American Coastguard cutters searched for survivors. The Beach Group Party, Captain Breach and three Other Ranks, had gone with the first flight of the Assault Battalion; their duty being to get acquainted with the general layout of the beach prior to the arrival of the Battalion.

At 0623 the Battalion loads from "EMPIRE BROADSWORD" and "EMPIRE BATTLEAXE" in a total of 20 L.C.A.s, with our 8th Brigade H.Q., the whole under Captain Sykes, R.M., were lowered. These circled round till joined by the leaders, L.C.I.s 228 and 229, and then in four Columns made for the shore.

Passed L.P. marking buoy at 0700 hours according to schedule. An uncomfortable journey, much spray coming inboard. H.M.S. "WARSPITE", on port bow, was firing steadily; but the wind carried away sound of guns for first half hour. Later we could see and hear many cruisers and destroyers firing. Bombers passed overhead and there was much rumbling from the land as they dropped their bombs. Fighters were patrolling the beaches. A single aircraft flew in from sea and from left flank laid very good smoke screen.

Troops in L.C.A. had cocoa and sandwiches during run in. Getting nearer shore the noise increased greatly and there appeared to be a thick belt of smoke along the whole seafront through which many fires glowed. Suddenly the beach came in sight and our eyes searched it to locate position. Luckily two houses, still standing, but knocked about and burning, which marked a hoped-for landing place, appeared slightly on starboard bow.

The L.C.A.s went into line abreast and drove on at full speed for beach, all troops sitting down and cox'ns closed down. I looked through slits in forrard shields. Suddenly the beach obstacles appeared half under water, many of them with Teller mines lashed to the top of them. Cox'n had to think quickly to avoid them and Sykes very calmly gave him advice as to steering. Beached safely narrowly missing a derelict tank at the water's edge. Put into about eighteen inches of water and plodded ashore. General impression of burning vehicles and boats, houses on fire above the beach, and a tremendous smell of explosive and burnt metal. Much noise of guns and small arms fire; but nothing appeared to be falling on the particular bit of beach while we were landing. When about forty yards up from the water's edge enemy guns opened from right front and shells whistled overhead and burst among craft beached—first shell appeared to land on ramp of the L.C.A. we had just left.

Companies moved up to head of beach where they were collected by Company Commanders and then moved forward. It was difficult to get clear picture of situation; but we found an A.V.R.E. prepared exit bridge and entered the house area. Here I met Second in Command of S. LAN. who told me that his Commanding Officer had been badly hit on the beach. Bullets and shells flying about in all directions. We moved forward and contacted a Company Commander of S. LAN. who gave me the situation and said that two Companies of their Battalion had gone forward to HERMANVILLE as intended. Battalion H.Q. approached assembly area with 'D' Company; other Companies on flanks. Snipers were firing on us from buildings behind and L/Sgt. Ling just in front of me was hit in thigh. Otherwise casualties at this stage were very light—only three wounded. Unfortunately the "Forward Officer Bombardment" attached to the Battalion, Capt. Llewellyn R.A., was wounded on the beach, so that we were without naval support for the day. This was unfortunate though not vital.

On arrival at the wood previously selected as the Battalion assembly area we found what we had suspected—so much had been cut that no decent cover was left. There was a sniper among the bundles of brushwood; but he was killed or made off at once.

Decided to move forward to the next cover about two or three hundred yards ahead as planned. On arrival here, an orchard, we were greeted by an officer and about five other ranks of a Canadian parachute unit who had been dropped over the wrong area during the night. They were very pleased to see us as they had had an uncomfortable time during the early hours, being bombed by our own people. However they were determined to go on with the battle and later joined 'D' Company for the morning.

A MARAUDER DURING THE EARLY MORNING OF "D" DAY FLYING OVER "QUEEN BEACH" WHERE 1ST BATTALION LANDED.

LEGEND:—B. BN. HEADQUARTERS LANDED ABOUT HERE.
D. ORIGINAL BATTALION ASSEMBLY AREA.
E. ACTUAL BATTALION ASSEMBLY AREA.
F. HERMANVILLE-SUR-MER.

At this point the Liasion Officer from C Sqn. 13/18 Hussars, Captain Wardlaw—reported in his tank with information that the Sqn. was on its way to us.

While waiting to collect the Battalion, information came over the air that the two bridges "RUGGER" and "CRICKET", over the ORNE had been captured intact. This was heartening news as it meant that the 6th Airborne Division had carried out its task in spite of the bad weather.

THE ADVANCE FROM THE BEACH.

All had reported and we proceeded to start our part of the operation proper; 'D' Company, less two platoons, moved off through the orchards in a southerly direction to a position from which they could get observation and bring fire on to the enemy battery at "MORRIS"—their advance was somewhat slowed up by the minefields in the orchards—thoughtfully marked "ACHTUNG MINEN", with a drawing of a skull and crossbones.

'C' Company moved off with the troop of tanks under Command in a S.E. direction towards the village of COLLEVILLE-SUR-ORNE, followed by Rgroup, 'B' Company, 'A' Company: L.O.B. remaining behind in the assembly area under Capt. Coppock. Cattle were grazing in some of the orchards, so we choose this as our route to avoid mines. Just after we left the assembly area an enemy multiple-barrelled mortar opened up on it; the bombs could be seen and made the most uncanny wailing noise.

We passed some of Lord Lovat's Commandos, who had just captured two pillboxes which lay to the North of the village; they had with them two or three frightened looking prisoners. They said they wanted to go and settle with 'that mortar' so we lent them a couple of tanks and they were not long in settling!

I met Lord Lovat at the north end of the village while his men were settling with the mortar—he looked as if he were out for a country walk—a little later he followed up through the village and struck off eastwards to cross the bridges over the River ORNE which had been captured by the Airborne Division during the night. These Commandos were carrying big loads and marched fast.

At this point 'D' Company came on the air and Major Papillon told me that 'C' Sqn. were in position on his right and were exchanging some shots with the strong point at "HILLMAN", but that there appeared to be no movement in the Battery "MORRIS". 'C' Company had by this time started clearing the village and as they were meeting no opposition I told Major McCaffrey, O.C. 'B' Company, that it was possible the enemy had already deserted the battery position; but to be prepared to put in his attack as arranged in case it was a trick. He moved his company quickly up into the village behind 'C' Company and directly he had elbow room moved out towards the battery.

'C' Company cleared the village very rapidly and the fact that it was done quickly but thoroughly, even though there was no opposition, spoke well for the great detail of the company plan. It was obvious that each platoon and each section knew exactly which houses or which side streets were its particular responsibility.

Meanwhile 'B' Company was preparing for its assault on "MORRIS", the Company commander deciding to blow the outer wire before calling for artillery concentration. However, just as the Bangalore torpedoes were being placed for this task, the white flag was put up and the garrison emerged from the concrete emplacements with their hands up; sixty-seven in all. These prisoners were brought back into the village by four highly delighted soldiers. They were in poor fettle, the battery having been an air target during the preliminary bombardment; a fair proportion were Poles.

'B' Company moved out of the enemy position as soon as they were satisfied there were no enemy left; it was as well that they did, as the Boche started shelling this area less than ten minutes after the garrison had surrendered.

Later he shortened his range and shells began to drop in the south end of the village which 'C' Company had cleared. Unfortunately 'A' Company who were following up preparatory to their attack on "HILLMAN" suffered some casualties, one section being almost entirely knocked out.

When about a hundred yards clear of the village another Canadian parachute officer met us, having also been dropped in the wrong place. He took me to a position from which to see the strong point "HILLMAN". Here, by peering over some standing corn, I could see the outer wire about 150 yards away; but only one steel cupola was visible.

THE ASSAULT OF "HILLMAN" BY 'A' COMPANY. JUNE 6TH.

Captain Ryley, Commanding 'A' Company, went off to make a closer reconnaissance; 'C' Company pushing one platoon forward to protect the reconnaissance and deployment of 'A' Company and another platoon through the orchards on the left where they could see the open country so as to form a defensive flank for the operation on that side. Thus with 'B' Company on the right 'A' Company was reasonably secure.

At the same time the platoon of 'D' Company with company H.Q. collected the breaching platoon which had been with 'B' Company; and waited in reserve at the top of the village.

The Battery Commander was now registering his guns on this enemy strongpoint and the Battalion 3-inch mortars were doing the same.

Just before 1300 hours Captain Ryley told me that he was ready and I laid on "GRAB" for 1310 hours giving this out over the air. At 1310 hours the H.E. came down, laid on by artillery, mortars and tanks; the breaching platoon with 'A' Company under Lieut. Russell, ready to move forward to the outer wire. Then with the lifting of the H.E. and under cover of smoke the platoon crawled forward through the corn; the Bangalore torpedoes were placed under the wire and blown. Next the mine clearance sheep tracking party made their three foot wide lane through the minefield and laid the white tape for the troops to follow. When these reached the inner wire, the Second Bangalore section came up and placed their torpedoes. Here Lieut. Russell had bad luck as the first initiating device to fire the torpedo failed to go off, and he had to go back and fire another one. This was successful and the breach was made. This platoon of 'D' Company carried out their task extremely well, working just as they had done on training many times before; but in this case they were within fifty yards or so of the enemy. They were then pulled back into company reserve.

The first assault platoon of 'A' Company then moved forward through the breach, crawling under cover along a narrow sunken lane which enabled the troops to get within about thirty yards of the outer wire.

The platoon got through the gap, the enemy opening up with machine guns; but the platoon went on into the trenches. These proved of little value, for when they moved again the Germans from their shelters and emplacements brought heavy machine gun fire to bear at short range. The enemy now had the gap in the wire taped and any movement brought bursts of automatic fire; casualties began to mount up. However, by use of 2-in. mortar smoke the second platoon got into the enemy's trench position; but were brought to a standstill like the first platoon. Captain Ryley was killed and Lieut. Tooley mortally wounded, also Corporal Stares, his leading section commander. It was not possible to bring these two latter in as no movement across the open was possible. Other wounded from the vicinity of the gap were dragged back through the corn to the sunken lane, where the stretcher bearers carried them back to the R.A.P.

By this time my carrier and the battery commander's tank had arrived; this gave us a 19 set, a link on the tank squadron net, and on the battery commander's tank, his proper communications to his guns, both of which were great assets. The smaller sets had not been working well: due to the great number in use over the area.

As there appeared to be no enemy anti-tank guns left in action in the position, I ordered the tanks up to the outer wire in order to give the troops close support.

At this time the 2nd Norfolks who were to pass through us, started to move out to the left and by-pass the position; as it was obvious that it would be some time before it was finally subdued.

The Divisional Commander came up to my O.P. and asked how we were getting on. On being told the situation he said, "Well, you must get it before dark; and in time to allow you to dig in on your consolidated positions. Enemy armour is about and they will probably counter attack at first light." I assured him we should succeed. He left with a cheery "Good luck."

The arrival of the tanks at the outer wire did not materially improve the situation; they prevented any enemy movement across the open, but they could not penetrate the emplacements or cover our men from the enemy machine gun fire. The steel cupola which was causing most of the trouble was not even penetrated by several rounds of 17-pdr. A.P. shot, though no doubt the occupants suffered from a severe headache. It was obvious that it would not be possible to capture the position unless the tanks went inside the wire to enable the infantry to get up close to the emplacements and winkle the Boche out. In the absence of enemy anti-tank guns this seemed a justifiable task for the Shermans, and accordingly I decided to make a vehicle gap and lay on a fresh attack with a short preliminary bombardment.

I ordered Lieut. Perry, who had taken over command of 'A' Company, to withdraw his men from the position to the sunken lane so as to get them clear of the bombardment. Then I ordered the R.E. officer, Lieut. Heal, to widen the gap to nine feet. This he proposed to do with a British Mark III mine buried deep; a job that would have taken at least an hour. It was only possible to work lying full length on the ground as any exposure drew machine gun fire.

Meanwhile the Squadron Liaison Officer and the battery commander went off in the battery commander's tank to look at the left of the position. They returned about twenty minutes later and the Liaison Officer sat down saying that he had a slight headache, as the tank had just gone up on a mine. The tank was in fact a complete wreck, one track being blown off and the tank completely burnt out.

The Brigadier arrived and I asked him for two Flails which would speed up the process of mine clearance and make a wider track. This he arranged to do. But we did not stop work on the gap, and this was just as well as the gap was open before there was any sign of the Flails. The Squadron Leader agreed to take a chance with the gap, even though the sapper had only been able to give it a 50-50 chance of complete clearance.

Time was getting on and I called for a preliminary bombardment of five minutes H.E. from the tanks and two batteries at rate four. When this lifted the tanks went through, negotiating the gap safely. The troops followed them up and set about cleaning up the complicated position:—one platoon from each of 'C' and 'D' Companies assisted 'A' Company with this task. It was a slow business and at the start the tanks drew away too far from the infantry; but were called back and then were of great assistance.

Whatever had been the state of the morale of the enemy we first encountered, there was no doubt that the men in this strongpoint had been told and were determined to fight to the end. They continued to fire from their emplacements while the mopping up was going on and in some cases had to be blown out of these emplacements with heavy explosive charges, which the Battalion pioneers were carrying.

When it appeared that resistance was decreasing and the situation under control, I ordered 'B' and 'D' Companies forward to their previously arranged consolidation areas, as it was essential that they should have as much time as possible for digging in before dark.

The last resistance on the strong point ended about 2015 hours and our men moved on as quickly as possible to get on with consolidation.

Just about this time, 2030 hours, we saw the most magnificent sight—the Air Landing Brigade coming. The sky seemed to be completely obscured by an enormous swarm of Dakota aircraft towing gliders. They came in in perfect formation right over our heads and released their gliders which turned through 180 degrees and came in to land away on our left. Following them up a few minutes later came a large number of Stirlings which dropped the containers of equipment; this was also most spectacular, the various containers were attached to parachutes of different colours.

The whole operation was done smoothly with complete absence of hurry and not a vestige of opposition. It was a great sight for the troops and an equally impressive sight for the German prisoners who did not seem to think it was quite fair.

'D' Company had in their consolidation area a farm. As the company approached it two snipers were encountered in the corn; and at the same time the C.S.M. said that he could see movement through a window of the farm about 250 yards away. He fired a round and someone fell down, whereupon the company set about tackling the farm as an enemy position. After a few bursts from a Bren group the white flag appeared and the bag this time was 2 officers and 48 other ranks. The Company Commander decided to stand back about 250 yards from the farm for consolidation in order to avoid the inevitable Enemy mortar fire which would come down. This proved to be a wise move as it was mortared on and off for about an hour without doing any damage to the company.

The two remaining hours of daylight proved sufficient to dig in, as the soil was sandy. The Anti-tank platoon were especially good; they got their guns dug in extremely well and quickly, doing the preliminary work on their pits by blowing 75 grenades.

The 3-inch mortars also dug in well and quickly and before dark registered the farm in front of 'D' Company as a D.F. task.

The Battalion 'stood to' from 2230 to 2330 hours after which patrolling for the night started.

Thus ended D-day, probably one of the most famous days in history and certainly an unforgettable experience in the lives of those who took part in it.

The Battalion losses for the day were 2 officers and 5 O.Rs killed, and about 25 O.Rs wounded. The gains were: all objectives taken, together with 270 prisoners including a Regimental Commanding officer.

The loss of Captain R. G. Ryley was the first of the many officer casualties the Battalion was to suffer. Ryley had joined the First Battalion from an O.C.T.U. in March 1941 and had risen on his merits to the Command of 'A' Company. He was one of the many examples that schoolmasters make first class officers. He had a sure understanding of his men and proved himself a very gallant commander in this his first and last action. When the leading platoon under Lieut. J. Powell was pinned down in the enemy trenches Ryley brought forward the reinforcements and organized and led the further unsuccessful attack. He was killed while returning for more help.

ROLL OF OFFICERS present with the First Battalion on "D" Day, 6th June, 1944.

Battalion H.Q.	Lt. Col. R. E. GOODWIN	(W)	Commanding Officer
	Major J. G. M. B. GOUGH	(W)	2nd in Command
	Captain H. K. MERRIAM	(W)	Adjutant
	Lt. A. C. L. SPERLING		Signal Officer
	Captain P. A. ROBINSON, R.A.M.C.	(K)	Medical Officer
	Captain H. G. WOODALL		Chaplain
	Captain P. W. SPURGIN		Quartermaster
H.Q. Company	Captain W. N. BREACH	(W)	Company Commander
	Lt. G. N. CASSON	(W)	M.T.O.
Support Company	Major W. D. GORDON	(W)	Company Commander
	Captain K. G. MAYHEW	(W2)	Carrier Platoon
	Captain H. C. ELLIOTT	(W)	Anti-Tank Platoon
	Lt. S. HEMINGWAY	(W)	Mortar Platoon
	Lt. R. J. GRAHAM	(W)	Carrier Platoon
	Lt. D. S. STEBBINGS	(W)	Anti-Tank Platoon
	Lt. M. M. RAMM	(W)	Pioneer Officer
'A' Company	Captain R. G. RYLEY	(K)	Company Commander
	Captain R. A. B. ROGERS	(W)	
	Lt. K. G. PERRY		
	Lt. T. J. F. TOOLEY	(K)	
	Lt. J. POWELL	(K)	

'B' Company	Major D. W. McCAFFREY	(W)	Company Commander
	Captain W. H. ARCHDALL	(K)	
	Lt. A. C. SANDERS	(W)	
	Lt. F. N. MATTHEWS	(W)	
	Lt. D. N. GARLE	(Evac. Sick)	
'C' Company	Major C. A. BOYCOTT	(W)	Company Commander
	Captain J. S. COPPOCK		
	Lt. E. A. TRIBE	(K)	
	Lt. M. L. WILSON	(K)	
	Lt. A. C. WOODWARD	(W)	
'D' Company	Major P. W. G. PAPILLON	(K)	Company Commander
	Captain A. H. CLAXTON	(K)	
	Lt. J. A. VAUGHAN	(W)	
	Lt. F. M. B. RUSSELL	(W)	
	Lt. G. WILDE	(W)	

(K) denotes - Killed. (W) - Wounded—during the whole Campaign.

THE BRIDGE HEAD.

JUNE 7th—JUNE 24th.

There is a great difference between an action planned with great precision on a well defined enemy position, and an attack on the unknown. As can be seen from the foregoing, even the assault of so formidable a barrier as the "Atlantic Wall" can go "like an Exercise" when every officer and man knows exactly what is required of him during every stage.

The subsequent fighting to enlarge the Bridgehead partook of the unknown and was in many ways the real test of the leadership and the soldierly qualities that had been built up during the months of training in the British Isles.

That night June 6th the Battalion dug itself in and "D" Day ended with patrols going forward to try and contact the enemy.

The other two Battalions of the 8th Brigade had lost heavily in the landing, and for the next few days the First Suffolk was attached to the 9th Brigade; forming a reserve for this formation on the 9th June when an attack was made on CAMBES - CALMANCHE - ST. CONTEST and MALON. This attack was only partially successful.

During this fighting Lt.-Colonel R. E. Goodwin with the Intelligence Officer, Lt. P. Keville, went forward to see the progress. As they reached the forward edge of a wood their Carrier was seen and hit by an 88 cm gun firing from the left flank. Keville was killed and Lt. Colonel R. E. Goodwin received a very severe wound in the shoulder. With great difficulty he was lifted from the Carrier and carried to safety, and thence evacuated by air to England. It is a tribute to surgical science and to his physical fitness that Goodwin was able by the end of the year to rejoin the First Battalion, and reassume command. The wound that he received would have proved fatal in almost every previous war.

The first four days had seen the taking and securing of the immediate bridgehead. But the enemy's resistance had hardened and it was unsound for the 3rd Division to attempt any further major operation on its own.

There was a pause for a fortnight for reorganisation and regrouping of forces against any enemy counter-attack and preparatory to the drive forward through the ring of containing enemy troops. Both sides settled down to a steady process of bombardment and patrolling, the gunners and the mortar platoon making the most of their orders to "hit the Boche as hard and as often as they could". A minebelt was stretched across the front of the Battalion area, which succeeded in disposing of sixteen cows, and was blessed as a particularly happy method of supplementing the rations.

A notably successful patrol, commanded by Lieut. Matthews, got right up to LA BIJUDE and brought back valuable information. During this period the Battalion lost one officer, Lieut. Tribe, and four other ranks killed, three officers and eighteen other ranks wounded.

THE CHATEAU DE LA LONDE.

JUNE 27th, 28th.

The 25th and 26th June were spent reorganizing and planning for the next move forward, the 8th Infantry Brigade having been ordered to capture LA LONDE, the CHATEAU DE LA LONDE, LA BIJUDE and EPRON, an area where fighting had already taken place. The capture of these localities was a necessary preliminary to breaking the enemy's salient in the centre of the CAEN sector.

Unfortunately our intelligence as to the enemy's strength and positions was faulty. It was believed that he was holding the ground with the 2nd Battalion 192nd Panzer Grenadier Regiment "very weak and hoping to be relieved shortly"; whereas the garrison of the CHATEAU DE LA LONDE alone comprised three companies of tanks amounting to 30 or 40 tanks, with a company of infantry, a platoon of sappers and the H.Q. company of the Panzer Regiment all fighting as infantry. Moreover an elaborate defence system had been prepared, probably well before "D" Day.

At 0730 hours on the 27th June the 49th Division was to begin a wide sweep on the right. The attack by the 8th Brigade would start shortly afterwards and was designed to capture LA LONDE, the CHATEAU DE LA LONDE, LA BIJUDE and the village of EPRON. At dawn the following day the 9th Brigade and the 9th Canadian Brigade immediately to the right of the 8th Brigade were to attack forward towards CAEN.

The Battalion's part in this operation "MITTEN", as it was called, was the capture of the final objective of EPRON after the preliminary objectives of LA LONDE, CHATEAU DE LA LONDE and LA BIJUDE had been taken by the South Lancashire and the East Yorkshire, the other two battalions in the Brigade.

The move forward out of CAZALLE started at 1600 hours on the 27th. In the corn fields behind and between the woods of LE MESNIL and LA LANDEL the Battalion came under enemy shell fire and paused until the first of the Brigade objectives should have been taken. The South Lancashires in their push forward were suffering heavy casualties from a large number of M.G.s on their left flank and their attack was held up. At 1720 hours they put in another attack with the aid of "Crocodiles". The situation was obscure. The artillery barrage was repeated and later a dense pall of black smoke rising from the area of the Chateau suggested that the flame throwers were in action. A series of red Verey lights were seen to go up near LA LONDE.

At 1800 hours a report was received that the infantrymen were pinned down in the centre of LA LONDE though some of them had reached the right forward edge of this farm. It transpired later that this was as far as the attack got. Enemy Mark IV tanks had been encountered round the CHATEAU DE LA LONDE.

At 2030 hours a Brigade "O" Group was called and the First Suffolk settled down for the night in its position in the cornfields. The Brigade Commander decided to attack the LA LONDE and CHATEAU DE LA LONDE area at first light on the following morning, 28th June, on a two battalion front, the 2nd East Yorks on the right, the First Suffolk on the left. If success was easy a quick follow up was to be made on the original axis of advance.

At 2230 hours the Commanding Officer, Lt.-Col. J. G. M. B. Gough gave orders for the attack in a barn in GAZELLE by the light of two hurricane lamps. A strong barrage was to come down on the enemy positions for eight minutes and then was to lift at a rate of 100 yards every three minutes. "B" Company and "C" Company were right and left forward Companies respectively. "D" Company was in immediate support and "A" Company in reserve. The 3″ Mortar and Anti-tank platoons were brigaded to assist the advance of the two Battalions, the Carrier Platoon was to act as a mobile reserve while one demolition team from the Pioneer Platoon was allotted to each of the forward Companies.

The approach to the position was over flat open corn fields except where on the right a single hedgerow ran in to the wall round the Chateau. This might be of assistance to "B" Company whose objective was the left part of the Chateau grounds. "C" Company, directed on to the cross tracks beyond the line of trees running out from the Chateau, the scene of many fierce patrol encounters, had only the wheat which stood little more than knee high for cover. Both forward Company Commanders asked for close support from several troops of tanks.

At 0407 hours the barrage came down and as it began to lift eight minutes later "B" and "C" Companies went forward. It was still fairly dark and under machine gun fire it was practically impossible to keep to any set Company plan. Major Boycott commanding "C" Company was wounded half way to the objective. The Company met strong cross fire from machine guns; but went on. Lieut. Woodward with the platoon on the left had only seven men left with him. He was joined by Lieut. Buchanan and one section of 13 platoon. On the right Lieut. Wilson, with 15 Platoon, had been killed in the last few yards of the assault. Captain Brown (Canloan, see appendix) now commanding the Company, took in the remainder of 15 and 13 Platoons with Company H.Q. on to the right of the Company objective. C.S.M. Lankester well up with the left party of assaulting troops was killed almost on the objective by machine gun fire. The enemy riflemen had withdrawn leaving their dead and wounded and a few frightened stragglers who were hauled out of a dugout and sent back as P.O.W.

"B" COMPANY IN THE ATTACK.

The following is an account by Major D. W. McCaffrey of the action of his Company, "B", in the attack.

The Battalion had no finer fighting soldier than this rugged determined leader. His Company had the greatest confidence in him and it was due in no small measure to his fine qualities that the three platoons, not far short of a hundred men at the outset, struggled through devastating fire to take their objective with but twenty four—all that was left. There to be overwhelmed by vastly superior enemy armament.

"During the afternoon of 27th June, 1944, whilst the Battalion was in a defensive position in depth at the village of GAZELLE, 'O' Group was sent for and orders issued for the evening.

"The South Lancashire was to attack and capture the CHATEAU DE LA LONDE; at 1715 hours First Suffolk and the East Yorks were to pass through the South Lancs' objective and attack first the village of LA BIJUDE, then the village of EPRON.

"At 1400 hours that day First Suffolk left GAZELLE and moved to the rear of LA LANDEL. On approaching the Rendezvous, my company came under enemy mortar fire and suffered a few casualties. We deployed and dug in, coming under quite a lot of shell and mortar fire probably meant for the South Lancs, who had started their attack. We could hear the noise of this attack and saw the wounded being brought back; but could see nothing. As usual, lots of rumours reached us, which we ignored.

"During the attack we saw the "Crocodiles" (Flamethrowers) for the first time, a troop of three supporting the South Lancs. But the Germans had dug in some tanks mounted with 88mm. guns; and after one had been knocked out, the other two Crocodiles withdrew into my Company area.

"At 1700 hours I received the order to "Stand Fast", so distributed the Company for defence in depth. At 2000 hours "O" Group was sent for to GAZELLE; here in a house the C.O., Lt.-Colonel Gough, was joined by the Company Commanders Prescott "A" Coy., McCaffrey "B" Coy., Boycott "C" Coy., Papillon "D" Coy., Gordon "Support" Coy., Elliott A.T., Hemingway Mortar Pln., Sperling Sig. Off. The C.O. explained that the attack on the CHATEAU DE LA LONDE by the South Lancs having failed a new attack at dawn would be made by First Suffolk and the East Yorks supported by the Div. Artillery and the Staffordshire Yeomanry (Sherman Tanks). Suffolk on the left and the East Yorks on the right, Yeomanry left flank protection and to engage the heads of the enemy in position at LEBISSY.

The "Start Line" was an imaginary line drawn east to west across the apex of a very pronounced triangle wood, the "Forming up" place for the two leading Coys. was a hedgerow about 500 yards from the "Start Line". Both Bns. were to pass the "S.L." at 0415 hours, 28th June.

"Owing to "B" Company's exposed position it was necessary for my platoon Commanders to issue orders from memory of the country in front. This was not difficult as we had been patrolling it nightly. At about 0100 hours I moved the Coy. to the F.U.P. Here we were to collect what food the Quarter Master could get for us, a most difficult task, as the whole Bn., less "C" Coy., had lost their cooking utensils when the ship carrying the "Assault Trucks" was sunk. Whilst static we had cooked in biscuit tins, by sections; now in default of food containers the Quarter Master, Captain P. W. Spurgin, sent up biscuits and tins of stew from the "Compo" ration and it worked out at one small tin between five men. This was very welcome as we had been nearly 24 hours without food.

"At 0355 hours the two leading platoons Nos. 12 and 10 under Lt. F. H. Evans and Lt. A. C. Sanders advanced from the hedgerow, I followed with my batman, one runner and the 38 set wireless man, who was controlling the Coy. group. My party moved slight'y ahead of and in the centre of my rear Pln. My Second in Command, Captain W. H. Archdall, I told to follow one bound behind with the 18 set and "S.Bs" to relay information to Bn. H.Q.

"We passed the "S.P." at 0415 hours, when we came under very heavy artillery and mortar fire which continued throughout the attack.

"My "Runner-Wireless" man and batman quickly became casualties. Minus my small staff, the wireless set being wrecked, and with the bad light and the noise, I lost control of the Coy., so decided to take command of the reserve Platoon, No. 11, which I led forward. A little later I became anxious, as I could see nothing of the two forward platoons. The enemy mortaring was very heavy and we had several casualties; but I realised it was quite useless to go to ground. At one point I found myself entirely alone. No. 11 Platoon being practically all casualties, so decided to move forward quickly and control the two forward Plns., who, I believed, were in front of me.

Whilst doing this, I happened to look to my right rear and was relieved to spot Cpl. Maddern leading about 20 men of 12 Pln, Lt. Sanders being wounded. I was still out of touch with 10 Pln. who should have been on the left.

We entered the wood of the Chateau where visibility was reduced to about 20 yards, and suddenly ran into a dug-in tank. We quickly took cover. Covered by the remainder I told Cpl. Maddern to stalk the tank. He was successful and dropped two grenades through the open hatch. We waited for a few minutes and then realised it was unoccupied. Continuing our advance we came under M.G. fire from our right flank and suffered several casualties. As the M.G. appeared to be in the area of the East Yorks objective, I left one man, under cover, to warn any troops approaching, and with the remainder, pushed on.

We reached a large hedge-row standing on a prominent bank which, I had been told, was the main enemy position. This we occupied without opposition apart from the heavy mortar fire from which we were still suffering casualties.

I organised a search along the hedge-row during which one German was killed, and five got away, making off to the right which made me think that their main position must be to my right flank, the East Yorks' objective. I then pushed on to my own objective and reached it with Cpl. Maddern and ten men. We had no "Anti-Tank" weapons as the P.I.A.T. men, whom I had grouped to come up with the Second in Command, for consolidation, had, I heard later, become casualties.

We set about digging in and whilst doing this a Canadian Officer, commanding a Platoon of the East Yorks, arrived on the scene with a few men. It took me some time to convince him that he was on the wrong objective and that the CHATEAU DE LA LONDE was not the village of LE BIJUDE. I directed him to where the East Yorks should have been and shortly after he had left I was joined by Lieut. F. H. Evans and about fourteen of No. 10 Platoon.

I decided to consolidate in as "Tank Proof" a locality as possible and positioned my small force of twenty four behind some thick trees on the forward edge of my objective, an orchard.

Evans had brought two Bren guns with his party and these I put on the flanks with my left flank echeloned back slightly in order to connect up by fire with "C" Coy.

I decided it was now time to put up the success signal, two green lights, and hope for A.T. guns and reinforcements. In case my signal was not seen, I sent back two Runners at about five minutes interval, to give the situation.

Shortly after I fired the success signal I saw two "Reds" go up between my Coy. and "C" Coy.'s objective. I realized that these must have been fired by the enemy, so got a Bren gun to open up on them and told Lieut. Evans to send a rifle group round the left flank after them. We then prepared to meet the counter attack that I thought would not be long developing. The men were in grand form.

We were counter attacked by six tanks who came straight at us.

I had previously given orders that, having no A.T. weapons, if attacked by tanks, we would lie low and only deal with any enemy infantry attempting to retake the position.

We were quite safe from tanks except on the left flank where there was an open gateway between the trees which I was unable to block. I hoped that if we kept quiet they would move round the flanks of the orchard and wood and so run into the Yeomanry and be scuppered.

The tanks came on and we held our fire. But not for long; thirty German infantry, who must have been withdrawing from the Chateau, came at us from the rear. We took them on and they went to ground about fifty yards from us. The tanks were now aware of us and three of them remained shooting their M.G.s at us from the front whilst three moved to the flank and caught us in enfilade with both small arms and H.E., firing as they advanced slowly through the gate.

Things became rather bad for us in our incompleted slit trenches when the Boche shouted "Kamerade Tommy" I saw the chaps nearest the tanks surrender, then others following suit.

When I saw that I had lost control I took a header into a large thorn bush, followed by Lieut. Evans who was near me.

The Germans searched the area; but we were not located. I then had the mortification of seeing some very brave men being marched off as prisoners. These men, although they were captured, upheld the traditions of the Regiment. Before reaching the objective, they had passed through a terrific enemy concentration of fire and had seen many comrades fall. They only surrendered when their own position was quite hopeless and they could do no more.

The enemy continued to hold the area where Evans and myself were hiding. After eight hours, during which time our own guns put down a concentration on the area, they withdrew about fifty yards and we succeeded in regaining our own lines.

I made my way to "D" Coy H.Q. and found Captain A. H. Claxton in command, Major P. W. G. Papillon had been fatally wounded, and his batmen killed.

I sent the information over the air from "D" Coy set, reporting that I was back; then set out for my own H.Q, where I found Archdall with twenty men busily consolidating on the left of "D" Coy. The enemy was mortaring us heavily and whilst I was there Pte Dix, the 18 set operator, was killed.

I handed over to Archdall and went back to the R.A.P. to have my wound dressed, stopping at Bn. H.Q. to report. Shortly after I had left them Captain Archdall and C.S.M. Broom were killed by mortar fire."

After the action Sgt. Moggridge of "B" Company described his experiences. These provide a commentary on the intermingling of units and the difficulty of control. They furnish a further proof that it was determination that won the victory. He said:—"As "B" Company went forward before dawn a succession of enemy red signal lights heralded a tremendous counter bombardment. Most of the men dropped flat in the two foot corn field, and there were heavy casualties. Then came the shout from the Officers "forward"; but already touch in the dark had been lost by many."

Arrived on their final objective Moggridge came back for reinforcements. He collected a band of six men of No. 11 Platoon and with six men of the East Yorks moved forward against the Chateau. Here he found himself up against two enemy tanks and here he was joined by three more of the Battalion who had been captured but had shot their captors and escaped. By this time Lt. Hemingway arrived and took command. The commander of one of the enemy tanks was killed, and both tanks withdrew. But the small party had suffered six men killed and two men wounded.

On the left Captain Brown who had succeeded to the command of "C" Company when Major C. Boycott had been wounded, had a narrow escape. He had come forward to arrange the consolidation of the ground which the Company had won, and was being harassed by enemy machine gun fire. Suddenly seeing two tanks he made his way across to them to ask for their support. A head rose from the turret of the nearer and each stared at the other in silence. Then the tank gun began to swing round and Brown bolted. Though chased back he managed to reach a German partially-made slit trench before being fired on. From a neighbouring post Lt. Woodward with a Piat disabled his attacker and the other tank withdrew.

Major A. H. Claxton takes up the story which Major McCaffrey has told. Claxton was Second in Command of "D" Company under Major Papillon and "D" Company, it will be remembered, was following in support of "B" and "C" Companies.

"At about 0300 hours on the morning of June 28th, "D" Company was aroused after spending a cold miserable night of fitful dozing. As is usual at such a time, tempers were not too good. It was dark. A heavy dew had saturated all equipment and clothing; but there was every promise that the day would be fine.

"The first British gun fired, followed by the rumble of others as the preliminary bombardment started up.

"By the time the Company was on the move the bombardment was well under way. Shells whined overhead in a ceaseless procession and we could hear ahead of us the dull crumps of German shells and mortar bombs exploding.

"There was something ominous about that dark morning. Occasionally there would be an absolute silence for about one minute, and the men who had been shouting conversation to one another would receive the incongruous order to "Keep quiet". Then as if by common agreement, the whole of the hellish fire would start again.

"We moved into the grounds of LE LANDEL where Major P. W. G. Papillon hurried forward to have a quick reconnaissance of the area. After a few minutes he returned and platoons were moved off to localities in the orchard to the S.W. of the LE LANDEL buildings. The ground had been torn by countless shells and branches of trees were lying about everywhere. Scattered about the place there were one or two very shallow slit trenches. Papillon, the Coy. Signaller and another man occupied one of these, the former sitting on the side operating the wireless set whilst the two men started to deepen the trench.

"I took the other wireless set about 15 yards away and with the signaller we started to scrape a shallow trench. About a minute later some 20 shells landed in quick succession behind us with terrific explosions. The air was filled with the "zing" of metal as fragments of the shells flew overhead. Dust, earth and stones rained down. All dug furiously. Then came a veritable deluge of shells right into the Company area, and it seemed impossible that anyone would remain alive. I heard the all too familiar cry for stretcher bearers. Hurrying forward I found Papillon lying on the top of his trench mortally wounded, Pte. Bradley, his batman, dead and the other two occupants of the trench slightly wounded. Cpl. Fordham and another S.B. managed to evacuate Papillon. This bombardment went on without cessation and we lost 12 more men, some killed.

"Lieut.-Colonel J. G. M. B. Gough told me over the air that "B" had reached their objective, and ordered me to take "D" along the axis of the advance used by the East Yorks and to clear the enemy from the Chateau by attacking from the right.

I put the Platoon Commanders into the picture. As we were about to cross the corn fields to the CHATEAU DE LA LONDE three German tanks appeared from behind the Chateau and opened fire; luckily a self propelled Anti-Tank gun, concealed in the orchard of LE LANDEL, opened fire and with its second round set the leading tank on fire; the others immediately withdrew.

We reached the CHATEAU DE LA LONDE, where I could get no information about the E. Yorks; but learnt that Captain Archdall of "B" Company was about 300 yards ahead.

Eventually I found him with about ten men lining a bank to the S.E. of the Chateau grounds. I passed many dead on the way and found the bank, which they were holding, was under continuous and extremely accurate mortar and shell fire.

Captain Archdall told me that Major McCaffrey had gone forward into the orchard to the south of the Chateau, with a platoon; but that he was not in touch with him. As the Chateau area had not been cleared it was possible that isolated Germans were still holding out there. I decided to clear the grounds and assault the Chateau.

This minor attack was carried out without difficulty, about 9 Germans being captured in the cellars of the house where they had been guarding some E. Yorks soldiers, who had been taken prisoner. No further Germans were seen, except wounded who quickly gave themselves up; we then consolidated our position, being subjected to artillery and mortar fire for the remainder of the day and indeed for many days to come."

The Anti-Tank gun platoon of six guns had been ordered to be in readiness to move forward to the CHATEAU DE LA LONDE area as soon as the attack by "B" and "C" Companies proved successful. During the night of June 27th their officers, Cpt. H. C. Elliott and Lt. D. S. Stebbings with Sgt. Hastings, the Platoon Sgt, had a hard time while the men were getting what rest they could. Stebbings had to find the 67th Anti-Tank Battery in the dark over a mile away, while Elliott during that night and the following day was reconnoitring all possible routes forward and trying to get personal contact with "B" Company.

"Is Captain Elliott all right ?" asked Stebbings of Sgt. Hastings at one time during the day's operations when the enemy fire had been particularly heavy.

"Yes," was the reply. "He was a few seconds ago; but he won't be much longer if he carries on as he is doing."

At dawn on the 28th, while McCaffrey was still in his thorn bush, and fixed there for some hours yet, and while "D" Company was moving forward to make good the ground which had already been won by "B" Company, every effort was made to move forward the guns of the Anti-Tank Platoon. There was a lane to the right of the wood the infantry had traversed but this was covered by the enemy 88mm., while the other side of this wood was open and under direct observation from the Chateau. The only alternative was to find routes through the wood which with its thick undergrowth and its many stout stone walls was difficult for the carriers to negotiate. Eventually the guns were got forward and by nightfall were dug in.

The evening was still with no breeze to stir the pungent smell of explosions. The neighbouring Chateau seemed to reek of death. Then a queer noise came from its interior; Stebbings and the Platoon Sgt. grabbing their arms walked to the steps of the house, and in the far corner of the hall found a badly wounded Boche.

The Battalion lost two most gallant officers in the action at the CHATEAU DE LA LONDE: Major Philip Papillon and Captain Archdall. Had Philip Papillon lived he would have risen high. He was a man of rare endowment. There was a spirited quality about his leadership that came to fruition during the few brief days in NORMANDY while he was commanding his company. He had the supreme gift in battle of inspiring confidence in all; imperturbability in voice and action, a complete disregard of danger. Scarcely any of his men had ever been in action, the enemy fire during the attack on the CHATEAU DE LA LONDE was very heavy, every eye watched Papillon walking about without haste, giving orders without excitement, and their self confidence rose to the level of his. As Lord Moran wrote of the death in battle that comes to so many: "Yet it is a fine free setting forth, this end in the field. It comes to a man in the spring time, before age and disease have soiled his body, and the traffic of cities has soiled his soul. He has lived his brief manhood among men, knowing what is best in them, and he has gone out untouched and undefeated by the petty strife of a world at peace."

The total casualties in this day's fighting were seven officers and 154 other ranks killed, wounded and missing.

CONSOLIDATION: 29th JUNE-12th JULY.

The situation remained tense for the next nine days. There was heavy shelling of the Battalion area, which could easily be viewed from enemy O.P.s to the left front in the LEBISSY woods, and multi-barrelled mortars were employed by the enemy. On 1st July Major Packe the Battalion's new second in command was killed in one of these "stonks."

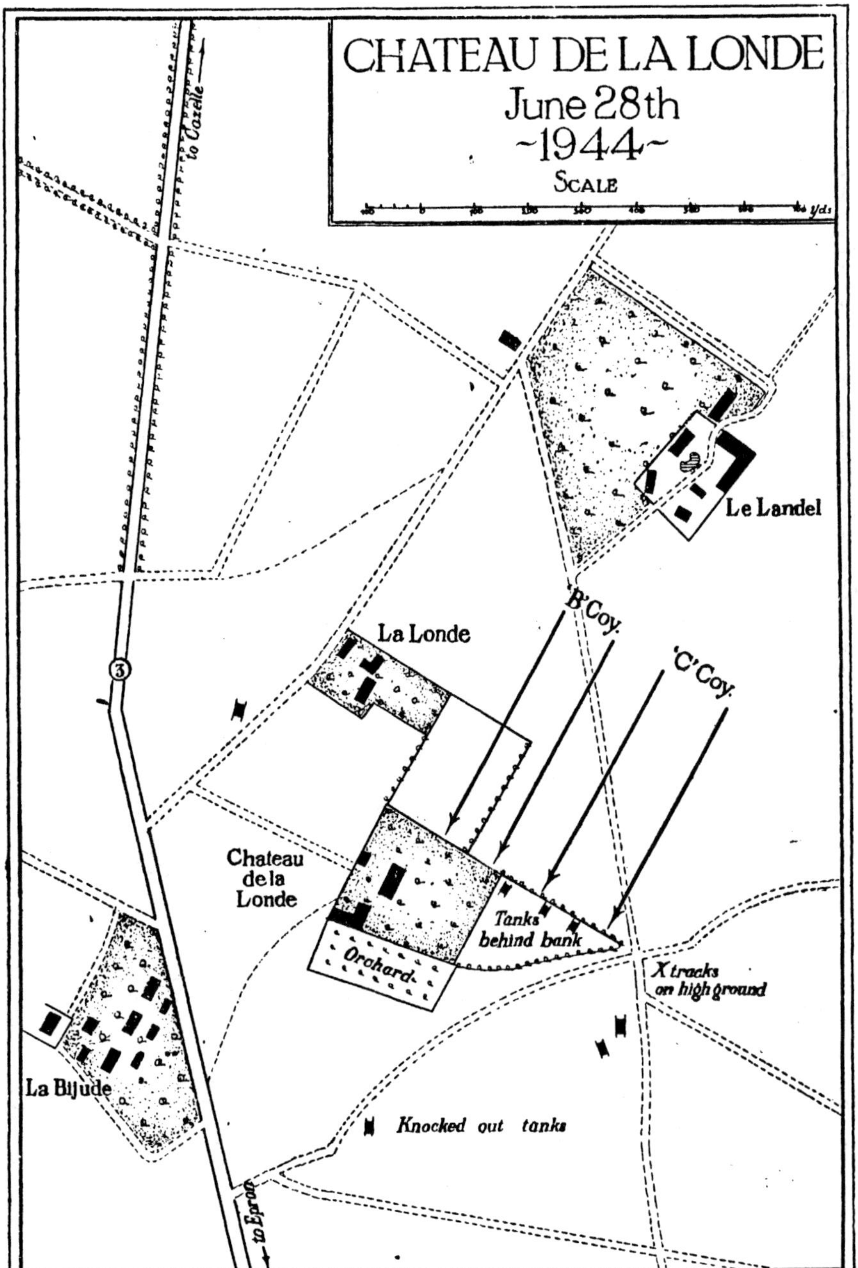
CHATEAU DE LA LONDE
June 28th
~1944~
SCALE
Yds
to Cazelle
3
Le Landel
La Londe
'B' Coy.
'C' Coy.
Chateau
de la
Londe
Tanks
behind bank
Orchard
X tracks
on high ground
La Bijude
Knocked out tanks
to Epron

IV

Meanwhile for another week the battalion held the Chateau. The enemy were continually engaged with artillery and mortar fire. One notable achievement was when the O.C. "D" Company, Major Claxton, personally engaged a machine gun post with a 2" Mortar. His second in command Lieut. Russell, observing and correcting from an O.P. in the roof of the Chateau. Two of the enemy machine gunners were driven out, one of them wounded and with half of his trousers shot away.

Throughout the period active patrolling was continued. Lieut. Peddar and 3 other ranks were killed on one of these patrols six days after Peddar had joined the battalion. On another occasion Lieut. Woodward, who had been awarded the Military Cross for his part in the attack on the 28th June, carried one of his men back to the R.A.P. half a mile and was found to have himself some fifty wounds in his body and legs.

Losses occurred almost daily; but within a month of "D" Day the battalion knew themselves to be seasoned troops, proud of their record and proud of each other. A Field Officer of a new division spoke of the men of the Suffolk Regiment as "steady old files," whose cheerfulness under shelling helped in keeping up the morale of his own men. On the 7th July the battalion was awarded a "grandstand view" of R.A.F. heavy bombers in action. The Chateau was on fairly high ground. CAEN was tucked away in a basin two miles ahead. Men came out of their trenches and talked excitedly. There was a crowd in the top of the Chateau. A huge pall of dust and smoke rose and obscured even the bombers themselves so that that night darkness fell over the CHATEAU DE LA LONDE half an hour before it was expected.

The 10th July was the first day since "D" Day that no shells fell in the Battalion area.

On the 12th July a memorial service was held in a garden of LA LONDE pockmarked by shell holes. So many men wished to attend this service that the number had to be limited. The service ended with the Roll of Honour read by the Commanding Officer, Lt.-Col. J. G. M. B. Gough, and the Last Post and Reveille. After every battle that was yet to come, after VIRE, TINCHEBRAI, OVERLOON, a similar memorial service was held; the Roll of Honour was read.

It is fitting that a tribute should be paid here to the Chaplain who had been with the First Suffolk in England and remained with the Battalion throughout the Campaign—The Reverend Hugh G. Woodall, C.F. Few, if any, who served with the Battalion will forget his inspiring character. Danger never prevented him doing what he considered his duty—sometimes visiting the forward positions, helping the wounded and dying at R.A.P., even on an occasion going out with a patrol. It was he who, with the help of the pioneers, undertook the burial of all the killed—friend or foe—after each fight.

He had his reward. Religion played a large part in the lives of these fighting soldiers. All his Church Services were voluntary and they were well attended.

Lt.-Col. H. B. Monier Williams writing home, enclosed a sketch he had made of the Chateau and said:-

"The CHATEAU DE LA LONDE is on the DOUVRES—LA DELIVERANDE—CAEN Road. It stands in wooded grounds approached from the north by a drive and avenue of trees which extends again to the south.

At the south end of the avenue is the Suffolk Cemetery. The memorial cross, which was made by the Pioneers of the Battalion, has been placed at the end of the grave and faces the Chateau. The cross had the regimental badge and the inscription beneath reads:-

"In memory of all Ranks—Bn. the Suffolk Regiment
killed in action on — June 1944."

On the plinth below is written:-

"They will never be forgotten".

Behind the cross are the graves of German soldiers who must have been buried prior to our capture of the locality.

The mound to the left is a trench with overhead cover and rifle slits facing south across the open fields. These were probably occupied by our men at one time.

To-day when I went there, it was some miles behind the present front line and peace and quietness reigned in place of the noise of battle. Some day the remains of these brave men will be removed to a permanent cemetery."

H.B.M.W.

"SUFFOLK CEMETERY." CHATEAU DE LA LONDE.

H.B.M.W.

CHATEAU DE LA LONDE.

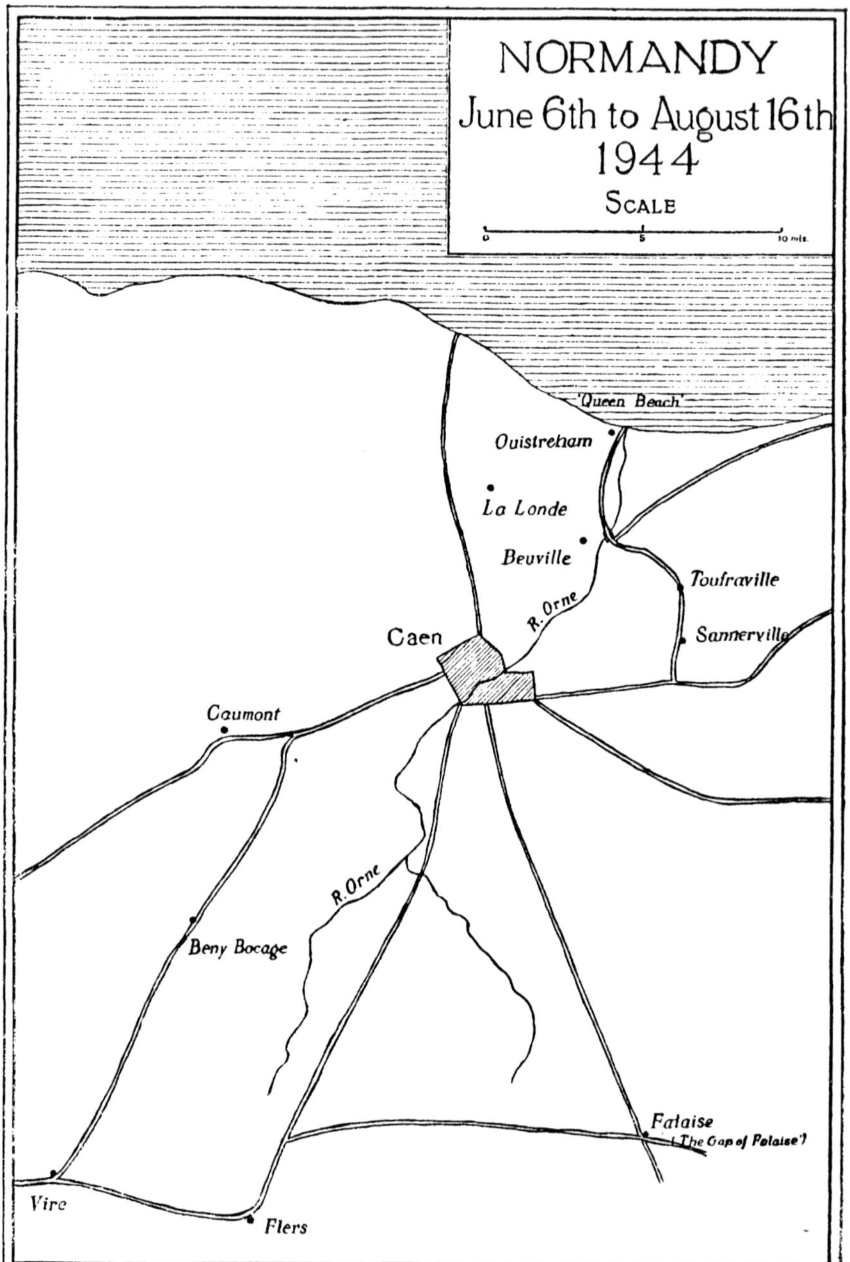
NORMANDY
June 6th to August 16th
1944
SCALE
0
5
10 mls.
'Queen Beach'
Ouistreham
La Londe
Beuville
Toufraville
R. Orne
Caen
Sannerville
Caumont
R. Orne
Beny Bocage
Falaise
('The Gap of Falaise')
Vire
Flers

CHAPTER FOUR.

FIRST BATTALION.

Breaking out of the Bridgehead—TINCHEBRAY—The Advance through France to Belgium—HAMONT and WEERT—Battles for OVERLOON-VENRAY—The Castle at GEIJSTEREN—A Rest at BOEKEL—The RHINE—Advance to BREMEN—Occupied Germany—Move to the Middle East.

BREAKING OUT OF THE BRIDGEHEAD.

17th JULY — 25th AUGUST.

The landing of the Allied armies on the coasts of NORMANDY on the 6th June 1944 is acknowledged as one of the major events in the war in EUROPE. It was the product of years of planning, of months of intensive, realistic training, of untiring research. The raids on the Northern and Western seaboards of EUROPE heralded it; the aerial reconnaissance planes of the allies foreshadowed it. It was called for by the Russians, it was hoped and prayed for by the peoples of occupied EUROPE, it was demanded in no uncertain manner by the British public. It was promised by the Government.

Speculation as to where and when it would be was long and continuous throughout these years. The slow realisation of its scale and grandeur brought the thrill of anticipation. But the thought of heavily loaded men stumbling ashore washed away idle imagination and brought all—most for the first time—face to face with the hard reality of German weapons in German hands.

Could the crossing from ENGLAND to EUROPE be made successfully? Even if possible would it entail terrible losses? There was no thinking person in England who was not gravely obsessed by the pros and cons.

There were many who had seen the problem from the other angle—from the defence of our own shores. The 1st, 4th, 5th, 7th, 8th Battalions of the Regiment had all had portions of the English coast to defend; in the months following DUNKIRK there had been great stretches of partially fortified sandy beach, very thinly covered by half-trained and inadequately equipped men; with insufficient reserves. Yet no invader had attempted a landing. Now, on the other side of the CHANNEL the "ATLANTIC WALL" was proclaimed impregnable. It was held by veteran soldiers with the most modern fortifications.

Well, it had been breached; with comparatively little loss. A great wave of thankfulness swept the country. A landing had been effected; the rest would be easy.

As has been described in the last chapter, the 3rd British Infantry Division—the "Iron Division" as it was called—had been one of the Assault Divisions, selected to make the landing. The First Suffolk had been in the Brigade acting as the spearhead of the landing on the coast; and following the two leading Battalions of this Brigade the Battalion had made good all its objectives. Very stiff Divisional fighting for four days—June 5th to June 9th had seen the taking and consolidation of the bridgehead to cover the beaches.

During these four days the Germans had brought up reinforcements and a further advance by the 3rd Division was not possible. During the fortnight following June 9th reorganization, consolidation and the building up of reinforcements and supplies from ENGLAND went on; meanwhile the Battalion sat entrenched in LE MESNIL wood from 10th June to 24th June.

Then, as has been described came the operation of the CHATEAU DE LA LONDE on June 28th, which can be included as part of the landing operations. In the neighbourhood of the CHATEAU the Battalion remained until 16th July.

The breakout from the Bridgeheads and the great sweeping movements which finally culminated in the utter defeat of the Germans followed inevitably. The enveloping advance of the Americans on the British right, the capture of CHERBOURG and the very heavy fighting round CAEN ended the first phase. The onrush through FRANCE to BELGIUM, HOLLAND, the breathing space on the GERMAN Frontier. The capture of ANTWERP and the mouth of the SCHELDT. Finally the advance across the RHINE and the capitulation of the Enemy.

It is scarcely an exaggeration to say that with the exception of the time immediately following the breakout—viz. from 14th August to 20th September—right up to the Cease Fire the First Suffolk was continuously engaged with the enemy; always under fire, always suffering casualties. The periods when the Battalion was withdrawn to reorganise and refit were astonishingly short, rarely extending to more than three or four days. An exact account of the movements of each Company would alone do full justice to the courage and endurance of all ranks throughout these long months. The story of any of the following engagements must therefore be multiplied a hundred-fold; the account of any act of gallantry must be pictured not only for the particular case but for numberless others.

The major events affecting the First Suffolk covers the fighting near CAEN in which the Battalion had two major engagements, at SANNERVILLE on 18th July and at TINCHEBRAY from the 12th to 18th August. Then came their rapid advance across the River SEINE, through FRANCE and BELGIUM, and the actions at HAMONT and WEERT on 20th, 21st September. The next major operation was the winter battle at OVERLOON-VENRAY lasting from 12th—18th October and the final fight at GOCH Woods on 27th February 1945.

The Battalion remained in the CHATEAU DE LA LONDE area until 16th July when on the night 16th-17th July it concentrated near the village of BEAUVILLE.

It was clear to everyone that big events were about to take place. The whole of the 3rd Division was now across the River ORNE as well as at least two armoured divisions. The C.O. issued orders at 1730 hours, 17th July, for an attack the following day. The 8th Brigade was to go forward behind the armour. The South Lancashire was to seize and hold an area of woods protecting the left flank; the East Yorkshire to capture the village of TOUFFREVILLE; the First Suffolk to capture the village of SANNERVILLE and exploit to BANNEVILLE, the final Brigade objective. The Battalion was to approach SANNEVILLE through TOUFFREVILLE unless the East Yorkshire was held up there, in which case it was to approach it from the right flank. The whole operation was known as "Goodwood".

On the 18th July a huge aerial bombardment by Fortresses, Lancasters and Halifaxes began, followed by medium fighter bombers; the sight of these and the sound of the artillery barrage considerably raised the spirits of the men. By 10.15 the Battalion moved off and proceeded down a track through the woods, under shell-fire until the village of ESCOVILLEX was reached. The ground was quite open, the only cover that afforded by standing corn, there were no hedgerows or trees. Batches of enemy prisoners were passed, for the most part so demoralised that they needed no escort; one shout and a point of the hand were enough to send them scampering down the track to our P.O.W. cages.

Occasionally British walking wounded passed in ones and twos. There was no sign of enemy in or about SANNERVILLE; though fighting was still in progress in TOUFFREVILLE.

About 400 yards from SANNERVILLE "A" and "D" Companies formed up and advanced into the village under artillery support, reaching their objectives without opposition. "B" and "C" Companies passed through, and consolidated on the southern edge of the final objective. Within the Battalion area were found six abandoned Nebelwerfers, a large 15 c.m. Infantry gun, two 7.5 c.m. infantry guns. Casualties were very light; two other ranks died of wounds, one officer and six other ranks were wounded and three other ranks missing. The battalion benefited greatly from the support of the heavy bombers, the enemy being very dazed and unable to offer any organised resistance. The ground was found pitted with huge craters to such an extent that bulldozers were needed to enable guns and vehicles to reach their consolidation area; even to walk amidst the rubble was hard work. At 1730 hours the 9th Brigade passed through on the way towards TROAN.

The following day the battalion closed up into a smaller area and awaited results from other formations in the battle. Active patrolling was carried out, Lieut. Perrett being particularly successful in bringing back information regarding the enemy. Next day, 20th July, torrential rain fell, and the whole battle came to a standstill. Once again the battalion had to spend eleven days sitting in dug outs and getting shelled.

The Battalion had now been for nearly two months at grips with the enemy. In these early days of the Campaign the officers had learnt that Active Service conditions are not the same as even the most realistic "Exercise." The landing in Normandy had been entirely successful, save only on the vital cookhouse side, the Battalion "Q" ship, as it will be remembered, having been sunk. This affected all ranks. During these two months the officers had messed with their men, the Section, Platoon or Company as the case might be; save only the C.O., his Second in Command and Adjutant who had a private cook—the faithful Perry, who unfortunately could not cook. This was the messing rule practically throughout the Campaign, except on those rare static occasions when a Central Officers' mess was possible. The messing and cooking then being in the hands of that sunny charactered man, Lce. Cpl. Low, who could cook most excellently even under the worst conditions.

Meanwhile the Battalion was admirably served by the Quarter Master, Captain P. W. Spurgin, a man who never failed the Battalion throughout the whole Campaign. It is the custom of the man in the front line to revile the man behind. The Quarter Master was a big man, he was reported in the days following "D" Day to have the biggest dug-out in NORMANDY, he was said to have fitted it with a billiards table ! Even Quarter Masters in modern war are not exempt; but when his dug-out was visited by a German "Stonk", those in front laughed.

As all knew, the Battalion was very well served, not only by the Quarter Master; but by all who worked under him. During these early days supplies generally came up by night with secret intent; but the low gears of the supply vehicles made such a noise that they could be heard for miles. On one occasion the Battalion Water Cart was hit, and little else could be heard in the battle area save the clattering of the empty cans and the curses of the water carriers as the spare truck bounced them over the shell holes. Yet the supplies always got through; even on the night when the R.Q.M.S., held up on the road, unwittingly made a flank movement across a mine field.

Often during these moves the exact location of the forward companies was uncertain; then the Company Q.M.S.s had the excitement of not knowing what would be round the next corner as they edged their way up the quiet NORMANDY lanes—quiet save for the noise of their own approach. How hard the M.T. drivers worked was not always known; they, under Lt. G. N. Casson, were a great team, an integral part of the Battalion. Lt. Casson was shortly after wounded and evacuated; he was coming forward to Battalion H.Q. when intercepted by a German patrol which had infiltrated. One of these he killed with his revolver before being wounded.

On the 31st July the First Suffolk recrossed the River ORNE to the neighbourhood of BEAUVILLE, remaining at four hours' notice to move. Here the Battalion in best battle dress and wearing their Minden Roses, spent the 1st August, 1944.

Lt.-Colonel Monier Williams, who had recently completed his Command of the 2nd Battalion in India, and was serving in the neighbourhood wrote an account of this Minden Day.

"On the night before, I asked my R.Q.M.S. to go round the village here and ask for roses—NORMANDY is full of roses this year, and the Nuns arranged to collect what was wanted. The result was a large armful of red, white, pink and yellow roses of all sorts, and, as the R.Q.M.S. said, 'They would have given me the whole garden if I had wanted it'.

"These I made up into three large bunches and on the afternoon of Minden Day I went over and laid them on the graves at HERMANVILLE as a tribute from their relatives and officers and men of the Regiment.

"After this, I went off to see the Battalion, who, thanks to the efforts of Major Smitherman, Suffolk Regt., Commanding the First Corps rest camp, were enjoying a real Minden Day.

"I was late arriving and heard that a Press photographer had been there already; but I found the Battalion filing in to the dining tents for their tea and cakes, with roses in their caps and looking so smart and clean, fit and well with their tails right up. Not all were County men; but they all belonged to the Suffolk Regiment and were proud members of it. Some of them had recently been in Burma, with a tale to tell of the Japs. They were all happy, and if the small supply of beer which had been collected could have gone further, it would have been an old time Minden Day. But instead, they went to the cinema and enjoyed their afternoon in rest and quiet.

"Lt.-Colonel Gough arrived later in the afternoon with operation orders, and the party had to terminate; the XII. Regiment going back to battle with roses in their head-dress."

TINCHEBRAY. 2nd AUGUST—15th AUGUST.

On the 2nd August the Battalion moved to CAUMONT; on the 5th to LA BENY BOCAGE, thence to LE RECULY; on the 8th to MONTISHANGER; on the 10th to a position overlooking VIRE in preparation for an attack on the gap South of FALAISE; this was now almost closed—but was being most stubbornly defended.

Here orders were received to co-operate in a large scale attack along the road VIRE-TINCHEBRAY-FLEURS, an American Division being on the right of the 3rd Division and the Guards Armoured Division on the left. The First Suffolk was the reserve Battalion of the 8th Brigade and was not expected to be in front line until the cross roads at point 279 had been reached.

The Battle commenced on August 11th and by 1600 hours that day the Battalion had reached L'OISONNIERE a mile behind the leading unit. On August 12th the E. Yorks was ordered to patrol to the crossroads Point 279 and at 1900 hours no enemy having been encountered north of this point, the First Suffolk was ordered to establish themselves in the locality point 279 preparatory to the rest of the Brigade moving to the high ground about 70.27. (See sketch map).

It was while orders were being issued for this advance that a shell landed in Brigade H.Q. Lt.-Colonel J. G. M. B. Gough was wounded and the Command of the Battalion passed to Major F. F. E. Allen, the Oxfordshire and Buckinghamshire L.I. There was great regret in the Battalion at the loss of Lt.-Colonel Gough; a Lincolnshire officer, he had most loyally and capably served the Suffolk Regiment. Throughout the Campaign the First Battalion was singularly fortunate in the senior officers of other Regiments who served with the Battalion; but none was better known or more respected than Lt.-Colonel Gough.

The Battalion had been under fire for the past 24 hours and for the next two days and nights was to be at close grips with the11/8th German Parachute Regiment, who were fighting desperately to cover the retreat of their army. Everything favoured the enemy; the country was very enclosed, the ground gently undulating, fields were small with high hedgerows and many trees. It was impossible to locate a skilful enemy; bold action by an attacker was essential. It was a supreme test for subordinate leadership, and the Battalion responded magnificently.

That night, August 12th, the advance was made with "A" Company on the right, "B" Company on the left. "B" Company reached their objective with little opposition, a German officer who shouted a challenge in English being killed by Cpl. Briggs. "A" Company were equally successful, due in a large measure to the fearless and skilful leadership of the Company Commander, Major John Prescott. He led his Company straight in to the Assault and after fierce fighting established it firmly on the cross roads. He then led two Platoons against an enemy in orchards and buildings on the right of the Company objective, cleared them out, took ten prisoners and was only halted by very heavy fire and grenades from a strong point 200 yards in advance. At first light on the 13th August he successfully attacked these buildings, personally using grenades and leading the house-clearing parties. One German officer and three other ranks were killed; one officer and a dozen men were captured; and the elimination of this strong point greatly facilitated the fighting later in the day.

The two forward companies had reached their objectives soon after midnight; at 0300 hours 13th August "D" Company moved forward with one platoon up as a fighting patrol. They came under heavy mortar and machine gun fire, and after a clash with enemy paratroops who were found in strength they established themselves in the rear of "A" Company.

With the daylight the wooded ridge to the left front overlooking the whole position gave the enemy an excellent observation line and any movement in the battalion area was immediately followed by accurate and heavy mortar fire. There was a steady flow of casualties throughout the day, including "B" Company commander and second in command, "A" Company second in command and almost the whole of the Anti Tank platoon headquarters. About midday "C" Company, section by section, took over the right flank between "A" Company and the Americans at LA FOUGUERIE. They succeeded in keeping out of sight of the ridge and were lucky to spend the rest of the day fairly quietly.

During the evening of 13th August, orders were received for an attack towards TINCHEBRAY by the First Suffolk and the East Yorks, right and left hand battalions, each supported by one squadron of Churchill tanks. The objective of the Brigade was Report Line "OIL", the First Suffolk having point 259 and the area around it. Within the battalion the attack was to take place with "C" Company right and "D" Company left. At "H" hour "B" Company was to advance and picquet the large wood (1, see sketch) to enable the two forward companies "C" and "D" to follow closely behind the artillery barrage and secure the first battalion objective, point 247, and the surrounding area on either side of the wood. After the capture of this Battalion objective, "B" Company was to clear this wood and to come into battalion reserve. "C" and "B" Companies were then to continue their advance right and left of the road respectively with "A" Company in support and "B" Company in reserve. Two troops of tanks were allotted to each forward Company, until darkness prevented their further employment.

All Company Commanders had managed to give their orders to platoon commanders; but in the short space of time between the end of the C.O.'s orders, approx. 1930 hours, and the barrage, at 2015 hours, in some cases the orders got no further. However the attack did not appear to suffer greatly thereby. Immediately the British barrage started the enemy answered with a strong counter barrage which caught "B" Company fair and square. All three platoon commanders, the C.S.M. and one platoon sergeant were killed, Lieut. Doree dying on his way to the A.D.S., and the other two platoon sergeants were wounded. However Captain Vaughan who had taken over the company when its commander, Major Duxbury, and second in command, Captain Calder, were wounded earlier in the day, managed to reform the remnants and crossing the road moved from hedge to hedge towards the objective in face of the enemy barrage.

"C" and "D" Companies went through to the first objective. In both cases co-operation with the tanks was excellent. A number of prisoners were taken and several enemy dead left, for loss of less than a dozen wounded. "C" Company under Command of Major E. L. H. Ward pushed beyond the objective and consolidated on a ridge of high ground (2) (see sketch), just as it was getting dusk. During this operation a previously unlocated enemy M.G. opened up from a hedgerow in front and fatally injured Captain Powell, who had shortly before been awarded the Military Cross for his work on "D" Day. The post was destroyed and the whole area had just been cleaned up when our own artillery began shelling it. The fire was quickly called off; but not before there had been several minor injuries and three men had been very severely wounded. There were several local counter attacks from the area of LES BROUSSES, all of which were beaten off.

In the meantime, "D" Company, having reached point 247 in the failing light, received orders to push on in the darkness as far as possible. Most of the Company had had no sleep for the two nights immediately preceding, and this and the continuous shelling of the past twenty-four hours, were having their effect. If the company made a short pause one or two fell asleep immediately. This added to the strain; for each man had to be woken noiselessly. After advancing 500 yards a new firm base was being established when a small party of Germans, one officer, 3 other ranks, was heard approaching. The leading section allowed them to pass and then took them prisoner from the rear. The leading platoon then advanced; when more Germans were heard approaching from two directions. The leading section opened fire on them and then dived into a ditch. Grenades were thrown by the Germans at their own men and in the confusion our section withdrew.

The Company again moved forward and by 0300 hours on August 14th was established at point 251, approximately six hundred yards beyond the Battalion's final objective.

"A" Company had followed up with Battalion H.Q. to a farm (see sketch). Support Company were slightly in rear. There had been no news of "B" Company's progress in their wood clearing operations and they had not come up into reserve.

Long before this, in fact before the completion of phase one, the attack of the East Yorkshires on the left had ceased to make progress; undeterred, the battalion's spearhead had gone on, constantly opposed by enemy fire; but coolly and efficiently dealing with the firers. By this time they had driven a wedge into the enemy's defences a mile deep and were holding what they had gained, although there were no troops on either flank to support them. Finding the progress of the First Suffolk had been too fast for the units on the flanks, the Brigade Commander ordered the Battalion to withdraw and consolidate astride the road. "C" Company moved astride the main road to cover the withdrawal of "D" Company who dug in astride the main road 701264. Casualties in "D" Company had been five dead and about twenty-five wounded.

Meanwhile "A" Company under Major Prescott was ordered forward to a position 200 yards short of point 259. In the dark and mist unknowingly they went too far. The leading Section under Cpl. Sellars captured a motor cyclist and one other prisoner. The Section was then joined by 7 Platoon of 10 men under Sgt. Barratt. 9 Platoon was ordered to clear the enemy from the gardens in their front, and 8 Platoon moved forward to the cross roads where they silenced a L.M.G. and pushed down the road.

With daylight the mist cleared and it was then realized that the Company had put their heads into a hornet's nest. 8 Platoon were in an orchard held by the enemy; these they proceeded to attack, capturing eleven prisoners. But when they pushed still further on they found more enemy in their rear. The enemy L.M.G.s sounded like Brens, and one N.C.O. disregarding the orders of his platoon commander stood up and shouted until he was hit: "Don't fire, we're Suffolks !" As the enemy in the orchard were estimated to be between thirty and fifty against the platoon's fifteen (including three wounded) it was decided to withdraw to the cross roads; where the platoon was reformed by the Company Commander, Major Prescott. Here Prescott organized a counter-attack on the orchard with 8 and 9 Platoons; leading them himself. 8 Platoon under Lt. Sindall attacked in front, while 9 Platoon, under Sgt. Cook which had moved up to the East of the cross roads and had come under heavy fire from the left and front, was ordered to make good the north of the orchard in support of 8 Platoon and to take on an enemy L.M.G. firing some 70 yards away. Covered by low angle H.E. and smoke from the 2" mortars 8 Platoon made the assault, and, notwithstanding the fire of another enemy L.M.G. pressed forward. The enemy stayed only long enough to throw a grenade before abandoning the gun. This position was over-run and also a third one fifty yards beyond which had been firing down the road.

A raw British soldier advancing up the road and seeing a German leave this last position, remarked: "There's a German walking down the lane ahead. What do I do ?" Needless to say, his rifle manipulation was no more rapid than his powers of deduction. Perhaps the moral of this story is that the Company was exhausted. They had driven the enemy before them. Had the fighting continued they would have summoned up the necessary strength; but now with victory they had no strength left to shoot at the enemy as he disappeared. So great is the strain of modern battle.

But as the battle died away, the hens of a neighbouring farm, who had taken cover temporarily, came out and the ducks followed. Posting adequate military protection, Prescott dealt with the situation. "Twenty minutes' break. Keep that white duck for me." At once all fatigue was forgotten, and a sack load of fowls went back to the cookhouse.

For these two actions Capt. Prescott was awarded an M.C., the citation reading: "By his fearless and skilful leadership he was an inspiration to his Company."

Bn. H.Q. in the farm was very heavily shelled and mortared, as was the whole battalion area. Once more these shells continued throughout the day; the stream of casualties was continuous. The night's work had produced some two hundred and fifty prisoners.

News of "B" Company began to trickle through from the R.A.P. The ranks of the company had been considerably thinned by the enemy's counter barrage, while the thickness of the wood, the darkness and the loss of all platoon commanders, platoon sergeants and the C.S.M. before the attack began made this normally hazardous type of operation particularly difficult and dangerous. The Company had entered the wood and, according to scraps of information received from casualties who reached the R.A.P., resistance had been severe. There was no reliable information as Captain Vaughan, the only officer present, had received severe head wounds, and with him nearly every man who had emerged from the wood was wounded and had been evacuated. Later the bodies of men of the Suffolk Regiment, with enemy dead, were found in all parts of the wood.

The enemy had stood and fought it out; the wood had been cleared and for the second time in two months "B" Company had taken its objective at the price of its own annihilation.

During the 14th August the artillery brought down heavy fire on to every possible enemy gun area to reduce the weight of shelling, which, as the most forward troops, the battalion was suffering. Towards the evening enemy shelling of the area did decrease.

The following letter was received by the Commanding Officer from the Brigade Commander :-

"Dear Allen,

"Very many congratulations on your good work last night. The G.O.C. is very pleased indeed. Please inform all ranks that it was a very good show and really shook the Boche. I am very sorry indeed that you lost so many officers and men; but I am quite sure that it has not impaired your splendid fighting efficiency.

Congratulations,

Yours sincerely,

E. E. E. CASS.

14th August, 1944. Commanding 8th Inf. Brigade.

An extract from a letter by Lt.-Col. Gough reads :-

"The Battalion got stuck into the Boche Paratroop Boys and set about them properly. I am told that the 3rd Division is quite the best in France and First Suffolk easily the best in the Division."

The truth of which latter statement no good Suffolk will for a moment doubt.

During the night of the 14th/15th August contact patrols kept touch with U.S. formations and other battalions of the 8th Brigade. By 0400 hours information from our forward patrols suggested a partial enemy withdrawal; though their rear parties were still in position.

At 09.30 that morning the N.C.O. i/c the battalion's water cart arrived at Battalion H.Q. a little late and somewhat excited. He reported that when he came forward earlier he had missed the track leading to the Battalion H.Q. and had gone straight down the road towards TINCHEBRAY. He had not realised his mistake until he arrived at the village of ST. QUENTIN DES CHARDONNETS. There he turned round quickly and hastily returned; but at no time had any enemy been encountered !

As a result of this unintentional reconnaissance a large scale attack by the South Lancashires, with armoured support was called off and instead Captain K. G. Mayhew, with one section of his carrier platoon, a section of anti tank guns and a platoon of "A" Company, was sent forward to search and clear the lateral road through LES CHARDONNETS, LA RUPARDIERE to BERNIERES, about four miles away on the left flank. Lt. Perrett had a similar command and orders to co-operate. The Kenforce and Perret Force as they were called, moved successfully, collecting from one hide-out five weary Germans, whose boots were worn through to their feet.

At 0830 hours 16th August the Battalion moved through TINCHEBRAY and along the road towards FLERS. At this time the resistance of the enemy on the whole front seemed to be crumbling and strenuous efforts were being made by the Allies to close what became known as the "FALAISE GAP". Contact with the enemy on the TINCHEBRAY front was in danger of being lost and so, though the battalion halted and consolidated at LA RIVIERE high in the hills three miles beyond TINCHEBRAY, a section of the carrier platoon was sent forward under Captain Mayhew to investigate. The patrol entered FLERS soon after 1200 hours. Captain Mayhew contacted the French resistance forces, released a Canadian pilot whom they had been hiding for two and a half months, and collected three prisoners from the German headquarters in the town. The whole town was "en fête" and the troops were showered alike with bouquets of flowers and kisses. The patrol was a little late in arriving back in the battalion area!

There followed hot summer days of rest and relaxation. Reinforcements arrived and the battalion reorganised. Since leaving VIRE casualties had totalled: killed, 4 officers, 25 other ranks; wounded, 10 officers, 129 other ranks.

On the 25th August a memorial service was held for those of the battalion who had lost their lives in the recent actions. On 28th August, Lieut.-Col. R. W. Craddock, D.S.O., M.B.E., The Buffs, was posted to the command of the battalion.

THE ADVANCE THROUGH FRANCE AND BELGIUM.

1ST SEPT. — 17TH SEPT.

The early weeks of September were spent either in training or in tactical moves. The advanced columns of the Allies having crossed the SEINE and enclosed PARIS, swept on. The American forces which had landed on the COTE D'AZUR pushed north through LYONS to join them in the heart of BURGUNDY and then side by side with them to dash for the BELFORT GAP and the VOSGES. As the Americans made for the MAGINOT LINE and the ARDENNES, the British were clearing ROUEN, AMIENS, LILLE, BRUSSELS and ANTWERP. The story of their progress trickled back. The wireless reported tumultous rejoicings and frenzied welcomes, and for a time there was a little disappointment felt in the battalion that they of the infantry, who had borne the burden and heat of the day, should miss the glory of its close, and the full realization of the pride of being part of the British Liberation Army. However before the month closed the battalion had done its own share of "liberating" and envy was forgotten.

The strength of the battalion at this time, Sept. 1944, was 925 all ranks casualties having been made up by reinforcements. The Company Commanders being:—Major Ellis, "A" Company; Capt. Calder, "B" Company; Major E. L. H. Ward, "C" Company; Capt. F. M. B. Russell, "D" Company; Capt. Halford, Support Company.

On 3rd September the 3rd Division moved across the SEINE, a journey of 130 miles. From FLERS the route passed along the hills of NORMANDY through ARGENTAN and L'AIGLE down to the river EURE at LOUVIERS and across the SEINE under the shadow of Richard I.'s great CHATEAU GAILLARD at LES ANDELYS. The road at intervals, and particularly near ARGENTAN, was

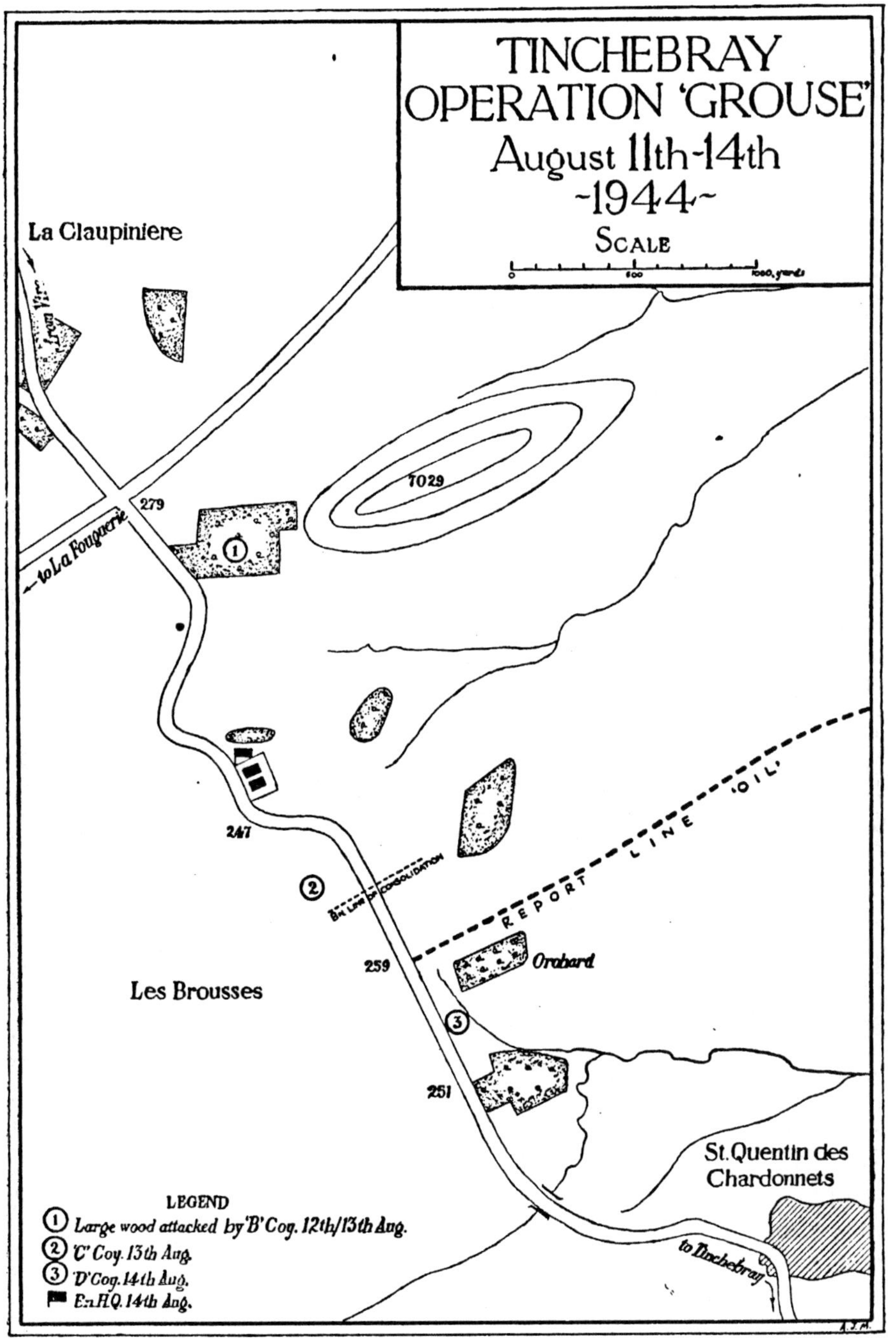
TINCHEBRAY
OPERATION 'GROUSE'
August 11th-14th
-1944-
SCALE
0
500
1000 yards
La Claupiniere
from Vire
279
to La Fougerie
7029
247
BN LINE OF CONSOLIDATION
REPORT LINE 'OIL'
259
Orchard
Les Brousses
251
St. Quentin des
Chardonnets
to Tinchebray
LEGEND
① Large wood attacked by 'B' Coy. 12th/13th Aug.
② 'C' Coy. 13th Aug.
③ 'D' Coy. 14th Aug.
Bn.H.Q. 14th Aug.

VI

littered with wrecked German vehicles, evidence both of the work of the R.A.F. and of the haste of the enemy's enforced retreat. The battalion was billeted north of the river SEINE in the little village of FARCEAUX, a comfortable spot where every man had the roof of a farmhouse or a barn over his head. On the 15th September, orders were given for a long move in two stages, the first stage being to the village of SOIGNIES between MONS and BRUSSELS, and the second being to the small town of PEER in NORTH EAST BELGIUM just short of the MEUSE-ESCAULT CANAL. The whole journey which was made by motor transport was marked firstly by the tremendous welcome given to the battalion in every town and village through which it passed, and secondly by the heartening sight of what must altogether have amounted to thousands of burnt out German tanks and lorries by the sides of the road. In places, and notably after the FRENCH-BELGIAN border, these extended for some miles, at intervals of not more than ten yards.

The MEUSE-ESCAUTL Canal was held by the enemy, and on arrival in this new area the Battalion "dug in" South West of the village of CAUVILLE, two and a half miles from the Canal. On September 18th, 'B' Company, forming a fighting patrol of full Company strength, combed the area forward to the Canal. As the Company was returning one of its parties was fired on by Germans hidden in a house. Lieut. Minton was killed.

HAMONT and WEERT.

18th SEPT. — 12th OCTOBER.

The 3rd Division was ordered to cross the MEUSE-ESCAULT Canal, the original plan being for the 9th Brigade to force a crossing at midnight 18th September and the 8th Brigade to extend this to include HAMONT. But the opposition beyond the canal was stiffer than expected and the plan was modified. A large wooded, marshy area was held by the enemy; this the East Yorks were ordered to clear, supported by the First Suffolk, who were then to capture HAMONT.

The East Yorkshires crossed at last light but by nightfall had made little progress. The First Suffolk followed and bivouacked for the night in the area of the bridge. Throughout the night the East Yorkshires doggedly continued with the clearing of the woods and by 0300 had completed their task. At 0400 20th September, the First Suffolk moved through their positions, shrouded in darkness and a heavy morning mist. The move towards HAMONT was uninterrupted and at the first houses a number of villagers loaded the leading troops with peaches, apples and pears. As the local estimates of enemy varied from none to one hundred the Battalion advanced as if the town was occupied. Companies were told to search their areas. There was a good deal of shooting and a steady stream of prisoners trickled in throughout the day as the Boche were winkled out of their various hiding places. The day's haul was sixty; but there were only three N.C.O.s. If they had not been deserted by their officers, this number of men might have organised the defence of the town and considerably hindered its liberation.

The Mayor, the Chief of the Gendarmerie, and the head of the underground movement were all most helpful in giving news of enemy movements in the outskirts of the town. The population could not do enough for the men. This enthusiastic reception was most touching. There was scarcely a house which did not bear its Belgian flag; no one was without a favour of some sort in the national colours. All our troops were presented with fruits and favours and the carriers bore garlands of flowers.

Pte. Hollis, killed that morning by shell fire, was given a funeral with full civic honours by the townsfolk. The coffin was draped with the Belgian flag and the hearse piled with flowers topped by a wreath inscribed: "Died for the liberation of HAMONT." The funeral procession must have run into hundreds.

At 1200 hours on the next day, 21st September, the advance continued. While the 9th Brigade fanned out to the left, the First Suffolk was to lead the 8th Brigade's advance on to the Dutch town of WEERT. At 12.30 "D" Company, Major A. H. Claxton, in the lead crossed the DUTCH frontier and began to move down a rough track over a desolate area of sand, scrub and fir plantations. The advance was uneventful until the leading troops moved forward of a small strip of wood at (1) (see sketch) when they came under fire from enemy positions on and near the railway embankment. A platoon of "D" Company was sent to clear the buildings at (2); but heavy fire prevented them reaching their objective. The C.O., Lt.-Colonel Craddock, therefore decided to put down artillery concentrations on the enemy positions on the left and in front, to lay 3 in. mortar smoke across the right flank and to attack frontally on the embankment with "D" Company.

As "D" Company disappeared into the haze the enemy spandaus opened up and it was impossible from advanced Battalion H.Q. in a strip of wood to discern the course of the battle. The C.O. and I.O. accordingly moved up. Their track ran through flat fields that were ideal for sweeping with machine gun fire and the men of "D" Company, seeing Lt. Colonel Craddock striding unconcernedly down the track wearing a peaked cap instead of a helmet, were greatly heartened.

As the attack went in a platoon of enemy was seen to be swarming over the embankment on the right into a house on the railway and a position nearby, about (3) see sketch. From these points their machine guns fired into "D" Company. The Battalion 3 in. mortars were immediately switched to the right; within a few minutes the enemy were seen running back whence they had come, one or two clutching their stomachs. "D" Company followed up to this house, which became a target for heavy enemy mortaring. "B" and "C" Companies pushed on and the battalion established itself across the railway. Meanwhile from 2000 hours onwards a series of explosions east and south east proclaimed that the enemy was destroying the canal bridges and his ammunition dump.

The "Citation" in which Major A. H. Claxton was recommended for an immediate M.C. for his leadership of "D" Company in this action is given in Appendix "A."

Once again, the welcome given by the townsfolk of WEERT was terrific. The Dutch flag; hats, frocks, sashes and favours in HOLLAND's national colour, orange, decorated everything and everybody. The leaders of the local resistance movement made themselves known to the C.O. near the site of the main bridge in WEERT and fixed a Battalion H.Q. and an unofficial "Liaison Officer" to act as interpreter. Information regarding the enemy's movements poured into battalion headquarters.

The Battalion settled down to hold the north of the canal for the next few days as it was impossible with the forces available to hold the whole of WEERT. Road blocks were constructed at the approaches to the bridges, now repaired, and mobile patrols were sent out. The following day Capt. K. G. Mayhew took out two sections of carriers and one section of three inch Mortars; a very successful mortar shoot was done on the enemy who were found digging in. On Sunday, 24th September, a much larger force, again under Mayhew, swept the west of the canal nearly as far South as the village of ELL. A small patrol led by L/Sgt. Ellis killed one enemy at the first bridge. The following day contact was made with the Belgian Independent Brigade.

For the next three weeks the First Suffolk was constantly in movement, first to protect the supply route through EINDHOVEN to NIJMEGEN, during which period they patrolled actively to maintain moral superiority over the enemy in the area; later they crossed the River MAAS and concentrated near MOOK within four miles of the German frontier. Although in reserve occasional shelling, especially at night, disturbed an otherwise not unpleasant period. So at any rate it seemed to those Companies who were lucky enough to be in positions near the river where for a time they were able to enjoy a little quiet canoeing.

At this time it is believed the intention of the Higher Command was to employ the 3rd Division as the spearhead for the assault on Hitler's Reich. But supply difficulties made an immediate attack impossible; and the role of the Division was restricted to the neighbourhood of the MAAS River. Although the great port of ANTWERP had been in British hands for a month, the islands of WALCHEREN and SUID BEVELAND and the southern bank of the SCHELDT estuary were still held by the enemy, thus rendering it unusable. This and the pertinacity with which the enemy held the CHANNEL ports and destroyed them before surrendering, greatly hampered operations. DIEPPE was not big enough for the supply needs of the force and the main bulk of the British supplies were still coming in to the prefabricated ports on the beaches of NORMANDY.

The Battalion had for a week its own experience of the maintenance problem when it lived in the main on captured German rations. These German rations were sorted out at the Q.M. Stores, where efforts were made, mainly by trial and error, to make loading lists comparable to our own tables. Some toothpaste tubes looked of comparatively small account until it was discovered that they contained cheese.

The swift thrust in early September towards the bridges over the two branches of the RHINE at NIJMEGEN and ARNHEM, even though later, supported and consolidated by the other Corps of the British Second Army, had nevertheless left a large tract of enemy-held land, including the islands of ZEELAND and the towns of BREDA, TILBURG and s'HERTOGENBOSCH. To enable the PORT OF ANTWERP to function properly and to give adequate security to the lines of communication radiating from it, the enemy had to be swept out of this area and thrown back across the MAAS. Responsibility for this task was taken over by the Canadian Army with certain United Kingdom forces under command. At the same time, however, the Eastern side of the front needed the protection of some easily defensible line and here, too, the obvious one was the River MAAS. It was on this side that the 3rd British Infantry Division was called on to function.

The First Suffolk arrived at RIJKEVOORT on 8th October. The following day the Officer Commanding, Lt.-Colonel R. W. Craddock, D.S.O., M.B.E., gave an inspiring address. It was a sunny afternoon and the whole Battalion sat in a field while Lt.-Colonel Craddock explained simply and clearly what lay before them. He spoke of the forthcoming battle, of the severe fighting that must come; but assured them that they would never be committed to action without the maximum help from all supporting arms, or without a good prospect of success. He spoke of what an Englishman's home and family mean to the soldier and of the supreme courage and endurance that this war required.

During by far the greater portion of the whole War the First Battalion was commanded by two notable Suffolk Officers:—Lt.-Col. F. A. Milnes and Lt.-Col. R. E. Goodwin; but during short periods, due to casualties in action, three officers:—Lt.-Col. J. G. M. B. Gough, the Lincolnshire Regiment; Lt.-Col. F. F. E. Allen, the Oxford and Buckinghamshire L.I.; and Lt.-Col. R. W. Craddock, the Buffs, had command. All three were outstandingly fine commanders and all, during their periods of command, became enthusiastically and wholeheartedly "Suffolk."

But of these three memorable leaders the finest probably was Lt.-Col. R. W. Craddock, D.S.O. The speech he made on the 9th October marked him out as a great man, knowing the men he commanded. True to his word he was indefatigable in visiting the forward positions till, later in the battle, falling a victim to a German mine, he was very badly wounded. Even so, with a shattered leg, he had crawled out of the mine field before being picked up, and he could still joke about the limb he had lost. His name was for long a legend in the First Battalion.

There was no doubt a special reason behind his speech. The Battalion had earned a great reputation; it was up to strength in all ranks; but it was no longer the same Battalion that had crossed on "D" Day; some of the reinforcements that now filled its ranks came from Divisions that had been broken up, others had seen no previous fighting, many had never been trained as infantry. For there was an acute shortage of manpower. But it was a "Suffolk" Battalion in spirit and heart that fought with such magnificent endurance and courage in the forthcoming battles. That it was so is an undying tribute to the quality of a great Regimental Tradition, invincible, unshaken by the chances and changes of the moment.

Major A. C. L. Sperling, one of the many war time officers with the First Battalion whose quality as a leader was outstanding, writing of this Battalion morale, says:—"On 'D' Day and during the succeeding weeks the Battalion was on the top of its form. A great team of officers, N.C.O.s and men had been built; men who knew each other intimately and were prepared to make sacrifices purely for the sake of the Regiment. After ugly casualties, reinforcements began to arrive. In October, 1944, in one draft there were 2 C.M.P.s, 5 R.A.M.C. stretcher bearers, a dozen from the R.A. and 4 tank drivers. Officers were drafted from a dozen different units. Yet, in time, all these diverse elements grew into our ways and became living assets."

"There were two outstanding factors for our high morale. One was the deep spirit of comradeship among the officers; the other was the spirit of mutual respect and admiration between the officers and men. The friendship between officers remains an outstanding memory. All officers from whatever Regiment were welcomed into the fold; but only too often

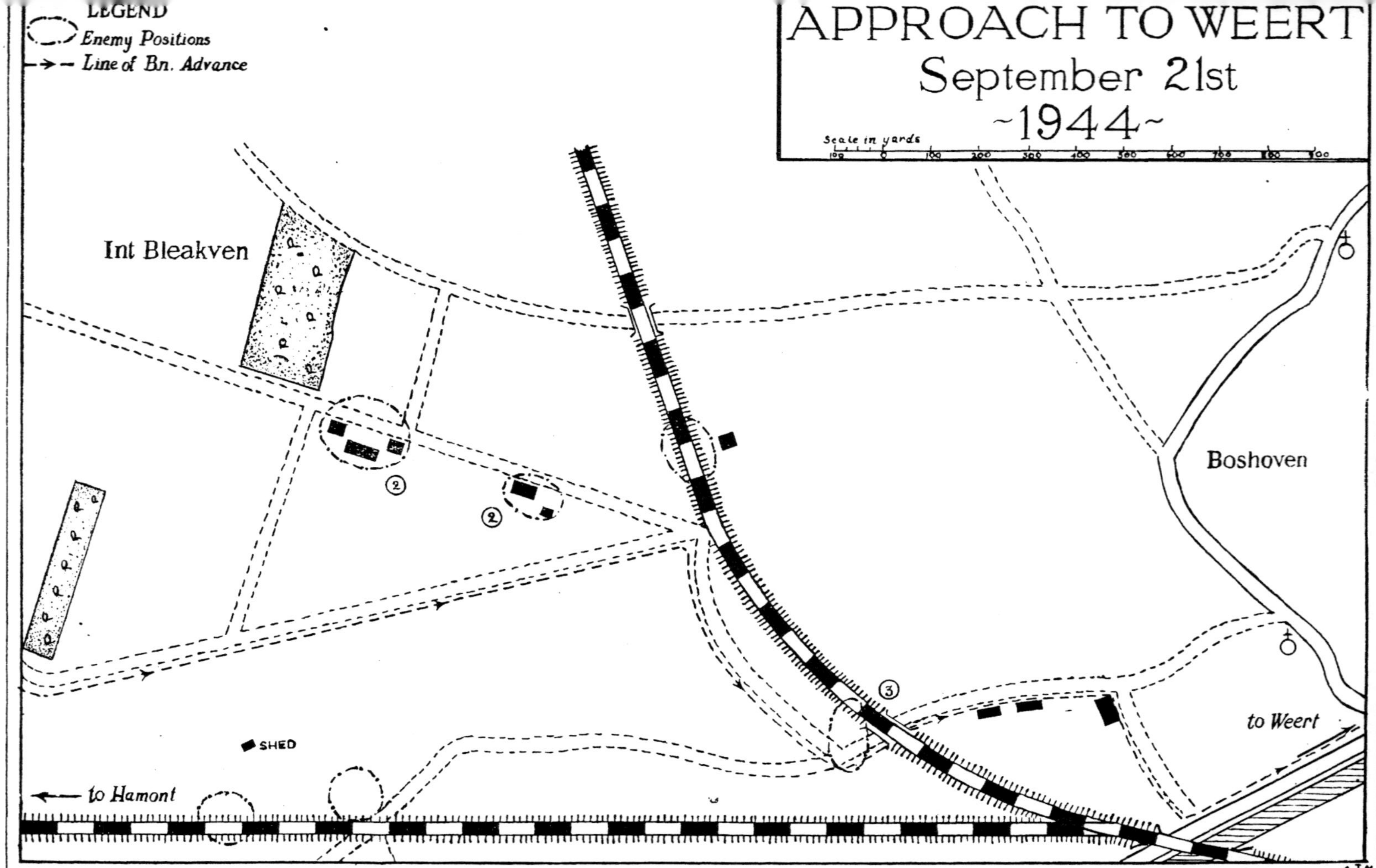
APPROACH TO WEERT
September 21st
~1944~
Scale in yards
100 0 100 200 300 400 500 600 700 800 900
LEGEND
Enemy Positions
Line of Bn. Advance
Int Bleakven
Boshoven
SHED
to Hamont
to Weert
2
2
3
A.J.M.

VII

subalterns would join one day and not be seen alive again. The spirit of comradeship among the officers of the First Suffolk, whatever their parental unit, was so strong that it became the one compensation for an otherwise highly unpleasant campaign."

Others with wider experience than Major Sperling comment on the moral effect of absorbing large numbers of men from untrained and sometimes static formations. For few men love fighting; all must be trained for it.

BATTLES FOR — OVERLOON — VENRAY.

12th October — 19th October, 1944.

Lt.-Colonel Craddock had outlined to the Battalion the probable course of events. The 8th British Infantry Brigade was to capture the village of OVERLOON, after which the 9th British Infantry Brigade was to pass through and capture the small town of VENRAY. Other divisions were to clear the areas to the South.

The battles for OVERLOON and VENRAY, which began at 1200 hours on the 12th October, were not won until 11.30 hours on 19th October. It was a week of fighting which will long be remembered in the 3rd Division. During this time the infantry attacked over many different types of ground; the flat open fields North of OVERLOON, with no cover except occasional ditches full of water and therefore ideal for enemy machine gunners in that village; similar conditions later in and around VENRAY; the thick woods South of OVERLOON; the mud round the BEEK which caused the ordinary infantryman to go on alone when the tanks, guns and vehicles had had to be left behind; and finally, the scrub and wooded sandhills West of VENRAY. It was a long slogging battle against an enemy who had prepared his defences well and was determined to stay and defend them. Furthermore, it was the first time that mines had been encountered in large numbers and the first time that Schu-mines had been encountered at all. During the battle in the VENRAY area the Battalion was reduced by almost a third of its strength in officers; casualties, killed and wounded, during this time totalled eleven officers and one hundred and seventy-two other ranks.

At 08.00 hours 10th October the Commanding Officer left Battalion H.Q. with several of the officers to reconnoitre the area of the future operations. Battalion "O" Group assembled in one of the forward Platoon positions in a cottage at (1) (see Sketch) and here, in spite of interruptions from heavy Nebelwerfer fire at intervals, plans for the attack were outlined, full orders being given out later. It was scheduled to take place the following day, "H." hour being 1100.

The plan was as follows:—

The First Suffolk would attack the right of the village of OVERLOON and capture the area South of it as far as the factory at (2) and the two orchards at (3). The attack was to be preceded by rocket firing Typhoons operating against OVERLOON, by a heavy artillery barrage and by medium machine gun fire. The start line was a lateral track (see sketch); the forward assembly area being in a big wood well to the rear of this line. The main axis of the attack ran along a track to OVERLOON. "B" Company, supported by one demolition team of the Pioneer Platoon was, to move down the main axis, clear the houses along the road between (4) and (4), and then hold this area.

"A" Company, supported by two troops of Churchill tanks, was to move on the right of the axis, via a burnt-out windmill, and capture the factory. "C" Company, also supported by two troops of Churchills, was to follow "A" Company and thence turn East to capture and hold the area of the two orchards at (3). "D" Company was to follow "C" Company to destroy the enemy in the area of the orchards round about (5). The Mortar Platoon was to take up a position near the start line ready for opportunity targets. The Carrier Platoon, less one section, was to establish itself North of the main road in the area (6) and provide right flank protection for the Battalion. The Anti-Tank Platoon as the battle progressed was to provide screens, first at (7), then in "B" Company area, and finally to send one section to each of "A", "B" and "C" Company areas. Crocodile tanks were available in Brigade Reserve if needed.

Owing to very bad weather the attack was postponed twenty-four hours. At 0730 hours on the 12th October the Battalion marched out of RIJKEVOORT. "H" Hour was fixed for 1200 hours and while the Battalion was drinking hot tea in the assembly area, medium bombers and Typhoons came over and attacked targets between OVERLOON and VENRAY. The weather had greatly improved.

Shortly afterwards "B" Company, and then "A" Company, moved out from the assembly area. There was spasmodic enemy mortar fire; but at first neither Company encountered much small arms fire. Progress was slow as the artillery barrage moved at a rate of one hundred yards in five minutes. By 1400 hours "B" Company seemed to be progressing satisfactorily and had sent back nine prisoners from Parachute Battalion Paul. It was impossible from advanced Battalion H.Q. to find a suitable O.P. for watching the progress of the forward Companies.

By 1400 hours it was difficult to get news of "A" Company, so the Commanding Officer went forward to find out the situation. "A" Company was in the area of the windmill and was held up by small arms fire from the right. Major Ellis, the Company Commander and half a dozen other ranks had been killed by sniping from this direction. The only other two officers in the Company had been wounded. C.S.M. Leatherland had assumed command of the Company (See Appendix "A"). Lt.-Colonel Craddock made a quick appreciation of the situation, checked up to see that "A" Company was in suitable positions, and returned to advance Battalion H.Q. which at this time was operating from the farmhouse at (8). Meanwhile "B" Company had reported that they were on their objective. The Commanding Officer ordered "C" Company to pass through "A" Company to their original objective, assisted as much as possible by "B" Company's fire. "A" Company was then to move behind "C" Company to the area of the factory. "H" Hour for this attack was fixed for 1530 hours.

The new attack went in at 1530 hours and an hour later "C" Company was progressing well. "A" Company left the area of the windmill and made for their objective. Shortly after 1630 hours "D" Company was sent forward on to its objective and by 1730 all objectives had been taken. In the second attack opposition had been light; but "A" Company had heavy losses in their initial push to the windmill area. Battalion H.Q. was set up in a farmhouse at (9) and all Companies consolidated for the night in their pre-arranged areas. Twelve of the enemy had been killed and sixty prisoners taken.

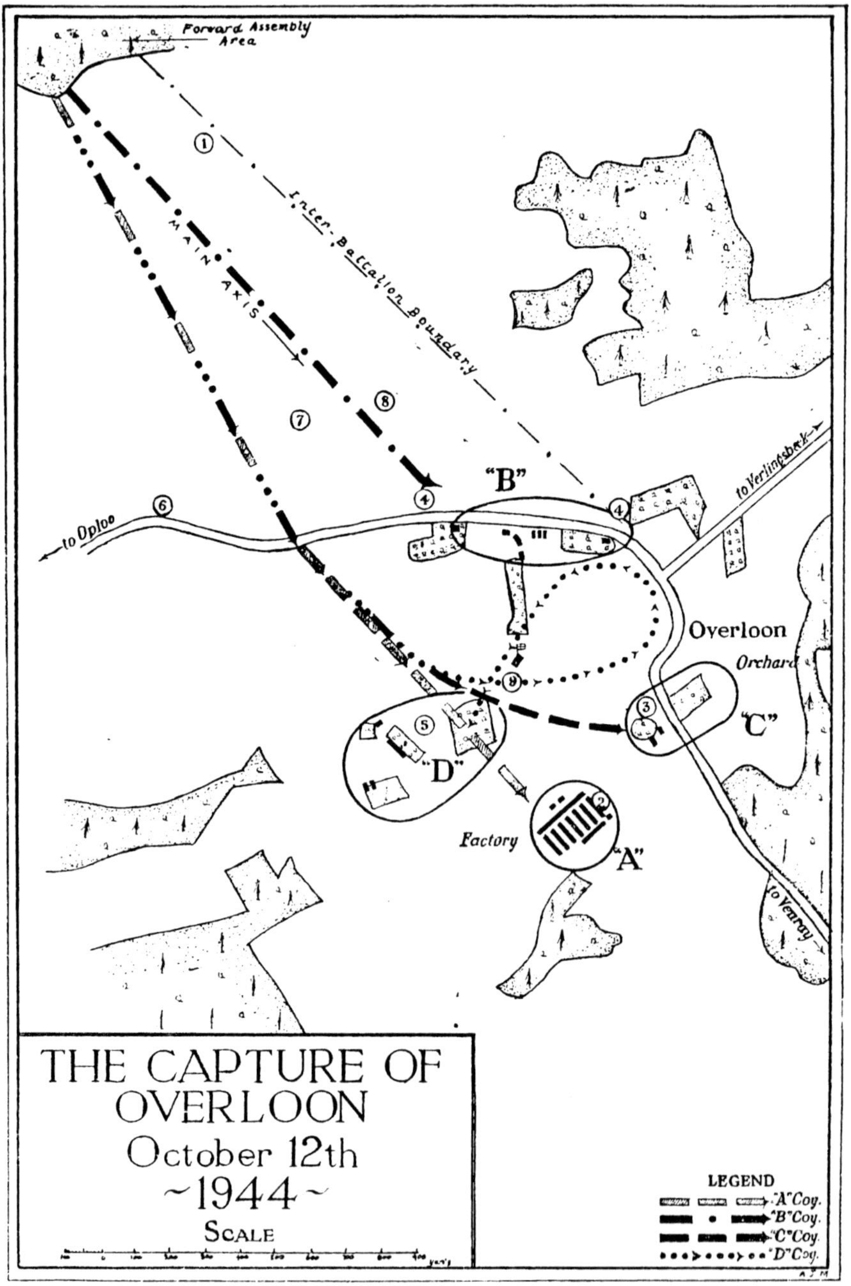
Forward Assembly Area
Inter-Battalion Boundary
MAIN AXIS
"B"
to Verlingsbek
to Oploo
Overloon
Orchard
"C"
"D"
Factory
"A"
to Venray
THE CAPTURE OF OVERLOON
October 12th
~1944~
SCALE
LEGEND
"A" Coy.
"B" Coy.
"C" Coy.
"D" Coy.

Night fell with the First Suffolk the most forward unit on this part of the front and, accordingly, during the hours of darkness and on the morning of Friday, 13th October, the Battalion area was subjected to fairly heavy shell and mortar fire. The areas particularly affected were the factory, Battalion H.Q. and "C" Company. Reconnaissance patrols were sent out by "C" and "D" Companies.

In the middle of the morning of 13th October, shelling and mortaring increased in intensity. The building that housed Battalion H.Q. was hit three times. At 1040 hours an enemy Battalion was suspected to be assembling for a counter attack in the woods to the South East of OVERLOON. Two Field Regiments of Artillery and a Squadron of Typhoon Fighter-bombers were ordered to deal with this threat. They did so very successfully. During the morning the welcome information was received that 9th Infantry Brigade was to drive through the large woods on the right of the Battalion and clear them while the 185th Infantry Brigade was to perform a similar task on the left. Both these tasks were completed by 1830 hours. On the night 14th/15th October, "B" and "D" Companies moved to the North side of the OVERLOON-VENRAY road; so that the Battalion was now firmly placed astride it.

Appendix "A" gives an account of the part played by Cpl. C. Bligh-Bingham in helping to keep open the lines of communication during this fighting.

On 15th October, shelling continued, but not so heavily, and the Battalion spent a fairly quiet day in its positions. This day orders were issued for the attack on VENRAY.

The First Suffolk which was the leading Battalion of the 8th Brigade, was ordered to advance down the OVERLOON-VENRAY road at first light on 16th October and make good "Line B" (see Sketch). The Brigade Commander would then decide whether the Battalion would continue in the lead or whether other Battalions of the Brigade would be passed through. The enemy was believed to be in strength between the MOLENBEEK and VENRAY, but it was thought that he had no troops west of the River.

The Commanding Officer's plan was for "B" Company to move at 0700 hours astride the main axis, to put two kapok bridges over the MOLENBEEK, cross over and establish a firm base. "C" and "D" Companies, each with a mine clearance team from the Pioneer Platoon, were then to pass through to "Line B"; "D" Company being on the main axis and "C" Company being on the right axis, (see Sketch map), "A" Company to follow in reserve at the Commanding Officer's disposal, as also the Carrier Platoon. The Mortar Platoon to engage opportunity targets. A Squadron of Churchill tanks supported the Battalion; these were to cross the MOLENBEEK by fascines placed by the AVREs and then to divide up, two troops going forward to support "C" Company, and two troops "D" Company. The Anti-Tank Platoon was to cross the MOLENBEEK as soon as possible after the tanks and remain at the Commanding Officer's disposal. F.O.O.s were with the two forward Companies.

At 0330 hours on the 16th October the Battalion marched out from OVERLOON to the forward assembly area, movement by night being helped by "Artificial moonlight."

At 0700 hours "B" Company moved out towards the MOLENBEEK carrying kapok bridging equipment. Half an hour later Flails began working on the main axis so that the tanks could follow. But the MOLENBEEK had been widened by the enemy to form a tank obstacle, the bridge over it had been destroyed and in the marshy ground mines had been laid. Moreover the recent rains had made the ground on each side of the track very soft and one flail got bogged.

"B" Company came under heavy machine gun fire; but pushed slowly forward while the mine clearing proceeded. Three AVREs, each with a large fascine to drop into the MOLENBEEK, followed the Flails. Unfortunately one of them was bogged before it reached the river bank, and another became immoveably stuck in the BEEK itself, while the third fascine was inadequate to bridge the river.

By this time "B" Company's Commander had been wounded and the Company advance had been held up. At 1000 hours the Commanding Officer decided to pass "C" and "D" Companies, with the kapok bridge, through "B" Company and over the BEEK. This decision was taken despite the fact that for some hours they would have to do without tank support, neither would the Battalion anti-tank guns and carriers be available if needed.

By 1045 both Companies had bridged the BEEK and one Platoon of each had crossed to the far bank. From then onwards wireless communication was poor and it was difficult to appreciate the situation. Progress seemed slow and heavy enemy fire was heard on the right. The whereabouts of the Platoon of "B" Company was not exactly known; but it was thought to be across the BEEK and about two hundred yards further on.

Lieut.-Colonel Craddock decided to go forward. He crossed the BEEK; but as he was walking over a corner of a field, which several men had traversed earlier that morning, his foot was blown off by a Schu-mine. This was a severe blow to the Battalion. In his comparatively short period of command, Lt.-Colonel Craddock had endeared himself alike to Officers and men for his outstanding qualities of bold leadership in action and complete disregard for his own safety; while at all times he showed a sympathetic understanding of the lot of the "private man". On several occasions his appearance among the forward troops at particularly difficult times had proved one of the main factors in the Battalion's gaining its objective.

For the second time the Second in Command, Major F. F. E. Allen, the Oxfordshire and Buckinghamshire Light Infantry, took over the Command of the Battalion under most difficult circumstances. It was raining hard, communications were non-existent, the wireless sets were waterlogged; the MOLENBEEK had proved itself a "task" obstacle and, unknown to Major Allen, the Battalion had just been ordered to push on without armoured support against a strong and determined enemy; "A" Company had no officers, the other Companies no more than two apiece.

Few men have had to grapple with a situation under more difficult circumstances. For the second time in the Campaign, Major Allen did so with calm assurance and led the Battalion to the conclusion of a costly but successful week's fighting into and beyond VENRAY.

"C" and "D" Companies were ordered to maintain their forward movement. At 1215 hours the flails began to clear a path to the MOLENBEEK on the left of the main axis for the tank bridge. It arrived three quarters of an hour later and work on it started immediately. By 1500 hours the bridge was in position and two Churchills had crossed; but both were bogged in the soft ground on the far side. A third attempted to cross; but sank in the mud immediately over the bridge. By 13.00 hours the Company Commanders of both "C" and "D" Companies had been wounded, and "C" Company had become split up.

Plans for the next stage of the attack were made with the Brigade Commander. At 1500 hours a new thrust was made by "D" Company on the left and "A" Company on the right. Artillery support had been arranged; but the three tanks that were bogged were only able to support the infantry with observed fire for the first few hundred yards of the attack.

Within a quarter of an hour wireless communication between Battalion H.Q. and all Companies had completely broken down. However, it was known that "D" Company had reached (1) (See sketch) the lateral track which was to have been the start line; also that "A" Company had passed through the thicket, and by 1600 hours was established at the houses at (2) in close contact with the enemy. There was no definite news of "D" Company; but they were known to have made progress North of the axis.

During this fighting Pte F. Barrett greatly distinguished himself; time and again in full view of the enemy and under heavy fire bringing wounded men back to cover.

The East Yorkshire Regiment now began to cross the BEEK in the Battalion area and to move well out on to the left flank.

At 1700 hours the Commanding Officer went forward to try to make contact with "D" Company. This he was unable to do as his party came under heavy fire; but the Company was shortly afterwards reported at (3), consolidating. By this time "C" Company had reorganised and Major Allen ordered them to patrol the thickets about (4) and to establish themselves in that area. "A" Company was ordered up to the village of HIEPT for a similar task. All three Companies remained in these positions all night. Battalion H.Q. moved up to the houses just beyond the start line.

Darkness fell and the Sappers worked hard on the bridge. By 2230 hours ration parties were able to bring up a hot meal and a rum ration, both very welcome for men who had been marching or fighting since 0300 hours that morning. In the day's fighting the Battalion had lost the Commanding Officer, Lt. Col.-Craddock, three Rifle Company Commanders and forty-five others either killed or wounded.

During the night 16/17th October orders were received from Brigade H.Q. for the continuance of the battle on the following day and at 0330 hours on the 17th October the Commanding Officer gave out his orders. The plan was substantially the same; "C" Company on the left and "A" Company on the right advancing along the same axis that were originally arranged. The 2nd East Yorks were to attack VENRAY on the left of the First Suffolk. The attack was to start at first light; this was later altered to 0900 hours. At that hour a five minutes Artillery concentration fell on the woods East of HIEPT and "C" and "A" Companies began to move forward. Shortly afterwards "A" Company reported that they were having difficulty in entering these woods, but that one Platoon had forced its way in. Meanwhile "C" Company succeeded in getting to the cross tracks on "Line B"; there it was held up by rifle and machine gun fire.

It was fortunate that in this situation the Battalion was at last joined by a Squadron of Churchill tanks and a troop of flails which had succeeded in crossing the MOLENBEEK some distance to the North. The flails set to work on the main axis and at 1130 hours one troop of tanks was sent to support "A" Company and one to "C" Company.

At 1230 hours "C" Company with tank support moved forward along the main axis; but they were held up by heavy fire from the woods and houses on the West of VENRAY. "A" Company also advanced along their axis; but it was against very strong opposition. At 1350 hours "B" Company was sent to follow up "A" Company. At 1415 hours the Commanding Officer, Major Allen, visited "C" Company in their forward position and decided to pass "D" Company through them to capture the wood about (5) which had proved to be the principal obstacle to the Battalion advance.

In the meantime the Brigade plan was changed and there was a pause. The South Lancashire were directed on to the Southern half of VENRAY, the First Suffolk to face right and clear the large wood at (5).

At 1600 hours "A" Company Commander, Capt. Halford, reported that he had withdrawn his depleted Company from the Western part of this wood, as the enemy was in strength and kept working round his flanks. At 1620 "D" Company moved to attack the North Eastern flank of the wood; while "B" Company was ordered to attack the North Western flank. Both Companies succeeded in entering the wood by 1715 hours.

By 1740 hours "D" Company had reached their objective and taken eleven prisoners; the enemy had been driven south of the road through the wood but were still in the woods south of this road. "B" Company reached their objective by 1800 hours and consolidated, having met no enemy; though they reported that they could hear them south of the road. Battalion H.Q. and "A" Company consolidated for the night at the cross tracks just north of the wood (5), "C" Company near the track junction to the east of the wood. The Commanding Officer went round and inspected all areas during the evening. By 2030 hours all was in order and the hot meal and rum ration had arrived.

During the night 17th/18th October patrols from "B" Company moved through the wood and made contact with "D" Company.

After desultory fighting during the morning of 18th October during which the Battalion further strengthened its position, at 1430 hours orders were given for a systematic clearance of all woods South West of the Battalion position marked (6) (see Sketch). "A", "B" and "D" Companies were employed; each was to clear an area to the Western extremity. Each had a troop of tanks in support and there were F.O.O.s with "B" and "D" Companies. "H" Hour was 1500 hours and phase one was completed by 1530. "A", "B" and "D" Companies then began the second phase of the attack. Within twenty minutes "D" Company had taken eight prisoners of Battalion Schwartz and "B" Company had taken prisoner one officer and six other ranks. All were too demoralised by the fire of the tanks to offer serious resistance. By 1700 hours both "B" and "D" Companies reported that they had completed their tasks and were returning. By 1745 hours the Battalion was consolidating for the night.

In this attack no casualties were suffered by any of the Companies and the total of prisoners for the day amounted to one officer and forty-six other ranks. Contact patrols between Companies and the South Lancashire, now in VENRAY, were made during the night. The whole of the town had by now been taken by the other two Battalions of the Brigade.

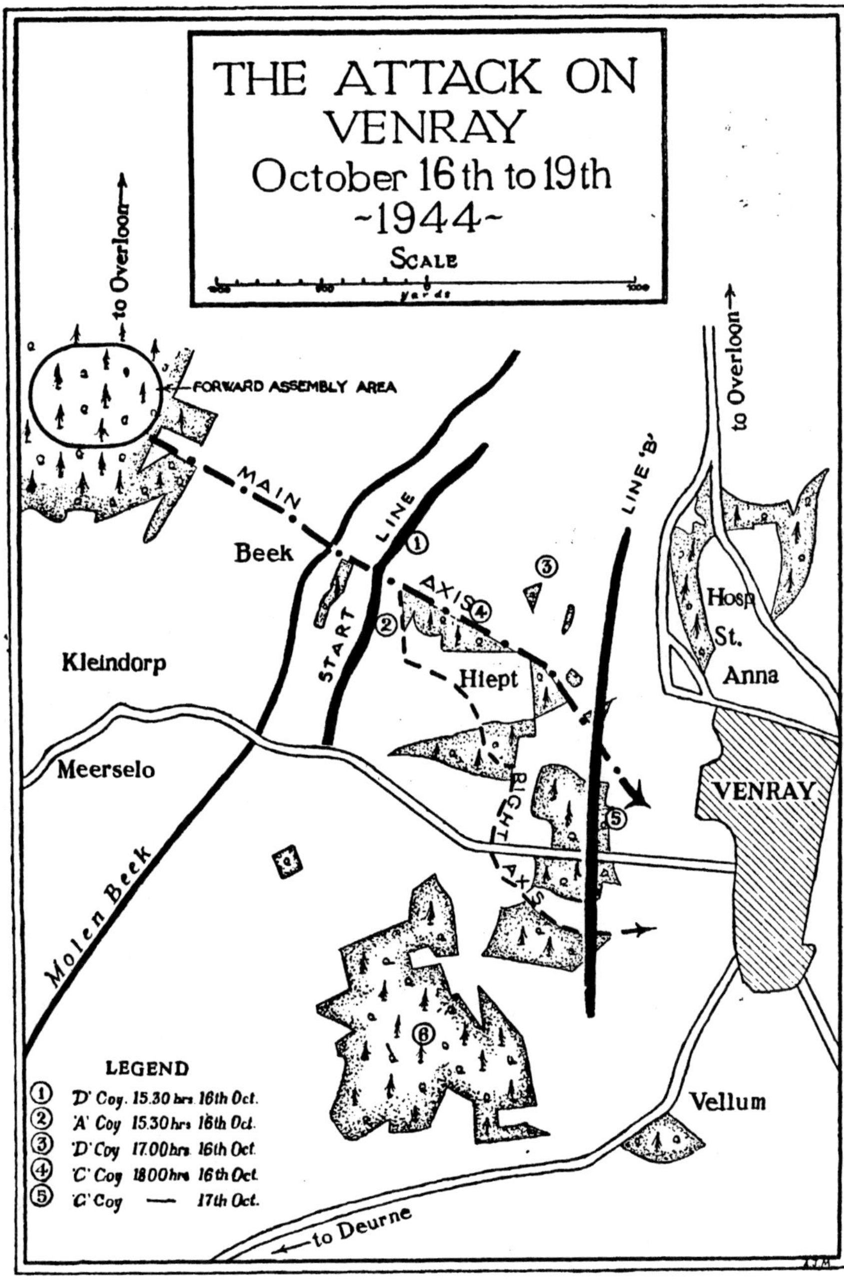
THE ATTACK ON VENRAY
October 16th to 19th
~1944~
SCALE
Yards
to Overloon
FORWARD ASSEMBLY AREA
MAIN AXIS
START LINE
LINE 'B'
Beek
Kleindorp
Hiept
Meerselo
Molen Beek
RIGHT AXIS
Hosp
St. Anna
VENRAY
Vellum
to Deurne
LEGEND
① 'D' Coy. 15.30 hrs 16th Oct.
② 'A' Coy 15.30 hrs 16th Oct.
③ 'D' Coy 17.00 hrs 16th Oct.
④ 'C' Coy 18.00 hrs 16th Oct.
⑤ 'C' Coy — 17th Oct.

At 0830 hours on the 19th "B" Company patrolled the area of the woods which had been cleared the previous evening, while "D" Company cleared the remaining woods south of the 26 Grid Line. At midday on the 19th October, on completion of its task, the Battalion was ordered back into Brigade and that afternoon moved into the Northern part of VENRAY. Here everyone was accommodated under cover, having dug tactical positions in case of an enemy counter attack. At VENRAY the Battalion remained resting and reorganising for four days. The mobile baths visited them, parties of men were sent on 24 hours' leave to the Divisional Club, and on 48 hours' leave to BRUSSELS. Intermittent shelling and mortaring of the area continued and the Battalion suffered casualties.

During all this fighting the difficulty of supply was very great. Deep muddy tracks made movement off the roads with a heavy truck a perilous proceeding. Only the real skill of the Battalion drivers gave the Battalion its unbroken record of maintenance. There was no harder working driver than Pte Noller and he, like most of the other M.T. personnel, experienced many near misses during this period.

Thus ended the attacks on OVERLOON and VENRAY, actions that could only have been brought to a successful conclusion by troops of the highest quality.

The casualties during this seven days battle amounted to 11 officers and 162 other ranks made up as follows:—

	Killed.		Wounded.	
	Officers.	O.Rs.	Officers.	O.Rs.
12th October ...	1	9	2	55
13th October ...		2	2	18
14th October ...		2		5
15th October ...				
16th October ...		3	4	37
17th October ...		2	1	20
18th October ...			1	9
TOTAL	1	18	10	144

On the evening of the 23rd October there was an unfortunate incident when the Standing Patrol of "A" Company, having captured a German reconnaissance patrol and were searching them, were themselves surrounded by a strong enemy fighting patrol and taken prisoner. Two signallers and two stretcher bearers who had hidden in a cellar escaped. An "A" Company Platoon went out immediately, but they were unable to catch the enemy patrol before it left the area.

Early on 26th October the Battalion left VENRAY and went back for one night to a rear area beyond OVERLOON, where it had no commitments, and was, at last, not under enemy shellfire. On the evening of the following day it came forward to ROUW; this, apart from some enemy shelling, was a fairly quiet area.

During the next month there was no major operation; but strong patrols, occasionally of Company strength, were constantly engaged with an enemy who was full of fight. Hardly a day passed without either shelling or mortaring of the Battalion area. Meanwhile the Battalion had been reduced temporarily to three rifle Companies, "A", "C", "D"; but "B" Company H.Q. and several senior N.C.O.s were kept to form the staff for a Battalion training cadre, so that all incoming drafts might pass through this Company.

On 7th November, Lt.-Col. R. E. Goodwin, D.S.O., returned to the Battalion after five months' absence, and resumed command. Lt.-Col. F. F. E. Allen was posted to the command of a Battalion of the 53rd Division. It was natural that alongside its welcome for its former Commanding Officer, the Battalion should feel sympathy for Lt.-Colonel Allen who, though of another Regiment, had through his four and a half months with the Battalion become accepted as a "Suffolk man". Twice he had been called on to take command in two of the most difficult battles of the campaign; those of the First Battalion who were there will remember his personal bravery and his firm but courageous handling of the unit alike on the TINCHEBRAY Road and in the woods near VENRAY. It is a pleasure to record that shortly after leaving the Battalion, while in command of another unit, he twice gained the D.S.O. for conspicuous gallantry.

Details began to emerge of the plan for finally clearing the left bank of the MAAS. The 3rd Division was to deal with the Northern part of the area, whilst other formations made the larger advances necessary to clear the enemy held territory up to the bank of the RIVER MAAS opposite ROERMOND and VENLO. Having already dealt with the OVERLOON-VENRAY area, the 3rd Division was already close to the river and so was not to take part in the advance until its later stages. Since the 8th Brigade was on the left of the Divisional front, there was some possibility, if the other attacks were successful, of the enemy withdrawing voluntarily in its area.

On 18th November there was a pronounced increase in the enemy mortaring; but by this time the Divisional Counter Mortar had pin-pointed most of the enemy positions and an Artillery target known as "Melrose" was arranged to deal with them. Target "Melrose" fired twice on 19th November; the enemy mortar fire which had been directed at "C" Company was much reduced. Unfortunately Major McKay, commanding "C" Company, was himself "Melrosed", receiving several wounds.

THE CASTLE OF GEIJSTEREN. 24TH NOV. 1944—DEC. 1944.

On the 24th November "A" Company was sent forward to search the area between the railway and the river MAAS. The whole area was reported clear except for the Castle on the bank of the river near the village of GEIJSTEREN. A civilian stated that there were about sixty Germans holding it. "D" Company, with two sections of 3" Mortars and a section of anti-tank guns, were sent up to join "A" Company. The whole force consolidated on the forward edge of a large wood three quarters of a mile from the river where it could dominate the area. The Commanding Officer decided to attack the Castle the following day, after it had been attacked by Typhoons and the Divisional Artillery.

There were two approaches to the Castle, which was almost surrounded by water as the MAAS was in full flood, one was by a road from GEIJSTEREN village, the other by a road along the river bank from MAASHEES. The road from GEIJSTEREN was covered by extensive flooding. The road from MAASHEES was not itself flooded though everything on either verge was; but it was in view from the other side of the river.

On the 25th, ten of the enemy were seen by a Standing Patrol in GEIJSTEREN. The Patrol opened fire and caused several casualties; four being later collected on stretchers by the enemy. It was decided that "D" Company should attack the castle at 1430 hours, at which time Typhoons would attack it with rockets and bombs, while the Divisional Artillery were to fire a concentration from H minus 10 to H plus 5. At the last moment a heavy hailstorm prevented the aircraft from taking part.

The Company advanced from the MAASHEES direction under cover of artillery. They came under heavy enemy shell and machine gun fire shortly after reaching the road and when they were still about six hundred yards from the entrance to the Castle. Here they were unable to deploy because of deep flood water; neither could they move forward. At 1630 hours the Brigade Commander called off the attack and Captain L. J. Thomas skilfully extricated his company. The casualties included two killed and ten wounded, most of them seriously. Corporal A. Fordham in charge of the Company stretcher bearers greatly distinguished himself in the collection and evacuation of the wounded. Although under heavy fire he showed exceptional courage and steadiness, attending personally to all the wounded.

Captain L. J. Thomas was awarded an immediate M.C. for the coolness and disregard of danger which he displayed under very difficult circumstances. Pte. L. Jaggard, the Company runner, was awarded an M.M. for conspicuous bravery during this fighting.

For the next four days the Castle was bombarded fairly continuously by Typhoon aircraft; by heavy and medium artillery; by tanks at close range and by mortar fire; while the Battalion snipers kept watch on it throughout the hours of daylight and claimed several victims. Great damage was done; but when a patrol of "D" Company again approached from the MAASHEES direction after dark on the 28th November, they were again unable to make headway owing to heavy enemy small arms fire. It was, therefore, decided to assault the Castle the following night from the South, crossing the flood water in assault boats. "C" Company was chosen for this operation. A bombardment by field artillery covered the noise of the carrying up of the assault boats.

The leading platoon, after crossing the flood waters, touched down at the North East corner of the Castle at 0150 hours on 30th November. A second platoon speedily joined them and the whole was searched. The enemy had withdrawn; though many of their weapons had been left behind. A Standing Patrol was left in the castle grounds.

The month of December 1944 was the quietest of the campaign for the First Suffolk. During December, January and the first week in February, the Battalion was holding the MAAS RIVER line.

The invasion of GERMANY, originally planned for October, was for the second time thwarted; this time by Von Runstedt's Ardennes offensive, which caused a complete redistribution of the Allied forces in LUXEMBOURG, BELGIUM and HOLLAND.

A REST AT BOEKEL. DEC. 1944 — FEB. 1945.

On the 3rd December the 8th Brigade moved back into the GEMEERT area. At this time the Battalion strength in all ranks was 960. This was the first time since it left FARCEAUX in FRANCE, on the 16th September, that the Battalion had been right out of the fighting area. It was quartered just North of GEMEERT in the little village of BOEKEL. There the week was spent in training, route marching and ceremonial drill parades.

BOEKEL was not far from HELMOND and there were opportunities of visiting cinemas, the Divisional Club and the Corps Rest Camp, situate in that town. But many men, after being so long away from civilian life, preferred to sit and make difficult conversation in something that was neither English nor Dutch with the hospitable local population.

No one is more insular than the Englishman; yet the British soldier is a past master at making himself at home with all classes in foreign countries. Perhaps an unconscious superiority complex is partly responsible for his friendliness. HOLLAND in the winter is a cold wet country, the DUTCH keep their houses warm; what more natural than that in every kitchen there should be an English soldier sitting before the fire. No diffidence about a language ever kept a soldier silent under such conditions; in every kitchen a lesson in the Anglo-Dutch language proceeded. No doubt where there happened to be a pretty girl she had a greater number of instructors.

There is a natural curiosity in the homeland about the FRENCH, BELGIANS and DUTCH. "Which did you like the best?" the soldier is asked when he returns. The FRENCHMEN of NORMANDY were the least welcoming; but they can hardly be blamed. Their villages and farms stood between two battle fronts; they could not be expected to open their arms to the men who were blowing their buildings to bits, robbing their orchards and hen roosts. The BELGIANS understood French, a link with many of the English; while the DUTCH were phlegmatic and spoke a language difficult to understand. But while that predisposed the officers in favour of the BELGIANS, no language difficulty made any difference to the men in the ranks, who could always make their wants known.

There is no greater mistake than to believe the more spartan a life the soldier lives, the better soldier he must be. Yet there are some misguided folk of this opinion. Both officers and men urgently need relaxation and the best of everything when it is available.

During the war every effort was made to provide for those needs; a 3rd Divisional Club and a 1st Corps Rest Centre were opened on the NORMANDY Beaches, and both accompanied the army on its moves forward. Here men had 24 hours' rest, out of shell fire, living in clean surroundings, getting a shower bath and eating good food. A mobile cinema and ENSA shows appeared in neighbouring barns during the semi-static periods, and the First Battalion at very short notice produced two very good concerts, thanks to Capt. E. Skelding. There were also all too rare "reunions" among the serving officers. It was in a house at NOOK in September 1944, where some sherry and champagne had been found, that a gathering of a few Suffolk officers took place. It deserves recording, for the Padre, Woodall, 'Hugh' Merriam, 'Ken' Mayhew, 'Nat' Breach, 'Alan' Sperling, 'Mike' Russell and 'Steve' Hemingway were the survivors of the officers who had landed with the Battalion on "D" Day. Twice before there had been gatherings; once after the fall of CAEN, in a tiny room of the CHATEAU DE LA LONDE, most of the officers of the Battalion pooling their supplies, had met and dined together. Then once again many months later after the battle of FLERS, on the chance occasion of the Adjutant's birthday, Major Merriam. They

RECOVERY OF 1ST BATTALION DRUMS. *Crown copyright reserved.*

Left to right—Pte. A. Day, L/Cpl. C. Clarke, Lt.-Colonel R. E. Goodwin, D.S.O., R.S.M. C. Tridini, L/Cpl. J. Hutchinson.

had lived together in England; but since then they had been in fierce fighting; losing many friends, comradeship meant much more to them at this Reunion.

The rest period ended with a march past, the salute being taken by the G.O.C. 3rd Division and later with the presentation by Field Marshal Sir Bernard Montgomery of the D.C.M. to C.S.M. Leatherland and M.M.s to C.S.M. Hawley, Cpl. Bligh-Bingham, L/Cpl. Linge and Pte. Clarke.

On 12th December the Battalion was again moved up to the MAAS. Capt. John Coppock, one of the veterans of "D" Day, provided one of the few incidents during this period. He dined one night in mid-December with Brigade Headquarters; and it is said that the Brigade H.Q. had some fine old brandy and some Dutch gin. On his return about midnight in a jeep he was ambushed by a German patrol who fired two bazookas. There was a blinding flash. The jeep swerved into a field. Coppock and his driver were thrown out, and made off swiftly on foot. A fighting patrol went out to investigate, found nothing; Coppock's account being received rather sceptically by his Company Commander. But next morning when Coppock made a personal reconnaissance he was able to substantiate his story by showing that one of the Germans had been killed by his own bazooka!

One very cold day on the banks of the MAAS at WANSSUM, with about eighteen inches of snow on the ground, the Brigadier, the Battalion Commander and the Company Commander visited forward platoons. An indifferent bridge over a swollen river had to be crossed. The Brigadier was allowed to go first, and nearly fell in. He was followed by Lt.-Col. R. E. Goodwin who, when almost safe, missed his footing and fell in head first—to the immense amusement of the Brigadier on one bank and the Company Commander on the other. There would have been no laughter had this happened in the German Army—but somebody would have been sorry.

At ROUBAIX in 1940, during the retreat from BELGIUM, the First Battalion compelled to abandon all surplus equipment, hid their drums. In December 1944 Captain W. N. Breach went back with Lance Corporals J. Hutchinson, F. Masson and Pte. H. Whitman to trace them. "I know what you have come for," said the Town Major. "Look behind you." Two of the drums were there, in perfect condition.

It was generally believed that the drums and other instruments had been hidden in a factory, the site being shown on a sketch in Breach's possession. The local F.F.I. at once organised a digging party; but only one other drum was found. The F.F.I. organization in this WATERLOS area, 800 strong, was commanded by a woman, Madame BARBIEUX, since honoured by General de Gaulle.

Two days were spent in Watrelos and the generosity and friendliness of the F.F.I. had to be "seen to be believed". The cemetery at Watrelos, which contained the graves of a dozen men of the Suffolk Regt. killed in 1940, was visited. Each year homage had been paid by the local people, though the Germans did their best to stop it—it was stated that 32 civilians were sent to concentration camps in Germany with sentences from 8 months to 5 years for being in parades paying homage to British graves in this cemetery.

During December the Battalion was billeted in or near the villages of HEGILSON, MEGELSUM and BLITTERSWICK. The night of 31st December/

1st January found the enemy in a nervy mood. A "feu de joie" went up into the air on the far side of the river and those of the Battalion who were awake enjoyed a "Brock's benefit."

The night 1st/2nd January a small patrol action afforded an opportunity for Major H. K. Merriam to gain a very well merited M.C. (See Appendix "A"). Major Merriam came out with the First Battalion as Adjutant, an appointment he had filled admirably until, the last surviving unwounded officer, he had been appointed to Company Command.

Early in January the Battalion area was heavily shelled; this continued several days. On the 6th January the Battalion was back in VENRAY; but on the 8th January they returned for an attack on WANSSUM WOOD, held by enemy who had crossed the River MAAS. For this attack "Kangaroos" (RAM tanks with turrets removed so that about 10 men could be carried in each) were available. "C" Company was detailed to attack, supported by "D" Company. The 7th January was spent practising loading and quick dismounting. At 0500 hours on the 8th January "C" Company in Kangaroos, "D" Company in Carriers, left VENRAY. Snow was freezing on the ground, and there was much skidding. Just before the attack a heavy snow storm obscured observation from the enemy position. The Kangaroos then went forward at speed right up to the edge of the wood; here some mines were struck as the infantry dismounted. The infantry quickly entered the wood and pushed forward to the point where the enemy had made his crossing, returning with twenty prisoners.

This was the first time the Battalion had seen or taken part in an operation with Kangaroos, and their success made a very deep impression on all ranks. They learnt that they must dismount quickly all round the vehicle, over the front and back as well as the sides if they were to avoid casualties. Seven of the Kangaroos struck mines and were disabled.

It was during this action that Lce./Cpl. R. Wise, a driver of a company carrier, gained a M.M. for his courage, steadfastness and devotion to duty.

Then the Battalion came back to VENRAY and on the last evening of their stay the Battalion Concert Party gave a successful performance in a large concert hall. On the 15th January "C" Company went to GEIJSTEREN, "B" to WANSSUM, "D" East of the MOLENBEEK, "A" Company in reserve near Bn. H.Q. in OOSTRUM, and "Sp" Company at OORLOO. This area was held for three and a half weeks, most of which time was fairly quiet. Standing Patrols were maintained along the river at night and occasional enemy reconnaissance patrols which crossed were engaged and driven off.

For the last eleven days of the month the ground was covered with thick snow; but on the 31st January came a thaw. The surfaces of all roads in the district were ruined and many became impassable to wheeled vehicles owing to great craters of mud.

On the night of 2nd/3rd February at 2300 hours, a fighting patrol of two Officers, Captain Harris and Lt. Gray, with Cpls. C. Coneybeare and five other ranks crossed the MAAS opposite GEIJSTEREN. After searching two houses approximately 1,000 yards beyond the MAAS, voices were heard approaching and twelve Germans, including an officer, who were carrying a rubber boat, were observed. Fire was opened on them at ten yards range and all fell to the ground, the majority probably being killed. Later, as the patrol was returning to the river, it encountered a post containing at least two machine guns and approximately eight men. This was engaged at a range of five yards and five of the occupants were either killed or wounded. After this second encounter it was found that Lieut. Gray was missing; Captain Harris and one other rank returned to look for him while the others under Cpl. Coneybeare, who had been wounded, returned to the boat. After waiting half an hour none of the three missing men having returned, the others re-crossed the river. Cpl. Coneybeare was awarded a M.M. for his fine leadership and courage in the handling of the patrol. At 0500 hours another patrol crossed the river to look for the three missing men. No trace of them was found.

This patrol was of the best possible type, mainly composed of young volunteers, extremely well briefed, alive to every situation; and they brought back excellent information. It was most regrettable that this highly successful action was marred by the loss of 2 officers and 1 O.R.

On the 7th February the First Suffolk proceeded to HAACHT, a small town between LOUVAIN and MALINES in BELGIUM. There many of the troops were billeted in civilian houses.

The Battalion spent 16 days in HAACHT. They were given a great welcome by the population and it is remembered by all ranks as the pleasantest fortnight between "D" Day and VE Day. The days passed in training and exercise. The training included the use of Stoomboats for river crossing, and practice in street fighting. Transport was provided to take each Company into BRUSSELS on one day each week. The outstanding feature of the period was the hospitality of the people of HAACHT.

On the 26th February the Battalion moved forward to take part in its last general action before the RHINE was reached. But although stiff fighting was encountered in the woods near GOOCH, it was the other two Battalions of the 8th Brigade that suffered the most casualties; particularly the East Yorks who had to undergo the full force of an enemy counter attack. As a result the 8th Brigade came into Divisional reserve; while the rest of the Division edged its way towards WESEL, while the enemy was hemmed into the loop of the RHINE, between WESEL, XANTEN and RHEINBERG.

It was in this fighting in the woods that Lance Sgt. J. Offord gained his M.M. Both the Platoon Commander and the Platoon Sgt. of 18 Platoon "D" Company had been wounded when Sgt. Offord took command of this Platoon and part of another Platoon. He at once staged an attack on a group of houses held by the enemy. Notwithstanding a mine field, accurate machine and rifle fire he led a charge, killing several Germans and capturing 25 prisoners. Sgt. Offord had landed with the Battalion on "D" Day and had twice been wounded.

THE RHINE.

FEBRUARY 1945 — MARCH 1945.

Before "the last good heave", as the Prime Minister called it, could be given to the now tottering structure of the REICH, several important preparations had to be made. The troops scheduled to make the assault had to be specially trained; the craft had to be brought up to the river; the ammunition, petrol, bridging and food dumps had to be established for the forward surge until the Army should find itself faced no longer with men wearing the Kokade and the Hohectabzeichen, but by those whose helmets bore the red star of SOVIET RUSSIA.

Some of this process could be watched by the Battalion from its new area at CALCAR, and for those who had made the "D" Day landing in Normandy, it afforded a pleasant occasion for restudying the administrative build-up necessary for an amphibious operation without any personal apprehension as regards the results.

Nevertheless, there were active tasks to be done as well. The whole area between the river and the main road from CALCAR to XANTEN had to be cleared of civilians, cattle and livestock; guards had to be kept at certain points in the area to see that they did not return and to deal with any enemy patrols who ventured across the river.

As the day selected for the RHINE crossing approached, movement of all vehicles was "frozen" so that there should be no hindrance for the battalions doing the initial crossing. Most of the Battalion tracked vehicles had been taken back into HOLLAND and those of the wheeled vehicles which were not vitally necessary to the Battalion area were moved to the neighbourhood of rear Divisional H.Q.

The preliminary barrage began at 1700 hours on the 23rd March and worked up in a crescendo, until at 2100 hours the first "Buffaloes," (amphibious tracked vehicles) carrying a platoon of infantry each, ran down into the river and crossed it. The Battalion had a "front row" view, especially of the Ack-ack tracer fire, known as the "Pepperpot", which played over the whole of the enemy's front line positions for an hour and a half until dusk approached. The following morning great fleets of gliders passed overhead, taking the Airborne troops scheduled to seize the crossings over the River IJSSEL.

For two or three days stiff fighting continued; then the crack came from which the GERMAN armies never recovered.

By the 28th March the main forces had crossed the RHINE and the Battalion moved up to the bank of the River. The same night it crossed, proceeding to the village of HALDERN. Scattered enemy remained in the area and several Companies produced one or two prisoners from the cellars and lofts of their billets and from the woods around them. The Pioneer Platoon was employed in clearing Regal mines, and the Platoon Sergeant, Sgt. Croft, who had been with the Battalion throughout the war, was killed.

ADVANCE TO BREMEN.

APRIL 1945 — MAY 1945.

The following morning the Divisional Commander addressed all Officers on the probable role of the Division. The 3rd Division was to follow up the Guards Armoured Division, consolidating its gains; available should any infantry task arise. BREMEN was the objective.

On the 31st March the Battalion moved, embussed, Northwards back into HOLLAND, through AALTON, to GROENLO, NORDHORN, ALTEN LINGEN on the DORTMUND-EMS Canal. As the "O" Group arrived, shells were falling in the village, the first that had been encountered since crossing the RHINE. The task of the Battalion was to safeguard the bridgehead while other units of the Division cleared the town of LINGEN. This town had contained a large German officer-training unit and stiff resistance was offered both in and beyond it. Active offensive patrolling was continued during the whole of the five days of the Battalion's stay at ALTEN LINGEN.

On the evening of the 10th April the Battalion left ALTEN LINGEN, passing through RHEINE, OSNABRUCK, past the DUMMER ZEE, to SULINGEN and on to BASSUM, a small town eighteen miles South of BREMEN. There it took up a defensive position surrounding the town. The whole situation was exceptionally fluid; pockets of enemy having been left behind by our forward troops. At one time the Division was responsible for protecting the left flank of the Corps area over a distance of approximately sixty miles.

On the 12th April two sections of the Carrier, Mortar and Anti-Tank Platoons were placed under command of "A" Company; which was now formed into a series of mobile striking forces. The first of these, commanded by Capt. R. A. B. Rogers, consisting of a Platoon in 15 cwt. trucks with one section of each of the Support Company Platoons, pushed up the road towards BREMEN and entered the village of NORDWOHLDE unopposed. At the same time a patrol of "C" Company with a section of Carriers moved up a parallel road to the village of DIMHAUSEN. Plans were made for the advance to BRINKUM. "A" Company were again to lead and Major H. K. Merriam, M.C., the "A" Company Commander, split his force into three parties. The first consisted of himself and Lieut. Garnham, commanding the Carrier Platoon, one section of the Carrier Platoon, one section of the Anti-Tank Platoon and one Platoon of "A" Company travelling in 15 cwt. trucks. The second group, a section of the Carrier Platoon, under Sgt. D. Ellis (See Appendix "A"), a section of the Mortar Platoon, and a Platoon of "A" Company in trucks. The third was similar; but a section of Anti-Tank guns replaced the Carrier Platoon.

These parties of "A" Company encountered road blocks and mines; on one occasion Lt. Garnham, jumping out from the carrier near a road block, heard a soldier say "You've jumped on a mine, Sir. I saw the ground move." This proved true, and the party proceeded to lift nine Teller mines; two of them being actually under the carrier.

By bold and skilful handling, first FHRENHORST and then NEINKONG were occupied; patrols from the remaining companies of the Battalion finding flank protection where necessary and occupying captured points. But as BRINKUM was approached, stiffer opposition was encountered. A section of the Carrier Platoon, commanded by Sgt. Sumner, was on this occasion in advance. About half a mile down the road one of the carrier commanders spotted a German soldier near a house some 50 yards away from the road. The section stopped and called on him to surrender. Instead of doing so he sent up a red verey light; whereupon three Brens of the section opened up on him simultaneously. He fell; civilians from the house carried him inside. The section continued up the road until heavy small arms fire met them from the area of a large road block (No. 1 Sketch Map). "A" Company and its supporting carrier sections dismounted (No. 2). Major Merriam ordered 7 Platoon round the back of houses on the left of the road and 8 Platoon to the right. Both were to try to get beyond the road block and deal with it from the rear; while the 3″ mortar Platoon engaged the cross roads. 9 Platoon and the Carrier sections remained in reserve. Progress was made, each part gradually moving along the backs of the houses, clearing them as they went. At this time very heavy nebelwerfer fire fell around

"A" Company and Lieut. Broadbent, commanding 7 Platoon, was severely wounded. As 8 Platoon, commanded by Lieut. Meredith, reached the last house on the right of the road before the cross roads, (No. 3) 7 Platoon and a skeleton Coy. H.Q. reached the group of houses opposite (No. 4). Major Merriam shouted orders across the road for the assault on to the cross roads "Penny". 7 Platoon, now led by Capt. Rogers, crossed the road and entered the corner house (No. 5), while 8 Platoon crossed in extended order on the right of it.

In the meantime Company H.Q. (No. 6) and C.S.M. Leatherland conducted a fire fight with the enemy in the house diagonally opposite them. Major H. K. Merriam, M.C., was wounded in the thigh by small arms fire, and a little later what was left of Company H.Q. withdrew. While 7 Platoon was at the corner house (No. 5), 8 Platoon saw a section of men approaching from the right. They had expected 9 Platoon to come from that direction and did not realise for some minutes that it was a group of enemy. As soon as this was realised they shot them up and drove them into the gardens on the North of the road. There was now a sound of considerable enemy reinforcements approaching and Lt. Meredith with 8 Platoon, not knowing that 7 Platoon was still in the vicinity, withdrew to the last house he had left (No. 3) which was in flames. Here the Platoon dug in while the Platoon Commander went back to Company H.Q. to find out the general situation.

"B" Company had been ordered forward on the left via the houses, B, up towards the lateral road at "Pea". Expecting stiff opposition near the cross roads, Major A. H. Claxton, M.C., led his Company further over to the left across open ground, only to come under fire at short range from farm buildings at "Pea". Claxton was killed, and though one of the Platoons reached the lateral road, the Company dug in round the houses. "D" Company, Major J. S. Coppock, consolidated in the area (No. 1); while Bn. H.Q., Support Company and "C" Company were about (No. 2).

Meanwhile, Lieut. Meredith returned to his Platoon and 9 Platoon were sent up to dig in round the houses opposite his positions on the left of the road (No. 4). There were sounds of "S.S." songs as the enemy occupied the right of the road and several enemy were heard digging in quite close on the left. Being too close to the cross roads for artillery support and not having enough men to make his present position tenable when daylight came, Lieut. Meredith asked permission to withdraw two Platoons of "A" Company 400 yards. This was granted and they dug in about (No. 1), close to the two Platoons of "D" Company.

In the meantime 7 Platoon under Capt. Rogers and Sgt. Foreman were still in the house beyond the cross roads (No. 5). They had seen the enemy reinforcements arrive and dig in all around them and decided to keep quiet until dusk before attempting to make their getaway. About one o'clock in the morning a German came up to the house and rang the bell. One of our men moved his foot; the enemy took alarm and a grenade was thrown in. Then the Germans appeared from all directions and threw grenades in through the windows. Capt. Rogers and Sgt. Foreman rallied the Platoon and they made their escape back to "A" Company area.

The road block (No. 1) was demolished at first light.

The following day an attack was planned to drive the enemy out of BRINKUM. The enemy holding the area were S.S. troops a battalion strong; with Companies disposed, one on the cross roads ("Penny"), one in

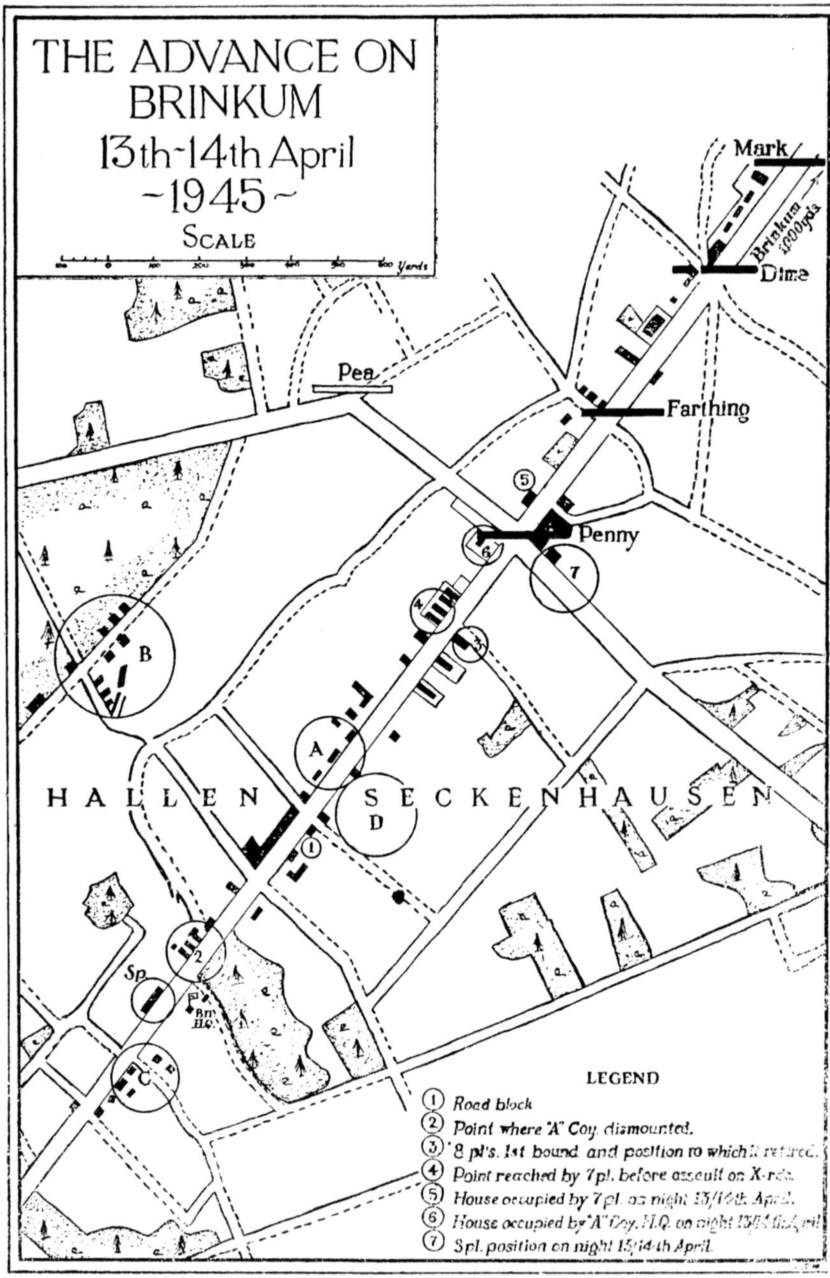
THE ADVANCE ON BRINKUM
13th-14th April
~1945~
SCALE
Yards
Mark
Dime
Brinkum 1000 yds
Pea
Farthing
Penny
B
A
D
C
HALLEN
SECKENHAUSEN
Sp.
Bn. H.Q.
LEGEND
1 Road block
2 Point where "A" Coy. dismounted.
3 8 pl's. 1st bound and position to which it retired.
4 Point reached by 7 pl. before assault on X-rds.
5 House occupied by 7 pl. on night 13/14th April.
6 House occupied by "A" Coy. H.Q. on night 13/14th April
7 8 pl. position on night 13/14th April.

Officers, 1st Battalion, Gutersloh, June, 1945.

Front row—Capt. (Q.M.) P. W. Spurgin, Majors H. G. Tomkinson, A. P. Bathurst-Brown, W. S. Bevan, Lt. Col. R. E. Goodwin, D.S.O., Capt. A. C. L. Sperling (Adjt.), Majors J. S. Coppock, R. A. B. Rogers, Capt. S. Hemmingway.

Second row—Capt. A. E. Lawrence, W. J. C. Ayres, A. J. A. Lacy, W. N. Breach, Rev. H. G. Woodall, Capt. J. B. Kent, Lts. A. C. Woodward, M.C., K. G. Perry, F. M. B. Russell, J. R. G. Perret, Capts. E. C. Skelding, R. J. Garnham.

Third row—Lts. F. W. Law, J. P. F. E. Warner, Capt. I. Morris (R A.M.C.), Lts. P. R. R. Boughton, M. H. McQueen, W. Lovelock, G. E. Halford, R. E. Meredith, B. H. Poppinger (Interpreter).

ERICHSHOFF, one in LEESTE and the fourth with Battalion H.Q. in BRINKUM. 185th Brigade was ordered to deal with the last three while First Suffolk captured the cross roads.

A considerable artillery programme was arranged and through the afternoon the enemy's answering shell fire fell fairly continuously in the Battalion area. "B" and "D" Companies began moving forward at 1445 hours, the former almost immediately came under small arms fire from positions between "Penny" and "Pea". The tanks engaged these places continuously; but were unable to silence the fire. Capt. Jones, commanding "B" Company, was killed with the leading Platoon. There it was pinned by accurate small arms fire.

In the meantime "D" and "A" Companies had come under accurate small arms fire. The Support Company group engaged enemy positions at "Pea" with 6-pdr., 3" mortar and small arms fire. One 6-pdr. H.E. round which struck the front of a building blew a German clean out of the back door !

Meanwhile two troops of Crocodile flame-throwing tanks had been sent for. As darkness was falling, at about 2015, the Crocodiles went into action, squirting flame into every house and trench they approached. They went right across the cross roads and on to "Pea". The enemy left his trenches and ran. The Battalion was wild with elation at the sudden change from complete deadlock to unqualified victory. But the cost had been high and amongst the casualties was "C" Company Commander, Major J. C. Vines, who received serious wounds from which he later died. Mopping up continued in darkness. "B" and "D" Companies were ordered forward; the latter keeping away from the main axis as the buildings there were on fire. They cleared forward to "Farthing"; "B" Company going forward with two Platoons to "Pea". All Companies consolidated for the night.

It was in this day's action that Major J. A. Coppock gained his M.C. An account of the skill with which he led his Company is given in Appendix "A."

At 0130 hours the following morning "A" Company were stepped up to "Dime". At first light the Company, supported by one section of Carriers and one section of Anti-Tank guns, moved up to the edge of BRINKUM. Light opposition was encountered. The position was held all day while 185th Brigade fought through BRINKUM.

During the battle before BRINKUM 31 prisoners had been taken and in the fighting on the 15th at least 30 enemy were killed. Battalion casualties were 2 Officers and 9 Other ranks killed, 4 Officers and 33 Other ranks wounded and 13 Other ranks missing.

The Battalion lost a very fine officer in the death of Major Claxton. Lt.-Colonel Craddock who commanded the Battalion and knew his worth wrote of him: "I always felt he was too selfless to survive the war. He was one of those who cared for nothing save what he considered his duty, and he was prepared to go to any lengths to do it. I pray there will always be men like him to carry on the torch." Claxton was an ex-Grenadier Guardsman and had been in the Brighton police. He served all his time with the First Suffolk, which he joined in January 1941. During training he had had the misfortume to lose an eye in a grenade accident; but he was very soon back with the Battalion. He was a most gallant man, who in the opinion of most earned a M.C. every time he went into action.

On the 21st April the Battalion moved into BRINKUM. From this village BREMEN could clearly be seen across the flooded fields.

The assault on the City began on 24th April, British Infantry Brigades crossing the flooded fields in "Buffaloes". The 8th Brigade were ordered in to finish the operation at dawn on the 26th April. The 1st South Lancashires commenced clearing as far as the railway from BREMEN to DELMONHORST and the First Suffolk finished the job off from there; no opposition was encountered. The Battalion advanced through the streets and gardens, watched by the local population. One German civilian pointed out an air raid shelter where 4 Officers and 9 other ranks were hiding. They surrendered without resistance.

On the 27th "A" and "B" Companies patrolled through STROM to MUHLENHAUSEN. At STROM two G.A.F. Officers and thirty three other ranks surrendered. Half a mile further on an Officer of a Labour Unit and twenty men surrendered; the Officer said he was willing to guide the patrol to MUHLENHAUSEN where more men were prepared to surrender. He took the carriers round the mines in the road and with the aid of a white flag a further 80 prisoners were taken.

This proved the last action by the Battalion. On the 8th May 1945 the First Suffolk was well in the heart of HANOVER. Here in BREMEN this Campaign ceased. The campaign which opened so strikingly against a vital, active enemy on the beaches of Normandy, fizzled out with that army stockaded in Allied prison camps and the Drums of the Suffolk Regiment proclaiming the victory in the heart of Hitler's Germany.

OCCUPIED GERMANY.

There was still much to be done by the armies in the field, even though the enemy had been decisively defeated and had accepted an unconditional surrender. When fighting is over the troops cannot sit back and take it easy, waiting for demobilization.

The First Battalion moved back from BREMEN to ENGER at the end of May, taking over responsibility for an area which included:- The Protection and internal security of the army lines of Communication; Assistance to the Allied Military Government Departments who were in charge of "displaced persons" camps; Battlefield clearance and the disposal of enemy war materials and installations; a search of the battlefield area. This, as can be well imagined, was a fairly large and comprehensive order.

Many points had to be guarded, including special road and railway bridges, vital locks and sluice gates, ammunition and P.O.L. dumps, large food stores, camps of all natures such as P.O.W., Displaced Persons, hospitals, prisons, concentration camps. The above were all of first importance; scarcely less so were the factories, warehouses and Government offices.

Fortunately Hitler's boasts of "were-wolf" organization had no substance in fact. There was only the most negligible sabotage—not always attributable to GERMANS. The enemy showed themselves, as after the 1914/1918 War, only too anxious to obey all orders.

But if the GERMANS were quiescent the large number of "Displaced Persons" and released prisoners provided plenty of incidents. It had been a common belief in many lands that when GERMANY was finally overrun

WARRANT OFFICERS AND SERGEANTS, 1ST BATTALION GUTERSLOH, GERMANY, JUNE 1945.

Back row—L/Sgt. Turpin, C.Q.M.Ss. Pleasance, Sturgeon, L/Sgt. Lucas, Sgts. Barwood, Lorrimer, Ellis, Blizzard, Fenn, Redding, Passey, Powter, Nice, Sumner, Plummer, C.Q.M.S. Pretty, L/Sgts. Eady, Gordon.

Third row—Sgt. Thomas, L/Sgt. Smith, Sgts. Rayson, Simons, Scholey, Eddis, Clayton, L/Sgt. Offord, Sgts. Dell, Rayner, L/Sgt. Ashman, Sgt. Francis, L/Sgt. Moohan, Sgts. Pryke, Wapples, Deyong, L/Sgts. Gilbert, Fleck, Sgt. Foreman, M.M.

Second row—C.Q.M.S. Keeble, C.S.M.s Croxon, Leatherland, D.C.M., Franklin, Capt. A. C. L. Sperling, R.S.M. Tridini, Lt. Col. R. E. Goodwin, D.S.O., Maj. W. S. Bevan, C.S.M.s Tyler, Hawley, M.M., Boast, Page, C.Q.M.S. Ablitt.

Front row—L/Sgt. Copsey, Sgt. Brocklehurst, L/Sgt. Newman, Sgts. Linkester, Goodchild, L/Sgt. Perfitt, Sgts. Jenkinson, Bradford, L/Sgt. Good, Sgt. Wordsworth, L/Sgt. Mead, Sgts. Oldman, Shear.

Officers and Other Ranks who visited the "Field of Minden" August 1st, 1945. The Memorial was erected by the Germans on the first centenary of the battle (1859).

by the Allies the millions of "Slaves", the forcibly enlisted workers from conquered countries and occupied lands, would take their revenge. None had a greater justification than the RUSSIANS. There were "incidents"; but to judge from the record kept by the Battalion in their area, they might have been much worse. There were cases of GERMAN farms being raided by RUSSIANS who had armed themselves; occasionally a man or woman was shot. During the month of June there were 25 "incidents"; but none could be classed as serious. In all cases the offenders were rounded up by the troops in occupation and if belonging to the people of EAST EUROPE were handed over to their respective Military Government Department for disposal. If the offenders were BELGIAN, DUTCH or FRENCH, they came before our own Military Courts.

While the Battalion was responsible for this area there was a continual movement of the Prisoners of War and the "Displaced Persons" back to their own countries; camps being opened for the "West-bound" and the "East-bound". In June the total number of these two categories was about 5,000; by far the greater proportion being East-bound—the actual figures were: RUSSIANS 880, POLES 1,604, HUNGARIAN 425, ITALIAN 1,624, YUGOSLAV 261—the remainder BELGIAN, DUTCH and FRENCH.

On June 22nd Lt.-Col. R. E. Goodwin, D.S.O., was appointed to the Command of a Brigade and left the First Battalion. Lt.-Col. F. A. Milnes, who had commanded the Battalion so ably in the retreat to Dunkirk and had since been promoted to the substantive rank of Lt.-Colonel, was posted to the First Battalion.

The fact of being in HANOVER and within 40 miles of MINDEN gave the Battalion a rare opportunity of celebrating the anniversary of the Battle on the 1st August, 1945.

Brigadier R. E. Goodwin and Lt.-Col. Monier-Williams joined the party of fifty under Lt.-Col. F. A. Milnes who set off for MINDEN on the morning of August 1st. A parade was held by the 1st Bn. K.O.Y.L.I. on the Adolf Hitler Platz. Here the First Battalion representatives were joined by Lt.-Colonel J. Yates and Major C. Boycott, and saw a very smart demonstration of Light Infantry Drill, which did great credit to that distinguished MINDEN Regiment. After the parade our party drove to the MINDEN Memorial, an uninspiring Gothic affair erected near the battlefield in 1859 to mark the first centenary of the battle. The monument records the fact that the combined effort of British and Germans "liberated" the town of MINDEN from the French invaders. The Regimental party was photographed in a group before the monument, and then moved to the battlefield itself.

The "stand" was chosen by Lt.-Colonel F. A. Milnes after much previous study of Regimental Histories and local German guide books, and was a piece of ground over which the 12th Foot must have moved in their assault. The battlefield as a whole is nearly flat, sloping gently and evenly downwards towards the town of MINDEN and the WESER River. The area where the opposing forces met is now considerably built over, and the EMS-WESER canal forms an obstacle which did not exist in 1759. It was therefore difficult to visualise the shape of the ground where the final assault took place. Nevertheless the Commanding Officer was able to point out most of the positions of the opposing forces, and to show their movements which led up to the famous fight.

During the following month the Battalion was represented at another celebration. The DUTCH honour anniversaries. One such was the liberation of WEERT, a small town of the DUTCH LIMBURG province, on September 22nd, 1944. That morning before sunrise the First Battalion, after a short engagement on the outskirts of the town, had marched in. Those who were there that day will not forget the genuine and rapturous welcome of the inhabitants. While for the next four days, unmolested by the enemy who were but two miles away, the rest of the Battalion shared this welcome and hospitality.

On September 22nd, 1945 an open invitation to the First Battalion to join in the anniversary festivities was received from the Burgomaster. Two three-tonners with two officers, 40 O.R.s and the Padre represented the Battalion. Capt. L. J. Thomas, M.C., who had been present at the liberation, being in command.

Every street was bedecked with flags; orange streamers hung from almost every house. The functions were delightfully informal. All gathered round the monument to three British airmen who had crashed at WEERT during the fighting. Here the Burgomaster, with the Dean and other officials, laid a wreath, made a short oration in Dutch, and then read a few words in English recalling the town's gratitude and not forgetting the sacrifice it had cost.

Then all flocked to the big medieval church in the Market Square for Solemn Benediction. Here the banners of the various organizations were grouped before the high altar; there were flowers everywhere, and a magnificent organ pealed out hymns of praise.

The crowd next gathered at the Town Hall. A loud speaker summoned the First Battalion contingent and as they pushed their way through the crowd they received an ovation. The Burgomaster, from the steps of the Hall, read a speech in English asking the Battalion to accept a Scroll and Silver Shield as a mark of the esteem in which the people of WEERT held the Suffolk Regiment. Captain Thomas replied on behalf of the Regiment.

MOVE TO THE MIDDLE EAST.

OCTOBER 1945 — DECEMBER 1945.

During the first twelve days of October 1945 the First Battalion was on the move from BELGIUM to the MIDDLE EAST, accompanying the rest of the 3rd Division. Their distination, EGYPT.

The advance party, 8 officers and 32 O.R.s under Major C. A. Boycott, flew from BRUSSELS to CAIRO. The main body accomplished the move in three stages:- a rail move to TOULON; by sea to ALEXANDRIA via MALTA; railway to TAHAG.

The two day journey through FRANCE was made in old German carriages, very crowded owing to the shortage of rolling stock; halts being made for hot meals en route. The converted French pleasure cruiser "Ville D'Oran" from TOULON carried four times as many personnel as in peace; while the Battalion travelled in goods wagons for the comparatively short journey ALEXANDRIA to TAHAG, near the SUEZ CANAL. Here a tented camp had been erected by the advanced party with the help of German P.O.W.

At TAHAG many guards had to be found by the Battalion to safeguard arms, equipment and personal kit from looters. The night guard for the Company being 1 Officer and 46 O.R.s.

The strength of the Battalion at this time was 990 all ranks. By the end of November this had been increased to 1,140.

The Battalion on arrival in Egypt from Western Europe had to be re-equipped; for only personal equipment had been brought from Belgium. This was successfully carried out by Lt. F. H. Wyartt, the newly appointed Quartermaster; Captain P. W. Spurgin having remained in Germany under the Military Government. About 50% of the Battalion, due for early demobilization, had also remained in Germany; these included a high percentage of officers, N.C.O.s and the many key men who do so much to make everything run smoothly. Reinforcements of 300 men were received from England; the majority coming from East Anglia.

Meanwhile the 3rd Division, with the exception of the First Suffolk, was dispersed to locations along the CANAL; the First Suffolk remaining under canvas in the desert, a pleasant and profitable arrangement, for it enabled the Battalion to assimilate the new comers.

Early in December 1945 the 3rd Division moved up to PALESTINE, the First Suffolk occupying for a fortnight a semi-permanent tented camp near NATHANYA, between TEL AVIV and HAIFA, and then moving to a similar camp about twenty miles to the north. While in PALESTINE more than half the Battalion visited many of the Holy Places, such as JERUSALEM, GALLILEE, NAZARETH and BETHLEHEM.

Thus ended six years in the life of the First Battalion; a span of time that may be reckoned as a peak period in its history. But the life of a Regiment is continuous; there have been many occasions in the past that might be compared with the years 1939-1945. A fragment of six years taken from Lt.-Colonel E. H. A. Webb's History of the 12th (Suffolk) Regiment in the days of Queen Anne, or at the time of Seringapatam, will not show such huge operations, such long drawn out fighting; but will tell of constant battles and skirmishes, of ceaseless moves by land and sea. In the days of old the climate and the conditions of life took almost as heavy a toll as battle casualties in modern war. Six years in the life of a Battalion is a very long period, scarcely an officer or man remains, but the Regiment goes on.

CHAPTER FIVE.

SECOND BATTALION.

RAZMAK—TOCHI VALLEY Operation—INTERNAL Security—Campaign in BURMA, 1944—ARAKAN—IMPHAL—"ISAAC"—END of Campaign.

RAZMAK.

NOV. 1939—OCT. 1940.

While the First Battalion returning in 1939 from MALTA to DEVONPORT was fully conscious of the war clouds hanging over EUROPE and the implications of air warfare, the Second Battalion under Lt.-Col. D. R. A. Eley, D.S.O., at MHOW had a horizon bounded by service on the Frontier at RAZMAK.

The declaration of war had little more outward effect than shortening the full names of officers to such aliases as "Sweat D......" or "Tommy A......" when their activities were announced in the Regimental Gazette—information that it is hoped sorely puzzled the ubiquitous Japanese Spy, checking up initials with names.

The Battalion left MHOW on November 25th, 1939, in two trains and arrived at MARI INDUS on 28th November; old soldiers at all times have not hesitated to describe in the tersest language long journeys by train in India. On the 29th November the move was continued by train to BANNU, and on the 30th by lorries for the last stage of the journey to RAZMAK. This was new country for the Battalion, most of whom were not a little alarmed at the pace the lorry drivers whizzed round mountain corners, suspending their loads over big precipitous drops of many hundreds of feet.

Extremes of temperature were experienced at MHOW and RAZMAK. At the latter blue noses and pink cheeks peeped through cap comforters and the first critical surprise at the sight of the long lean natives dressed in every conceivable cold weather fashion was modified by the reflection that the thermometer showed many degrees below zero.

The Battalion relieved the Leicesters, who, while not concealing their joy at departing, said engagingly: "You'll like it here; you get so fit." RAZMAK may be salubrious; but life in a perimeter Frontier camp has some of the limitations of prison restriction.

With the Spring of 1940 reinforcements arrived from the I.T.C. at BURY ST. EDMUNDS. They brought first hand news of the Home Front, to dissipate the rumours which during the winter had been almost the sole topic of conversation. They also brought, and it is worth quoting what was said at the time: "An odd type of garment known as 'Battle Dress' which they assure us is considered 'comme-il-faut' at Home. This assertion we are inclined to take with a pinch of salt."

Officers, 2nd Battalion, Razmak, 1940.

Standing—2nd Lt. F. D. Ingle, 2nd Lt. B. J. Newton, —— Lt. K. E. J. Henderson, 2nd Lt. C. W. Swannell, Capt. G. T. O. Springfield, Capt. R. J. Hildesley, 2nd Lt. P. E. V. Richards, 2nd Lt. Risal Singh, 2nd Lt. P. B. Forrest, 2nd Lt. A. Mathiesen.

Sitting—Capt. W. P. Ferrier, Capt. W. S. Bevan, Major J. Yates, M.C., Major H. W. Dean (Adjt.), Lt. Col. D. R. A. Eley, D.S.O. (C.O.), Major (Q.M.) J. H. Hill, Major R. Q. March, Capt. R. B. Freeland, Capt. A. C. C. Hill.

The "Laissez faire" attitude among the great majority of people in England during the winter 1939/1940, had a more confident note in RAZMAK. This can be summed up in a letter from one of the Companies:—

"The present situation in Europe has cast a spell over the whole world; even we, at a remote Post of the Empire, feel it too, and are wondering what is going to happen in the Spring. Of course it is a foregone conclusion there will be 'great guns to go'; Adolph, with his expectations, aggressions and idle dreams of being a world conqueror, will go up in smoke. To think we young soldiers won't be in at the kill; but contending with an occasional "Tack-dum" from out of the blue. However, since most of our veterans are being posted to the U.K. for duty, we hope to be well represented."

Frontier life is monotonous when the tribesmen are busy cultivating their land and haven't time to bother with the "Gora log". But the monotony was ended with the Battalion going out "on column".

It is always active service on the Indian Frontier, and Frontier tactics have been perfected in the course of almost ceaseless campaigns against the warlike peoples who inhabit these desolate mountainous regions. Unfortunately this warfare has bred a limited military outlook. Once upon a time in the days of "Small Wars" INDIA was the nursery of the British Army; with the birth of "Great Wars" a much wider education has been necessary. But a British Infantry Battalion serving on the Frontier has much to learn from the men who have lived and fought there for generations; woe betide those who do not take to heart every lesson. Mistakes outside the camp perimeter must be paid for no matter how strong the column, or how limited the objective. The Frontier is a fine school for elementary soldiering. The time the Second Battalion spent at RAZMAK in 1940 and later in the TOCHI VALLEY in 1941 was full of Frontier warfare lessons; well learnt and carried out by officers and men.

Selected officers and men of the Battalion had been given instruction in mountain warfare before they reached the Frontier; but first practical experience was when the Battalion went out with the "RAZCOL" from 14th to 21st July, 1940. The RAZMAK Column consisted of the Second Battalion with three Indian Infantry Battalions and auxiliary forces and was primarily intended for practical training; but the operations included the destruction of tribal towers in ASAB KHEL and MUSAKI villages as reprisals for the wounding of the Resident earlier in the month.

The following officers were at this time serving with the Second Battalion:—

Bn. H.Q. and H.Q. Company.

C.O.	Major H. B. Monier-Williams, M.C.
2 i/c	Major J. Yates, M.C.
Adjt.	Major H. W. Dean.
Q.M.	Major (Q.M.) J. H. Hill.
Intelligence	Lieut. S. D. Jackson.
Spt. Pl.	2/Lt. A. Mathieson.
Tpt.	2/Lt. B. J. Newton.
Sig.	Cpl. K. Mason.
R.S.M.	R.S.M. F. Nice.

A Company.

2/Lt.	... ...	A. F. Campbell.
2/Lt.	... ...	R. J. Hildesley.

B Company.

A/Capt.	... ...	W. S. Bevan.
A/Capt.	... ...	G. T. O. Springfield.
2/Lt.	... ...	P. E. V. Richards.

C Company.

Capt.	... ...	R. B. Freeland.
A/Capt.	... ...	O. C. Horne.
2/Lt.	... ...	P. B. Forrest.

D Company.

A/Capt.	... ...	A. C. C. Hill.
2/Lt.	... ...	F. D. Ingle.

Attached to Wazindist H.Q. RAZMAK and Brigade H.Q.

2/Lt.	... ...	K. E. J. Henderson.
2/Lt.	... ...	C. W. Swannell.
2/Lt.	... ...	B. Birchmore.

On Leave.

		Lt.-Col. D. R. A. Eley, D.S.O.
Majors	... ...	R. Q. March. S. H. Atkins.
Lts.	... ...	G. W. Gilbert. W. P. Ferrier.

On the 14th July the Column moved from RAZMAK to RAZANI, 14 miles. The 11th Sikh formed the advanced guard, the Second Suffolk moving with 'B' and 'C' Companies through the line secured by the 11th Sikh to establish further piquets for the Column, and being finally withdrawn through the 2nd Gurkha Rifles, who formed the rear-guard. 'C' Company, in piqueting the high ground DUN and DAS came under fairly heavy fire, lost one man killed, and was held up temporarily. Heavy rains soaked the Battalion before it reached camp; where a Battalion perimeter camp had to be dug. There was some sniping during the night.

The next day the Second Suffolk formed the advanced guard. All four Companies were employed on piquets. There was no opposition during the very hot morning. The 10th Baluch and the 2nd Gurkha Rifles extended the Second Battalion piquets to camp at DOSALI, where the Column went into an existing stone wall perimeter camp. 'B' Company had a long day, their piqueting included Hill 70. There was considerable sniping at the camp piquets at dark, and some shots at the camp.

On the third day the Battalion formed the rear guard. This entailed taking over the whole of the last night's camp and withdrawing the piquets of other units before the Column left. There was no opposition and the Battalion reached DAMDIL Camp without incident; Major Yates with Company and Platoon representatives going forward along the route and selecting successive positions for occupation.

That night a march was made by the 2nd Gurkha Rifles, 10th Baluch and 11th Sikh to surround the villages of ASAB KHEL and MUSAKI by morning daylight. The Second Suffolk, less 'A' Company, remained in Camp. 'A' Company proceeded with Column H.Q. on this night march. The villages had been evacuated by most of the inhabitants; but a few hostiles were brought in and four Towers were destroyed. It rained very heavily late that day; all bivouacs were flooded, those in the low ground and re-entrants being washed out.

The next three days were occupied with the return to RAZMAK. During this operation there was spasmodic enemy sniping. On the last day, 21st July, in the move from RAZANI to RAZMAK the Second Suffolk formed the advanced guard. 'C' Company made good "GREEWOODS' CORNER"; but 'D' Company, advancing up the spurs beyond, came under heavy sniping fire. 'A' and 'B' Companies were also engaged piqueting hills and the whole Battalion had a long day's operation before the hills were finally cleared and the Column re-entered RAZMAK.

These operations would not be worth recording, save that they illustrate the difference between "Small Wars" and "Great Wars." WAZIRISTAN presents a grim tangle of precipitous mountains through which the few roads wind. Every yard of the road is commanded by rocky fastnesses from which agile sharpshooters can fire in safety into the long columns of men and animals. Our Columns move out, 'piquet' the heights on either side of the road, burn the strong-points in enemy's villages, and return. There is 'sniping' from the time the Column leaves until it returns, and the strong-points are promptly rebuilt. But more military roads are constructed and more peaceful civilization gradually seeps in.

Such is a "Small War". The enemy shoots straight; but he has only a rifle. He enjoys the fighting; but only as a local sport. He fights no pitched battles; for the results would be decisive defeats. There are very few casualties on either side.

The Second Battalion that gained a "distinguished" in this elementary test was to be examined later in frontier warfare under "Great War" conditions. BURMA also is a tangle of precipitous mountains; but instead of these being bare, standing out in stark reality, they are hidden by almost impenetrable jungle. Eight miles is a goodly distance for an advance on the NORTH WEST FRONTIER; eight miles was to be considered a goodly distance in BURMA—under infinitely worse conditions. The enemy were no isolated snipers; but a fanatical nation armed with the most modern weapons, and trained to the highest pitch in "Jungle" Warfare. The weather in BURMA knows no limitations; there are no NORTH WEST FRONTIER torrents followed by a drying sun; but the deluging monsoon. The malaria of TOCHI has to be mutiplied almost a hundredfold, while the mosquito is reinforced not only by every imaginable insect that lives in fetid marshes and dark forests, but by larger beasts. The best trained unit on the NORTH WEST FRONTIER had to start from scratch before it learnt to fight successfully in BURMA.

While in RAZMAK, the Battalion helped in quelling a fire which destroyed half the RAZMAK Bazaar before it was brought under control. It was here that Corporal S. Gaught, in charge of the Garrison Military Police, received a special commendation from the C-in-C Northern Command.

He organised a bucket party and climbing on to the verandah roofs of threatened shops succeeded in preventing the fire from spreading. His action was carried out in intense heat and at considerable personal risk.

In 1940, at the end of a year's tour, the Battalion was not sorry to turn its back on the "Romance" of the Frontier and in war time phraseology "Occupy a new address in a well populated town." Their leave taking with their relief had been hearty; but there were few regrets at departing from the monastic outpost RAZMAK. The old soldiers passed on the same tall stories to the new ones that took over; then mounted into their lorries and looked at the distant hills they had piqueted whilst on Column; and once again gripped the sides of the vehicles as they whizzed round the bends of the mountain passes.

The Battalion left RAZMAK for RAWAL PINDI at the end of October 1940 with a fine reputation. The Brigade Commander wrote:— "I want to thank you and all your officers and men for the splendid spirit you have shown—you have the satisfaction of knowing that you will leave a very high reputation behind you. We are all going to miss you badly."

TOCHI VALLEY OPERATIONS.

OCT. 1940 — JAN. 1942.

At RAWAL PINDI the Second Suffolk was called upon for an unusua duty—to quell an incipient mutiny in a wartime Native Regiment which had no British officers. The causes were trivial; but the situation was temporarily out of hand. A show of force restored order; the Battalion furnishing a Guard of Honour with a Cavalry Escort to conduct the Native Commanding General on to parade. Here the defaulting unit was ordered to lay down its arms—and did so.

Lt.-Col. D. R. A. Eley, D.S.O., completed his Command in December 1940 and was succeeded by Major H. B. Monier-Williams, M.C. During the Spring of this year demonstrations of tanks, lorries and guns operating over broken ground, and of aircraft dive-bombing were given to four officers and fifty men of the Battalion, a very limited form of training compared with that being undergone by the First Battalion in England. During their training the Second Battalion proved their physical fitness in marching by covering 35½ miles in 12½ hours.

From June to September 1941 the Battalion was employed once again on Frontier Service. There had been trouble in the TOCHI Valley during the previous six months and reprisals were organized against the inhabitants who had been sheltering the "hostiles." The posts at BOYA and DATTA KHEL were besieged, and no supplies could be got to them, save by air.

The 1st Indian Infantry Brigade moved via MARI INDUS to BANNU and thence by road to MIRANSHAH, where two companies of the Second Suffolk, composed of recent drafts, went out on practice road protection duty, suffering one or two casualties from snipers.

The TOCHI Valley operations opened in earnest on 4th July. The 1st Indian Infantry Brigade at AHMED KHEL being responsible for keeping open the L of C with "TOCOL", operating in the central part of the valley from DEGEN, and with "RAZCOL" moving up to the relief of DATTA KHEL.

For a month the Battalion remained at AHMED KHEL helping to keep the road open for four days a week, suffering occasional night sniping and a few shots during the day. The heat was intense and there was a good deal of sickness. At the end of this period they helped to clear and search the villages on the South side of the River TOCHI.

During these operations the Battalion was visited by the Commander in Chief, General Sir Archibald Wavell, who in a message to the Commander of the force said:—"Let all troops know how favourably I was impressed by their bearing and evident keenness."

During the last days of July and the beginning of August the Battalion continued with road protection duties and with the destruction of towers, the village of DILPURA being completely destroyed. During these duties the troops made the most of an abundance of fruit growing in the valley; grapes, pomegranates and plums were eaten as soon as ripe—or before. The 1st Indian Infantry Brigade left the TOCHI Valley on 14th August but continued operations in the LOWER DAUR area. On 20th August it moved to KASURI for the further destruction of villages and particularly IPI. By this date malaria was at its worst, no less than 50% of the Battalion had been evacuated. The heat and hard conditions of campaigning had proved exceedingly trying. On the 26th August the Brigade moved back by IDAK to MIRANSHAH and DARDONI where a perimeter camp was made and tents, etc., were brought from BANNU to bring the Battalion to F.S. Scale once again. On the 28th September the Battalion returned to RAWAL PINDI.

No limelight is thrown on operations like the above; especially when a world war is in progress. There had been no spectacular engagements and very few casualties; but the duties had been long and monotonous, nights in bed were few and far between, administrative duties and fatigues had been heavy and the sick rate had taken an exceedingly high toll. The Battalion fully deserved the congratulations it received from all in Command. All ranks had maintained their cheerful attitude and splendid discipline.

Back in RAWAL PINDI training was resumed and it is worth noting that in November 1941 two 3″ and one 2″ mortars were received, and training commenced. But while these made their belated appearance men from the Battalion, anxious for active service, were departing to join the 151st Parachute Battalion and other formations.

Infantry is the arm that wins victory. It has been called the "Queen of Battle." But in India on occasions infantry is required to keep the peace, a wretched role. The History of the Second Battalion during this Second World War was:—A tour on the Frontier, a creditable part in the TOCHI Valley Campaign; a short spell of training in RAWAL PINDI; a long spell at "Internal Security"; an all too brief time at Jungle Warfare; the BURMA Campaign.

Had the majority of the officers and N.C.O.s who had been with the Battalion in RAZMAK remained with the Battalion throughout these months and years the outstanding efficiency of the Unit would have been preserved. But they did not. With every change in role large drafts including most of the best of all ranks were drained away, their places being filled from anywhere. On one occasion when the Second Battalion and another British Battalion were within 30 miles of one another each received a draft of 200 men belonging to the other, the drafts having arrived from home on the same transport. No representations to "Higher Authority" could get this "Babu" Blunder altered.

There is almost always another side to any question. India might well complain that in the great expansion of Imperial armies she came off worst. The best officers and N.C.O.s remained with the Battalions in England. Those who served in India at the outbreak of the War were the only source for the Army's expansion. It was said that you could not go to any of the big establishments throughout India without finding men of the Suffolk Regiment—pulling their weight.

But when the Second Battalion finally embarked on the BURMA Campaign it had lost a large proportion of the well trained and experienced officers and men who had done so well on the Frontier.

"INTERNAL SECURITY"
JAN. 1942 — OCT. 1943.

In January 1942 at RAWAL PINDI the role of the Battalion was stated to be:—

Tribal Warfare on the N.W. Frontier.
Warfare on the N.W. Frontier against a modern enemy.
Local Internal Security.

Internal Security has always been one of the duties of our Army in India; but during 1942-1943, it was a vital necessity and the behaviour of the troops so employed was of the greatest importance, for the Japanese armies were on the frontier of India and the enemy was making every effort to foster Fifth Columnist activity.

In March, 3 officers and 30 other ranks of the Suffolk and Cambridgeshire Battalions who had been sent away from Singapore before the capitulation joined the Battalion. About the same time the Battalion was ordered to prepare a draft of 5 officers and 100 O.R.s for service in BURMA and these at once started intensive training.

In April the Battalion moved to LAHORE. Here Internal Security became of primary importance. In August the Battalion was called out at very short notice and the Area Commander congratulating them wrote:— "It was very heartening to see how keen you were to get down to business; the duties have been strenuous; but it is gratifying to note how willingly you have co-operated with the Civil and the Police and how cheerfully you have got on with the job. Internal Security duties are in some ways bad training for war and are liable to form bad habits; different situations call for different methods."

The Companies employed had been actively engaged. Villages had been burnt, fines collected, roads and railways patrolled. Fire had had to be opened more than once. On one occasion two officers, Lt. B. B. Coward and Lt. Denton, were attacked by a mob.

In September the Battalion was again employed on Internal Security duties, moving by rail from GORAKHPUR to AZAMGARH, with Companies at SYZABAD, AZAMGARH and MAU, LUCKNOW, GORAKHPUR and BHATNI.

The Battalion was thus scattered over an area of approximately four hundred square miles of the UNITED PROVINCES on railway protection and

I.S. duties. Platoon training was carried out in the intervals of the road and rail patrols.

The following letter was received from the Superintendent of Police, GORAKHPUR by Major S. H. Atkins, temporarily in command:—

"Thank you so much for your letters. I am afraid I have personally done nothing to deserve all the pleasant things you have written. As you say there has been the most complete co-operation between you chaps and us and it has been a real pleasure working together. Poor Ennion is at his wits end to know how to meet all his commitments."

The Commander in Chief sent the following telegram:—

"I greatly appreciate all you have done, your firmness, restraint, devotion to duty under circumstances of great strain and difficulty in present disturbances. Action in aid of Civil Power is always a distasteful duty for a soldier but you have tackled this task as a soldier should. We are NOT yet clear of these troubles, but I have faith in your resolution and determination to deal with future situations which may arise. You may rest assured you will have as always my full support in whatever may be required of you."

The following letter was written by the Commanding Officer to The District Commissioner, GORAKHPUR:—

"Dear Sir,

Now that the companies of The Suffolk Regiment have been withdrawn from your district, I am writing on behalf of All Ranks in the Battalion to thank you and all your staff and the many civilians who have been so kind to us all.

Since August—when the Regiment arrived to assist in restoring order—we have covered a good deal of the District and everywhere we have found nothing but kindness.

The various local populations have entertained the Battalion on many occasions, at what must have been considerable expense to them. This entertainment was greatly appreciated and it is difficult to know how we can repay their hospitality.

If we have created an impression of good-will among the population of your District, I feel that we have done our duty as a small cog in the wheel to bring India back to peaceful conditions.

Yours most gratefully,

H. B. MONIER-WILLIAMS.

The following answer was received from the GORAKHPUR District Commissioner's Camp:—

"Dear Sir,

I acknowledge with thanks your letter dated 4th December, 1942. The Companies of The Suffolk Regiment stationed at various places in the GORAKHPUR Division created a most friendly atmosphere and their friendliness was appreciated by the public and officials. Whatever little the public and the officials did for them, was in appreciation of their treatment of the people. The assistance that they gave in restoring order was of very great value. It was with regret that the news of their transfer was received by the people of the places where they were stationed.

Yours sincerely,

WAJABET HUZZAIN."

In October 1942 the Battalion was once more together at LUCKNOW.

The winter months of 1942-43 had not been all wasted; the Battalion was becoming more up to date. As one man wrote:—"We have had a three days' outing just before Christmas, one of the first times that we have been out as a Battalion. It was a start of perhaps bigger things; but we still have a lot to learn which you blokes at home have known for some time. We haven't had a real chance before; but we will be all right before long, whatever they say about us."

Some had been teaching themselves novel ways of crossing rivers. 'C' Company under Capt. P. E. V. Richards boasted that "they could cross any river with only a charpoy, a bundle of grass, or a new type of water wings." While 'B' Company under their "naval" Company Commander, Capt. R. G. B. Daws, were "building boats with a couple of pieces of bamboo!"

But though the spirit was willing the means were not forthcoming, as none knew better than the Mechanical Transport officer, who, although he had a "very decent medley of vehicles to look after, either had too many men and no vehicles, or vice versa."

Early in 1943 the Battalion Command changed. Lt.-Col. H. B. Monier-Williams, M.C., was given employment in the European Theatre of War, his place being taken by an officer of another Regiment, whose stay was comparatively short.

In April of this year the Battalion was concentrated at FYZABAD with indications of a fresh start and the possibility of future employment in BURMA. It was a good training area, reorganizations and re-equipment were put in hand. But once again Internal Security intervened. While in May a draft of 150 trained old soldiers was detached to another Regiment, and this draft included 14 full-rank N.C.O.s who could be ill spared. This was followed in September by the loss of 22 more senior N.C.O.s on "repatriation."

But by this time it was certain that the Battalion was for BURMA, and this created a great wave of enthusiasm. The Battalion was in the RANCHI area for final intensive training in jungle warfare. A fairly hectic time was spent, tents being luxury items and a thick bush the acme of comfort. It was the Monsoon Season, when crawling through paddy fields and nearly drowning in the process, trying to keep dry with only a ground sheet against the pouring rain, and the building of Basha huts was a trying experience.

Once again the Command of the Battalion changed, Lt.-Col. H. R. Hopking, O.B.E. taking over. His arrival was the best possible tonic at this special time. He at once set to work to fit the Battalion for the strenuous time that was ahead of them.

THE 1944 CAMPAIGN IN BURMA.

The War in EUROPE engrossed the attention of the people of the British Isles from 1939-1945. The distant war in ASIA and the PACIFIC was only of secondary interest. Yet it is possible that an even higher degree of individual courage and endurance was required in the Campaign in BURMA than anywhere else in the World War. As was said "No one will ever write of the long marches, lonely patrols and bloody battles save with profound admiration of the courage, endurance and supreme devotion to duty of the troops who fought and fell here in such large numbers at the far off post of honour."

No appreciation of the part played by the Second Battalion is possible without a description of the country and a brief survey of the operations. A sketch map is shown facing page 167.

INDIA throughout the Centuries has been protected from invasion from the East by the great mountain mass, the "Roof of the World" which from its impenetrable heights in the North extends in a tangled confusion of precipitous jungle covered hills Southwards throughout ASSAM and BURMA to the sea.

There were no metalled roads through the mountains to connect INDIA and BURMA. The best of the very few tracks that led across the passes ran from the IRRAWADDY Valley at KALEWA, by IMPHAL to DIMAPUR on the CALCUTTA-LEDO Railway. It was along this almost impassable route that most of the 200,000 refugees made their way from BURMA to INDIA; followed in March 1942 by General Alexander's army, fighting a retreat against greatly superior Japanese forces.

Another track, of great importance later, went from MYITKYINA to LEDO. These, and one or two other rough paths, could not be traversed during the Monsoon period save by small bodies of men inured to the greatest hardships.

In 1942, and most of 1943, there was constant patrol and out-post fighting. During this period a metalled road was made from DIMAPUR through KOHIMA, IMPHAL to the frontier at TAMU. By this means our troops in contact with the Japanese were reinforced and maintained. At the same time the American General Stilwell pressed on with the construction of a road South from LEDO.

In 1942 the Japanese with greatly superior lines of communication had advanced from RANGOON. They had established themselves in strong positions on the CHINDWIN River and had cut the BURMA Road. Further South they had made their way into ARAKAN and had occupied AKYAB.

There had been no major operations since the retreat in March 1942; but General Wingate in 1943 made his first raid into Burma; small columns of his force crossing the CHINDWIN and penetrating 200 miles into enemy country. These columns were supplied from the air. The boldness displayed, the difficulties overcome, the information gained were of inestimable value as a model for future operations.

In October 1943 Admiral Lord Louis Mountbatten took over command of land, sea and air forces in SOUTH EAST ASIA; and the Allied land formations on the 700 mile front stretching from LEDO to ARAKAN were increased to three weak Corps:— the XXVth in the North; the IVth in the Centre about IMPHAL; the XVth in the South. The whole being formed into the 14th Army under General Slim.

The Allied front at this time formed three distinct Sectors. The Northern Sector based on LEDO with the American General Stilwell in command; the Central Sector on the IMPHAL Plain based on DIMAPUR; the Southern in ARAKAN. The Northern Sector was among the highest mountains of all. Here during 1942 and 1943 the Americans had built up a chain of airfields and the famous LEDO Road. By the end of 1943 with United States trained Chinese Divisions they were driving on to MYITKYINE and the old BURMA Road; one of the main objectives of the campaign being to link up with our distant ally, CHINA, by the old BURMA Road. Between the Southern and Central front stretched for 200 miles the CHIN Hills, the LUSHAI Hills and the ARAKAN Tracts.

The greater portion of this immense battle area, extending from the HIMALAYAS to the BAY OF BENGAL, is covered with jungle hills rising to 8,000 feet; one of the wildest, most impenetrable areas in the world. Moreover any advance into BURMA has to be against the grain of the country, the mountains and swift flowing rivers all running North-South, thus constituting a barrier and not a route between INDIA and the EAST.

The Orders from the Supreme Commander, Admiral Lord Louis Mountbatten, to General Slim, Commanding the Fourteenth Army, for the 1944 Campaign were to hold the Central and Southern Fronts, while in the North to advance to the line MOGAUNG-MYITKYINA.

These Orders could best be carried out by attacking the line of communications of the Japanese forces opposite LEDO, on the Northern front; at the same time engaging and holding the Japanese forces on the Central and Southern Fronts. It came to pass that the Japanese moved first and as events turned out their unsuccessful operations in the South and then the centre greatly facilitated the Allies' plan.

The Japanese operations opened on the 3rd February 1944 with an attack in the South, planned as a surprise, on the 7th Division of the XVth Corps. Fortunately General Christison, commanding the XVth Corps, had received warning through a captured message, and had made a redistribution of his command. But even so there was very severe fighting for 17 days before the Japanese attack was repulsed; the fighting in this area continued till June. Although the enemy frontline strength had not exceeded 8,000 men, his defeat here had a great effect on the following operations; for he had counted on this attack drawing reinforcements from the Centre Sector, against which he had massed 100,000 of his best troops.

On March 17th, three Japanese Divisions in three Columns crossed the CHINDWIN River and attacked the Centre Sector with the object of capturing the IMPHAL Plain and cutting the British Line of Communication to the North. This was intended to be a prelude to the invasion of INDIA. They severed the main supply road from DIMAPUR to IMPHAL; but the effect was nullified by British and American aircraft continuing to supply the beleaguered garrisons. Meanwhile the XXXth Corps under Lt. General Montagu Stopford, with the 2nd Division hurriedly brought from INDIA, and reinforced by air by the 7th Division, co-operated with the IVth Corps at IMPHAL who had been temporarily reinforced by the 5th Division.

By March 30th the Japanese were round KOHIMA and it was not till May 14th that they were driven back from the neighbourhood of this town. By June 22nd the attack on the Central Sector was defeated; but the fighting on the ground won by the enemy in their first advance continued until mid July, their last man being driven over the Indian frontier on August 25th. The defeat was by this time decisive; very few of the 100,000 who had attacked escaped.

While the fighting proceeded in the Centre Sector, in the North General Stilwell continued his move South; nineteen weeks of continuous fighting, while the road followed him like his shadow.

On March 5th, this year, General Wingate made his great flight over the enemy lines. With 12,000 men, two thirds of whom were British, and 1,200 mules, he landed 150 miles behind the Japanese lines in very rough open country on which air strips had to be constructed; losing only 121 men in the landing. Then, after stubborn fighting, his force finally joined up with General Stilwell. On 17th May, MYITKYINA was captured; but the area was not completely cleared until August 3rd.

Thus the Campaign of 1944 was completely successful on all three fronts. Our casualties were approximately 10,000 killed, 2,000 missing, 27,000 wounded; while it is estimated that at least 50,000 Japanese were killed, and few of the remainder escaped.

That is a very brief outline. The Second Suffolk were in the 123rd Indian Infantry Bde. of the 5th Indian Division belonging first to the XVth Indian Corps in the ARAKAN, then for a short time to the IVth Indian Corps at IMPHAL. They thus took part in the actions on the Southern and Central Fronts during 1944.

The XVth Corps, as part of the General Plan, had to make the enemy fight on as broad a front as possible. The MAYU range of mountains dominated this Southern battle area; the 5th Indian Division was South West of this range, the 7th Indian Division to the South East, the crest was shared by both. But to link these two Divisions, and to improve their communications to the Coastal belt, roads had to be built to replace the existing trails and rough passes. One of these passes was a mule track, the GOPPE pass, the other the NGAKYE DAUK pass, better known under the name "Okeydoke". Sappers and Miners with bulldozers and pneumatic drills accomplished a wonderful piece of work in making these rough trails passable by motor transport.

In January, 1944, the offensive containing action of the XVth Corps ordered by General Slim precipitated the Japanese plan, who saw that their time table for the invasion of INDIA would be upset if the British on the ARAKAN front were not quickly defeated.

Tanahashi, the Japanese Commander in ARAKAN, confident that he could easily do this, attacked on the night 3/4th February, with all his available force, keeping only one Battalion in Reserve. He even brought up gunners without their guns, intending to use them with the guns he expected to seize from the British.

Captured documents had warned General Christison, who broke off his attacks, concentrated for defence and, by a secret move of his tanks, reinforced the 7th Division east of the MAYU Range.

The Japanese, by a forced march of 33 miles, swept on to the MAYU Heights and sealed off the so-called 7th Div. Administrative "Box" at SINZWEYA. This "Box" had become a Corps Administrative Area containing some 8,000 administrative troops, pioneers, sappers, ordnance and medical units, mule companies and native road builders. Six thousand Japanese, with 4,000 forming an outer ring, hurtled into the attack, anticipating an easy victory. A soldiers' battle raged; all inside the "Box" fought like veteran infantry. The attack was held.

Meanwhile Tanahashi pressed on round flank and rear towards the GOPPE pass; he was turned here by a small, gallant mule company; but crossed the range between the GOPPE and "OKEYDOKE", reaching the road connecting the 5th and 7th Divisions and destroying British stores and bridges. Here he dug in. It looked as if he had gained a substantial success. The Tokyo press announced a great victory; a British army destroyed in one thrust; the march on DELHI begun. For the attack on the Southern Front had a direct relation to the main attack that was to be made on the centre.

But Tanahashi had left out of account the Allied Air Force. He believed that if British air fighters appeared they could be wiped out. Within ten days of the first challenge to our "Spitfires" 65 Japanese fighters had been destroyed for the loss of 3 "Spitfires," while from the outset of the battle large air-defenceless troop carriers were safely supplying the beleaguered British garrisons.

ARAKAN demonstrated the truth of Wingate's saying:

"The vulnerable artery is the L of C winding through the jungle. Have no L of C on the jungle floor. Bring in the goods, like Father Christmas, down the chimney."

The Japanese had set ten days for the successful accomplishment of their Southern task in the ARAKAN; they had carried ten days' rations, the ten days were up, and nowhere had the British fled or been overwhelmed. The forward Brigades of the 7th Division and one Brigade of the 5th Division had inflicted heavy casualties and had prevented the enemy either supplying his own troops or withdrawing his casualties. Moreover the Japanese were tiring.

Although the Allied troops in this Southern Sector were surrounded and their L of C cut the enemy had no means of supplying food or ammunition, or of evacuating the heavy casualties they were suffering in their "bunkers" and "fox holes" from the Allied Air Force. The diary of a Japanese Intelligence Officer recorded how one Brigade group had gone seven days without rations, living on wild yams and water; while elsewhere the enemy was reported so short of food that he was eating monkeys.

A British counter attack was staged and pressed home in a pincer movement from both sides of the MAYU Range; the enemy's stranglehold on "Okeydoke" was broken. The first major victory in BURMA was won. It is estimated that the Japanese lost nearly 7,000 of his finest troops, killed, in this fighting. What was even more important, the British and Indian soldiers established their superiority man for man over an arrogant enemy.

The Prime Minister in a special message to Lord Louis Mountbatten said:

"The enemy has been challenged and beaten in jungle warfare. His boastfulness has received a most salutory lesson."

The Second Suffolk helped to contain the Japanese by an attack on a position named "Bamboo" during the first phase of the fighting on this Southern Front. In February after the Japanese had attacked, the Battalion occupied an extended front and by successful aggressive action deceived the enemy as to their weakness. In March they took their full share in the attack which finally defeated Tanahashi's force. Later in the month the Second Suffolk while still in front line was pulled out of the successful counter attack on the Japanese in the ARAKAN, and flown to IMPHAL with the rest of the 5th Division.

The Japanese Supreme Commander had hoped that the attack on the British Southern Sector would result in the British Centre Sector being called upon to support the Southern and thus open the way for Japanese success when they in turn attacked the Centre. But the opposite resulted, the enemy failure in the ARAKAN enabling the 5th and 7th Indian Divisions to come to the assistance of the Allies in the IMPHAL plain.

This Central Battle started on March 17th, when a Japanese army of 100,000 of their finest troops, very lightly equipped, crossed the CHINDWIN River on the first stage of their invasion of INDIA. Their object was to cross the Mountains beyond the CHINDWIN and destroy the Allied Advanced Base at IMPHAL. Then, securing the IMPHAL-KOHIMA supply road, to sweep on to the ASSAM-BENGAL railway and cut the Line of Communication to the Northern Front and thus sever all communication between INDIA and CHINA. The way would then be free for them to enter INDIA.

Speed was essential; they must reach IMPHAL and KOHIMA before Allied reinforcements could arrive. Five days after crossing the CHINDWIN River the Japanese stood on the INDIA-BURMA frontier.

It is not necessary here to describe how the 17th Indian Division was successfully withdrawn 160 miles from the South towards IMPHAL, fighting hard all the way; and how the 20th Indian Division also came back from the East from UKHRUL to the same rendezvous.

Together they were besieged in IMPHAL, from which some 50,000 non-combatants had been evacuated, mostly by air. Meanwhile another Japanese punch was directed on KOHIMA.

For the second time this year the Japanese believed they had won the Campaign; for the second time they were defeated by air supremacy. The fall of IMPHAL was announced in TOKYO on March 30th, and of KOHIMA in April. But though the road was cut, their fierce assaults had been always beaten back with the heaviest loss, our tanks in particular exacting a heavy toll. Throughout the battle of IMPHAL the men of the IVth Corps serenely stuck it out.

KOHIMA had a more anxious time. There were no more than 3,500 men to hold this gateway to INDIA. The Japanese attacking were vastly superior in numbers. For fourteen days this gallant force held on, the whole garrison being under constant fire from the Japanese batteries on the ridges surrounding the plain. Several times the Japanese, fighting their way into the town, thought they had won, only to be driven out again.

Then the arrival of strong reinforcements of the 7th Indian Division with the 2nd British Division and Lt.-General Sir Montagu Stopford of the XXXth Corps arrived, and KOHIMA was relieved. Not a building was left undamaged, most were rubble; the gallant garrison of grimy-bearded riflemen were almost completely exhausted. The XXXth Corps swept on; but it was not until the middle of May that the last Japanese was driven from the network of "bunkers" he had constructed round the town. He had lost 4,000 killed. An officer who had fought on Hill 60 in 1914-1915 declared that the Battle of KOHIMA was more terrible.

Down in IMPHAL the Japanese had completely failed in their attack on the IVth Corps.

By the 22nd June the IVth and XXXth Corps had joined hands and pressed East on UKHRUL, the biggest burial ground for Japanese in the length and breadth of MANIPUR. Thence the Japanese were driven back beyond the CHINDWIN River from where they had started. With his L of C blasted from the air, his retreat became a major disaster. Everywhere his condition deteriorated; the legend that the Japanese soldier could live on a daily handful of rice was disproved. They had the rice; but the many stragglers and deserters who fell into our hands were suffering from acute beri beri and covered with sores. They crawled dying to the feet of the giant marble and gold leafed idols in the Buddhist temples to end life.

While these battles on the Southern and Central Fronts were being fought, General Stilwell continued to push forward on to his objective, the line MOGAUNG-MYITKYINA, which he reached after hard fighting on the 3rd August. Men of Wingate's airborne force having stood a siege for 78 days in road blocks on the way to MYITKYINA.

Such in brief outline was the campaign of 1944 in BURMA in which the Second Battalion Suffolk Regiment took a full share.

Too often when we read Military History we are content with the bare outlines of a Campaign, such as the above. The problem seems simple, it can be stated in a few lines, the veriest novice can give an answer. To such, there does not appear anything very clever or outstanding in Stonewall Jackson's Campaigns in the Virginian Mountains; rather it seems to be Banks's elementary stupidity. So we might argue of General Slim; History so often reduces the flesh and blood of a Campaign to a bare inanimate skeleton and forgets all the palpitating details that made it an almost insoluble problem.

Particularly is this true of the Campaign in BURMA. As was said; the country constituted a Logistical nightmare, the logistics meaning all those Administrative problems that must be solved before a plan can be made and an army put in motion to carry out that plan.

Lines of Communication—roads, transport, supplies—The Road. What a story could be written on the construction of the roads that, quite apart from the air lines, were so essential for tactical victory in BURMA.

The way had to be first hacked through virgin forest, thorny scrub, bamboo and elephant grass, graded over towering ranges, supported across swamps and rivers; ceaseless work in a climate that during the monsoon season could exceed 10 inches of rain in the day. Chinese, Chins, Indians, Nepalese all cut, hauled and piled. Black, brown, yellow and white men all worked shoulder deep in the swirling streams, or deep in mud. All had to be prepared to fight at any moment; for there were constant Jap raids coming in from the jungle, when tools had to be dropped and rifles seized.

As the trail was blazed and the jungle cleared, the bulldozers came forward shovelling, pushing, levelling, and behind the bulldozers the highway builders, blasting, metalling, bridging, grading. Many thousands of non-combatant troops were employed. These workers on the bridges included elephants. An elephant could lay a plank with the precision of a carpenter—and, as was stated, he could lay off work with the same precision. There were some elephants who "downed trunks" dead at 5 p.m. winter or summer, showing that the difference in the light had nothing to do with their decision.

Then on the newly made roads came the transport. 50,000 vehicles moved daily through the jungle, over the mountains, across the rivers, through dust clouds and monsoon mud. An average of 77 miles a day was maintained by the motor trucks from railhead to forward areas during the worst months of the year. Supplementing the motor vehicles were mules from INDIA, AFRICA and the U.S.A. and donkeys from SOUTH AFRICA.

For thanks to Major General Snelling, the Major General for Administration, half a million fighting men and 300,000 coolies were kept magnificently supplied with every necessity and a great many luxuries.

Supplies were only one of the administrative questions that had to be answered before the plan could be decided. The medical question was another. For every casualty in action there were ten from malaria. In this Campaign the jungle was everywhere. Trackless, immense, it not only had an overpowering effect on the minds of all, it was as dangerous as it was frightening. Wild beasts and snakes, fearsome stinging insects, leeches, lice, and ticks, malaria and dysentry. Malaria has conquered armies and can cripple empires, nowhere had this sickness been more prevalent than in the ARAKAN. This was an enemy that could not be stamped out; but thanks to the skill of the Medical Services and to "Malaria discipline" it was eventually so reduced that 90% of the men suffering returned to duty within three weeks.

Casualties in battle could not be so drastically reduced. The jungle enclosed them; wounded men had to be carried on stretchers over the most difficult country for as much as ten miles. Everyone with experience of campaigning on the Indian Frontier knows the necessity of evacuating the wounded; they could not be left in BURMA to Japanese mercy; for they had none. One of our men was found gagged with his own field dressing and with his own bayonet through him from side to side.

It was air mastery that above all brought about Japanese disaster; blasting their L of C while so greatly lightening the strain on our own. But here again the jungle had to be conquered. Landing grounds could be prepared behind our own lines; but to an audacious mind like Wingate's landings must be made behind the enemy's lines on unknown ground. There is no space in this History to describe the landing of gliders flying by night, unlighted and unescorted, over the 7,000 feet mountains, 150 miles into BURMA, and landing on clearances that air reconnaissance had reported might bear an initial landing. A great adventure that became a model for the airborne assault on EUROPE. Many gliders crashed; one with a bulldozer ploughed into the wall of the jungle at sixty miles an hour; its wings were torn off, its fuselage cleared of the wreckage, rushed on, while the pilot and co-pilot were flung into the air and landed unhurt. "I planned it just that way," said the American pilot. That was the spirit that made our air force invincible.

The Japanese were expert in jungle fighting. They had studied the technique before the war started and they put their training and experience into deadly effect against our untrained troops defending SINGAPORE. Their armies in BURMA were fortified by war experience and by the moral effect of their victories. They believed themselves the greatest fighters on Earth, and in this belief gave full play to their uncivilized savagery.

Credit must be given to the enemy for fanatical bravery; but there were other matters which will damn them. The Japanese soldiers fighting in BURMA had been taught that every man opposed to them, whether wounded or in hospital, should be killed. In the ARAKAN battle when the enemy overran a medical dressing station, they burst in howling like dervishes and killing all. This brutality was not due to the heat of battle. Forty-eight hours later, after the fight was over, a Senior Japanese Officer entered and ordered all wounded and orderlies to be massacred. Six doctors were lined up and shot in cold blood.

But as the Campaign proceeded, so their morale changed. Occasionally a suicide Japanese Squad would attack by day; but generally they chose the night and then came through the thick jungle uttering weird animal calls to intimidate our men and keep in touch with one another.

It is a tribute to the Allied soldiers that starting so badly yet they learnt to beat the Japanese in the tactics in which he was a master. The side which has the higher skill gains supreme confidence and becomes almost unbeatable. At the outset of this Campaign the Japanese had conquered the jungle, and the jungle was a psychological factor of supreme importance.

Jungle warfare has a technique differing from all other forms of warfare. It is a war of patrols, of small parties separated from their comrades, forcing their way through and over the most difficult country in the world to find and attack some strongly protected post. It calls for endurance, dauntless courage; quick decisions must be made, great risks must be taken, and failure may well mean death. These patrols had to be out from two to seven days. Each man carried upwards of 70 lbs. in his pack additional to his rifle, ammunition and tools; the days were intensely hot, the nights cold, the dawn dew was as heavy as a small shower and it remained damp till 10 a.m. Each man in turn hacked a way through the jungle; a jungle where silence might be vital, yet dead pieces of bamboo went off like pistol shots and big dead teak leaves made quiet stepping impossible.

The CHIN hills where the Second Battalion saw service first were 2,000 to 8,000 feet in height, with unusually steep sides, full of gorges and precipices; there were streams and thick jungle in the valleys, growing thinner as the sides were climbed. In parts the route would run through elephant grass 12 feet high, which cut into the skin and kept out such fresh air as there might be.

At night double sentries were posted—for the jungle was full of sound: birds with unbirdlike notes, deer, hyena, and sometimes tiger; while by day or night the ticks and leeches proved their tenacity. The mosquito was everywhere; veils, gloves and mosquito cream all had to be used against this universal enemy.

When the Second Battalion entered the BURMA Campaign the Japanese were still confident in their superiority over the Allies. They fought with fanatical courage; attacking without regard to loss of life and in defence holding on to their positions until all were killed.

The Second Battalion was to have considerable experience of the enemy's skilful defensive tactics during the next eight months. It was based on concealment. Strong positions were selected and heavily fortified with concealed and camouflaged "Bunkers." These were small redoubts with overhead log and earth cover, to hold from four to six men on the forward or reverse slopes. "Fox Holes" for single look-out men, sometimes connected by trenches with the main position, were pushed out to the flanks. Generally the Japanese remained silent in these hidden jungle positions until the attacker was under their close fire. Occasionally they covered their front by snipers in trees, who withdrew after holding up the advance; they very rarely used patrols in defence. They made great use of LMG and MMG fire and grenade discharges.

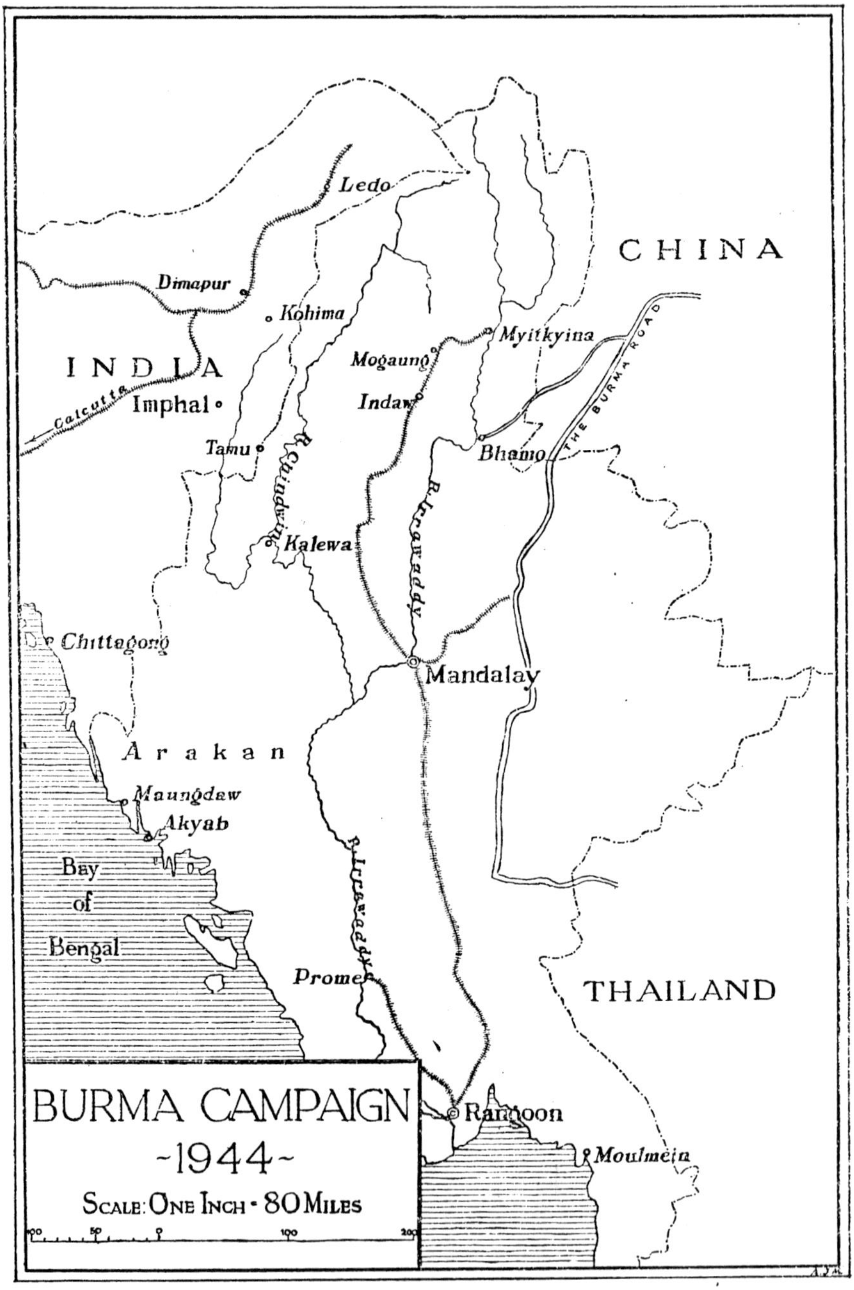

CHINA
INDIA
THAILAND
Ledo
Dimapur
Kohima
Imphal
Calcutta
Tamu
R. Chindwin
Kalewa
Mogaung
Myitkyina
Indaw
Bhamo
THE BURMA ROAD
R. Irrawaddy
Mandalay
Chittagong
Arakan
Maungdaw
Akyab
Bay of Bengal
Prome
Rangoon
Moulmein
BURMA CAMPAIGN
~1944~
SCALE: ONE INCH = 80 MILES

Strong offensive patrols were necessary before an attack could be launched on a prepared Japanese position in order to pinpoint the "Bunkers" and destroy these by supporting fire from the ground or the air.

But perhaps the chief reason for the final success of the Allies in the attack over this most difficult country was the co-operation of tanks with the infantry. Many feats judged impossible were carried through in BURMA notwithstanding jungle, monsoon and mosquito—one of these feats was the movement of tanks up and down the astonishingly steep and rocky slopes.

ARAKAN.

OCTOBER, 1943 — FEBRUARY, 1944.

After a short period of training, unsatisfactory owing to scarcity of men and a shortage of equipment, the Second Battalion was ordered in October 1943 to mobilize; this was followed by a final stage in Jungle training.

On the 19th October the Battalion embarked on the S.S. "Ethiopia" at MADRAS and four days later disembarked at CHITTAGONG, whence they set out on a week's land marching to join the 123rd Brigade of the 5th Indian Division in the forward area.

The heat in the ARAKAN was still intense, for the monsoon had just finished; the day and night traffic to the front was unceasing, while the dust added to the severe strain during this move to TUMBRU on the India-Burma frontier.

Here they were fortunate to have a clear month to concentrate on their uncompleted training. This included an N.C.O.'s Battle Course and practice with all weapons on ranges constructed by the companies. At the same time representatives were sent to forward units of another Division to get practical battle experience.

In November the Battalion moved forward to WAYBYIN, in Brigade Reserve; where they were employed on long range patrols in the foot-hills of the MAYU Range. It was here that the Guerilla Platoon under Lieutenant D. Lee Hunter began the first of a long and successful series of patrols. This platoon had been formed from volunteers and selected men in the Battalion and did very good work. From the outset they had the confidence of the local people by taking out medical stores and rendering first aid, so that the villagers were always willing to help and to give information about the Jap. No better choice could have been made for a Guerilla Platoon Commander, Lee Hunter, a young officer of the Royal Norfolk Regiment, had an instinctive grasp of this kind of warfare. It is estimated that he led at least fifty long distance patrols; these he handled with great boldness and skill; the results were markedly successful, very heavy casualties were inflicted on the enemy while his own losses were negligible.

The ARAKAN is a narrowing peninsula divided in two by the rugged spine of the MAYU Range, which rises to 2,000 feet. The low lying areas had been paddy fields; but since the Jap occupation of BURMA in 1942 and the unfortunate ARAKAN campaign of the previous year, many of the villagers had fled and much of this fertile land was derelict. The coastal plains are broken up by numerous "chaungs" or tidal estuaries running into the foothills of the range and forming a maze of water obstacles. Jungle clad pimples and chains of low hills sprout out of the plains, these features become more bold and bulging until finally they merge into the lower slopes of the MAYU Range itself. Apart from the paddy fields, the whole area is thick jungle and secondary growth, impassable save along the rare tracks. The MAYU Range is covered by impenetrable jungle; the lower slopes clothed with densely matted bamboo and bush, thinning out into trees and more open scrub towards the higher features; while at the rocky precipitous top of the ridge vegetation is sparse.

The jungle has a particularly sinister atmosphere on first acquaintance, a factor not to be ignored. The overwhelmingly dense vegetation causes a feeling of oppression, heightened by the insistent background of unfamiliar noises; the calling of the jackal; the strident whistling and scraping of crickets; the quacks and croaks of jungle frogs and toads; the rustling and chirping of myriads of nocturnal creatures and thousands of other disquieting murmurings and rustlings. The dense growth seethes with animal life, each denizen contributing its quota to the unceasing cacophony of sound. There is an ever present subconscious dread of snakes, which the newcomer to the jungle expects to find lurking behind every blade of grass and hanging from every tree. He hears the barking deer with their peculiar and almost human cough; starts at the jungle cats with their unpleasant hissing.

It is not surprising that the raw soldier attuned to our English country music is at first nervous and jumpy. It takes time to get conditioned to this jungle environment, during which hardening process most men waste ammunition firing at ghostly noises and imaginary enemy. This state of mind was known as "Jungle jitters." As an example of "Jungle jitters" a certain officer is quoted, who, while lying in his "juggah," suddenly became aware of two bright eyes glancing at him through the undergrowth. Thinking it a bear and taking no chances, he whipped out his pistol and emptied it into the bushes. The two "eyes" continued to twinkle unblinkingly; being stars they could not do otherwise.

The 123rd Indian Infantry Brigade line ran north of MAUNGDAW across the MAYU RANGE, covering the MAUNGDAW-BUTHIDAUNG ROAD. The Second Suffolk in conjunction with operations on their right and left was ordered to capture a series of features which were known to be strongly held.

The advance against this position was a slow and laborious process, limited to the speed with which approach tracks could be cut. Animal tracks through the jungle had to be hacked or enlarged, forward patrols establishing themselves while the track was widened, or sometimes realigned when a chasm intervened. Mules followed the track makers, then the "jeeps," until finally sappers, bulldozers and coolies completed a 15 cwt road. Thus it was not until the middle of January that the Battalion was ready to launch its attack.

The first objective of the Battalion was a conical feature named "BAMBOO"; a small hill matted with dense bamboo and undergrowth that lay beyond a deep "Chaung."

On January 2nd 1944 while the forward tracks were being cut, the Guerilla platoon was sent forward to reconnoitre an under feature called "Wrencat" on the approach to "BAMBOO". They crossed a "Chaung" climbed the ground beyond about 700 yards from "BAMBOO" and signalled that they had seen no enemy. Next day they were followed by "D" Company

TYPICAL ARAKAN COUNTRY.

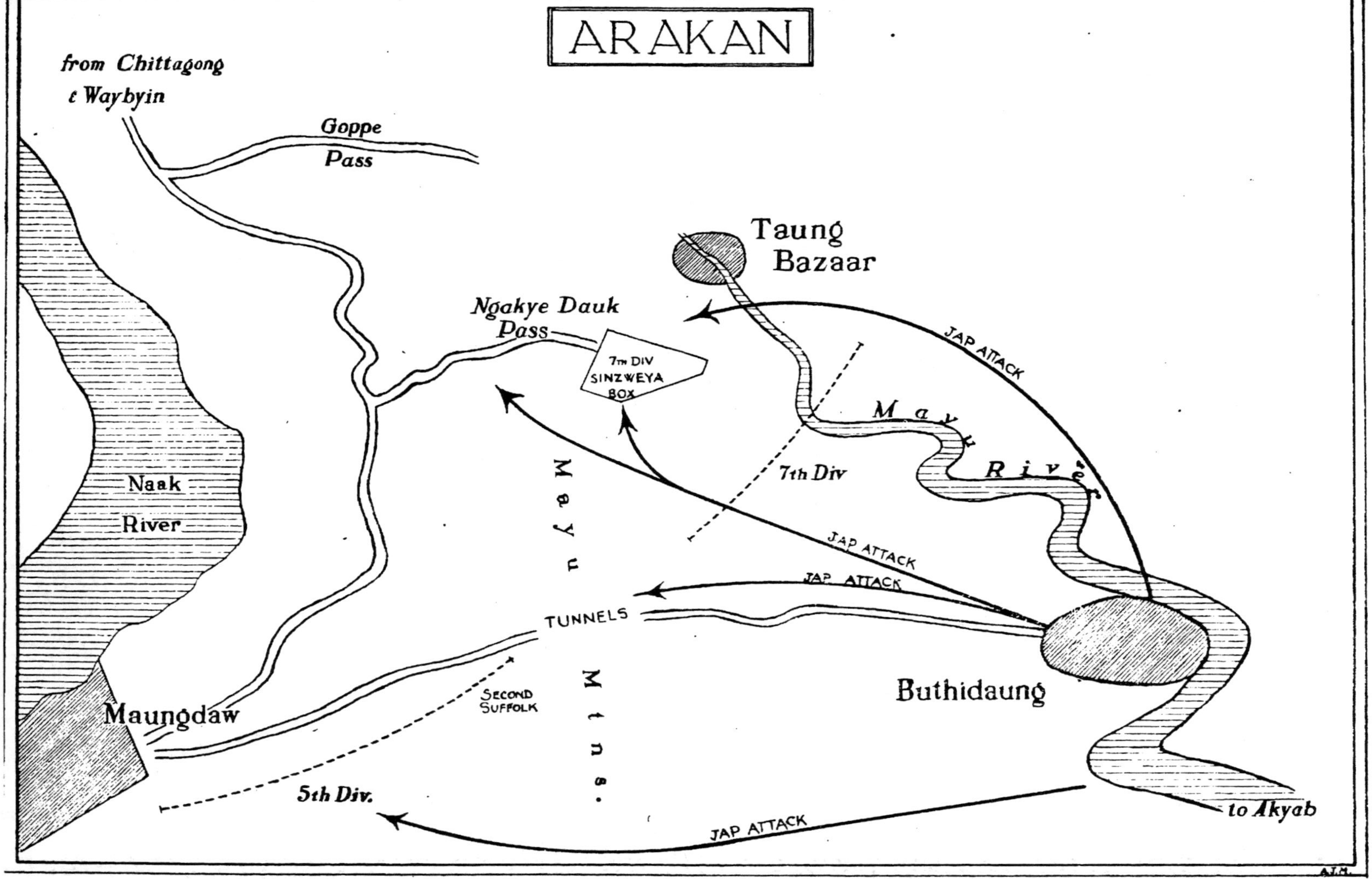
ARAKAN
from Chittagong
& Waybyin
Goppe
Pass
Taung
Bazaar
Ngakye Dauk
Pass
7TH DIV
SINZWEYA
BOX
JAP ATTACK
Mayu River
7th Div
Naak
River
Mayu Mtns.
JAP ATTACK
JAP ATTACK
TUNNELS
Buthidaung
Maungdaw
SECOND
SUFFOLK
5th Div.
JAP ATTACK
to Akyab
A.J.M.

XII

who, interpreting the message that no enemy had been seen as information that there was no enemy to see, moved forward in single file and strung out. When the head of the Company reached the neighbourhood of the Guerilla platoon an "operation" group was assembled. Then the storm broke from "Wrencat," the enemy opening up on the Company "operation" Group; with grenades, discharger fire, mortar and machine guns on the men behind whose movements had been clearly visible.

Fortunately darkness, for it was late afternoon, and inaccuracy of fire saved the Company many casualties. But it was an unfortunate start to operations by a raw unit and emphasized how much the Battalion had to learn.

It was here that Sergeant R. Brown of the Guerilla Platoon got a chance to show his quality. In spite of the extremely heavy fire directed on the Company, Sergeant Brown with an L.M.G. silenced three of the enemy machine guns and although an enemy "cut off" party started to shoot up the rear of his position he continued firing and silenced two more machine guns. He then successfully retired under cover of darkness. Sergeant Brown was awarded a M.M. for this action.

It was not until January 24th, after heavy artillery preparation, that "A" Company, commanded by Major D. Gray, moved forward to capture the objective. Good progress was made, one platoon assaulting "BAMBOO" while another platoon gave covering fire. The assaulting platoon reached a position 30 yards from the summit, where they came under heavy and concentrated fire from Jap bunkers on "BAMBOO" and supporting features which had not previously been located. The company suffered casualties and was unable to get further forward, so consolidated on a subsidiary feature, a part of the objective, where they were still under mortar, grenade discharger and rifle fire. "A" Company was now in close contact for further detailed planning, based on the information they had gained of the Jap defences.

Next morning the Commanding Officer, Lt.-Col. H. R. Hopking, after reconnaissance, decided that "C" Company, commanded by Major P. E. V. Richards, should capture a feature to the rear of "BAMBOO" whilst "A" Company gave supporting fire on to "BAMBOO". This feature was reached without opposition; but on "C" Company occupying it they came under heavy automatic fire from unlocated bunker positions. Richards, up with his forward platoon, was hit and the attack came to a standstill. While Major P. E. V. Richards was being pulled back under cover he was again hit by a Jap sniper and killed.

"C" Company with its casualties withdrew from the exposed position to "A" Company's position, where both Companies were constantly under grenade discharger and sniper fire, during which a grenade hit Major Gray, who died while being evacuated. Next morning "C" Company endeavoured to occupy a position to the right of "BAMBOO" which had been giving trouble and from which a further attack could be launched. This attack was again unsuccessful, the defences proving too strong; Captain Mitchison, commanding "C" Company, was wounded by grenade and evacuated, and Captain P. B. Forrest went up to take over command of "C" Company, as the company's third commander within a week.

The following day, while the 1/17th Dogras on the left attacked, a platoon of "A" Company assaulted "BAMBOO" and reached the summit after knocking out two bunkers and killing several Japs. But the enemy in position on the reverse slopes brought such heavy mortar and grenade discharger fire to bear that the platoon was forced off the summit, slithering down its precipitous side to the bottom. On their left the Dogras attack had also failed.

The following congratulatory message was received by the Second Suffolk as a result of their fighting on "BAMBOO" in the Arakan.

"The Brigade Commander wishes to congratulate Suffolk on the gallantry displayed in to-day's operations, which could be witnessed by all. The spirit of the troops was in accordance with the best traditions of the Suffolk Regiment."

While the following message was received by the Brigadier, 123rd Indian Infantry Brigade:

"The Army Commander and Div. Comd. are very proud of the magnificent show put up by your Battalions during the past four days and again to-day. It was beyond compare. Please give wide circulation to this message."

The action against "BAMBOO" cost the Batalion two fine Company Commanders: "Dicky" Richards and Major D. R. Gray of the 5th Royal Norfolk. Major P. E. V. Richards had been with the Batttalion practically the whole of his short service; during those few years he had made his mark as a young officer of outstanding personality. His one ambition was to get into action. His men were devoted to him and would have followed him anywhere under the most adverse conditions; his inspiration and leadership setting a magnificent example. In the annals of a Regiment a short but heroic career in war is not forgotten for many years.

Major Gray was a fine officer who made a hazardous escape from SINGAPORE.

Two more Military Medals were awarded during this action. One went to Lance Corporal Salter (later killed in action). During the retirement he located an enemy machine gun. He went back; three times he temporarily silenced it, thus enabling his platoon No. 7. to retire without casualties.

These frontal assaults against strong and consolidated bunker positions, supported as they were by equally strong flanking positions, had been costly; it was decided that the Brigade on the right should launch an attack against the flank and the rear of the Jap defensive line from the direction of MAUNGDAW.

It was now early February; but before this new plan could be put into effect the situation on the east of the MAYU Range had undergone a rapid change. The Japanese had launched their bold plan to cut the "Okeydoke" Pass from the direction of TAUNG BAZAR; as a result the 123rd Brigade, less Second Suffolk, was switched north, the Second Suffolk taking over the whole front previously occupied by the Brigade.

At the end of February Major E. G. W. Browne joined the Battalion from special employment elsewhere in BURMA taking command of "A" Company. On the 26th February he made the three days journey by train, road and boat from COMILLA to where the Battalion was holding positions in the foothills of the MAYU range just north of MAUNGDAW. Writing of the Battalion at this time he says: "Road journeys were at this time most

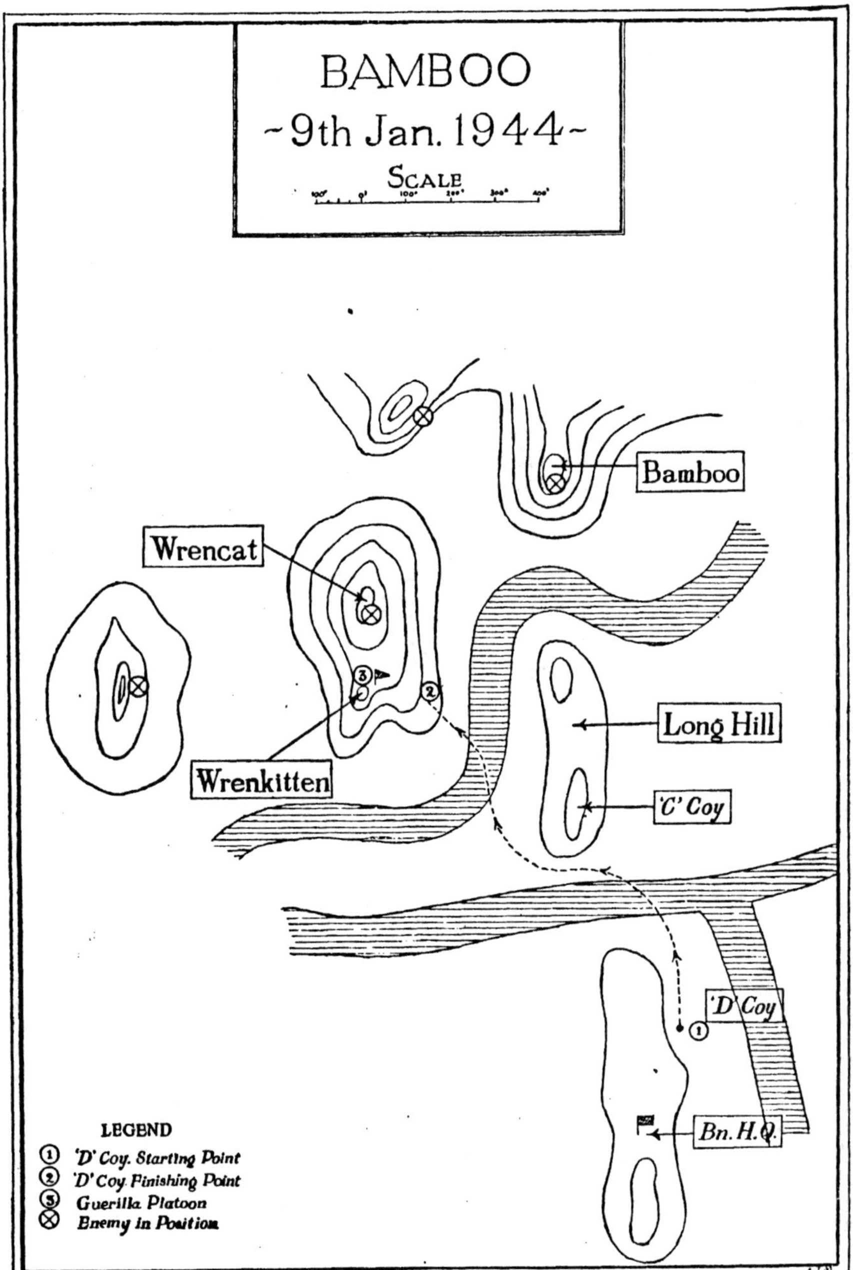
BAMBOO
~9th Jan. 1944~
SCALE
Bamboo
Wrencat
Long Hill
Wrenkitten
'C' Coy
'D' Coy
Bn. H.Q.
LEGEND
'D' Coy. Starting Point
'D' Coy. Finishing Point
Guerilla Platoon
Enemy in Position

XIII

unpleasant, the dust some four inches deep, rising in a stifling fog and making the men look like cobweb covered ghosts."

"The Battalion occupied a wide front with company localities on dominating hill features. The hills were very steep with knife like crests. Positions were hollowed out of the hill sides and platforms built up. Except in a few clearings ground visibility was restricted to a few yards. Everywhere there was dense scrub, growing to a height of ten to twelve feet, mostly of elephant grass or bamboo. Water was all this time plentiful; but was beginning to dry up."

"The climate was hot by day, but reasonably cool at night; malaria was taking a rather heavy toll. The fighting had died down; the opposing forces being at extreme small arms range (700 to 800) and saw very little of each other. The enemy fired a few shells; patrols went out, mortars and machine guns opened whenever the enemy showed himself."

"An inexperienced unit would have had lively nights as the area was stiff with small bears, deer and other game which could have been mistaken for enemy patrols. Elephants had been in the area; but had cleared off."

As has been told the Japanese attack on "Okeydoke" failed to eliminate the British forces, so that the Japanese although they had cut the lines of communication of the British Indian forces were themselves compelled to retire when they ran short of food and ammunition. The failure opposite the 7th Division resulted in the Japanese retiring from the front of the Second Battalion, who, following them up, took, amongst other hills, the fateful "Bamboo", which had cost them so many casualties.

While engaged in this advance, and while still in contact with the enemy, the Battalion was withdrawn; the Japanese were now attacking the Central Sector of the Allied line, and though no one but the Officer Commanding and his Adjutant knew, the Battalion, with the rest of the 5th Indian Division, were to be moved by air to reinforce this front at IMPHAL.

The Battalion had been in continuous contact with the Japanese for four months; an unsuccessful period it may have seemed to many officers and men. But in fact, they had proved their stubborn quality; they started lacking experience and training, they ended veterans, confident in their superiority in every respect to the Japanese.

IMPHAL.

MARCH 1944 — MAY 1944.

Military Science advances with great strides during war, when nations are engaged in a life or death struggle. What is a hazardous attempt at the outset is of no account a few months later. The movement of formations by air is an example. That a Battalion of the Suffolk Regiment complete with transport should have been flown over 200 miles of impenetrable jungle from one battle area to another, would have been regarded before this war as a great historical event in the History of the Regiment. Accounts from some participating in this move describe it as "uneventful," "the country just a mass of jungle covered hills with no sign of habitation." While another's only comments are that the move came so unexpectedly that a special cinema entertainment had to be cancelled; but fortunately there was time for the beer that went with it to be consumed.

Though the Battalion took this move in its stride, it was a remarkable episode in our Regimental history. The Battalion was taken in 3 ton lorries driven by West Africans to DOHAZARI 90 miles away, railhead on the CHITTAGONG L of C; the next day they were given their Plane Serial Numbers, the distribution of personnel, weight and stores, and at 1800 hours that evening, March 18th 1944, proceeded to the aerodrome. Slowly the Dakotas, British and American, with pilots from all over the Empire, came. As soon as one arrived it was loaded up and departed. There was no air escort. Everything went smoothly and without fuss.

This move was organised overnight and the load tables worked out on a hypothetical number of planes of varying carrying capacity. Looking back to that Sunday morning there can be no doubt that it was a fine achievement to emplane a whole battalion, including its mules and jeeps, in a matter of a few hours without previous training or rehearsal. This was their first flight for the majority of the men, but there were no signs of nervousness. Perhaps they were steadied by the outward appearances of unconcern by all taking part.

After an hour or two of peaceful flight over the wild and rugged INDO-BURMA border, where the failure of an engine meant almost certain destruction, the Battalion reached the IMPHAL Plain, circling and losing height to land. The town of IMPHAL looked very peaceful and orderly, with its regular compounds and fine open spaces, forming the centre of a tablecloth mosaic of paddy fields. Landing at the air strip, the men were quickly out of the planes and moving in M.T. down the PADEL Road. The people of IMPHAL gave them a great welcome.

The differences between the ARAKAN and MANIPUR were striking. Here were fine macadam roads with no dust, a civilized atmosphere, fresh, clean and orderly, a spacious and open country with long views and fine vistas to the distant mountains.

It was early spring, with a wealth of strange flowers and blossoms, The Ma..ip.uris seemed to symbolize the differences from the ARAKAN, for they too were sturdy, clean and cheerful, taking pride in their appearance. A refreshing change from the dirt and all-pervading shabbiness of the ARAKAN and its inhabitants.

Here again were many of the little pimply hills up-cropping from the plains, and it was towards a group of these that the Battalion was moving to dig the first of many defensive positions against the threatened attack on IMPHAL. These hills on the PADEL Road were covered with sparse low scrub, and occasional pineapple plantations; into the distance in all directions stretched long uninterrupted views of plains. In front of their defensive line was an expanse of low-lying flooded ground, a fine blue colour, very inviting; it was not long before the whole battalion was swimming and paddling, revelling in this opportunity of washing the last traces of the ARAKAN dust from their bodies. After a few days the Battalion was once again on the move—a move that was to continue without an appreciable break until the Japs had been finally driven out of MANIPUR.

By the end of March 1944, the Japanese threat to IMPHAL and to the L. of C. from DIMAPUR through KOHIMA had rapidly developed. The

Crown copyright reserved.

THE IMPHAL AIRSTRIP ON WHICH THE 2ND BATTALION LANDED AFTER ITS JOURNEY FROM THE ARAKAN.

leading elements of three enemy divisions had been in contact with our patrols covering the tracks leading west from the CHINDWIN and were attacking our outposts in the TIDDIN AREA, forcing them steadily back towards the INDIAN Frontier. KOHIMA itself was threatened, and orders had been given for the evacuation of its hospitals. KOHIMA was a strong natural fortress, a bastion on the only road to INDIA and the railhead at DIMAPUR. Further south the Japs advancing on UKHRUL were developing the threat to IMPHAL. The situation was daily and rapidly becoming more serious.

In order to meet these two vital and simultaneous threats it was decided that the Second Suffolk should move at once to the defence of KOHIMA; while the other two battalions of the 123rd Indian Brigade remained to meet the enemy advance on IMPHAL.

Travelling by night 21st/22nd March, the Second Suffolk moved by motor transport to KOHIMA, arriving there in the early hours of the next morning. It had proved a hair raising drive with Indian drivers over a most tortuous road. One of the drivers was a Pathan who had fought against the Battalion on the Frontier while at RAZMAK. At KOHIMA they prepared the defence of one of the main spurs on which the town is centred, the Hospital Spur, later to become well known as the scene of very heavy fighting, but at this time peaceful enough with its fir trees and profusion of flowers.

By the beginning of April, the Japs had advanced to within striking distance of the IMPHAL-KOHIMA Road and the Battalion was warned that this road might be cut at any moment. Then orders were received that another brigade of the 5th Indian Infantry Division had arrived at DIMAPUR, and that the Second Suffolk would rejoin their own brigade at IMPHAL. The battalion, less two companies, immediately started back there, the remaining two companies rejoining a few days later and just before the Japs got astride the road.

In the IMPHAL area the enemy advance from UKHRUL was developing rapidly and the Battalion took up a defensive position some 17 miles from IMPHAL on the mountain road, where it debouched into the plains. UKHRUL had already been seized: our parachute brigade there was fighting a fierce delaying action against greatly superior numbers, retiring on to the 3/2nd Punjabi Battalion of the 123rd Brigade. It was not long before the position of this latter unit became extremely difficult and although heavy casualties were inflicted on the oncoming masses of the Japs they found themselves penned in a huge natural amphitheatre with the Japs sniping and directing mortar fire into the bowl from the dominating heights. The administrative personnel in the area had been evacuated, the large stores and equipment dumps were destroyed, and then the 3/2nd Punjabis withdrew through the Suffolk positions, strong but only partially prepared on the saddle of the hill.

This line was too far out from IMPHAL and the Second Suffolk retired to a defile guarding IMPHAL from the east some ten miles from the town. Here they took up a position to the north of the road, with the 1st/17th Dogras to the south. The Punjabis going into reserve.

The enemy had suffered very heavy casualties and had to regroup and reorganize; so that an unexpected and welcome lull of nearly a fortnight enabled our men to prepare well sited defensive positions with extensive belts of wire and mines. Strong patrols kept in touch with the enemy.

During this time the Battalion helped to bring in 300 head of cattle and 38 lorry loads of rice, equivalent to 40 tons; the villagers having fled to the safety of the town.

During this lull a platoon under Lt. T. E. Watt, maintaining a forward standing patrol, lay up for the night in some scrub, and woke next morning to find themselves in the midst of a Company of Japanese. Discretion is the better part of valour. They endeavoured to slip away unobserved. But the Jap officer raised the hue and cry and as they broke cover Watt found himself chased by the enemy Commander, a fellow over six feet tall, brandishing his sword, while the rest of his company stood and stared. One or two parting shots and our patrol was clear.

The 1/17th Dogras on the Brigade right took the first brunt of the Japanese attack. With a great deal of noise and shouting the Japs charged the Dogras defences en masse, only to run into wire and concentrated fire. They were easily beaten off with very severe casualties. The Jap at this time was bursting with huckstering pride, imagining that he had only to show himself in strength, make known his redoubtable presence by cat-calls and other wild noises, and a benumbing chill would turn to water the hearts of all those who did not happen to be born "Sons of Heaven". Then these lesser mortals would flee in terror, abandoning their arms and stores.

These tactics were outdated. The Jap attacking company dropped back on its heels and dug in under the noses of the Dogras. When light came their position was not enviable. After severe mortaring they decided to make a get-away across the open paddy fields, but they were met by concentrated fire from the tanks, which had come round behind them, and it is doubtful if there were more than two or three survivors. This was the first and last time that the Japs ventured into the open in the IMPHAL PLAIN—it had been a very costly lesson.

The position which the Second Suffolk held was a high feature named the "MOUND"; a steep and rather bare mountain consisting of a large mound with a small pimple on its northern perimeter. "B" Company, under Major P. J. Hill, had constructed an elaborate system of defences, with communicating trenches, fire bays and dug in sleeping quarters. The company held the mound excluding the pimple, which lay some 100 yards outside the perimeter. Extensive belts of wire from 15 to 25 yards in depth surrounded the whole position and crossed the small saddle separating the mound from its neighbouring pimple.

The Battalion held the rest of the ground extending to the main road with "A" Company, Major Gordon Browne, behind the ridge in reserve responsible not only for its own protection; but for most of the Battalion long distance patrols. These patrols absorbed at least a third of the Company strength and went 12 to 15 miles into the very difficult country to the north East. This reserve company was also being continually called upon for strong fighting patrols closer to the front.

The approaches from the hills lying to the north and north-west were densely wooded and parties of Japs could approach close to the position unobserved. An attack on the "MOUND", dominating the road and the defile, was expected, and on April 9th without warning a Jap company attacked strongly from the direction of the pimple. They can have made no previous recce and were completely surprised by the thick belts of wire concealed in the grass. "B" Company's first warning was the sound of the Japs tumbling and tripping into the wire. They were immediately engaged by heavy fire from the Battalion Brens and the attack was broken. That night the Japs made several other attempts from other directions, only to meet the same fate, and in the morning a number of dead were picked up in the wire including an officer, whose magnificent sword was presented to the Commanding Officer, Lt.-Col. H. R. Hopking, O.B.E.

The Japs dug themselves in under the lee of the pimple and safe from our fire remained there for some days. In an unsuccessful attempt to drive them off Lt. T. W. Watt gained his M.C. carrying a badly wounded man to our lines under heavy fire. It was not until fire bombs, improvised with the aid of the Sappers from oil drums, were employed that the enemy was cleared from the neighbourhood of the pimple.

The Jap now tried, by probing the Battalion defences, to outflank the position from the north; to circumvent this the Battalion occupied and held against several small attacks the whole chain of hills running north from the "MOUND" position.

"A" Company with 2" mortars and two machines gun manned by Ghurka paratroops moved out on the night of 13/14 April to occupy one of these positions to the north. A pitch black night; and as the company moved off stray bullets whined overhead from the direction of Brigade H.Q. which a Japanese patrol was attacking. The Company carried food, ammunition and water for three days, the men being loaded up to about 80 lbs. apiece. Their objective was an unoccupied hill some 4 miles away and involving a climb up an almost perpendicular slope of about 1,500 feet. This slope was jungle covered, and the approach had to be made in single file.

The advance had started at midnight and by day light, 0530, the hill had been reached and occupied, though the heavy weight carried by the men proved a great strain and many had been on their hands and knees climbing. There the company consolidated.

"C" Company who had followed "A" Company pushed on with a flank attack on the Japanese who were still engaged with "B" Company on "MOUND", and in this attack were supported by the fire of "A" Company. But they failed to dislodge the enemy.

That night the Japanese from a position further north of "A" Company made an attack on "A" Company. There was a loud Bang as they exploded a booby-trap that had been laid, followed by wild yelling and shouting as the Japanese charged up the slope. They arrived just where they had been expected, and had a very warm reception. Shot and shell fell everywhere for a short space. Then silence and "A" Company heard the enemy dragging dead and wounded away. Only one grenade was thrown during the rest of the night—a tribute to the good state of the Company's nerves.

The next night was quiet; but there was another attack on the night following. During these fights the gunners were particularly good in the accurate fire support they gave, when ever it was needed.

Meanwhile another battalion of Japs out-flanked the positions and established themselves on the NUMSHIGUM feature, which lay between Second Suffolk and IMPHAL. This feature, from which the Japs had driven a company of an Indian battalion, was vital to the defence of IMPHAL and accordingly the 1/17th Dogras with tank support were ordered to retake it. They were completely successful; the tanks making history by climbing gradients which had hitherto been considered impracticable. In this action almost the whole Jap battalion was wiped out.

This battle was the turning point of the fight for IMPHAL. As the Japs swung to the defensive our troops took the offensive. The 123rd Indian brigade moved into the IRIL Valley in May 1944 and commenced to oust the enemy from the heights on either side. After a series of arduous and successful small scale operations to winkle out the small detachments of Japs in this mountain fastness, it was decided to dislodge the Japs from their main positions astride the main IMPHAL-KOHIMA Road.

One of the most successful of these minor operations was the raid on a mountain village, SABANG, by a fighting patrol from the Second Battalion Guerilla Platoon. During the night 7th May Captain D. Lee Hunter and 13 men from his Platoon set off into the mountains and next day had reached a position overlooking this village.

There was considerable enemy movement there and Lee Hunter manoeuvred his patrol so that by midnight they had reached the outskirts of the village of 20 native huts or "bashas". They were not challenged, so crept up to a "basha" where a light was seen. Inside were several sleeping figures wrapped in blankets on the floor; these were sprayed with tommy gun bullets and three hand grenades thrown in for good measure. The silence was changed into a wild din, the sound of a wooden clapper spreading the alarm. The patrol quickly withdrew and slipped quietly out of the village.

Next morning the patrol was divided into two groups—a Bren group to give covering fire for a raiding party into the village. A number of Japs were seen digging, and a party of over a dozen sitting round a board playing some kind of game. Both bren guns and a tommy gun were fired into the party at the board, who were all killed or wounded. The diggers ran off into the jungle. An enemy M.M.G. engaged the Bren group; but when its fire was returned it ceased. Then the covering patrol moved towards the enemy casualties; but this time came under heavy fire, one man being killed.

During this action the raiding party approached the village where they engaged eight Japs who scattered at once. The raiding party entered the village and ran through it, firing into the "bashas" as they went. A party of eight Japs ran out of one; but as soon as they were engaged with tommy guns, ran in again, leaving several casualties behind. The raiding party left the village and returned to their previous rendezvous. From here a party of five Japs under a Warrant Officer with binoculars was seen; when they came within point blank range fire was opened and all were killed. More Japs ran out and there was some wild firing during which the Guerillas withdrew to their rendezvous.

The Bren group not having returned, the original raiding party withdrew to the next rendezvous back, where they were joined in the evening by two of the Bren group, the remainder returning early the following morning. It was estimated as a result of this very successful raid that about 30 Japs were killed or wounded; our casualties being one man killed.

For this exploit, and for his outstanding leadership on many previous patrols, Capt. D. Lee Hunter was awarded the M.C.

During this period the Command of the Battalion changed, Major K. C. Menneer succeeding Lt.-Colonel H. R. Hopking, O.B.E. The importance

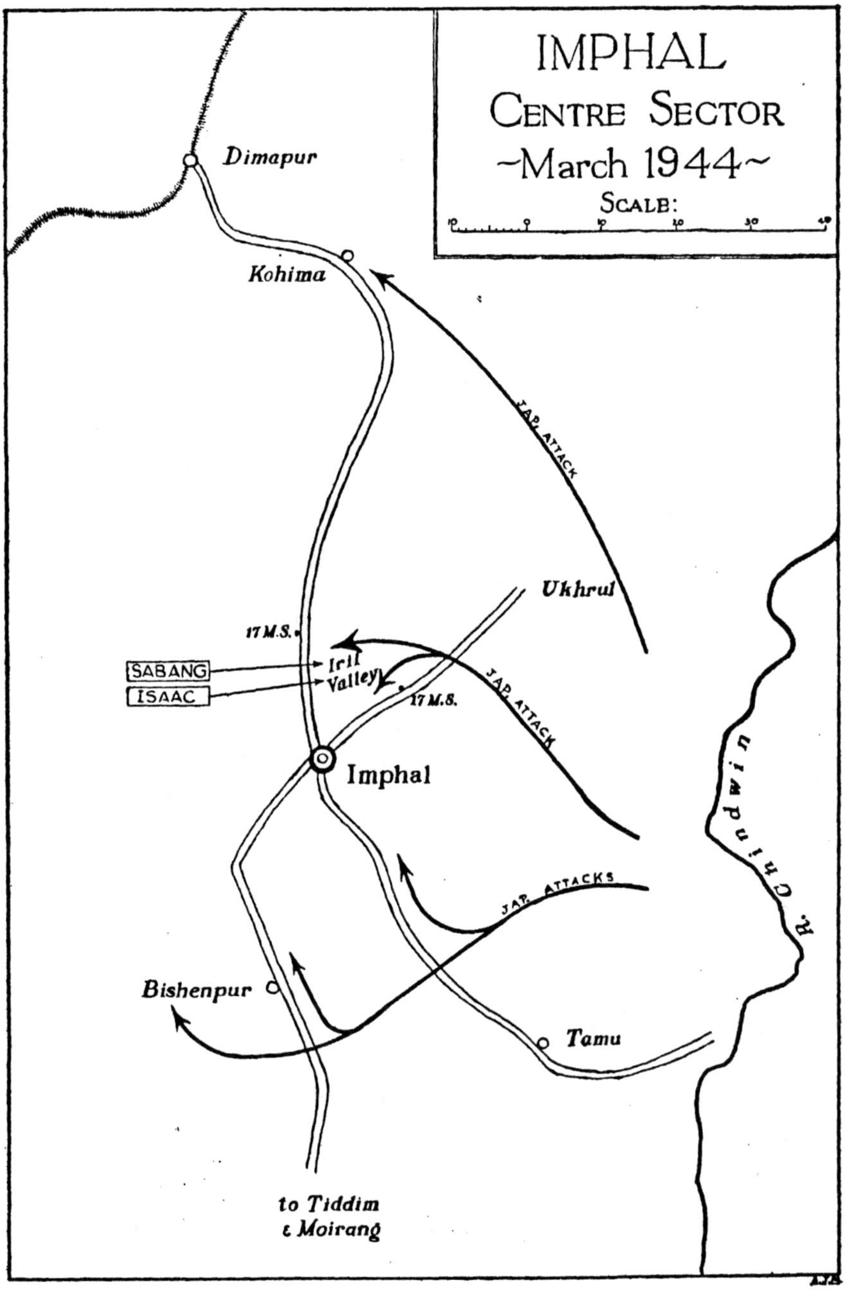
IMPHAL
CENTRE SECTOR
~March 1944~
SCALE:
Dimapur
Kohima
JAP. ATTACK
Ukhrul
17 M.S.
SABANG
ISAAC
Iril
Valley
17 M.S.
JAP. ATTACK
Imphal
R. Chindwin
JAP. ATTACKS
Bishenpur
Tamu
to Tiddim
& Moirang

THE IMPHAL—KOHIMA ROAD.

of this change and the circumstances require some explanation. Lt.-Colonel Hopking considered that insufficient time was given him to reconnoitre by patrols the enemy's positions which he had been ordered to attack, that in consequence men's lives were being needlessly lost. As a protest he asked to be relieved of the Command of the Battalion.

The only man who can decide how quickly an attack must be made and what time can be allowed for reconnaissance is the responsible Commander who orders it. It is no part of this History to suggest which was right in this instance; but the effect of this change in Command was of outstanding importance to the Battalion. Lt.-Colonel H. R. Hopking during the seven months that he had commanded had earned the affection and respect of all his officers and men. He had taken over the Command when the Battalion was in urgent need of training and administration and in the very short time available he had set it on its feet. He took it into battle and both his Brigade and Divisional Commander paid a tribute to his unfailing courage in action.

In early May, 1944, the Battalion was given a rest for 10 days. The Battalion had been in the front line since 20th December, 1943, and during these four months there had only been two days when it had been possible to dispense with a "Stand to".

About a quarter of its existing strength had joined during the last fortnight and there was a serious shortage of senior N.C.O.s; the last draft that the Battalion had received consisted of 170 men with only one Sgt. and two Cpls. Most important of all there was a deficiency of Platoon Officers, while preparations were made for a drive north along the KOHIMA Road. The operation entailed an encircling move through the thick jungle to seize the high ground covering the first defile north of IMPHAL and to establish a road block near the 17 M.S. on the IMPHAL-KOHIMA Road on a precipitous and jungle clad spur. A study of air photos of the area showed the terrain to be densely wooded with many cliffs and deep ravines. Officers' patrols were sent out to select a route, and an unused track was discovered which it was hoped would lead unseen to the objective, which had been called "PYRAMID."

In conjunction with this encircling movement, one of the first of a series of "left hook" operations which were to pay such handsome dividends in forcing the Japs out of their bunker positions, the 3/2nd Punjabis were to engage and harass the enemy astride the road.

This flanking move had to take place at night, as the first stages were across open paddy fields. The difficulties of maintaining contact in the dark throughout a long column are great, and it was decided to form a crocodile in single file, each man keeping close contact with his neighbour front and rear; the head of the crocodile being led by Intelligence personnel, who had "recced" the route. In addition, a route marking party was to set up a shaded lamp marking the entrance into the jungle from the paddy fields, and post guides to mark with white paper the jungle track. So, at dusk on May 12th, the mile long "caterpillar" started easing its way into the night.

Progress was inevitably slow and laborious, with many halts at nullahs, streams and other obstacles. By midnight all was going well; the Battalion had crossed the open into the jungle, the lamp and the guides serving their purpose, while in the thick jungle the danger of their tenuous thread being snapped by some prowling Jap patrol was much less, for although the noise of the moving column was considerable, the persistent insect throbbing made other sounds inaudible more than 25 yards distant. At pre-arranged times the whole column halted to rest and adjust loads. During one of these halts a loud crashing and thrashing of under-growth was heard, and men were seen running in all directions off the track. Then the disturbance as suddenly subsided; some wild cattle had been stirred and had charged through the column, knocking men right and left.

A lot of time was lost before the column could be reformed, for the seat of the trouble had centred among the coolies carrying food and ammunition. Then the column again advanced; progress was very slow, the country grew wilder, more rugged and difficult. The sky became overcast, the moon as it rose was shrouded in thick black clouds. Vivid flashes of lightning illuminated the wild scene as the head of the column felt its way across the rocks and boulders of the river bed and climbed the steep shoulder of the mountain on its far bank. The storm closed in and the column was blanketed in a deep shroud of blackness which from time to time was startlingly torn apart by the ever more frequent stabs of lightning. In the pitch blackness a halt was called; until the storm cleared it was impossible to see the path or track. So the Battalion was closed up into a rough box on the shoulder of the mountain and there awaited the passing of the storm or the coming of the day. The rain lashed down with a great pelting and roaring, soaking everyone.

The first light of dawn enabled the column to wind forward again; but far behind the time schedule, only half the distance having been traversed. With daylight, wet and tired, a good speed was set; by ten o'clock the guide thought they were close to their objective. It was decided to halt and form a defensive box. In broad daylight the straggling formation was not in a state to move against a vital feature which quite possibly was defended by the Japs.

In a defensive position the Battalion tucked in its tail and remained hidden. But uncertain as to its exact location.

The next day the leading company "A" moved off early; but quickly ran into an unreconnoitred Japanese position and was held up. Patrols were pushed out and by nightfall their own location had been determined; the Battalion meanwhile returning to their last night's camp.

Orders were received from the Brigade to push forward to the main road at M.S. 17 and at the same time seize "PYRAMID". Caterpillar formation was again formed, this time in light fighting order with fewer porters. The going was slow and difficult across a deep precipitous ravine with very steep cliffs; the country was wild and rugged and it was not until the late afternoon that the Battalion reached the adjacent feature to their objective, it was hoped unseen by the enemy. Unfortunately their approach had been observed.

An attack was staged. After scanty reconnaissance and without supporting fire the Battalion walked straight into unknown trouble and suffered heavy casualties.

As "B" Company, under Major P. J. Hill, which was in advance was seen by the enemy advancing on "PYRAMID" a few shots rang out followed by long bursts of LMG and then MMG.

The leading platoon of "B" Company had reached "PYRAMID", and was inside the Japanese defences, pinned to the ground. This leading unit was in a trap anchored by cross-fire of automatic. The commander, Lieut. C. W. Stephens, was killed, and his platoon suffered many casualties.

Meanwhile "B" Company was badly placed; parties of Japs endeavouring to get between them and the remainder of the battalion. This enemy encircling move was nipped in the bud by "C" Company from an adjoining ridge where they were able to shoot down the Japs who had climbed up in the trees in the nullah between the two companies.

"B" Company was ordered to withdraw after evacuating their casualties; a tricky manoeuvre; but successfully completed. "A" Company was also withdrawn, both companies passing through a defensive screen formed by "C" Company and "D" Company. During this withdrawal Captain D. R. Anslow, commanding "D" Company, was shot through the head by a Japanese sniper and instantly killed.

The situation this late afternoon was not easy. The Battalion was many miles—jungle miles—forward of their own troops and had a number of wounded. Rations and ammunition were limited. With "C" Company as their rear guard, they moved back to the south side of the ravine which they had crossed early that morning. With the burden of wounded men retirement was painfully slow and laborious; but the Japs made no serious attempt to follow. Thence the Battalion was ordered to Mile Stone 16, establishing themselves there, while the Dogras operated further north beyond the "PYRAMID" defile, which the Japanese evacuated soon after their positions had been pin-pointed and subjected to artillery fire. This was the only occasion on which all casualties were not successfully evacuated.

"ISAAC"

JUNE, 1944.

By the end of May the Monsoon had broken. Fortunately during the advance the Battalion had overrun an abandoned Allied Ordnance dump and had reclothed themselves. They had also salvaged a considerable quantity of canvas tarpaulins; but in spite of this, conditions were becoming increasingly bad and the strain was felt by all. Soaking rain, hard work, poor rations were pushing the sick rate up to a high percentage. For days on end there was no fresh food, not even potatoes; only bully beef and biscuits. Fit men were always hungry; sick men couldn't stomach the food. A large number of the men had chronic diarrhoea.

This sick rate had become a matter of real anxiety. Many men had to be evacuated, and the strength of companies was much reduced; a high proportion of those remaining were unfit and under normal circumstances would have been sent to hospital. Daily changes were taking place in the Battalion strength. It will be remembered that the First Battalion before the battles of OVERLOON—VENRAY had received many drafts from other Divisions and even gunners who had no previous service in Infantry. The changes in the Second Battalion were even more drastic; besides the losses due to casualties there was a constant flow on repatriation to the United

Kingdom. Officers and Senior N.C.O.s whose service and experience were invaluable served all too short a time with the Battalion, while the reinforcements of all ranks that flowed in came from strange units often without the essential training in jungle warfare.

Everything, in comparison, favoured the First Battalion; they had a solid core in the quality of their leaders, and could absorb all who came. The First Battalion physique remained magnificent, whereas sickness had greatly undermined the strength of the Second Battalion. There was no reserve in India of tried, experienced officers to fill the senior gaps. The Second Battalion entered the next phase of the Burma Campaign very heavily handicapped.

Meanwhile the Monsoon came down in all its fury; tracks that had been inches deep in dust, became mud, slush and waterways. Digging was an impossibility, for holes became sump pits; it was only the thickness of the jungle that afforded cover from the enemy as well as the weather.

The difficulties of supply to the many sub units into which the Battalion was split became a major problem, gallantly tackled by the men behind. Throughout the operation at IMPHAL and until the main road was finally opened, supplies had come by air, going forward by mule from the Battalion base. The men in front owed much to those who brought the loaded mules forward through the thick jungle and teeming rain, starting at daybreak and barely getting back to camp till night fell. They owed much to the mules, those indispensable animals who will not do what they do not want to do. It is essential to get the right side of a mule's mentality; as every mule leader knows. Neither did the Acting Quartermaster, Sgt. Cropley, or the Battalion cooks fail in those hard days; many a cow, a pig or water buffalo that "might have slipped on a land mine" helped to swell and vary the rations.

The Japanese attack on the Centre Sector about IMPHAL-KOHAT had failed. But he still occupied the strong positions which he had fortified along the high ridges running East of the KOHIMA-IMPHAL Road. It was courting an overwhelming disaster for the enemy to remain there, for his communications were vulnerable from the air. It was well for the allies that he did so, for his armies were eventually annihilated.

At one point on this Japanese line was a dominating feature which had been named "ISAAC." Early in June the Second Battalion was directed against it, and the fighting to take this position proved the biggest operation of the Battalion during the Campaign.

On the 31st May the 4/8th Gurkhas had overrun and captured a Japanese platoon in a bunker position on hills named "HARRY" and "TWIN PIMPLES". The Gurkhas had endeavoured to exploit this success on to "ISAAC" without success.

The Second Battalion was ordered to relieve the 4/8th Gurkhas on the 2nd June and destroy the Japanese on the "ISAAC" feature and then exploit north. The sketch maps give a panoramic view of "ISAAC" from "HARRY" and show in detail the entrenchments held by the Japanese.

The immediate necessity was to gain the fullest information of the Japanese strength and disposition; to locate his bunkers, to discover what guns he had, to study his habits, and find his communications. An "O.P." was established on "HARRY" and at night listening posts were pushed forward on to the "TWIN PIMPLES", while for the next four days fighting patrols

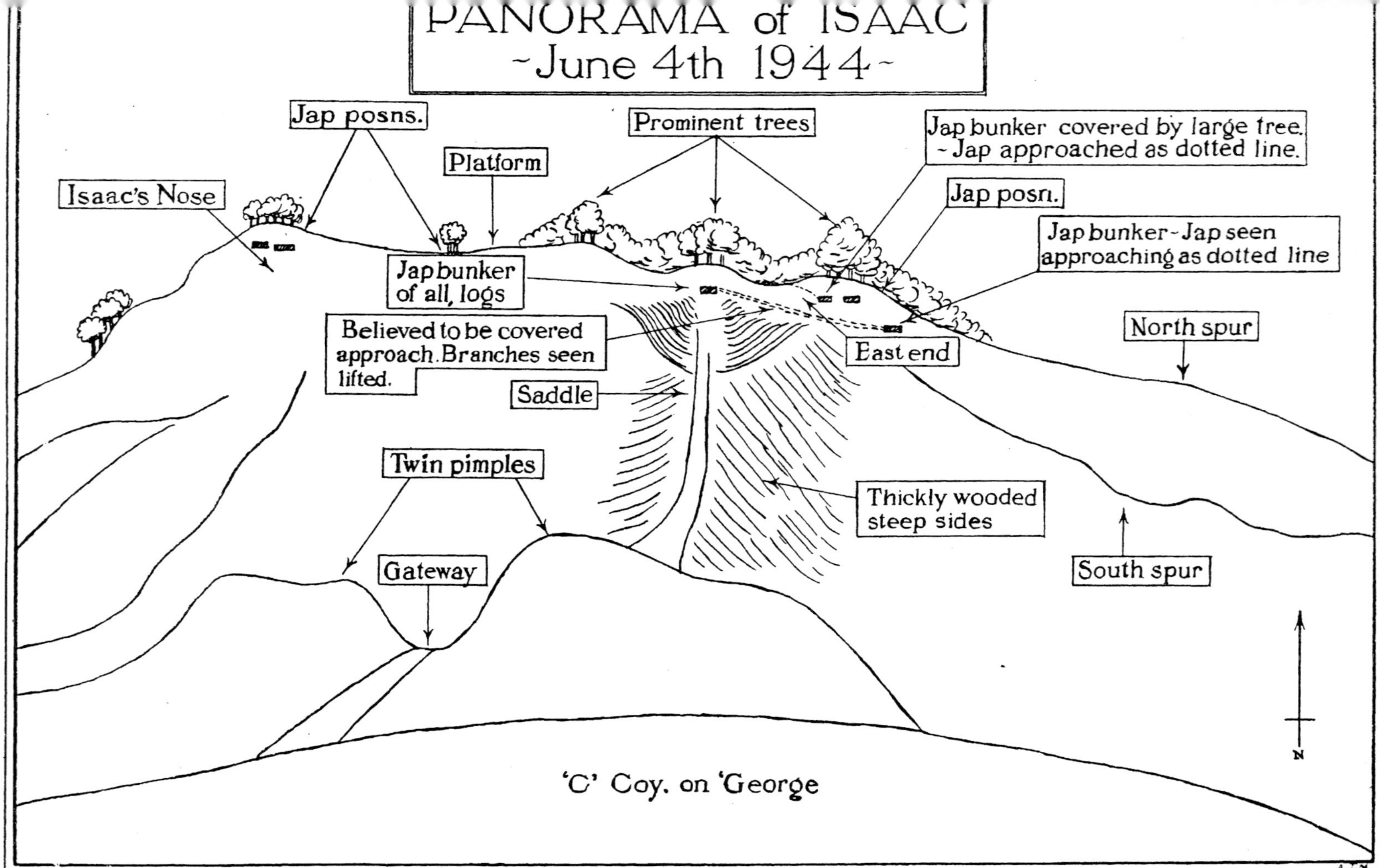
PANORAMA of ISAAC
~June 4th 1944~
Jap posns.
Platform
Isaac's Nose
Prominent trees
Jap bunker covered by large tree.
~ Jap approached as dotted line.
Jap posn.
Jap bunker ~ Jap seen
approaching as dotted line
Jap bunker
of all logs
Believed to be covered
approach. Branches seen
lifted.
East end
North spur
Saddle
Twin pimples
Thickly wooded
steep sides
Gateway
South spur
N
'C' Coy. on 'George

were probing. During this time every endeavour was made to find routes and to bring forward the four supporting tanks of the 3rd D. G.s. While on the 5th and 6th June, after a magnificent piece of work, a 6 pdr. Anti-tank gun was hauled into position on "HARRY" from which it fired with great effect. Co-operation between infantry and tanks in this most precipitous country was invaluable and extraordinarily difficult. An attack must progressively advance; but at times the infantry would forge ahead while their armoured support was held up by impenetrable obstacles; on other occasions the exhausted infantry would find it temporarily impossible to keep up with their collaborators. The fighting during the three day and night attacks on "ISAAC" showed how gallantly and doggedly each endeavoured to do their task.

On June 3rd a sniper on "HARRY" killed a Japanese on "ISAAC." Bunker positions on "EAST END," "PLATFORM" and "ISAAC'S NOSE" were pinpointed. These bunkers were a few feet below the crest, made of logs covered with turf and dead branches and the loopholes were clearly visible. Two fighting patrols moved out to the East of "ISAAC" without locating any enemy. On June 4th a reconnaissance patrol was sent to find a suitable "forming up place" to the East of "EAST END"; but reported that the country was too difficult and that the attacking troops would not be sufficiently fresh to assault up the steep slope to "EAST END." Another patrol moved from "SOUTH SPUR" to "NORTH SPUR" and killed two Japanese on the reverse slope.

On June 5th two patrols went out; one of these tried to view the reserve slopes of "ISAAC", but were prevented by the thick jungle; the other which stayed out all night below the crest of "CENTRE BUMP" confirmed the occupation of "ISAAC'S NOSE" and "CENTRE BUMP." It was on this night that the 6 pdr. of 221 Anti Tank Battery was hauled by teams of 30 men half way up one of the Spurs in rear to the perimeter camp of "B" Company.

During the same afternoon the four 3rd D.G. Tanks attempted to move up on to "HARRY." They did not succeed; one of the tanks being lost over the Khudside, the other three harbouring further down in the Battalion H.Q. area.

On June 6th a patrol east of the "SADDLE" found a better route to a "forming up place" under "EAST END". It was estimated that the assaulting troops could be in a position there and ready to assault within fifty minutes of leaving "HARRY." A Medium Shoot on "ISAAC'S NOSE" knocked out one Bunker. During this day the 6 pdr. Anti Tank gun was brought into position on "HARRY" while the work was continued of getting the tanks forward. They finally reached "HARRY" by 0800 hours on June 7th.

On June 7th at 0830 Battalion Tactical H.Q. moved up to "HARRY," while "C" Company (less one Platoon) under Major P. B. Forrest moved from "HARRY" to the Forming up place.

At 0930 the leading tank moved out along "SADDLE" closely supported by the remaining platoon of "C" Company and accompanied by a mine clearing detachment. No opposition was met until the leading tank reached the junction of "SADDLE" and "ISAAC," but at this point the Japs opened up with MMG and LMG from forward positions on "EAST END" and from a Bunker on "PLATFORM."

The mist had now cleared sufficiently to enable the anti-tank gun to fire on "ISAAC." The shooting was accurate and effective and all the known bunkers were quickly neutralised. Two MMGs in area "TWIN PIMPLES" and two on "HARRY" were also firing to good effect according to the Time Programme.

The leading tank continued to climb the slope to "EAST END" blasting out bunkers with 75 mm shells, and silencing, with Browning fire, positions covering the line of advance; the infantry meanwhile working forward with great spirit towards the crest.

As the leading tank climbed the final steep slope up to the right mound of "EAST END" it ran against an anti-tank ditch, a 3ft. step in the side of the slope. In spite of many attempts the tank was unable to negotiate this obstacle; nor could it engage the positions behind the large bunker, covering the top of the ditch, which had already been knocked out.

Meanwhile the infantry had worked forward of the tank and the leading section, accompanied by the Company Commander Major Forrest and Lt. Yonge, got into position behind the knocked out bunker.

While this was going on, the platoon on the right had reached the top. L/Cpl. Shanks, working with great dash, knocked out one bunker by throwing a grenade inside; but was unable to make any further progress.

Heavy automatic fire from the left front was now directed on the leading sections of "C" Company, and the Japs realising that the tanks were in difficulties threw over hand grenades and grenade discharger bombs, causing serious casualties. Lt. Yonge was killed by a burst of LMG fire. The leading men dropped back behind the crest to shelter from this fire.

The situation at this time was a platoon well up on the right and another platoon well up on the left, the whole of the basin area between them being protected from small arms fire. In these circumstances the sappers were called forward to build a track up the re-entrant between these right and left mounds comprising "EAST END."

While this work was in progress the second tank attempted to get to the right of the anti-tank ditch—but came up against a tree which it could not knock over and dropped back into the basin.

The sappers made good progress, cutting down large sized trees to afford a grip for the tracks. As the track was carried forward under the noses of the Japs on the crest, the sappers themselves came under fire and lost one killed and two wounded.

"C" Company being unable to advance until the tanks could co-operate, a platoon of "A" Company under Lt. Tomkinson was sent forward to work round to the left on to the crest between "EAST END" and "PLATFORM." This platoon succeeded in linking up with the remaining platoon of "C" Company under Lt. Haygarth and together they reached the crest. Here they came under MMG fire from "ISAAC'S NOSE." Lt. Haygarth was wounded and his platoon had many casualties. "A" Company platoon was withdrawn to the Company in "SADDLE" area.

The tank track was reported ready about 1600 hours and the third tank made several attempts to move forward; but owing to a faulty engine was unable to progress. By this time, 1700 hours, it was decided that no more could be done that day. "C" Company was ordered to hold and consolidate their positions covering the basin. One platoon of "D" Company had been sent forward to assist in this task as "C" Company had been

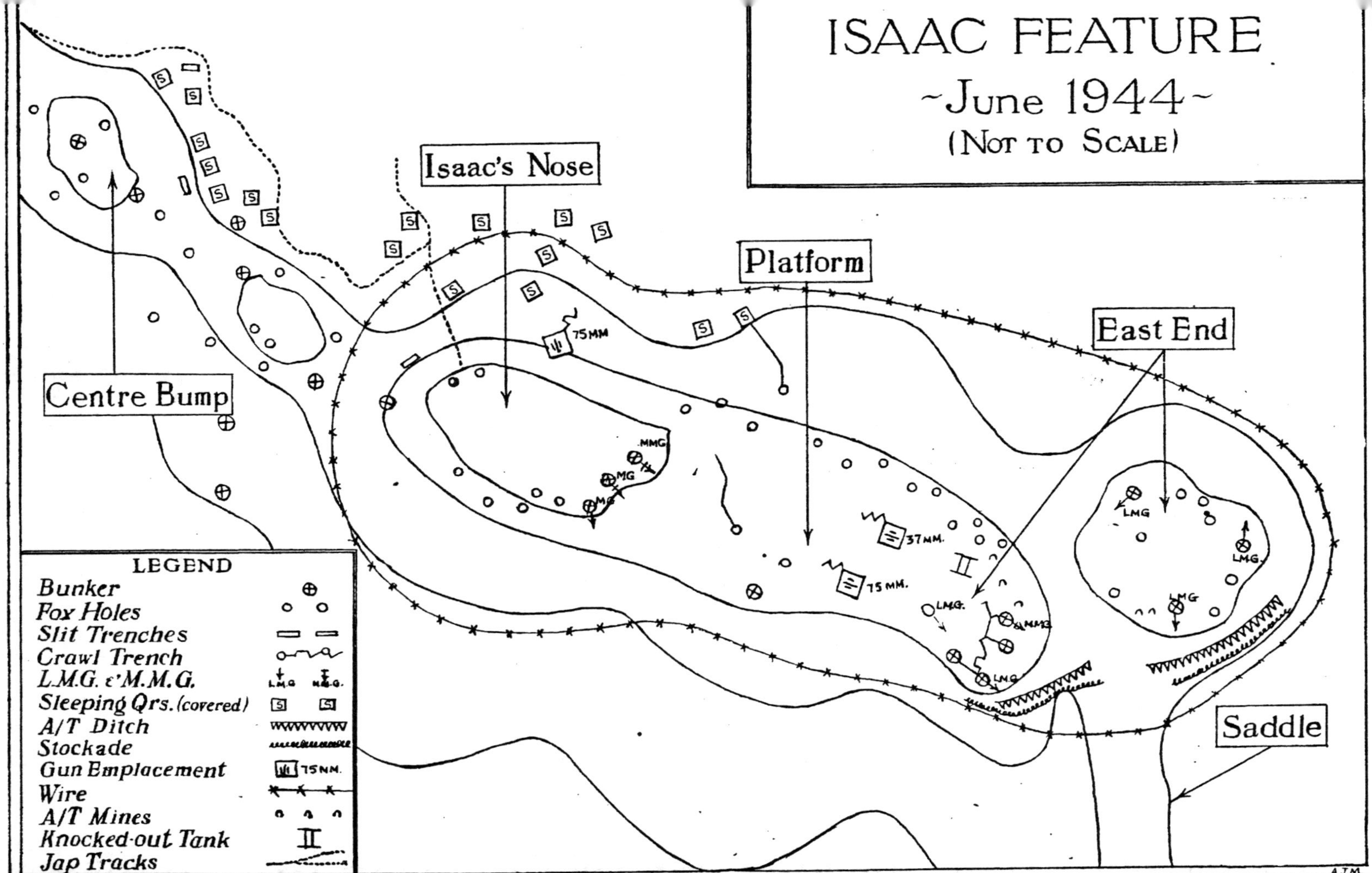
ISAAC FEATURE
~June 1944~
(Not to Scale)
Isaac's Nose
Platform
East End
Centre Bump
Saddle
75MM
MMG
MG
MG
37MM.
75 MM.
LMG.
MMG
LMG
LMG
LMG
LMG.
LMG
A.J.M.
LEGEND
Bunker
Fox Holes
Slit Trenches
Crawl Trench
L.M.G. & M.M.G.
L.M.G.
M.M.G.
Sleeping Qrs. (covered)
A/T Ditch
Stockade
Gun Emplacement
75MM.
Wire
A/T Mines
Knocked-out Tank
Jap Tracks

seriously depleted. Casualties were Lt. Yonge and eight men killed and 27 men evacuated wounded. The fighting strength of "C" Company was little more than 40, with the Company Commander slightly wounded in the leg.

"A" Company in the "SADDLE" area was ordered to relieve "C" Company in the positions gained. This relief was completed by 1800 hours and "C" Company moved back to "GEORGE," behind "HARRY" where a well deserved hot meal was awaiting them.

"A" Company at once got to work to improve and dig positions; tools and wire were on the tanks and by nightfall the Company was dug in and wired. During the night both Japs and ourselves were hard at work, the Japs being heard digging and chopping wood. Harassing fire was brought down on many occasions during the night; but it was doubtful if it had much effect, as each time the flash of the gun was seen or the pop of a mortar was heard the Japs shouted out a warning to take cover. On our side of the hill the sappers were improving the track on the new alignment. Logs were cut in the "HARRY" area and these were carried forward and placed in position. By morning the track was completed.

An airstrike on "PLATFORM" and "ISAAC'S NOSE," to be indicated by mortar smoke, was arranged for 1100 hours and at this time "A" Company was to assault and capture the "EAST END" positions with tanks. But the Japs fired smoke into the area occupied by our troops, and the air strike was cancelled.

"A" Company's attack went in as arranged, the leading tank moving up the new track without difficulty. As it had surmounted the steepest and most difficult part of the new track and started working up along the crest it was met by a volley of small arms fire. When it came well on to the crest of the left mound a large cloud of white smoke and phosphorous was seen to burst on its tail and a heavy explosion was heard. The tank immediately stopped, began smoking and was seen to be on fire. Three of the crew baled out, the remainder were killed inside the tank or while attempting to get out, including Lt. Cole, the troop Commander. A 75 mm in a gun pit on the reverse slope had got a direct hit on the tank at point blank range. At the time the tank was some 20 yards ahead, having outpaced the accompanying infantry.

"A" Company, Major Gordon Browne, attacked again that afternoon; but on reaching the crest between "EAST END" and "PLATFORM" the Company came under heavy fire from MMG and grenades from positions on the reverse slopes. The Company withdrew below the crest and consolidated on the further ground gained.

"D" Company in the area "TWIN PIMPLES," with one platoon in the area of "A" Company H.Q. on the "SADDLE" was ordered to take over the forward positions of "A" Company. "A" Company to remain in the "SADDLE" area. This relief was completed by 1800 hours. "D" Company was ordered to continue pressing throughout the night to get a footing on the crest of "EAST END" now that the position of certain fox-holes covering the crest between "EAST END" and "PLATFORM" had been located.

Fighting patrols from "D" Company went forward. One of these from the right of "EAST END" found the Japanese evacuating their positions. A number were shot as they got away, some falling over the khud. "EAST END" was quickly cleared and "D" Company were then ordered to continue West towards "ISAAC'S NOSE."

This success on the right had been sufficient, in conjunction with the previous heavy fighting, to turn the scale, and by first light on June 9th the Jap were seen evacuating their positions. "EAST END" was quickly cleared and then "D" Company continued West to "ISAAC's NOSE." The enemy evacuation of this latter feature was orderly; but his position on "EAST END" had been hastily abandoned and large quantities of equipment were left behind. It was estimated that he lost 51 killed; our casualties were 14 killed, 45 wounded.

Thus after three days' fighting the operation against this vital feature was crowned with success.

The Divisional Commander's congratulatory message read:

"Your success was due to your determination to succeed."

The Japanese position on "ISAAC" had been extremely strong. Many bunkers on the South slope had been effectively destroyed by our supporting fire; but many more on the crest and slightly below and beyond the crest line were untouched. All were inter-supporting, and even the one man fox-holes were linked up with the main defences. The enemy had paid great attention to camouflage, with the result that many of his defences were unlocated and caused us heavy casualties.

So brief an account as the foregoing can give little idea of the skill and courage that gained success at such comparatively little cost unless the conditions of this BURMA fighting are understood. The immensely difficult country put the highest possible tax on the endurance of every man before he had even got in touch with his enemy. Each section, platoon or patrol had to work independently, the value of the whole depending on each individual effort. How well these parties fought would require a fuller account than is possible here. The tank that falls over the Khud side, the tank that breasts the rise and is knocked out, the patrol of "D" Company that establishes itself on the right flank, the endurance and gallantry of Lance Cpl. Shanks, who, on the first day of the attack, bombed and destroyed an enemy bunker under heavy fire, are examples of these vital factors. The gallantry and skill with which "B" Company was commanded by Major Forrest merited high praise; he deservedly gained the [illegible].

Among the booty captured on "ISAAC" was a Japanese flag, now a Second Battalion trophy. The days have long since gone when "Colours" were carried in action. They were the rallying point of every battle in the past; but the spirit they inspired still lives on in the field today. The Pennant that led the tanks of the 142nd Regt, once the 7th Suffolk, is enshrined at the Regimental Depot in Bury St. Edmunds. The Churchill tanks of this unit bore the names of our Battle Honours. The Maple Leaf, the emblem of the Canadian Army, was added at their request as a special distinction. Each of the Carriers of the First Suffolk on "D" Day commemorated a Suffolk Battle.

After the capture and consolidation of "ISAAC" other battalions from the Brigade continued to clear the ridge northwards, as part of the operations for opening the MANIPUR road.

The monsoons were now at their height, and with the whole battalion on the east side of the MANIPUR River, the problem of supply over the temporary mule suspension bridge became very difficult. Mule convoys could

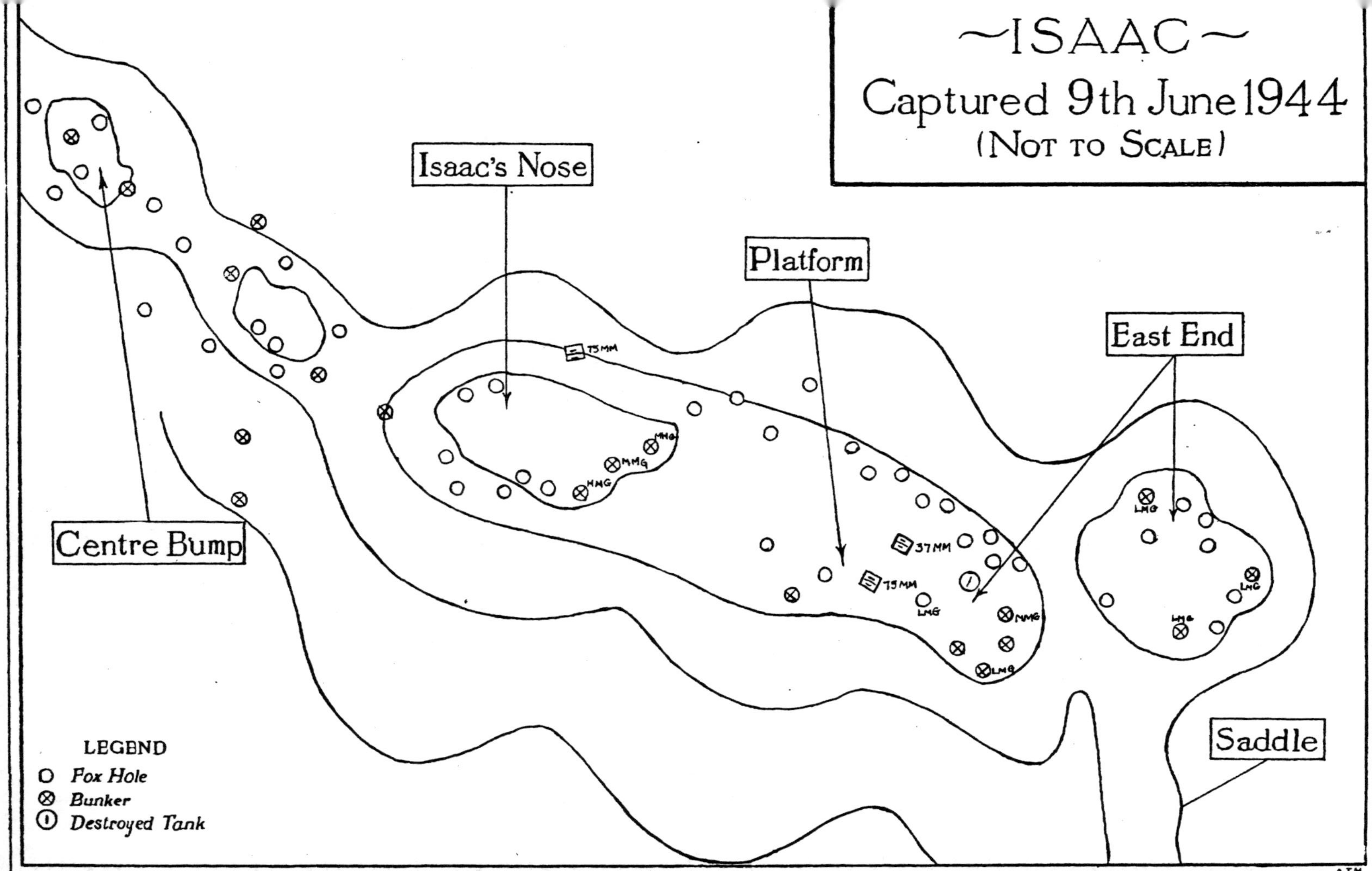
~ISAAC~
Captured 9th June 1944
(NOT TO SCALE)
Isaac's Nose
Platform
East End
Centre Bump
Saddle
75MM
37MM
75MM
MMG
MMG
MMG
LMG
MMG
LMG
LMG
LMG
LMG
LEGEND
Fox Hole
Bunker
Destroyed Tank
A.J.M.

scarcely negotiate the slippery mountain tracks which were frequently impassable for days. The river was rising rapidly and as the operations had been brought to a successful conclusion the Battalion was ordered to return over the river. Most of the heavy mortar and signal equipment, heavy stores and reserve ammunition was ferried across, the suspension bridge being appreciably submerged and shortly after being swept away. The rain had set in hard; no mules could make the journey to the companies on the hills, and the exhausted, bedraggled men, plastered in mud, had to man-handle their kit and stores to the river bank where they were ferried across on an improvised cable trolley.

The Second Suffolk was in reserve when, towards the end of June, the final move to clear the road by a wide outflanking move was made. Once again the Battalion formed a long "caterpillar" for the trek through the jungle foothills. Once again they found themselves on the spur of the foothills overlooking the road; on the 22nd June they were able to watch the tanks of the 2nd Division clearing up the final obstacles, while the Dogras were descending from the West. All felt the surge and thrill of this scene and a sense of personal pride, not unmixed with relief, that the siege of IMPHAL had been concluded.

The Brigade consolidated in a deserted basha camp near the road and began to make itself comfortable. The Battalion, in spite of the continuing heavy rain, had been allocated a good area where every man could be accommodated in the dry.

* * * * * *

END OF THE CAMPAIGN.

The rest was of short duration. Captured operation orders showed that the Japanese had been reinforced and were preparing to launch a new attack for IMPHAL from the South. The Second Suffolk was despatched from the North of IMPHAL to the South to counter the enemy threat to the rear of the 7th Division.

A position half way between BISHENPUR and IMPHAL was occupied and consolidated; wide ranging patrols were pushed out; but by the time the rest of the Brigade had followed the Battalion it was realised that the Japanese plan had been no more than wishful thinking.

It was July and the time was ripe to drive the Japanese right out of the IMPHAL Plain. The Battalion assisted in this operation by occupying features in the hills south of the SILCHAR track in the rear of Japanese positions, helping to convince the enemy that the game was up. It fell to them to start the chase of the enemy out of the IMPHAL Plain and down to TIDDIM and beyond 25 miles down the road to the village of MOIRANG.

Heaped on the roadsides and in the villages were abandoned ammunition dumps, equipment, rifles and all the impedimenta of war. Great quantities of these stores were in good and new condition and all had been hastily abandoned. Near the village of MOIRANG the Battalion had their last brush with the enemy. "D" Company, commanded by Major K. E. J. Henderson, entered the north end of the village during the afternoon and one of his patrols brushed a party of 10 to 20 Japanese who attempted to get into a position. After several of the Japs had been seen to fall a two inch mortar was directed on them, and a fighting patrol went out to finish them off. During the night the remaining Japs attempted to slip out and rejoin their comrades, but walked into "B" Company; only two escaped.

While Minden Day, 1944, was being celebrated by the First Battalion in a Normandy village from which the men were hurriedly recalled to action and went with Normandy Roses in their hats; it was held by the Second Battalion on a number of separate peaks in the forest clad hills of BURMA where they also wore red and yellow roses. Here some were visited by the Corps Commander, Lt.-General Sir Montagu Stopford, the Divisional and the Brigade Commanders.

Here is "B" Company's menu to prove that conditions were looking up!

06.45 Gunfire.

08.00 Breakfast. Porridge, sausages, bacon, beans, fried bread, butter, marmalade, tea.

13.00 Lunch. Cheese fritters, pickles, baked rice pudding, tea.

17.00 Supper. Roast N.Z. lamb, baked potatoes, onions. Peach and pineapple pie. Bread, butter, tea. BEER.

No one could say that the Quarter Master and his staff had not done their share. But above all how magnificently the Air Force had performed. The purr of the engines of transport planes had become the permanent background to life in Burma. Two or three times a day the Dakotas would circle round, dropping supplies and ammunition by parachute—or where possible coming down on the landing strips. The skill and courage of the young pilots was above all praise, maintaining this supply even through the Monsoon, previously believed impossible.

These planes had enabled all our forward operations to be maintained. During the rains the troops had to carry a minimum of three days' rations, being put on to half rations when this minimum was reached; yet the longest period during which no supplies could be flown was only five days, while the 'dropping' became increasingly accurate; so that it was said that "P for Peter" could drop the manifest on to the office table.

Conditions during these last stages of the fighting beyond IMPHAL proved better for the Second Battalion. The main road as L of C meant the provision of all natures of ammunition with which to pound the enemy positions; drugs were got up for the sick; some fruit, vegetables and eggs could be purchased locally. But the area was excessively wet, leeches were all too plentiful, and the mosquitoes were unique—they could bite through almost any clothing and under favourable conditions up to ten would be biting at the same time. Fortunately they were not malarial.

But the long spell was telling on the men. Hospital admissions were up to 60 or 70 a week, mostly general debility and some with Malaria, Dysentery and Scrub Typhus. At one time there were only six fighting officers with the Battalion and two rifle companies of 80 men each in place of four of 130 each.

At the end of August the Battalion was withdrawn from General Reserve to a rest area in IMPHAL, its strength then being 7 officers, 350 other ranks.

Although the Battalion was to go forward again on the L of C it was to see no more fighting.

The casualties from 1st November 1943 until 17th August 1944 had been:—

	Killed in action	Wounded in action	Reported Missing	Evacuated to Hosp.	Returned from Hosp.	Total New Drafts.
Maj. ...	2	2		3	1	2
Capt. ...	1	1		4	3	3
Lt. ...	1	8		8	9	9
2/Lt. ...	2	2				8
C.S.M. ...				2		2
C/Sgt. ...				2		3
Sgt. ...	3	4	1	37	18	1
Cpl. ...	2	14	1	103	73	12
L/Cpl. ...	2	12		80		
Pte. ...	65	106	7	1,360	1,069	556
Total Officers	6	13		15	13	22
Total O.Rs.	72	136	9	1,584	1,160	590

Killed, Wounded & Missing: Officers 19. O.Rs. 217.
Not returned from Hospital; Officers 13. O.Rs. 424.
The Officer casualties were:—
Killed:—
Major P. E. V. RICHARDS Killed on "BAMBOO."
Major D. R. GRAY Killed on "BAMBOO."
Capt. D. R. ANSLOW Killed on "PYRAMID."
Lieut. M. J. J. YONGE Killed on "ISAAC."
2/Lieut. C. W. STEPHENS Killed on "PYRAMID."
Wounded:—
Major P. J. HILL On "PYRAMID."
Major K. E. J. HENDERSON In MOIRANG.
Capt. G. A. MITCHISON On "BAMBOO."
Lieuts.: INMAN, DUNCAN, LAWRENCE, GLOVER, HASTIE, HAYGARTH, TOMKINSON, GILBERT.

Christmas was spent in the IMPHAL area; but with the new year of 1945 a forward move was made as Line of Communication troops. Very weak in numbers, little could be given them to do. The Battalion was first at KALEWA on the CHINDWIN RIVER and then moved forward to SHEWBO, a few miles West of the IRRAWADDY. From this neighbourhood, in March 1945, the Battalion was flown out of the operational area, back into INDIA to LAHORE.

An Officers' Mess reflects the qualities of the outstanding members; it may change in character many times during a war. But a Sergeants' Mess in an Infantry Regiment is a constant factor, changing scarcely at all in peace or war; built as it is on Regimental tradition. This was peculiarly true of the Second Battalion; there was a constant change in the personnel, many newcomers from other Regiments, yet the spirit was always "SUFFOLK."

The Regimental Sergeant Major C. Jasper, writing to me from BURMA, said:—

"At the present moment I'm afraid that many of the men of this Battalion are far from 'Suffolk' in respect of birth; but all are working as we have always done, as one happy family, and the newcomers are quick to take to the ways of the old time 'Suffolk'; which as you I'm sure are well aware, has a peculiarity of its own."

There were many who should be enumerated; some whose names constantly recur in the stories of the Campaign. One such is Sgt. Harry Cropley, the Sgt. Cook. Even the Americans spoke of the Sgt. Master Cook as "a great guy."

There was an occasion when the Sergeants' Mess was in happy proximity to a canal with a local atmosphere of mango trees and water buffaloes. A small family of monkeys attached themselves to the Mess, and to Sgt. Harry Cropley in particular—no doubt with an eye to the main chance. They lived in one of the mango trees over his Messing Store and to get a better view of the Master Cook and his methods they pulled the tiles off his bunk for four days in succession. It may be that this perfidy on the part of an "honorary member" decided the Sgt. Cook to take a short leave of absence—the first he had had for eighteen years. Surely a Regimental Record.

Here are the names of some of the Senior N.C.O.s in the Second Suffolk who for a long or short time did their share; C.S.M.s "Nobby" Clark, Aldous, and Kingston, Gardiner, Day, Shanks, Allum, Randall, "Stan" Winter, "Tommy" Warren, "Paddy" Duffy, "Titch" Bunce, "Busty" Byam, Chapman, Bembridge, Mortlock, Sorrell, Hunter, "Freddy" Peck, "Whistler" Pryke, "Tim" Mead, "Spud" Turner, Nice, Jarrold, Alder, Ward, Branch, "Kate" Kerridge, Gilbert Garnham, Isaacson, Revell, Durrant, "Peter" Brown—their name is legion, all members of that infinitely valuable Sergeants' Mess, some mounting from Corporal's rank, some arriving from the U.K., some returning from leave or employment elsewhere. The miracle was:—the ceaseless change of personnel, the unchanging quality. To recount the merits of anyone is to describe them all; an unvarying loyalty to the Regiment, an inexhaustible sense of humour, bound up in the best qualities of wartime brothers in arms.

C.S.M. Crandall, rejoining the Second Battalion in BURMA, from the Lincolns, writes:—"There's nothing like being at home with all the old faces" and then he adds:—"It's hard for one to write long letters as there is nothing much happening these days!"

Neither must those who gallantly lost their lives in action such as Sgt. Brown, M.M., Sgt. J. E. Bates, Sgt. D. F. A. Steele and Cpl. E. Long be forgotten.

With peace in 1945 the Battalion was once again back in LAHORE and with peace the Command of the Battalion changed from Lt. Col. K. C. Menneer to Major H. W. Dean, who had started the war as Adjutant of the Second Battalion. The Regiment owes a debt to Menneer of the 4th Suffolk. He learnt his wartime soldiering with the First Battalion, returning from DUNKIRK with them, and serving under Lt. Col. F. A. Milnes at home. Then for a short time he was Second in Command to Lt. Colonel Victor Oborne and to Lt. Colonel R. E. Goodwin. He succeeded Lt. Colonel H. R. Hopking, O.B.E., in BURMA and during the War he was probably longer with the Second Battalion than any other officer. The continuous changes that took place in the Battalion can be judged when it is said that when Lt. Colonel H. W. Dean took over there were but four men:—R.S.M. Jasper, R.Q.M.S. Isaacson,

Sgt. Cropley and Bandsman Serle, still serving with the Battalion who had been there when he was Adjutant at RAZMAK.

The War against Japan ended with the complete surrender of the enemy. The Second Battalion Suffolk Regiment had done their full share in the BURMA Campaign—itself no small contribution to this final downfall. British Infantry had once again proved their worth, no matter where called upon to fight. To quote the words of the Commander-in-Chief the South Eastern Asia Command:—

"In this theatre it is incontestable that the infantry have been the basic and most important arm on which success or failure has depended. When the infantry were poor, we lost, when they were up to their job we won. This does not mean that the contribution of other arms, tanks, artillery, etc., was not of immense value; but of itself it would have been of little use without good infantry. Infantry were and will remain in an Eastern Theatre the foundation of any land force, and the measure of its effectiveness."

CHAPTER SIX.

4th and 5th Battalions.

April, 1939 to October, 1941—The Soldier—Voyage to Singapore—Battle of Singapore—Prisoners of War—Changi—Burma Thailand Railway—Third Phase.

April 1939 — October 1941.

The years 1926—1939 as far as the 4th Suffolk was concerned can be counted as years of stringency, frustration and unceasing difficulties. It was solely due to a succession of fine Commanding Officers:—Colonel E. P. Clarke, Colonel H. R. Hooper and Lieut. Colonel E. C. Rands, assisted by Adjutants from the Suffolk Regiment:—Captain D. R. A. Eley, Captain H. W. Dean and Captain E. R. D. Elias that the Battalion maintained its efficiency and was fairly well up to strength.

The Spring of 1939 marked a belated realization by the Government that unless drastic action was taken war would be inevitable. One of the results was the decision to duplicate the Territorial Army. The 54th East Anglian Division was to double its strength and throw off the 18th Division. In this way the 4th Suffolk, at that time a portion of the 163rd Brigade, was to form the 5th Suffolk. This was ordered in April 1939; the split between the old and newly formed units being fixed for October, 1939.

The 5th Suffolk had been disbanded in 1921 after a distinguished War Record in Gallipoli, Palestine and Egypt in 1914/18. It had been a West Suffolk Battalion with H.Q. at Bury St. Edmunds and it was wisely decided to recruit a new 5th Battalion from more or less the same area. The 4th Battalion therefore handed over officers and men from Hadleigh and Sudbury, and recruiting started with Lieut.-Colonel J. F. Harter, D.S.O., M.C., late the Royal Fusiliers, as the first 5th Suffolk Commanding Officer, Major Phillip Wilson being his Second in Command. The H.Q. of the new Battalion for the time being were at Ipswich with the 4th Battalion.

County Recruiting Meetings were organized and held in:—Ipswich (Lord Cranworth); Felixstowe (Lord Woodbridge); Eye (the Mayoress); Bury St. Edmunds (the Mayor); Sudbury, Hadleigh, Bures (Colonel Sir Charles Rowley, Bart.); Boxford (Colonel D. C. L. Corry, M.C.); Needham Market (Major P. C. G. Hayward, M.B.E.); Stowmarket (Captain J. M. Cobbold, D.L.); Botesdale (J. Holt-Wilson); Mildenhall, Haverhill, Steeple Bumpstead, Ixworth, Clare (Major-General Lord Loch). The wonderful success of these meetings was due to the co-operation of all the Regular and Territorial Army, the large firms, the Local Governments, the Press and Cinemas.

The success was outstanding. Within a month of the order to increase their strength the Mayor of Ipswich received a congratulatory telegram from the Secretary of State for War which read: "I should be grateful if you would send my heartiest congratulations to all ranks in the Territorial Army in the Town of Ipswich on their completion of the expansion of their Units." Ipswich and East Suffolk had raised 1,000 men in a month.

A month later BURY ST. EDMUNDS and WEST SUFFOLK reported completion of recruiting, thereby establishing a record for T.A. recruiting in England, 2,060 men were raised in Suffolk during the first two months.

The 5th Suffolk was at once formed and, raw though it was, joined the 4th Battalion, at FULMER from the 15th July to 29th July, in camp, 1939.

In July, 1939, Lieut.-Colonel E. H. W. Backhouse, commanding the 1st Suffolk at DEVONPORT, had been nominated to command the 54th Infantry Brigade of the 18th Division, when, in October, this new formation should come into being. But in August he was ordered to take over forthwith. He found the 163rd Infantry Brigade at NORWICH with six battalions; there the Brigadier handed him over the 4th and 5th Battalions with the 4th Royal Norfolk to form the nucleus of the 54th Brigade.

That month, on August 23rd, warning messages were issued that telephone and key positions were to be manned continuously. On September 1st the order was given to mobilize the Territorial Army; companies assembling the next day at their embodiment centres. On September 3rd War had been declared.

Thus the history of 1914 was repeated. Peace time policy since 1918 had starved the Territorial Army of equipment and Regular personnel; now when fear suddenly loosened the purse strings the order had been given to double its strength. Did the politician really believe that during the peace a Territorial Army fit to take the field in any form existed, or was he content to be hoodwinked into this feeling of security? The volunteers who served before this second World War, and the citizens who joined during the first months of fighting, knew that inefficient rulers had once again repeated the disastrous mistakes of the first World War; but with far less excuse.

The 4th and 5th Battalions were admirably officered with the best possible senior Territorial officers from Suffolk; the men who commanded their companies at the outset were with few exceptions with them to the end of the war. But in the early days they needed a backing. The material they handled was all raw. The young officer and the junior N.C.O. absorbed into the Regular Battalion during a war quickly learn their trade in the everyday life of the Battalion; their counterparts in mobilized Territorials have not the same atmosphere as a background.

Even a Territorial Battalion that has had a long and continuous history and been fully equipped has much to learn in war time to catch up with a Regular Battalion; both in field tactics and more particularly in administration, for morale depends on the well being of the rank and file.

The difficulties that both the 4th and 5th Battalions suffered during the first months of the War must not be minimized. At the outset the strict medical examination resulted in the discharge of many keen and efficient N.C.O.s and men at a time when they could be least spared. While their intake, instead of being trained soldiers, as with the Regular Army, consisted of raw recruits.

It is true that in April, 1939, the National Service Act had been passed, by which all young men were compelled to register and were called up for six months training at the Depot. At the end of which period they had the option of joining the Regular Army or continuing for the next four years in the Territorial Army. Militia, they were called, and the first batch had arrived at BURY ST. EDMUNDS in July, 1939. But none of these came in the early days of the war to the 4th and 5th Battalions.

Prior to the war, and for some months subsequent, the 4th and 5th Suffolk were dependent on their own exertions to secure recruits. They started the war up to Establishment; but the wastage necessitated reinforcements. The first received by the 5th Battalion was in October, 1939, a party of 52 untrained Militia recruits. This resulted in the formation of a new company, "R," for recruit training. Two further drafts of 100 and 88 untrained men were received in February, 1940. Not until June, 1940, were men who had completed their training at one of the Infantry Training Centres to be the only reinforcements received by either Battalion.

In June, 1940, 109 men were received by the 5th Suffolk from the Bedfordshire and Hertfordshire, followed by 150 from the Lincolnshire I.T.C. these latter for First line reinforcement. But while the actual proportion of "Suffolk" men gradually decreased to about 50%, when the two Battalions finally embarked and landed at SINGAPORE, a very large proportion of the remainder came from East Anglia. Moreover the officers and senior N.C.O.s were overwhelmingly from the County of Suffolk.

Early in October, 1939, both Battalions, as has been stated, had intakes of raw recruits; first class material and extremely keen. But their arrival was a heavy commitment; for the 4th and 5th Suffolk were hard at work training, and giving special attention to the teaching and selection of N.C.O.s. Fortunately Lieut. Colonel H. R. Gadd, D.S.O., M.C., at the I.T.C. BURY ST. EDMUNDS came to their aid. He not only printed a full and detailed training programme for recruits, but he drew up suitable N.C.O. cadet courses. Thus helped both Battalions gave their recruits sound primary training.

On September 17th, 1939, the 54th Infantry Brigade commenced life as a separate entity; H.Q. were opened at IPSWICH where also was 18th Divisional H.Q. under Major-General Dalby.

The location of the two Battalions was:—4th Suffolk: Battalion H.Q., IPSWICH; "A" Company, FELIXSTOWE; "B" Company, BAWDSEY; "C" Company, LEISTON; "D" Company split up for guard duties.

5th Suffolk:—Battalion H.Q., BURY ST. EDMUNDS; "A" Company, BURY ST. EDMUNDS; "B" Company, EYE; "C" Company, HADLEIGH; "D" Company, HAVERHILL.

As early as December, 1939, an 18th Divisional School was opened at CROMER for Company Commanders with demonstration Units from the Battalions. Parties of three officers and forty men per unit were also sent over to the B.E.F. in France for temporary attachments, and there was a constant stream of officers and other ranks to courses of instruction. But ammunition was scanty, ranges non-existent; one of the many extraneous duties of the Battalion being to construct ranges. The 5th Battalion made one at PALLING in December 1939, another at HORSEY in February, 1940.

On 1st November, 1939, the 18th Division was ordered to concentrate in Norfolk. 4th Suffolk H.Q. and "D" Company moved to BECCLES; "A" and "C" Companies to LOWESTOFT; "B" Company to LODDON. 5th Suffolk H.Q., HORNING; "A" and "B" Companies, MUNDESLEY; "C" Company, STALHAM; "D" Company, ACLE. Training improved; for on the move the Battalions were relieved from guarding many vulnerable points.

The 54th Infantry Brigade had been made responsible for the coast from LOWESTOFT to MUNDESLEY, the 4th Royal Norfolk in GREAT YARMOUTH and the 4th Suffolk in LOWESTOFT having these special localities to defend.

Major E. R. Daglish had command of the troops for the defence of LOWESTOFT. These consisted of "A" and "C" Companies and a 3 inch Mortar detachment, 4th Suffolk, 419th Field Battery R.A. (6 guns), a detachment of sailors. This Command was responsible for resisting all landing operations and for the defence of LOWESTOFT against an enemy attacking from any direction.

There was however little danger of an unheralded seaborne invasion in those early months of the war; but it was possible that the enemy might drop parachute troops and even attempt to seize a port. The "Broads" it was thought might be used by enemy seaplanes or flying boats. Defensive measures were therefore adopted to deal with these contingencies.

But while the intention, if such a landing was made, was to "drive the enemy into the sea" the means were lamentably weak. There is an order from the 5th Battalion which reads:—"Transport:—Pending the issue of First Line transport each Company must be ready to requisition any that is available at the time. **Not** to be done now."

In December the Command of the 18th Division passed to Major-General B. C. T. Paget, D.S.O., who held it until June, 1940, when he was transferred to H.Q. Home Forces. The organisation and training of the Division profited greatly from General Paget's exceptional ability.

By June, 1940, both Battalions had reached the stage when Company training had made real progress and carriers, signallers and other specialists were becoming really efficient.

During the Spring 1940, there were occasional temporary moves. The 4th Battalion finally moved their H.Q. to LANGLEY PARK with "B" and "D" Companies at RACKHEATH PARK; "A" Company, ST. OLAVES; "C" Company, SCOTTOW.

In June, 1940, Lt. Colonel A. A. Johnson, M.C., succeeded Lt. Colonel E. C. Rands, T.D., in command of the 4th Suffolk, Lt. Colonel Rands going to organize and command the 70th (Young Soldiers) Battalion, a fine Battalion Commander to whom the 4th Suffolk owed much.

Prior to this in July, 1940, Lt. Colonel L. J. Baker, M.C., succeeded Lt. Colonel J. F. Harter, D.S.O., M.C., late Royal Fusiliers, who was promoted. The 5th Battalion had been particularly fortunate in having so distinguished an officer as Lt. Colonel (later Major-General) Harter to command them during the first critical year of their existence. Their quality was in no small measure a reflection of his sound judgment and exceptional gift in commanding men. Lt. Colonel L. J. Baker, M.C. had already distinguished himself in the retirement to Dunkirk.

In September, 1940, Captain E. T. Sykes succeeded Captain M. Hely-Hutchinson as Adjutant, two valuable officers who gave first class service to the 5th Battalion.

The tragedy of DUNKIRK in June, 1940, had immediate repercussions on the 18th Division. The danger of invasion became a reality. The task of defending the long Norfolk coast line had to take precedence over training. The 54th Infantry Brigade had been allotted a stretch of 25 miles which included LOWESTOFT and excluded CROMER; the 4th Battalion near LOWESTOFT and the 5th Battalion near HORSEY each had approximately four miles of beach. The defensive works that had previously been made were now greatly strengthened; fresh trenches were dug, pill boxes built, beach obstacles constructed, mine fields laid, and the men learnt how to dig, wire, lay mines and also to look after themselves in the field.

In June, General Paget left the 18th Division, the command being eventually filled by Major-General M. Beckwith-Smith, who remained with the Division until SINGAPORE.

During the Summer that followed the evacuation of our army from DUNKIRK there was an understandable state of tension on and near the vulnerable stretches of the coast line of England. This is reflected in the precise irrevocable orders issued to the double sentries on road blocks; none but the most carefully "briefed" German Agent had a chance to pass unstopped.

There were occasional "alarms". In June, 1940, enemy ships were reported on the move. Followed by a report that enemy ships were "off the coast"—the report, in the excitement of the moment, omitted to say what coast. During these days there were many air raid warnings and some bombs; but fortunately no casualties in either battalion.

At the beginning of the war unit transport had been very scarce; by the end of the year 32-s ater buses were available to transport reserve units when and where required.

By the end of 1940, Home Defence Units were sufficiently trained and equipped to take a place on Coast defence and allow formations such as the 18th Division to be withdrawn for more extensive training or operations. As a consequence late in October the 4th Battalion concentrated in the neighbourhood of GORLESTON Holiday Camp and about the same time the 5th Battalion moved H.Q., "B," "C" and "D" Companies to NORTH WALSHAM; "A" Company, SWAFIELD HALL.

On 1st November, the 4th and 5th Suffolk moved by road to the ST. NEOTS and CAMBRIDGE areas respectively. Here they spent two and a half months revising what they had learnt, and training up to Company exercises. Courses for officers, N.C.O.s and specialists were much needed and increasing numbers were sent. Equipment and transport began to arrive in larger quantities. The Battalions were taking shape.

While in the ST. NEOTS area the 4th Battalion was located: Battalion H.Q., ST. NEOTS; "A" Company, TETWORTH; "B" Company, COCKAYNE-HATLEY and WRESTLINGWORTH; "C" Company, HAYLEY ST. GEORGE; "D" Company, WIMPOLE HALL. The 5th Battalion was in the immediate vicinity of CAMBRIDGE.

In December, 1940, the 18th Division had orders to mobilize ready to proceed overseas. It had been decided that this partially trained division should be sent to EGYPT there to complete its training. As a preliminary the Division was sent to SCOTLAND; the 4th Suffolk going to STOBBS CAMP and the 5th Suffolk to HAWICK in January, 1941. Here the two Battalions mobilized up to full strength in men, equipment and vehicles. Training was pushed on in spite of the severe winter weather; constant Company, Battalion, Brigade and Divisional Exercises being held, some lasting three to

OFFICERS, 4TH BATTALION, OCTOBER, 1941. *Photo—Vivian of Hereford.*

Back Row—2nd Lt. K. R. Issott, Lt. H. F. Archer, 2nd Lt. L. D. Humphrey, Lt. J. H. Scrimgeour, Capt. R. G. De Quincey, 2nd Lt. S. E. Scott, 2nd Lt. J. B. Day, Lt. T. E. Scaife, 2nd Lt. T. Peacock, 2nd Lt. J. M. Bebb, Lt. B. H. Gubbings.
Second Row—2nd Lt. M. B. Perkins, Lt. G. M. Plumbly, Capt. M. H. Vinden, Capt. C. V. Lewes (M.O.), 2nd Lt. P. H. Bennett, 2nd Lt. J. E. Wilson, 2nd Lt. M. C. M. Arrindell, 2nd Lt. N. I. Lock, 2nd Lt. B. J. Clarke, Capt. R. H. Willett, 2nd Lt. E. S. Smith, 2nd Lt. E. Pryke.
Third Row—2nd Lt. J. C. Clarke, 2nd Lt. R. A. Holmes, Capt. L. Tuck, 2nd Lt. J. Taylor, Lt. D. A. Wise, Capt. B. H. Walker, Lt. E. T. Bennett, 2nd Lt. T. E. Cork, Capt. R. H. Hollamby, 2nd Lt. F. A. Barnsley.
Front Row—Capt. J. Foster Haigh (C.F.), Capt. G. H. Clarke, Major J. A. Brown, Major S. G. Flick, Lt. Col. A. A. Johnson, M.C. (C.O.), Major W. J. Hollowell, Capt. J. Wysock Crundall, Capt. F. G. Davies, Capt. A. E. Mitchell (Adjutant).

four days. For the first time all men were exercised in classification practices and in Field Firing.

It was exceedingly hard work. STOBBS CAMP under nine inches of snow and occasional blizzards is not much fun. But the kindness of the inhabitants and the really good discipline of the Battalions made the time bearable and at times enjoyable.

Embarkation leave was taken. But as the weeks slipped by it was realized that there had been a change of plan. In the light of after events, what a tragedy this change of plan proved for the 18th Division.

In April, 1941, orders were received for the 18th Division to relieve the 5th Divison in LANCASHIRE. With H.Q. 54th Infantry Brigade at BLACKBURN, 4th Suffolk was billeted in a Bleaching Mill at WHITEFIELDS, near MANCHESTER and the 5th Battalion near Lord Derby's home at KNOWSLEY PARK.

On 16th August the Brigade moved to HEREFORDSHIRE, the 4th Suffolk to the Cathedral town of HEREFORD, the 5th Suffolk to LEOMINSTER, their last station before departing overseas. Embarkation leave, inoculation, the final drawing of mobilization items of equipment occupied September and October. By the middle of October both Battalions were complete in men and material; confident in themselves that they could deploy, attack, consolidate quickly and efficiently.

Both Battalions saw a great deal more of England than is indicated in the above locations. There were constant large scale exercises:—LUDLOW, WORCESTER, BLACKBURN, SWANSEA, ANGLESEY amongst many other places came within the range of all or some of the Battalion units. While in August, 1941, the 5th Battalion had a welcome change from soldiering when they went to assist the Leicestershire farmers with their harvest. The 4th Battalion followed their example in September.

While the principal training of the two Battalions had been to fit them to take their place in Brigade and Divisional operations overseas, attention was also given to the possibility of home defence. There was always the danger of enemy air or seaborne invasions, and the possibility of large scale sabotage of home installations. Plans were made and practised of large scale operations in which the Division with other large formations took part, and others in which the 54th Infantry Brigade operated independently. Home defence did not depend only on the Field Force Divisions; but also on area troops and Home Guards. The 54th Infantry Brigade Units had therefore to make themselves acquainted with all the local formations with whom they might have to act. They had also, as in May 1941, in LIVERPOOL, to give assistance in clearing the debris after heavy bombing attacks.

THE SOLDIER.

The foregoing is a bare outline of the history of the 4th and 5th Suffolk from September, 1939, until the Winter of 1941. The colour is provided by the following accounts by officers and men of the events as they saw them during these two years.

This is a letter from a man during the latter portion of the year 1940, after DUNKIRK:—

"It was while holding this long bleak coast that a message was received to be prepared for a possible enemy landing. Many will remember watching and waiting in the wind and rain, then sleeping in the positions we had dug Unfortunately our only view of a German was a dead one, whom we found on the doorstep next morning, washed up by the rough sea."

Wide stretches of coast were covered in those days; as much as four miles to a Company in some parts. Real hard work was put in by the Battalion, and there were no complaints. As one man said; "Ah, we got on fine down there. Bags of Stand-tos and Stand-downs, lights flashing on and off, air-raids and bombs, everything to brighten our little lives. It wasn't exactly a holiday; but we can say that we spent summer by the sea, with a vengeance!"

Then came the move to Cambridgeshire in the late Autumn in 1940. The first sight of a new billet described here will be reminiscent to many.

"I shall never forget the dismal scene. The Dower House, with the wardrobe lying prone in the mud. The "Slough of Despond" surrounding the Cookhouse. The 'ornamental lake' guarding the entrance to the Company Office. The lack of sanitation; the faint aura of Scotch whiskey. Culminating with an unknown siren at point blank range at midnight, causing our venerable Company Commander to sit bolt upright in bed and impale his head violently on the corner of a painted dresser."

Later he writes:—"We have now got on much friendlier terms with the mud into which, however, half the by-products of an asbestos factory and a Platoon truck were sunk without any visible trace whatever."

A few weeks later the same writer was able to say:—"Life goes on. The skeleton of elegant, graceful structures appear outside the Company office to the husky incantation of wild gypsy songs from central Europe; even when the cement-mixer is going you can smell spring as it comes to the upper reaches of the Moldau. The Triplex stove at the Cookhouse has had a baby."

In SCOTLAND at the beginning of 1941 the gibe made by a writer of the 4th Battalion that the 5th Battalion always got the best of the deal when the Brigade moved seems to have been true for correspondents with the 5th Battalion wrote:—

"We are now well installed in a place where sirens are only heard when they are tested, and folks are very hospitable; it is definitely a very good spot. Social life is well to the fore, three picture houses, dancing nearly every evening, numbers of Canteens, and two well-known Clubs available for the troops, all within a few minutes."

By the Spring of 1941 both Battalions had swept South across the border and invaded the suburbs of Northern industrial towns.

It was the visit to help clear up the debris in Liverpool after an enemy bombing raid that inspired this letter:—

"In days of old, clad in satin doublets with lace cuffs, proud as peacocks, gay as larks, men went to war, leaving their weeping women behind them. It's different now. The men get together quietly and unobtrusively; a great many clear-eyed women put on khaki or blue. Instead of the Army it's the civilians who are tasting Fascist bloody-mindedness. And sometimes when you ask for leave it strikes you hard that it is they who ought to get it, not you. They are living like badgers, inhaling shrapnel and fire; whilst a great many of us are catching up on that sleep we missed before September, 1939. They have just got to take it lying down, and are proud, because, living in the capital towns, they have been singled out to provide the Roman Holiday of 1940. It's no fun for us, for our 'bit' seems very small at this time. We owe them a great deal, and if we do half as well as they are doing when our turn comes, there will be no need to flip a coin for the final score."

The last move of the two Battalions, before they were to leave ENGLAND on their disastrous expedition, was to HEREFORD. Here the 4th Battalion was billeted in the immediate neighbourhood of the old Cathedral town, the 5th Battalion in villages outside. The Battalions had always made themselves welcome wherever they had been; but probably this HEREFORD country was the most popular of all.

A correspondent in the Carrier Platoon of the 5th Battalion writes:—

"Everyone is pleased with our new quarters in the West of England, amongst the apples and cyder, cows and red sand stone. It is such a wonderful change to see a green field and apple orchards; for at one period it was thought we should never see these again.

"We amused ourselves one Sunday doing battle with the Home Guard. I rather fancy more eating of buns and drinking of tea was done than fighting the invader, for every time we stopped for a moment or two some kind lass ran out with jugs and plates full of good fare. I must say the West country folk certainly rival our friends in Scotland for handing it out.

"From what I've seen, the rabbit season has started and is now in full swing, judging by odd skins that are found within a stone's throw of No. 3 Section Hut. Would Lockwood know anything about this? No, of course not. Just like the pheasants and eggs at Ormesby; no one found them: they just landed in the pot by accident."

The 4th Battalion made many friends in HEREFORD. Here is a description from one of them:—

"In this lovely market town, with a view of the Cathedral while dressing, we established a beautiful home from home. In the lush meadows there is a continuous rustle of Ovaltine in its first stages. Even the girl at the ironmonger's looks as if she has never touched anything but Grade "A" milk all her life. Meanwhile, in the narrow streets, khaki and light blue jostle side by side and many a lonely soldier's arm has thrilled to the touch of a female respirator or the hot breath of a small landgirl who knows her onions."

It would seem, reading the peaceful records of the two Battalions from the time they settled down as units to the last days at HEREFORD that their principal time had been spent in Sport:—football, cricket, golf, tennis, water-polo, boxing, fencing, cross-country running, and the periodical athletic meetings. They excelled in all, not only the Battalion representatives, but Platoon teams as well. The football team of the 4th Battalion deservedly won the Divisional Cup at Molineaux Park, the home of Wolverhampton Wanderers, where they beat the 1st Cambridgeshire Regiment in the final by 4-2 after a great game.

But behind this Sport could be seen the steady progress in training, mounting in tempo as the Battalions became better equipped and more efficient.

Minden Day, 1941 had come and gone. Then there was a week of many inspections, culminating on October 22nd in an inspection by His Majesty the King, who spoke to the Company Commanders and had a few words with some of the N.C.O.s and men.

Though the men did not yet know it, the Division was under orders for Service overseas. Both Battalions came to a Special Service in Hereford Cathedral, the Sunday before they sailed.

VOYAGE TO SINGAPORE.

OCTOBER 29th, 1941 — JANUARY 29th, 1942.

The officers with the 4th and 5th Battalion The Suffolk Regiment were:—

4TH BATTALION THE SUFFOLK REGIMENT.

Lt. Colonel	A. A. Johnson, M.C.
Major	S. G. Flick, Second in Command.
Major	J. Brown, "D" Coy Commander. (Killed in action).
Major	G. H. Clarke, "C" Coy Commander.
Major	W. Hollowell, "A" Coy Commander (Missing, believed killed).
Captain	F. G. Davies, "B" Coy Commander.
Captain	R. G. de Quincey, Carrier Commander.
Captain	B. H. Gubbings, Quartermaster.
Captain	R. S. Hollamby.
Captain	A. Mitchell, Adjutant. (Died as P.O.W.)
Captain	L. Tuck.
Captain	M. H. Vinden. Signalling Officer.
Captain	B. H. Walker.
Captain	R. H. Willett. Transport Officer.
Captain	D. R. Wise.
Captain	J. Wysock-Crundall. H.Q. Coy. Commander.
Captain	Foster-Haigh. Chaplain to the Forces. (Died as P.O.W.)
Captain	Lewis (R.A.M.C.). Medical Officer.
Lieutenant	H. Archer (Missing, believed killed).
Lieutenant	M. C. M. Arrindell (Escaped and later served with 2nd Battalion).
Lieutenant	J. M. Bebb.
Lieutenant	F. Barnsley (Killed in action).
Lieutenant	E. T. Bennett.
Lieutenant	P. H. T. Bennett.
Lieutenant	J. C. Clarke.
Lieutenant	B. J. Clarke.
Lieutenant	T. Cork (Died as P.O.W.)
Lieutenant	J. B. Day.
Lieutenant	R. Holmes (Killed in action).
Lieutenant	L. Humphrey (Killed in action).
Lieutenant	K. R. Issott.
Lieutenant	N. Lock (Killed in action).
Lieutenant	T. Peacock.
Lieutenant	M. Perkins (Killed in action).
Lieutenant	E. Pryke.
Lieutenant	T. E. Scaife.
Lieutenant	J. H. Scrimgeour. Intelligence Officer.

Lieutenant	S. Scott (Died as P.O.W.)
Lieutenant	W. Watson (Died of Wounds).
Lieutenant	J. Wilson (Killed in action).
Regimental Sgt. Major	D. Tubby.
Regimental Q.M.S.	C. Butcher.
Q.M.S.	A. Baker, M.M.

5TH BATTALION THE SUFFOLK REGIMENT.

Lt. Colonel	L. J. Baker, M.C.
Major	C. J. M. Watts, Second in Command.
Major	G. N. H. Mayes. H.Q. Coy. Commander.
Major	J. H. Harrison. "C" Coy. Commander.
Captain	E. T. Sykes, Adjutant.
Captain	M. Hely-Hutchinson. "D" Coy. Commander.
Captain	G. M. Oliver. "A" Coy. Commander.
Captain	R. S. Wood. "B" Coy. Commander.
Captain	P. N. Fletcher. (Escaped).
Captain	R. M. Oliver.
Captain	N. A. Brown (Killed in action).
Captain	C. C. Wells. Transport Officer.
Captain	P. D. A. Clarke. Intelligence Officer.
Captain	R. R. Fewell.
Lieutenant	W. W. Cook.
Lieutenant	W. W. Soames.
Lieutenant	S. J. Masters. Carrier Platoon Commander.
Lieutenant	H. A. G. Collins.
Lieutenant	G. G. Moir. Mortar Platoon Commander.
Lieutenant	F. W. Yorke.
Lieutenant	I. P. Watt.
Lieutenant	D. I. C. Hopkins.
Lieutenant	J. Munnings.
Lieutenant	J. R. Edney.
Lieutenant	F. Hughesdon. Signalling Officer.
Lieutenant	K. P. Meade.
Lieutenant	L. J. Tedder.
Lieutenant	J. N. Westren.
Lieutenant	R. C. G. Clarke.
Lieutenant	H. F. Goodsman.
Lieutenant	G. Richardson.
Lieutenant	A. H. H. Base.
2/Lieutenant	P. W. H. Smith.
2/Lieutenant	A. D. Bayfield (Killed in action).
2/Lieutenant	W. L. Clarke.
2/Lieutenant	P. R. Peachey.
2/Lieutenant	D. G. Jones.
Lieutenant	J. G. Griffiths. Quartermaster.
Captain (C.F.)	D. E. Davidson.
Captain (R.A.M.C.)	F. E. de W. Cayley.
Regimental Sgt. Major	D. F. Wakefield.
Regimental Q.M.S.	J. Wade.

On 29th October, 54th Brigade H.Q. and the 4th Suffolk embarked at Liverpool on the S.S. "Andes"; the 5th Suffolk on the S.S. "Reina del Pacifico." The remainder of the 18th Division, less its transport, being in other transports, the whole moving in convoy on its great adventure.

An escort of British destroyers covered the convoy half way to HALIFAX, being relieved in mid Atlantic by a strong American fleet which included a battleship, an aircraft carrier, "The Ranger," cruisers and destroyers; although America was not at this time at war with Germany. HALIFAX was reached on November 8th where the "Andes" and the "Reina del Pacifico" lay out all day in perfect autumn sunshine, memorable after the foggy days in the Atlantic. Early next morning the 4th and 5th Suffolk transhipped to the U.S.T. "Wakefield."

The "Wakefield" was to be the home from home of the two Battalions for more than two months, and they were fortunate. She was a magnificent transport, fitted to carry 4,600 troops; these included the whole of the 54th Infantry Brigade, the 18th Divisional H.Q. and the 148th Field Regiment. Few will forget the friendliness, kindness and efficiency of her officers and crew, particularly her Commander, Captain Scammell. It is pleasant to think that she and her sister ships in the convoy escaped eventually from Singapore.

PORT OF SPAIN, TRINIDAD, was reached on the 17th November; the convoy remained until the 19th November. Shore leave was not permitted. Thence they sailed down the Venezuelan Coast, crossed the Equator east to CAPE TOWN, arriving there on the 9th December. From the 9th December to 13th December all ranks were able to stretch their legs and enjoy the hospitality of the Cape.

At the Cape the troops received an outstanding welcome from the local residents. The mornings were spent by the troops route marching; the rest of the day was devoted to sight seeing. At midday lines of cars waited at the dock side to give officers and men the best of holidays that many had ever had. Field Marshal Smuts had welcomed the Anglo American convoy in a speech at KELVIN GROVE, and General Beckwith-Smith personally thanked the Lord Mayor and the South African Women's Auxiliary Services for their great share in the reception to the men. He was informed that the people at Cape Town had been much impressed by the uniformly good behaviour of the troops.

While at Cape Town news came of the sinking by the Japanese of H.M.S. "Prince of Wales" and H.M.S. "Repulse." But the destination of the 18th Division was still unknown; most believing that it would be SUEZ, though some guessed SINGAPORE.

The convoy sailed out of TABLE BAY at 1600 hours 13th December, the 4th and 5th Suffolk having no absentees. "General Quarters" was ordered as the ships moved through the mine fields. The escort consisted of the British Cruiser "Dorset" and 6 U.S. destroyers. Christmas was celebrated on board; dinner including roast turkey, braised Virginian ham, American Christmas cake, candied carrots, etc.

BOMBAY was reached on 27th December; next day the Battalion disembarked and travelled by train over the Western Ghats to AHMEDNAGAR where after a dusty march they were encamped. Here two weeks were spent getting fit after the long sea voyage. The strength of the 5th Battalion at this time was 40 officers, 889 other ranks.

But the situation in the Far East had been rapidly changing; once again the 4th and 5th Battalions embarked on the U.S.S. "Wakefield." At 1300 hours, 19th January, 1942, the convoy left BOMBAY. Later that day it was known that the 18th Division was bound for the South West Pacific area where the 53rd Infantry Brigade had already preceded them. The escort was H.M.S. "Caledon," for the first five days, later she was relieved by H.M.S. "Glasgow," H.M.S. "Durban" and H.M.S. "Dane."

On 27th January H.M.S. "Exeter" with three destroyers took the place of H.M.S. "Glasgow."

As soon as SINGAPORE was announced as the destination of the 18th Division pamphlets on jungle warfare were issued and all ranks endeavoured to learn something about the conditions of fighting that lay ahead of them. The news was not encouraging; but spirits were high.

On the 28th January the convoy was unsuccessfully bombed by a single hostile plane in the BANKS STRAIT. The ships were then proceeding in line:—H.M.S. "Exeter," U.S.S. "West Point," H.M.S. "Electra," U.S.S. "Wakefield," H.M.S. "Encounter," H.T. "Duchess of Bedford," H.M.S. "Express," M.V. "Empire Star," H.M.S. "Dane," H.T. "Empress of Japan," H.M.S. "Durban." That night the three fastest ships were sent ahead under the cover of darkness for SINGAPORE:—U.S.S. "West Point", U.S.S. "Wakefield," and H.T. "Empress of Japan," the U.S.S. "Wakefield" drawing into the lead. By 29th January, 1942 they docked safely at Singapore.

BATTLE FOR SINGAPORE.

JANUARY 29TH TO 15TH FEBRUARY, 1942.

The Battle for Singapore, as far as it concerns the 18th Division, falls into two phases. First:—January 29th, when the main portion of the Division landed, to February 9th; during which phase the Division occupied and held a portion of the island defences. Second:—February 10th, when the Japanese breached the defences opposite the A.I.F. to February 15th, when the garrison capitulated. The whole period was only 17 days.

There were considerable administrative difficulties during the first phase; but except for some shelling the 18th Division had a breathing space to take stock of their situation.

The U.S.S. "Wakefield" had berthed on January 29th; the 4th and 5th Battalions at once disembarked and were taken by M.T. to a tented camp on the Tempines Road—the Australian lorry drivers giving their passengers a most gloomy account of the retreat down the mainland.

That same day, January 29th, the Commander in Chief decided to evacuate the mainland and withdraw all his forces for the defence of the Island. The mainland was to be cleared by midnight January 31st at which time the mainland causeway would be destroyed. The Right Northern Sector of the Island was allotted to the 18th Division; the 11th Indian Division (including the 53rd Infantry Brigade) 3rd Corps was to occupy the coast on the left of the 18th Division up to but exclusive of the Causeway which was held by the Australians.

By the evening of the 31st January the 4th and 5th Suffolk were in position facing across the narrow straits. Both Battalions as well as the rest of the 18th Division were short of full equipment, this not being completely cleared from the sea transports until 8th February.

The defensive front taken over by the 54th Infantry Brigade is shown on the sketch map. The 4th Suffolk on the right stretched from Fairy Point to Sewage Farm. "D" Company right, "C" Company centre, "A" Company left, with "B" Company reserve at Hill 85. With the forward companies were five 75 M.M. Beach guns and two searchlights. The 5th Suffolk on the left was responsible for the Pungol Peninsula and placed "D" Company at the forward point of the Peninsula, with "C" Company in support. "A" Company being on the right beach and "B" Company in reserve. The 5th Suffolk had three 75 M.M. Beach guns and two searchlights forward with "D" Company. The 4th Royal Norfolk was in Brigade Reserve. The front was extensive and consisted of some open beach and long stretches of mangrove swamps. After the first few days officers of the Singapore local forces who spoke Malay and Chinese were sent to the Battalions to act as guides through the mangrove swamps and to deal with the inhabitants, many of whom were still in the area. The mangrove swamps were then found to be far from impassable as had been previously believed.

The orders for defence were to hold the beaches at all costs, reserves to counter attack if need be. The defences were constructed for all round defence and a small amount of defensive material including wire was brought forward. A naval patrol operated in the Straits and some very erratic light motor craft were available for reconnaissance by the infantry. There was a daily Divisional Conference; Brigadier E. H. W. Backhouse, the 54th Brigadier, visited the Battalions daily, and the defences made good progress.

On the 5th February, "D" Company, 5th Suffolk, came under shell fire for the first time, and suffered some casualties. Meanwhile fresh 18th Divisional Troops had been landed in Singapore and the Divisional front was strengthened by guns and composite formations. The 54th Infantry Brigade being allotted a machine gun Company made up from the 9th Northumberland Fusiliers and 125 Anti-Tank Regiment R.A., and also two Companies 18th Div. "Recce" Battalion lightly armed as infantry.

On the night February 8/9th away to the west, the storm broke. The second phase had started. The Japanese after a short but heavy bombardment effected a crossing on the Australian front, on the north-west corner of the Island where the distance from the mainland was scarcely half a mile. The troops were thin on the ground, exhausted after their long fighting withdrawal down the Peninsula, while the thick country near the landing made defence difficult. The enemy penetrated to a distance of one or two miles.

During the next two days the Japanese pressed on towards the Causeway and the two vital reservoir lakes, Pierce and MacRitchie. The 12th Indian Infantry Brigade having failed to stem the tide the 18th Division was called upon to provide a force from its reserve units. This (Tom) force, under the Command of Lt.-Col. L. C. Thomas, D.S.O., O.B.E., M.C., included the 4th Royal Norfolk from the 54th Infantry Brigade; the 4th Suffolk stretching its defence line still further and the Divisional R.A.O.C. leaving their technical duties to become two Rifle Companies.

February 11th brought more disquieting news. The left of the 11th Indian Division was exposed, the Japanese were almost at the Causeway and were infiltrating towards the Reservoirs and SINGAPORE. Once more, a "Force" was scraped together—this time the 4th Battalion was quickly taken off the beaches and hurriedly sent to join "Massey" Force; to cover the Northern flank of "Tom" Force and also safeguard the vital SINGAPORE town water supply.

The 4th Suffolk moved early on the morning of the 11th February finding a considerable uncontrolled congestion of military and civilian traffic on the road. Their "RECCE" unit was the first to arrive at the cross roads S.E. of MacRitchie Reservoir and from here it was sent to face north in the direction of Thomson Village. But when the rest of the Battalion arrived at the cross roads it was ordered to connect with "Tom" Force in the neighbourhood of Swiss Rifle Club Hill.

Unfortunately before these orders were given the R.A.S.C. Company which had transported the 4th Suffolk had been dismissed. The Battalion had therefore to march, and with indifferent maps and in exceedingly enclosed country they lost their way. Beyond the made up roads stretched rubber plantations and the jungle, the local maps were inaccurate as to the rough tracks.

Eventually the Battalion arrived in the neighbourhood of Swiss Rifle Club Hill after a march of some 12 miles. Lt.-Col. A. A. Johnson, M.C., was with a small advanced party which ran into the Japanese on the hill and was forced to withdraw after suffering a few casualties. Lt.-Col. Johnson then contacted the O.C. "Tom" Force and the O.C. 4th Royal Norfolk who was at "Tom" Force H.Q. and it was decided that the 4th Suffolk should prolong the "Tom" Force line.

It was dark before Lt.-Col. Johnson succeeded in picking up his companies; and in the dark he formed a rough line, his left on the Bukit Timar Road, his right near the Club House on the Golf Course. "B" Company, Captain F. G. Davies and "D" Company, Captain J. Brown were on the right under the 2nd in Command, Major S. G. Flick; while on the left were "A" Company, Capt. L. Tuck and "C" Company, Major G. H. Clarke. There was a gap between these two wings and behind the gap came the Battalion H.Q. and the H.Q. Company, Major W. Hollowell.

After midnight that night February 11/12th the Battalion received orders to push on before light on to the original objectives Swiss Rifle Club Hill.

It is difficult to see how this order could have been carried out in the dark or even by day under the existing conditions. For by daylight one company endeavouring to get in touch with "Tom" Force had been caught by enemy infiltrations and was temporarily held up by snipers and mortars; while another company in the dark had had a brush with a post occupied by our own troops.

Nevertheless at dawn an unreconnoitred attack was made on to Swiss Cottage Rifle Club; but with little or no success. "D" Company had a number of casualties including the first officer to be killed—Lt. F. Barnsley.

Later that day, February 12th, the 4th Suffolk was ordered back to the right of the new perimeter in rear of Adam Road, where it was temporarily in reserve behind the 1st Cambridgeshires.

On the morning of February 12th the 5th Suffolk was the only Battalion in the original 54th Infantry Brigade Sector; other units there were R.E., R.A.S.C., and R.A.O.C., armed and serving as infantry. Meanwhile to the West and North-West of the Island the situation was now so critical that the Commander in Chief decided to abandon the northern beach defences; and the 18th Divisional Commander was directed to take over the MacRitchie Reservoir Sector of the new and unreconnoitred perimeter defence of SINGAPORE.

Brigadier Backhouse with the remains of his 54th Infantry Brigade came across forthwith and took over the command of "Tom" Force. The 5th Suffolk moved by M.T. through the chaotic streets of SINGAPORE to an area near the junction of the Mount Pleasant Road with the Bukit Timah road. Here Lt.-Colonel Baker that night established his headquarters and placed two of his 5th Suffolk companies in position in the deserted houses, one of which had been the Commander-in-Chief's peace time residence.

Next day, February 18th, Brigadier Backhouse established his command on a front of nearly two miles which extended along Adam Road, past the Bukit Timah cross road, down Farrer Road. Beyond his right were the 1st Cambridgeshires and the 4th Suffolk. On his left, there was first a gap and then some Australian troops.

To hold this front he had the 4th Royal Norfolk and 5th Suffolk with ten other units, including three Indian Battalions. These latter Battalions had suffered heavily on the mainland and had since been reinforced by the rawest recruits, while some of the others were of doubtful value except for static defence.

That morning, 14th February, the 5th Suffolk moved forward and took over the defence of the important cross roads Bukit Timah—Adams Farrer roads. Lt.-Colonel Baker established his H.Q. in Raffles College and held his front with "A" Company on the right, "C" Company in the centre at the cross road, "D" Company on the left. Here they took up a strong position and held firm till the 15th February, suffering only sporadic fire and bombing from the enemy. But the 4th Royal Norfolk, on their right, who had had 48 hours' continuous fighting, were subjected to mortar and artillery fire by night and day.

During the morning, 13th February, the 1st Cambridgeshires extensive front stretched as far as the MacRitchie Reservoir north of the cross roads, the 4th Suffolk being behind this line. This was considered to be more than the 1st Cambridgeshires could safely hold and during the afternoon a re-grouping was ordered, the 4th Suffolk being directed to take over from the Reservoir inclusive to Hill 95, an important hill which had been the scene of earlier fighting, having been temporarily lost and recaptured by the 1st Cambridgeshires. The relief was ordered for 2300 hours 13th February; but the 4th Suffolk was not in position until 0300 hours 14th February.

At 1800 hours 14th February the Japanese suddenly put down a heavy artillery and mortar attack on the 4th Suffolk front, following this up with tanks from the golf course. A heavy attack was directed on Hill 95 and by 2000 hours the 4th Suffolk, having suffered heavy casualties, fell back on the Mount Pleasant road, closely followed by Japanese infantry. Here they consolidated among the houses and gardens. This night with the 1st Cambridgeshires, they came under the Command of Brigadier Backhouse.

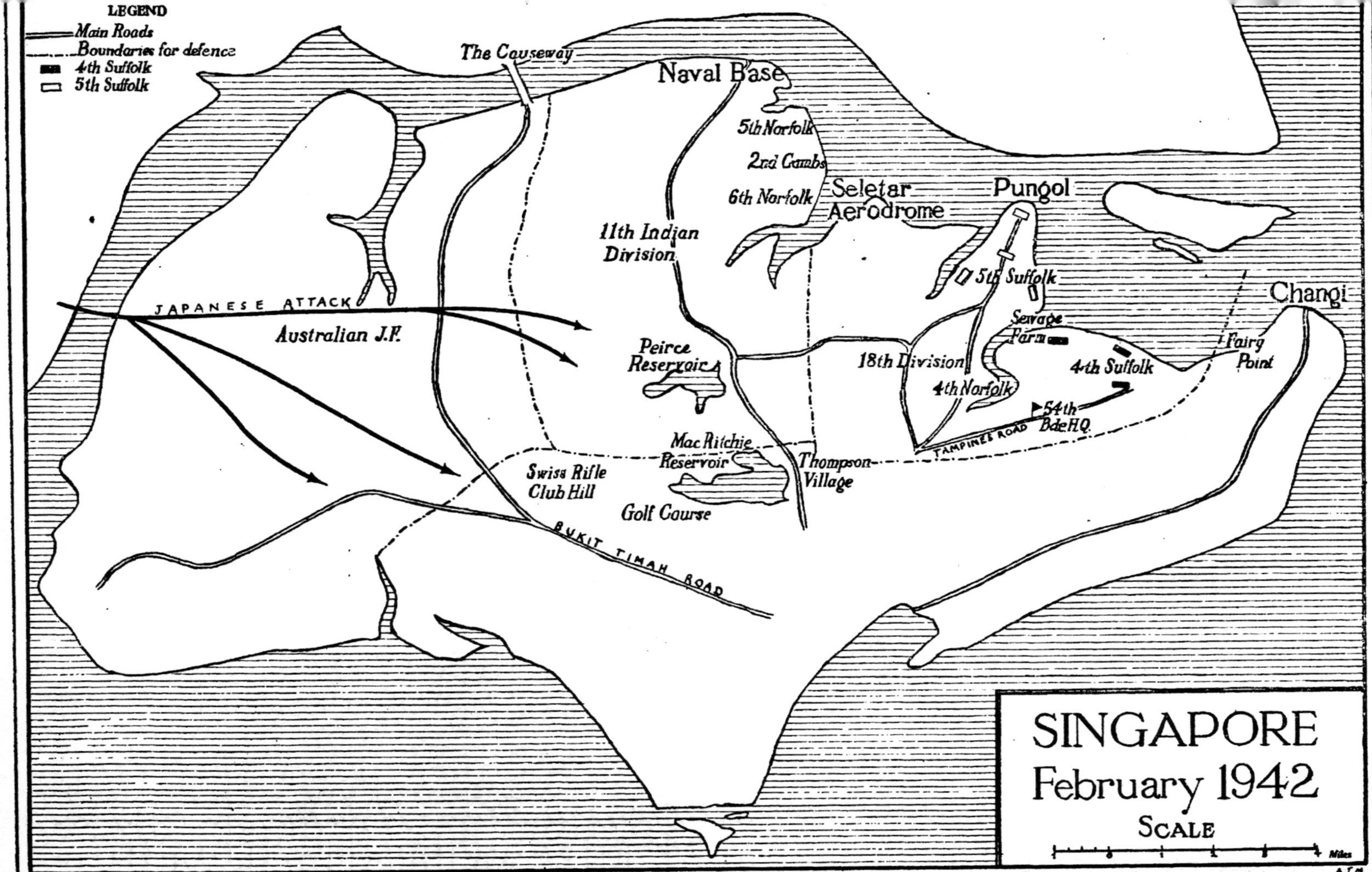

LEGEND
Main Roads
Boundaries for defence
4th Suffolk
5th Suffolk
The Causeway
Naval Base
5th Norfolk
2nd Cambs
6th Norfolk
Seletar Aerodrome
Pungol
5th Suffolk
Changi
11th Indian Division
JAPANESE ATTACK
Australian J.F.
Peirce Reservoir
18th Division
4th Norfolk
Sewage Farm
4th Suffolk
Fairy Point
54th Bde HQ
TAMPINES ROAD
Mac Ritchie Reservoir
Thompson Village
Swiss Rifle Club Hill
Golf Course
BUKIT TIMAH ROAD
SINGAPORE
February 1942
SCALE
Miles
A.J.M.

Meanwhile the 1st Cambridgeshires under Lt.-Col. G. G. Carpenter, D.S.O., had held firm in their original line on Adam Road where they had been subjected to heavy enemy pressure; for the retirement of the 4th Suffolk had left the 1st Cambridgeshires right flank completely exposed. The reserve company "B" of the 5th Suffolk was sent at dawn, 15th, to Lt.-Col. Carpenter to help him close this gap; but in the difficult enclosed country "B" company's attack faded away. The 1st Cambridgeshires notwithstanding held their vital position on the Adam Road throughout the 15th February.

The battle continued during the night 14/15th February and on the morning of the 15th the Japanese continued their progress on the 4th Suffolk on the Mount Pleasant Road. Lt.-Col. A. A. Johnson, M.C., Commanding the Battalion was wounded; the Command being taken over by Major S. G. Flick. The enemy succeeded in establishing himself well forward; but by midday the houses were cleared of the enemy—partly due to the bravery of Sgt. Salter of the 85th Anti-Tank Regt. R.A. who almost single-handed brought one of his guns into action at point blank range against an occupied building.

At about 1100 hours the order was issued that firing was to cease on the Bukit Timah Road as at 1130 hours, a party bearing a white flag would pass through to the Japanese lines.

Captain G. M. Oliver (Geoff) Commanding "A" Company with his brother Captain R. M. Oliver (Bill) as second in Command was at the Bukit Timah cross roads when the white flag arrived. "Bill" has written the following account four years after the event.

"Sunday, the 15th February, 1942, Singapore Island was a day of brilliant sunshine, and devoid of any tropical showers, which happen so quickly in that part of the world.

The 5th Battalion had moved up into the front line on the evening of Friday, 13th, and "A" Company had taken over its sector from a Company of a Dogra Regiment on the main road which runs North and South across the Island from SINGAPORE to JOHORE, a secondary road crossed the main road immediately in our rear.

These cross roads we called the Bukit Timah cross roads.

We had spent a very irritating Saturday night, as the Japanese had been mortaring us a little, and the infernal crackers in their mortars exploded a good time after the bomb had burst, and sounded just like rifle shots. As we were new to the game we could not quite make them out, and kept wondering if we were being sniped; it was bright moonlight. So we were very glad to see the dawn; things quietened down a bit. We had our breakfasts undisturbed and had seen that everybody was all right. I think I had just been over to see the Company Commander of the Unit on our right flank, when at about 1100 hours I noticed a number of cars approaching Bukit Timah cross roads from SINGAPORE. To my horror, I saw a white flag flying on the right hand side of the car, and a Union Jack on the left. I remember one optimist to whom I had been talking, said—"The Japs have surrendered."

I immediately ran round a little hut on to the road, where I could see better. I think there were three cars, two carrying flags. An Officer stepped out of the first car, and came up to me and told me to remove the road blocks on the main road, running up to Johore, which we were covering.

This, I may add, had been prepared only two days previously, and we had road mines, and all sorts of presents in it for the Japs should they choose to try and break through.

So to receive an order like this from someone whom I did not know, who had come from a car carrying a white flag, made me angry, suspicious, and not a little worried, all at once, and I think my only retort was "What the b-----y hell are you doing with those flags ?" I was then thinking of Fifth Column, as rumours of Fifth Column activities had been very rife. I then drew my revolver, and rammed it into this Officer's ribs, and it was only then did I notice his rank, he was a Brigadier.

I was very suspicious indeed by now, and I wondered if I ought to shoot him then and there; but luckily by then the occupants of the other cars had come up—I think there were eight of them, including one civilian—and this man said, "Do not shoot Brigadier Newbigging, he is Brigadier, General Staff, at General Percival's H.Q." I think my retort was "Who the hell are you ?" I believe I withdrew my revolver from the Brigadier's ribs, and pointed it at the civilian. He replied, "I am Hugh Fraser, the Colonial Secretary." He then went on to say, "Brigadier Newbigging has the surrender terms for the Japanese from General Percival." With that I again put my revolver into the Brigadier's ribs, and demanded to see them. He produced an envelope, and I saw it was addressed to "Nippon." I then demanded his identity card, and was shown it. It seemed in order to me. Then he told me I had no right to stop him, as he was Percival's envoy to the Japanese, and once again ordered me to remove the road block. This I refused point-blank to do and murmured something about "he and others ought to be shot," as I was still thinking in terms of Jap Fifth Column. But I was getting a little worried, as to what I ought to do, as we were not in telephonic communication with Battalion H.Q. and I was just going to send for the Company Commander when he appeared on the scene, and the Brigadier told him the same story as he had told me.

I then suggested to Geoff., the Company Commander, that I ought to go back at once to Battalion Headquarters, and inform the C.O. This he agreed to, and I went off in our one remaining truck, as hard as ever I could go.

By now I was very agitated indeed, as I was beginning to think there might be something in it after all, and we really were surrendering.

I arrived at Battalion H.Q. and told the C.O. the awful news. He at once telephoned the Brigade, and I heard it confirmed by the Brigade Major over the telephone.

My orders were to go back and remove the road blocks to enable the party to go on its way. But as I neared the Company position I was rather amused to see the party walking up the road, with the road block still in position.

Geoff had evidently satisfied himself as to their identity, and allowed them to proceed; but refused point-blank to remove the road block, as he had had no orders to that effect from Battalion H.Q. And the last I saw of them were eight little figures disappearing up the road, carrying two white flags and two Union Jacks."

Thus ended the battle for SINGAPORE. There was a bitter feeling of frustration among the fighting men of the 18th Division. A Division

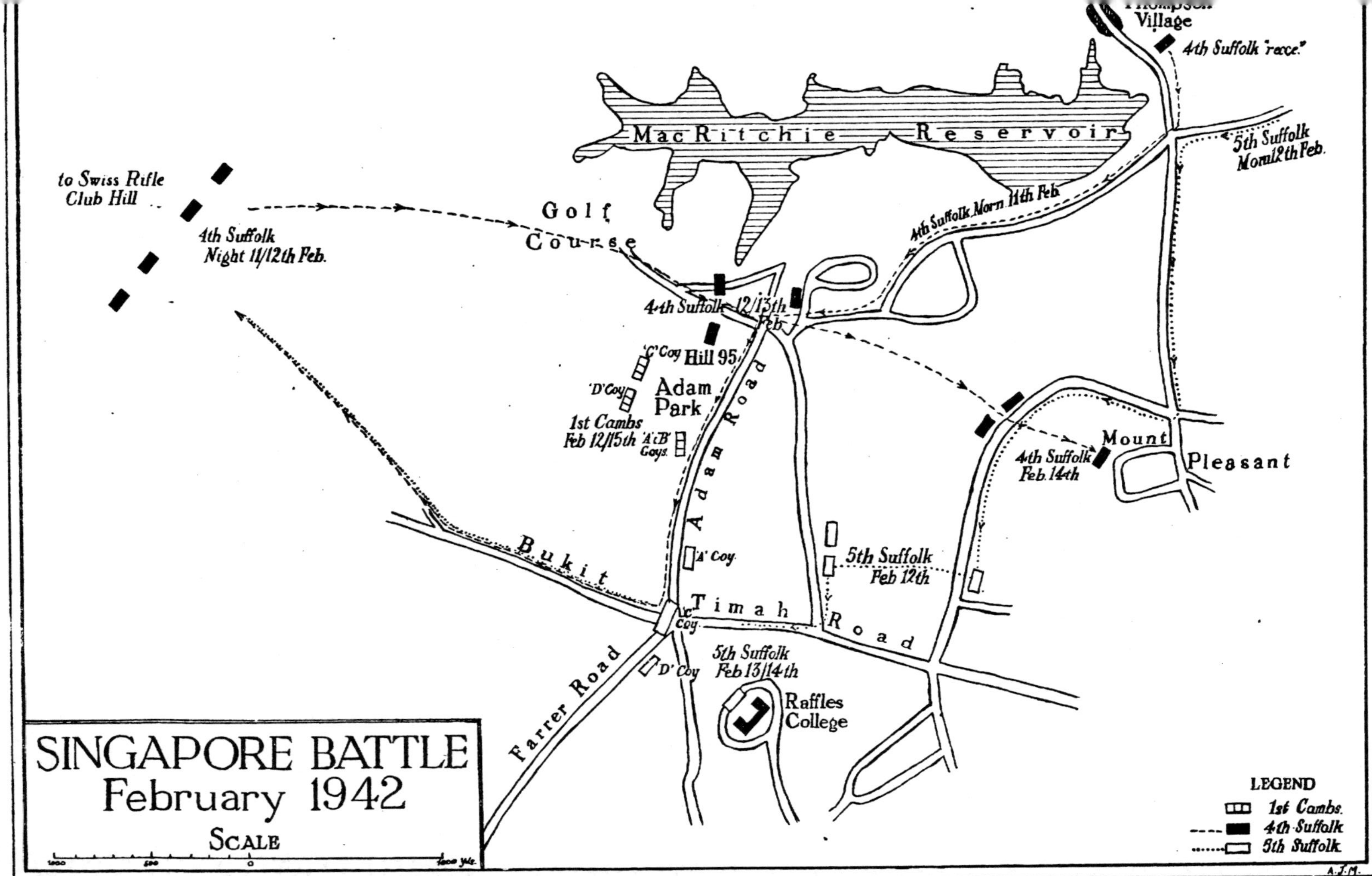
SINGAPORE BATTLE
February 1942
SCALE
1000
500
0
1000 Yds.
LEGEND
1st Cambs.
4th Suffolk
5th Suffolk
MacRitchie Reservoir
Village
4th Suffolk "recce."
5th Suffolk Morn 12th Feb.
4th Suffolk Morn 11th Feb.
to Swiss Rifle Club Hill
4th Suffolk Night 11/12th Feb.
Golf Course
4th Suffolk 12/13th Feb
'C' Coy
Hill 95
'D' Coy
Adam Park
1st Cambs Feb 12/15th
'A' & 'B' Coys.
Adam Road
Mount Pleasant
4th Suffolk Feb. 14th
5th Suffolk Feb 12th
'A' Coy
Bukit Timah Road
'C' Coy.
'D' Coy
5th Suffolk Feb 13/14th
Raffles College
Farrer Road
A.J.M.

presumably landed as a forlorn hope; untrammelled by an exhaustive retreat; fresh, inspired, ready to match itself against a victorious but by no means superior or invincible enemy. A Division that actually was never employed as a Division when the battle came; but was scattered not even by Brigades but by Battalions, and sometimes by Companies, under strange Commanders.

The full story has yet to be told; when all the facts are known. But in the final tale the accounts of the individual Battalions will have small space. The knowledge that the 1st Cambridgeshires fought a great fight; the belief that the 5th Suffolk, had they been equally tested, would have equally responded; the realization that the 4th Suffolk had a raw deal. For the 4th Suffolk was pushed "into the blue" on the 13th and here in the enclosed country they were subjected to Japanese superiority in tactics; snipers up trees, crackers from aircraft and artillery in their rear sounding like rifle shots, infiltration—and they were fighting with no clear objective. A gruelling battle baptism.

An even sterner test was yet to come. Captivity. How magnificently the officers and men responded is known to all.

The final order to "cease fire" came soon after 1600 hours on 15th February. Before this the 5th Battalion, one of whose companies had withdrawn on an order from the Officer Commanding 4th Norfolk, concentrated at and around the hill on which Raffles College stands.

Thus after two and a half years' training, the battle experience of the 4th and 5th Suffolk ended with seventeen days' fighting. The 4th Battalion had lost, killed or died of wounds, 7 officers and 93 other ranks; the 5th Battalion 2 officers and 32 other ranks. But the casualties in the 18th Division in no way represent the measure of the test to which the Battalions were put.

PRISONERS OF WAR, CHANGI.

FEBRUARY, 1942—OCTOBER, 1942.

The troops who capitulated at SINGAPORE spent three and a half years in Japanese hands. During this long period they suffered an incarceration that will for ever brand the honour of Japan.

The three and a half years can be roughly divided into three phases: The first: nine months at CHANGI and other camps on the island of SINGAPORE; here conditions though hard were bearable. The Second Phase: from October 1942 till the middle of 1944, when the Japanese were building the BURMA—THAILAND Railway through jungle and over mountains to link Bangkok with their front in BURMA. Every available prisoner of war was employed at work on this railway, with complete disregard to life or suffering. The Third Phase: when, the Railway completed, many of the prisoners who still remained alive were moved to Japan. The conditions on board the ships were atrocious; many ships were sunk by American bombers or submarines.

Throughout the greater portion of the captivity no attempt was made by the Japanese to mitigate the conditions of existence; instead, a savage hatred and gross callousness added to the prisoners' lot and accelerated the very heavy death roll.

The food was the bare minimum to keep the fittest and toughest alive; yet when captivity ended, Red Cross parcels that had been stored for months and perhaps years were found in Japanese possession. A loin cloth was often the only article of clothing for the men at work on the railway, while boots, shoes and hats were very scarce. Their own ragged blankets were their only covering for men who slept sometimes in the open, often in leaky tents during Monsoon weather. Medical stores were either deficient or far below requirements; scourges of cholera and all the tropical diseases swept the insanitary camps; yet the sick undernourished men were made to continue at work under the blows of their guards.

In the sharpest distinction to this malignity of the Japanese stands the temper of their prisoners. The East Anglian Territorial Battalions closed their ranks and stood firm. The officers shared all with their men, pooling their pay, proving their quality; the medical officers were untiring in their labours to relieve the sick; the chaplains played a noble part; the cooks spared no efforts; the signallers risked much to obtain news and pass it round. Battalion Records of the men were kept, though all writing materials were forbidden. There was magnificent discipline.

The British character under adversity was pre-eminent. The good temper. The unfailing sense of humour; that most wonderful British heritage. The unselfishness. The optimism. H.E.P., an officer in the 5th Bedfordshire, wrote:—"It was not all black. Just as the jungle scenery often made a beautiful background for the hard work that had to be done, so did the wonderful good humour of everybody help to off-set the unpleasant deeds of our captors." Those who have read the stories of the prisoners of war will feel that "unpleasant deeds" is a very mild description.

There have been many epic stories of the world war; many outstanding feats of gallantry and endurance. But have even the greatest of these exceeded the steadfast courage of the units on the BURMA-THAILAND Railway? For it is not danger that so fully tests the quality of a man as disaster.

In one respect the men of these Infantry Battalions had an advantage over their comrades in the other branches of the Army. They belonged to a Regimental family. Time and again the inestimable value of this link is proved in the story of the 4th and 5th Battalions.

The following record of the captivity is compiled from accounts by Lt. G. G. Moir, Major C. J. M. Watts and particularly from the diary kept by Capt. R. G. de Quincey. This diary was a wonderful achievement; for all writing materials were strictly forbidden by the Japanese, who would not have hesitated to inflict the severest penalty had they known. It was a diary prompted by the Battalion desire to keep in touch with all its officers, N.C.O.s and men; to render them help wherever they might be, to bring final news of them to their relations at home. It did all this. It is a record of the marches, the camps, the labour throughout the building of the BURMA-THAILAND Railway; the streaming rain, the sun's heat, the sickness, the death and burial; the food, the clothing, the pay and in mitigation of all this, the home made amusements.

On the capitulation at SINGAPORE Major S. G. Flick collected as many of the 4th Battalion as possible into a house in Mount Pleasant Road, where they remained for two days. Thence they went to CHANGI. The strength at this time was 18 officers and 432 O.Rs., during the next fortnight the 4th Battalion strength rose to 28 officers and 746 O.Rs.

Meanwhile the 5th Battalion had also been assembled at CHANGI. At this stage everyone was very downhearted. Why, they said, were we thrown into a chaotic campaign that was already lost? It was a bitter blow for such eager men to know their services had been wasted. Most men lay down on the concrete floors with nothing to do and wishing to do nothing. During this difficult period General Beckwith-Smith set a magnificent example to everyone in the 18th Division; adding to the respect and admiration of all who came into contact with him.

During the first few weeks of imprisonment, most were too tired and too hungry to take advantage of the temporary laxity of Japanese control. There was much sickness, chiefly dysentery, due to the sudden change from European food to a scanty rice diet.

After three weeks' rest at CHANGI, prisoners of war were sent into SINGAPORE to clean up debris and work in the docks. They passed Japanese lolling in their shirt sleeves on the verandahs of European houses; but however much the enemy swaggered, he failed to impress. During these visits the men managed to scrounge books and kit which later were to prove invaluable.

The period from February till October, 1942, was by far the easiest part of the captivity. The hot days passed to the accompaniment of unending conjectures as to "How long will it be before we are free"; for none had yet settled down to the professional long term prisoners of war they were to become. At this time the Japanese were still out to get a good Press in the world's newspapers. There was condescending talk by them of "BUSHEDO," their vaunted code of chivalry, and many "PRESENTOS" of looted stores. When the war was going less well the same word "PRESENTOS" instead of indicating charity became, in prison parlance, a beating.

In March and April parties of the 4th and 5th Suffolk were sent out from CHANGI to labour camps outside. The largest of these parties numbered about 2,000 under Brigadier E. H. W. Backhouse and included Lt.-Col. L. Baker with 18 officers and 600 of the 5th Suffolk, 6 officers and 250 of the 4th Suffolk. They were camped in the neighbourhood of Bukit Timah Golf Course, where they remained until they proceeded to THAILAND. Here their principal task was to construct on the hill overlooking the golf course a road and shrine to commemorate the Japanese who had fallen in the battle.

At this Camp, in addition to dysentery and malaria, the first onset of diseases due to vitamin deficiencies developed. These included tropical ulcers, ringworm and other skin complaints. In time it was no common sight to see a man's chest and back completely covered with ringworm. Many were affected by cornelia ulcers of the eyes.

In June Lts. Bennett and Peacock with 61 O.Rs. of the 4th Battalion were sent to Bang Pong to build camps for the main labour parties which, though it was still unknown to them, were to follow later to construct the BURMA-THAILAND Railway.

Minden Day, August 1st 1942, was celebrated by those who remained in CHANGI. Capt. R. G. de Quincey gives the following account.

"Minden Day, 1942 turned out to be a thoroughly enjoyable day under the circumstances:—

Battalion Parade at 0845 hours with 106 on Parade, a March Past, the C.O., Lt.-Col. A. A. Johnson, M.C., taking the Salute.

Hospital Visit by C.O. and Adjutant. Each patient received roses and cigarettes.

An Arts and Crafts Exhibition in the 5th Suffolk Library, 37 entries of high standard. C/Sgt. Torell got the 1st prize.

Cricket v. 5th Suffolk. Football v. 5th Suffolk. Football: Officers v. Batmen.

Dinner attended by Brigadier Backhouse and 5th Suffolk officers.

Concert arranged by Padre Foster-Haigh including "The Maiden Ghost"; Thomas, "Impersonations"; Mr. Botten's, Cards; the Padre's singing; the Male Choir, etc.

Greetings from and to all Working Parties in SINGAPORE, hoping next Minden Day will be under happier circumstances !

No grumbles, in fact men's main criticism was:—'Why, when P.O.W.s, did we get fresh eggs whereas last year, when free, the P.R.I. gave us only egg powder ?"

On 16th August Japan Party "B" left SINGAPORE. This included all full Colonels and above. The British troops lined the route to say goodbye, and cheered.

These Senior Officers included Brigadier E. H. W. Backhouse, the former Commander of the First Battalion. Fortune, which plays so large a part in the Active Service careers of soldiers, has rarely been so unkind. Backhouse had been with the 2nd Suffolk in the great rearguard fight at LE CATEAU in 1914, and had remained a prisoner of war in Germany for the rest of the Campaign. Now, after an equally short Active Service experience, he was once again a prisoner, through no fault of his own. On each occasion he had his foot on the ladder and opportunity was only required to show his worth and his ability.

On the 19th August an Inspection was held for the new Japanese general i/c all P.O.W.s., Malaya, Major General Fukuye. A route lining parade and a harangue by the General to the effect that he would be as kind and lenient as possible in accordance with the conventions of the Japanese. "All rather boring and tiring, though somewhat relieved by the antics of a persistent dog !" according to de Quincey.

Rumours had been current for some time about Red Cross ships, and the first concrete proof was issued on 20th August, the men receiving:—

1½ lbs. Jam.
13½ ozs. Soap.
4½ ozs. Sweets.

and enough maize to last one month for every man.

September 1st, 2nd and 3rd will be remembered as the Selarang incident. The prisoners were confronted with an ultimatum to sign a form that on their honour they would never try to escape under any circumstances. This they refused to do. As a result all the camp, 15,000 strong, were ordered to collect in the Selarang Barracks, comprising some 14 blocks and a square. Guards with machine guns were placed around. No food was supplied, other than what they had brought with them. After three days, with a threat that the medical cases would be brought in, and the medical authorities stating that there would soon be large loss of life, the Commander decided that the P.O.W.s should sign under duress. Thus from 1500 hours on the 2nd September 1942 until 1300 hours 5th September, 15,000 men were in an area of 7.65 acres; or 2,000 men to the acre.

De Quincey commenting on the "Incident" says:— "Suffice it to say that the troops behaved absolutely magnificently and appeared more at ease then the numerous Japanese and Sikh Guards.

We managed to get eight of our worst cases into hospital before the move, which took place at 1500 hours, and had to be completed by 1800 hours. An amazing procession, comprising every conceivable type of article: bats, chickens, all sorts of beds, footballs. Traffic control overwhelmed.

On the 3rd day serious illness had increased by 200%, chiefly dysentery, owing to the open latrines, which were being dug day and night in the centre of the square.

National Day of Prayer on September 3rd.

Forms signed night of 4th September 'under duress'.

Everyone got back to CHANGI, mostly a race down the hill. All officers' trunks had been turned upside down and ransacked: little missing. Probably dirty work of Sikh guards or those few O.R.s who had voluntarily signed their paroles and stayed in CHANGI."

It was just after this period that the three senior officers in the camp were compelled to witness the shooting of six British P.O.W. for attempting to escape.

At this time the Japanese commenced paying officers in cash $20 a month (except 2nd Lts.). Later this became $30 for Captains and above, $25 for Lts. and $10.85 for 2/Lts. Officers had to sign for gross rates of pay per month: Lt.-Col. $220, Majors $170, Captains $122.50, Lts. $10.85. From these amounts were deducted, with the exception of Lts., $60 a month for food, accommodation and clothing, and the amount paid in cash. The remainder was "banked" by the Japanese for distribution to officers at the termination of the war. This was, as an English speaking Jap officer explained, "in accordance with World rules."

Actually these gross amounts were deducted from officers' pay by the War Office month by month but at the end of the war refunded in full as the W.O. considered officers had not received value for money.

In October parties from SINGAPORE started to go up the mainland by train en route for THAILAND. The record of the moves of the 4th Battalion is:—

Capt. Tuck, Lt. Clarke and 47 O.Rs. of "A" Company; Sgt. Bailey and 12 O.Rs. of building Battalion moved on 15th October.

1st Bukit Timah party of 4 officers (Davies, Willett, Scaife and B. J. Clarke) with 121 O.Rs. moved en route for Banpong on 17th October.

Rest of Bukit Timah Party, 2 officers (Vinden and Day) and 51 O.Rs. moved on 24th October.

The remainder under Lt.-Col. A. A. Johnson left CHANGI on 31st October.

New boots had been issued to all. Red Cross hats to nearly everyone. As much Red Cross supplies as possible were carried; but a fatal error was made when it was ordered that on no account would any cooking pots and pans be taken.

Captain R. G. de Quincey gives a summary of the imprisonment at CHANGI:—

"On re-organising after the Battle, at CHANGI, many officers and men were very depressed and lethargic, and it became necessary for these to be shaken up, to regain their self-respect, smartness and even cleanliness. To achieve this men were ordered to shave, ordered to go bathing, given drill parades, had to salute, etc., etc.; gradually this "brassing up" took effect, and many listless persons began to get interested in what was going on around them. C.S.M. Thirkettle was a great help and disciplinarian.

The highest praise and respect was due to the G.O.C. Major General Beckwith-Smith, for his energy and example; it was with much regret that we saw him depart for Overseas on 16th August, 1942. The news of his death from diphtheria at a P.O.W. Camp in FORMOSA came as a horrible shock to all.

P.T. was compulsory and there were remedial P.T. Classes for medical and badly developed patients. Sport became very popular, especially football, hockey and cricket. Padre Foster-Haigh did very well in the entertainment line in concerts, and formed a popular Sunday night concert with good music and songs. The 18th Division formed a theatre and put on some very good shows. It had opened on 11th July, General Beckwith-Smith's birthday, with an excellent performance of the "The Dover Road."

Education was run on good lines, with three different standards:—(1) University Classes, (2) Secondary Education, and (3) Unit Classes. Practically all subjects were tackled, Languages, Economics, Agriculture, Bookbinding, M.T. Lt. Bebb was outstanding in our unit, both as an Economic expert and in organising talks and entertainment for our sick. The Padre instructed in Theology and Major Flick in Agriculture.

There was a definite religious fervour and revival in CHANGI, and great credit is due to the Padres.

The Canteen started slowly; but was running well with good stocks when we left.

Mr. Botten was "Daddy" to our officers, a first class cook and a wizard with his cards. We were very glad when he volunteered to come up country with the Battalion.

So CHANGI was not such a bad place after all, and we lived on "Rumour Hill" and could gaze out to sea, sometimes thinking, always hoping and often wondering—'Why ?'."

With more of the P.O.W. up country, CHANGI was emptied of all possible officers and men fit for work. The remainder of the two Battalions were left under the command of Major J. H. Harrison, 5th Suffolk, the numbers being swelled to 150 at Christmas by the return of unfit men from SINGAPORE camps who had not proceeded to THAILAND.

Here in CHANGI the officers lived in an old Chinese Attap house. A good garden under Lt. D. Hopkins and Sgt. R. Dunningham was started, providing many vegetables, while the excellent library of 750 books originally collected by Lt. G. Moir and Sgt. Howarth, with a small reading room, became a favourite resort.

Major Harrison writes the following account of life at CHANGI from October, 1942, until the end of the war:—

"In 1943 the work became harder. . . . .At Christmas, 1943, some of the survivors returned with the news of the appalling death rate on the BURMA-THAILAND Railway.

During May, 1944, the whole camp was moved to the CHANGI Civic Gaol and neighbourhood. The Hospital, some 1,600, went to KRANJI 20 miles away. Churches were removed complete from the old camp and re-built in the new. The services were always well attended and many found there great help and consolation during their captivity.

With the working parties out all day the only entertainment to celebrate Minden Day, 1944, was a concert in the evening, plus one bun with the Suffolk Colours on it per man.

So the months went by with news from home usually only eight months old. On Christmas Day, 1944, a whole holiday had been obtained and every-one forgot other days. The happiness, courage and spontaneity shown was unbelievable. The cook houses had saved up and gave us of their best and that night no man went to bed hungry.

February, 1945, proved a black month with two big cuts in rations, leaving us with only half a pound of rice per day. The doctors gave us six months to three years; we started to lose further weight month by month. At Easter a small consignment of Red Cross supplies, one parcel to one man, got through. By skilful use in the cook house they lasted ten weeks. The greatest praise is due to those Signallers who got the news each day. There were many rumours but it was possible to get the truth, and so we heard of the end of Germany.

Then that glorious Saturday morning in August when we heard that Japan was capitulating. A moving ceremony was the hoisting of the Union Jack once again on the Tower of CHANGI Gaol. We knew now, as never before, that under it there was freedom, fairness and justice. The kindness of the Royal Navy in entertaining us on their ships will never be forgotten.

So the eighty-six of us released on the island embarked in different transports for home, with great memories of many cases of kindness and courage."

* * * *

THE BURMA-THAILAND RAILWAY.

OCTOBER, 1942—AUGUST, 1944.

The following brief record of the work of the 4th Suffolk on the BURMA-THAILAND Railway is quoted from the diary of Capt. R. G. de Quincey, supplemented by personal accounts of Lt. G. G. Moir and Major C. J. M. Watts of the experiences of the 5th Suffolk.

3rd Nov. 1942. We steamed out of SINGAPORE at 1730 hours, a dull and tiring journey of five days up-country on the West coast route.

Food three times a day at various stations, generally stew, fetched in our scanty containers, and usually served in a hurry, especially at KUALAR LUMPUR, where we had incidents with the Japanese, accompanied by the usual slappings. The higher up MALAYA the more we were able to buy such things as pomolos, cakes and biscuits. Later in THAILAND we were troubled by Thais attempting quick "snatches and grabs" from the trucks, but they generally received clouts on their skulls. Such incidents relieved the monotony.

4th November. Arrived at BANPONG at 0700 hours.

6th November. Left BANPONG for "up river." Moved by M.T. 35 miles to CANBURI.

7th November. Left CANBURI early, after an unpleasant incident with a Japanese W.O. who insisted we should take cooked rice as Haversack Rations, although most men had no containers to carry such food—in months to come we were less fussy. We crossed the MEKLONG by motor boats, and marched 5 Kilos to our future abode, CHUNGKAI.

This camp held about 6,000 British troops. Biggest blessing was being able to bathe in the river, where many men learnt to swim. About 350 All Ranks lived in each Attap hut. The Attap hut was supported on a bamboo framework and covered with a thatch of palm. It could be weather proof when well made; the Attap huts occupied by the P.O.W. were never weather proof. A gangway ran down the middle of each hut with a raised floor on each side, on which the men slept. Sometimes the central gangway became a ditch of mud and water, while the platforms were always alive with bugs.

The work allotted was the continuation of a metre gauge railway to join THAILAND and BURMA. To open up the hinterland of the country as the Jap Camp Commander stated. The first task was to make a large embankment: this was hard and monotonous work, especially to men unused to a tropical sun. Parties were formed and divided into two, half filling baskets or "bangis" with earth and half forming a chain and passing the baskets to the embankment. Work ended at about 1800 hours and then everyone collapsed into and recovered in the blessed river.

Daily ration scale:

Rice, 20 oz.	Sugar, 2/3 oz.
Veg., 20 oz.	Tapioca, 2 oz.
Tea, 1/10 oz.	Meat $3\frac{3}{4}$ oz.
Salt, 1/3 oz.	

20th November. All Battalions allowed to reform into their own Units as far as possible.

No. 4 Bn. under Lt. Col. L. J. Baker, M.C., 5th Suffolk.
No. 5 Bn. under Lt. Col. E. L. V. Mapey, 2nd Cambridgeshire.
No. 8 Bn. under Lt. Col. A. A. Johnson, M.C., 4th R. Norfolk and 4th Suffolk.

We became No. 8 Bn. organised as follows:—

Bn. H.Q.	Lt. Col. A. A. Johnson, M.C.
	Major S. G. Flick, 2nd i/c.
	Major Bowman, Adjutant.
	Lt. J. M. Bebb, Messing Officer.
H.Q. Coy.	Major Everitt, R.A.O.C.
1 Coy.	Capt. Tundridge, 4th Norfolks.
2 Coy.	Capt. Clarke, (PMC), 4th Norfolks.
3 Coy.	Major G. H. Clarke, 4th Suffolk.
4 Coy.	Capt. F. C. Davies, 4th Suffolk.

In addition there were about 30 attached spare officers, mainly R.A.O.C. and R.A.S.C.

21st NOVEMBER. The "Task System" of work was introduced; one day's holiday a week provided the allotted task was finished: otherwise work on the 7th day. At first it was considered a good idea; but as the men's strength and resistance ebbed, we realised we had been fooled again.

9th DECEMBER. Sick rate very heavy, nearly 50%, chiefly Deficiency Cases of all types, diarrhoea and malaria. The food is still poor; desperately cold at night: many men without blankets: and to make matters worse the sale of kit to the Thais was punished with flogging.

The "Officers Crisis". At CHUNGKAI the Japanese Commander held weekly conferences with the British Battalion Commanders. This Japanese Commander demanded that Officers should work, the British refusing to agree as contrary to the Geneva Convention. The Japanese Commander fixed 20th December as the date for parading for work, saying that extreme measures would be taken in the event of refusal.

The British Battalion Commanders decided that on this parade officers should refuse to work, and that this refusal should be maintained until loss of life seemed imminent.

On the parade on 20th December the order was given to the Battalion Commanders to fall the officers in for work. They shook their heads and said they could not. "But it is an order" said the horrified Japanese interpreter. The Japanese Commander said nothing and shortly after found it convenient to absent himself.

Finally the Korean guards were called out with rifles to surround the officers. They were issued with ammunition and ordered to load.

At this stage the Battalion Commanders decided they must give way. There had been much feeling in the Camp on the subject; some arguing that they should continue to refuse at any cost.

26th JANUARY, 1943. Paraded at 0900 hours for a move to BARNKAU.

Marched 8 kilos. At WAN RAN bad rations and evil huts; but good cookhouse and bathing facilities, and the best market at any camp on the Railway.

27th JANUARY. A terribly hot and tiring day's march, made woise by our guides losing the way. Arrived WAN TIEKIN in late afternoon and found Col. Baker and 5th Suffolk there, so we were again well received.

28th JANUARY. A hot and dusty march along a track to BARNKAU, some 5 Kilos. We found the camp situated round a School and Temple with pleasant trees and grass, and a large village in the vicinity. The camp was only half built, there being five large huts, of which two were unfinished and only one had bamboo beds in it. Hence there was a great deal of initial scrounging and improvising. Excellent bathing facilities; rations at first small but later improved with many pigs. Capt. Anger ran an excellent Canteen—eggs were always plentiful—and Sgt. Wiffen ran the shop. There were many herds of cattle about, but the price of a bullock rose from about $15 to $135. The Thais on the whole were friendly and set up a few native shops in the camp, but their prices were generally more expensive than the Canteen's.

8th FEBRUARY. "Sword Display" by Lt. Kiriarma and his C.S.M. over the heads of Major Buchan and Capt. Biass, for returning to camp early without finishing an impossible task. Incidents increased as time went on and it is impossible to record them, especially as face slapping and bashing were generally more degrading than hurtful.

17th FEBRUARY. 'Doc.' Lewis (Capt. Lewis, R.A.M.C.) gave everyone their second Inoculation against Cholera: also tried out a stiff Plague Inoculation on himself without dire results.

Higher rates of pay introduced: W.Os 40; N.C.Os 30; Ptes and L/Cs 20 cents. Men now give two days' pay to their Messing and Officers contribute to a Sick Fund.

27th FEBRUARY. Officers Bridge Party finished their task and went up country to TAKILIN. We got back Bennett, Peacock and English, the former having fixed some ingenious "No booto" racket.

11th MARCH. No. 8 Bn. left BARNKAU for WUN TOW KIN, to spend a rest period, during which we evacuated all our worst Sick to CHUNGKAI, including Majors Bowman and Clarke, Lts. Bebb, Peacock and English, R.S.M. Tubby and C.S.M. Mann. Major Flick led a purchasing commission over the river and bought an expensive water buffalo which escaped and was eventually brought to earth by rifle fire from a Japanese sentry.

29th MARCH. Left WONTOWKIN at 0900 hours for "Jungle" Camp. When passing BARNKAU a wheel came off the engine and held us up for some time. When we eventually arrived at the end of the line at ARROWHILL it was pitch dark.

30th MARCH. Left ARROWHILL early. We had an astonishing march round a ledge, and came into WANPO CENTRAL and found Lt. J. C. Clarke and Sgt. Richardson of A. Coy, who were running a Canteen for Capt Ruck and his party, whom we found at our next stop, WANPO NORTH. They had been here all the time. From here we were taken by motor boat round another ledge to a small camp, which we called "Jungle Camp." This camp was in a disgraceful condition; excreta everywhere, many bad sick, many ramps, striking prevalent; the men commanded by Indian Army Officers, neither of whom saw eye to eye.

2nd APRIL. Major Flick went down to WANPO CENTRAL for Canteen goods. Lt. Peel-Yates, East Surreys, the Canteen Officer, was very successful in this line, especially with a Thai called Pong, who behaved generously, bravely and efficiently with our needs, even supplying us with "Bird Seed" (batteries) for the wireless sets. He cashed Col. Johnson a large cheque, the money from which was later to save many lives of our sick men. Rations improved and the men were well fed; but the work was very long and hard (drilling and blasting) and there were many incidents and strikings.

5th APRIL. The Doc. (Chief Cook), Ben (fireman) and de Quincey (stooge) are cooking hard and running the Officer's Mess.

14th APRIL. Issued with a few Dutch clothes.

24th APRIL. No. 8 Bn. marched to TARSAO, en route for Camp 203 Kilo. Capts. Barrett and Bardwell received a bashing en route for failing to help in shoving a truck out of a ditch.

25th—27th APRIL. Rested at TARSAO. Many Dutch troops straggled through; a pitiful sight.

28th APRIL. Left TARSAO at 0830 hours. Flick stayed behind with jaundice; I decided not to be left behind and borrowed Major Flick's stick for the 7 days' march ahead of us. Much praise is due to the men for marching up so cheerfully and always in a compact body; fortunately Lt. Col. Johnson was allowed a free hand in halts. We marched for 40 mins. and rested for 20 mins. I think I can truthfully say that this party under Col.

Johnson easily put up the best show. All heavy baggage had been left behind at TARSAO. Later we received some, but much was damaged or looted.

Marched 13½ Kilos and arrived at TONCHAN CAMP.

29th APRIL. Left TONCHAN. Marched 8 Kilos to a Staging Camp in a clearing.

30th APRIL. Marched to KANU No. 3 Camp, a well constructed camp run by Australians; rations very bad.

1st MAY. Marched 11 Kilos to KINSAYHUK, a very bad camp. The Dutch cooked for us; the British were not helpful. We were left to sleep in the open: it rained most of the night, but most preferred to sleep out owing to the numerous bugs and rats inside the huts.

2nd MAY. Marched 16 Kilos to RIN TIN—a horrible march.

3rd MAY. Marched 19 Kilos to HINFATO, where we found a mixed British and Dutch Camp.

4th MAY. Marched 10 Kilos to BRENCARDA.

5th MAY. Marched 17 Kilos through hilly country to Camp 203 KILO, on the river's edge.

No. 8 Bn.s casualties during this whole march were only 4 sick. Much singing en route, especially "The Perambulator" and "Cockadoodle Doo"; the leading lights were L/Cpls. Woombs (4 Norfolk) and Kersey.

N.B. On arrival after marching seven days without solid food, with fever, jaundice and malaria, I regret I lay down and said I wanted to die. My friends decided otherwise!

203 KILO CAMP was on a good sandy site by the side of the river. To start with rations were very bad; there was a great shortage in tents; the guards were difficult. There was however a first class bathing beach.

12th MAY. Rations were only:—

Tea	.055 oz.	Veg.	5.2 oz.	Sugar	.4 oz.
Oil	.24 oz.	Salt	.5 oz.	Dried Meat	14 oz.
Rice	23 oz.	Fish	.8 oz.		

16th MAY. No. 8 Bn. present strength; 7 officers and 248 O.Rs. First batch of Mail arrives from England, etc., mostly dated June and July, 1942.

26th MAY. Our first Cholera suspect, viz., Pte. Wilson, 4th Norfolk. Although the Japanese said he had Cholera, our doctors did not think so. 'Doc' Lewis pulled him through.

3rd JUNE. 45 deaths from Cholera at Base Camp.

21st and 22nd JUNE. Cholera for 8th Bn., a very unpleasant period. On the 21st Pte. Bryant (4th Norfolk) contracted it, died and was burnt that night. On 22nd L/Cpl. Moseley, our Medical orderly, developed it and died that afternoon; and Pte. Jarmay (4th Norfolk) did likewise. Great credit during this period is due to 'Doc' Lewis and especially to Pte. Constable who saw a great friend die and walked out of the infected area that night without a stitch of raiment to his credit! He was made to burn even his Salvation Army Flag! Pte. Constable ran many devout and well attended services.

We heard of the death of Sgt. Owen at HINDATO. We had tried very hard to get milk and money down to him and I was refused permission to walk down there. When a man got stranded in a strange camp, away from the Unit, he often failed to pull through. Owen had always shown himself a first class N.C.O.

28th JUNE. A good concert, with Frankie, Major Woods, Jock Allen, 'Doc' Lewis, Lt. Hardy, etc.

14th—20th JULY. It rains in earnest. Rations fall off, no surplus cows and no fresh vegetables. A few boots and shorts arrive and we now have "No booto" officers.

1st AUGUST. Minden Day. Each Suffolk man given 10 cigarettes. At night 'Doc' Lewis does some conjuring and Frankie and Major Flick make a noise.

5th AUGUST. 5th Suffolk party came in very late and all through the night, utterly exhausted and looking pretty ill: it had rained incessantly and they had had to swim and wade a great deal. Much difficulty was experienced in getting them all into Camp, as the night was pitch black and the track a shambles of half finished bridges and cuttings. Capt. Davies was up all night and eventually went out on a rescue party with R.S.M. Meredith.

6th AUGUST. 5th Suffolk party left at 1400 hours, somewhat rested and dried. Col. Johnson won the day over some bad sick of theirs, who were allowed to stay behind eventually, but not before two very sick men who were lying on the ground were brutally kicked; they both died a few days later.

22nd AUGUST. 8th Bn. marched to KAMERON PAR. All ranks had been given some form of footwear before leaving, but many lost them in the mud, especially any plimsolls. March included such obstacles as bridges ('Doc' Lewis never tackled one, preferring to swim; Major Mead and L/C Furk both fell off!), ravines, waterfalls, virgin jungle and mud. Thousands of natives all over the place. KAMERON PAR one mass of mud: no tea: men tried to sleep in leaky tents, officers on barges.

23rd AUGUST. Arrived at 226 KILO CAMP.

203 KILO CAMP had proved a good camp on the whole, except for the very hard work and long hours on the Railway. Many sick, but evacuation scheme came into play. Definitely it is now a case of endurance and the survival of the fittest. From all accounts conditions and especially the rations at CHUNGKAI are now sufficiently good for the light sick to get well, but are inadequate for the bad sick.

Both Col. Johnson, Camp Commander, and Capt. Davies, Camp Adjutant, dealt successfully with the Japanese, and earned the praise and respect of the men.

29th AUGUST. Officers pay slightly altered. Food and accommodation reduced from 60 dollars to 20 dollars, but the balance gets banked; and all officers, irrespective of rank, get 30 dollars a month.

7th October. Embankment and bridging work ends: tools are cleaned on the 8th: henceforth work will be quarrying, maintenance and ballasting.

16th OCTOBER. Second batch of letters arrive.

25th October. Official opening of the railway. Jungle Concert here.

13th NOVEMBER. We get pretty low with Oil and Sweetenings. I bought a sack of sugar for $240 (probable cost about $20) at KINBURI.

27th NOVEMBER. I go to TOMAJO and see Lt. Scaife who had seen Capts. Hollamby and Walker evacuated from NICKI. A very grim picture painted; we lost 2 officers (Rev. F. Haigh and Lt. Cork) and 111 O.Rs up there out of about 180. (Later proved to be many more).

Sgt. Bloomfield, 4th Suffolk was at TOMAJO. Writing of the Rev. Haigh he says "The Padre was magnificent in comforting the men. He was singing a few hours before he died from Cardiac Beri-Beri.

28th NOVEMBER. Death of Pte. Upson. Funeral attended by 7 officers and 20 O.Rs. of the 4th Suffolk. Service taken by Col. Johnson. (There are many similar entries in the diary).

27th DECEMBER. Xmas is over. Considering the circumstances, the food, sports and entertainment were excellent. Xmas Day included Carols, Treasure Hunt, Magic, Sports, and a most amusing Pantomime, especially noteworthy for Freddie Thompson and a cow.

1944. 1st JANUARY. An enjoyable day with good food, sports, etc., but the 2nd version of the "Suffolk Pub" had to be postponed because Pte. Smy, the "Leading Lady," was ill with malaria. We had 20 All Ranks, including Pte. Wright ("A") as guests from KRIANKRI for 3 days: also Capt. Angus' bitch "Sally" who afforded Markwell and various onlookers much fun in the "rat" line.

20th JANUARY. Healths improving, except for much fever about. Swimming and Basketball popular, sports held in both. The mail arrived up to letter M, about a year old.

4th FEBRUARY. Red Cross issue of a goodly size, including games, and canteen goods.

The six months spent at 226 KILO CAMP was, under the circumstances, one of the best run and happiest camps in THAILAND. The work and conditions were very hard to start with but everything possible was done until eventually the accommodation was good and especially clean, the men's spirits very high, entertainment plentiful, and the messing well run. The chief disadvantages:—the dread of cholera and later maglignant malaria.

1st MARCH. Train journey to CHUNGKAI.

2nd MARCH. Arrived CHUNGKAI. There are about 300 4th Suffolk here, mostly reasonably fit. All our officers have been good in welfare and Lt. Bebb especially noteworthy in Messing. Sgt. Horrex, camp Carpenter, especially praised for making double bass for an excellent orchestra led by Norman Smith and Cliff. The cemetery is very large with over 1,300 graves. Lt. Col. Johnson, Major Flick, Davies and Self are put into an Officers fit "Red" Bn. of about 200 strong—future obscure!

10th MARCH. The 1st Overseas (Japan?) Party leaves. We sent 44 O.Rs including C.S.M. Challess, Sgt. Woodruffe and L/C Wilkes, who took a copy of the Bn. Casualties with him. They went off—a very cheery party all in Winter clothes, ranging from Gordon Trousers to Airforce Coats. A word of praise should be inserted here for Pte. Snell, who has at all times done the dirty things in and around hospital. He is the mascot of all the Bn.

2nd APRIL. Gordon, O. R. returns to this camp from 6 months' imprisonment in SINGAPORE JAIL, and reports that Sgt. Jackson, Cpl. Evans and L/C Dawkins were all involved in a NICKI Escape Party, and as a result were serving life sentences there. Those three had escaped, hidden in a cave, and lived on the country until recaptured.

23rd MAY. A few Red Cross Supplies came in to-day on the scale of one parcel between 5½ people.

6th JUNE. 300 O.Rs went up country to KINSYDK with 3 officers under Capt. Aylwin for repair work.

7th JUNE. Second Japan Party left in good health and dress. We lost 'Doc' Lewis and 53 O.Rs.

24th JULY. Much fever, especially Dengue.

14th AUGUST. We celebrated Minden Day, postponed on account of floods, as best we could with extra cooking and an amusing concert at which the chief stars were:—Smy, L/Cpl. Kersey, Markwell, R.S.M. Tubby, C.S.M. Bailey, Cpl. Smith, Snell, Sgt. Wiffen, Capt. Gubbings, Cpl. Thorpe, Lieut. Bebb and his Cookhouse Staff (who forgot their words). The Camp Swingtet assisted and gave a good rendering of "Speed the Plough."

23rd AUGUST. The Japanese order that all dogs are to be killed or they will shoot them. This was done.

17th SEPTEMBER. The Japanese caused all watches, rings, lockets, medallions, gold and silver articles of value, to be registered. These articles fetch a high price in the Black Market with the Thais, and most prisoners think rightly that it is better to have dollars in cash which can be converted into eggs for the benefit of the sick, than keeping sentimental possessions. The Japanese are also troubled about the loss of kit, and as usual there are numerous bashes. As a result each Bn. is given a Quarter Master who has to be responsible for the issue and checking of clothing.

20th SEPTEMBER. The Japanese are denuding the camp of fit men and are sending them up country. The usual procedure is for the Japanese doctor, who in private life was a horse quack, to pick out those people considered to be the fittest. In Col. Johnson's Bn. I, as Adjutant, go round with paper and pencil pretending to be very impressed with respective choices; then after he has left, our own medical officer holds a British Sick Parade and picks out those men who were really the fittest. The Japanese considered a man as fit unless he had a visible complaint such as:—Ulcers, Yellow Jaundice and Beri-Beri swellings.

Space has not permitted more than the above brief extracts from de Quincey's diary. John Coast in his most graphic book "Railroad of Death" tells in great detail the tragic sufferings. He summarises the conditions at the end of April, 1943, as follows . . . .

"Before we enter on this fatal stage of our journey, let us recapitulate the normal position that the troops and officers were in. We had now been prisoners for fifteen months. The men had been doing daily hard coolie work in tropical weather, on insufficient rations with little or no medical attention, and on fourpence a day for anything up to fourteen months. There was hardly a man who had not already been in hospital and most of them were already familiar with malaria, dysentery and vitamin deficiency diseases. They probably on average were one to two stone underweight and in a very poor state of resistance. Already the total kit of the average troop might be made up as follows; an old hat; a pair of boots with leaky soles and of course no socks; a "Hap-Happy" in which he worked; perhaps a patched pair of reserve shorts his only "smart" garment—no other clothes at all. Then there would be a water bottle with a worn out cork; a mess tin and spoon; a ground sheet out of which the proofing had vanished, and which was sticky, smelly, and leaky; two sacks, or perhaps an old blanket; a pack to carry this in; and possibly a share in a mosquito net; these were the sum total possessions of the average British soldier, and many had far, far less.

"The officers were more fortunate . . . . . out total kit might consist of an old valise; one blanket, plus a sacking or home made cushion which made up our bedding; a mosquito net and an old stinking ground sheet or gas cape; mess tin, knife and spoon; one good, one bad shirt; one good, one bad pair of shorts. Some sort of boots, and a much darned pair of old grey socks.

That would be about the lot, much more would, anyhow, have been impossible as we were our own porters.

From this it is clear that the motley gang that was now off on the real trek up country was already pretty depleted in food, clothes and bedding, and most important of all, in physical resistance to disease."

* * * * *

The story of the 5th Suffolk during the building of the Railway is taken from accounts written by Major G. G. Moir, Major C. J. M. Watts and Capt. E. T. Sykes.

In October, 1942, the 5th Battalion moved up from SINGAPORE to THAILAND by train. The four days' journey to BAM PONG in Thailand will remain a memory of remarkable discomfort; thirty men were crammed into each small enclosed truck, so that it was impossible to lie down or indeed move at all. The food issued was plain rice; and they would have been in poor shape by the end of the journey had they not just received the first and only complete Red Cross issue of rations from home. The natives were friendly in Malaya, occasionally giving them fruit. Apart from the acute personal discomfort, the most distressing aspect for the prisoner travelling was the impossibility of protecting his very limited kit from damage—kit on which his future comfort entirely depended. The floors of the truck were often awash with water or covered with coal dust; anything breakable was almost certain to be trampled on before the journey was over.

After a harangue by a Japanese general, who warned them that they were about to work hard on the great BURMA-THAI railway, they moved by truck to CANBURI, and then by foot to the next camp up the MEE KLONG river, CHONGKIA. Here in November, 1942, the two parts of the Battalion were reunited under the Command of Lt. Col. L. J. Baker, as No. 4 Battalion, and worked either on the embankment or quarrying, living in bamboo huts thatched with 'attap' made of palm fronds.

Although there were still those amongst them who, incurable optimists, maintained that they had only another three to six months of imprisonment to endure, most by this stage had ceased to believe the false prophets, and were adjusting themselves to what they realised must be a long stay. They obtained a little news from reading between the lines of a Japanese-controlled newspaper, the "Bangkok Chronicle," printed in English, and from illicit radio-sets concealed in bamboo or water bottles.

In January, 1943, No. 4 Battalion moved up the line on foot to WIN TOW KIN. The Japanese Commander was an indolent man who disliked unnecessary trouble between his Korean sentries and prisoners; so for the two months they were there, hittings and beatings up were rare. But the Japanese engineer detachment who were responsible for overseering were a "boorish and jungly crew."

It became clear that work would increase on a rapid crescendo as they moved further up-country, and the more urgent the task the more truculent became the attitude of the engineers and guards. Blows with bamboo-sticks and pick-helves were quite normal at the next camp, BAN KO, where to the ill-treatment meted out by the engineers was added slappings and indignities from the Korean guards. If the work on the embankment fell short of the week's schedule, men had to work through the night and then out again at the usual hour next morning.

Various types of vitamin deficiency were prevalent; as a result there was much diarrhoea, beri beri, and tropical ulcers. It was therefore with great relief that they heard in March they were to move down country again to CANBURI, to work on ballasting. The march—about 30 miles in 2 days with full kit in a temperature of over 100°—was gruelling. But the two months' stay in CANBURI during March and April of 1943 afforded a welcome respite from the jungle routine of work. Rations were better, and there were contacts with the outside world, principally through the agency of the friendly Thai trader, Boon Pong, who supplied them with canteen stores and occasional news.

The BURMA-THAILAND railway was in April completed as far as TARSAO, more than 100 kilos up river. But the worst part through the mountains above TARSAO had to be finished before the end of the year in order to link up with the BURMA side. Rumours had come through of the enormous casualties to the Prisoners of War working on the line; casualties caused by malaria, dysentery and beri-beri.

It was therefore with sinking hearts that they departed in May, 1943, from CANBURI, to fill the gaps in the labour force up country. Their only consolation was that they had been able to stick together as a Battalion for so long, and they would all be in it together.

No. 4 Battalion under Lt. Col. L. J. Baker travelled by train to railhead, crossing the terrifying recently-constructed viaducts through the gorge of WUN YI and WUN PO. As each half of the train reached the centre of the viaduct, it stopped. The men were ordered to get out and push. An unpleasant experience, for there were only the sleepers to stand on and a drop of about 70 feet to the river below. The line was like any other Japanese production, gimcrack and temporary; but it worked. When the men reflected on the number of tree trunks that had been pushed surreptitiously into the embankment, it was hardly surprising that with rain the line tended to subside!

The Battalion, about four hundred strong, marched for four days to MARTONA via KINSYOK. MARTONA camp was a strip of wet jungle waiting to be cleared for the erection of tents. Their task was bridge-building, and after a few days they split up into two smaller working camps each about a company's strength, retaining the original camp at Martona as a base for the sick, whom the Japanese would not allow us to evacuate, however ill.

The wet monsoon weather was starting and the track through the jungle, along which the line was to run, rapidly became a sea of mud. The Japanese officer in charge was one Lieut. Taramoto, a young engineer of malevolent appearance and strong anti-British prejudices. The Fifth Suffolk had met him before at CHUNGKAI, where his favourite slogan had been: "The best cure for dysentery is work." His callousness and utter ruthlessness in attaining his ends were to be the cause of many Suffolk deaths. The men had been told many times that they must be prepared to make sacrifices in order to get the railway through according to schedule; more than a quarter of the Battalion made the final sacrifice during 1943.

Lieut. Moir gives a normal day's work as:— "Parade at 8 a.m. March several miles to work through deep mud, many being bare-footed by this time. Pull all day on the ropes of the pile driver, often in pouring rain; or work high up on the scaffolding, hauling logs into place by hand. Home about 8 p.m. There was only one break of an hour in the middle of the day. It was not uncommon to see a man fall off the scaffolding from sickness or sheer exhaustion, often aided by a kick or blow from the Japanese engineers. Our diet was boiled rice, three times a day with dried vegetable, which was invariably rotten. The brutality of the Japanese knew no bounds."

The crowning disaster was a severe outbreak of cholera, introduced by the crowds of Tamils who struggled past the camps on their long trek into the hills to fill up the rapidly diminishing ranks of British and Dutch coolies. Many of these Tamils died by the wayside, and their bodies lay for days unburied, reeking of disease.

Once the epidemic had got under way in the jungle camps there was no stopping it. Capt. Cayley, the gallant and indefatigable doctor of the Battalion, had to walk many miles a day along muddy tracks to visit all his patients; but even so shortage of supplies made it impossible to give them the intravenous injections of saline which alone might have saved their lives. Of the first ten who contracted the disease in the 4th Battalion, everyone died. Lieut. Moir writes:—"Out at work, one became used to the sight of men dropping out, the dehydration process rapidly draining their limbs until only the bones showed through, like so many living skeletons. The Japanese seldom allowed such cases to be taken back to camp until the day's work was over. Most had had malaria several times; probably dysentery, either amoebic or bacillary, or both, and certainly tropical ulcers in plenty, so resistance was at a low ebb.

Just before this camp was left the Jap Medical Orderly from Group H.Q. (he was made this because he had a brother who was a medical student) arrived in the camp and demanded some surgical instruments from Captain Cayley; no doubt to sell. Cayley refused and continued to do so even when severely beaten on the face several times with a wooden clog. While being struck he packed up the instruments in a determined and defiant manner which only increased the force of the blows. But the gallant Cayley kept the instruments.

"At MARTONA CAMP the sick (the cholera cases were isolated) had no more sleeping accommodation than anyone else, and there was just room for them to lie on their backs with no interval between each man. There were usually 50-60 extreme cases who looked like death, and the medical orderly had periodically to scrutinize each man to see if he were still alive. With so many suffering from diarrhoea and dysentery and in such a weak condition that they were unable to reach the open latrines in the mud and dark, the scene and stench at daybreak was appalling. Excreta lay in the open all around the tents and an officer who was not working or a man who was not so ill as the others had to go round and bury or cover the refuse before the flies made their appearance. It was with difficulty that sufficient numbers could be found to dig the graves and carry the bodies to the grave."

The C.O. and any officers available had to assist not only with the burial service but in digging and filling in graves and carrying bodies.

In August, 1943 orders came for a fortnight's march further up country through the swollen rivers and sodden jungle to KONKWITA.

Two days after arrival at Konkwita cholera started again. With the close proximity of all so called tents and shacks, the mud, the impossibility of men being able to reach the latrines at night, and the low state of everyone's powers of resistance, the outlook seemed grim indeed. However, after 14 cases it stopped miraculously. Why? No one knew, but possibly because in addition to all food, drink being boiled, everyone was compelled to dip his mug, tin and spoon into boiling water the moment before he drew his food.

About 200 men who had been too ill to march to Conkwita were sent down country by barge to KINSYOK which had now become the railhead. KINSYOK CAMP was under the command of Lieut. Sejuki, who "used to laugh heartily on being informed of the daily death-roll." "The huts here provided no shelter from the rain, and no fit men were in the camp. Men with severe dysentery or malaria or with ulcers which displayed the bone had to carry sacks of rice, or cholera cases to the isolation hospital a mile away; others had to work in the cookhouse by day and do cattle guards by night, and finally to provide burial parties for their more fortunate comrades who had preceded them into the grave. These sorry conditions were terminated by a two-day train journey down to CHUNGKAI. But their effect was evinced by the daily toll of 5th Suffolk deaths in the base hospital which went on without intermission for the whole duration of our stay in that camp."

Lieut. Moir writing of Lt. Col. Louis Baker says:—"It is safe to say that Col. Baker's high example, which had always been at hand to infuse new life into us during the battle, was an even greater help through the years of imprisonment. He succeeded in holding the greater part of the Battalion together until 1944, and was one of the very few Commanders who remained on the THAI-BURMA Railway from 1942 until its completion. He insisted on completing the nightmare march up-country from MARTONA with his men although he was suffering from malaria and beri-beri. The sight of his tall figure striding along the column up and down SIAM helped many who felt they could not any longer keep going."

During these first three months on the railway, out of the 400 5th Suffolk under Lt. Col. L. J. Baker, 70 died, 170 were evacuated—and many of them died, 160 were ordered forward to KONKWITA.

Lieut. G. G. Moir in the foregoing account of the life of the men of the 5th Suffolk at work on the THAILAND-BURMA Road takes the story as far as the move in August, 1943, from KAMBURI to KONKWITA. Major C. J. M. Watts describes in detail this march.

Major Watts was with the Battalion on its arrival at MARTONA and describes the overcrowded condition of the leaky huts, the primitive cooking arrangements, with the small dirty stream which had to be used for cooking and washing. During this period it would rain continuously for four or five days and nights, then fine for two days before it started again. The embankment was a sea of mud and clay; many men's boots had the soles sucked off. Speaking of the working parties he says: "If the working party numbers could not be found all the sick were paraded in the evening and a Korean private soldier inspected the sick and ordered out to work as many men as he required to make up the numbers."

On August 1st (Minden Day 1943) 360 British and Dutch, so-called fit men, began the march north. It had been raining steadily for days and we marched carrying everything we possessed, along the embankment, up to our ankles in mud, with a steady rain descending and increasing the weight of our packs and bundles. At the end of the first day's march we were offered six small tents for the 360; these tents had been used by Tamils and they were far too foul to use, so all bivouacked in the jungle. It rained all night. The second day was a repetition of the first.

"On the third day we reached an area of railway embankment where no bridges had yet been built. Streams and rivers were flowing through large gaps. The first stream was only up to our waists, the second came to the shoulders of a 6-ft. man. Towards the afternoon we came to a really big river, 30 yards wide and 15 foot deep. A few rafts of bamboo were found, and some men placed their kit on these and swam across, pushing the raft; but many could not swim. Eventually a submerged tree was found. The trunk was about five foot under water and it was an extemely perilous crossing; but by the aid of good swimmers who trod the water each side of the trunk, men were enabled to cross. It was an extremely wet and straggling party which eventually got that night to Tarkinun camp.

"TARKINUN was occupied by 4th Suffolk under Lt. Col. A. A. Johnson, M.C. Here everything was laid on for us. Major Flick and the other 4th Suffolk officers saw to the feeding and housing of the men, and had guides on the track all night guiding stragglers to the camp. Everyone was dead beat and we shall never forget the wonderful reception and kind treatment by the 4th Suffolk. The last of our party, who had sick men with them who could hardly walk, arrived at 0730 on the following morning.

"We moved out the following day, leaving behind three men, who all died from cholera. At our next staging camp there had been thirteen deaths from cholera that day and we were not allowed in. The night was spent on the road, extremely wet and cold. Then on again the next day, the rain still streaming down. Most by now had discarded a great part of their kit as it was too heavy to carry. Nearly everyone was suffering from red and blistered feet; no one had dry socks or boots during the whole eight days' march.

"That night we camped at KAMARON PAR. The last two miles was a stretch of churned up mud that came half way up our legs; many men fell out, dead beat, and had to be left behind. The next stage was CRIAM CRI, with an enormous mountain to cross—up and up, sometimes on hands and knees. Finally, as dark fell, many men were benighted on the mountain side, unable to find a way down in the dark. The last and final day was comparatively easy going, and the party, everyone many pounds lighter in weight, and all suffering from either dysentery, malaria or Beri Beri, staggered into CONKWITA, our destination. Tents had to be pitched, firewood collected, and the exhausted cooks produced some rice for our supper.

"We were allowed one day's rest to get the camp straight, and then work on the railway began again. During the whole march we only had two Japanese guards with us, and they took no notice of us or our difficulties; they had quite enough difficulties themselves ploughing through the mud. We moved in 'go as you please' fashion and the column was generally about two miles long. Food on the journey consisted entirely of rice and dried vegetables and hot water. Sometimes it was rice only."

At MARTONA CAMP with the teeming rain dripping from the jungle leaves, the continuous mournful cries of the many monkeys and the ever increasing cholera cases and deaths it was no wonder that here one seldom heard anyone laugh.

Captain E. T. Sykes, another of the 5th Suffolk officers, finishes the tale of this march. He describes how on arrival at CONKWITA the Japanese set the Prisoners of War to cleaning the camp site and then to pitching the leaking wet tents, the best of which were at once appropriated by the guards. He ends this account:—

"Next morning the Japanese called for working parties on the railway and the sick and officers left in the camp tried to make it habitable; not easy with 6 inches of mud on a steep hillside. That afternoon the sick who had fallen out at KRIANKRI the previous day arrived by forced march.

"On such a gruelling march impressions were a bit blurred. We did not then know of the landings in Italy or Sicily. The incessant rain, mud, the longing to discard rain-sodden and sweat-sodden shirts and shorts; leaky boots, two daily meals of rice and dried vegetables, exhaustion, thirst, all filled one's mind almost to the exclusion of all else. Thirst was a real problem. The river and streams were extremely risky without boiling, one saw so many dead Tamils in them. The staging camps were usually short of wood for boiling water and we considered ourselves lucky if we started each day with a pint of boiled water in our water-bottles. Many collected rain water in mugs or mess tins as they walked along. The rain was frequently so heavy that a mess tin was half full in a few minutes."

Of the 165 British under Lt. Col. Baker (5th Suffolk and 1 Leicesters) who set off from MARTONA, 68 finished the march. The remainder eventually arrived on foot or by barge, with the exception of six men of 5th Suffolk who died at one or other of the staging camps.

Thus were the Prisoners of War treated by their captors, the Japanese. Here is an extract from the official letter to them from Lt. Colonel Yanagida, the Japanese Commander of No. 2 P.O.W. group, dated 16th December, 1943:—

"Taking the opportunity of the stage now reached in the completion of the Railway, I, the Commander of the Group, fully appreciate the services rendered by your people. At the same time, I trust you will appreciate you are getting fair treatment by the Japanese and I expect you to take care of your health so that you will be fit enough and prepared for the task that may be allotted to our group at some future date."

* * * * *

THIRD PHASE.

AUGUST, 1944 to AUGUST, 1945.

The great majority of the Prisoners of War had been concentrated on the construction of the BURMA-THAILAND Railway. When this was completed only small numbers were retained for its maintenance, the remainder were scattered to Japan and Japanese occupied territories. During this period the officers were finally segregated from their men.

No complete account of either the 4th or 5th Battalions is possible owing to the great number of small detachments into which they were split. Descriptions of the life of one or two of these parties in Japan must be multiplied many times over.

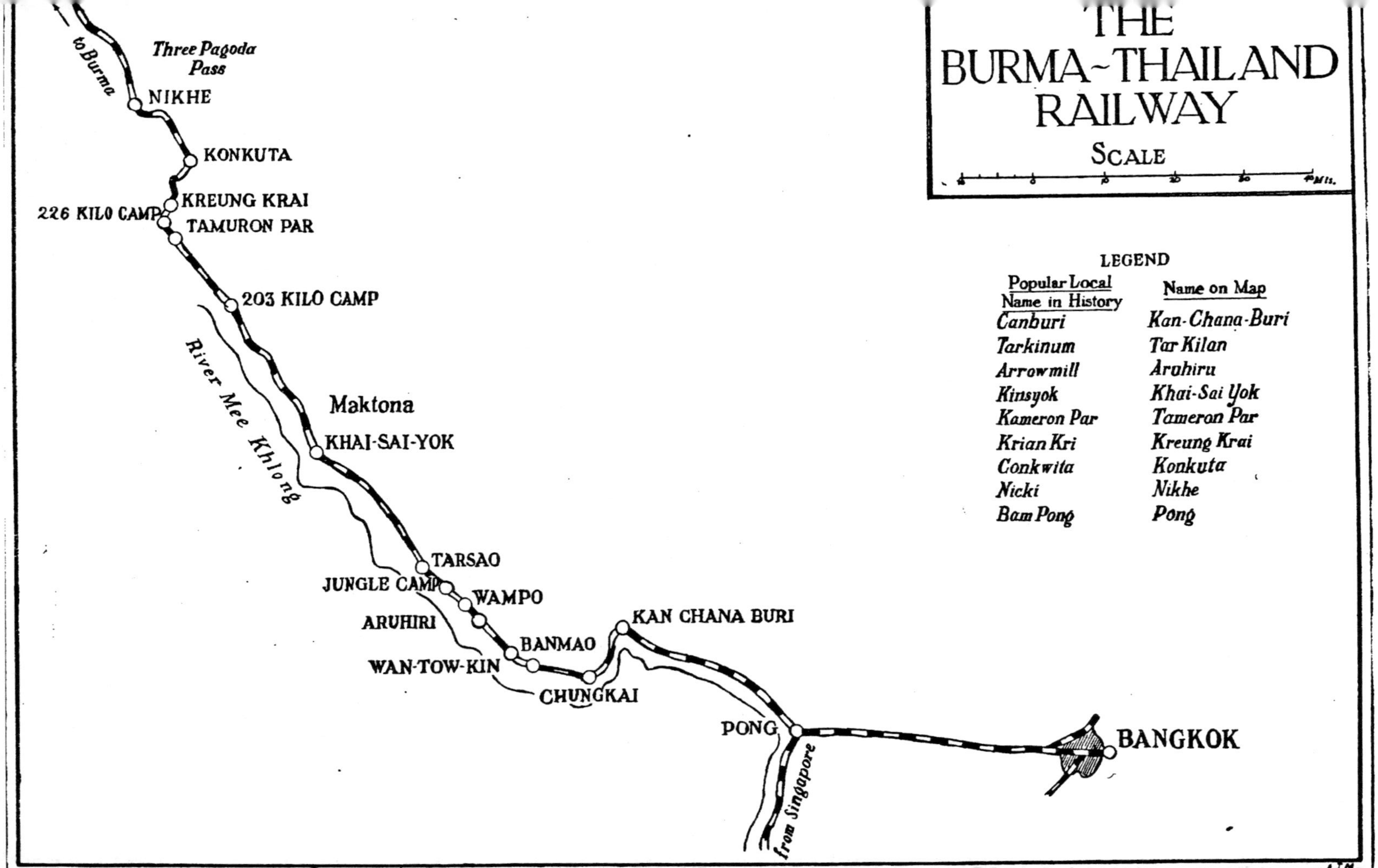
THE
BURMA~THAILAND
RAILWAY
SCALE
Mls.
LEGEND
Popular Local Name in History | Name on Map
Canburi | Kan-Chana-Buri
Tarkinum | Tar Kilan
Arrowmill | Aruhiru
Kinsyok | Khai-Sai Yok
Kameron Par | Tameron Par
Krian Kri | Kreung Krai
Conkwita | Konkuta
Nicki | Nikhe
Bam Pong | Pong
to Burma
Three Pagoda Pass
NIKHE
KONKUTA
KREUNG KRAI
226 KILO CAMP
TAMURON PAR
203 KILO CAMP
River Mee Khlong
Maktona
KHAI-SAI-YOK
TARSAO
JUNGLE CAMP
WAMPO
ARUHIRI
BANMAO
WAN-TOW-KIN
CHUNGKAI
KAN CHANA BURI
PONG
from Singapore
BANGKOK
A.J.M.

But hard as the life was for these Prisoners of War in Japan, the voyage there in Japanese transports was far worse. Moreover, Allied bombing was now added to all the other dangers and disasters.

Capt. R. M. Oliver, 5th Suffolk, writes the following account of a voyage from SINGAPORE to SAIGON in a Japanese P.O.W. Transport.

"At the beginning of July, 1944 about 204 4th and 5th Suffolk, together with about 1,000 others, left NONPLADUK (near BAMPONG) camp in Siam for Japan.

"We travelled to SINGAPORE, 30 to the truck with our meagre baggage and after five days and five nights arrived on 5th July tired, thirsty, hungry and sore. We then marched to the RIVER VALLEY Camp, the transit camp for P.O.W.s waiting to go to Japan.

"There was no food in SINGAPORE, and rations were very bad—rice 'pap' for breakfast, boiled rice with a few tapioca chips in it for lunch, and rice with a little dried fish at night. I think the fish ration was about ½ oz. per man per day, including the head and tail.

"In January, 1945 about 300 Cambridgeshires left our party for Saigon. We finally left on February 2nd; our party included the Dutch, a small Australian party and ourselves—about 2,500 P.O.W.

"We marched to the docks and found we were all to travel together on one ship; but to make matters worse there were 750 Javanese coolies on board already. The ship was the old Dutch 'Fuij Nord', built in Rotterdam in 1909, tonnage 3,500.

"The Japanese had attempted to rig up the 'between decks' with bunks to hold 300, but by forcing people below, and knocking them down with rifle butts, they managed to crowd in 600, and there just was no room for anything. To make matters worse, the 'Fuij Nord' had a very large deck cargo of lorries, steam rollers, hen coops, and all the rubbish and filth that only can accumulate on Japanese ships. So after they had crammed as many as possible into the holds, the remainder had to stay on deck, and get where they could. Men were sitting on the derrick booms, up the mast, anywhere.

"There were no washing facilities; the only place we could wash was the salt water hose, which was used for washing out the food containers. This meant waiting in the queue for hours. The latrines were little wooden boxes slung over the side, and necessitated long hours of waiting.

"We were allowed ½ pint of tea twice a day, and two rice meals. As we only had one-third of the hatch covers off, the heat was stifling; when the tubs of rice came down from the cookhouse, it made the atmosphere in the hold very nearly unbearable. We were bathed in sweat all day long and found the shortage of liquid very distressing.

"No one died, but several people were very ill from heat stroke and dysentery. Ten Javanese coolies died on the voyage. They were a poor unfortunate lot, in an awful condition. They had been tricked into this slave gang by the Japanese. A ship sailed up a river to a village in Java, and advertised free Cinema shows. Of course, all the natives went, so it went on all the week, until Saturday, when the Japanese advertised a special show for men only. The men attended. The Japs locked the doors and set sail. That was how the Japanese obtained their native labour.

"We sailed from SINGAPORE Roads on February 3rd, with two other merchant ships, and three Japanese warships. On the night of the 6th

February we suddenly heard a bang, then lots of bangs in the distance. About four or five hours later we heard them again. At dawn we discovered we were the only ship left in the convoy—those on deck told us they had seen the other two ships torpedoed. Later on one Jap warship appeared—what had happened to the other two I do not know. Fortunately, we were the only ship in the convoy carrying P.O.W.

"Next night as it got dark we were amused to see the Japanese sergeants come out of their cabin with their ridiculous swords and attache cases, and climb up on the boat deck into a life boat.

"Next day we entered the river and arrived at SAIGON about 2000 hours. I have never seen troops get off a ship quicker than they got off that 'hell' ship."

Pte. Powell of the 5th Suffolk travelled from SINGAPORE in a convoy of twelve ships, escorted by two destroyers. This convoy ran into a typhoon—some of the P.O.W. were on the top deck, while the greater number were battened down below when they had to fend for themselves for three days.

Another convoy had nine ships, all of which were reported as hit and sunk by American bombs.

A prisoner on board one of these ships writes:—

"Our ship received three direct hits, broke her back, and sank very quickly, taking the majority of people on board with her. The behaviour of everyone aboard at this time was outstanding. There was no panic and everyone did exactly as they were instructed.

During the whole voyage the doctors, assisted by volunteer orderlies, did excellent work. Three major operations were carried out by "Doc", Capt. C. V. Lewis, R.A.M.C., attached 4th Suffolk, in the hold, with absolutely no equipment except what they could make themselves, and I am glad to say that all three were successful. I would particularly like to mention that most of the medical orderlies came from volunteers from the Suffolk and Cambridgeshire Regiments. Of these, L/Cpl. Bedford, L/Cpl. Price and Pte. Crowson, B.A., and Cambridgeshires, Pte. Savage and L/Cpl. Beckett, 4th Suffolk, and others did a most splendid and thankless job of work, which all will remember with gratitude.

Lt. J. Scrimgeour with a party of the 4th Suffolk, including Capt. Mitchell and C.S.M. Rowse and Cpl. Varden reached JAPAN in May, 1943; where they were moved to a small fishing village and employed preparing an aerodrome. He says: "We procured the news here by means of a Japanese wireless set sold to us by the Japanese, which had been used in their own office!" Later they were moved to MURORAN on HOKKAIDO ISLAND, where, under Lt. Hirate, beatings were frequent.

In February, 1944 all the officers in JAPAN were moved to HAKCDATE Camp, the H.Q. Camp of HOKKAIDO ISLAND. Here Scrimgeour joined up with Capt. Mitchell and several other Suffolk, including Crane, Self and Leggett.

While they were in this camp the Japanese Commandant was replaced by another. This man was a fluent linguist. He interviewed every man in the camp, improved food and general conditions, and stopped all beatings. Letters from home were received here and another small amount of Red Cross stuff, also American parcels and a few clothes.

"In June 1945 100 British officers were moved to MITSOSHIMA in the Japanese alps. Capt. Mitchell and Capt. Scrimgeour were in the same party and found in this camp Sgt. Thorogood and two other 4th Battalion men and several 5th Battalion men. Capt. Scrimgeour writes:—

"This camp was without doubt the worst we had experienced. Appalling living conditions, bad food—seaweed being the main item, no books or recreational facilities, and with the advent of one, Sgt. Watanabe, from TOKYO, the treatment became atrocious. He made a dead set at officers—none felt themselves safe from his fist."

"The treatment in the homeland," he adds, "was definitely worse than SINGAPORE."

Meanwhile those who had remained in THAILAND were getting their first experience of allied bombing. Once again Capt. R. G. de Quincey's diary can be quoted. On the 28th November 1944 he went down with Lt.-Col. A. A. Johnson to TAMAKAN, a camp well administered by the Australians.

Capt. de Quincey writes:

"28th NOVEMBER. Although reasonably fit, I went down on this sick party to remain with Col. Johnson so as to keep the Bn. records going. On arrival at TAMAKAN I found it necessary to bury the diary I had been keeping and the remaining notes are written from memory.

"The Australians gave us a grand welcome when we came in and their hospitality and kindness at all times was greatly appreciated. They had much more kit, clothing and money than any of the British; but they are by nature good scroungers and improvisers. They were good in standing up to the Japanese.

"At about 2000 hours on the night of our arrival we experienced our first air raid. It was a beautiful evening and 21 planes were seen to be flying down the length of the river. Everyone stood still; the Japanese mistook them for their own planes until the very last moment, when their A. Guns, which were protecting the TAMAKAN concrete bridge which had taken one year to build, opened fire. Bombs were released. Some fell on an A.A. post where one gun was destroyed, four fell in the camp resulting in 18 casualties. We suffered no casualties in this raid. I, like a fool, ran the wrong way and ended up quite near enough to the last crater, with one foot in the cookhouse fire and the other in a red ants' nest, and a Dutchman lying on top of me, being sick ! Discipline was good throughout. The camp authorities demanded that slit trenches should be dug. The Japanese replied that their own Anti-Aircraft guns were quite sufficient protection for us. Later however they consented.

6TH DECEMBER. I got a Red Cross blanket and it is marvellous to be warm again, especially as it is very cold at night.

10TH DECEMBER. Much air activity. A raid over the Camp. Everyone appears to be rather nervous, especially those who are low in health.

10TH JANUARY, 1945. Small Pox breaks out in the camp.

6TH—12TH FEBRUARY. Officers are definitely going to be segregated and sent to CANBURI. I think I can truthfully say that the vast majority of O.Rs. were extremely disappointed at the officers being segregated; there is no doubt that the communal spirit played a large part in keeping the men together and their spirits high.

CANBURI was a new camp for officers of all nationalities. In charge of us were some very bad Japanese officers, N.C.O.s and Korean guards. Especially bad were the Camp Commandant, Capt. Najuchi and the Adjutant Tagasaki (nicknamed 'the frog'). Sgts. Mura and Shimoga:— the 'Boy Bastard', the 'Undertaker' and 'Scar Face'.

Surviving Suffolk officers from outlying camps came into CANBURI. Among them Capt. Tuck who had been with 4 Group up river; the men of "A" Company were particularly proud of him; and Capt. Vinden who had also been up country with 4 Group joined here. He had got into trouble with the Japanese when found with a wireless set, and had received a severe beating up which resulted in a serious mastoid operation. Vinden had been evacuated very sick to NAKAMPATON where he did magnificent work for all members of the Suffolk Regiment.

At KANBURI we were lucky in having an excellent wireless set, run by the Webber brothers, Malayan volunteers. There was very little outside contact with the Siamese, so as many Suffolk officers as possible went with outside working parties to get news of our men.

In mid June the Japanese were becoming worried about the war in BURMA. We were told that the P.O.W. officers were to build themselves a new camp in the jungle the other side of BANGKOK. An advance party was called for of 400 of the fittest officers.

28TH JUNE, 1945. The advance party left in the train at 1.0 p.m. being played out of the camp by the band: 'Bounce my brother, ten to a loaf'. The 4th Suffolk officers with this party were:—Capts. Davies and de Quincey, Lts. Webb and Mathews.

29TH JUNE. Arrived at NOMPLADUCK. The engine developed trouble here, and we were delayed for about six hours. Whilst waiting in a siding we obtained our first sight of how the Japanese treated their own wounded soldiers. Although we couldn't have looked fit ourselves, these Japanese front line troops were utterly exhausted, diseased, hungry, lousy, defeated and disillusioned. Not the slightest care was being taken of them: if they were not strong enough to get on to a train they were left to die by the side of the track. We saw many similar pitiable cases on this journey, and you got the astonishing spectacle of British prisoners giving good food and money to their hosts.

30TH JUNE. Arrived at BANGKOK Subsidiary Station. There were 26 O.Rs. here, controlled by a bad Japanese officer with very strict discipline. We were not allowed to contact these O.Rs.; but needless to say, we did. The Siamese were very friendly and used to give us the victory sign.

3RD JULY. Our party was split into two. We went on the first party with 'The Frog'. Arrived outside BANGKOK Station at 4.30 p.m. and left at about 6 p.m. The bombing had been extremely efficient here. Found ourselves marching with full kit at 1 a.m.

4TH JULY. Marched about 16 kilos that night and rested by the side of the road with hundreds of mosquitoes. Continued to march next day when we ran into a torrential rain storm, and our loads became twice as heavy. One Dutch officer fell out and was carried for two hours by his best friend on his back. They both 'passed out' about 50 yards short of our destination. We arrived at 2 a.m., quite exhausted, to find neither tea nor water for us. 50% of the officers had very bad feet.

6TH JULY. I went out in charge of the first officers' working party of 100 to the site of our new camp in the middle of the jungle at the foot of the KORAT HILLS about 2 kilos off the road. Here during the next few weeks we made a road through to the main one, kept the same in repair, cleared the jungle, carried bamboos on our shoulders about 25 kilos a day, got up in the dark, went to bed in the dark, often had to volunteer to work in the night, were always hungry, never worked so hard in our lives and always got wet at night in leaking tents which were meant for 12 persons, but had a minimum of 32. In fact conditions were extremely trying; but there was a magnificent spirit and always tremendous humour.

12TH AUGUST. We knew that something was going very seriously wrong with the Japanese guards. The Korean guards told us that Russia had declared war on Japan. 'The Frog' however continued to be unpleasant. Capt. Neguchi arrived on the 13th and immediately put four officers outside the guard room in the sun to sit there. Two days he later released them and said: "After all, we are all officers."

It was in this camp that we learnt of the capitulation. We flew all our flags which we had kept hidden for so long. We remained in this jungle camp for some days, getting into touch with Suffolk troops in their different camps and sending them money. Then we were flown from BANGKOK aerodrome to RANGOON en route for Home.

The full story of the sufferings and bearing of these two Suffolk Battalions during their long captivity inevitably brings to mind that East Anglian line:—

"If it was'nt for hope, the heart 'ud surely die."

The casualties in the two Battalions in the Battle of SINGAPORE and the subsequent captivity were:—

FOURTH SUFFOLK.

	Officers.	O.Rs.	Total.
Killed in Action	5	74	79
Died of wounds	2	9	11
Missing at Sea (en route for Japan)	—	58	58
Died whilst P.O.W.	3	283	286
Missing at Singapore	3	21	24
To X List	—	4	4
To Other Units	—	2	2
Total	13	451	464

FIFTH SUFFOLK.

	Officers.	O.Rs.	Total.
Killed in Action—Died of wounds	2	32	34
Died while P.O.W.		271	271
Total	2	303	305

Of the deaths from disease in the Fifth Suffolk there were:—
Beri Beri, 61; Cholera, 52; Dysentery, Diarrhoea, Malaria, etc., 92.

Of the 271 who lost their lives, 144 came from Suffolk and Cambridgeshire, the majority of the remainder came from East Anglia.

CHAPTER SEVEN.

THE CAMBRIDGESHIRE REGIMENT.

Commanding Officers—The Years Between—The First Battalion—The Second Battalion—The Escape Party—Epilogue—Honours and Awards

HONORARY COLONEL.

MAJOR-GENERAL R. M. LUCKOCK, C.B., C.M.G., D.S.O.

COMMANDING OFFICERS 1939—1945.

1st BATTALION.

LT.-COL. F. N. D. DRAKE DIGBY, T.D., D.L.

LT.-COL. H. P. SPARKS, M.C. (later MAJOR-GENERAL).

LT.-COL. G. G. CARPENTER, D.S.O.

2ND BATTALION.

LT.-COL. E. T. L. BAKER, O.B.E.

LT.-COL. I. G. OWEN.

LT.-COL. H. P. GARDHAM. (Later Brigadier).

LT.-COL. G. C. THORNE, D.S.O.

LT.-COL. E. L. V. MAPEY, T.D.

NOTE. Between the 13th and 15th February the Battalion was commanded first by Major A. B. Grant Stephen and after his death by Major P. T. Howard.

THE CAMBRIDGESHIRE REGIMENT.

Peace is cradled in the Fen, in the fields and open sky,
Peace of spire and carven stone, of the wailing plover's cry,
Peace for which our fathers bled, and for which they chose to stand
Valiant in the gate of Death that their blood might buy the land.
Scattered in the dust of earth are the hands that gave their toil
For the taming of the plain, and the warding of its soil;
Cambridgeshires in Cambridge earth, Cambridgeshires in foreign ground,
They arose and left their homes when they heard the challenge sound;

They are calling, "Leave the Fen,
Though you fight as one with ten
Laugh and quit yourselves like men,
Sons of the Cambridgeshires."

"THE YEARS BETWEEN"

Reduced after the 1914—1918 War to its original strength of one Battalion, the Cambridgeshire Regiment formed part of the Corps of The Suffolk Regiment with which there were many strong ties. This alliance was brought about for administrative reasons, but in point of fact the association was much older; in the latter part of the 19th century, the volunteer battalions raised by the two counties formed a single Corps, while in 1917 the 3/1st Cambridgeshires had amalgamated with the Reserve battalion of the Suffolks to form a joint reserve unit, and in the following year the 1/1st Cambridgeshires absorbed the remnants of the disbanded 7th and 8th Suffolks; the 11th Suffolk battalion, in addition, was raised entirely from Cambridgeshire.

For the next eighteen years the Regiment lived the normal life of a Territorial unit, forming part of the 163rd Brigade of the 54th (East Anglian) Division and earning a reputation for range work and boxing. Major-General R. M. Luckock, C.B., C.M.G., D.S.O., succeeded Field Marshal the Earl of Ypres as Honorary Colonel, having already a strong association with the Regiment as a native of Ely and a former commander of the East Anglian Division.

In the 1938 reorganisation the Regiment returned to the 162nd (East Midland) Brigade, to which it had belonged twenty four years previously. When in 1939 the call came to double the Territorial Army, it was promptly answered, and in a few months the Regiment was over strength on the authorised establishment of two battalions and a cadre; the recruiting drive had been brilliantly planned, and was largely carried out by serving members, together with a number of energetic local civilian liaison officers. Despite the fact that annual training coincided with the harvest, the Regiment mustered 1,500 men at Dibgate Camp, and within a few days after their return home the threat of war became reality.

When war came there were three things that the Regiment could do efficiently—mobilise, signal and shoot.

THE FIRST BATTALION.

ON the 25th August, 1939 "Key Parties" were called out, and in a few days the battalion was embodied; many adjustments of personnel with the 2nd Battalion were necessary, and were completed by the 9th September. The Battalion was then distributed in the following locations:—

Battalion H.Q. with "H.Q." Company and "A" Company at Cambridge.
"B" Company (Linton, Sawston & Gamlingay detachments) at Linton.
"C" Company (Bourn, Caxton & Melbourn detachments) at Caxton.
"D" Company (Newmarket & Soham) at Newmarket.
Regimental Cadre at Bury St. Edmunds.

The battalion formed part of the 55th Infantry Brigade of the 18th Division.

Training started under company arrangements, but shortage both of qualified instructors and of equipment, coupled with lack of administrative experience and little transport, were severe handicaps which made themselves felt for many months; nevertheless, much elementary work was done and the standard of physical fitness considerably improved. Shortly after the outbreak of war, both "A" and "D" Coys. had to take over airfield defence duties at Duxford and Newmarket for some weeks. In November, the Battalion concentrated for the first time at Weeting Hall, near Brandon, but was only complete for a few days, and from this time until the end of June, 1940, two to three companies and even odd platoons were continually on detachment for defence duties. The airfields provided for during this period included Feltwell, Marham, Honington, Stradishall, Docking, Great Massingham and Sutton Bridge, and owing to the extent of this work there was little time for recreation or training; the duties were monotonous, and in the severe winter arduous; reliefs were few and far between. It was unfortunate that only Territorials were available for this work, with the result that their very necessary training was sorely handicapped; the "higher authorities" seemed to assume that the training of officers and men was proceeding normally all the while, and this naturally led to trouble later on when they were sadly disillusioned. This might have been foreseen.

Meanwhile, first at Cambridge and later at Newmarket, the first drafts of conscripts were being trained by a selected staff of Officers and N.C.O.s, and the results were a tribute to the drafts and their mentors; on completing their training they were sent to the Battalion to fill the gaps made by the posting away of those who were unfit or "immature"; the removal of the latter class was a great loss to the Battalion and an extremely ill-advised move, as the subsequent history of many of them showed. The C.O. fought hard but vainly to retain them, while the men themselves were dejected at this forcible removal from the Regiment which they had joined as volunteers; they were inclined to regard it as a breach of faith on the part of the War Office.

At the end of the year, Lt. Col. H. P. Sparks, M.C. took over command from Lt. Col. F. N. Drake Digby, T.D., and R.S.M. Phillips received a commission as Quartermaster; C.S.M. Cole became R.S.M.

With the passing of Winter, it became possible to concentrate on range work at Thetford, and such companies as were free of airfield duties were able to get down to serious training for a time. Further calls on the Battalion for technicians for newly formed specialist units were replaced by drafts from the I.T.C. Blandford, who were very much under trained.

Prior to the war it had been supposed that the Cadre would train conscripts and draft them to the two battalions; but for reasons unknown it was disbanded on arrival at Bury and carefully selected N.C.O.s and men marked for rapid promotion found themselves engaged on all manner of duties, including service in the Officers' Mess. It was unfortunate that, if they were not required at Bury, they were not returned to their own units which needed them badly.

In July, 1940, the Battalion moved to take over a sector of coast in 2nd Corps area. The line was inclusive from Palling to Bacton, and for the first month was held by two companies, with the reserve companies guarding the crossings over the North Walsham—Dilham canal and H.Q. at North Walsham; later, the canal was taken over by another unit and three companies were put in the line; Battalion H.Q. with H.Q. Company and the newly formed Mobile Group moved to Happisburgh, and the reserve company, equipped with cycles, was quartered near Bacton.

TELEPHONE, WHITEHALL 9400

WAR OFFICE,

WHITEHALL,

LONDON, S.W.1.

15th October, 1941

My dear Russell

I am glad to hear you are going down to say goodbye to your Regiment and should much appreciate it if, in doing so, you would wish them good luck and Godspeed from me.

As Colonel of the East Lancashire Regiment, I am also particularly interested in the Cambridgeshire Regiment. The 30th East Lancs. was, after all, the Cambridgeshire Regiment up to 1881, and there is in your Regimental Chapel in Ely Cathedral a stand of our colours, which is in your safe keeping.

It is difficult to predict anything in this war-wracked world, but of one thing I feel quite certain. That in any duties the Cambridgeshire Regiment may be called upon to perform, all ranks will acquit themselves in accordance with the highest traditions of the Army.

Wishing them the best of good luck in whatever may lie ahead.

Yours ever

Jack Dill

Major-General R.M. Luckock, CB., CMG., DSO.,
"Brockland",
Saltwood,
HYTHE,
Kent.

A LETTER FROM GENERAL SIR JOHN DILL, G.C.B., C.M.G., D.S.O., CHIEF OF THE IMPERIAL GENERAL STAFF, TO MAJOR-GENERAL R. M. LUCKOCK, C.B., C.M.G., D.S.O., HONORARY COLONEL, THE CAMBRIDGESHIRE REGIMENT.

The "Invasion scare" was now beginning, and in foggy weather and during the frequent alarms all positions were constantly manned in strength; wire obstacles and defence posts were erected along the ten mile front, and minefields laid in many places. Troops were not allowed more than 500 yards from their battle posts, so that life became monotonous as well as hard. But spirits remained high, and the visits of H.M. The King, the Prime Minister and Mr. Eden during this period were much appreciated. The only training here was carried out by the Mobile Group and the reserve company, but did something to counteract the deadening effect of too much coast defence.

At the end of September, Lt. Col. G. G. Carpenter took over command, and C.S.M. Saunders became R.S.M. A month later, the Battalion was relieved and moved back to Wymondham with a counter attack role. Training in M.T. movement to likely "invasion points" took first precedence.

Early in January, 1941, the Battalion proceeded north to Galashiels for intensive training and mobilization for overseas service. Battalion and Higher Formation exercises occupied four to five days in each week, and everyone worked furiously to carry out the training which should under normal circumstances have been completed in the first six months of the war. The schemes were of great variety and interest, and the hilly country and bitter weather provided a good test of endurance. New equipment was received; in a short time the Battalion was moulded into a fighting instrument worthy of its commander's ability.

The arrival of khaki drill clothing raised thoughts of the Middle East at an early date; but plans were changed and in April a move was made down to the Midlands, where after a preliminary dispersal the Battalion was concentrated in a tented camp at Arbury Park, near Nuneaton. During the continuance of training, the pitiful ruins of Coventry and Nuneaton were a grim reminder of the purpose before the unit. The operational role was a varied and arduous one, and long M.T. moves were made through the Midlands into Yorkshire and Wales, one such involving 400 miles of movement and exercises.

Spare time was limited, but it was possible to organise a Tattoo which was produced on August 31st; an audience of 15,000 attended the single performance, which achieved a success beyond the wildest hopes of the organisers. By this means the £500 raised to endow a cot in the Nuneaton Hospital was a tribute to the hospitality of the citizens and their fortitude under bombing.

A few days later, the Battalion marched into Whittington Barracks at Lichfield where the traditional military atmosphere and amenities were appreciated. Within a month orders for overseas service were again received and this time there was no cancellation. Khaki drill was once more issued, equipment and stores checked, and final drafts completed the establishment; H.M. The King came down to inspect the Battalion, and on the 25th anniversary of the Capture of the Schwaben Redoubt it paraded with Colours, Band and Drums before the Honorary Colonel and past Commanding Officers; two days later, the Bishop of Ely paid a farewell visit. Even now the Battalion still maintained its Territorial tradition and outlook, and a high proportion of Officers, N.C.Os and men had been serving since the pre-war days. Morale was high.

* * * *

After entraining at Lichfield on the 27th October, the Battalion embarked at Liverpool in the liner "Orcades" and sailed to join the rest of the Divisional Convoy in the Irish Sea. There was some surprise at the smallness of the escort, until the unexpected arrival of half the U.S. Navy a few days later explained matters. The convoy proceeded across the Atlantic to Halifax, where the whole Division re-embarked in U.S. transports; the Battalion, together with the remainder of 55th Brigade and other odd units, was now on board the U.S.S. "West Point," the former luxury liner "America." The convoy route then led through the Caribbean to Trinidad, and thence across the South Atlantic to Capetown; as one old soldier aptly remarked "Just like the ruddy Army, going to South Africa via America!"

The memorable visit to Capetown passed all too soon, and the convoy was again on the move, headed for Bombay. In the middle of the Indian Ocean the two battalions of the Regiment parted company, as the 53rd Brigade transport left the convoy and headed west to Mombasa. The next meeting was to be on the battlefield; but meanwhile there was much speculation as to which of the two would be the first in action and in which theatre of war.

On arrival in Bombay, the Battalion entrained for Ahmednagar, which was reached on New Year's Eve; but there was little time to unpack and settle into Keren Lines, for training was in full swing once more within 24 hours of arrival there. However, the stay in India was destined to be brief; by the 17th of January the Battalion was at sea again. There was now no doubt about the final destination.

The Division reached Singapore on the 29th, by which time the Japanese air attacks were working up to their peak; there was news of the 2nd Battalion, which was reported to have been cut off on the mainland and to have suffered severe casualties.

The Battalion first moved into requisitioned houses in the Ketong area of Singapore, and then took up positions to the south of, and covering, Seletar airfield; later, the perimeter defences of the airfield were taken over. The first reinforcements of the whole Brigade were formed into a reserve battalion. But by this time, the enemy were firmly established on the island, and the situation to the West had become critical. Accordingly, on February 11th the Battalion again moved and in the afternoon dug positions covering the junction of Thomson Road and Braddell Road.

No one had any clear idea of what was happening in this area; but during the night useful information was obtained by Capt. Derby and Lt. Newman, who carried out an extensive patrol round Bikut Timah, in the course of which Newman was wounded, the first casualty. At dawn the next morning, "B" & "C" Coys. went off as an independent force to hold the Pipeline running through between the Peirce and MacRitchie Reservoirs; it was essential to prevent any enemy infiltration in this area, since such would have cut the lines of communication with 53rd Brigade operating north of Nee Soon village, and also would have threatened the right flank of 54th Brigade to the west of the Broadcasting Station.

The independent force achieved its main object and also made a successful attack on the enemy. In the early afternoon, a Japanese battalion was discovered near the north-west end of Peirce Reservoir, and Capt. Gurteen with "B" company promptly advanced his L.M.Gs and 2" mortars and opened fire at a range of 450 yards. The enemy were taken completely by

HIS MAJESTY VISITS THE AREA HELD BY 1ST BATTALION, THE CAMBRIDGESHIRE REGIMENT, AUGUST, 1940.

Left to right—LT. COL. H. P. SPARKS, M.C., COMMANDING 1ST BATTALION, BRIG. W. M. OZANNE, M.C., COMMANDER 55 INFANTRY BRIGADE., H.M. THE KING, LT. GEN. E. A. OSBORNE, C.B., D.S.O., G.O.C. 11 CORPS, MAJ. GEN. M. BECKWITH-SMITH, D.S.O., M.C., G.O.C. 18 DIVISION.

surprise and were routed with heavy loss in an action which lasted only ten minutes. During the night, Derby with a "C" company patrol moved westwards and destroyed an enemy post which in daylight had been firing with mortar and L.M.G. into positions held by 54th Brigade. They then received orders to withdraw to Thomson Road at dawn.

Soon after the departure of this independent force, the Battalion had come under the orders of 54th Brigade, and moved to the west, finally digging in on the Adam Park estate, where it was soon in action; the front was very extended, but was kept constantly patrolled in the hours of darkness; for the time being the enemy kept their distance.

On the morning of the 13th, the independent force, on its way to rejoin the Battalion, located the enemy to the west of Lornie Road; a sharp action followed, and the 3" mortars, sent up to support, did a map shoot at 1,500 yards which for accuracy and effect could not have been bettered. The enemy appeared to be trying to get round the right flank of 54th Brigade, but were decisively checked.

Meanwhile, the Reinforcement company had rejoined the Battalion, against which enemy attacks were developing; "A" company, on the right, was heavily engaged and the Reinforcement company counterattacked in support to relieve pressure. The situation was kept well in hand; but many casualties resulted, amongst them two company commanders, Marriott and Newson who were both mortally wounded. The return of "B" and "C" from the independent force duties considerably improved the position; but fighting was continuous along the whole front. The enemy failed to make any impression on the line and sustained considerable losses in their attempts. The Battalion mortars were switched from sector to sector and did excellent work on Japanese assembly positions, while fire from the guns of the 118 and 148 Field Regiments was of the greatest assistance.

Elsewhere however, the situation was now deteriorating: on the left, the enemy were barely held on the Bukit Timat cross-roads, whilst on the right they finally crossed Lornie Road on the afternoon of the 14th, thus cutting the Battalion's communications.

Casualties were steadily mounting and could no longer be evacuated, while Capt. Phillips with his "B" Echelon could no longer get through with water, food or ammunition; but from time to time, individual vehicles were able to break through with vital supplies and information. During this very critical period Capt. A. Barber, M.C., R.A.M.C., who had formerly served as Battalion M.O., somehow contrived to bring in a convoy of six ambulances to evacuate casualities. Unfortunately, before any evacuation could take place, the Japanese succeeded in setting fire to all the ambulances and also the R.A.P., which were completely destroyed, though the wounded were removed to safety. Capt. Barber then gave invaluable help to the Battalion M.O., Capt. M. F. Smith, who with his medical staff had had no rest for several days.

By midday on the 15th, the enemy had broken through to the left of the Battalion line and were pushing into the City of Singapore itself in the Mount Pleasant Road area, well to the rear of the Battalion; in front of the line Japanese tanks were seen massing for an assault, but six were put out of action by mortar fire, and for the time being the danger passed. On the right flank the pressure increased and was becoming more difficult to counter. Artillery support could no longer be counted on, and the Battalion mortars, which had been brilliantly handled and gallantly served by their crews, were no longer in action; one by one these weapons were destroyed, fighting to the last in a hell of burning grass and buildings, with their ammunition exploding around them and the bodies of their crews lying in the wreckage. They made a splendid end.

As the afternoon passed, enemy tanks again moved across the front, and now there was no weapon left to deal with them. But as evening drew near, enemy pressure slackened, firing died away and the front became strangely quiet. The reason for this lull became apparent when news finally reached the Battalion that the order to cease fire had been given two hours before.

THE SECOND BATTALION.

Originally formed in June, 1939, the 2nd Battalion finally became a separate entity when embodied on the 1st September of that year; it was not, of course, purely a battalion of new recruits, for with the reorganisation of the Regiment on a "geographical" basis those companies of the 1st Battalion which existed in the northern half of the county were transferred over to the 2nd. On the outbreak of war, Battalion H.Q. moved from Cambridge and joined Headquarters Company and "C" Company at Wisbech; "A" Company was at March, "B" at Ely and "D" at Chatteris.

To begin with, shortage of equipment, arms, clothing and boots, with a lack of instructors, considerably hampered the companies in their efforts to turn themselves into full-time soldiers, but the task was tackled with great keenness by everyone and the fullest use was made of the limited instruction available. On November 1st the Battalion concentrated for the first time as a complete unit at Melton Constable in Norfolk, and was shortly afterwards transferred to the 53rd Infantry Brigade of 18th Division, thus parting company with the 1st Battalion which remained in 55th Brigade. At the end of the month a further move took place to Holt, where companies were assigned a variety of billets including a condemned school and a disused chapel. Here the first Christmas of the war was spent, chiefly memorable for the generous gifts of cigarettes, woollen comforts and luxuries sent by the people of Cambridgeshire, and also for a large-scale influenza epidemic.

In January, 1940, the Battalion marched to a new station at Stiffkey, on the coast, which being a hutted summer camp by design, received the full benefit of the extremely severe weather of that winter; the camp was on the edge of the salt marshes and everything froze solid. Heavy snowfalls disrupted communications throughout the district, and companies were employed in clearing roads and digging out railway trains until better weather enabled a start to be made on platoon and company training. Guards were also supplied to various V.P.s in the neighbourhood.

In the meanwhile a cadre of officers and N.C.O.s was sent from the Battalion at Wisbech, who were drafted to the Battalion as soon as their primary training was complete; these new drafts were of first class material and were badly needed to fill the gaps caused by the withdrawal of "category" men.

With the Spring, training began to get well under way; but the invasion of the Low Countries resulted in the Battalion being allotted an operational role and other considerations had to be shelved in a hurry. The unit took over the defence of a sector of coast and responsibility for a number of airfields as well. The size of the task necessitated the dispersal of companies over an enormously wide area, and like the rest of the small garrison of Britain at that time the 2nd Battalion found itself holding the equivalent of a Divisional front. "A" & "B" held the coast between Salthouse and Cley, with Battalion H.Q. and H.Q. company behind them, while "C" was at Fakenham and "D" distributed between King's Lynn, Docking and Hunstanton; it took all day to distribute mail round the whole unit. At this time a Mobile Group was formed within the Battalion for patrol and airfield assistance duties, and they were really the only people who got any training at all, the remainder spent every day and many moonlit nights furiously digging and erecting defences to the detriment of seaside amenities.

In July the Battalion moved back into Brigade Reserve and was at last able to get down to training again while stationed at Melton Park and later in Gresham's School, Holt. While at the latter station it was inspected by the Prime Minister, who appeared to be satisfied with its appearance.

While in reserve, the unit held a mobile counter attack role and was allotted a number of double-decker buses for this purpose; in the numerous exercises which took place along the coast, many headaches were caused by the problem of how best to camouflage these enormous Eastern Counties vehicles in flaming scarlet; the drivers also had a peculiar habit of disappearing before a practice alarm.

In August, coast defences were again taken over, this time at Sheringham and West Runton; here the Battalion sustained its first air attack, but suffered no casualties, though some were rudely awakened from their Sunday afternoon siesta. Finally, the defensive role of the Battalion ceased, and it was moved inland to Houghton Hall, Raynham Hall and nearby villages, where the second Christmas was spent in greater comfort.

With the move of the Division to Scotland early in January, 1941, the 2nd Battalion was sent to Dumfries. It was expected that orders would be given to prepare for service overseas, but these failed to materialise and the unit settled down to intensive company and battalion training over new and formidable country, followed by Higher Formation exercises in severe weather. Considerable hospitality was shown by the Provost and citizens of Dumfries, and the Battalion came into contact with the Free Norwegian Army stationed in the same town. Unfortunately the Norwegians had more money, and this gave them an unfair advantage in the eyes of the local maidens.

In April the Division moved down into Western Command, and the 2nd Battalion took up quarters in Crewe Hall, Cheshire. The summer was principally occupied by Divisional exercises carried out over large distances into Lancashire and Yorkshire. In addition, time was found for field firing on Ruabon Mountain in Wales and company camps at Plas Power, near Wrexham. In August, companies were dispatched to carry out defensive wiring tasks on the north Wales coast and to help with the harvest in Leicestershire. Assistance was also given in the evenings to local Home Guard units in Crewe, and large-scale co-operation exercises with Home Guard, Civil Defence and other units took place in Crewe, Birmingham and Carlisle.

In October, orders were at last received to prepare for foreign service, and on the completion of mobilization the Battalion was inspected by H.M.

The King in the grounds of Crewe Hall. Last minute visits were also made by the Bishop of Ely and the Honorary Colonel of the Regiment, who brought with him a personal message from the C.I.G.S.

On October 31st the Battalion sailed from Gourock in the Free Polish vessel M.V. "Sobieski" and joined the 18th Division convoy off the Irish coast; on arrival at Halifax, N.S. the Battalion re-embarked in the U.S.S. "Mount Vernon" and began the long voyage to Capetown.

* * * * *

On leaving Capetown, the Divisional convoy continued on its way to India; but the "Mount Vernon" carrying the 53rd Brigade, parted from the other ships and put into Mombasa on Christmas Day; Mombasa was found to be about the hottest spot yet known; there were few facilities for amusement except bathing, and even this resulted in severe sunburn for most people. However, after three days the brigade was on the sea once more, and it was soon known that its destination was Singapore.

On January 13th the "Mount Vernon" arrived at Singapore in the middle of an air raid, for which the ship was meant to be the target; but a sudden squall of heavy rain and mist providentially concealed the vessel and the aircraft unloaded elsewhere instead. In heavy rain the Battalion disembarked and proceeded to a makeshift camp on the Bukit Timah racecourse which consisted largely of mud, expecting to spend some weeks in re-organising and training after the long voyage. However, owing to the critical situation on the mainland, these illusions were rudely shattered and the unit was rather unceremoniously pushed into the battle on the 16th, without having time to unpack. It was attached to 15th Indian Brigade and despatched to Batu Pahat in north Johore to relieve a composite Leicester-Surrey Battalion (the "British Battalion") and prevent the enemy occupying the town and its airfield. Within a few hours of arrival on the mainland, the first casualties were sustained from dive-bombing attacks.

The first few days in Batu Pahat were spent in active patrolling; contact was soon made with parties of enemy who had landed on the west coast behind the Battalion positions and were threatening communications. Before long, the main enemy forces driving south from Muar had built up a considerable force round Batu Pahat on the north bank of the river and began to attempt to break into the town. The British Battalion was brought back from reserve to reinforce the small garrison of the town which consisted of the 2nd Battalion, a company of the Malay Regiment and a battery of the 155 Field Regiment. Even with the addition of the British Battalion it was a very small force to hold a place of the size of Batu Pahat and meet attacks from every direction. In the meanwhile, the enemy continued to land troops behind the defence line, and before long the defenders found it necessary to form a complete circle, which was perforce only thinly held in parts. The Japanese then attacked the troop positions of the Field Regiment, taking them by surprise; a company each from the British Battalion and the 2nd Battalion had to be sent to disperse the enemy and rescue the guns. This was done with the loss of one gun only.

Having failed in their attempts to take the town by direct frontal attack, the enemy next sent out a flanking force to work round to the south-east and cut the Ayer Hitam road, the principal line of communication with the rear.

His Majesty inspecting 2nd Battalion, The Cambridgeshire Regiment, October, 1941.

Left to right—Major L. J. W. Seekings, ———, Lt. Colonel G. C. Thorne, His Majesty The King.

They succeeded in doing this on the 22nd, ambushing part of the 2nd Battalion's "B Echelon" and destroying a number of vehicles; the R.Q.M.S. who was in charge of this convoy was wounded, but managed to escape from the trap with two of his trucks. From this day onwards, no further food or ammunition could be delivered to the Batu Pahat garrison and life became rather austere.

The enemy now began to feel their way towards the town by the Yong Peng road, after crossing the river some miles outside the defence perimeter. The garrison was by now so hard pressed for men that this road could not be effectively patrolled so far from the main defences, since all available reserves were in daily use attacking enemy infiltration parties nearer to the town itself. But though the Japanese were thus able to effect a crossing of the river, they soon ran against "A" Company's positions astride the north-eastern entrance to Batu Pahat. They were promptly driven back into cover each time they attempted to break through. Similar attempts to cross the Muar Road Ferry in the harbour area of the town were held by "B" & "C" with the assistance of the gunners.

The last remaining line of communication with the besieged garrison was the coast road to Benut; but unprotected vehicles could not be sent up by this route since enemy landing parties some miles to the south were known to have reached the road and prepared blocks in places.

On the 23rd, orders were received by wireless for a withdrawal from Batu Pahat to a position some miles down this coast road, where it was intended that the garrison should halt and fight a delaying action to cover the establishment of a further defence line through Benut. Soon after nightfall the complete force broke off action and withdrew from the town without difficulty; the Brigade formed up on the coast road with its vehicles and began the march south, headed by the last three armoured cars remaining to it, and with its guns disposed in the column.

No sooner had the move commenced than a further signal was received cancelling the withdrawal order and ordering the force to reoccupy the town and hold it for a further 48 hours to enable certain British units on the East coast to be extricated first. It is profitless to question why and how mistakes such as this are made; from the wider tactical point of view it may be but a small error and unimportant, but to the garrison of Batu Pahat it was an extremely serious matter. Had no withdrawal order been given in the first place, the town could have been held indefinitely without any trouble, since the defenders were well placed in carefully chosen and prepared positions on which the enemy had made little or no impression as yet; now, however, they had in pursuance of orders withdrawn from those positions which thus fell to the enemy without the necessity of fighting for them. The garrison had thus to recapture Batu Pahat by force before it could be held for the further period, and the enemy had now all the best positions in the town.

The reoccupation of the town was effected by a night attack, delivered by the 2nd Battalion with the assistance of two companies of the 5th Norfolks, which with their Battalion H.Q. had been sent up to reinforce the Brigade just before the coast road became impassable. The attack was successful; though the enemy held grimly to Hill 127, an important feature, and were only dislodged from this after a series of company assaults in the course of which "B" company commander, Capt. Cutlack was mortally wounded, and a number of officers and other ranks killed and wounded.

Throughout the 24th, the Japanese made a sustained effort to retake Batu Pahat and pressed heavily on the defenders from all sides; the brunt of these attacks was borne by the 2nd Battalion and casualties began to mount up. Street fighting developed in several quarters of the town and confused close-quarter actions prevented the use of artillery to support the hard-pressed infantry; but the Battalion mortars were in constant demand. In the course of the day "A" Company captured an enemy infantry gun.

On the night of the 25th the Batu Pahat force, having fulfilled the demand made upon it, finally withdrew down the coast road to the village of Senggarang, where it was found that the last way out of the trap had been already blocked and the force was surrounded. An enemy landing force had erected blocks across the road and prepared strong positions to prevent a break-out.

From dawn on the 26th until 1630 hours in the afternoon continual attacks were launched against these blocks in the hope of being able to clear the road to allow the ambulances and other vehicles of the Brigade to pass through; but in vain. Once again, the brunt of this action was borne by the 2nd Battalion, and every man of the unit was thrown into the fight, including cooks, drivers, signallers and batmen; the opening of the road was a matter of desperate necessity, for the Brigade was still carrying with it the accumulated casualties of the last four days' fighting in the town, for whom there was no chance of evacuation to hospital.

The enemy positions were well chosen, the only way of attack lay over marshy ground, thickly wooded, with every clearing covered by light and heavy automatic weapons. By reason of the limited visibility in this type of country the use of artillery to support the attacks was quite useless and even mortars were employed with difficulty. Up to their knees in mud and water and hampered by the thick vegetation the companies struggled to reach their objectives, suffering heavy casualties from the concealed weapons of the enemy; destroying one post after another only to find that the Japanese position was planned in depth with every position covered by another. While the battle was in progress, the guns and transport in the village itself were constantly attacked by Japanese aircraft and threatened by infiltration parties who closed in on the houses, armed with machine guns and mortars. Behind the Post Office, the Field Ambulance staff worked under great difficulties, being continually under fire.

When finally it was found to be impossible to open the road for the passage of vehicles (there were found to be no fewer than six blocks and ambushes between Senggarang and Ringit) the Brigade Commander gave orders to destroy all guns and transport and to attempt to break out through the jungle and link up with the nearest British forces, who were believed to be at Ringit or Benut. A bitter decision had to be made—such of the wounded as were too ill to be moved were to be left in the village under the care of two doctors of the 168 Field Ambulance. When the 2nd Battalion Padre heard of this, he elected to stay with them and share their fate.

When the "break-out" order was given at Senggarang, the Battalion was widely deployed amongst the swamps on both sides of the roads with every man in action. As a natural result, it was impossible to collect the scattered sub-units into a complete Battalion in the time given in the order; however, in companies, platoons, sections and groups of every size and sort, under their respective officers and N.C.O.s, the great majority of the Battalion

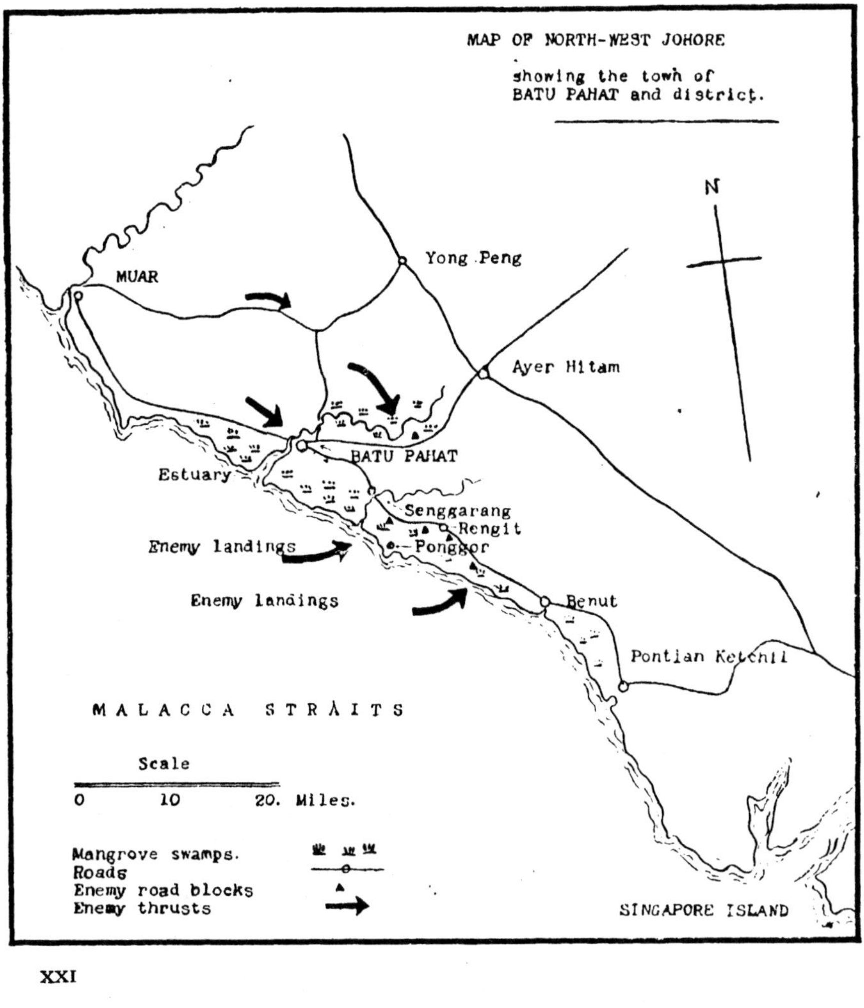
MAP OF NORTH-WEST JOHORE
showing the town of
BATU PAHAT and district.
N
MUAR
Yong Peng
Ayer Hitam
BATU PAHAT
Estuary
Senggarang
Rengit
Enemy landings
Ponggor
Enemy landings
Benut
Pontian Ketchil
MALACCA STRAITS
Scale
0 10 20. Miles.
Mangrove swamps.
Roads
Enemy road blocks
Enemy thrusts
SINGAPORE ISLAND

XXI

managed somehow to break out of the enemy ring and make their way back to Singapore, 70 miles distant.

The story of the adventures of the many parties who found themselves alone in the jungle, desperately weary and hungry, hampered with many walking wounded in need of assistance, and constantly harried by enemy ambushes on the few practicable tracks and river-crossings, would alone be sufficient to fill a book. One can only say that by the qualities of great endurance, faith and unconquerable cheerfulness these men won through; mud-covered, exhausted, their clothing in rags they came back, their weapons in their hands, the strong helping the weak. Some marched through swamp and jungle till they contacted British units in Benut or south of that town, others found sampans and paddled down the coast, while a large group of 9 officers and 400 men were taken off by naval craft from a fishing village on the coast. All those who escaped were sent on to Singapore in the hope that there would be sufficient survivors to reorganise as a Battalion again.

But there were many who did not come back, and these were killed or captured in the trap or succumbed to their wounds and exhaustion in the mud of the mangrove swamps.

As the survivors returned, the Battalion was able to reorganise and re-equip at a temporary camp on Serangoon Road outside Singapore. As the days went by and more and more of the "missing" turned up, each with stories of wild adventures to tell, the spirits of all ranks rose high and the Battalion had its tail up as never before.

The rest of the Division had now arrived on the Island and contact was made with the 1st Battalion again. But this rest period lasted a bare five days, after which the unit found itself once more in the line, taking over a sector of coast to the east of the naval base. Here there was a complete lack of any sort of defence works, and much digging and wiring was involved, principally by night and often under shellfire from the enemy batteries across the Straits; any movement by day drew artillery and mortar attention. Here the Battalion returned to 53rd Brigade. Air attacks increased in intensity daily.

Shortly afterwards, as a result of the Japanese landings on the west coast of the island, the 53rd Brigade was ordered to carry out a withdrawal in stages to the south, to conform with the movement of the left of the general line. This operation was successfully concluded although at one time the enemy cut the road behind the Brigade, and nearly caused a second Senggarang. Final positions were taken up on the evening of the 13th February to the north of Braddell Road, but owing to darkness the positions could not be thoroughly reconnoitred the same evening and information of the positions of other units was scanty. The same evening, the C.O. with a small party of officers and other ranks of the Battalion was ordered away from the island on an official "escape party," and in spite of his forceful protests to Brigade was compelled to leave his Battalion. Major Stephen took over command.

Soon after midnight, the enemy attacked the Battalion line in several places, and a force which had outflanked the Brigade came in from the left and assaulted Battalion H.Q., which though mustering only some 15 all ranks, fought back stoutly and thus contained a complete enemy company on its own. Confused and bitter fighting ensued in the darkness, and the Battalion found itself assaulted from front, flanks and rear. The C.O. was killed while manning an L.M.G., and the Adjutant with several of the Battalion H.Q.

staff met their deaths in a gallant attempt to drive back the enemy with the bayonet. All communications were cut, and part of the defence line was temporarily overrun, but Major P. T. Howard took command of the Battalion and at dawn the line was reformed and the gaps closed; the enemy withdrew into cover and seemed to have exhausted his strength for the time being.

The following night further attempts were made by strong enemy patrols to find a weak spot in the defences, but these were countered and the line held. Throughout the 15th the Battalion continued to hold its ground though its left flank was now in danger and communication with the rear was no longer possible.

In the late afternoon the Brigade Commander came in person to deliver the order to cease fire, lest this should be disbelieved.

* * * *

THE ESCAPE PARTY.

The 2nd Battalion Escape Party consisted of Lt.-Col. Thorne, Capt. Page, Capt. T. A. D. Ennion, Lieut. Squirrel, C.S.M. Randall, and Ptes. Bray, Clarke, Desborough, Hunt, Squires, Powell, Pells and Johnson. These were the only men of the Regiment detailed for this venture, since the 1st Battalion did not receive the order until too late for it to be complied with.

On leaving the Battalion this party made its way to Brigade and there joined similar parties from 5th and 6th Norfolks, afterwards proceeding to the docks; here it was found that shipping was not available for the whole Divisional party, and the greater part were returned to the Y.M.C.A. building to wait for the next night. Here Lt.-Col. Thorne was informed of the true nature of the "special" mission for which he and his men had been selected, and he and they at once asked permission to return to their unit, only to be informed that they were under orders to escape and must do their best to obey the order.

During the evening of the 14th the Y.M.C.A. building came under heavy shellfire and received several direct hits. When the 53rd Brigade party reported to the docks after dark they again found no ships, and received a message to the effect that they were to attempt to find boats and make their escape unaided. The night was spent searching the docks for seaworthy craft, and with the coming of daylight this task was hampered by continual air and artillery strafing. Finally on the afternoon of the 15th, the party embarked 41 strong in a ship's lifeboat and began to row in the rough direction of Sumatra.

After crossing over the Straits of Malacca and calling in at several islands for supplies and information, at one of which the lifeboat was bartered for a decrepit motor launch, the party reached Sumatra. Here they were taken in buses over to the west coast and conveyed by ship to Java. After a few days only in Java they were put aboard a small flat-bottomed river steamer and taken to Ceylon, being attacked with torpedoes on the way, but escaping by reason of the vessel's light draught.

And in the story of this party there is again a tragedy. While waiting in the Y.M.C.A. on the 14th, before making their escape from Singapore, Lt.-Col. Thorne was taken from them and ordered to join a number of

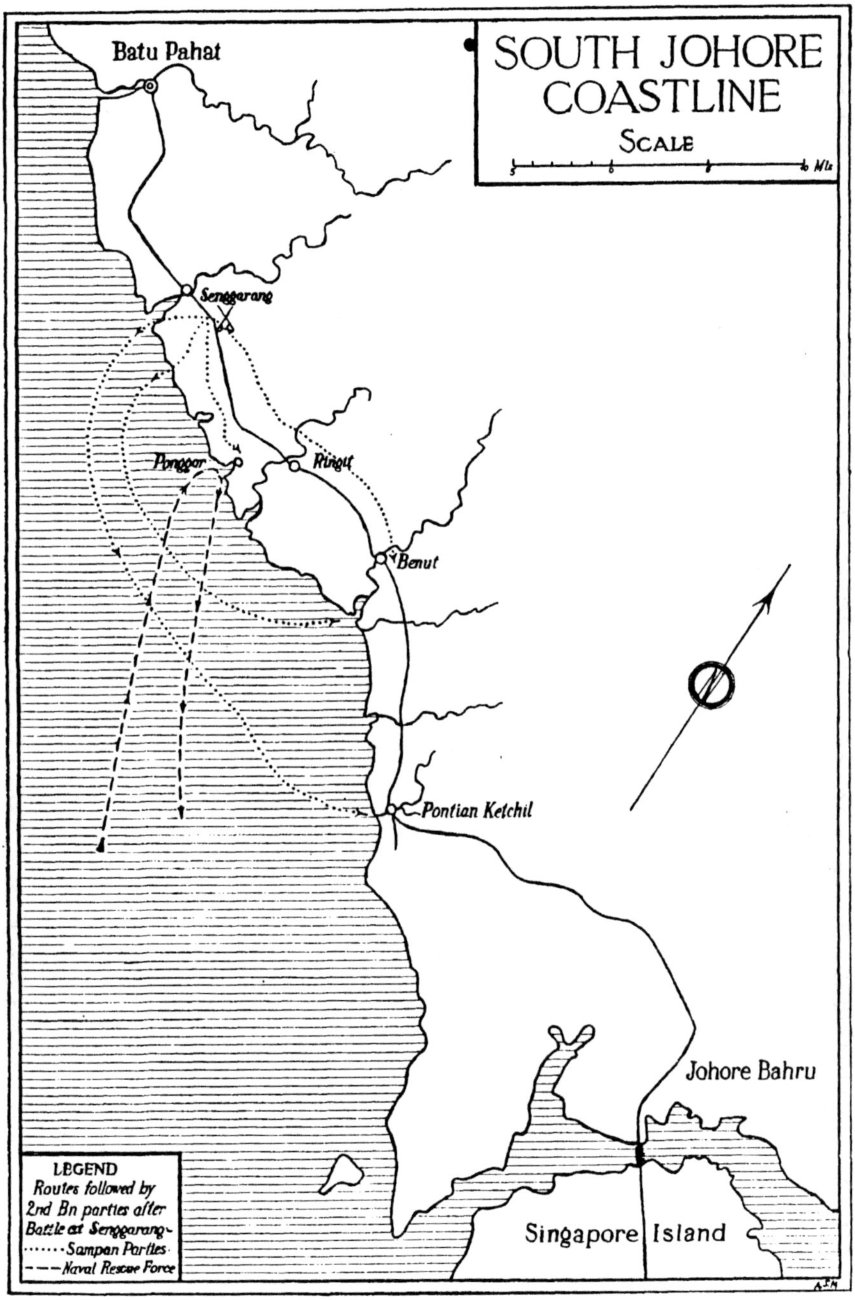
SOUTH JOHORE
COASTLINE
SCALE
Batu Pahat
Senggarang
Ponggor
Ririgit
Benut
Pontian Ketchil
Johore Bahru
Singapore Island
LEGEND
Routes followed by
2nd Bn parties after
Battle at Senggarang
Sampan Parties
Naval Rescue Force

XXII

senior officers who were to be evacuated first; regretfully, Thorne said good-bye to the other Cambridgeshires, and was sent off almost at once. He was never seen again. When the rest of the Battalion "Escape Party" finally reached Ceylon, they made every endeavour to rejoin their C.O., but could find no trace of him. After extensive inquiries amongst other Officers and men who had reached safety, they learnt that he had arrived in Sumatra and had there been embarked in a vessel which was believed to have been lost in the Indian Ocean with no survivors.

The news of the loss of Lt.-Col. G. C. Thorne did not reach those of his Battalion who were in captivity until long after, when one of the few letters to arrive fom home gave information that he was reported missing; even then, there was still hope that he might somehow have survived and been made prisoner somewhere in the East, but as the war drew to its close that hope died away. The best tribute that can be paid to the memory of this well-loved Commander is this, that whenever in the slave-camps of the East two members of his Battalion were met together they asked each other if there was news of the C.O. For those of us who served under him, he is remembered as he was on that morning at Senggarang, tired, hungry and grimy as the rest of us, standing on the open road in full view of the enemy block, smiling and cracking jokes to cheer us on into battle, his helmet as usual forgotten.

* * * *

EPILOGUE.

In this second World War the Cambridgeshire Regiment went into battle for only a very short space of time, and took a small share in an ill-fated and disastrous campaign in a remote corner of the Empire. It was not numbered among the conquering hosts that finally overcame the forces of darkness, and it made no triumphal progress through liberated countries into the lands of the oppressors. Instead, it was sent in to fight for a lost cause and its fate was certain before ever it landed on that far shore. There were no laurels to win, only death and chains.

Yet in that brief action which preceded the Tragedy of Singapore both battalions carried out the tasks assigned to them and were not found wanting. They stood fast where they were ordered to stand; they were surrounded and were not dismayed, and they attacked the enemy with confidence at every possible opportunity. They gave rather more than they received.

During the 1914-1918 War it had become a tradition in the Regiment to expect to be assigned the hardest tasks and the most thankless, and to go into them gladly without fuss and without self-advertisement, in the spirit of Leonidas; the year 1942 gave to the sons the opportunity of observing the tradition of their fathers.

When the shadows closed in on the city of Singapore, the survivors of the two battalions, united for the first time since that last camp of 1939, were cut off from the world for three and a half bitter years. The history of those years was written in the jungles of Siam, on the infamous Burma Railway, on the airfields of New Guinea, in the mines of Japan and in the packed holds of prison ships. It is a tale of disease, degradation, cruelty and death, and much of it is best forgotten. But it also brought forth some things that should never be forgotten: cheerfulness, comradeship, unselfishness and bravery, and such are the qualities that a regiment may be proud to find in its members whether in victory or in ruin. Though it was not for us to win laurels on the battlefields of the world, yet perhaps after all we won a victory of our own, for each man overcame selfishness and brought out the good that lay in him for the benefit of his comrades in misfortune. Wherever fate led them, Cambridgeshire men stuck together and the strong did their utmost for the sick and dying. They also learnt a loyalty which was not limited to their own Regiment alone; many took it upon themselves to suffer that others might have better treatment, and of these the name of Lt.-Col. E. L. V. Mapey, O.B.E., T.D. will be remembered.

Until the end of 1943 a large number of the survivors of the Regiment managed to keep together in two of the main working parties; one of these Cambridgeshire parties while working in Singapore contrived to build a wireless set and obtain regular news from the outside world. When moved to Siam they smuggled with them a large store of radio components out of which a certain officer of the Royal Corps of Signals, encountered in Chungkai, was able to construct five secret sets for distribution to various camps along the river. One of these sets was retained and worked by this Cambridgeshire party, No. 5 working Battalion, from Chungkai to Takanun and assisted greatly in maintaining morale at a high level. On one occasion at Wan Tai Kien, an officious guard discovered the existence of this instrument, but was fortunately in need of a wrist watch, so those responsible for working it escaped the usual fate of discovered radio operators and were able to preserve the set into the bargain.

When the Japanese commenced the sending of parties of prisoners overseas to Japan and Formosa the splitting up of the men of the Regiment began, and from 1943 onwards they were scattered all over the Pacific. Some of the prison ships were torpedoed on their way, and most of their human freight met death at the hands of their own people; in one such sinking one officer and 90 men of the 2nd Battalion alone were lost. And among those left in Siam there were soon casualties from Allied bombing attacks on the railway.

Throughout the captivity accurate records of all deaths and burials were constantly kept, although such things were of course forbidden. Whenever a party containing Cambridgeshire men left for some remote or unknown destination, the senior officer, N.C.O. or private made himself responsible for recording the fate of his party; if he died, the next senior took over the job, and so it went on. List of casualties were buried in tins, hidden inside bibles and sewn up in shirts, and miraculously all these records survived, though many of the authors did not. In this way the fate of almost every man of the regiment was known as soon as these documents came back to England at the end of the war.

There are many who deserve to be remembered for their work in those days of misery, but special mention should be made of the medical staffs of the two battalions, in particular of Sgt. Easingwood for his work in the cholera epidemic at Takanun at a time when he himself was a sick man. Nor shall we forget Noel Duckworth, the Padre of the 2nd Battalion, of whom it has been well said that he was a true servant of his Master.

And then after the long years came the day of liberation, and the survivors began the journey home from the furthest corners of the Far East. Some by plane, to Rangoon and India, some by ship to America, others to Australia and thence to Southampton and Liverpool. It was perhaps fitting that one of those ships which carried them home again should be our old friend the m.v. "Sobieski," on which the 2nd Battalion had set sail for Halifax so long ago in 1941.

It was a very wonderful homecoming, and it was made even happier by the deputation from the Territorial Army Association of Cambridgeshire, which, dodging back and forth with great rapidity, met every ship at both ports to welcome home each member of the Regiment and arrange transport to his own doorstep.

Regimental offices were at once established at Cambridge, Ely and Wisbech and survivors of the headquarter staffs of the two battalions volunteered to spend their leave compiling records and answering inquiries. With the help of the T.A. Association this work was soon well under way. Each returning group of ex-prisoners as they reached home sent in their casualty lists to one of the regimental offices, and within a few weeks complete returns for both battalions were supplied to the Infantry Record Office, Part Two Orders were published up to date and plans of the various cemeteries in Malaya and Siam submitted to the War Office. Many hundreds of inquiries were also dealt with.

* * * *

Throughout the days of captivity a plan had been maturing in the minds of several members of the Regiment, and had been discussed at length in Chungkai in 1944. On the 17th February, 1946, this plan was put into execution; a "Cambridgeshire Weekend" was held, to which everyone who had served in either battalion during the recent war was invited; they came in their hundreds. On the Saturday, a separate reunion took place for each battalion, the 1st in the Cambridge Drill Hall, and the 2nd in the Wisbech Corn Exchange. In each town, as the men arrived, they were registered at a battalion office, allotted accommodation in the town if they needed it, and presented with a souvenir book containing the history of the Regiment in the 1939-45 war. Records were prominently displayed so that everyone might know what had happened to his friends and give such information about the missing as he might have. There was a vast supply of food, and an equally vast supply of beer. The Commander of the East Anglian District and the Mayors of the two towns welcomed their battalions home on behalf of the county, and this was followed by a first-class ENSA concert at each reunion. And then, of course, everyone renewed old friendships and talked far into the night.

On the following day the two battalions were brought by special trains to Ely, together with members of the Old Comrades Association and the relatives of many of the fallen, and marched up to the Cathedral for a Service of Thanksgiving and Remembrance to which many guests and friends of the Regiment had been invited. The address was given by Padre Duckworth and the Bishop of Ely delivered a charge to the Regiment. Over 3,000 people were gathered in the great Cathedral, which made a magnificent setting for a very memorable and moving service.

After the service the two battalions marched through the streets of the city and the salute was taken by the Honorary Colonel of the Regiment; it was a day of brilliant Spring sunshine, and the route was crowded with spectators from the towns and villages of the county.

Mobile canteens supplied the entire parade with food and drink, and special trains and buses then began the task of returning the members to their homes, some of them lay as far afield as Scotland and Northern Ireland.

The organisation and expense entailed by this weekend reunion was considerable, and the project could never have been attempted without the generous assistance given by the Lord Lieutenant, the Mayors and citizens of Cambridge and Wisbech, the Old Comrades Association, the W.V.S., the T.A. Association and many others throughout the county.

* * * *

A second opportunity for a reunion occurred on the 29th of September, later in the year, when the Honorary Freedom of the Borough of Cambridge was ceremonially conferred upon the Regiment in recognition of its services over many years in the cause of freedom. Every member of the Regiment since 1908 received an invitation to attend the parade, and some 1,500 were able to take part. Three uniformed parties were formed as escort to the Colours, which were followed by the Singapore Drums in the place of honour. The remainder of the parade, to the number of 1,000, were in mufti, wearing their decorations. Led by the drums of the Cadet Battalions affiliated to the Regiment, the parade marched through Cambridge to the Market Place, where the silver casket containing the scroll of the Freedom was presented by the Mayor to the Honorary Colonel. The flag of the 1st Battalion, concealed from the Japanese during the captivity, flew proudly from the tower of Great St. Mary's church during the ceremony. When the Honour had been conferred, the Regiment, led by its Colonel with ten of its past commanding officers at the head, marched past the Mayor and through the principal streets of the town. The entire Regiment was then entertained to tea by the Mayor, Aldermen and Burgesses of the Borough of Cambridge, and the proceedings ended with a party arranged by the Old Comrades Association in the Drill Hall.

* * *

HONOURS AND AWARDS FOR SERVICES IN THE FAR EAST.

1. MALAYA AND SINGAPORE, 1942

D.S.O.	1
Bar to D.S.O.	1
O.B.E.	1
M.C.	2
D.C.M.	1
M.M.	1
Mentioned in Despatches	11

2. AS PRISONERS OF WAR, 1942—1945

M.B.E.	1
British Empire Medal	1
Mentioned in Despatches	4

Many Officers and Other Ranks of the Regiment served on other fronts, including Norway, France and Belgium 1940, Middle East, Crete, East Africa, Sicily, Italy, Burma and North-West Europe 1944-1945; unfortunately, the record of awards made to members of the Regiment for these campaigns is not yet complete, but the list includes the following :—

M.B.E.	2
D.C.M.	1
U.S. Bronze Star	1

CHAPTER EIGHT.

THE SEVENTH BATTALION

AND

142ND REGIMENT, R.A.C.

Training in England—Early Operations—Tunisia—Medjez el Bab; Djebel Ang—Medjez el Bab, Gueriat el Atach—Medjez el Bab, Djebel Bou Aoukaz—Victory in North Africa—The Italian Campaign—The Adolf Hitler Line—Advance to Florence—The Gothic Line—Till Disbandment.

THE 7th Battalion, Suffolk Regiment was formed in May 1940, being made up to strength in the months following the evacuation from DUNKIRK from the surplus infantry reinforcements in training centres and Holding Battalions available in England.

The 1st Suffolk had served in the B.E.F. and had suffered heavy casualties in the retreat. On its return to the United Kingdom the Battalion was immediately reformed; but a number of the original officers and men were posted to the Infantry Training Centre at BURY ST. EDMUNDS and were available to form the nucleus of further battalions. A small but strong cadre of officers and N.C.O.s with recent battle experience came to the 7th Battalion.

The Commanding Officer, Lieut.-Col. R. H. Maxwell, had commanded a Company of the 1st Battalion in France. Others who joined the Battalion included Major S. D. G. Robertson, also a Company Commander in France; Captain R. P. Newcomb, who had done very well with the carrier platoon; Captain C. Boycott, later to become Adjutant of the 7th Battalion; and Captain G. N. R. Stayton. Among the officers were some with many years' service as warrant officers, whose value to the infantry Battalion it is difficult to over-estimate; in particular, Lieutenants E. C. V. Williams and G. Ward. The Warrant Officers and N.C.O.s included Regimental Sergeant Major J. Weevers, R.Q.M.S. Golding, C.S.M. J. Daley, and Sergeant C. Stiff; both the latter subsequently became R.S.M. There was also a number of most valuable junior N.C.Os. and other ranks from the First Battalion, such as Corporal A. G. Reedham and Private E. Haylock. Lieutenant (Q.M.) W. H. Johnston, M.B.E., the Bedfordshire and Hertfordshire Regiment, was Quarter Master. The great majority of the rank and file came from East Anglia, and were men of the 26-28 age groups.

The raising and early training of the Battalion took place in Warwickshire, under manifold difficulties. Equipment of all kinds was extremely scarce; only seventy rifles were available, loaned by the Birmingham University Officers' Training Corps. These had to be passed round daily between companies, it being of paramount importance that every man should be proficient in weapon training in the minimum time. Recruits had to carry

THE 7TH BATTALION MARCHES PAST THE V CORPS COMMANDER (GENERAL MONTGOMERY), 1941.

their civilian respirators for such a long time before service respirators were issued that they got for the Unit the nickname of "the string and cardboard Suffolks", a name they encountered on several occasions in after years.

The Battalion's first move was to WIMBORNE in DORSET, and by the beginning of 1941 it had assumed its first main operational role—beach defence. Stationed around POOLE HARBOUR it was responsible for the construction and manning of beach defences of STUDLAND BAY, from SANDBANKS, east of the Harbour mouth, to OLD HARRY ROCK, not far from SWANAGE. The Battalion remained responsible for this task until November, 1941, except for one month spent on Southern Command exercises.

The 7th Suffolk was a Unit in the Vth Corps, commanded by General (later Field-Marshal Sir Bernard) Montgomery. In the Vth Corps a very high standard of efficiency was required.

Maxwell proved an ideal commanding officer. Unperturbed by the manifold difficulties he proceeded slowly and surely, choosing his subordinate officers and N.C.O.s with the greatest care, promoting the men in whom he had complete confidence and relegating to home employment those who were no longer up to the physical or mental standard. Under him the Battalion developed all the finest qualities of the Suffolk Regiment, in fact the County tradition grew so strong that although it was shortly afterwards converted into a unit of the R.A.C., it never until it was finally disbanded considered itself anything but "Suffolk". Throughout its existence the Suffolk Badge was worn.

I had, during this period, an opportunity of visiting the 1st, 7th and 8th Battalions and I was impressed by the differences in these three Battalions. The 1st Battalion had the background of a fine record in Belgium. It had been blooded under the existing Commander, Lieutenant-Colonel F. A. Milnes. It was confident in itself; almost too confident. The 7th promised to be magnificent; it was climbing step by step, believing in its leaders and most of all in its Commanding Officer. The 8th, with perhaps the finest men of all, was being driven too fast; it was trying to run before it could walk.

They were anxious days; the three Battalions were full of untrained officers, N.C.O.s and men, while beyond the Channel a victorious fully equipped enemy was waiting to invade. It was a race against time. Under such circumstances the importance of the Battalion Commander cannot be over-estimated. The future splendid record of the 7th Battalion had its firm foundation in its training under Lieutenant Colonel R. H. Maxwell. Maxwell was the exception to the rule that you can never be quite sure before he is promoted whether a promising man will succeed as a Battalion Commander. He had all the qualifications; experience, self-reliance, personality; a quick brain, a wide vision, a vivid vitality that struck sparks in the most phlegmatic. He was a Commander, he told whoever might be visiting him what he intended to do. He was prepared to pick any man's brains, to accept loyally any orders; but whatever he did had the strong flavour of his own decision. That is as it should be; to create we must add something of our own individuality to the ideas of others.

Fortune favours one Commander more than another, giving to one a finely tempered weapon which needs no more than skill in its use; to another metal that has still to be forged. Maxwell was slowly but surely shaping his material. As events turned out Fortune was most unkind to him. If an enemy mine in TUNISIA, long after the battle had been won, had not severely wounded Maxwell, he would assuredly have risen from Brigadier to Divisional Commander and higher.

Apart from the manning and maintenance of beach defences, work had been concentrated on infantry training, as the 7th Battalion was expected to take its place in a front line infantry division. But this was not to be. The Mark IV "I" Tank, subsequently named the "Churchill", had been designed and put into production at high speed; it is said that the first experimental model was completed ninety days after work on the blueprint had been begun. By the summer of 1941 these tanks were beginning to come off the production lines, and there was the problem of finding units to crew them. The 7th Battalion had been formed to absorb into infantry units the large number of potential reinforcements which were dispersed about the country. Now the time had come to reform them from infantry into new units of the Royal Armoured Corps.

The process of converting the Battalion began in 1941. Since an Army Tank Battalion is numerically smaller than an infantry unit, some selection was possible. When this had been done N.C.O.s and men were sent to the A.F.V. School at BOVINGTON and LULWORTH for training as gunners, drivers and wireless operators. Courses of a more general nature were organised for senior and junior officers. All through the summer of 1941 large numbers of officers and other ranks were away on these courses, while the 7th Battalion, working on a skeleton basis, continued to fulfil its operational role on the beaches, including the erection of anti-tank scaffolding.

By the autumn all initial courses were completed, and the Battalion moved to WESTGATE-ON-SEA, where, in November, the formal conversion took place; the 7th Suffolk ceased to exist, and the unit became the 142nd Regiment, Royal Armoured Corps. It joined the 25th Army Tank Brigade, commanded by Brig. T. Murray, and throughout its history it remained in the same formation.

Tanks began to arrive immediately. A few "Matildas" were first used for training; but within a few weeks a number of "Churchills" were received. A regimental school was established, and individual training continued throughout the winter of 1941/42, tank crews first being trained in their particular task, and subsequently in the duties of all the other members of the crew. By the early spring of 1942 collective training on a crew and troop basis was commenced; this stage culminated in the first field firing exercise of the Regiment, held during April, 1942, at LINNEY HEAD, PEMBROKESHIRE.

Squadron training commenced with the South Eastern Command exercises held in May 1942. In Exercise "Tiger," the Regiment worked for the first time as a whole, and may be said to have got through its "teething troubles." In the worst of weather conditions much was learned that was of value to all ranks:—the difficulties of road movement, particularly at night; co-ordination with the transport echelons; the problems of water and of petrol; the troubles of distant reconnaissance; the need for thoughtful "harbouring." It is not too much to say that the Regiment emerged from

SKELETON ORGANISATION 142nd R.A.C.

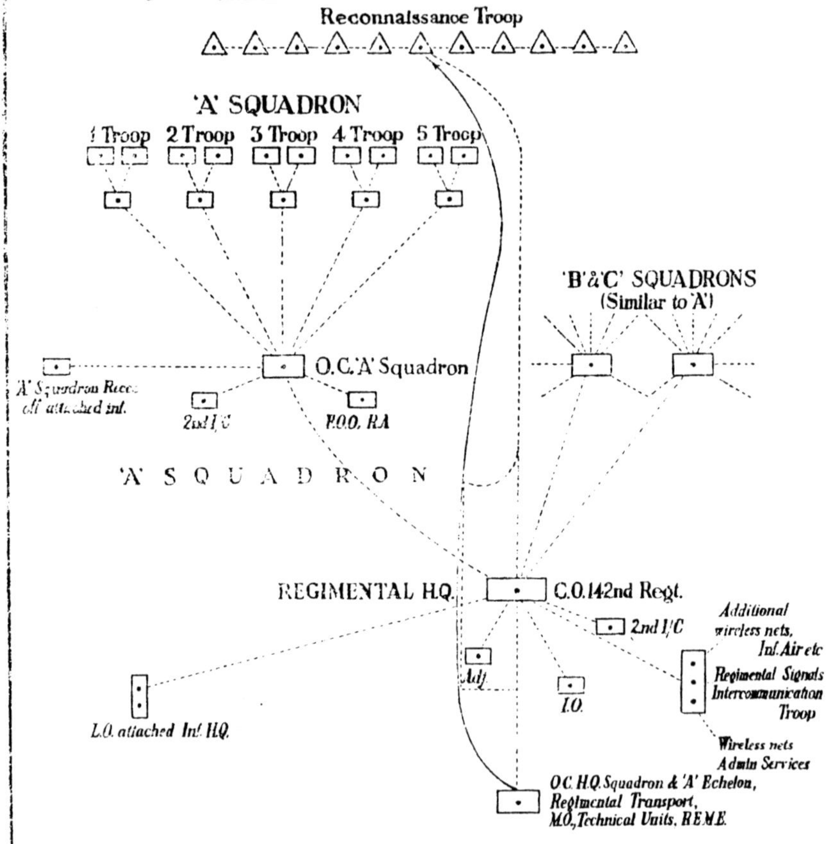

LEGEND

Regimental H.Q. (fighting element)	4 Churchill tanks (C.O., 2I/C, Adj., I.O.)
'A' 'B' 'C' Squadrons HQ	3 Churchill tanks (O.C. & 2I/C) Close Support Tanks with (F.O.O.) 3in Howitzers
Four Troops in each Squadron	3 Churchill tanks in each troop (Subaltern, Sgt, Cpl.)
Crew of each Tank	5 Men (Driver & Co-driver, Commander, Gunner, Wireless Operator)
HQ Squadron:-	
Reconnaissance Troop	11 Light tanks (General Stuart tanks) allotted as required
Intercommunication Troop	9 Scout cars

All administration & supply personnel, all attached units – Royal Signals, R.E.M.E.

'A' Echelon	18 Vehicles – supply, admin & tank repair purposes

OFFICERS, 142 REGIMENT, R.A.C., 1941.

Back Row—Left to Right: Lts. J. E. Forrest, J. H. A. Dudin, Howard, R. C. Rowe, R. O. Prentice, Harris, A. H. J. Paddick, M. J. F. Shaw, C. V. K. Lister.
2nd Row—Lts. J. Paul, J. W. Salmons, W. H. Payn, A. G. A. Jaques, C. A. Pogson, Ball, Clewes, Robertson, Smith, J. Austin.
3rd Row—Lts. Wilcox, Hudswell, Holt, A. T. V. Borrett, G. N. R. Stayton, Capt. Evans (Chaplain), Capt. Mackenzie (M.O.), Capt. Everett, Lts. W. Ross-Taylor, Norrish, Churchill.
Front Row—Capts. I Sanderson, G. Ward, Majors F. Roper, G. R. Heyland, S. D. G. Robertson, Lt. Col. R. H. Maxwell, Capt. D. O. Roberts, Majors F. G. L. Lyne, R. P. Newcomb, Capts. Gardner Johnston.

exercise "Tiger" as a homogeneous whole, each part understanding and appreciating the work done by the rest.

It reaped the full advantage of this sound groundwork during the following summer months at WORTHING. Here as an integral portion of the 43rd (Wessex) Division it trained over a large portion of the South Downs, the Squadrons of the 142nd training individually with Companies of infantry. During this period the Regiment was re-equipped with the new "Churchills" carrying the six-pounder gun.

SKELETON ORGANISATION

142ND R.A.C.

It is taking a long step forward to give here a diagram showing the skeleton organisation of the 142nd Regiment, for this diagram shows the Unit when it was waiting in October, 1943, on the Coast of North Africa to embark on the Italian Campaign. It was somewhat different in the summer of 1942. But the framework was the same; throughout the war there were constant reorganisations.

As will be seen from the diagram there were three fighting Squadrons "A," "B" and "C". The Churchill tanks had a BESA M.G. in the front hull and a six pounder and BESA M.G. coaxially mounted in the turret. Each tank was fitted with wireless for command and short range within the troop and also a telephone for communication within the tank. Each tank also had wireless for communication with the infantry with whom they were co-operating.

The Headquarter Squadron was the home of all the remaining components of the Regiment, including the Reconnaissance troop of eleven light tanks, known as "Honey" tanks. Prior to the Italian Campaign this Reconnaissance troop had been equipped with "Carriers."

There were several re-organisations during the war. During the Italian Campaign, two troops in each of the fighting Squadrons were re-equipped with Sherman tanks in lieu of the Churchill. The Sherman had a 75 mm gun instead of the six pounder. Later in this Campaign, after the capture of the Hitler Line, the fighting Squadrons were reorganised on a four troop basis, this re-organisation being based on manpower consideration, and not for tactical reasons.

The 142nd R.A.C. in its H.Q. Squadron contained a large Regimental echelon of wheeled vehicles with all the attendant administrative and supply personnel of the Regiment and such others as the M.O. and his staff and the Regimental Technical Adjutant and his mechanical experts. This Squadron formed the home for attached other arms, i.e., Royal Signals Troop and R.E.M.E. Light Aid Detachments.

The essential role of the whole formation was close support of infantry: with this object it had been trained and to this end in the North African and Italian Campaigns it was employed. Thus in the Squadron organisation the Squadron Reconnaissance officer in his scout car was usually attached to the H.Q. of the Company or Battalion which the Squadron was supporting; while very often the Regimental Commander would have to be at Battalion or Infantry Brigade H.Q., moving with a half tracked wireless vehicle and scout cars in attendance.

The 142nd R.A.C. formed part of 25 Tank Brigade of which the tank regiments were:—

The North Irish Horse.
The 51st Royal Tank Regiment.
142nd Regiment, Royal Armoured Corps.

Other units who remained with the 25th Tank Brigade practically the whole of the war were the 142nd Field Regiment (Devon Yeomanry) R.A. and No. 5 Light Field Ambulance. Apart from these the Brigade had its own complement of services including Ordnance, Signals, R.E., R.A.S.C. and R.E.M.E. making it a complete self-contained entity and in effect a miniature armoured division but without any infantry of its own. It could therefore be placed under command or in support of any infantry division, and, being so self-contained could be, and was, rapidly transferred from the support of one infantry formation to another whenever occasion or operational necessity so required.

Reverting once again to the Regiment on the South Coast of England it can be said that in one year since the conversion of the 7th Suffolk to the 142nd R.A.C. the unit became fit for active service as a tank unit. The Suffolk Regiment at this time (1942/43) had three first line units in training, for very different roles. The 1st Battalion had to take its place as one of the first line highly specialised infantry formations that at some time in the future would have to cross the seas, land on the strongly defended coast of EUROPE and defeat a veteran enemy. The 2nd Battalion already in INDIA, was earmarked for BURMA, where jungle warfare would require skill and endurance on a scale hitherto believed impossible. The 7th Battalion had had to super-impose on its infantry training and instincts the imagination and wide horizons of armoured warfare. All three were undergoing intensive training to fit them for their future active service roles and all three gained renown when at a later period they came to grips with their enemy.

Meanwhile the other front line units, the 4th and 5th Suffolk, with the 1st and 2nd Cambridgeshire, on whom also the hopes of the Regiment had been set so high, had been engulfed, through no fault whatever of theirs, in the tragic disaster of the capitulation of Singapore.

In July, 1942, Lt.-Colonel R. H. Maxwell was promoted to command the 25th Army Tank Brigade, a high tribute to an infantry officer. Lieutenant Colonel A. S. Birkbeck of the Royal Tank Regiment was promoted to succeed him in command of the 142nd Regiment. Any successor to Maxwell would have had a difficult task to win the same place that he had held in the Battalion. It is a tribute to Lt.-Col. Birkbeck that he was immediately accepted as one of the Regiment, and it is not too much to say that before he had been with his new Unit more than a few months he undoubtedly became the most popular figure in it. All ranks had confidence in his fairness, and above all, in his personal interest in them, their military efficiency, and in their individual welfare. Alec Birkbeck, as he was known to his officers, was regarded in the Mess very much as an elder brother, and worthily upheld the traditions of a Regiment with which he was quick to identify himself.

A few weeks after he had taken over orders were received to mobilise the Regiment to go overseas. Full equipment was issued, first line reinforcements received; but some weeks later the Regiment was stood down. It then moved with the 25th Army Tank Brigade, to MUNDFORD, Norfolk, where the Brigade joined the First Division. Combined tank and infantry training was carried out, and ten days were spent at MINEHEAD, SOMERSET, on field firing exercises with the new six-pounder.

The order to mobilise came once again just after Christmas, 1942, when the Regiment had been at HEVENINGHAM HALL, near HALESWORTH in Suffolk, for a few weeks.

EARLY OPERATIONS IN TUNISIA.

JAN. 1943—MARCH 1943.

The reason for this second mobilization and subsequent move overseas can be traced in the following summary of events in North Africa:—

In the first week of November, 1942, an allied expedition, planned and executed with the greatest secrecy, had arrived off the coast of North Africa. A great Armada carrying British and U.S. troops entered the ports of CASABLANCA, ORAN and ALGIERS. After the landing an immediate advance on TUNIS and BIZERTA was made.

The Germans were completely surprised; they had no troops in Tunisia. But they reacted with their usual promptitude. Detachments from Rommel's army in LIBYA were despatched; the ports and airfields in TUNISIA were seized; troop carriers from SICILY and sea transports from ITALY were put into immediate commission and until the final capitulation in NORTH AFRICA in 1943 German reinforcements of all natures continued to arrive.

A great effort was made by the Allies to take advantage of the initial surprise, and seize TUNIS. Had this been successful the early complete annihilation of Rommel's army would have been assured and many months of bitter fighting would have been saved. But the distance of ALGIERS, our nearest port, from TUNIS is 700 miles, and although MATEUR on the road to BIZERTA and the commanding ground beyond MEDJEZ EL BAB on the way to TUNIS were reached by the last week of November, 1942, they could not be held. Then the rains came, and a stalemate ensued.

In England optimistic hopes followed the great news of the surprise landing of the Allies and disappointment was expressed that further spectacular results were not achieved. Comparisons were made between the operations of the Desert Army under Montgomery and this new North African Force and the criticisms showed how little was known of the conditions. History will show how very near that great Division, the 78th, backed up by "Blade force," and by other formations, came to success; what big risks were accepted by all concerned; and how magnificently these untried units fought.

TUNISIA differed in every particular from EGYPT and LIBYA. Sea communications and the coast road were the only lines of supply between EGYPT and TRIPOLI. The vast desert that flanked the coast was the illimitable manoeuvre area across which movement could be made in any direction by troops that were desert trained. TUNISIA, the new theatre of operations, was a country of great rocky mountains through which a few main roads of great strategical importance wound their way, over passes, and through defiles, and by valleys that were luxuriant and highly cultivated. Operations were confined to the neighbourhood of these few roads.

Much had been made in the early news of the size of the invasion fleet that had so successfully crossed the seas; it was believed that this must contain a great army of fighting men. Actually there were only a few thousand front line troops landed in NORTH AFRICA in November. The proportion at the front to the men on the lines of communication in the Great War of 1914/18 had been about one to every two. But in the war in AFRICA there were now at least four men on the supply lines for every man in the front line, so great was the requirement of ammunition, equipment and all the needs of modern war.

Great convoys followed the first Armada, one of them in January, 1943, carrying the 142nd Regiment; gradually our front line strength in NORTH AFRICA was built up. But in the first three months from November, 1942, we were very weak everywhere. When the gamble to seize TUNIS failed it became a dour struggle to hold on to our gains and still keep probing at the enemy's position.

Strategy is constant in all wars; but tactics are dependent on the changing conditions of modern equipment. The earlier battles of EGYPT and LIBYA had been fought with tank formations in the forefront. In 1943 minefields and anti-tank guns made it necessary for the engineer and the infantryman to probe the enemy's positions and to find a way through which massed tank formations could burst. The 142nd Regiment had a role with the rest of the 25th Tank Brigade of supporting the Infantry and Engineers in this probing. The 142nd Regiment lacked nothing in training but there is a great difference between what we are told and what we learn by experience. The army that landed in November, 1942, and in the subsequent months was opposed to veterans. It is a great tribute to its training that the men adapted themselves so quickly, that so few mistakes were made and that eventually they had a full share in the enemy's decisive defeat.

During the two months November, December, 1942, prior to the arrival of the 142nd in ALGIERS, the Allies had pushed forward towards BIZERTA and TUNIS.

"LONGSTOP" HILL, on the road to TUNIS, had been captured, recaptured and finally relinquished; but MEDJEZ EL BAB, just south-west was held. And MEDJEZ EL BAB, the junction of many roads, was accepted as the one vital point that must be held, vital not only for the capture of TUNIS; but for eventual co-operation with the Desert Army.

Meanwhile between November, 1942, and February, 1943, as reinforcements continued to arrive in NORTH AFRICA, the original front which had only included the northern roads to MATEUR and MEDJEZ EL BAB now extended southwards. LE KEF became important for from LE KEF main roads stretched to SOUSSE and SFAX. South of LE KEF the road junction at KASSERINE carried the direct route to SFAX, while another road went south to FERANA and GAFSA. These road junctions and the passes beyond them were of the greatest importance both to the Allies and to the Germans for the coming trial of strength. But while the Allies succeeded in reaching and holding the road junctions, the Germans were in possession of the main passes through which these roads debouched.

In the fortnight following the order to mobilize it was found possible to give everyone some embarkation leave. Security precautions with the Regiment were redoubled; all badges were removed, side caps were issued in place of berets and when the unit finally entrained on January 19th, 1943, all ranks wore in their caps the grenade badge of the Royal Artillery.

The 142nd Regiment sailed from GOUROCK on board the "Durban Castle" on January 24th, 1943. To the men on the transports the voyage seemed dull and uneventful. It was anything but dull and uneventful to the escorting ships. Great "packs" of enemy submarines were constantly operating against convoys. Although the 142nd Regiment landed at ALGIERS complete, their tanks and transports which had proceeded separately had been attacked and the other units of the Brigade had suffered loss.

The following were with the 142nd R.A.C. when they sailed from ENGLAND to NORTH AFRICA:—

Regimental H.Q.	Lt.-Col. A. S. Birkbeck	Commanding Officer.
	Major S. D. G. Robertson	Second-in-Command
	Captain W. H. Payn	Adjutant.
	Captain C. Austin	Liaison Officer.
	Captain J. Auger	Technical Officer.
	Lt. and Q.M. W. H. Johnston, M.B.E.	Quartermaster
	Lt. R. J. Loewe	Intelligence Officer.
	Lt. J. Salmons	I/c H.Q. Troop.
	Lt. R. J. Paul	I/c RECCE Troop.
	Capt. the Rev. Evans	Chaplain.
	Lt. D. C. Watson	Medical Officer.
	Capt. G. Fitt	R.E.M.E.
	Lt. C. A. Pogson	Signals Officer.
H.Q. Squadron.		
	Major R. P. Newcomb	Capt. E. C. V. Williams.
"A" Squadron.		
	Major G. R. Heyland.	Capt. J. Austin.
	Captain R. O. Prentice.	Lt. R. Rowe.
	Lt. Shaw.	Lt. Ross Taylor.
	Lt. A. H. Dodson.	Lt. Smedley.
"B" Squadron.		
	Major F. G. L. Lyne.	Capt. I. H. Sanderson.
	Capt. H. Norrish.	Lt. P. B. Harris.
	Lt. A. Borrett.	Lt. A. J. Paddick.
	Lt. Wilson.	Lt. H. R. Adams.
"C" Squadron.		
	Major F. W. Roper.	Capt. G. Ward.
	Capt. W. Marriott.	Lt. A. G. Jaques.
	Lt. Clewes.	Lt. Forrest.
	Lt. Aylward.	Lt. Lister.
First Line Reinforcements.		
	Capt. A. H. S. Moser.	Lt. Fletcher.
	Lt. Butcher.	

The Regiment disembarked at ALGIERS on February 1st, being met by Brigadier R. H. Maxwell, who had flown out.

As at the port of embarkation, stringent security measures were taken in Africa. At ALGIERS the quays had been closed and screened for three weeks prior to their arrival.

On landing the Regiment marched seventeen miles to billets, but within forty eight hours orders were received to proceed to PHILIPPEVILLE by sea. Leaving a party at ALGIERS under Major G. R. Heyland to unload some of the tanks, the main body sailed on 4th February on board H.M.S. "Princess Beatrix" and landed at PHILIPPEVILLE on February 5th. Ten days later, February 15th, all tanks arrived by sea and had been unloaded and stood camouflaged in a wood; all movement from the docks taking place at night.

The intention of the First Army Commander, Gen. K. Anderson, had been for the 25th Tank Brigade to concentrate in the area of LE KEF, where guns could be shot in and a certain amount of training carried out. Accordingly an advance party had been dispatched on February 11th, and in the following days movement to the concentration area commenced by rail and road transport, the tanks being completely enshrouded in tarpaulins. But during the first fortnight of February the strategic situation in North Africa had been changing.

Rommel had made a skilful withdrawal opposite the Eighth Army, sending the bulk of his armour to secure TUNIS, BIZERTA, and the CAP BON PENINSULA. A portion of this armoured force had turned inland along the road from SFAX and a serious situation had developed. The First Army front was only of skeleton strength; the Americans to the South of the First Army had been defeated at SBEITLA and had had to withdraw beyond KASSERINE. It had become necessary to concentrate all available forces to stem a further German advance.

The original intention had been to hold the newly arrived "Churchills" for operation later when their concentrated strength might have had decisive results; but under the circumstances they had to be called upon for immediate action. Consequently within twenty-four hours of arriving in the concentration area west of LE KEF, the 25th Tank Brigade Commander issued a warning order that there might be an urgent call for tanks on the BOU ARADA front, and "C" Squadron, commanded by Major F. W. Roper, was placed at thirty minutes notice to move.

The order to move up was received next day, 17th February, and the twelve tanks already unloaded were sent forward, the remainder of the Regiment being ordered to follow as soon as possible. Roads were cleared of all other troops for the free passage of the very large "Tank transporters" carrying these tanks. "C" Squadron came under the command of "Y" Division, an *ad hoc* British formation created to control units on the BOU ARADA front.

By late afternoon the position clarified. The enemy was attempting infiltration wherever the passes of the WESTERN DORSALE permitted the use of armour, and was working along his front from right to left, in a southwesterly direction. The Army Commander was concerned lest he should now break through in the area of SHEILA and SBIBA astride the main road running north to LE KEF. LE KEF itself was a vital communication centre both for the south and the MEDJEZ EL BAB front; consequently all available anti-tank defence was to proceed south forthwith. Tanks of the 25th Tank Brigade were ordered to move as they became available, with the exception

Crown copyright reserved.

CHURCHILL TANKS OF 142 REGIMENT, R.A.C. PREPARING FOR ACTION NEAR THE SBIBA—SBEITLA ROAD. THESE WERE THE FIRST "CHURCHILLS" TO BE USED IN THE WAR. TANK "MINDEN" ON RIGHT.

of "C" Squadron 142nd Regiment which would remain on the BOU ARADA front.

The collection and organisation of tanks for this rush move was no easy matter. Apart from the "B" Squadron tanks halted east of LE KEF on the road to BOU ARADA, which were now recalled, there were others arriving from the north of the town on transporters. As the latter reached the concentration area after several days' exposed travel, they were ordered to prepare for action immediately; refuelling and stowage of ammunition had to be commenced as soon as the tank had left its transporter. To add to these difficulties, heavy rain was making the narrow roads very treacherous, many transporters slipped off the edges and became ditched; one, indeed, skidded badly in LE KEF and became wedged across the road, thereby turning the town into a bottle-neck for several hours. However, by night-fall a composite force of twenty-four tanks was marshalled and moved off under the second-in-command, Major S. D. G. Robertson.

The Churchill tank won its spurs for mechanical efficiency during this march southwards. Twenty-four tanks arrived at SBIBA without any mechanical breakdown. Some of these had come straight off their transporters without time for minor adjustments; while the few "B" Squadron tanks that had set out for the BOU ARADA front moved on their tracks without a hitch a hundred miles in twenty-four hours. Above all, credit is due to the tank commanders and drivers who were faced with their first night drive in AFRICA under most difficult weather conditions.

At a conference on the 21st February, the 6th Armoured Divisional Commander, Major General C. Keightley, outlined the task of the Regiment as a counter-attacking force, with the 1st Guards Brigade, against a possible enemy advance along the SBEITLA-SBIBA road.

At mid-day, 21st February, orders were received for two troops of tanks with a platoon 2nd Coldstream Guards and some R.E., to advance through the Forward Defended Localities and occupy a long feature to the east of the SBIBA-SBEITLA road.

The action commenced at five o'clock in the afternoon; a smoke screen, artillery support, and diversionary action on both flanks having been arranged. Some initial success was achieved; several machine gun positions and possibly some light anti-tank weapons being knocked out. On reaching the crest the tanks observed nothing on the next ridge and started to reconnoitre the dead ground below them. Two tanks of the troop on the left were knocked out by medium and heavy anti-tank weapons firing at very short range. A third was hit by a 50 mm. anti-tank gun at close range; but the commander, Sergeant Powell, succeeded in extricating it, although badly wounded in the legs. He was subsequently awarded the Military Medal for his gallantry in this action. On the right, the tank commanded by Cpl. B. Wright was hit and set on fire; the remaining two of the troop being withdrawn safely by Lieut. M. J. F. Shaw.

Casualties were discouragingly high in this first action by the Regiment; out of a strength of thirty-five all ranks, three were killed, four wounded, eight unaccounted for. The results achieved were disappointing. But viewed in perspective, the action achieved a distinct measure of success. The knowledge that there was heavy British armour present on the front probably deterred the enemy from thrusting along the SBEITLA-SBIBA road. In fact, the next day he abandoned his position and devoted his attention unsuccessfully to the KASSERINE PASS.

The night that the enemy withdrew southward our troops were withdrawn to the north, Lieut.-Col. A. S. Birkbeck commanding the rear-guard to cover the withdrawal of the Infantry and Derbyshire Yeomanry. The Regiment now came under command of the 34th U.S. Division with a similar defensive role in the area of ROBAA, some miles to the north of its previous position.

Meanwhile a force of tanks under Major G. R. Heyland had been posted on the road running west from ROBAA to act as a stop in the case of an enemy breakthrough in the area of THALA; but was shortly afterwards withdrawn. A detachment was also ordered to MAKTAR in a similar role to the West, and remained detached for several days without being engaged.

The Regiment was at this time disposed in support of all three Allies; the main body of the Regiment was under the Second American Corps, the majority of "B" Squadron was with the French Nineteenth Corps at MAKTAR, while "C" Squadron, at BOU ARADA, was operating in conjunction with "Y" Division, a temporary British formation. Moreover, the transport Echelon, still in the original concentration area at LE KEF, had been held for local defence; for the possession of LE KEF was a matter of considerable moment.

Brig. R. H. Maxwell had been entrusted with this responsibility, and some of the tanks that had arrived since the departure of the Regiment had been held here by him. But by the 24th February LE KEF was no longer threatened, and the Regiment gradually concentrated near ROBAA, with the exception of "C" Squadron, which continued to fulfil its operational role at BOU ARADA.

Circumstances made it imperative that the 142nd Regiment should be split up and employed on detached operations. Although as an Army Tank Battalion it had been trained and organised so that Squadrons could operate independently, the ideal aimed at had been to employ it as a unit. But the skirmishes had proved the quality of the training and the ability of the Squadron Commanders to adapt themselves to battle conditions. All ranks learnt that tank fighting in TUNISIA was not a case of charging at opposing tanks with all guns firing; but a skilful jockeying for position on the unexposed side of a hill, the avoidance of the plain on the one hand and hill crest on the other. The value, in short, of the "Hull down" position.

Evidence was given by German prisoners taken in these first actions of the great moral effect on the enemy of the unexpected appearance of the Churchill tanks, so much more powerful than any that had previously been seen on the allied front. There is no doubt that the sight of the Churchills had a most inspiring effect on our own infantry.

"C" Squadron had been in position on the BOU ARADA front for approximately a week, in support of the 38th Irish Infantry Brigade and the first Parachute Brigade. The attack came on February 26th, when the enemy advanced to capture EL ARUSSA, and roll up the allied positions south of the line EL ARUSSA-BOU ARADA. The 1st and 3rd Parachutist Battalions of the Hermann Goering Jaeger Regiment, supported by a company of tanks, attacked.

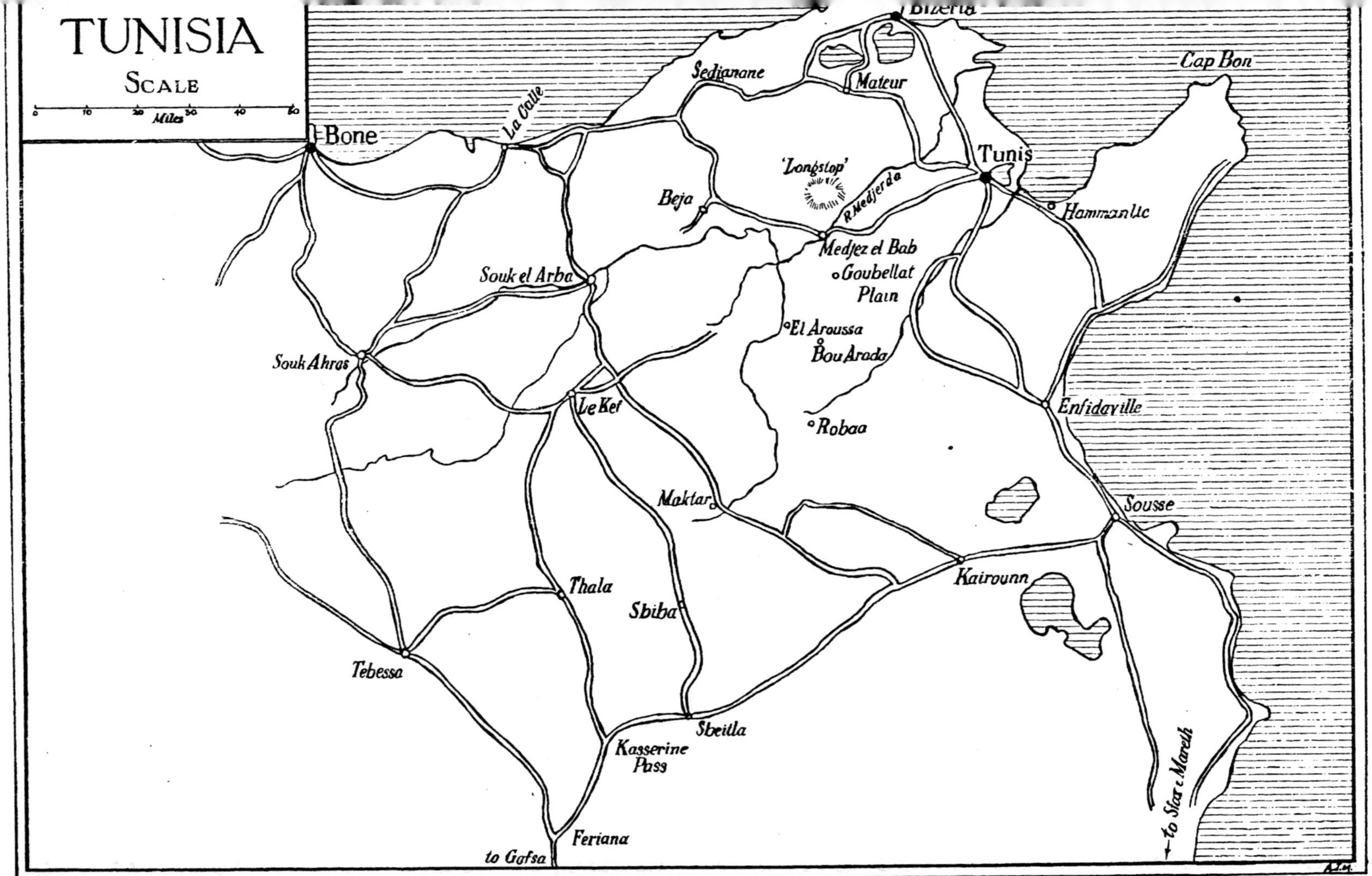
TUNISIA
SCALE
0 10 20 30 40 50
Miles
Bone
La Calle
Sedjanane
Mateur
Bizerta
Cap Bon
Tunis
Hammanlic
'Longstop'
R. Medjerda
Beja
Medjez el Bab
Goubellat
Plain
El Aroussa
Bou Arada
Robaa
Souk el Arba
Souk Ahras
Le Kef
Maktar
Enfidaville
Sousse
Kairounn
Thala
Sbiba
Tebessa
Sbeitla
Kasserine
Pass
Feriana
to Gafsa
to Sfax & Mareth

"C" Squadron, under Major F. W. Roper (less two troops detached under Capt. G. Ward), moved to the flank. Contact was made by Capt. W. Marriott, the tank reconnaissance officer, who was able to get the leading troop of tanks into a good fire position just in time to engage the enemy tanks. Four enemy tanks were set on fire and a further three were disabled; one 88mm. anti-tank gun was destroyed. "C" Squadron continued to hold the position until the evening unsupported by infantry; it then withdrew to its original harbour. One Churchill tank had been knocked out and could not be recovered by nightfall, so it was destroyed. No personnel casualties were sustained during the action.

Meanwhile the two troops detached under Capt. G. Ward fought a successful separate action slightly to the east, in support of the R.I.F. and the Inniskillings.

The German attempt proved a complete failure; apart from his tanks he lost about eight hundred prisoners. Had he captured EL ARUSSA and then turned south, he could have advanced south west and threatened the French Nineteenth Corps from the rear. Major F. W. Roper was awarded the D.S.O. as a result of this successful action by "C" Squadron.

MEDJEZ EL BAB—DJEBEL ANG.

MARCH, 1943—17TH APRIL, 1943.

The operations of the 142nd Regiment of North Africa fall into two parts. The first, as already described, when the Regiment was constantly split up, squadrons, and even smaller units, being sent to widely separated localities to operate with other detached formations. The second, when the Regiment was concentrated and fought as a unit. The first part had lasted during February and March; then came a short period near MEDJEZ EL BAB when reorganisation was possible. The second part included intense fighting during most of April.

The change came when that great Commander, General Alexander (later Field-Marshal Sir Harold Alexander), General Eisenhower's deputy, had taken over Command in North Africa. He sorted out the confusion, grouping the different Allied formations; the U.S. Corps in the South; the French in the South Centre; the British First Army in the Centre and North. A distribution that as the Desert Army advanced along the coast he changed by moving the U.S. Corps to the North and concentrating the British First Army in the Centre.

His plan was, once the MARETH line was broken, to drive the enemy from "LONGSTOP" on the MEDJEZ EL BAB sector and make his decisive thrust with his massed armour down the valley to TUNIS.

It was five months since the Allies had landed in North Africa, nearly four months since the Guards had captured and recaptured LONGSTOP HILL. In the interval the Germans, fully alive to its vital importance, had converted it into a very strong position. Defence for men, mortars and guns had been constructed, all approaches had been mined, and it was supplied with water, food and ammunition. LONGSTOP could not be ignored, or masked. It commanded with its guns and its garrison both the approach roads to TUNIS.

During the first three days of March, 1943, the Regiment concentrated and moved north to the MEDJEZ EL BAB sector, where it became responsible for several counter-attack tasks. These were rehearsed with the co-operating troops; but during the month activity was confined to patrols. Thus the Regiment was free to complete its reorganisation and overhaul its tanks and vehicles.

It was not until April that warnings were received of further operations. In the east, the Eighth Army had broken the MARETH LINE and was moving up through EASTERN TUNISIA. The western Tunisian front had been mainly quiet since Rommel's armoured probings of the Allied line earlier in the year had been stopped; but there had been some fierce fighting at SEDJANANE, where his attempts to get astride the main coast road running west to BONE and the Allied supply base had failed. The remainder of the front had been stabilised, and ran more or less south from the coast to BEJA; here it turned eastwards towards MEDJEZ EL BAB, which formed the head of the Allied salient. Thence the line ran down through the GOUBELLAT PLAIN; the villages had farmsteads of which were patrolled by both sides. The Allies had during this time been building up forces in preparation for the final assault.

The possession of the MEDJEZ EL BAB salient was of great tactical value to the Allies. Besides including the bridge over the RIVER MEDJERDA on the road to TUNIS, the town formed an important centre uniting the roads from BEJA and LE KEF with those running east to TEBOURBA and TUNIS and that running southward along the edge of the GOUBELLAT PLAIN. This Allied salient was strongly held by infantry, supported by the tanks of 142nd Regiment.

Exceptionally rugged mountainous country lies to the North east of MEDJEZ EL BAB and commands all the plain running East from this town to TUNIS. "LONGSTOP" was by no means the only feature; many miles of craggy fastnesses lay between it and MEDJEZ EL BAB from which the enemy could be driven only after very stiff fighting. Across the RIVER MEDJERDA more ridges extended from this mountain mass into the plain.

This strong series of natural positions formed the basis of the German defence line on the central front, and was regarded by the enemy as his "Siegfried Line of Tunisia." He had appreciated that the valley of the MEDJERDA was the gateway to TUNIS, and by the fortification of the natural line described above he hoped to stultify our possession of MEDJEZ EL BAB.

"LONGSTOP HILL" was the key to the enemy position; but several direct assaults in the past, although temporarily gaining control of the feature, had failed to secure it permanently. It was now decided to attack the western end of the ridge north of the BEJA-MEDJEZ EL BAB road in the neighbourhood of DJEBEL ANG, 2,000 feet high; if secured the "LONGSTOP" feature could be dominated from higher ground, and possibly its supplies cut off. A plan was made to attack these hills by the 78th Infantry Division, supported by two Regiments of the 25th Army Tank Brigade; the North Irish Horse and 142nd Regiment.

For the first time the Regiment was to be employed as a unit, previous action having been on a squadron or a composite squadron basis. It was also the first time that there was opportunity for detailed reconnaissance, so that careful plans could be made with co-operating arms. The Regiment was to support the 11th Infantry Brigade with two squadrons, "A" and "C"; "B" Squadron to remain behind for counter-attack duties.

Tanks 142 Regiment, R.A.C., in Medjez el Bab Sector. Typical country over which "Churchills" had to fight.

The first briefing was on April 3rd, and four full days were available for reconnaissance and planning. During this period plans were made from observation posts overlooking the BEJA-MEDJEZ EL BAB road, for this road was commanded by enemy artillery. Reconnaissance Officers patrolled with the infantry to report on the suitability of certain tracks for Churchill tanks. Troop Commanders were shown the ground which concerned them, and as far as time allowed this was also arranged for individual tank commanders and drivers.

The plan was to assault the ground north of the BEJA-MEDJEZ EL BAB road, and capture the villages of TOUKABEUR and CHAOUACH, both known as enemy centres. On the right, "A" Squadron would support the 5th Northamptons, on the left "C" Squadron the 2nd Lancashire Fusiliers. The enemy units holding the ground were mountain troops from AUSTRIA, whose morale was not expected to be high.

The attack was timed for first light on April 7th. On the right the 5th Northamptons and "A" Squadron met with partial success; but their central and left objectives were not reached; an enemy strong point on a small feature nicknamed "the Pimple," effectively prevented the clearing of the reverse slopes of rocky hills generally known as "Recce Ridge." A 50 mm. anti-tank gun knocked out five of our tanks.

On the left instead of moving through with the 2nd Lancashire Fusiliers "C" Squadron was compelled to assist "C" Company of the 1st East Surreys, who had suffered heavy casualties, to gain a low ridge nicknamed "the Oyster." The Squadron suffered heavy mortar fire all day; but without much damage. During the day reconnaissance was carried out with the 2nd Lancashire Fusiliers for an attack on the original objective, known as "Sugar Loaf Hill." But owing to the late hour and the possibility of minefields, the attack was postponed to the next day. In spite of limited tactical success, the day had produced a reasonable bag of prisoners.

The operation was virtually completed next day when "C" Squadron with the 2nd Lancashire Fusiliers, captured "Sugar Loaf Hill" and shot up enemy infantry leaving CHAOUACH. TOUKABEUR was entered by a company of 1st East Surrey, supported by the three fit tanks of Regimental Headquarters. "A" Squadron also successfully completed their task in conjunction with the 5th Northamptons.

Major G. R. Heyland and Lt. A. Smedley were each awarded the Military Cross for their part in these operations.

On April 9th the attack was carried forward with fresh formations, a footing being finally gained by the infantry of the 78th Division on DJEBEL ANG where they were subjected to many counter attacks; but held their ground.

This had been the Regiment's first experience in the vital fighting for a springboard in the hills round MEDJEZ EL BAB. CHOAUACH, their objective, lay just below the summit of a rocky crag and the winding narrow track that led to it passed by cultivated valleys and through rock strewn hills, the tops of which were often knife edged in formation. There were golden orioles, brilliant masses of wild flowers, azaleas down in the valleys and above them steep crags that it seemed impossible that a Churchill could negotiate. But the tanks did magnificently, crawling up hills foot by foot, covered with dust and smoke from enemy mortar fire, coming through unscathed and turning their guns on to the enemy machine gun nests. It was due to their unflinching persistence that the infantry succeeded.

The enemy had not believed this country possible for tanks: consequently, whenever a Churchill could be manoeuvred into a firing position among the crags the moral and material damage inflicted produced a rich dividend, even though the tanks might suffer severe mechanical strain and might even have to be abandoned.

Meanwhile the 142nd Regiment had been withdrawn from the fight and for the next four days was able to attend to their maintenance and recovery of damaged tanks. Only one Section of carriers with seven tanks under Captain G. Ward remained in the fighting line until April 19th.

While the above operations were being completed Units of the 1st Division and the 142nd Regiment moved by night on the 18th-19th April across the RIVER MEDJERDA to an area South West of MEDJEZ EL BAB.

MEDJEZ EL BAB.

GUERIAT ES ATACH.

19th April — 25th April.

From MEDJEZ EL BAB the River MEDJERDA winds its way north east to TEBOURBA. To the West LONGSTOP and the mountains rise to DJEBEL ANG. On the East of the River is a range of hills DJEBEL BOU AOUKAL and DJEBEL ASOUD divided mid-way by a gap nicknamed the GAB-GAB GAP. This range commanded the plains over which the Commander in Chief had planned to make his decisive drive by MASSICAULT to TUNIS. This drive could not be made until this range of hills was in Allied hands.

Before these two hills, DJEBEL BOU AOUKAL and DJEBEL ASOUD, each a tangled mass of rocks, could be attacked, much preliminary fighting was necessary to drive the enemy from the succession of bare hills near MONTARNAUD FARM within a few miles of MEDJEZ EL BAB and from his entrenchments at GRICH EL DUED. But the enemy appreciating the Allied intentions, decided to forestall them with a spoiling attack. The point he chose was to the south of MEDJEZ EL BAB, where several gaps in the hills afforded an approach to the MEDJEZ EL BAB — BOU ARADA road.

His attack opened at 2330 hours on April 20th with not less than six Battalions of Infantry and seventy tanks. His first objective was BANANA RIDGE, a long hill some 5 miles South East of MEDJEZ EL BAB held by our foremost troops. The enemy advance rapidly overran this position and the artillery positions in the rear; but the night was dark and the Allied casualties were slight, the infantry remaining in their slit trenches. The Germans on the other hand lost heavily.

At first light on April 21st the enemy put in his main attack, on the GOUBELLET-JEDJEZ Road. He was ignorant of the strong Allied concentration into which he thrust.

The news of the German attack on the night of April 20th was quickly received by the 142nd Regiment. At midnight, April 20/21st "B" Squadron, which mustered fourteen fit tanks, was sent to act as a stop against any enemy force advancing across the GOUBELLAT plain towards MEDJEZ EL BAB. Major F. G. L. Lyne, the Squadron Commander, took up a position on a

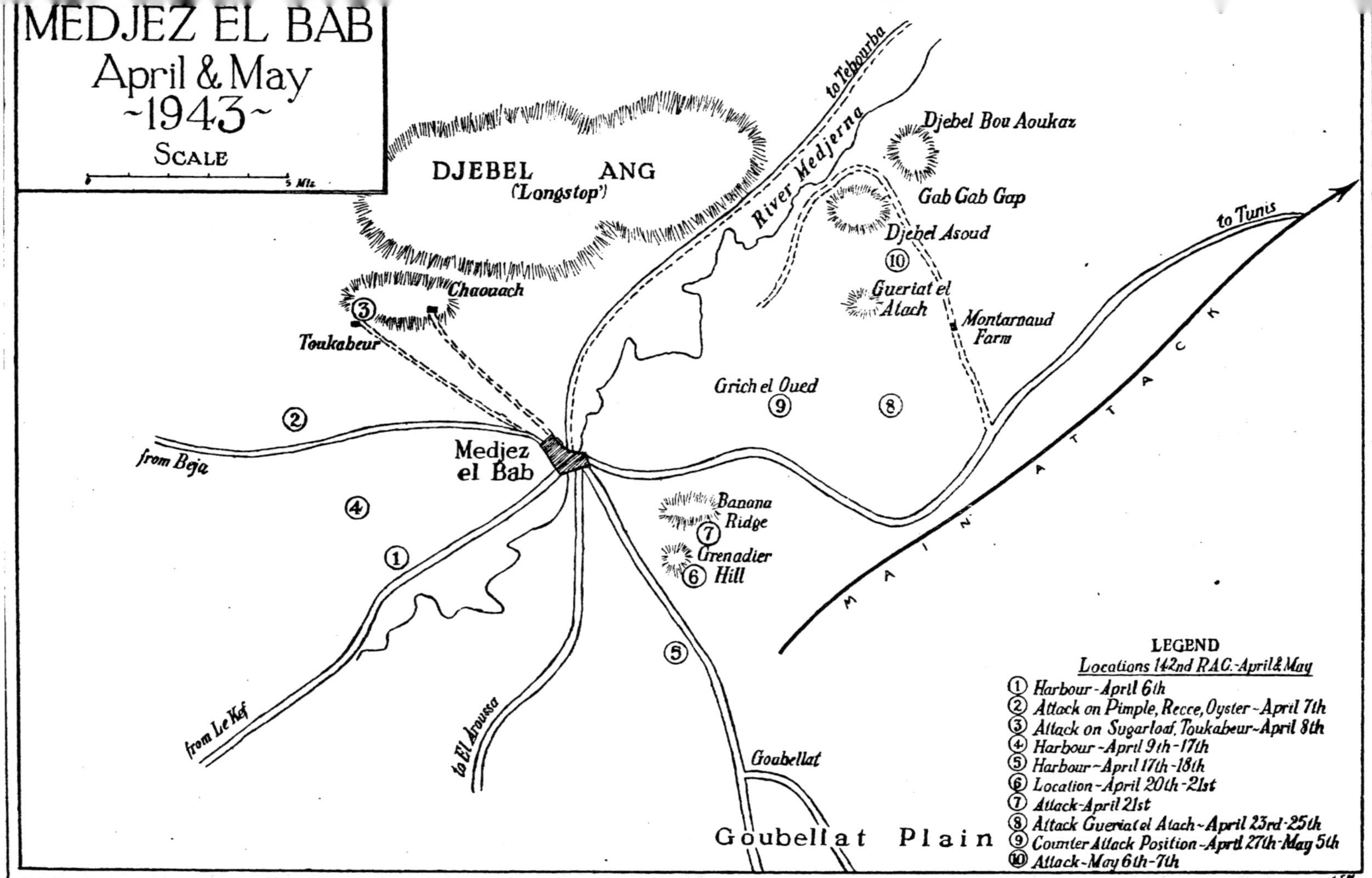
MEDJEZ EL BAB
April & May
~1943~
SCALE
5 Mls
DJEBEL ANG
('Longstop')
Chaouach
Toukabeur
River Medjerna
to Tebourba
Djebel Bou Aoukaz
Gab Gab Gap
Djebel Asoud
Gueriat el Atach
Montarnaud Farm
Grich el Oued
to Tunis
MAIN ATTACK
Medjez el Bab
from Beja
from Le Kef
to El Aroussa
Banana Ridge
Grenadier Hill
Goubellat
Goubellat Plain
LEGEND
Locations 142nd R.A.C.-April & May
① Harbour-April 6th
② Attack on Pimple, Recce, Oyster-April 7th
③ Attack on Sugarloaf, Toukabeur-April 8th
④ Harbour-April 9th-17th
⑤ Harbour-April 17th-18th
⑥ Location-April 20th-21st
⑦ Attack-April 21st
⑧ Attack Gueriat el Atach-April 23rd-25th
⑨ Counter Attack Position-April 27th-May 5th
⑩ Attack-May 6th-7th

crest overlooking the road, south-west of "GRENADIER HILL." At first light April 21st, enemy infantry and anti-tank guns disclosed their presence by firing at our tanks. Enemy tanks were also observed at about eighteen hundred yards range, and were engaged. They did not return fire; but attempted to withdraw behind the smoke of some burning huts. Five of the enemy tanks were destroyed, and two further ones knocked out on minefields. The enemy anti-tank gunners scored some hits on the "B" Squadron tanks, setting one on fire and damaging two others. Lieut. P. B. Harris was severely wounded, and his wireless operator, Corporal Beale, was killed. The crew of Captain I. H. Sanderson's tank, which was hit and set on fire, baled out successfully with two seriously wounded; a supernumerary member of the crew, a pet cockerel, which had mounted the tank unnoticed, survived the action and baled out with the remainder—to fall to the mess-tin in which a neighbouring gun crew were preparing a meal.

"C" Squadron, coming up on the right of "B" Squadron, attempted to advance on BANANA RIDGE; but ran into a minefield. They retired to find an approach further to the south east while Lieut.-Colonel A. S. Birkbeck, whose tank successfully negotiated the minefield, proceeded alone to make a reconnaissance. The attempt to reach BANANA RIDGE from the Southern end was abandoned as a commanding feature had been occupied by parachutists from the Hermann Goering Jaeger Regiment, with snipers and machine gunners.

Our attack ultimately developed towards the northern end of BANANA RIDGE, a plan being made for "A" Squadron to support two companies of the 3rd Grenadier Guards in an attack on the feature. Unfortunately communications had been broken, and "A" Squadron advanced alone. Enemy infantry were found dug in on the reverse slope; these were cleared out with the assistance of the 1st Duke of Wellington's, which was contacted in the neighbourhood. "A" Squadron finished the day by towing in two abandoned German tanks. which were in running order.

Arrangements were being made for all the tanks to drop back and refuel, when information was received of further enemy tanks "trailing their coats" on the right. Major S. D. G. Robertson reconnoitred the ground and found the going impossible for attack. But a troop of "C" Squadron, under Lieut. C. V. K. Lister, was sent to assist a company of the 1st Loyals recover a feature where a detachment had been cut off. Lieut. Lister's Troop engaged an enemy machine gun post successfully and the 1st Loyals recovered the position, taking fourteen prisoners.

By 1600 hours, April 21st, BANANA RIDGE was again in our hands and the Regiment was released. It returned to its harbour area, where it formed a close laager in case the enemy attack was renewed. Shortly afterwards a message came from Brig. R. H. Maxwell that all plans for the original major attack would stand. The Germans spoiling attack had proved a complete failure; although in a document subsequently captured the enemy stated that as a result of his operation the First British Division was incapable of mounting a full-scale offensive for another fourteen days.

The first stage of this Allied major attack was the capture of GUERIAT EL ATACH on the way to MONTARNAUD FARM. The 142nd Regiment was in support of the 2nd Infantry Brigade; "A" Squadron with the 1st Loyals,

"B" Squadron with the 6th Gordons, "C" Squadron in Reserve. The ground was steep but not impossible for tanks.

Final orders were issued on April 22nd, and at 0230 hours the tanks moved off under wireless silence, in the order "A" Squadron, "B" Squadron, Regimental Headquarters, and "C" Squadron. The brigade route passed through the basin beneath the steep ridges, where two days before the enemy had broken through, and thence over BANANA RIDGE and across the TUNIS road. The track ran in places through narrow defiles; but carefully planned schemes ensured that no congestion occurred through breakdowns, and a special team of officers and the Infantry brigade Light Aid Detachment kept the track clear and marshalled vehicles across the TUNIS road, which formed the start line. During this approach march one tank, commanded by Lieutenant A. T. V. Borrett, blew up on a pile of Hawkins grenades. At 0200 hours, 23rd April, the TUNIS road was crossed. Here "C" Squadron remained in reserve; shortly afterwards the "A" echelon—essential petrol and ammunition, and the armoured recovery vehicles, under command of Major R. P. Newcomb—came up to the forward slopes of BANANA RIDGE. Regimental Headquarters remained at the point of divergence where "A" Squadron forked left to support the 1st Loyals, and "B" Squadron went to the right with the 2nd North Staffords.

"A" Squadron had been unlucky in the latter part of the approach march, the track was very rough, and it finally mustered only seven tanks, the remainder having shed tracks on the way. It was decided that the Squadron should occupy the objective of the 1st Loyals at first light. Accordingly at 0530 hours the tanks advanced and reached the objective four strong; two had been disabled on a minefield and a third carrying the Forward Observation Officer of the artillery had been hit; the driver, Tpr. Taylor, being killed and the artillery officer severely wounded. Nevertheless the four tanks of the Squadron dominated the crest until the infantry arrived and consolidated. By midday touch with the 24th Guards Brigade on the left was effected.

During this time another of the tanks was disabled; but its Commander, Lieut. A. H. Dodson, proved of the greatest value during the subsequent fighting. Casualties among the infantry had been very high, Battalion Headquarters had struck a minefield, and the Officer Commanding had been killed. Communications were disorganised, and for a long time Lieut. Dodson's tank provided the only live link. From his own observation, and from information received from the 1st Loyals, he was able to pass targets and corrections back over his wireless to be relayed to the artillery; thus enemy positions over the crest of the position were engaged. During the afternoon the enemy attempted to counter-attack, and two enemy tanks took up hull down positions. Lieut. Dodson's immobilised tank remained alone in support of the 1st Loyals and engaged the enemy until it was hit, the driver, Tpr. Leacock, being killed. The part played by Lieut. Dodson during this action was of great value and won him a well deserved Military Cross.

During this fighting Regimental Headquarters from a central position had engaged the attacking enemy, knocking out one tank. But the German counter-attack was pressed home and the Loyals were driven off the position they had gained. "A" Squadron had meanwhile re-organised, recovering several of its damaged tanks, and it supported by fire a reserve Company of the Loyals who succeeded in reaching and holding a position on the flank of the ground lost.

Meanwhile the 24th Guards Brigade on the left had advanced with the 145th Regiment in support; and on the right flank "B" Squadron, operating with the 2nd North Staffords, had found a position on point 151 from which it could support the infantry on to their objective, GUERIAT EL ATACH point 174. The infantry were at first forced back, but subsequently regained the position, with the assistance of "B" Squadron, and then at their request Major F. G. L. Lyne, the Squadron Commander, attempted to get into hull down positions. But the top of GUERIAT EL ATACH, a small plateau, made it virtually impossible to reach the crest without exposing the tank, or to get into a hull down position behind it. Moreover, as was known from the air photographs and defence overprints, the enemy had strongly fortified the ridge with anti-tank guns and had it well covered by mortars. Two tanks which exposed themselves in attempting to get into position behind the crest were immediately knocked out. Major F. G. L. Lyne, "B" Squadron Commander, endeavouring to support them from hull down position lost two more tanks from the enemy anti-tank and mortar fire. The remainder of the Squadron stayed up near the infantry below the crest, firing as opportunity offered. They were in this position throughout the morning and afternoon, and at about one o'clock assisted the 1st Duke of Wellington's in a successful counter-attack on point 174 which had been temporarily lost.

Meanwhile the 6th Gordons on the right of the 2nd Infantry Brigade front had occupied a feature slightly to the rear of the main brigade objectives. Lieut. R. J. Paul, Commander of the Reconnaissance Troop, was with them as liaison officer, and at 1330 informed Lieut. Col. A. S. Birkbeck that tanks were approaching from the south east. The Divisional Commander's permission was given for "C" Squadron to take up a position on the extreme right, on the southern slope of point 151. Here a Mark VI (Tiger) tank was engaged and an anti-tank gun hidden in the corn was knocked out.

At the same time the Commanding Officer prepared for any counter-attack that might develop from this right flank. Two troops, commanded by Lieuts. C. V. K. Lister and J. E. Forrest, were detached from "C" Squadron, a troop was found from "A" Squadron, commanded by Lieut. R. C. Rowe, while a few tanks were withdrawn from "B" Squadron. This composite Squadron, under command of Major S. D. G. Robertson, moved over to the right to cover the plain beyond. Although the Squadron did not have to meet any counter-attack, it was heavily attacked with mortars and dive bombers during the afternoon. The ground over which it was operating was thickly mined; the first victim being Major Robertson's tank, which threw a track that had been previously weakened by a mine. With assistance from Lieut. Forrest's tank crew repair work continued under heavy mortar fire. An enemy Mark IV tank appeared on the crest of 174 while the task was in hand, and was engaged by Lieut. Forrest. The enemy succeeded in blowing off the first bogey of his tank, but was thought to have been itself destroyed.

The remainder of the Squadron found targets for themselves in enemy mortar positions until at six o'clock the Commanding Officer called on the tanks to rally on him. In returning two further minefield casualties occurred; the tanks commanded by Lieut. Lister and Sgt. Lienhard blew up, and then Lieut. Forrest's, which had been already damaged and was coming in last.

By 1800 hours that day, 23rd April, the first objective, points 151 and 156, had been reached and held; but the main feature of GUERIAT EL ATACH, point 174, off which the Loyals had been counter-attacked, remained strongly held by enemy forces on and behind the crest; our infantry never having gained more than a precarious hold on its slopes. Enemy tanks, although they had been reported in large numbers were unwilling to counter-attack over the knife-like edge of the GUERIAT EL ATACH plateau, where they would expose themselves to our tanks and anti-tank guns. Conversely our own tanks were immediately picked off when they had shown themselves on the top. Without tank support the infantry were held up by numerous machine gun positions.

The remaining fit tanks had concentrated towards the centre for replenishment of fuel and ammunition. Major F. G. L. Lyne had three "B" Squadron tanks, while with the tanks withdrawn from the right, together with repaired minor casualties, there was the basis of a small squadron grouped round Regimental Headquarters. These were placed under the command of Major F. W. Roper, D.S.O.

Light was beginning to fail. If the main feature GUERIAT EL ATACH 174 was left as it was, the enemy could utilize the night to strengthen his position. It was therefore decided to put in an attack at last light with the 2nd Sherwood Foresters, of the 3rd Infantry Brigade, supported by tanks, to gain control of the crest. The Commanding Officer of the Sherwood Foresters was forward; but the Battalion was six miles to the rear; co-operation was impossible before dark. But the Commanding Officer 142nd Regiment appreciated that the tanks must go forward although unsupported by infantry. The composite Squadron under Major Roper, numbering in all fourteen tanks, including Regimental Headquarters, was therefore drawn up to proceed up the track to point 174. The Commanding Officer, Lt. Colonel A. S. Birkbeck, led the attack himself.

The Squadron moved off as the light was going, and passed through the lines of the 1st Duke of Wellington's, which, greatly reduced in numbers, was holding on to its positions just below Point 174, the nearer slopes of GUERIAT EL ATACH. As soon as the tanks were observed by the enemy, intense machine gun and anti-tank gun fire was directed both on to the crest of the position 174 and the flank of the advance. Even so, Birkbeck and his tanks did succeed in getting far enough forward to engage the enemy tanks. Some damage was inflicted on the enemy, several of his tanks, including one "Tiger," being knocked out; but within the first few minutes the Commanding Officer's tank had been hit and was blazing. The gunner, Tpr. Poulson, succeeded in getting out; but Lieut. Col. A. S. Birkbeck, with the remainder of his crew—Sgt. Reedman, L/Cpl. Peacock, and Tpr. Elsom, were all killed.

It was now quite dark, and the dust caused by the tanks lay in the air like a blanket. Considerable confusion might have ensued had not Major Roper noticed a blazing vehicle near the track up which the force had come. Over the wireless he gave the order to tank commanders to turn about and make towards this, following the direction of the enemy tracer fire directed on point 151.

All can picture the "Forlorn Hope" in a battle of a byegone age; the small band of very gallant volunteers who took so big a risk in leading the way. The attack, led by the Commanding Officer of the 142nd, Lt. Col. A. B.

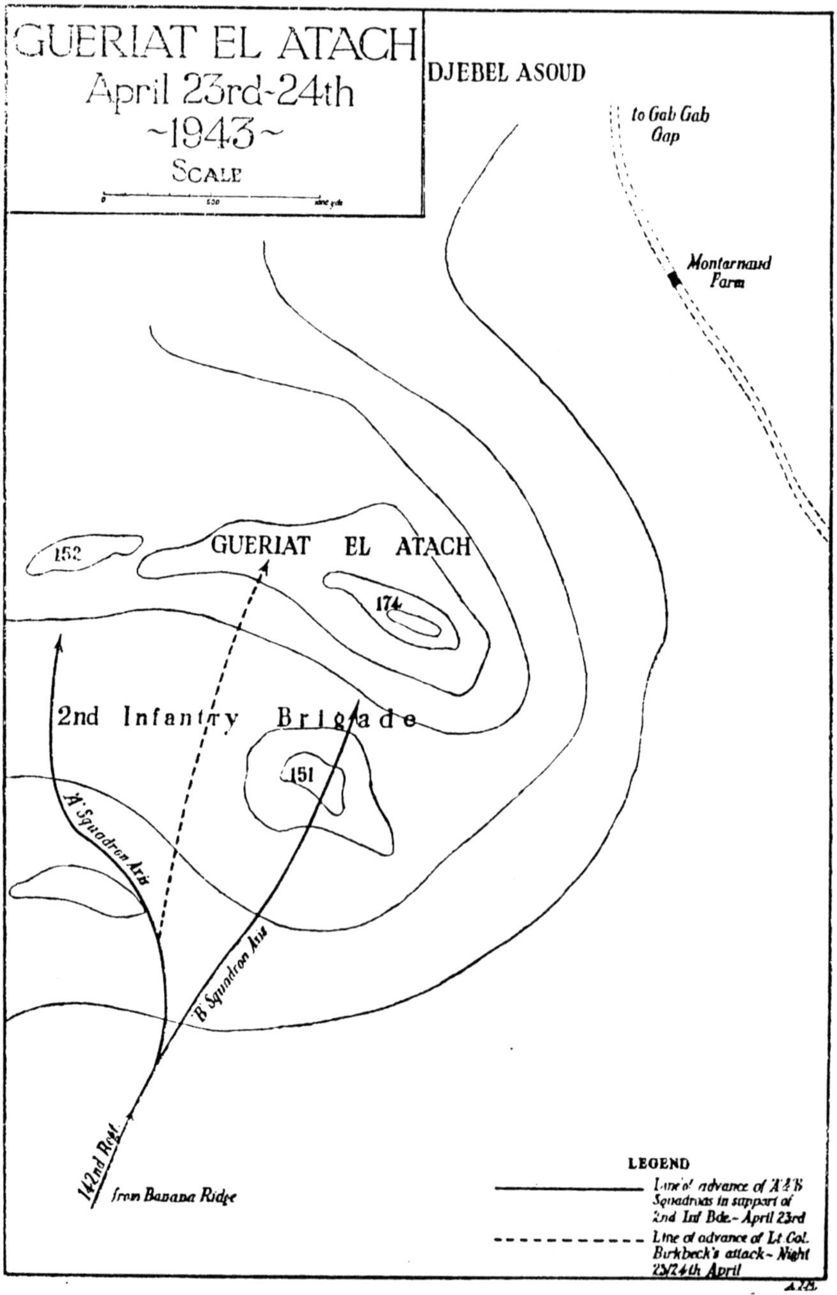
GUERIAT EL ATACH
April 23rd-24th
~1943~
SCALE
0
500
DJEBEL ASOUD
to Gab Gab Gap
Montarnaud Farm
152
GUERIAT EL ATACH
174
2nd Infantry Brigade
151
'A' Squadron Axis
'B' Squadron Axis
142nd Regt.
from Banana Ridge
LEGEND
Line of advance of 'A' & 'B' Squadrons in support of 2nd Inf Bde.- April 23rd
Line of advance of Lt. Col. Birkbeck's attack- Night 23/24th April

XXVI

Birkbeck, can be compared to the finest of these valiant assaults. None knew better than Alec Birkbeck the hundred to one chance he took when in his tank, flying the Suffolk pennant, he led the way to the attack.

His tank was the target for every enemy weapon, already trained on this vital summit. But he knew that even if his tank was lost there was a possibility that this vital hill could be taken and held by those who followed and so save the inevitable casualties of another daylight assault.

The attack failed, but not before it had inflicted loss on the enemy and so contributed to ultimate success. His pennant was recovered and is held today by the Suffolk Regiment in proud memory of a very gallant officer of the Royal Tank Regiment.

The tanks that remained mobile withdrew to the TUNIS ROAD, where replenishments were brought up and the fit tanks were again organised into a composite squadron by Major S. D. G. Robertson, who assumed command of the Regiment. By morning this force numbered sixteen tanks.

At 0300 hours, 24th April, the 142nd Regiment was ordered to support the 3rd Infantry Brigade at first light, but this was later cancelled.

Major F. G. L. Lyne, commanding the composite Squadron, moved back at first light to an open laager behind BANANA RIDGE and completed his re-organisation. Meanwhile a reconnaissance was made by Brig. R. H. Maxwell and Major Robertson and it was decided to make another attack on GUERIAT EL ATACH in co-operation with the 2nd Sherwood Foresters; the tank element being the composite Squadron under Major Lyne, with a Squadron of the 48th R.T.R., both under the control of Major Robertson. The tank wirelesses were hurriedly adjusted to a new frequency—enemy interference on the air on the previous day had been very heavy.

The advance followed the same track as previously, some fire from field artillery and mortars being encountered. The Officer Commanding Sherwood Foresters asked for tanks on his right flank, and some of the 48th R.T.R. were diverted; but before these arrived the infantry gained the positions on the crest of GUERIAT EL ATACH that had been held previously.

Meanwhile the Infantry had lost touch with the tanks. Lt. R. Loewe, the Intelligence Officer, who was accompanying the Infantry Officer in his scout car with a wireless link to Major Robertson, was away finding a suitable tank route; when he rejoined the infantry on the crest they were being heavily counter-attacked by enemy infantry and tanks. One enemy tank had actually got in to a hull down position on the track where it crossed the top of GUERIAT EL ATACH and was making use of this to very good effect. If the infantry were to hold on, the support of tanks was essential. Wireless communication broke down; but connection was re-established on foot by Lieut. Loewe. He left his position and covered the open ground to our tanks though completely exposed to enemy fire. He was subsequently awarded the Military Cross for his gallantry. Major Robertson, who had already lost six tanks in a minefield, succeeded in leading a force of approximately nine tanks round the right of point 151. He engaged the enemy; and at least two enemy tanks were knocked out.

By 1800 hours, April 24th, the situation was stabilised; the Officer Commanding the Sherwood Foresters reported that his Battalion could hold the crest for the night without tank support. Accordingly the remainder of Major Robertson's command, consisting of ten tanks under Major Lyne and five from the 48th R.T.R., fell back and remained at their forward rally ready to support the Sherwood Foresters if required. Soon after midnight the force withdrew a few hundred yards; replenishments were brought up. Maintenance of the tanks was not completed before 0200 hours the 25th April. That morning the tanks, which had gone forward at dawn remained in position subjected to continuous fire from mortars and artillery.

After midday April 25th attempts were made to locate an enemy tank firing on the infantry from the right. As the infantry casualties were high, Major Lyne decided to repeat the manoeuvre that had proved successful on the previous day—moving round from the right. Six tanks were observed, but proved to be dummies. Our tanks drew heavy anti-tank fire from guns sited near MONTARNAUD FARM, and were forced to withdraw; on reaching their previous position they again came under considerable shelling. Shortly afterwards the Squadron was relieved.

Major F. G. L. Lyne received the D.S.O. for his part in the foregoing operations.

The highest praise is due to the crews who manned the tanks of this composite Squadron. Like the remainder of the Regiment, they had been engaged either fighting or reorganising almost continuously since April 21st. They had been directly supporting the infantry for two days, and had spent considerably more than twenty four consecutive hours inside their tanks.

So ended this phase of the operation. It was now a question of maintaining composite Squadrons as tanks and crews became available.

MEDJEZ EL BAB.

DJEBEL BOU AOUKAZ.

April 26th — May 6th, 1943.

On 26th April, a Composite Squadron under Major F. W. Roper, D.S.O., once more returned to the GUERIAT EL ATACH fighting. It was now realised that suitable fire positions on this feature could not be found, and that if tanks attempted outflanking movements in this neighbourhood they immediately drew fire on to themselves and the infantry. It was decided to keep them to the rear as a counter-attacking force. Although rumours of the approach of enemy tanks were current throughout the day no attack materialised; at darkness the Squadron returned to its echelon in the regimental lines.

On April 27th the 142nd Regiment moved up to a location in the area of GRICH EL OUED to be in a jumping-off position for the next phase and prepared to counter-attack should enemy armour infiltrate through the GAB GAB GAP.

At 1430 hours on April 28th the enemy made his expected attack. It began with some artillery fire and smoke put down in the area occupied by the tanks and neighbouring gun lines. The composite Squadron, under Major G. R. Heyland, took up a defensive position: but no enemy tanks came within their range.

The same positions were occupied the next day, April 29th, a second squadron, commanded by Major F. W. Roper, D.S.O., reinforcing. As before, the enemy attempted infiltration soon after midday, but with larger forces, and succeeded in establishing an anti-tank position. Major Heyland's Squadron was therefore ordered to advance to protect the right flank of the

6th Gordons. At about 1700 hours, Major Heyland saw a force of enemy tanks of about two squadrons' strength come through the GAB GAB GAP into the valley. He pushed forward; but his tanks ran into a minefield, and three were blown up. After dark the enemy withdrew leaving a number of disabled tanks behind him, but he succeeded in recovering them during the night.

During the night plans were made to send two squadrons, one from each of the regiments, to relieve the garrison of the 1st Irish Guards, isolated on a feature of DJEBEL BOU AOUKAZ. This advance was to be unsupported by either infantry or artillery over unreconnoitred ground: it was to go in at first light so that preliminary reconnaissance was impossible. At the last moment it was cancelled. The task was subsequently carried out during April 30th by the 5th Gordons and a Squadron of the 48th R.T.R.

The Regiment spent April 30th in its counter-attack positions; but had no call. A good deal of work had by now been done by the regimental fitters and the Light Aid Detachment, 42 tanks were assembled for action and the Regiment was reorganised on a three squadron basis. On the same day, Major S. D. G. Robertson, who had commanded the Regiment since the death of Lieut. Col. A. S. Birkbeck, was confirmed in the rank of Lieutenant Colonel, Major F. G. L. Lyne was appointed 2nd in command, "B" Squadron being taken over by Captain I. H. Sanderson.

The next few days were quiet. On May 2nd an intercepted enemy message indicated an immediate attack; on May 4th enemy tanks again attempted to penetrate the GAB GAB GAP, but were repulsed. Meanwhile close liaison and planning was in progress with the 4th Indian Division for the second phase of the main operation due on May 6th.

On May 3rd, the Guards had obtained a precarious foothold on a small peak on the South West corner of DJEBEL BOU AOUKAZ but the remainder of it was strongly held by the enemy. The "BOU," with its precipitous rock and boulder strewn heights and its deep stone nullahs, presented an apparently impossible task to tanks; but a daylight reconnaissance and a night patrol of the 3rd Grenadiers, accompanied by Capt. R. O. Prentice and Lt. W. Ross Taylor, reported the ground, although exceedingly rough and steep, not impossible.

The 3rd Infantry Brigade was ordered to attack, while "A" Squadron with a Company of 2nd Sherwood Foresters seized high ground to cover the two possible approaches for enemy counter-attack. The operation was timed for 1700 hours May 5th, the evening before the main attack.

At zero hour the 14 tanks of "A" Squadron moved off, line ahead, with the Company of infantry alongside to remove boulders. Each tank carried 6 coils of barbed wire for use by the infantry, and four of the tanks towed 6-pounder anti-tank guns with crew and ammunition. The area was found littered with bodies and wrecked German tanks from battles of the preceding days.

The tanks at first made use of a wadi for cover, but beyond the wadi were subjected to heavy fire from machine guns and artillery, and the anti-tank gunners who were riding on board the tanks had to dismount, losing fifty per cent. casualties. The tanks experienced much difficulty in finding a way over to the plateau, above which rose their objective. Two tanks broke their tracks and another was knocked out by mortar fire. But by

1900 hours, when dusk was falling, the remaining eleven tanks, together with two anti-tank guns, had reached the base of the position.

Further progress in the dark being impossible, a close laager was formed, and the crews stood to. The infantry had suffered considerable casualties. A reserve company of 2nd Sherwood Foresters, as local protection for the tanks, arrived soon after midnight. Meanwhile the tanks, whose position was known to the enemy, were subjected to fire from all directions, including some from six-barrelled mortars.

At first light, May 6th, the laager was broken, and the advance continued. There was a good deal of opposition; but in conjunction with the infantry a large number of prisoners was taken. The solid armour-piercing shot of the tank guns proved very effective against the dug-in enemy, who suffered from the splintering of rocks. After the infantry had consolidated, the Squadron withdrew to laager.

This operation of "A" Squadron links the First phase of the battle for Tunisia with the Second and decisive phase.

Brig. R. H. Maxwell had previously visited all Squadrons and explained the importance and the scope of this operation. The 142nd Regiment (less "A" Squadron) was to advance on May 6th along two routes in support of the 7th Indian Brigade, whose objective was a number of undulating features to the South of DJEBEL BOU AOUKAZ. When these were secured the armoured thrust on TUNIS would commence, and the 7th Armoured Division, which, like the 4th Indian Division, had come round from the Eighth Army to the First Army for the *coup de grace*, would pass through and up to the central track through MOBTARNAUD FARM on the left of the Regiment.

It is a tribute to the planning of this operation that it was carried out without a hitch. As the tanks and infantry moved up they encountered scarcely any opposition; the ground, pitted with shell holes, gave evidence of the efficacy of the artillery barrage. By midday the infantry were digging in securely on DJEBEL BOU AOUKAZ and the great stream of vehicles of the 7th Armoured Division began to pour through. It was a wonderful sight for units of the First Army, who had never yet seen large formations of tanks manoeuvring over open ground after the manner of the Western Desert. Aircraft were in great strength. By afternoon the battle had been won, and the 142nd Regiment fell back to a rear rally, the supply Echelon came up, and tank crews knew that for the first time since April 19th they could rely on an undisturbed night.

VICTORY IN NORTH AFRICA.

May, 1943 to April, 1944.

Enemy resistance west and south of TUNIS had been broken; but there still remained a good deal of mopping up to be done. Squadrons were detached in support of various formations, and it was not until May 10th that they were together again at AINE EL ASKER, a small village to the south of TUNIS.

But almost immediately "B" Squadron was off again with the 5th Indian Brigade, and "C" Squadron with the 7th Indian Brigade. "B" Squadron with the 1/9th Ghurkas collected a large number of prisoners, including practically a whole tank battalion. Two troops of "C" Squadron were engaged by enemy anti-tank guns and Lieut. J. B. Aylward had his tank disabled but continued to engage the enemy until the firing gear of his sixpounder gave out and his Besa machine guns ceased to work.

During that night, May 10th, emissaries under a white flag arrived in the lines of the 1st Royal Sussex to negotiate a surrender of the 86th Regiment. With this Regiment several thousand other enemy troops gave themselves up.

Lieut.-Col. S. D. G. Robertson was with "C" Squadron when a German staff car drove up, flying a white flag. It contained two senior German officers, Col. Nolte and Col. Stolz, from the Headquarters of Col. Gen. von Arnim, the German Commander-in-Chief; with them was Gen. Kramer, the Commander of the Afrika Korps. They bore a letter from Gen. von Arnim to Lieut. Gen. Anderson, Commanding First Army. Lieut. R. J. Loewe, the Intelligence Officer of 142nd Regiment, R.A.C., was called upon to act as the British interpreter at 4th Indian Divisional H.Q.

The letter from Gen. von Arnim was handed to Lieut. Gen. C. W. Allfrey, the Commander of the 5th Corps. In it, the German Commander-in-Chief stated that, his supplies of ammunition being exhausted, he was prepared to ask for surrender for all troops under his immediate command.

The definition of the last phrase caused trouble. The German officers, when pressed, were unwilling to commit themselves beyond saying that means of communication had more or less completely broken down. Lieut. Gen. Allfrey made it clear that he would only accept the unconditional surrender of all Axis troops remaining at large in NORTH AFRICA; further, he would expect immediately complete details of all remaining enemy minefields. Col. Nolte would not give a definite answer. The whole party then proceeded to the Headquarters of Gen. von Arnim at St. Marie du Zit, south of the great rock of DJEBEL RESSASS. Gen. von Arnim admitted that the only troops whom he could now claim to have under his immediate command were his own staff and his headquarters; such communications with his formations as had not been destroyed by the advancing Allies had been sabotaged by the German forces themselves. He added that formations and units, now cut off from him, who had the ammunition, should continue independent resistance. German Army Headquarters surrendered.

The Regiment now concentrated in some pleasant olive groves near HAMMAM LIF. Here it was within easy reach of TUNIS, and had magnificent bathing facilities—greatly appreciated after the sweat and grime of the last days of the battle. Major Gen. Tooker, Commanding 4th Indian Division, visited the Regiment and addressed all ranks. His visit was a fitting end to a most happy partnership between the Regiment and the 4th Indian Division.

On Sunday, May 15th, a parade service was conducted by the Regiment's Padre, the Rev. P. Thomas, C.F., a memorial prayer was recited for the fallen members of the Regiment and the Roll of Honour read. The victory parade of the Allied Forces in TUNIS followed on May 20th. Two troops of the 142nd Regiment took part in the march past. Other troops of the Regiment formed the flanking guard for the saluting base; while a Squadron under Major R. P. Newcomb lined part of the route.

The decorations awarded for services in the concluding stages included the D.S.O. to Major F. G. L. Lyne, for his action with a composite Squadron on GUERIAT EL ATACH. Staff Sgt. A. G. Campbell, R.E.M.E., of the Regimental Light Aid Detachment received a Distinguished Conduct Medal for his work in recovering tanks among the minefields during the battle.

Brig. R. H. Maxwell held an inspection of the Regiment to mark the close of the campaign; addressing all ranks he summarised the history of the Regiment since leaving England, and pointed out the part played by them in the victory gained.

It is a tragedy that the story of the Regiment in North Africa should be marred at the end by a most regrettable disaster. On May 26th, a large party from all units in the Brigade set out to visit the battlefields in the area of MEDJEZ EL BAB; much could be learnt from a discussion of the tactics on the ground, particularly when examined from the positions occupied by the enemy. After a visit to LONGSTOP HILL, where the part played by the North Irish Horse was explained, the party adjourned to GUERIAT EL ATACH, where the story was taken up by Lieut. Col. S. D. G. Robertson. Here an anti-personnel mine was set off. Eight persons were killed, four of them members of the Regiment—Lieut. Col. Robertson, R.S.M. Daley, R.Q.M.S. Bennett, and Sgt. Lienhard. Those seriously wounded included the Brigade Commander, Brig. R. H. Maxwell, and Capt. G. Ward. Robertson's death was a great loss to the Regiment. One of the best, regimental officers at the outset of the war, he had proved his worth as Second in Command to Maxwell. Cool and determined in action, he had all the promise of proving himself a first-class Commanding Officer.

Lt.-Colonel F. A. Dow, Royal Tank Regt., was posted to the Command of the 142nd Regt.

The months that followed can be briefly told. The 25th Tank Brigade moved to AIN MOKRA, near BONE where recreational transport and bathing was arranged on a generous scale. Leave was granted to Rest Camps near the sea, but this was overshadowed by the grant of leave to England to over a hundred men for a short holiday. Moreover a large number of troops was required as escort for the thousands of prisoners who had been taken in the latter stages of the Tunisian campaign, and the 142nd Regiment supplied a proportion of their personnel. Vacancies were given first to compassionate cases, and then by lot, and the parties were granted several weeks' leave on arrival in the United Kingdom. They ultimately rejoined the Regiment in September and October.

Further training in tank and infantry co-operation was carried out in August in a series of exercises appropriately named "Concord." Unfortunately forest fires were started over a large area, and strenuous efforts were called for by troops to get them under control.

In September, 1943, the Regiment moved back to TUNISIA, for a further period of training on the Eastern side of the CAP BON peninsula with the 24th Guards Brigade and with units of the 1st Free French Division. At the same time preparations were in hand for remobilising the Regiment to go to Italy, where the campaign had now been well begun. By the end of November the Regiment was back again with the remainder of the 25th Tank Brigade near BONE. At the end of the year courses commenced for officers and N.C.O.s on the 75 m.m. tank gun, with which, in some form, the Regiment expected to be equipped shortly.

Early in 1944 the 142nd Regiment took part in a wireless exercise in wheeled vehicles which took them as far south as BISKRA on the edge of the desert. The lessons which were learned were passed on to the fighting personnel in a series of miniature exercises carried out during February.

BONE offered few amenities to the troops; but much was done in Camp to combat the monotony. A commodious and well equipped canteen, the envy of all the Brigade, was built by the Regiment, while their prowess at boxing formed the backbone of the victorious Brigade team.

There were several changes in Command. Major F. G. L. Lyne, D.S.O. left to command an armoured reinforcement Regiment, his place as Second in Command being taken by Major P. W. C. Colan, M.C., Major J. Austin commanded "A" Squadron, Major R. C. Easton, M.B.E., "B" Squadron; Major Moser "C" Squadron; and Major "Taffy" Williams the H.Q. Squadron. Capt. M. J. Shaw had succeeded Capt. Payn as Adjutant, the latter having gone as Staff Captain to the Brigade. The Rev. D. R. Tarleton, C.F., became the Unit Chaplain and remained with the Regiment until its final disbandment.

THE ITALIAN CAMPAIGN.

April, 1944.

The Regiment finally moved from North Africa to Italy in the Spring of 1944. The move was welcomed. The Regimental Commanders and later the Regimental Intelligence officer, with other officers of the Brigade, had visited the Italian front during the winter. Their first hand knowledge of local conditions, such as roads and complications thereon caused by enemy demolitions, as well as the experience of Italian battle conditions, stood their Regiments in very good stead.

The History of the Regiment in ITALY can be described more briefly than the story of its activities in AFRICA. Its interest is no less; but its campaign importance is of a more modest nature. When the Regiment had reached AFRICA, the Brigade of which it formed part, and the Sixth Armoured Division, comprised virtually all the armour on the Allied side in Tunisia; the French had some obsolete tanks and the few American ones were all light. Thus the presence of a Regiment, or even a squadron, of Churchills on any part of the front often had a decisive effect.

The position was changed by the Spring of 1944. Tank production had increased; the problem was not to find tanks, but to find the men to man them. There were sufficient armoured units in Italy, in the Fifteenth Army Group—which included all the Allied forces under General Alexander—to give armoured support on a fairly generous scale to any formation. The significance of a Regiment of Churchills was no longer notable.

The problem facing Kesselring, the German C-in-C in Italy, differed from Rommel's in North Africa. Kesselring could not consider any major offensive action. His policy was dictated, a slow withdrawal northwards containing as many Allied troops as possible; but he had with him some of the best remaining German troops, including the 15th Panzer Grenadiers and several Parachute units.

The enemy had prepared three strong positions on which to make a stand. The southernmost, known as the Gustav Line, was based on Monte Cassino and the River Garigliano. This was an immensely strong natural position, the assault and defence of which had been the favourite study of the Italian General Staff for years. Some ten miles in rear of this lay a second line, known as the Adolf Hitler Line; after which the road to Rome was clear. No further major defensive position had been prepared before the Line from Pisa to Rimini in the North, sometimes known as the Gothic Line.

The physical conditions of the country made the role of the Regiment fundamentally different in Italy from that in North Africa. In spite of the development of cross-country travelling by armoured vehicles, the possession or command of roads is a paramount consideration to any commander. It is only where roads are non-existent, as in the WESTERN DESERT, and, to a lesser extent, in NORTH AFRICA, that an Army will get used to the idea of blazing its own trail. In mountainous ITALY the road problem is paramount; for the roads often constitute the only possible path for vehicles. They have been cut on the wooded slopes of steep hillsides, where the gradients, the gullies, and the thick vegetation often make it impossible for them to be by-passed. The dividend in delay that the enemy could secure in the Italian Campaign by skilfully placed road demolitions was great.

The opportunities of fully deploying tanks, or anything at all except infantry were rare. Thus combined Tank and Infantry tactics frequently resolved themselves into the organisation of a column to proceed along the roads in line ahead, the composition and arrangement being varied according to type and intensity of the opposition expected. Only occasionally could a light formation be sent ahead for distant reconnaissance or to make contact.

The move from AFRICA to ITALY was accomplished without incident. The port of embarkation was BONE, which was conveniently near to the Regimental area. The main body of the Regiment embarked on the S.S. Ville D'Oran on 18th April, 1944, and arrived at Naples on 20th April. On arrival the Regiment crossed to the East side of ITALY.

An encouraging incident occurred en route. As the tank trains were passing through CASERTA, General Alexander happened to notice the tank trains waiting on a siding and paid an informal visit. He recalled the Regiment's association with Brig. R. H. Maxwell, and asked to be remembered to him.

After proceeding by train to BOVINO, the Regiment went into a concentration area south of LUCERA, near to FOGGIA. Here outstanding deficiencies, which had not been available in AFRICA, were drawn, and the Regiment was brought up to full scale of equipment. Units of the 1st Canadian Infantry Brigade, which formed part of the 1st Canadian Division, were affiliated to the 25th Tank Brigade for a few days, combined training. The units of this formation were The Royal Canadian Regiment, The Hastings and Prince Edward's Regiment, and the 48th Highlanders of Canada. The Canadian Brigade was commanded by Brig. D. C. Spry. Most cordial relations were established at once, at all levels, and it became obvious that the partnership was to be a happy one.

Little time was available for combined training; within a few days both formations were concentrated on the Western side of ITALY. The Regiment was given an area North of MADDALONI, near CASERTA, on the banks of the RIVER VOLTURNO near the village of SOLOPACA.

The Allied offensive began on the night of May 11/12th, the intention being the capture of ROME and to continue the advance to the North.

The two main roads, all other roads were indifferent, were the VIA CASILINA, Route 6 which runs past the foot of MONTE CASSINO, and the VIA APPIA, Route 7 which connects NAPLES with ROME via the sea coast.

The Allied front, prior to the offensive, ran south from CASSINO, held by the enemy, along the Eastern side of the RIVER GARI, to its junction with the RIVER LIRI; then it followed the RIVER GARIGLIANO. The enemy held the Northern banks; but the Allied Fifth Army with French troops on its right flank had gained a footing on the Northern bank of the GARIGLIANO.

The Eighth British Army lay opposite CASSINO, and the orders given were to cross the RIVER GARI, break the GUSTAV LINE and exploit if possible as far as and through the ADOLF HITLER LINE some 10 miles to the rear.

Two main formations were detailed for this exploitation. On the right, along Route 6, the 6th Armoured Division, on the left the 1st Canadian Division supported by the 25th Tank Brigade. The objective of this latter formation was the Southern sector of the ADOLF HITLER line from PONTECORVO to Route 6.

After very heavy artillery preparation, the Engineers threw Bailey Bridges across the RIVER GARI and the GUSTAV LINE was breached. The 142nd Regiment meanwhile had moved up immediately in rear of the front line and harboured north of the village of MIGNANO.

On the evening of 15th May, after a daylight reconnaissance by the Commanding Officer and Squadron Commanders, the tanks crossed just north of the junction of the GARI and the LIRI into the appendix formed by the two rivers. At first light next morning the advance began, each tank squadron in support of one of the Regiments of the 1st Canadian Infantry Brigade. During the first two days no major opposition was encountered; the enemy was concerned only to cover his withdrawal to PONTECORVO, having done what he could in the way of improvised demolitions. He covered his retirement with a screen of infantry supported by self propelled guns; these the tanks had no difficulty in dispersing; though some tanks became casualties to infantrymen armed with anti-tank grenade. There were a few casualties, Lt. Kimber being killed.

Supply was the major difficulty. The poor track north of the RIVER LIRI was the only road axis; but tracks were made by Bulldozers, and the Regimental Echelon under Major E. C. V. Williams kept well up behind the fighting troops.

By May 17th the Regiment had reached PIGNATARO which the enemy held for a few hours. By the night May 19th the Brigade group was within sight of PONTECORVO, a bastion in the ADOLF HITLER Line. Here a movement was commenced to rush the HITLER Line.

But Brigadier Tetley, who commanded the 25th Tank Brigade, represented to the G.O.C. Canadian Division the need for more detailed reconnaissance by the tanks and their own supporting Engineers. An anti-tank ditch was visible on air photographs forward of PONTECORVO; very little being known of the strength of this obstacle. It was agreed to postpone the assault.

THE ADOLF HITLER LINE.

22nd MAY — 24th MAY.

There were several changes of plan; but it was finally decided that the 142nd Regiment would support the 1st Canadian Infantry Brigade in its attack up the track to PONTECORVO with "C" Squadron on the right supporting the 48th Highlanders, "B" Squadron in reserve with the Royal Canadian Regiment; and "A" Squadron on the left with the Hastings and Prince Edward Regiment.

The attack was to be made on the 22nd May; but before it started the Regiment was ordered to find a detachment of Sherman tanks of about half a squadron to support the Reconnaissance Regiment of the Canadian Division in an armoured reconnaissance to the South of PONTECORVO where the German defences rested on the RIVER LIRI. This move did not meet with immediate success; three tanks being put out of action. Among the casualties killed were Sgt. Bugg, Troopers Maurice Roberts, Houghton, R. Miller, all original members of the 7th Battalion.

The tanks had been knocked out by an anti-tank gun of the latest type —the Panther Turret. This was a 75 mm. gun in a revolving turret fixed to a steel lined concrete casemate, the casemate being below ground level. Only the turret showed; a small and very difficult target to locate in the undergrowth. There was a line in depth of these Panther Turrets in the Hitler position, interspersed with anti-tank guns all sited with great skill. Supplementing these in the defence were tanks, self-propelled guns and extensive minefields.

After the failure of the armoured reconnaissance, at 1030 hours the main attack was launched. Stubborn resistance was met. The village of PONTECORVO stands on a commanding rise: its forward slopes concealed many anti-tank weapons and this effectively held up the attacking tanks. "C" Squadron, supporting the 48th Highlanders of Canada, experienced great difficulty in crossing the anti-tank ditch, although the Engineers had blasted passages in it. Here the O.C. "C" Squadron, Major A. H. S. Moser, was wounded. The few remaining fit tanks joined by nightfall "B" Squadron, many of "C" Squadron tanks remaining out for the night under the command of Capt. R. J. Paul.

"A" Squadron, in support of the Prince Edward Regiment, had moved forward at 10.00 hours ready for the second phase of the battle which did not materialize. However at 19.00 hours they were ordered forward by the G.O.C. 1st Canadian Division and their support enabled the infantry to penetrate the enemy defences. "A" Squadron withdrew to harbour at 2100 hours.

Next day, May 23rd, the main assault was launched on the HITLER Line from PONTECORVO to beyond AQUINO. All units of the 25th Tank Brigade were engaged; the 142nd on the left facing PONTECORVO, the 51st R. Tanks in the centre, the North Irish Horse on the right opposite AQUINO. The remainder of the line on the right was attached to the Sixth British Armoured Division. On the left beyond the RIVER LIRI the French troops in the rugged mountains had already made progress and from the heights could look down on the battle raging in the river valley.

"B" Squadron had moved at dawn, contacting the 48th Highlanders and advancing with them at 0800 hours. They covered the infantry advance against stiff enemy resistance with close support and heavy fire. The expenditure of ammunition was great; Squadron Sgt. Major Lovett using all the batmen, cooks and other employed men that he could find, and under heavy H.E., mortar, and small arms fire, built up a forward supply from which the tanks replenished. At 1930 hours the enemy put in a strong counter-attack supported by tanks and self-propelled guns and covered by an artillery barrage. This counter-attack was successfully beaten back; "B" Squadron ending the day at 2115 with a bag of one 75 mm. PAK 43, one 75 mm. Panther Turret, one 50 mm. A/Tk. gun, one inf. gun and many machine guns.

"A" Squadron, further to the right, supporting the Prince Edward Regiment did not move forward until 1500 hours; from then until 2100 hours steady progress was made. Their attack included the capture of 263 prisoners.

On the right flank of the battle the 6th Armoured Division had made a break through as far as the AQUINO aerodrome. The Derbyshire Yeomanry had shot up a host of enemy transport here, but had been forced to withdraw when counter-attacked as the infantry had been unable to get up and consolidate. Further to the right, the Polish Corps had fought a very stubborn battle against Parachute troops for the possession of MONTE CASSINO; they eventually captured their objective after sustaining very heavy losses. On the left, the Fifth Army had met with considerable success, and the Goumiers, or Mountain troops from French Morocco, were scouring the thickly wooded mountains of the MONTE AURUNCI to mop up isolated enemy pockets of resistance; at the same time the French Artillery was lending its support to the Canadian Division by firing on to PONTECORVO from beyond the RIVER LIRI. During the fighting ground troops received close support from dive bombers, a wave of these making a successful attack on the barracks to the North of PONTECORVO. Late in the afternoon, it was realised that the enemy's resistance had collapsed and that he was pulling out from his defences.

The ADOLF HITLER Line had been lost by the enemy; but its possession was valueless if the battle was to stop there. Immediate pursuit and exploitation was essential. The fighting Squadrons were in no condition to continue the advance; but the Reconnaissance troop of Stuart Tanks had not yet been engaged. A force was made up of the 4th Princess Louise's D.G., (the Canadian Reconnaissance Regiment) and the 142nd Reconnaissance Troop. Lt. R. J. Fletcher was also attached to the 142nd Troop with three Sherman Tanks for close support.

A start was made before nightfall. Some opposition was encountered in the course of the next day, May 24th, from mortars and self-propelled guns situated in the farms which lay to the north west of PONTECORVO, and the Shermans played their part in "winkling out" the enemy; but by the evening after the break through the enemy was in full flight.

This had been the Regiment's first battle on Italian soil; Major R. C. Easton, M.B.E., the commander of "B" Squadron, was awarded the D.S.O. for his part in the battle, and his reconnaissance officer, Capt. A. T. V. Borrett, the M.C. S.S.M. G. Lovett, who had done such valuable work in maintaining the supply of ammunition to forward tanks, was awarded the Military Medal.

On the 30/31st May the advance proceeded up the LIRI VALLEY to CAPRANO, where the Germans had blown the dam and bridge over the great reservoir and speed was checked while the Royal Canadian Engineers completed a Bailey Bridge some hundred feet long. Thence the route ran parallel to Route 6, in a north westerly direction to CAPRANO and the woods beyond and then on to the edge of the great plain which adjoins the road to FERENTINO.

On June 3rd the 142nd Regiment was encamped West of FERENTINO when the 1st Canadian Division received a report that the American Fifth Army had broken out of the ANZIO Bridgehead. Elements were reported on the way to ROME, while a main break had been effected along Route 7 and towards VALMONTONE. It was important to get early confirmation and establish contact with Fifth Army troops to the north west. Lieut. J. Butcher and the Reconnaissance Troop were despatched forthwith with orders to attempt to find a route across country, through the wooded area that lies West of Route 6. Lieut. Butcher was given a Canadian flag, with orders to break it from his aerial mast if he sighted any American armour. This flag is now at BURY ST. EDMUNDS, the depot of the Suffolk Regiment. The going was by no means easy, but by the next morning he had regained the main road, and reported that he was halted by a serious demolition half way between FERENTINO and VALMONTONE. While he was attempting to construct a way across, by digging and the use of some captured demolition charges, a jeep drove down to the demolition from the further side, carrying an American quartermaster; and thus the 142nd Regiment's Reconnaissance troop had the signal honour of effecting the junction between the Eighth Army and the Fifth Army.

The news was immediately passed back by wireless to Eighth Army Headquarters, and Lieut. Gen. Sir Oliver Leese, the Army Commander, was soon on the scene. He congratulated the Regiment, and Lieut. Butcher in particular, on the part they had played respectively; but he was anxious that more formal contact should be established with the forward troops of the Fifth Army. Lieut. Butcher was therefore ordered to proceed along Route 6, as soon as a crossing could be effected, to establish contact with the French on the Fifth Army's right flank. Lieut. Butcher proceeded to VALMONTONE, where he reported to the French officer commanding.

The following messages were received at the end of the ADOLF HITLER battle:—

From Commander 1st Canadian Corps to Commander 25th Army Tank Brigade:

"Canadians owe a debt of gratitude to the 25th Tank Brigade which has fought so magnificently with us to-day. The courage and determination of all ranks has been beyond praise."

From Commander 1st Canadian Infantry Division to Commander 25th Tank Brigade:

"Canada will be proud forever of a battle which its 1st Canadian Division has won to-day. Through the courage and determination of all ranks of the Division and their British comrades of the 25th Tank Brigade this Hitler Line has been broken in the face of bitter opposition, and the enemy has been dealt a blow from which he will not soon recover. The final victory is nearer, let us press on and complete our task."

Major-General G. C. Vokes, D.S.O., Commanding 1st Canadian Infantry Division, instructed that he would be pleased if all ranks of the 25th Tank Brigade would wear a maple leaf emblem in token of the part played by the Brigade in assisting the 1st Canadian Infantry Brigade to breach the ADOLF HITLER Line.

The offer was gratefully accepted. A silver Maple Leaf was added to the black diabolo which formed the 25th Tank Brigade sign.

A valuable memento was presented to the 142nd Regiment by the Royal Canadian Regiment in the shape of a silver cigarette box, engraved with the crest of the Royal Canadian Regiment with the following inscription below:—

"Presented to 142nd Regiment, R.A.C. (Suffolk Regiment), by the Royal Canadian Regiment, to commemorate the battles of the GUSTAV and ADOLF HITLER Lines, Italy, 1944."

The Commander of the French Forces who from the high ground beyond the RIVER LIRI had seen the fighting, sent the following message to the Commander, 1st Canadian Division:

"I send my greetings and congratulations to your magnificent fighting men. From here we can see the enemy smarting and cringing under your lash. I wish particularly to congratulate your gunners on their skill, their efficiency and speed in engaging targets, your fearless tank crews and your admirable infantry. You have done great things in this valley."

Lt. Colonel F. A. Dow, Commanding the 142nd R.A.C., issued the following Special Order:—

On the occasion of the breaking of the ADOLF HITLER Line, many messages of congratulation and appreciation, thanks have been passed both to the Regiment and to the Brigade for their support of the 1st Canadian Division.

These messages you have all either seen or have read to you, and there is little I can add to the glowing tributes paid to you by the Canadians.

Not only in the difficult attack on the ADOLF HITLER Line itself, but also in those trying days of the earlier advance to contact, you have been faced with a new type of fighting in a particularly nasty type of country.

The fact that you have victoriously and cheerfully overcome all the difficulties with which you were faced has given proof of your grim determination and guts that will eventually lead us to complete victory over the Hun.

The Commanding Officers of the Royal Canadian Regiment, the Hastings and Prince Edward's Regiment and the 48th Highlanders, have all been full of praise of your support, and I thank you all—tank crews, transport echelons, signals, fitters, repair and other services, for your share in the work that has earned this praise.

I am extremely proud of the Regiment.

As you know, the Brigade has been asked by G.O.C. 1st Canadian Division to wear the Maple Leaf in recognition of this great day

In addition, the Commander 1st Canadian Infantry Brigade has asked me if we would carry on the tanks and vehicles of this Regiment their Brigade Insignia.

On behalf of you all I have gladly accepted this honour.

The job of clearing the enemy out of Italy has begun. Let us, with our Canadian comrades, continue with the same speed and determination to annihilate him.

Good Luck to you all.

F. A. Dow,
Lieut. Colonel,
Commanding, 142*nd Regiment, R.A.C.*

Field,
26th May, 1944.

THE ADVANCE TO FLORENCE.

On June 5th the advance was resumed for the next objective, the road TERNI—RIETI, some 60 miles North of Rome; the 142nd Regiment being transferred to the 6th British Infantry Division of the 13th Corps. The Regiment was allotted to the 12th Infantry Brigade.

The Brigade Group turned north to TIVOLI, by-passing ROME, and moved up the axis of a second rate road with few parallel tracks, passing through very rough country. The weather had turned wet and detours from the road meant bogged vehicles. The route led through PALAESTRINA; on June 7th TIVOLI was reached. Here the Regiment had a glimpse of the dome of St. Peter's, forty miles away across the plain.

Next day, June 8th, with the Regimental Reconnaissance Troop in advance, PALOMBARA was reached; here demolitions made the route impassable and an enemy self-propelled gun reinforced an enemy machine gun that was firing on the column. Casualties were suffered, including Lieut. Butcher, who was killed while bringing his tanks forward. All the crew of Capt. R. O. Prentice's tank were either killed or wounded, he alone escaping unhurt.

While the infantry were pushing forward through the undergrowth a detour down a steep narrow track was found for the tanks and by next morning the advance was continued, first along the valley of the TIBER and then due north towards TERNI.

Communications now became a serious problem; the range of the wireless sets was insufficient for the distances covered and was moreover seriously reduced by the mountains. The Signal Officer, Lt. A. H. Dodson M.C., had to organise a system of relay stations using his signal Sgt. R. Latheron, and the Intelligence N.C.O., Cpl. W. Schooling, to act as Step-up Stations.

On June 11th, the Regiment was transferred to the 8th Indian Division and with this formation passed North of TERNI through BEVAGNA to FOLIO.

The pace was too hot for the Churchill tanks, which moreover urgently needed maintenance, for the Regiment had been continuously at 24 hours' notice or less, so that no major repair tasks could be undertaken. Consequently on June 15th, the two Sherman tanks from each Squadron were united into a Sherman Squadron under Major P. W. C. Colan, M.C., the Churchills dropping out of the pursuit temporarily.

Close on the heels of the retreating enemy the advance was continued to SPELLO and thence to SANTA MARIA DELIGI ANGELI, a village in the plain close to ASSISI. SANTA MARIA contains a large Basilica which houses the original Chapel of St. Francis. This the Germans had marked as neutral;

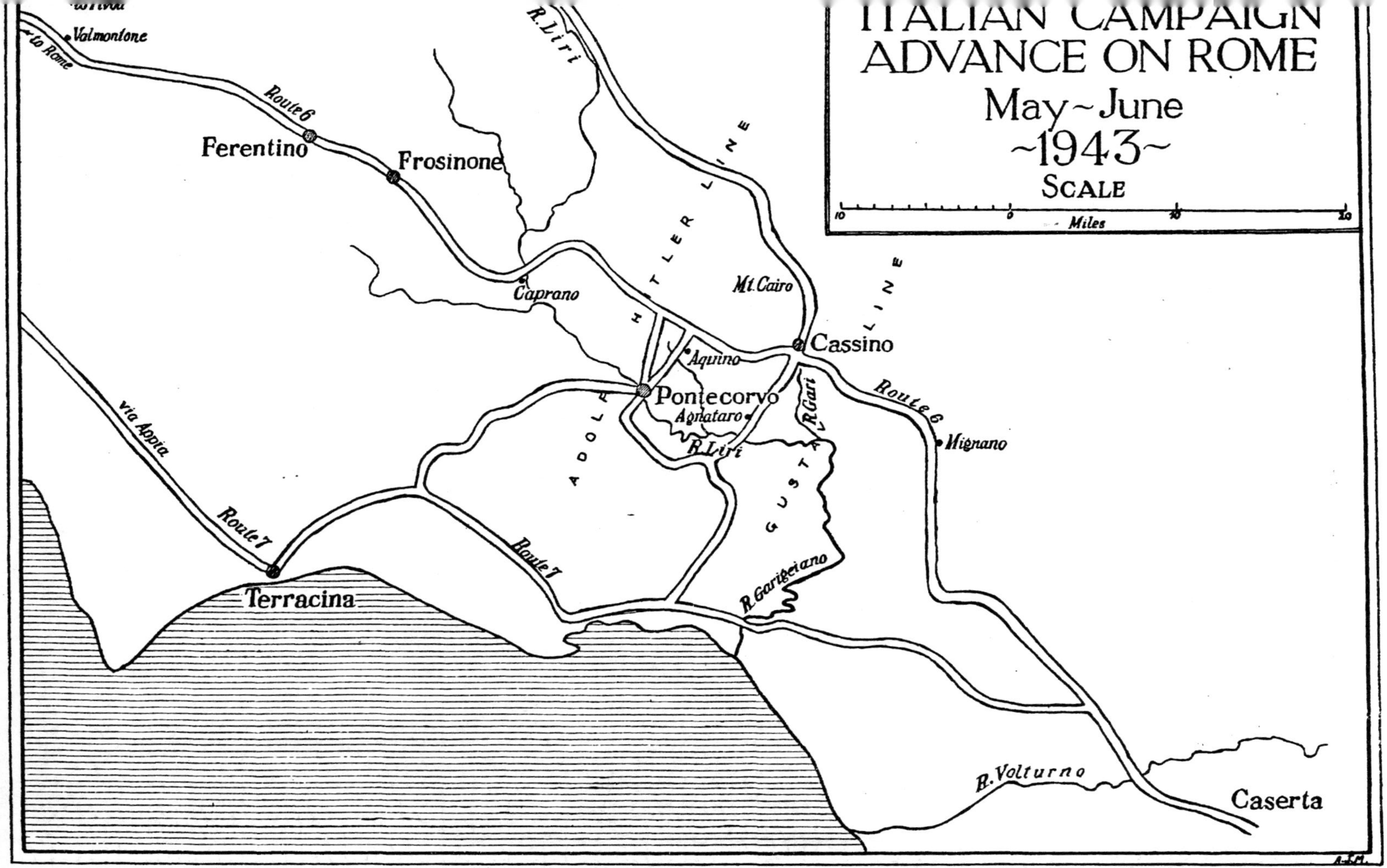
ITALIAN CAMPAIGN
ADVANCE ON ROME
May ~ June
~1943~
SCALE
10
0
10
20
Miles
Valmontone
to Rome
R. Liri
Route 6
Ferentino
Frosinone
HITLER LINE
Caprano
Mt. Cairo
Cassino
GUSTAV LINE
Aquino
Pontecorvo
Agnataro
R. Gari
Route 6
Mignano
R. Liri
ADOLF
via Appia
Route 7
Terracina
Route 7
R. Garigliano
R. Volturno
Caserta

but when it was behind the Allied advance the first enemy ranging shot fell on the Dome, fortunately causing little damage.

The advance continued in heavy rain. Just north of BASTIA on June 18th the Regiment supported the 1/5th Ghurkas and 6th Lancers against an obstinate rearguard action. That night, in BASTIA, they were relieved by the North Irish Horse. Since the beginning of May the Regiment had been continuously employed.

By June 22nd, the Regiment was concentrated near NARNI, some 50 miles north of ROME, at 108 hours' notice. Here the long overdue tank overhaul and major maintenance was put in hand.

Praise has constantly been given to the tank crews. It had also been thoroughly earned by the fitters, gun fitters, electricians and all the other mechanical and technical staff of the unit and Light Aid Detachment, who throughout the campaign had kept the tanks fit for action, working continuously at recovery and repair. It was their enthusiasm, skill and keenness that enabled the Regiment to do whatever was required of them.

It is no light matter to keep a Churchill tank fit with its 40 tons of armour, tracks, engines and machinery, guns and equipment, complicated electrical and hydraulic systems, wireless sets, telescopes, periscopes and all the innumerable items and components which go to make up the gear and equipment of the modern Armoured Fighting Vehicle. The fighting crew are primarly responsible for the maintenance of their tank; but expert help or advice from the technical Regimental Staff or the Light Aid Detachment was always available the moment anything went wrong, or was suspected of going wrong.

While at NARNI, 30% of the Regiment were transported each day to ROME. The city was still in the first flush of relief and excitement following liberation. The streets were full of teeming crowds; shops, cinemas and hastily, but well organised canteens provided welcome attractions for all ranks.

During this time the Reconnaissanee Troop was reorganised, with a troop of three Sherman tanks for close support, the remaining eight light tanks being formed into three patrols, with a Commander's tank and a rear link tank.

On July 22nd, the Regiment left NARNI and moved North West of AREZZO to join the advance. The break through which followed CASSINO and the fall of ROME had spent its impetus. Magnificently as the Engineers had done in constructing Bailey Bridges and clearing minefields, their task was ever mounting as the advance continued. There was an ever increasing difficulty in bringing forward supplies now that the main bases were some hundreds of miles behind the front line; while the petrol expenditure was out of all proportion to the normal. The most careful staff work, the best of road discipline, failed to prevent long delays on the mountain roads. Company Commanders and Provost Officers had to act ruthlessly, if necessary pushing a break down vehicle off a road and over a precipice to keep the traffic moving. The time had come to build up stocks forward, to complete the railway repair and wait for the petrol pipe line to be completed.

Meanwhile the Germans were still retiring north, but as the hills afforded them greater opportunities, the intensity of their rearguard actions increased. Kesselring's plan was to hold back the Allies until he was ready for them in his next prepared position, north of Florence, where, between PISA and RIMINI, he had reinforced a position already naturally strong. This was called the GOTHIC LINE. By now the enemy's own administrative difficulties were immeasurably greater than our own. Captured documents told of a petrol shortage so serious that vehicles were ordered to coast down gradients wherever possible; while the physical categories of many of the enemy in the front line were extremely low—some not having the full use of their limbs.

This was the situation when the 142nd Regiment was ordered on July 25th to rejoin the 4th British Infantry Division, to support the 12th Infantry Brigade through the mountainous CHIANTI country towards FLORENCE. An extremely poor axis of advance was allotted. The road system in this area was based on a single secondary road, and for some distance this had to be shared with the 24th Guards Brigade. So difficult was the country that frequently it was a question of manoeuvring only one or two tanks into a position to help the infantry, and it had to be decided whether a tank if it broke down on a vital track might not be in a positive danger. For the tanks had frequent steering difficulties, and their tracks broke.

The advance was only two days old when a misfortune befell the Regiment. The Commanding Officer, Lieut. Col. F. A. Dow, had set out early in the morning to look for an observation post, and to establish a tactical Headquarters for use jointly with the Infantry Brigade Commander. He had stepped out of his jeep and together with his Intelligence Officer was investigating a suspicious corner when a mine was set off, which wounded the C.O. badly in the groin. The Second in Command, Major P. W. C. Colan, M.C., thereupon assumed command of the Regiment, and Major R. C. Easton, D.S.O., M.B.E., returning from leave that evening became second in command. Easton handed "B" Squadron over to Capt. R. O. Prentice, his former Squadron 2nd in command.

The enemy was determined to hold on to FLORENCE and the crossings of the RIVER ARNO for as long as he could, and in the neighbourhood of the last big hill before the city the Regiment encountered the fiercest opposition since PONTECORVO. Four days fighting continued in the hilly country, "A" and "C" Squadrons supporting the 6th Black Watch and the 1st Royal West Kents, while to the west, "B" Squadron and the 2nd Royal Fusiliers were trying to get forward along the road. Opposition from mortars was very heavy; if a tank was damaged in the open it immediately drew all their fire. Thus, a tank commanded by Sgt. Macdevitt, broke down on the edge of a precipice, and the enemy mortarmen attempted to blast the route underneath the tank.

Casualties in tanks and personnel were considerable. Lieut. J. S. B. Ivey was killed by a mortar bomb which landed on the turret of his tank, and Sgt. O'Connell lost an arm when his vehicle was attacked by a tank hunter with an anti-tank grenade. It was impossible to move tanks back for relief; when crews were exhausted they were relieved by fresh crews.

The Reconnaissance Troop light tanks took supplies of ammunition, petrol and rations forward to the tanks.

During this fighting, Lieut. R. C. Rowe, the commander of the Regimental Headquarters Troop, distinguished himself by getting tank support to the infantry through very thickly wooded country; he was subsequently awarded the Military Cross.

Eventually, by August 1st, Minden Day, the enemy was forced to withdraw from his commanding ground and further advance up the road was then possible. But strong opposition and heavy shelling was encountered from the little village of STRADA which was taken on August 2nd by the 2nd Royal Fusiliers, supported by some tanks under Capt. R. O. Prentice. Here two enemy counter attacks were beaten off. Lieut. J. E. Forrest was wounded.

On August 3rd, Major A. H. S. Moser with "C" Squadron attempted to capture the river bridge of GRASSINA before the enemy could blow it up. But the enemy fought fiercely, and self-propelled guns in his position caused many casualties to tanks and personnel; Major Moser being seriously wounded.

Here Lieut. Cinelli, the Italian liasion officer who was with Major Moser was wounded. Some months later a letter was received from Marshal Messe, Chief of the General Staff, the Italian Army, expressing appreciation that this officer had been so promptly evacuated before our British wounded, to prevent the possibility of his falling into German hands.

In this action a Sherman tank commanded by Lieut. H. B. Ridgeway was hit and set on fire, Ridgeway being killed with Troopers Newton and Parnham. The driver and co-driver, though wounded, succeeded in escaping. The casualties were quickly evacuated by the Regt. Medical Officer, Capt. D. C. Watson, R.A.M.C., who under heavy fire coolly went forward and collected them.

This gallant officer and his party of batmen stretcher bearers travelled in rear of and in the closest proximity to the tanks engaged in battle and every man in the Regiment went into action knowing that if anything happened to him the M.O. would very quickly be on the spot, however difficult the circumstances. Captain Watson received the M.C. for his gallantry throughout the campaign.

The following day, August 4th, the enemy pulled out of his position, retiring the 3 or 4 miles to the RIVER ARNO. On August 10th, the Regiment was moved back to the area near PERUGIA. The Regiment had little to show for its strenuous advance through extremely difficult country. But without armoured support the task of the infantry would have been far harder, more protracted and casualties much greater.

THE GOTHIC LINE.

August 28th — October 17th.

The Regiment stayed only a short time at PERUGIA; but wasted none of it, working from dawn to dusk on maintenance. By August 28th a move was made to the Eastern side of Italy, to the village of MONTEFELCINO, some 15 miles South West of FANO on the Adriatic Coast. Here it was on the VIA FLAMINIA, Route 73.

Here Lt. Colonel G. A. E. Peyton, O.B.E., assumed command in place of Lt. Colonel P. W. C. Colan, M.C.

Lt. Colonel Peyton, writing to me at the time, said:—

"I am writing to introduce myself on taking over Command of your 7th Battalion. It is an honour and a privilege of which I feel very proud.

I only hope I will do all that is required of me by such a grand lot of chaps, imbued as they are obviously with great Regimental and County spirit . . . . The Regiment went into action three days after my arrival and got very high praise from all for the part they took. I can claim none of the credit for myself; but they did go well."

The Regiment was placed in support of the 138th Infantry Brigade of the 46th Division, a portion of the 5th Corps. The plan of operations was for the 8th Army to break the GOTHIC LINE, exploit to the North, and secure the passes into AUSTRIA. It was hoped that Marshal Tito would be able to co-operate in the North West parts of JUGOSLAVIA.

Actually the Italian Campaign could not be completed until the Spring of 1945, mainly on account of most adverse weather conditions. There was very heavy rain; water courses became impassable, and mud made both offensive and administrative movements extremely difficult and very slow.

Thus Kesselring was able to hold the Allies South of the APPENINES until the Winter 1944 came to his aid; the possibility of his then being outflanked along the road BOLOGNA—PIACENZA and the plain of RAVENNA being impossible owing to flooding.

The first objective of the Brigade Group was the crossings over the River Foglia; a strong defensive position, part of the forward area of the GOTHIC LINE. An advance had commenced on August 29th; but except for giving supporting fire on August 31st, there had been no fighting. August 31st was spent on reconnaissance; Lt. Clark and Sgt. Braunton with a party of R.E. reconnoitring the approaches and sweeping for mines after dark.

The assault on September 1st was successful. "A" Squadron crossed the River Foglia and by 1400 the attack on the high ground beyond commenced. Two troops of tanks headed the assault followed by infantry and the remainder of the Squadron. The first objective "COW" was taken and consolidated, twenty prisoners being captured. "B" Squadron supporting the 2/4th K.O.Y.L.I., followed and were equally successful against the next objective, "HORSE," which was secured by nightfall.

"C" Squadron, in rear, lost three tanks from a skilfully concealed A/Tank Gun.

The following day, September 2nd, a further advance was made by "A" and "B" Squadrons against considerable gun opposition; enemy mortar and shell fire being very heavy. By 1600 hours six tanks had pushed through to MARIA DEL MONTA where a large body of enemy surrendered without fighting. "C" Squadron had minor clashes while supporting the 6th Lincolns.

At 1930 hours that day the Regiment sustained a serious loss. Major R. C. Easton, D.S.O., M.B.E. and the Intelligence Officer Lt. R. J. Loewe, M.C. having dismounted from their tank were walking across to the C.O.'s tank when a large calibre enemy shell struck Sgt. Bishop's tank. Both officers were seriously wounded by shrapnel; Major Easton dying the following day and Lt. Loewe being incapacitated for further service. Both these officers had given invaluable service throughout the Campaign.

On September 3rd the North Irish Horse relieved the 142nd Regiment, after a substantial break into the crust of the Gothic Line had been achieved.

The success of these three days' fighting disclosed that the enemy's GOTHIC LINE defences were still incomplete. There were many Panther

Turrets in course of preparation, but few were ready for action; while the large number of disabled enemy tanks, S.P. Guns and anti-tank weapons proved that he had done his best to hold the line with his mobile troops. If the attack had been made a month later, far greater difficulty would have been experienced.

From September 3rd to September 11th the roads were cleared while the 1st British Armoured Division carried forward the assault. But by this time the enemy had strongly reinforced this flank of his line, and no break through, as had been hoped, was effected. The 1st Armoured Division suffered heavy losses in the neighbourhood of GEMMANO and only gained a limited amount of ground.

During this time Major J. D. Ellerbeck was posted as Second-in-Command and Lt. R. G. Whittington became Intelligence Officer.

On the night September 9/10th the Regiment moved to MONTEFIORE, just South of the River CONCA and West of the high ground GEMMANO. The Regiment came under Command of the 139th Inf. Bde. and on September 13th "C" Squadron supported the 5th Forresters in an attack on the Southern side of the River Conca towards the GEMMANO feature. The tanks, despite considerable ground difficulties, got to within 400 yards of their objective and assisted the infantry in a successful assault.

On September 15th "A" Squadron was in action from 0400 hours until 1800 hours, supporting the 2/5th Leicesters in an attack on high ground about the village of MONTE COLOMBO. During this fighting Lt. J. A. Truman was killed.

A short description of this fight is given, as it is typical of the many infantry tank actions in which the Regiment was engaged.

A warning order had been received by 1800 hours the 14th September and on this "A" Squadron was moved forward under the 2nd i/c; Major J. Austin, the Squadron Commander, preceding to the Inf. Bde H.Q. for orders. At 0700 hours September 15th the Squadron Commander and the Inf. Coy. Commanders were making their reconnaissance from high ground which gave a view of the objectives, and it was decided that three infantry Companies should leap frog on the the final position while two of the three Churchill troops of "A" Squadron would support the successive leading infantry companies, the remaining Churchill troop with the Sherman troop following in support. Inf. Coy. Commanders and Troop Commanders then contacted one another to ensure the fullest co-operation.

The tanks and infantry advanced from fire positions to fire positions, one Churchill troop going forward, sometimes one tank at a time, supported by the fire of the others, the infantry and tanks being within a hundred yards of one another during most of this advance. But the ground was worse than the distant reconnaissance had suggested, one Churchill was lost by "bellying", another turned on its side in a steep ditch, a third lost its track.

The attack of the first two Companies was successful; but the third Company, after successfully making the final assault lost touch with Battalion H.Q. where the "A" Squadron Liaison Officer was. This Company was forced to retire by heavy enemy pressure and it was not until touch was regained that a reserve Company with tank support regained the position. Then the tanks remained on the flanks while the infantry consolidated.

Throughout this little typical action neither the infantry nor the tanks had sufficient knowledge either of their own troops on the flanks or of the enemy's positions, with the result that the fullest flanking use could not be made by the tanks to help the infantry forward. This action was also an example that there is a time limit to the employment of tanks. Many tanks were kept running for nearly 15 hours, and at the end they were short of ammunition and nearly out of petrol; this was largely due to the leading Company having lost touch with its Battalion H.Q., causing a delay of some three hours.

The next day, September 15th, "B" Squadron successfully supported 128th Inf. Bde. in a continuation of the attack on a village called MONTESCUDO. Two troops of "C" Squadron supported the 1/4th Hants on September 16th. This advance was continued during the following days under similar conditions; the ground was always difficult and the resistance stubborn. The independent republic of SAN MARINO was entered on September 19th.

By September 20th the Regiment had reached VALLECHIA. Here the weather took a decided turn. Torrential rain prevented any further advance for the time being; until September 23rd when a Composite Squadron under Major R. O. Prentice supported the 5th Foresters and 2/5th Leicesters in an unsuccessful attempt to force a crossing over the River MARECCHIA. Four tanks managed to get across; but had to be withdrawn, after Trooper F. Stone had been killed and eight others wounded.

Next day, September 24th, a Composite Squadron under Major A.T. V. Borrett, M.C., crossed this River and during the next four days the advance continued. On September 28th, among other casualties, Lt. Hersant was killed.

September 29th found the Regiment on the RIVER RUBICON, where further torrential rain brought the advance to a standstill.

A Brigade Rest Camp had been established at PESARO on the ADRIATIC. Leave parties were sent to this camp to give the men short spells of rest after their long and continuous spells of action. Officers also made use of the Rest facilities at RICCIONE, offered by their old Canadian Comrades.

On October 17th the Regiment was once again placed under the 12th Division and moved via SANTA ANGELO to BARDIA, a small village on Route 9.

TILL DISBANDMENT.

OCTOBER 17TH, 1944—JANUARY 22ND, 1945.

From August to October, 1944, the 142nd had been grimly struggling through the most difficult tank country. Mountains with rough tracks had meant fighting an unending succession from one small ridge to the next. Now the enemy's flank had been turned by the 8th Army and a firm footing had been gained at the South Eastern end of Route 9, that straight road that runs from RIMINI through FORLI, FAENZA, BOLOGNA to the RIVER PO. Here was a first class supply route over a dead flat plain, an inviting prospect for an armoured break through. A theatre in which the enemy would have little chance to form a defensive line until the RIVER PO was reached.

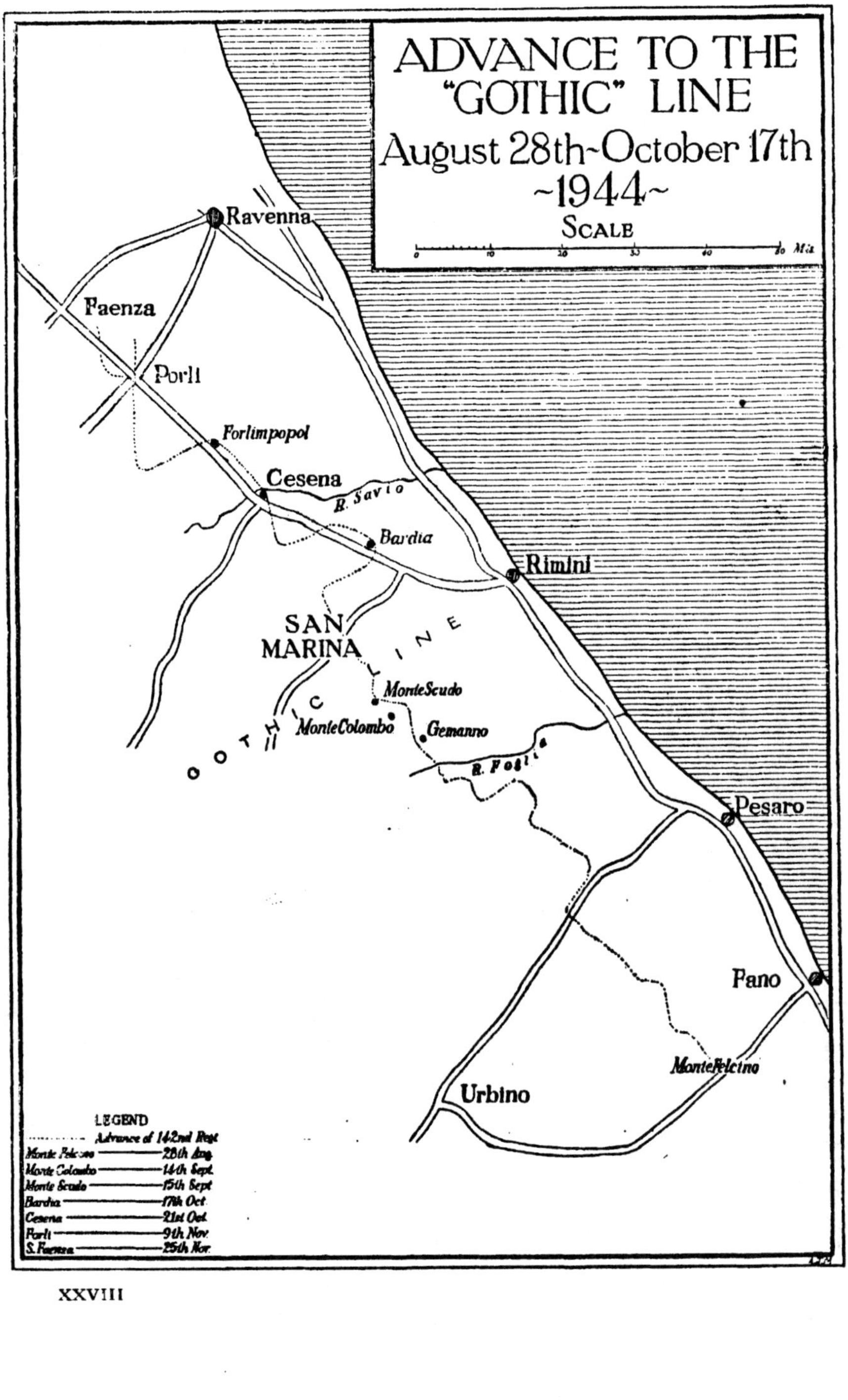
ADVANCE TO THE "GOTHIC" LINE
August 28th–October 17th
~1944~
SCALE
Ravenna
Faenza
Forli
Forlimpopol
Cesena
R. Savio
Bardia
Rimini
SAN MARINA
GOTHIC LINE
MonteScudo
MonteColombo
Gemanno
R. Foglia
Pesaro
Fano
MonteFelcino
Urbino
LEGEND
Advance of 142nd Regt
Monte Colombo — 14th Sept
Monte Scudo — 15th Sept
Bardia — 17th Oct
Cesena — 21st Oct
Forli — 9th Nov

But the flank had been turned too late. The weather which had been quickly deteriorating, became very wet indeed. Innumerable rivers and watercourses bifurcate the plain; inconsiderable obstacles in dry weather, brimming over now and major obstacles to progress. The ground between the water courses rapidly became waterlogged and practically impassable for tanks. The Campaign speedily resolved itself into a succession of big and little actions for river and stream crossings.

The difficulty of getting a 40 ton tank across an obstacle is obvious; much was done to overcome these difficulties by the provision of specialized equipment. A Churchill tank without its turret was "decked" and carried a large ramp in front and astern, ready to turn itself into a bridge when its ramps were lowered. Such Churchills were called "ARKS". In the case of a wide stream one or more would be run into the bed of the river while the rest crossed in single file over their recumbent comrades.

These "ARKS" belonged to the Assault Regt. R.E. attached to the 142nd Regt. as required.

Other Churchills became "Fascine Carriers," the great fascines they carried on the tip of their turrets slid down the runners into great ditches or small streams making a foundation for a pathway. Many of the 142nd Tanks became Fascine Carriers.

On October 17th the Regiment at BARDIA under the 12th Division moved forward for the next major operation, the crossing of the River Savio at CESENA.

Night reconnaissances were made of possible crossing places by officers of the Reconnaissance troop working with infantry patrols; but it was evident from the heavy enemy shelling that the attempt would be difficult. During the night October 19/20th a crossing was made a few hundred yards south of the main demolished bridge and a limited bridgehead was established; but without tank support. By first light October 21st an ARK bridge had been effected and over this "A" and "C" Squadrons were ordered to move. Two troops of "C" Squadron and one tank of "A" Squadron succeeded before the ARK became damaged.

Opposition on the far side of the River was encountered; enemy tanks pinning down one small force in the limited bridgehead. Five hours later the remainder of "A" and "C" Squadrons were able to cross. The Infantry and tanks then proceeded to dislodge the enemy, who had many M.G. posts in the buildings in the vicinity. During that night, in spite of great difficulties, two "honey" tanks managed to cross the river with supplies, petrol and ammunition.

There was heavy fighting throughout October 22nd; heavy enemy fire of all natures pinning our small force. That night replenishments had to be ferried across the river.

On October 23rd "B" Squadron with a Squadron from another formation crossed by the ARK, which although showing signs of weakening had stood the strain. But when the last tank had crossed, it was decided that it was unsafe. At daylight, October 24th, the force made a successful assault on the enemy who was compelled to abandon the river line.

All troops engaged in this action deserved the highest praise for endurance and courage, particularly those who were engaged on the ark bridge over the river, which was constantly under very heavy fire. In this fighting Lt. M. D. Malone was wounded; three troopers were killed and two wounded.

On October 24th the Regiment was released from the 12th Division and retired to CESENA. During the next week there was torrential rain.

On November 1st the Regiment moved 7 miles N.W. of CESENA to FORLIMPOPOLI where it was brigaded with the 28th Inf. Bde to force the crossing of the River Ronco and the capture of FORLI, an important town on Route 9.

On November 6th "A" and "B" Squadrons supporting the 2nd Somerset L.I. and the 2nd King's respectively made a flank crossing and assisted in clearing FORLI; many enemy casualties and a number of prisoners resulted during the next few days while the enemy's positions were being probed.

After FORLI the next objective was FAENZA, the approach to which had to be made across a number of difficult water obstacles. Operations commenced on November 22nd, bridgeheads being secured over the River Cosina.

The last operation of the 142nd Regiment was on the night of November 25th, when it took part in a shoot, bringing harrassing fire down on enemy positions in and about FAENZA.

Although the operations after September, 1944, have had to be described briefly, the part played by the Regiment is reflected in the honours conferred on all the Squadron Commanders. Major John Austin ("A" Sqn.) and Major R. O. Prentice ("B" Sqn.) each received the M.C. Major A. Borrett ("C" Sqn.) was awarded a Bar to his M.C. Major E. C. V. Williams ("H.Q." Sqn.) received the M.B.E. and was Mentioned in Despatches.

On November 29th the Regiment was back in FORLI, and the following day at a Regimental Parade the Commanding Officer told all ranks that the Regiment was to be disbanded. He told them that he had had a personal letter from the C.-in-C., Field-Marshal Sir Harold Alexander and he read to them the message from the Army Commander. He explained to them that their disbandment was a matter of the greatest regret to all the authorities, but was due to a shortage of man power; that the 142nd Regiment, R.A.C. and the 145th Regt. R.A.C. (formerly a Battalion of the Duke of Wellington's Regiment) had been selected for disbandment solely because they were the two junior tank Regiments in the theatre, both having formerly been Infantry Battalions.

Captain A. H. Dodson, M.C., the last Adjutant of the 142nd Regiment who has supplied the details of all the Italian Campaign, writes as follows:—

"This news came as a sad and bitter blow to all ranks. It was regarded as a misfortune of the greatest magnitude that the 'happy family' should be broken up and not be able to add further honours to its proud fighting record. It may be recalled that the campaign in Italy ended on 2nd May, 1945, with the first unconditional surrender by any of the German armies engaged in the war.

"On December 1st, 1944, the Regiment paraded in a cinema at CESENA for an address by Lieut.-General Sir R. L. McCreery, K.C.B., K.B.E., D.S.O., M.C., the Commander Eighth Army, who stressed the brilliant record of the Regiment and his great regret at the necessity to break up the Regiment.

Officers of Regimental Headquarters and H.G. Squadron, 142 Regiment, R.A.C., November, 1944.

Standing, Left to right—Capt. (Q.M.) Johnson, M.B.E., Capt. Sewell (R.E.M.E.), Lt. H. R. Adams, Italian L.O., Capt. R. J. Paul, Lt. Whittington, Capt. C. Austin, Lt. R. I. Brown, Capt. C. Lister, Lt. D. Martin, Capt. D. C. Watson.

Seated, Left to right—Capt. A. H. Dodson, M.C. (Adjt.), Lt. Col. G. A. E. Peyton, O.B.E. (C.O.), Maj. J. E. Ellerbeck (2 i/c), Maj. E. C. V. Williams, M.B.E.

"On 3rd December Major-General H. L. Birks, D.S.O. (Major-General Royal Armoured Corps, Allied Force Headquarters) visited the Regiment and spoke to all officers concerning plans for the future of personnel.

"The Brigade Commander, Brig. J. Noel Tetley, D.S.O. also spoke to all ranks on parade.

"On December 18th the Regiment moved from FORLI to CAMERINO, a small town hidden away in the mountains South West of ANCONA. Preparations for a bumper Christmas were put in hand. The cooks excelled themselves and no effort was spared to provide every possible form of entertainment. Italian civilians and the town authorities did everything they could to help to shew their gratitude to the liberation forces. A modern cinema was put at our disposal and an ample supply of films. An army pantomime performed for two nights. ENSA provided a concert party. A Regimental Dance was held in the Teatro Phillipo Marchetti and the Italian civil authorities welcomed personnel of the Regiment to many of their Christmas functions.

"A message received from the Colonel of the Suffolk Regiment was published in Regimental Orders:—

> 'I have had a long letter from General Birks, giving me the latest news of the '7th'. I have told him how grateful I am to him for watching the future welfare of officers and men.
>
> 'If it is not too late please tell all how immensely proud we have been of their exploits—from start to finish, and how truly we consider they have earned the General's praise as 'Second to none'.
>
> 'The history of the Unit will make one of the greatest chapters in our Regimental History.'

"After Christmas the Disbandment Order arrived, and departures of drafts of personnel became a daily event. A hold up occurred when the Regiment was snowed up for eight days, but after extricating ourselves and moving to MACERATA some 30 miles away, disbandment proceeded apace and ultimately on 22nd January, 1945, the remnants of the Regiment departed to the Royal Armoured Corps Depot at RIETI.

Captain Dodson concludes:—

"It is not for me, who was privileged to serve with the Regiment, to comment on its accomplishments. I can however testify to the affection which all ranks had for the Regiment and the heavy hearts occasioned by its dissolution. All had the greatest interest in the Suffolk Regiment, despite the change in the name of our own unit in 1941. We felt the same allegiance to the Suffolk Regiment as if we had at all times remained a unit thereof and knew our unit was held in the same esteem by the Suffolk Regiment. When the unit first embarked for overseas service in January, 1943, 70% of the personnel of the unit were former Suffolk infantrymen. At the dissolution of the unit the proportion was still as high as 50%, despite the toll of time and battle."

MESSAGE FROM THE ARMY COMMANDER
TO ALL RANKS
142ND REGIMENT, ROYAL ARMOURED CORPS.

The Commander-in-Chief has written to your Commanding Officer telling him of his great regret that your splendid Unit has got to be disbanded and that the shortage of man-power is the reason for this decision being taken. I want to endorse all that the Commander-in-Chief has said, and to add to it my own personal regret that the traditions and loyalties that have grown up in five years of war service must now be dissolved.

I well remember the enthusiasm and efficiency you at once showed in training for your new role when in Kent. You had the honour of being the first Churchill tank Regiment in action, when a squadron, in the SBIBA gap, after a long forced march on tracks, helped American troops to stop the right wing of Rommel's armoured thrust through the KASSERINE Pass. This successful action was soon followed by heavy fighting in the TUNIS Plain, when the Regiment fought with great gallantry, determination, skill and endurance. The reward came when you supported 4th Indian Division in the historic break-through attack of 9th Corps, which led to the fall of TUNIS and the end of the AFRICAN Campaign. In ITALY during the great offensive battles of 1944 you have played a distinguished part with several different Infantry Divisions, from the LIRI Valley right up to FLORENCE, and finally in the assault on the GOTHIC LINE and the advance into the Po Plains. This is a magnificent record, and one of which you can all be justly proud.

Times have changed since the early days of the war, and final victory is certain. But it is not yet achieved. Victory can be hastened only by the greatest exertions on the part of us all, and I know that I can rely on All Ranks to fight as hard and as well in the future to finish the job off quickly as they have in the past with the 142nd Regiment, Royal Armoured Corps.

R. L. McCREERY,
Lieut.-General,
Commander, Eighth Army.

It is a matter of real regret that the fortunes of the officers and men of the disbanded 142nd Regiment during the rest of the Campaign cannot be recorded. There had been a great spirit of comradeship within the Tank crews, the Troops, the Squadrons and the Unit; this was fully appreciated by the Commanders in the Army and every effort was made to ensure that the officers and men were kept together as much as possible by units in the formations they subsequently joined.

No Battalion of the Regiment has a finer record in this War. Whatever they were required to do they did efficiently and enthusiastically. Wherever they went they gained fresh praise.

Their casualties in action included among the officers:—

KILLED IN ACTION.

23rd April, 1943	Lieut-Colonel A. S. Birkbeck.
17th May, 1944	Lieut. B. J. Kimber.
8th June, 1944	Lieut. J. Butcher.
28th July, 1944	Lieut. J. S. B. Ivey.
3rd August, 1944	Lieut. H. B. Ridgeway.
14th September, 1944	Lieut. J. A. Truman.
28th September, 1944	Lieut. A. R. Hersant.

DIED OF WOUNDS.

3rd September, 1944	Major R. C. Easton.

KILLED ON ACTIVE SERVICE.

26th May, 1943	Lieut.-Colonel S. D. G. Robertson.

DIED ON ACTIVE SERVICE.

3rd September, 1943	Captain W. J. Auger.
24th March, 1944	Major R. P. Newcomb.

OTHER RANKS.

NORTH AFRICA—1943-44.

Killed in Action	26
Died of Wounds	8
Died on Active Service	3

ITALY—1944.

Killed in action	31
Died of Wounds	6
Died on Active Service	2

CHAPTER NINE.

SECOND LINE BATTALIONS.

Eighth Battalion—Sixth Battalion—Ninth Battalion—Thirtieth Battalion—Thirty-first Battalion—Seventieth Battalion.

8th BATTALION, SUFFOLK REGIMENT.

MAY, 1940—JUNE, 1946.

THERE is a fortune of war that follows Battalions no less than individuals. A fortune that transformed the newly raised 7th Battalion Suffolk Regiment into a tank unit, in which guise under the title of the 142nd Regiment, R.A.C., it gained great renown for the Regiment. A fortune that launched the newly raised 8th Battalion, but instead of guiding it into the stream whence it might serve in any part of the world, anchored it in home waters. Of the five Battalions, the 1st, 4th, 5th, 7th, 8th Battalions the Suffolk Regiment serving at home in the summer of 1940 probably the finest men, physically and mentally, were in the ranks of the 8th Battalion. Yet 8th Battalion was fated to see no active or foreign service during the whole war.

Throughout the war officers and men continually departed, some individually, some in drafts. The individuals joined those branches of the Service which called to the adventurous—Commandos, the Air Force; the drafts were despatched to other units—and not always to units of the Regiment. Their places were taken by untrained officers and men. But for many months hopes ran high in the Battalion that they would eventually take their place as a first line unit.

The War History of the Battalion is therefore brief. But although Active Service, which is the highest incentive to comradeship, was of necessity wanting, yet the standard of discipline, training and *esprit de corps* never fell below the high level of the Suffolk Regiment. This in no small measure was due to Lt.-Colonel E. R. Daglish, posted to command the Battalion in early 1941 and remaining with it until the end of 1944, then once again Commanding until the final disbandment in the Spring of 1947.

The 8th Battalion Suffolk Regiment was formed at Bury St. Edmunds on the 28th May, 1940, under the title of the 50th Holding Battalion, Lt.-Col. J. S. D. Lloyd being appointed to the command. In June and July it was brought up to strength by intakes of militia men.

On the 17th August the Battalion moved to the Saxmundham area in an operational role, which necessitated four weeks' digging and wiring in the middle of a 12 weeks recruits' training course. Incidentally this recruits' training course included four weeks very sketchy field training. There were several officers serving with the Battalion who could remember an identical state of affairs in the early days of the War in 1914, when hurriedly raised and untrained units were despatched to the East Coast to deal with a possible invader.

While at Saxmundham the Battalion was ordered to carry out Platoon and Company training; Lt.-Colonel Lloyd protested that this was expecting the Battalion "to run before it could walk."

On the 8th October the Battalion was reorganised as the 8th Battalion Suffolk Regiment. 100 other ranks of low medical category were removed, as well as a large proportion of the Senior Warrant and N.C.O.s who were physically unfitted for this work. The 8th Suffolk now had a magnificent contingent of men; though the larger proportion of N.C.O.s were young and inexperienced. But there still remained R.S.M. Pallant, R.Q.M.S. Tuck, C.S.M.s Tyler, Holloway, Bacon, as well as other Senior N.C.O.s such as Short, Cook, Freeman, Matthews; a sheet anchor to a new unit.

On the 14th October the 8th Suffolk moved to Walton-on-the-Naze and Frinton, where in due course it formed a unit of a Coast Division. Here the Battalion was almost immediately set to work at field fortifications which Lt.-Colonel Lloyd noted were unlikely to be completed before the end of January 1941—and which were in fact never finished.

In March, 1941, Colonel E. R. Daglish succeeded Lt.-Colonel Lloyd. At this time the Battalion was in the 223rd Infantry Brigade under Brigadier Sir Alexander Stanier, Bt., the Brigade being a part of the Essex Division under Major-General J. Priestman. Capt. D. Perrens was Adjutant, an officer who subsequently greatly distinguished himself in the Air Force; Lt. A. Bacon was Quartermaster and Major H. R. Hopking came as Second-in-Command.

Lt.-Colonel Daglish making a note at the time writes:—

"Nearly all the officers, N.C.O.s and men were entirely inexperienced and had had very little training; but they were all extremely keen; most of the other ranks were from the big call up in July, 1940. The men of the Battalion as a whole must have been some of the very best of the country's man-power. The majority were of ages from 24 to 28; keen, intelligent, cheerful and ready to learn anything.

"The Battalion sector was from about half a mile south of Frinton to North of the Naze—a front of about four miles. All four Companies were forward on the beaches. There were no other troops in depth in that sector except for a battery of medium guns."

For the next two months the Battalion was engaged the whole time in field works and defences, including the erection of steel scaffolding, and was allowed to take only a very few hours off a week for weapon training, which was badly needed.

A feature in the construction of these defences was their frequent alteration. All senior officers from the Army Commander and Corps Commander downwards had their views on the siting of section posts, and after their frequent visits corresponding 'adjustments' usually had to be made !

"One wondered whether the time taken up digging and wiring had been balanced with the time which was so urgently needed to teach the men to shoot straight."

At this time the officers serving with the Battalion were:—

Lt.-Colonel E. R. Daglish	Commanding Officer
Major H. R. Hopking, O.B.E.	Second-in-Command
Captain D. F. Perrens, D.S.O., D.F.C.	(later Squadron Leader, R.A.F.) Adjutant
Major O. K. Leach	
Major C. E. Neep	
Captain S. J. Tufnell	
Captain J. W. Stevenson	
Captain M. G. H. Style	
Captain H. W. Bond	
Captain A. J. W. Clarke	
Captain W. C. Smith	
Captain E. T. Lummis	
Lt. N. J. D. Turner	
Lt. K. L. Fawdry	
Lt. S. Whatling	
Lt. S. E. Sneezum	
Lt. J. Cooper	
Lt. G. C. Roberts	
Lt. L. G. Thomas	
Lt. E. J. King	
Lt. F. C. Layne	
Lt. R. C. M. Yates	
Lt. R. A. Halstead	
Lt. P. W. Nice	
Lt. D. F. Rowe	
Lt. E. J. W. Smith	
Lt. J. F. Earp	
Lt. K. Chapman	
2nd Lt. S. Moore	
2nd Lt. N. H. Harris	
Capt. A. F. Bacon	Quartermaster
The Rev. C. J. Soar, C.F.	Chaplain
Capt. B. S. Quinn, R.A.M.C.	Medical Officer.

In May, 1941, the Battalion came back to a Camp near Colchester for a month's training. An invaluable month for the Companies, who for the first time lived and trained together and were able to work up a Battalion spirit. In June it returned to Walton and Frinton. But in July the Battalion, with the Brigade, was relieved from Coast defence duties and moved to Mill Hall near Epping wh re it was issued with full W.E. Equipment and transport and at last was able to train.

It was now that the chequered nature of the early work showed itself. The Battalion had never had a chance to get down to the ground work. It had been directly ordered not to delay on individual training; but to intersperse this basic work with section, platoon and higher exercises. The result was that on field training there was bad handling of weapons. It is a short sighted policy to attempt to run before learning to walk.

Nevertheless, good work was now done. The men were keen and enthusiastic, they became physically fit and the team spirit was obvious.

"B" COMPANY, 8TH BATTALION (LT. NICE) MARCHING PAST THE PRIME MINISTER (THE RT. HON. WINSTON CHURCHILL), 1941.

There is a letter from a man in the Signal Platoon which shows this essential state:—

"Considerations of the personality of groups can be left to the social and political theorists. All that I know about it is that one night in a quarry, like 'The Ship that Found Herself', our Platoon became a whole. Flung together by chance (working through her chosen instrument, the War Office) Bob and Sandy and Tom and Les and Bill, whose birthday it was, and the rest, became integral to the Signal Platoon. They ceased to be just men put in a pattern that is given a name. It says much for the Sergeants and their sturdy assistants, the Corporals, that, more permanent than we mere six-week sojourners, they yet do not remain apart. On that night we were all suddenly subsumed into the greater whole.

"And things have stayed that way. Unfortunately, our Signal Officer, looking boyish and hugely enjoying the game, is now translated to hospital. We will remember Sgt. Freeman's extraordinary staying power on the march; Cater, a radio set on his back and an endlessly reiterated 'Chatanoogh Choo-choo' on his lips; Jolley with jokes that always promised to be funny; Wolley, so addicted to a curious game called 'Slippery Sam'; Harris, unable to get up in the morning without seeing to it that everyone else got up too. To report them individually would need a book; to choose a few out of all, when all deserve notice—that cannot be done.

"So we must say only that, ploughing across country whose early autumn is so full of potential Breughels and Constables and Van Goghs, with radio sets or lamps or buzzer units, the Signal Platoon is, like all signal platoons, its own cheerful and definitely superior self. But with a difference springing from all the people who, that night, gave it life of its own. This Signal Platoon is the one we shall remember, and its heart is high."

Meanwhile the 223rd Infantry Brigade had become an independent Brigade Group and was part of G.H.Q. reserve. The 8th Suffolk had counter-attack roles on two local airfields—North Weald and Stapleford Towney.

Higher training followed and the brigade was used on several exercises as enemy to other divisions in various parts of East Anglia. There was an advantage in belonging to an independent brigade group, all got to know the working R.A., R.E., and R.A.S.C. There was the same unit of R.A.S.C. to lift, the same R.A. battery co-operating. The 8th Suffolk became quick and 'handy' in action. It was therefore a great blow when it was suddenly ordered to draft 200 O.R.s to the 18 Div., just before the latter left for the Far East to be engulfed at Singapore.

Shortly afterwards the Battalion received a direct intake of about 150 recruits. A special training company was formed and the men were drafted into other companies after 12 weeks' training.

The following is a letter from one of these 150 recruits, written at the time:—

"What ideas any of us may have had about the Army in civil life, whether founded on old soldiers' stories or standing music hall jokes, have been pleasantly dispelled. At our assembly depot there seemed to be no 'moustachioed' Sgt. Major bellowing here or roaring there; but a reception committee of grinning drivers, prepared to take us off "somewhere" into the countryside.

"Our first few days in the Army proved to be, for most, a pleasant surprise; the greater part of the time seemed to be spent in either parading for meals or visiting the M.O. for medical inspections, needle stickings, etc. against some horrible disease or other, with 48 hours off duty 'to take the taste away'.

"After three weeks our boots no longer feel as though they are screwed on our feet, and even if the parade ground does resemble the Himalayas, we have learnt to drill and drill well on it ! Furthermore, we know all about kit inspections, hut inspections, and realise how important they are in the prosecution of the war effort. We have seen the N.C.O.s in their pleasant moods and their less pleasant moods, and occasionally the officers. In fact, we are beginning to learn, like good soldiers, not to ask, even ourselves, 'Why ?' But to get on with the job."

In May, 1942, the Brigade moved to Suffolk and the Battalion was quartered at Orwell Park, about three miles S.E. of Ipswich. Company, Battalion and Brigade training continued. By this time divisional battle-schools had been started and all officers and as many N.C.O.s as possible were put through the courses. There is no doubt that the results obtained from these invaluable schools were most satisfactory. The junior leaders gained in self confidence, quickness in giving out orders, and learned a technique in handling their platoons and sections, or their carrier and mortar platoons and sections. It taught them various "strokes" which they could play as definite answers to the problems the enemy set them. Above all it taught them what to expect in battle, how, if need be, to screw their courage to the sticking point.

In July the Battalion moved to Felixstowe in relief of another unit in the Brigade, and took over a semi-beach role. In August the brigade moved to the Buckinghamshire area and the 8th Suffolk was stationed at Berkhamsted. At the end of this month the 223rd Brigade was broken up.

On the 4th September the Battalion entrained for Lincolnshire and joined the 143rd Infantry Brigade in the 48th Div. H.Q. was at Raithby, near Spilsby, and all Companies were detached in Spilsby and other nearby villages. Several more large drafts left the 8th Suffolk about this time.

In October, 1942, the Battalion departed for a camp near Mansfield and had a week's training in co-operation with tanks—its first experience. This would have seemed much belated if Lt.-Colonel Daglish had not by now known, unofficially, that his Command was likely to be committed to a training and drafting role. The 48th Division to which it was now attached being a "Home Establishment" Division.

From Mansfield there was a move to Flying-Dales Moor in Yorkshire for a week's field firing, and then a march of 102 miles back to Spilsby in five days.

In November the 8th Suffolk went to Skegness and took over a coastal sector of about 5 miles. There was a certain amount of field work to be done but the urgency of coast defence was now greatly lessened and the Battalion was able to carry out some useful training as well; while the night patrols required on the coast were now far fewer.

The unit came back to the Spilsby area in January, 1943, and now the 48th Division was brought under the new Reserve Division organisation, with the role of regular training and drafting.

8th Battalion Rapid Fire Team, 1941.

Back row—Ptes. Wilding, Mayling, Sibley.

Centre row—Pte. Thurston, C/Sgt. Gilbert, Sgts. Hawes, Miles, Ptes. Partridge, Spurr, Cpl. Gooch, Pte. Turner.

Front row—C.S.M. Aldous, Sgt. Driver, Lt. Bond, Capt. McCaffrey, Lt. Col. Daglish, Lt. Bacon, R.S.M. Pallant, C/Sgt. Elliston, C.S.M. Tyler.

Battalions in the Reserve Div. organisation were reduced to a W.E. of a cadre of administrative personnel and instructors, and received intakes of Corps trainees from I.T.C.s for eight weeks:—a preliminary week, five weeks' training and two weeks' embarkation leave. After this, the drafts were "kitted" up and sent off as ordered.

The 8th Suffolk had to draft away all Medical Category 'A' personnel, except those who were required for the instructional staff. The administrative staff of the Battalion had to be below medical category A.1.

As Lt.-Colonel Daglish writes:—

"Thus a very fine and fit formation was broken up. This was a great disappointment to all ranks who felt that their keenness and hard work had been wasted. All had been enthusiastically anxious to fight as a Battalion. For over a year they had worked well together and felt confident that they could have given a good account of themselves if they had been given the chance. Moreover, only a small proportion of the Category 'A' personnel who had to be drafted away found their way to the 1st and 2nd Battalions of the Regiment."

As a Battalion of a Reserve Division the 8th Suffolk took intakes from No. 3 I.T.C. at Bury St. Edmunds and from the I.T.C.s at Norwich and Colchester. This was changed later, so that the intakes were limited to those of the Suffolk Regt. and the Bedfordshire and Hertfordshire Regt. from No. 3. I.T.C. only. The five weeks' training was good and hard and included section and platoon training; in the fifth week all trainees did exercises which included being "shot over" by artillery. There is no doubt that when the trainees were drafted to field force units they were very fit indeed and seemed confident.

The Battalion remained in this role at Spilsby from Jan. '43 to July '44. There was then a reorganisation of Reserve Divisions, and the 8th Suffolk moved to the Blakeney area in Norfolk, to the 47th Division, and continued in the same role.

In October, 1944, Lt. Col. Daglish handed over the Command to Lt. Colonel J. R. Harper of the Hertfordshire Regiment.

Throughout the war the Regiment had been uniformly fortunate in the Commanding Officers it had furnished for its Battalions. Without exception they have one and all been imbued with the highest Regimental traditions. With all of them it has been "the Regiment first"; and this spirit in the Commander has been of inestimable value to his Battalion.

Lt. Col. E. R. Daglish was no exception to this rule. Hard working and conscientous he never let the disappointment of commanding a second line Battalion detract from the high standard he set himself. Thanks to him the many hundreds of men who passed through his hands were all proud to have at one time been members of the 8th Suffolk.

Lt. Colonel E. R. Daglish was posted to Command No. 3 Holding Battalion; but in the autumn of 1945 he was once again appointed to the Command of the 8th Suffolk and relieved Lt. Colonel Harper at Blakeney. The 8th Suffolk had been selected for retention temporarily in the post war Army and was under orders for reorganization and service in the West Indies. Meanwhile the Battalion moved to Shrublands, near Ipswich.

Here, with only a small cadre of the Battalion, Lt. Colonel Daglish received drafts from many different Regiments and a large complement of young officers. But the material was good and he had the backing of Majors R. M. Marsh, G. R. Heyland, M.C., and P. B. Forrest, M.C., with Captain F. D. Ingle as Adjutant. While the Senior Warrant and N.C.O.s included many Suffolk regular soldiers, among them being C.S.M. Duffy, who had made a great name for himself in the 2nd Battalion. Much preliminary work was however necessary before the Battalion could reach the standard of a War Service Battalion.

The 8th Suffolk remained at Shrublands until March, 1946, when it embarked at Tilbury in the S.S. MATAROA for Jamaica with "B" Company under Major R. M. Marsh for Bermuda.

Neither the voyage nor the arrival in Jamaica was void of incident; some of the West Indians on board, serving with the R.A.F., proving anything but co-operative. However all ranks of the Battalion behaved with exemplary forbearance on the voyage and there was no serious incident. But shortly after their arrival at Kingston, a second transport steamed into the Bay carrying 1,200 West African R.A.F., as well as British wives and families; a warning had been received that there had been trouble on board and that some of the R.A.F. had mutinied.

On account of the insubordinate behaviour of the troops, most of whom were armed, Lt. Colonel Daglish took four platoons of Infantry with him and was prepared to board the ship, which had refused to come alongside a special wharf. However a naval frigate ensured that the berthing order was carried out and then the detachment of the Suffolk Regiment carried out the search for arms among the native troops. Little was found, for arms and some grenades had been thrown into the harbour.

In the official report it was stated that "the discipline, bearing and restraint of the 8th Suffolk was admirable"; while two Lance Corporals, Able and Jones, who had been on board during the voyage, were officially commended for their good and cool behaviour on the trip.

The 8th Suffolk quickly settled down to the life of the West Indies; its diverse elements seasoned into a fine Battalion taking its full share in all the local activities, while every opportunity was given Lt. Colonel Daglish to bring the training ot the various sub-units up to a high pitch of efficiency.

In February 1947, the Battalion was relieved and embarked on the S.S. "Carthage" for home. From Southampton the Battalion was moved to Shrublands, near Ipswich, where the Battalion was finally disbanded in March 1947.

6TH BATTALION.

The 6th (Home Defence) Battalion The Suffolk Regiment expanded into the 9th, 30th, 31st and 70th Battalions as the war proceeded.

Chronologically the dates of these changes are as follows:—

August 1939. Formation of the 6th Battalion from National Defence Companies.

September 1940. Formation of the 70th (Young Soldiers) Battalion from the young soldiers serving with the 6th Battalion.

November 1940. 6th Battalion becomes the 1/6th and the 2/6th Battalions.

December 1940. 2/6th Battalion becomes the 9th Battalion.

December 1941. 1/6th and 9th Battalions become the 30th and 31st Battalions.

December 1942. The 30th Battalion is absorbed into the 31st Battalion.
January 1943. Disbandment of the 70th (Young Soldiers) Battalion.
April 1946. Disbandment of the 31st Battalion.

Before recounting the history of the 6th Battalion and its successors, mention must be made of its forebears.

In 1938 approval was given to raise County Groups of National Defence Companies. Under Lt.-Colonel H. R. Hooper, O.B.E., M.C., T.D., assisted by an adjutant and a small mobile recruiting squad formed of volunteer workers, the County was divided into recruiting areas, and in due course "No. 7 Group" was raised. The conditions for joining were:—Previous army service; between 35 and 50 years of age; a Five Pounds Bounty upon enlistment. The duties:—Guards and Anti-Sabotage Service at vulnerable points. Mobilization:—on outbreak of war.

The haunts and habits of the old soldier being well-known, contact was easy; a plain spoken "notice" not infrequently displayed in the window of the "Local," invariably drew a number ready to serve again. The conditions of enrolment, simple and practical, were explained from impromptu platforms, a waggon, a tumbril, sometimes the Tap Room table. The response was gratifying and immediate. Attestation papers were completed, followed by medical examination by the local Medico. The oath once again taken, time permitting there was a short sing-song—and so home.

Thus 8 officers and 600 other ranks were enrolled in Suffolk previous to the outbreak of war, becoming No. 7 Group of the National Defence Companies, administered by the Suffolk Territorial Army Association and affiliated to the 4th Bn. The Suffolk Regiment. Similarly 8 officers and 300 other ranks were enrolled in Cambridgeshire.

In August, 1939, the 6th Battalion was formed by absorbing the above National Defence Companies of Suffolk and Cambridgeshire. Lt.-Colonel H. R. Hooper, O.B.E., M.C., T.D. was appointed to the Command with Captain A. W. Neve as his Adjutant. The Battalion Headquarters were at Portman Road Drill Hall, Ipswich.

Here Lt.-Colonel Hooper, assisted by the 4th Battalion, made the necessary arrangements for transport, clothing and equipment as far as resources were available, and for the despatch of the various detachments to their battle stations. These stretched from Darsham R.D.F. Station in the North to Duxford R.A.F. Fighter Aerodrome in the South, a distance of approximately 100 miles; within the boundaries of Suffolk and Cambridgeshire his Command took over the anti-sabotage duties of all aerodromes, airfields, R.D.F. Stations, bomb dumps, petrol installations, dock installations, wharfage facilities at Harwich, Parkeston, Ipswich and Felixstowe—involving long tours of duty, monotonous, exacting, often in lonely and remote areas, with little chance of relief. So numerous were the commitments that during the first months of the war alternate nights in bed were the rule, and not the exception. It speaks well for the quality of the "old soldier" that nothwithstanding the severe conditions under which they served they stood up to the strain remarkably well; sickness during the exceptionally hard winter of 1939-1940, when many were under canvas or in tin huts and sheds, was very low.

The diary of the early months shows that the 6th Battalion Commander was continually travelling; inspecting, recruiting. His visits included Stradishall, Bury St. Edmunds, Mildenhall, Leiston, Dovercourt, Claydon, Barnham, Duxford, Bassingbourne, Cambridge, Debden, Honington, Hadleigh, Felixstowe. It was not perhaps surprising that an order was issued that any officer of the unit must be able to ride a motor bicycle.

Meanwhile the organization of the Battalion had been taking shape. Company H.Q.s were established:—"A" Company, Ipswich; "B" Company Bury St. Edmunds; "C" Company, Saxmundham; "D" Company, Dovercourt; "E" Company, Cambridge; "F" Company, Bawdsey; "G" Company, Ipswich.

By the end of 1939 the strength was 30 officers, 694 other ranks; on the anniversary of the Battalion formation it had risen to 63 officers, 1,604 other ranks.

The ages of the Battalion were remarkable; they ranged from a little over 14 years to 67 with a definite preponderance to the latter. It was estimated, six months after formation, that the average age was 52. But though this, on paper, may detract from their value, an inspection of the Battalion gave a different impression. I visited them in Ipswich in November, 1939. They were undoubtedly old; but a high proportion of the N.C.O.s and the old soldiers had seen active service in most parts of the world; the pick were in every sense an "old guard". There was moreover a solid core of Regular Company Sgt. Majors and Quartermaster Sgts., all of the Suffolk Regiment.

But a Home Service Battalion, even of old soldiers, needs a specially selected Battalion Commander and the fine start which the 6th Battalion made during its first year of the war was due to Lt.-Colonel H. R. Hooper, O.B.E., M.C., T.D. Harold Hooper was a man of robust character, of outstanding personality, with a fine record in the 4th Battalion during and after the last war. Among his many activities he had no more absorbing interest than the country men of Suffolk; none knew or loved them better. No one could give so vivid a picture of the East Anglian or speak his dialect so convincingly; the man who followed him in an after dinner speech in Suffolk was in sorry case; for the whole room would still be rocking with laughter that had been uproarious. No better choice for command could have been made, for here was a Suffolk man compact with all the outstanding Suffolk qualities; a man who had proved himself a capable soldier. All his Command knew that their well being was in the safest hands; knew too that the unit they belonged to would earn the respect of all higher Commanders.

Early in the war the Battalion was faced with a new problem; the reception, clothing, equipping, training and administration of large numbers of "young soldiers" drafted at short notice from the blitzed areas of London. These were formed into Companies under officers and N.C.O.s from the Battalion, separate billets being requisitioned. The numbers of these "Young Soldiers" soon rose to between 600-700 and under War Office instructions they were formed into the 70th (Young Soldier) Battalion, the Suffolk Regiment, under the Command of Lt.-Col. E. C. Rands, T.D.

In November, 1939, the three Companies at Bury St. Edmunds, Saxmundham and Cambridge were formed into the 2/6th Suffolk under Lt.-Col. V. L. de Cordova, M.C. who established his H.Q. at Bury St. Edmunds.

The officers serving with the two newly constituted Battalions were:—

1/6th BN. THE SUFFOLK REGT.

H.Q.

Lt.-Col. H. R. Hooper, O.B.E., M.C., T.D.
Major H. D. Wise, M.C.
Capt. K. R. Basham (Adjutant)
Lt. B. H. Gubbings (Quartermaster)

"A" Company.

Capt. D. J. Grant.
Lt. F. E. Whalley.
Lt. C. R. Knight.
Lt. A. G. Douglas.
Lt. R. A. Newman.
Lt. H. Manvel.
Lt. T. M. Houghton.
Lt. C. G. L. Marriott.

"B" Company.

Capt. W. A. Spence.
Lt. F. A. Saunders.
Lt. S. C. Barker.
Lt. L. P. Eagle.
Lt. C. Verden.

"C" Company.

Capt. J. Burton.
Lt. F. G. Firman.
Lt. G. Classey.
Lt. H. Wilcox.
Lt. C. E. Ward.

2/6TH BN. THE SUFFOLK REGT.

H.Q.

Lt.-Col. V. L. de Cordova, M.C. (The King's Own Royal Regt.).
Lt. E. J. Hawkins (Adjutant).
Lt. C. J. Kent (Quartermaster).

"M" Company.

Capt. F. S. Beauford.
Lt. H. R. Scoggins.
Lt. F. C. R. Hancock.
Lt. L. M. Shepherd.
Lt. E. E. Reed.

"N" Company.

Major J. W. Langford.
Lt. E. C. Crust.
Lt. H. A. Langdon.
Lt. F. Shipman.
Lt. W. R. Mathews.
Lt. B. W. Silk.
Lt. S. C. White.

"O" Company.
Major H. F. Ling.
Lt. O. W. Lane.
Lt. R. S. Robinson.
Lt. H. J. C. Wood.
Lt. T. W. P. Hawkes.
Lt. H. R. Shepherd.

In January, 1941, the 1/6th Suffolk left Suffolk for Corsham in Wiltshire to guard important depots. Here the Companies of the Battalion had a better chance for training and "C" Company under Major L. C. Crick, M.C., became the training company.

In March, the Army Commander, Lt. General the Hon. H. R. L. C. Alexander (later Field-Marshal Alexander) inspected the Battalion and expressed himself as well satisfied, instructing Lt.-Col. Hooper to convey this to all ranks.

But although every effort was made to improve the training, local conditions made this difficult, and equipment was still short. It was not until March, 1942, that L.M.G.s and M.M.Gs were issued to the Battalion.

* * * *

THIRTIETH BATTALION.

By September, 1941, the strength of the Battalion had risen to 50 officers and 1,237 other ranks; but a fresh redistribution was taking place within the Battalion separating the fit Category A man from the unfit Category B and under. It was at the end of 1941 that the 1/6th Suffolk became the 30th Battalion, a Category unit, receiving only men of Category B who were unfit for front line service.

Meanwhile the proportion of Suffolk men with the Battalion had been changing. At Ipswich most had come from the County; but at Corsham large reinforcements had been received from other units including 200 from a West Yorkshire Bn. While new men were constantly arriving, drafts of the original recruitments were leaving, most going either to the C.M.P. or the R.A.S.C.

The year spent at Corsham had been popular with all ranks, a Battalion spirit had grown up and proved a solid basis for the change that was about to take place, for by the end of the year the Battalion was mainly composed of younger men of a higher medical category.

In June, 1942, the Battalion left Corsham and moved to Kingsbridge in Devon for coast defence. The Battalion, younger and fitter than when first formed, now underwent the progressive training of a unit in the Field Force. Exercises with the Regular Army and Naval Units within the Command brought a new life and interest to the officers and men.

For two years the 30th Battalion had suffered all the grave disadvantages of being split up; now it was at last possible to start a central officers' mess. At the same time a Battalion Sergeants' Mess was opened under R.S.M. G. E. Weavers, and at once displayed the open handed hospitality that comes so naturally to Suffolk Sergeants' Messes.

It is a great advantage not only to the individuals but to the Battalion as a whole when both officers and sergeants can be collected, respectively, under one roof. The large majority of the Sergeants' Mess were Suffolk soldiers, and included:— R.Q.M.S. "Mongy" Marsh, C.S.M.s "Spud" Turner, "Put" Gilbert, "Darkie" Gilbert, J. Hackett, T. Dallimore; C. Sgts. J. Perry, J. Barnes, "Bill" North, "Tubby" Wyartt, "Fiddler" Sayers; Sgts. A. Reeve, A. Culley, J. Bloomfield and W. Hyde. Almost every senior member of a Sergeants' Mess has a nickname, a name that he has generally gained in some lower rank and that sticks to him throughout his service. It is perhaps a peculiarity of the Services and a sign of that friendly spirit that unites all together.

In August, 1942, Lt.-Colonel H. R. Hooper, O.B.E., M.C., T.D. handed over the Command of the Battalion to Lt.-Colonel H. R. Hopking, O.B.E.

In September the Battalion was transferred first to Weymouth and then to Wareham and Studland. In October they were at Yeovil and a month later their disbandment commenced.

During the Battalion's War Service they worthily upheld the best traditions of the Regiment. Wherever they served their formation Commander spoke highly of their qualities and their discipline, their willingness to do everything that was asked.

The Battalion was finally absorbed into the 31st Battalion on 16th January, 1943.

9th & 31st BATTALIONS.

When in November, 1940, the 6th Battalion became the 1/6th and 2/6th Battalions, The Suffolk Regiment, the H.Q. of the latter Battalion remained in Ipswich for a month and then moved to Fornham St. Martin, near Bury St. Edmunds, with Company H.Q. at Bury St. Edmunds, Saxmundham, Ipswich—Cambridge being handed over to another unit shortly after the formation of the new Battalion. A month later the 2/6th Battalion became the 9th Battalion The Suffolk Regiment.

In June, 1941, Lt.-Col. V. L. de Cordova, M.C., was succeeded by Lt. Col. H. D. Wise, M.C. Once again the Regiment was fortunate in this appointment of Battalion Commander. Lt.-Col. Wise was a fine disciplinarian with a particular interest in the welfare of his men. Knowing full well the value of tradition, he made his Battalion an integral part of the Regiment. Many N.C.O.s and men temporarily unfit came to the Battalion from first line units, some arrived with an openly expressed wish to get out and back to their own comrades. But none left without an acknowledgment of the quality of the Commander and the Battalion they left behind.

The 31st Battalion was, under the existing stringent medical classification, unfit for first line fighting; but if the men's feet or their lungs were impaired, their spirit was not.

The 9th Suffolk became the 31st Suffolk in December, 1941. But prior to this date, they, like their sister Battalion, the 30th Suffolk, had been gradually sorting out the fit and the unfit men. 327 A.1. men had been transferred to the 30th Essex; from whom they received 242 men Category B; while at the same time they transferred all their Category C men to a Warwickshire Battalion.

In August, 1941, the Battalion was transferred from Ipswich to Digswell Welwyn, in Hertfordshire, where it absorbed 529 other ranks of the 7th Bn. Bedfordshire and Hertfordshire Regiment. In July, 1942, it moved to Ingatestone. Here the Battalion was split up between Ingatestone, Claydon, Faulkebourne, Purfleet, Corringham. At Ingatestone the Battalion received 8 W.O.s, 28 C/Sgts. and Sgts., 38 Cpls. and 141 Ptes. from the 30th Battalion, when this latter unit was finally disbanded, the majority of whom were Suffolk men.

At this time Lt.-Col. Wise had with him Major H. S. Davidson, the Border Regt. as Second in Command. Capt. F. Calver was adjutant and "Jim" Golding was Quartermaster, two invaluable men in their respective spheres. Calver was a "live wire," while Golding, imperturbable in character, brought twenty years regular army experience to his work. The 31st Battalion was also lucky in having a large proportion of old Suffolk soldiers among their Senior Warrant and N.C.O.s, among whom were R.Q.M.S. W. Waxham, C.S.M. F. Clarke, C. Flynn, H. Crainge; C.Q.M.S.:—G. Clarke, C. Davis-Mann; Sgts.:—W. Adlam, W. Clare.

In February, 1943, the Battalion was reorganised into a H.Q. Company and four Companies with an establishment of 817 other ranks. The excess numbers then serving with the Battalion being transferred to the 30th Bedfordshire and Hertfordshire. Later in the year, in September, the 31st Battalion embarked at Glasgow for foreign service in North Africa.

Prior to the departure of the Battalion the Command of the Battalion changed, Lt.-Col. Wise being succeeded by Lt.-Col. C. L. Wilson, M.C., of the Essex Regiment.

In September, 1943, under the command of Lt.-Col. C. L. Wilson, M.C., the Essex Regiment, they moved by train to Glasgow and embarked on the troopship Almanzora, sailing in convoy on the 12th September.

Accommodation on board was very crowded for at the last moment the 30th Royal Norfolk was added, a ship having sprung a leak in dock. On the 23rd September the Battalion disembarked at Algiers and marched to the racecourse at Hussein Bay.

The Battalion remained here one week loading and unloading stores in the Docks, with one interval of light relief when 50 men of "B" Company accompanied the Special Investigation Police in a raid on the native quarter where large quantities of W.D. equipment were discovered.

On 1st October, 1943, the Battalion entrained at Maison Carree station, for Bizerta; coaches being provided for the officers and Warrant Officers, cattle trucks for the men. The journey took four days and four nights, and it was noticeable how quickly the men settled down to the strange conditions, cooking their meals on the platforms at the halts. The Battalion detrained at Bizerta on 5th October, 1943, and proceeded to the Texas Concentration Area.

Here the Battalion took over:—The Texas area, a concentration area for troops in transit from Africa to Italy and elsewhere; the Texas P.O.W. Camp; the Houston area, and assembly area just outside the Karouba and La Pecherie Docks; the "Survivors' Post," a small transit camp for escaped allied P.O.W., shipwrecked Merchant Seamen, and refugees from occupied countries.

The Texas area and the Texas P.O.W. Camp were administered by "A" Company; the transit Camp by "B" Company; the Houston area by "C" and "D" Companies, while the "Survivors' Post" was looked after by H.Q. Company.

The Battalion was kept busy for in the short time between mid-October and the end of November, 1943, no less then 376 Units passed through the areas for Italy, the tally for the month of November in the transit Camp being 860 officers, 12,143 other ranks. But after the First Division had passed through in December, 1943, pressure grew less.

In February, 1944, there were four weeks of almost continuous rain and violent gales. The whole area was deep in mud, and on some days the gales were so violent that tents were blown down as soon as they were erected. In spite of this the men worked with constant cheerfulness, allowing for the British soldier's historic privilege of grumbling. Many men who had scarcely boiled an egg in their lives were working about 14 hours a day cooking meals for the troops in transit.

By the end of February the transit work in the camp had largely ceased. Early in March the Battalion was relieved from all further duties in these Camps and was detailed to take over train guard duties from the 264 Train Guard Company, Pioneer Company.

Their future duties were explained by Lt.-Col. C. L. Wilson, M.C., to the Battalion. He told them that not only were large amounts of stores and huge dumps left in Africa when the Allied armies invaded Italy, but as the main S. Italian ports had been so badly damaged, it was necessary for a long time for stores and ammunition arriving from overseas to be landed at Algiers, then moved by rail to Tunis and Bizerta, and shipped on small vessels which could enter the battered harbours. The main N. African line carrying these stores goes for most of the way through a wild country, with small railway stations and inhabited by a fairly thick population of Arabs; the N. African Arab is the most skilful thief in the world. Thus the role of the train-guard was not unimportant.

The move began on 9th March, 1944, and Bizerta was left in pouring rain, with the country all round water-logged and one mass of mud. Battalion H.Q. went to Hamman Plage, a small seaside place between Tunis and the Cap Bon Peninsula; this during the advance on Tunis had been the scene of a decisive battle; "A" Company were with Battalion H.Q., garrison company for Tunis, with a good many commitments, including the garrison guardroom and a mobile platoon to prevent sabotage at the various dumps. The train guards were divided between "B," "C," "D" Companies; their duties began with the line on the Algerian frontier and were eventually extended as far as the Port of Bone. Each train that contained goods of military importance was accompanied by a guard, usually 1 N.C.O. and 3 Ptes; static guards were maintained at key stations. A good many attempts at theft were prevented and there were some exciting episodes of which the following are typical:—

L/Cpl. Howes with a guard of "D" Company, were checking up wagons at Sidi-el-Hemessin, when they sighted a mysterious person disappearing under the train, and on coming closer recognised him as the brakesman on wagon 54612. The guard commander and guard then jumped onto an open wagon near at hand to observe him; on reaching Oued Mangras they found he had broken the seal of the wagon and already had his hand on the contents. He jumped down and tried to escape but was caught.

L/Cpl. Bradshaw of "B" Company took over a train at Ghardimaou to which two trucks were added just before it left the station. The guard commander and 2 sentries, Pte. Savill and Pte. Peacock, went to check the two trucks, but the train started off and the three men managed with difficulty to scramble on the truck next but one to the two in question. After a little while they heard noises coming from the truck which contained timber, and saw planks being thrown out by five men inside the wagon. L/Cpl. Bradshaw handing his rifle to one of his guard proceeded to clamber along the swaying train and boarded the truck with his bayonet in his hand. He shouted to the five thieves, and one jumped over the end of the truck. The remaining four shewed fight, one pulling out what appeared to be a knife from under his blouse. L/Cpl. Bradshaw thrust at him with his bayonet and resistance ceased. The other three attempted to jump off the train, but L/Cpl. Bradshaw was successful in frustrating that attempt and tied them up securely, until they were handed over to the French police at Soul-el-Arba. The fifth man who jumped off when the 'show' started had apparently hung on to the underside of the wagon, and when the train stopped at Oued Melij he ran away.

The G.O.C. directed that the N.C.O. and guard of the train be congratulated on their excellent work, and stated that their action reflected great credit on their keenness and enthusiasm.

In June, 1944, the 31st Suffolk entrained at Tunis reaching Algiers on the 19th June. Here they embarked on the corvette Maigot. This was the first time this vessel had been used as a troopship; conditions on board were very overcrowded. The corvette was picked up by a large convoy, most of which was bound for the Middle East, and from which they separated off Bizerta, landing at Naples in the afternoon of 22nd June. They proceeded to the Afrigola Staging Area, about 8 miles outside Naples. An unsatisfactory place, dusty and fly-ridden, and also infested by the inhabitants of the local and dirty town, who were prepared to do anything from washing clothes or cutting hair to selling fruit and religious medals, to say nothing of making off with any kit if they had the chance. After a few days a considerable number of men were in hospital with a variety of sandfly fever.

During the following month the Battalion was employed on P.O.W. escort duties, and it was believed that they would move to Ancona or Leghorn as soon as these places were captured. But much disappointment was felt when in mid-July the 31st Suffolk was ordered to proceed at once overseas. The Battalion embarked at Naples on the S.S. Takliwa on 16th July, reaching Gibraltar on 21st July, where on the following day they relieved the 2nd Bn. Royal Scots, "H.Q.", "A", "C" and "D" Companies moving into Buena Vista Barracks, "B" Company into the Slaughterhouse Area to act as Outpost Company. An advance party had previously flown from Naples, under command of Major H. S. Davidson, 2nd I/C.

After the more active service atmosphere of N. Africa and Italy, coupled with their disappointment at not being sent on the job which they had expected, the Battalion found some difficulty in settling down to the peacetime and spit-and-polish life of Gibraltar, every officer and man having

WARRANT OFFICERS AND SERGEANTS, 31ST BATTALION, GIBRALTAR, 1945.

First Row—C.S.Ms. J. Cox, A. Newton, O.R.Q.M.S. H. Brown, R.S.M. A. Guerin, Lt. Col. C. L. Wilson, M.C., R.Q.M.S. A. Rix, C.S.M.s. E. Vincent, E. Avis, P.S.M. A. Freear.
Second Row—Sgts. J. Hampford, E. Hinnels, L/Sgt. F. Surman, Sgt. J. Smith, C/Sgt. C. Sillett, L/Sgt. H. Southall-Owen, Sgts. R. Dutton, A. Graham (R.E.M.E.), C/Sgt. W. Streets, L/Sgt. A. Wills.
Third Row—L/Sgt. J. Lynch, C/Sgt. H. Paxford, Sgt. R. Robbins, C/Sgt. A. Adlam, C/Sgt. P. Rogers, Sgt. H. Page, Sgts. C. Gardner, H. Latham (A.C.C.), E. Roworth, R. Morgan.
Back Row—L/Sgts. F. Claydon, N. Goldberg, Sgt. H. Gladwin, L/Sgts, F. Andrews, G. Stratton, D. Kersey, Sgt. L. Griffiths, Sgt. F. F. Hazell, R. Buxton, G. Walker, S. Reeve, A. Hazell.

looked forward to a more active role. However, apart from routine and ceremonial duties, such as various guards, including the Governor's guard, and the ceremony of the "KEYS," much hard work was done by the men of the Battalion on working parties in the tunnels of the rock, helping in the various jobs of construction and maintenance, in loading rations from the various store-rooms and on the quays for shipment overseas. On all occasions they won special praise from the units and organisations for whom they worked.

After VJ Day, Education took the place of tactical training. It was carried out on a highly intensive programme, designed to prepare men for return to civil life. It proved highly popular and very few men returned to "civvy street" whose minds had not been broadened, or whose hands had not regained some of the skill lost during their Army service.

Letter from His Excellency the Governor of
Gibraltar to Lieut. Colonel C. L. Wilson, M.C.,
Commanding 31st Battalion, The Suffolk Regiment.

My Dear Wilson,

Your tour of duty on the Rock is nearly over and you will shortly be leaving for home. I would, therefore, like to take this opportunity of thanking you for the good work your Battalion has done whilst stationed in Gibraltar, and to congratulate you on the high standard of discipline that has been maintained; also on the successes the unit has gained in the world of sport.

Your Battalion has served here through a difficult period: it arrived a year and a half ago when the more interesting role that Gibraltar had played in the war was over and there remained little but the ordinary routine work of a garrison unit.

You have the satisfaction of knowing that, by your efforts, you have done much to restore the amenities of Gibraltar, resettle the civilian population, and thus to make the stay of those units who follow after you more pleasant.

Whatever the future may hold in store for the Battalion, I wish you one and all good fortune and good luck and may you have a very happy Christmas and New Year re-united with your families at home.

Yours ever,

R. EASTWOOD.

The Brigadier wrote :—

My Dear Wilson,

On the eve of the disbandment of 1st Gibraltar Brigade H.Q. and of my departure for the U.K., I wish to place on record my appreciation of what your Battalion have accomplished since their arrival in Gibraltar in July, 1944.

They have worthily carried out their task, not only of holding the Fortress, but also of maintaining the high reputation of the Regiment and of the Army which they represent. That task is now to be handed over to others.

I have been particularly impressed by the exemplary behaviour of the Battalion and by the way in which they have fully entered into the sporting activities on the Rock.

I wish to thank you and all ranks for your loyal support and for all you have done while on the Rock; it has been a pleasure to work with you.

May I wish you all a very happy Christmas and a safe return to your homes and families.

Yours sincerely,
R. B. L. PERSSE.

On December 17th, 1945, the Battalion embarked on H.M.T. "Duchess of Richmond" for home. A strong S.W. gale made "The Duchess" take control of the pilot as he tried to leave harbour. She rammed the Detached Mole in no uncertain manner. It was a tense moment, and more than one soul aboard had fleeting visions of the Birkenhead incident repeating itself in the Regiment's history. Nothing so serious developed fortunately, and after ten days in dry dock a successful second effort to leave resulted in the Battalion arriving at Liverpool on January 2nd, 1946. Its arrival coincided with the coldest spell of Winter, which everyone felt keenly.

After three months at Wimbush Camp, Saffron Walden, the Battalion was disbanded on April 8th, 1946.

Very few of those who had left England 2½ years previously were still with the Battalion on the date of its disbanding, most having returned to civilian life. Only the C.O., the Q.M., and Lt. F. Monk, among the officers, remained till the end, and amongst the W.O.s and N.C.O.s, C.S.M. Sillett, C.S.M. Roworth, Sgt. Tarplin, L/Sgts. King and Wright, Cpls. Harvey, Salmon, Thomas, Griffiths and L/Cpls. Norton and Phillips.

The "Release Scheme" had already robbed the unit of some of its oldest members, including the Regimental Sgt. Major Guerin, R.Q.M.S. Rix, C.S.M. Dallimore, Lance Sgts. Lynen, Surman, Ptes. Green, Carr, Phillips, to mention only a few who had departed by the "Blighty Ferry."

Lt. Colonel C. L. Wilson, The Essex Regiment, writing of the Battalion he commanded so ably says:—

"During its existence the Battalion carried out work which, not spectacular or thrilling perhaps, was yet of great importance to the war effort. Whatever job it undertook, whether sitting in the Fens awaiting a Hun invasion; whether chasing and capturing thieving Arabs; whether cooking meals for thousands of troops, or mounting a ceremonial guard at the Convent, the Battalion entered into the job with all its heart.

"In work and play the high traditions of the Regiment were well maintained, whilst conduct and behaviour of all ranks was exemplary. The letters of appreciation from C-in-C.s and formation commanders were well and truly merited.

"It is not possible here to single out individuals responsible for the reaching of this high standard—they are too numerous. When everyone's heart is in the job it comes about naturally.

"To all officers and men from the highest to the lowest rank must the credit go for creating and maintaining a fine Battalion."

* * * * *

70th BATTALION.

The 70th (Young Soldiers) Battalion, another offshoot of the original 6th (Home Defence) Battalion, was formed at Ipswich on the 19th September, 1940, under the command of Lt.-Col. E. Cyril Rands, T.D., an officer who had previously commanded the 4th Suffolks.

A separation of the "young" soldiers from the "old" soldiers was clearly necessary and had been anticipated by Lt. Colonel H. R. Hooper, who had formed separate companies for administration and training. There was at this time a great influx of "young" soldiers; many who were anxious to start their soldiering before their age group was called up; others who had been "bombed out" in London and had nowhere to live. The Young Soldiers included youths of all ages, classes, manners and habits.

A formation such as this required carefully selected officers and N.C.O.s. Unfortunately during the summer of 1940, following Dunkirk, specially selected officers and N.C.O.s were practically non-existent, all available being ear-marked for first line and defence units. Lt.-Colonel E. C. Rands, T.D., had therefore a particularly hard time during the six months that followed the formation of his unit. That he succeeded so admirably is very greatly to his credit; the 70th (Y.S.) Battalion Suffolk when he finally handed over the Command in October, 1941, received high praise as a unit from its Higher Commanders.

The following were the Senior Officers with the Battalion on and shortly after formation:—

Lt. Colonel E. C. RANDS, T.D.	C.O.
Major G. S. CUBITT	2nd in Command.
Capt. H. J. TAYLOR	Adjutant.
Capt. W. STUBBINGS, D.C.M.	Quarter Master.
Capt. J. A. BUTTERFIELD	Commanding "A" Company
Capt. F. GARLAND	Commanding "B" Company
Capt. G. W. ANGELL	Commanding "C" Company
Capt. T. O. M. FFOULKES	Commanding "T" Training Company.

Within a very short time of formation the Battalion was split up; Companies being detached for the defence of aerodromes in the vicinity. These included Martlesham, Honington, and Wattisham. In order that training could proceed concurrently "T" Company remained in Ipswich, officers and men being attached to it periodically from the Companies on defence duties. Meanwhile many officers and N.C.O.s were despatched to the various "Command" Schools of Instruction.

The organization and training of a New Army in an island fortress such as England would be a comparatively simple business if there was no more than the British Isles to be considered. Unfortunately throughout the War there was a continual and very heavy drain of officers, N.C.O.s and men to all the theatres of war across the seas. Even the front line units suffered heavily from the constant departure of their trained men. Units such as the 70th Suffolk had to take the leavings and give whatever was demanded. The 70th Battalion was only in existence from September, 1940, until December, 1942, but during this time it had 73 officers, none of whom were casualties due to enemy action.

Nevertheless the Battalion made steady progress in training; what it may have lacked in knowledge it made up for in enthusiasm. It celebrated Minden Day annually, and it showed its quality at inter-unit competitions, winning the Hertfordshire Area Boxing Tournament for Young Soldiers and securing in May, 1941, at the Armoured Lorry School:—

First and Second Place with the Lewis Gun.
First Place on the Rifle Range.
First Place for Care of Arms and Equipment.

While in October it was first of all units in the area in an athletic contest.

In October, 1941, Lt. Colonel E. C. Rands, T.D., was succeeded by Lt. Colonel J. W. Josselyn.

Shortly after this change in Command, Battalion H.Q. and the Training Company moved from Ipswich to Felixstowe; while here two platoons from each of the detached Companies came in for a three weeks' course with the Training Company. The whole Battalion was concentrated at Felixstowe for one month in January/February of 1942.

A year later the Battalion was disbanded—20th January, 1943. It can be fairly said that during their service, the 70th Battalion pulled their weight. That this was so was due in part to their enthusiasm; there will always be enthusiasm in youth, but it can be damped if it has not the best possible leaders. That it survived the teething stage must be put to the credit of Lt. Col. Rands, and later to the Command of Lt. Colonel Josselyn. Josselyn was admirably fitted to a Young Soldiers' Battalion; with a fine disregard of "paper", and an excellent head, he ignored his office and concentrated on his Young Soldiers.

CHAPTER TEN.

THE HOME GUARD, THE ARMY CADETS, THE A.T.S.

The Home Guard—The 2nd Cambridgeshire and Suffolk Bn. H.G.—The Isle of Ely Battalions H.G.—The 11th Suffolk Bn. H.G.—The Army Cadets—The A.T.S.

HOME GUARD.

THROUGHOUT our history our Country has been the land of the free. Believing ourselves superior to all other people we have never been particularly interested in them or their affairs; but when they have tried to impose their will on us and restrict our freedom to do as we wish, then the whole nation has risen.

When the Romans maltreated the Early Britons in East Anglia the Iceni under Queen Boadicea rose and fought until they were finally exterminated. A thousand years later the fen men of Cambridgeshire followed this example against their Norman oppressors; while in the interval between these two great invasions the Anglo Saxons carried on a practically ceaseless war against the invading Danes. During all these centuries the people of our land could rarely pit equal strength or organization against their enemies; but they were always animated by their passionate love for freedom.

There has been no invasion since the Norman Conquest; but we have had enemies comparatively as superior as those early conquerors; the Spaniards with their Armada; Napoleon, the master of Europe; Hitler. Sea and air power has saved us from invasion; but behind this has been the character of a people who count all lost if they have not the freedom of their forebears.

The Home Guard embodied this spirit. The Home Guard was the lineal descendant of the army that rallied round Alfred the Great, the trained bands of Elizabeth's days, the Volunteers in the time of Napoleon.

But while the same incentive animated all the national risings against an invader, the machinery to bring it into force has undergone constant changes. The feudal system of the Middle Ages gave place to the County Sheriffs, and these in turn were superseded in Queen Mary's reign by the Lord Lieutenants, who up to the time of the outbreak of war in 1939 were responsible for raising armies in the event of apprehended invasion. In 1940 a change was once more made and the Lord Lieutenants were only required to co-operate in the formation of the new great national defence army.

In May, 1940, Mr. Eden, Secretary of State for War, broadcast an appeal for a Citizen Force, to be called the Local Defence Volunteers. The appeal was made in particular to those who lived in villages and small country towns, for the force at this time was required to help deal with parachute troops who might be dropped by the enemy to disrupt communications behind the main defensive lines. All British subjects between the ages of

17 and 65 were invited to join as a "Spare time job," and were told to give their names in at their local police station.

Since the outbreak of war England, Scotland and Wales had been sub-divided into 19 Military Areas under the peacetime Five Commanders in Chief; there were also twelve newly created Regions under the Ministry of Home Security. The L.D.V. was in a sense a Home Security Formation; but it came under the Military Authorities for training and operations, its administration being undertaken by the Territorial Army Association. It was to be a democratic citizen force raised on the principles of equality of service and status—a design which in due course was changed when it became the "Home Guard," framed on the lines of the Army.

The first step was to select the leaders, and organise the force on a village and town basis into Sections of 10 men, grouped into Platoons and Companies—of varying strength, with no fixed establishment. No country in the world is better provided with potential leaders. Zone and County leaders were quickly chosen throughout Suffolk and Cambridgeshire. The Lord Lieutenants of Suffolk and Cambridgeshire nominating:—Colonel W. P. Cutlack, C.B., T.D., D.L. for the Isle of Ely: Colonel W. N. Phillips, D.L. for Cambridgeshire; Major-General G. Fleming, C.B.E., D.S.C. and Colonel W. A. B. Daniell, C.B.E., D.S.O., T.D., D.L. for Suffolk. These selected the Company Commanders for their areas. The highest formation at this time was the Company; but these proving too numerous, within a year Battalions of Home Guard were formed.

The appeal for men was received with enthusiasm; great numbers joined. All old soldiers, Regular or Territorials, who were able to do so gave in their names, and there were as many others who had no previous training. The old soldier was not always the more valuable of these two classes; he was not always so ready to adapt himself to new conditions and Home Guard needs; for it was neither necessary nor possible for the new force to become a machine such as the Army. But in those cases where the old soldier was good, he was invaluable.

The original conception of this national reserve of men raised to defend their homes, training in their spare time, un-hampered by "red tape" regulations, costing a minimum amount to the country, inevitably changed as the infant Hercules grew. "Red Tape" never actually hampered its growth, the "spare time" was a hopeless misnomer, and the expense slowly mounted; but throughout, the character of the Force remained the same; it was eminently British, proving, especially in East Anglia, that a Volunteer Force can always be raised and led—but never successfully driven.

At the outset 2/6 per rifle was allowed. This was shortly increased to 20/-, and it mounted from 22/- to 30/- annually; while out of pocket expenses, such as travelling and subsistence, were paid by the Government. Even so the final cost per man never exceeded £3 a year—a fortieth of what the Regular Soldier during the war cost the nation.

It was easier to raise the men in May, 1940, than to equip and arm them. At first an arm-band with L.D.V. was the only distinguishing mark from the civilian; while the defensive weapons ranged from sporting rifles to old time carbines with a minimum of ammunition. But by July the sporting rifles and the .303 Rifles were being replaced by the American .300 Rifles, with 20 rounds of ammunition, and in November, 1940, American Lewis guns were arriving.

Until September, 1940, the men wore denim overalls and field service caps; but from that date boots, great coats, Regimental badges and steel helmets were being issued. It was not until 1941 that web equipment was available.

Meanwhile there had been no halt in the training, based on static conditions. As the time passed so the defensive armament increased, with corresponding efficiency. Last of all came an appreciation of the importance of the administrative side; that not only must ammunition be replenished, but food must be available and cooked.

Early in 1942, compulsory service in the Home Guard was instituted. It might have been expected that this would have completely changed the character of this great Voluntary force. It did not. Although it brought into the ranks a certan number of men who had not previously done their share, the majority who joined from that date onwards were fine material.

At its formation and throughout the war there was a distinction and a difference in the constitution and character of the Regular Forces and the Home Guard, a difference which was marked in the official titles they bore; the Regular Forces were: "Battalions, the Suffolk Regt.", while the Home Guard were "Suffolk, Cambridgeshire or the Isle of Ely, Battalions Home Guard."

No history of the Suffolk Regiment which covered the war period 1939 to 1945 would be complete without reference to the share taken by the Home Guard, who were, practically without exception, Suffolk or Cambridgeshire men, wore the Regimental Badges and attained a high degree of efficiency. Had the Home Guard of the Eastern Counties been called upon to defend their homeland they would have proved their worth.

THE SECOND CAMBRIDGE AND SUFFOLK BN. H.G.

It would be impossible to refer here to all the Home Guard Battalions, a list of which is given on pages 324, 325; the following accounts of some must be accepted as in general applicable to all.

The Second Cambridge and Suffolk Battalion Home Guard can be specially referred to because owing to a tactical weakness in the boundary between Cambridge and Suffolk about Newmarket and Mildenhall two neighbouring units of Suffolk and Cambridgeshire were combined. "WE ALSO SERVED", an account of the Cambridgeshire and Isle of Ely Home Guards, can be quoted:—

"In England the parish and County spirit are strong. It would be wrong to say that there was any animosity between the men of Suffolk and Cambridgeshire, but they were cousins rather than brothers, and sometimes distant cousins at that. Possibly the Suffolk man with his deep distrust of all new fangled ways had come to associate Cambridgeshire with its University Town and the spirit of progress; while Cambridgeshire considered its neighbours insular and uncouth. Perhaps the explanation is a simpler one. Like all good East Anglians, they regarded each other as "them foreigners." The fusion of the two units was most successful and proved one more link between the two Regiments.

A still better reason for the quality of this Battalion lay in the choice of its Commanding Officer. His appointment showed that the men in the County knew their business. I met Lt.-Col. J. Taylor in the summer of 1943 and he told me the story of the creation of the Battalion.

The telephone rang. "Joe, we want a Home Guard Battalion, and you are the man to command it. Officers ? Pick them yourself."

There was a magnificent leaven throughout the Home Guard; but there was of necessity some who could not, or did not, pull their weight. As was said by another Home Guard unit: "One of the problems in all Home Guard units was the old soldier. Either he was very good indeed, but wanted his own way in almost everything; or he took the view that he'd done all that twenty years ago, and had nothing to learn."

In December, 1944, I was staying with Lt.-Colonel J. Taylor to attend a "Conference" of his Battalion officers at Mildenhall. We drove to the Battalion Meeting along the straight Cambridgeshire roads which stretch to a boundless horizon past the wide fields. An endless tramp for regular soldiers returning from Newmarket. We picked one up. "I always give lifts to soldiers," said Lt.-Colonel Taylor. "I never heard a complaint from any of them. I ask 'em about their officers, their N.C.O.s, their grub."

We passed through Mildenhall in the dusk and pulled up under the lee of the School wall, out of the icy cold wind. The great school hall was flanked by two long lines of tables; there was a high table joining these two and a table facing us at the far end, for the "Vice."

We sat down 120 officers. There were fewer grey heads than I expected; but when the "Conference" began the faces turned towards the speaker were lined and weather-beaten; forty years and upwards must have been the age of most. What a dinner for War time: turkeys, pheasants, real sausages, hares, chickens and the rest to match. There were speeches, straight and to the point, and stories that called a spade a spade. When all had eaten and drunk they spoke freely and frankly on Home Guard matters, and got answered.

It was an impressive gathering, such as might have assembled to fight the Danes, or against the Spaniards in Queen Elizabeth's time, or to defeat a Napoleonic invasion. Each man has had his niche in this war; the young to the front line units, where at 40 a Battalion Commander is too old; the old to the Home Guard, where a Lt. Colonel at 60 could be in the prime of life as a Battalion Commander. It isn't age—save when physical fitness is essential—its the vitality and character that matters when the fighting will be a matter of hours and not of days.

"He's a great character," said the District Commander to me, "and he's got a damned good show." It's the fighting spirit that boosts up the men in the ranks—not the technical knowledge of the Commander. It isn't sufficient that the men are put in the right place to fight, they must have had the fighting spirit breathed into them.

Next day in the Newmarket Cinema the District Commander addressed the whole Battalion—preceded by prayers from the Chaplain. "The men like it," Taylor told me. Here was a good forceful Regular soldier putting the role of the Home Guard across. The probability of an enemy invasion by sea had passed; but there remained the possibility of enemy paratroops when our army had landed in Europe—and what if the Home Guard aren't ready to do their bit as the Garrison of England? What if the invasion of the Continent is a failure because Divisions had to be brought back from France to deal with an enemy air borne raid, murdering and destroying?

* * * * *

THE FIRST AND SECOND ISLE OF ELY BATTALIONS H.G.

The First and Second Isle of Ely Battalions are another example of the best type of Home Guard unit in which organisation and administration kept pace with training. It was fitting that this should be so in Hereward's country, where nine centuries earlier Home Guards had been the last men in England to defend their land against the Norman invaders, as thorough-going oppressors as the Germans have proved to-day.

No L.D.V. formations were quicker off the mark than these units, thanks to an organization under Colonel M. C. Clayton, D.S.O., which had been eminently successful in raising the 2nd Battalion Cambridgeshire Regiment in April 1939. When Mr. Eden made his broadcast appeal the response was immediate; within a quarter of an hour first applicants were arriving at the local police stations. Section leaders, instructors, orderly room staff were listed, and at a meeting in the Corn Exchange on the 19th May, the 800 who attended were at once formed into sections, graded and training started.

The role for the L.D.V. at this time was defined as:—

Manning observation points from dusk to dawn to give warning of hostile paratroop descents.

Endeavouring to shoot the paratroops before they landed, and failing that, to mop them up before they had a chance to collect their arms and become organized bodies.

This latter would have been no mean achievement! While the former, before it was modified, meant riding long distances on bicycles whenever the siren sounded.

In August, 1940, Colonel M. C. Clayton, D.S.O., took over the multitudinous sections of the North Western portion of the Isle of Ely, which were then formed into Company areas and became the First Isle of Ely Battalion, wearing the Cambridgeshire blue-black-blue flash on their shoulders; while the South Eastern portion of the Isle of Ely became the 2nd Battalion under Colonel W. P. Cutlack, C.B., T.D., D.L., who had previously been the zone organizer, with Major Posth as Second in Command, and later, Commander.

When the Battalion organization was started, training was stepped up, and the Home Guard as they were then named welcomed mobile training as a change from holding road blocks. Imaginary paratroops were chased over open country, orchards were searched.

But arms and uniforms were still short. The disadvantage of this is emphasised in a story told by the First Isle of Ely:—

"Late one night an L.D.V. Corporal with L.D.V. armlet, civilian overcoat and bowler hat, armed with a 12 bore gun, held up a regular officer at a road block. The officer refused to prove his identity. Whereupon the Corporal retorted: 'It's O.K. by me, Sir; you can stop here until a real officer comes along—that is if one comes before I go to work at 6 a.m. Bill, just take this ——— along, and lock him in Payne's cowshed'."

* * * * *

ELEVENTH SUFFOLK BATTALION HOME GUARD.

Much of the following is taken from the published records of the 11th Suffolk Battalion Home Guard.

The 11th Suffolk Battalion Home Guard was an off-shoot of the 9th Suffolk Battalion Home Guard when the latter became too unwieldily for convenient control. The defence of Ipswich was then subdivided between these two Battalions. The 11th Suffolk Battalion is yet another example of the value of a Commanding Officer. Lt. Colonel H. C. Howes, Commanding the Battalion, knew every officer and practically every N.C.O. by name, he could put a Christian name to most, in a Battalion which reached 1,900 officers and other ranks. He was not an obscure deity; every man knew him, and under him the unit became Battalion conscious. The 11th Suffolk Battalion had however two advantages over some other East Anglian Battalions:—Ipswich is of a size that engenders a nodding acquaintance; and Ipswich was a likely enemy objective. From the outset the men knew one another and almost to the end they had an incentive to become efficient.

The men who composed a Battalion such as the 11th Suffolk Home Guard were a great fellowship. A man of the Battalion wrote at the end of the War as follows:—

"A general survey of all our strivings, difficulties, disappointments and triumphs leaves certain impressions which will never be forgotten. What a list of names would be included if we attempted a list of every member who put all he possessed into the task asked of him! The Home Guard has sometimes been referred to as the 'Great Unpaid'; but little reference has been made to those in all ranks whose duties involved them in real domestic inconvenience, and, frequently, in monetary loss. Every change of defence positions, every alteration of training procedure, involved large numbers in drawing up maps, re-writing instruction programmes, reorganising their squads, re-siting their weapons, perhaps more digging, more routing of patrols, new accommodation for Stores, Rest Quarters; all this at a time when every man in the Company was 100% engaged on essential war work. But far from damping enthusiasm, it seemed to give fresh impetus to training and planning. It must not be inferred that we were always convinced by the explanations given by "High Command" as to the necessity for all these changes in our arrangements; but orders were loyally carried out. Any work in connection with preparing defence positions was always done with the best of humour. A man might be swinging a hammer in the Smiths' Shop all the week; yet he attacked hammering in stakes for barbed wire with the greatest zest all day Sunday. Shovelling sand in the Foundry might be 'work,' whereas digging a Machine Gun Post was good fun if a H.G. duty. Pioneers and Butt Parties could always be relied upon for cheerful service.

'B' Company can look back with pride and satisfaction to the good spirit and tireless co-operation which always existed.

So much for the good will of the men; what sort of soldiers did these men become? They were East Anglians; they had been formed for the defence against invasion, and if invasion came their territory was likely to be the first objective. There is no question that all the Home Guard Battalions of Suffolk, Cambridgeshire and the Isle of Ely aimed at the highest possible efficiency. From the earliest days Battalions and Companies drew up 'Proficiency Tests,' consolidated and standardized in 1943 by the War Office. There was no eye-wash about these Tests; the man who passed and wore the proficiency badge had a trained soldier's innate knowledge of the rifle he fought with, the grenade, the Northover or the Spigot mortar.

I recall a Home Guard parade in 1944 during the National Savings Week devoted to 'Salute the Soldier.' The average age of the men taking part was 45. After a drill demonstration in the numerous weapons with which they were armed, the platoons proceeded to cross a stiff obstacle course in an attack on a defended house; thence they followed the beaten defenders across an unbridged river and drove them from a wood. It was a set piece; but the physical test was severe. The obstacle course included barbed wire entanglements, a ten foot wall, a defended house that had to be escaladed, a river to be crossed by ropes—while the operation was enlivened by thunder flashes and explosive charges. A thousand Dominion soldiers watched the exercise, and their praise was unstinted."

The efficiency attained is all the more remarkable when it is remembered that the way had been tortuous. The early months of training were thickly spread with 'Tokens.' A writer in the 11th Battalion aptly describes this state:—

"What a feeling of frustration this work invokes in the Home Guard breast! Token road-blocks, token weapons, token mines, token trenches, and even token rations and token reinforcements—all these were common-place in the early stages of our career. The Home Guard needed consider-able imagination in those days, and sometimes a generous endowment of good humour in order to take the will for the deed.'

We remember an exercise in which most of the road-blocks consisted of such devices as a tape stretched across the road or a plank balanced precariously on a couple of tubs, so perhaps it was hardly surprising that 'enemy' tanks, generally Bren Carriers as 'tokens', heartlessly swept them aside in their attacks on our positions. On such occasions there might be a solitary Home Guard standing exposed to the wintry blast, because his Weapon Pit only existed in the imagination, while he himself represented a Squad in token. It was rather trying, too, for a party of men to stand for hours in a private garden, or outside a Pub. because their 'Rest Quarters' had no substance in fact. There were sometimes compensations, for No. 1. in the L.M.G. team often had to carry a rifle as token for a B.L.A. Certainly token ammunition was more portable and less dangerous than the real thing.

In due course, real weapons, solid road blocks and reinforcements in flesh and blood made their appearance, a token in themselves of the actual strength of the national defence against the invader."

When the tokens were made good what an armoury had to be mastered. It is worth enumerating some of these weapons if only to emphasize how much the Home Guard differed from the Trained Bands, the Militia, the Volunteers of other days and other wars.

The following extracts are taken from a review of the Home Guard weapons and were written by Capt. B. B. Beaumont, the Weapon Training officer of the 11th Battalion.

"Looking back over the recent years of Weapon Training in the Battalion it is remarkable to recall the variety of weapons at our disposal.

The Rifle naturally formed the basic weapon of the H.G. While many of the older seasoned soldiers of the 1914-18 war were at first prone to a preference for the British Lee-Enfield .303 with a "U" back-sight of their younger days, our American P.17 Rifle with the aperture back-sight, slowly but surely became popular.

To many the 36M. Grenade was an old and trusted friend—a 24-oz. Anti-Personnel Grenade, thrown by hand or projected from the P.17 rifle fitted with a Discharge Cup.

The first specialist weapon to make its welcome appearance was a Browning Heavy Machine Gun, again American, water-cooled, a 250-round Belt Feed, firing .300 ammunition, operated by a team of three or five when available, and capable of direct or indirect fire. The tripod mounting was in all probability responsible for more casualties to personnel in the shape of crushed, bent or bruised digits than any other weapon used. No animal could tie itself up into such knots as did this triple universal-jointed swine.

The Field Force 'Bren' had its counterpart in the 'B.A.R.' (Browning Automatic Rifle). This also was American make, firing .300 ammunition and loaded with a magazine of 20 rounds. Although an automatic weapon, very accurate performances could be relied upon when using it as a single-shot rifle.

The Thompson Gun was soon replaced by the more renowned "Sten," a short range weapon of decidedly cheap appearance; but it performed its role most efficiently. Here was the weapon to accomplish those aggressive and demoralizing bursts of fire that Street Fighting and House-entry Battle Platoons needed.

An early weapon to engage enemy light armour, was the 'Northover Projector,' resembling a telescope on a tripod, and in design a Breech Loading Smooth Bore weapon on a 4-leg mounting. With a range of 200 yards, it was limited to selected defensive positions, such as road approaches. It fired a Glass Bottle 24-oz. projectile containing self-igniting phosphorous in liquid rubber. On registering a hit, and this was a probability rather than a possibility, an inevitable fire resulted that seemed almost unquenchable, together with an atrocious choking smell.

Towards the end of 1941, 'Explosives' were being issued and by the end of 1942 there was a great variety. The 'Blacker Bombard,' later known as the 29 m.m. Spigot Mortar, was the weapon used for firing these so-called explosives. Primarily an anti-tank weapon, discharging a 20 lb. bomb filled with special explosive, either from a semi-portable or a fixed concrete pit mounting, with a range up to 450 yards, it was operated by a team of three or five. It was hailed as a long-felt want in the defensive role; its secondary use was anti-personnel, when a 14 lb. bomb of the fragmentation type was fired with a range up to 800 yards. The 20 lb. bomb was capable of knocking out heavy armoured vehicles; many will remember the decided 'wallop' and the resultant devastation at the target end when this bomb

By permission from "The Lion Roared his Defiance."

THE SMITH GUN.

scored a hit in an Area Competition held in 1943 near Dunwich, where the 11th Battalion defeated all other Suffolk Battalions. At 150 yards range the No. 1 in the team scored five direct hits, the maximum obtainable, on a British Tank travelling at 15 m.p.h. across his front in a total run of 300 yards.

A lighter and more portable anti-tank explosive was the No. 68 Grenade. This was a projectile for use against a less armoured type of vehicle and for street fighting against barricading. It was a 2 lb. Percussion Grenade fitted with a 'finned' tail unit for true flight purposes and was projected from the P.17 rifle in a somewhat similar manner to the 26 M.

In the hand projected class of grenades, three types were in use—known as the No. 73, No. 74 and No. 75. The No. 73, sometimes called the 'Thermos Flask', was a 4-lb. percussion grenade somewhat difficult to throw and therefore limited to a range of 10-15 yards. This short range and instant detonation ensured the greatest agility in taking cover after throwing this lump of awkwardness.

The No. 74, the 'Sticky', had a glass bowl stocking covering with a layer of bird lime substance. It had peculiar habits. Originally intended for 'placing' or 'pitching' at moving enemy mechanisation, neither the intention nor the grenade really 'stuck'; moreover it required delicate and prolonged handling to coax detonation. With its time fuse grenade it was better as demolition charge for 'mouse-holing' in street fighting. There was an occasion of certain 'Stickies' at Bromeswell 'Flying off the Handle' after having been primed, with a resultant scatter for 'cover.'

Lastly, the No. 75, a 'Grenade-cum-Mine.' It could be laid as a small mine trap, or thrown into the path of oncoming vehicles, or used in pairs as a Pole Charge for entry gaps in street fighting. It could be threaded on ropes for dragging across enemy tank approaches or placed in track suspensions of stationary tanks.

There was also another Field Force anti-tank-mine—the Mk. II, which lent itself well to the construction of booby traps.

Soon after the formation of the 11th Battalion H.G. an issue of the 3-in. O.S.B. Gun, commonly called the 'Smith Gun,' was made. It was by far the heaviest weapon yet encountered, mounted between two large diameter disc wheels and towing an ammunition trailer. When arriving at its selected firing position it could be overturned on to one of its wheels, which then served as its firing base. Three types of projectiles were in use, varying from 10-lb. 3-in. Mortar Bombs to 6-lb. Anti-Tank Shells.

A rather belated arrival was the Field Force 2-Pdr. Anti-Tank Gun—a quick firing, breech loading weapon for use against the lighter armoured enemy vehicles.

From the outset a system of Weapon Training on Field Force standards was inaugurated, covering little more than the essentials for war. Much of the earlier somewhat tedious teachings of 'Mechanisms' was omitted, but there is little doubt that that much publicised 'Sole Object of Weapon Training—a kill'—could have been obtained."

There must be many in the Home Guard who could confess to a secret regret that the Home Guard were never tested in battle, a confession that they would no doubt qualify by selecting some lonely locality where no civilians would suffer. They were the descendants of the 'thin red line', extending as innumerable dots in every direction throughout East Anglia. Had invasion come they would have signed their names on the dotted line."

But apart from this one regret; all testify to the benefits of soldiering. The following extracts from contributions to the 11th Battalion H.G. "Souvenir" will be echoed by most:—

"On looking back upon four-and-a-half years as a Home Guard, I find that certain conclusions have formed themselves in my mind.

We Home Guards were always civilians. We did our best work when left to our own devices and made most progress when we relied upon ourselves. We had all the talent we wanted and we could always improvise. When it came to technical matters we had the experts; if it was instruction that was needed, we had the teachers. We were united and we understood each other. We were keen to emulate the Army, but I doubt whether military methods of administration and control represented the best means of exploiting our enthusiasm and peculiar composition.

Anyhow, the Home Guard provided astonishing evidence of how much the willing horse can pull and it has been a precious and unforgettable experience."

Another writes:—

"It is not easy to write of one's experiences or opinion of the Home Guard without accentuating grievances or exaggerating benefits.

Before the war, most of us middle-aged men were getting into a groove. The Home Guard, if it did nothing else, got us out of the rut, enabled us to meet lots of fresh people, and gave us the opportunity of acquiring a broader outlook.

Most of us dislike military discipline; but it was necessary in the Home Guard, and no one was really the worse for it. Drill annoyed many of us intensely and speaking personally neither in this war nor the last was the barrack square my spiritual home.

Most of my training required a certain amount of physical agility which showed up my limitations cruelly. Vaulting gracefully over stiles, jumping ditches and crawling noiselessly through thick gorse were never among my accomplishments, and my efforts in this direction must have caused considerable annoyance to those following me, as well as endless exasperation to my instructors."

Another describes his experiences:—

"After I had decided I ought to be a member of our great organisation, I can honestly say my one regret was that I did not enrol sooner.

I soon found that parades far from being boring as I had feared, stimulated my interest; but three evenings a week at Portman Road, plus a Sunday morning were about enough! It was after being detailed to my Company that I began to appreciate the feeling of comradeship, which I'm sure exists among all Platoons. I remember how, besides Officers and N.C.O.s, veteran members would be helpful in any way which would make me feel 'at home.' I was thus enabled quickly to settle into my new job.

There were many occasions and incidents, mostly pleasant and interesting, some, to me, boring and unnecessary, which have made up my activities; but I would sum up by saying that I have gained much of value from my association with the Home Guard. I have made new friends and acquaintances; it's pleasant to give one's C.S.M. a cheery 'How do' on the way to business. Previously we must have passed each other hundreds of times, and not a word between us. I've gained self-control, for surely, to exercise authority, however slight, is to learn how easily it can be abused. I've observed, too, the value of team-work between all members."

One Home Guard writes:—

"If one fact emerges from the experience of the present war, it is the readiness of men and women from all walks of life to unite together without promise of payment or reward to do service for their Country; amongst these the Home Guards have done their share.

Now the 'Stand Down' has come and we take stock of our possessions —boots, battle-dress, etc. etc. Yes, but what else? Health is better, for some of us have left behind pounds of 'superfluous' with which we were burdened in 1940. We have learned that there is something better than crouching over a fire, however nice, on cold, crisp nights; since we have turned out in all weathers in warm battle-dress on training parades, and enjoyed it.

Our circle of acquaintances has grown considerably, doubtless some hitherto strangers have formed lasting friendships, but all of us, even if we only know one another facially, will always pass a cheery time-of-day whenever we chance to meet, each contact bringing with it a remembrance of Home Guard days. We have surely learned that outside our immediate circle there are many fellows of sterling quality with whom one would not feel apprehensive in time of trial or danger.

Finally we would say 'Thank you, Home Guard,' for these experiences which would never have been ours but for your helping us to discover ourselves."

Finally let me quote what the wife of a Home Guard said:—

"What has the Home Guard meant to me? Apart from being wholeheartedly glad that my husband was one of the original L.D.V.s, as time went on I found myself taking a personal interest in the 'domestic' affairs when on Exercises, of two platoons at least. The nearness of our house to a Platoon H.Q. and easy means of access by way of the back garden, meant on different occasions, soup making in bulk for transport at dead of night to snowbound warriors; Home Guards 'about the house' manning the telephone and acting as runners; the sitting-room handed over to a Platoon Cmdr. and his 2 i/c (the fire came in handy, incidentally, for drying their rain-soaked socks); a Home Guard cook in the kitchen, brewing vast quantities of tea, which camouflaged figures with blackened faces came, in twos and threes, to fetch. Had the evacuation of the civil population taken place, the house would have been given over to the Home Guard, primarily for use as a cookhouse, and, at a practice, I marvelled at the efficiency and thoughtfulness of the L/Cpl. Cook in charge. Neither speck of mud nor flick of cigarette ash was allowed over my threshold, and had I had to leave my home, I should have gone with an easy mind, happier that my house was in his care than had it been standing empty.

As a needlewoman, I shall long remember how unwieldy was the bulk of a battle-dress blouse and greatcoat when it came to the sewing thereon of stripes and flashes, and how exasperating it was to find that, in spite of meticulous measuring and pinning beforehand, the wretched things never looked quite straight when the stitching was finished!

My husband's health has never been better; he has not been able to lay even a common cold at the door of being soaked to the skin and chilled to the bone, while performing H.G. duties. Has he benefited in other ways? Yes, in many, as do all men who are provided with a fresh interest and follow it keenly. Certainly, I have heard quite a few honest British grumbles about this, that, and the other on the H.G. during the past four years, but he would be the first to admit that, most of the time, he has experienced exhilaration from, and enjoyment in the work and training and to the comradeship in the Home Guard; above all, he owes a better understanding of and a more tolerant attitude towards other men's problems and outlooks on life."

The 'Peak' strength of the Home Guard Battalions of Suffolk, Cambridgeshire and the Isle of Ely was approximately 50,000 all ranks; the total number who passed through the ranks during the War Years being in the neighbourhood of 100,000.

The following is a list of the Battalions and other Home Guard units raised, with the names of their Commanding Officers:—

1st Suffolk Bn. Home Guard.
Brig. Gen. Sir T. D. Jackson, Bt., M.V.O., D.S.O.
Lieut. Col. H. H. Chandor, O.B.E.
Lieut. Col. H. B. A. Adderley (now Lord Norton).
Lieut. Col. The Lord Somerleyton, M.C.

2nd Suffolk Bn. Home Guard.
Lt. Col. H. M. Lawrence, D.S.O., O.B.E.
Lieut. Col. S. J. M. Sampson, M.C., T.D.

3rd Suffolk Bn. Home Guard.
Lieut. Col. E. C. Walker.
Lieut. Col. The Lord Erskine, G.C.S.I., G.C.I.E.

4th Suffolk Bn. Home Guard.
Lieut. Col. E. P. Clarke, D.S.O., T.D.
Major H. E. Connop.
Lieut. Col. Hon. A. N. A. Vanneck, M.C.
Lieut. Col. B. F. Taylor, V.D.

5th Suffolk Bn. Home Guard.
Lieut. Col. E. R. Wyatt, C.B.E.
Lieut. Col. D. G. Wigan.

6th Suffolk Bn. Home Guard.
Lieut. Col. F. L. Tempest, O.B.E., M.C.
Lieut. Col. A. Bass.

7th Suffolk Bn. Home Guard.
Lieut. Col. D. Ovey, D.S.O.

8th Suffolk Bn. Home Guard.
Col. W. A. B. Daniell, C.B.E., D.S.O., T.D., D.L.
Lieut. Col. A. P. Dene, C.M.G., D.S.O.
Lieut. Col. Sir T. P. Larcom, Bt., D.S.O.
Lieut. Col. C. E. Colbeck, M.C.

9th Suffolk Bn. Home Guard.
Lieut. Col. Kingsley Reavell.
Lieut. Col. H. D. Wise, M.C.

Photo—H. I. Jarman.

No. 8 (A.R.P.) Platoon, "A" Company, 2nd Battalion, Suffolk Home Guard, June, 1942.

Back Row—Pte. F. O. Codling (R), Pte. E. W. Williams (R), Pte. D. Baldwin (R), Pte. B. G. Candler (C.C.), Pte. J. L. Nunn (C.C.), Pte. G. W. Radford, (A.F.S.), Pte. B. A. Willingham (W), Pte. J. W. Honeybell (R), L/c. R. E. Dewell (C.C.) Pte. E. V. Bradbrook (R), Pte. P. C. Cook (R).
Centre Row—Cpl. S. E. Palmer (W), L/c. E. C. Green (R), Pte. H. W. Allen (W), Pte. F. J. Ross (W), Pte. S. P. Gardiner (W), Pte. E. J. Atkin, (A.F.S.), L/c. E. G. Slark (W), Pte. A. R. E. Hooper (A.F.S.), L/c. G. A. Bradley (W), Pte. T. Dorling (R), Pte. L. R. Driver (R), L/c. F. C. Harwood (R), Cpl. E. A. Haxton (C.C.) Pte. H. C. F. Beard (R), Pte. P. J. Hayhoe (W).
Front Row—Pte. F. E. Bentley (W), Cpl. F. D. Whitewick (R), Cpl. W. H. Ward (W), Cpl. E. V. Butt (W), Sgt. E. W. Lovick (W), Major M. S. Chase (O.C. "A" Coy.), Lt. Harvey G. Frost (R), 2nd Lt. E. A. Borley (W), Sgt. E. H. Lack (W), Sgt. G. Simms (C.C.), Sgt. W. H. P. Cullen (W), Cpl. H. A. Winterton (W), Pte. B. Bougin (R).

(W. Warden. R. Rescue. C.C. County Control. A.F.S. Auxiliary Fire Service).

10th Suffolk Bn. Home Guard.
Lieut. Col. R. J. Armes, C.M.G.
Lieut. Col. K. A. Crockatt, M.C.

11th Suffolk Bn. Home Guard.
Lieut. Col. H. C. Howes.

2010 Suffolk H.G. M.T. Coy.
Major R. H. Bremner.

2018 Suffolk H.G. M.T. Coy.
Capt. O. J. Barnard.

1st Cambridgeshire Bn. Home Guard.
Lt. Colonel J. M. Bryan.

2nd Cambridgeshire and Suffolk Bn. Home Guard.
Lt. Colonel W. J. Taylor.

3rd Cambridgeshire Bn. Home Guard.
Lt. Colonel O. B. Foster, M.C.

4th Cambridgeshire Bn. Home Guard.
Lt. Colonel R. H. Parker, M.C.

5th Cambridgeshire Bn. Home Guard.
Lt. Colonel (Vice Admiral) W. Lake.
Lt. Colonel G. F. Dale.

6th (34 G.P.O.) Cambridgeshire Bn. Home Guard.
with Companies at Cambridge, Norwich, Bedford, King's Lynn and Luton.
Lt. Colonel L. L. Tolley.

7th Cambridgeshire (Mobile) Bn. Home Guard.
Lt. Colonel John Grace.
Lt. Colonel D. Mackenzie.

8th (University) Cambridgeshire Bn. Home Guard.
Col. K. D. B. Murray, C.B., D.S.O.

1st Isle of Ely Bn. Home Guard.
Lt.-Colonel M. C. Clayton, D.S.O.

2nd Isle of Ely Bn. Home Guard.
Colonel W. P. Cutlack, C.B., T.D., D.L.
Lt.-Colonel Posth.
Lt.-Colonel C. E. Cross.

3rd Isle of Ely Bn. Home Guard.
Lt.-Colonel G. W. Walker.

101st Cambridgeshire A.A. Battery Home Guard.
Major B. F. Pratt.
Major S. J. Moss.

2007th Motor Transport Company Home Guard.
Major Dickerson.

The 7th Cambridgeshire (Mobile) Battalion Home Guard started with a number of men who were anxious to put their cars and motor cycles at the service of the country. By July, 1940, there were 145 names on the roll ready to act as a mobile reserve whenever required. Later the Battalion was organised as four Rifle Companies, including two cyclist companies.

The 8th (University) Cambridgeshire Bn. Home Guard existed before the war as a contingent of the Senior Training Corps, a function which was expanded during the War, the 1,200 University Members forming a part of the local Home Guard and being made up into five units (Engineers, Artillery, Armoured Corps, Signals and Infantry).

The Honours and Awards included:—

C.B.E.

Colonel W. J. C. Lake, Sector Commandeı, Cambridge.
Colonel W. A. B. Daniell, D.S.O., T.D., D.L., Zone Commander, Suffolk.

O.B.E.

Colonel H. H. Chandor, Sector Commander, Halesworth.
Lt.-Colonel M. C. Clayton, D.S.O., D.L., Commander 1st Isle of Ely Bn. Home Guard.
Lt.-Col. W. J. Taylor, Commander 2nd Cambs. & Suffolk Bn. Home Guard.
Colonel F. L. Tempest, M.C., Sector Commander, Ipswich.

M.B.E.

Major G. B. Batch, 6th Cambs. Bn. Home Guard.
Major G. L. Boyle, T.D., 5th Cambs. Bn. Home Guard.
Major F. B. Brooke, M.C., 1st Cambs. Bn. Home Guard.
Major J. C. W. Francis, 2nd Cambs. and Suffolk Bn. Home Guard.
Major C. E. Cooper, 6th Suffolk Bn. Home Guard.
Major W. A. Wylie, 10th Suffolk Bn. Home Guard.
Capt. J. Jopling, 4th Cambs. Bn. Home Guard.
Lt. C. R. B. Draper, 4th Suffolk Bn. Home Guard.
C.S.M. J. Parker, 1st Isle of Ely Bn. Home Guard.

B.E.M.

Sgt. A. King, M.M., 4th Cambs. Bn. Home Guard.
C/Sgt. J. Baxter, 101 (Cambs.) A.A. Battery, Home Guard.
Cpl. R. Buck, 3rd Isle of Ely Bn. Home Guard.
Sgt. S. A. Gautrey, 1st Cambs. Bn. Home Guard.

There were also a large number of Certificates for Gallantry or Good Service granted to the men serving in the Battalions.

ARMY CADETS.

There were Cadet units in the Napoleonic era, existing as elementary training units for the Regular Army. But it was not until 1859 that a voluntary movement for cadets was started, largely associated with schools and other institutions, which movement in due course has blossomed into the present Army Cadets.

During the first World War 1914-1918, the strength of these Cadet units rose to 100,000; but the financial crisis of 1931 resulted in a withdrawal of Government recognition and the Army Cadets were threatened with extinction. Fortunately a small Cadet Committee formed in each county in 1934 kept the Cadet spirit alive.

In December, 1941, the Army Council decided to expand the existing Army Cadet Force and the Lord Lieutenants were asked to form County Cadet Committees to administer the Force; the Committees formed in 1934 were absorbed into these new Committees and gave invaluable assistance. By 1943 membership of the Army Cadet units had risen to over 180,000 and the units were no longer confined to schools and institutions. Open units were formed which enabled any working lad, who felt so inclined, to prepare himself for the Army. This resulted during the war years in a vast and rapid expansion which eventually included youths from 14 to 18 from all walks of life.

The birth of the Army Cadet Force in Cambridgeshire and the Isle of Ely took place in December, 1941; but for many years there had been a Cadet Corps at Wisbech Grammar School. This was a "closed" unit of about 120 cadets, forming part of the school and recruiting no members from outside. This unit formed the nucleus of the 1st Isle of Ely Cadet Battalion, its company commander, Capt. L. G. Anniss, becoming the new Lieutenant-Colonel. The ex-members of this school unit played a notable part in the great war of 1939 to 1945, sending a total of over two hundred to the Armed Forces.

The Lord Lieutenant of Cambridgeshire, Mr. Charles Adeane, appreciated that the leadership of youth was the specialised task of the schoolmaster; he therefore summoned the leading schoolmasters of Cambridgeshire and the Isle of Ely to meet him at the Guildhall at Cambridge on the 28th January, 1942, to discuss the outlines of the new Force. The schoolmasters declared themselves heartily in support of the Cadet movement and it was decided that Home Guard Battalion Commanders should be invited to nominate Battalion and Company commanders for the Army Cadet Force and to give them every encouragement in recruiting. As a result the 1st and 2nd Isle of Ely Cadet Battalions, the 7th (Borough of Cambridge) Cadet Battalion and the 2nd Cambs. & Suffolk Cadet Battalion, together with the 1st, 3rd and 4th Cambridgeshire Cadet Corps, started recruiting.

The 1st and 2nd Isle of Ely Cadet Battalions, under the command of Lt.-Col. L. G. Anniss and Lt.-Col. C. J. E. S. Fendick were raised in the areas of the 1st and 2nd Isle of Ely Home Guard Battalions, covering respectively the areas Wisbech and Whittlesey on the one hand and March, Chatteris, Ely and Haddenham on the other. The 2nd Cambs. and Suffolk Cadet Battalion under Lt.-Col. A. F. Fuller was moulded on 2nd Cambs. & Suffolk Battalion Home Guard. The Borough of Cambridge unit was affiliated to the 7th Home Guard Battalion, and was raised under Lt.-Col. D. R. Counsell; but later changed its affiliation and title to the 5th Battalion. The remaining unit, later to become the 4th Cambs. Cadet Battalion, under the Command of Lt.-Col. M. C. Burkitt, began as three separate corps in the areas of 1st, 3rd and 4th Cambs. Home Guard Battalions respectively. Its territory covered the whole County of Cambridge, less the Borough.

The expansion of the Army Cadet Force in Cambridgeshire was exceedingly rapid. The original "ceiling" of 300 allotted by the War Office was quickly raised to 1,000 and again in a few weeks to 1,500 and 2,000, and a total strength of just under 2,000 was attained by July, 1942. There were external reasons for this rapid recruitment. The war was at its worst, or so it seemed to Cambridgeshire and the Isle of Ely, for in February, 1942, Singapore had fallen and two Territorial Battalions and a Field Company from the County had been made prisoners. The primary object of the Army Cadet was to get through his Pre-entry training, to join first the Home Guard and then the Field Force. The outlook of the cadet at this time is well illustrated by the case of the boy in the 1st Isle of Ely Cadet Battalion who misappropriated the papers of a soldier on leave and joined up in his place. He succeeded in serving as a soldier for seven weeks, two of which he spent under punishment for the absenteeism of the soldier whom he had impersonated. The experience did not appear to diminish his enthusiasm as an Army Cadet.

Training during the first year, 1942, was rudimentary with little beyond foot and arms drill under instruction from the Home Guard and with weapons borrowed from them. The Home Guard was naturally reluctant to lend rifles to be "thrown" about by cadets. In July and August, 1942, the first annual camps were held, 1st Isle of Ely going to Stow Bardolph, 2nd Isle of Ely to Burwell, 2nd Cambs. and Suffolk to Elveden and the 7th Cambridge to Newmarket, while the 4th did not concentrate as a Battalion but held a series of company camps rather more on the lines of Boy Scouts. These Battalion camps were primitive judged by later standards but, even so, they provided valuable experience. But it was evident that in future Brigade camps would have to be held and that the organisation would have to be centralised. The first summer concluded with a Brigade Parade at Ely Cathedral attended by 1,400 of all ranks. At the close of 1942 Lt.-Col. D. R. Counsell 7th (Borough of Cambridge) Cadet Battalion was succeeded in command by Major S. A. Earl.

This year saw the genesis of the boys' club in the Army Cadet Force of the County. In September Mr. Randal Keane of the National Association of Boys' Clubs addressed a gathering of officers at Cambridge and again at March, and early in 1943 the Isle of Ely Cadet Bn. opened their Club at North Brink, Wisbech, and the 2nd Cambs. & Suffolk Cadet Bn. opened another at Waterwitch House, Newmarket. These clubs were at that time little more than off-duty meeting places and canteens. The principle of the Boys Club was to be realised later, but at least a beginning had been made and the Ministry of Education supported the venture with a considerable grant.

In August, 1943, the first Brigade camp was held at Babraham and was attended by 93 officers and 974 cadets; the Army giving the fullest assistance. In addition to the high standard of catering, the Army ration was at that time on a very generous scale. The experiment of a Brigade camp was an undoubted success. The boy realised that he was part of a big organisation and a strong *esprit de corps* and rivalry between units was at once apparent. From this first Brigade camp the lesson was learnt that the annual camp must contain the holiday element and that over-organisation must be avoided.

By the autumn of 1943 the sweeping series of Russian victories, the defeat of Italy and the imminent invasion of the Continent had all combined to give an impression that the war was as good as won. This was reflected in the attitude of the Home Guard whose strength was largely influenced by the prospect that an invasion of the Continent might provoke a last and desperate riposte from the Germans. The numbers of the Army Cadet Force also took a downward trend, only checked by the incorporation of 17-year-olds who, up to that time, had not been allowed to serve in the Army Cadet Force because they were eligible to volunteer for the Home Guard. It was at this time that the County Cadet Committee, inspired by the War Office, issued a directive that the short-term object was to make a soldier, the long-term object of the Army Cadet Force was to make a better citizen; from this time onwards the long-term object was increasingly borne in mind.

In the year 1944 the second Brigade camp was held at Babraham. The other main feature of 1944 was the announcement of the interim accommodation scheme under which County Cadet Committees were to be given a number of huts and a sum of money with which to erect them where required. But the scheme took effect slowly, and during the first months of 1945 only some half dozen huts were erected, chiefly in the area of the 1st Isle of Ely Battalion.

1945 was probably the most critical year of the Army Cadet Force; its officers were in many cases overdriven men, some of them holding many appointments and nearly all finding it increasingly difficult to keep pace with the demands and enthusiasm of youth. The victory over Germany produced a natural desire to relax and the stand-down of the Home Guard at the end of 1944 tempted many boys to put off khaki like their fathers. But the County Cadet Committee had a stroke of good fortune in the discovery that the Combined Training Centre at Inverary, Scotland, would be available for annual camp. This announcement came at an opportune moment, when everyone was in need of a holiday, and the response among the cadets was marked. 1,264 of all ranks attended, travelling in three special trains to Scotland. To boys who had lived all their life in the Fens it was a wonderful experience to be plunged into the wooded Highlands of Scotland; there were one or two who had never before been in a train and some were heard to say that, if they had to return home at once, the thrill of crossing the Forth Bridge had made everything worth while. The average rainfall for Inverary is 124 inches, or nearly one third of an inch a day; but luck held, for ten consecutive days there was blazing sunshine, thus breaking a record of fifty years. The War Office sent an Army Kinema Section to Inverary to record the camp and the film "Work Hard—Play Hard", shown all over the British Empire and in the United States, proved one of the best recruiting agents for the Army Cadet Force.

While at Inverary the news of the final defeat of Japan was received and amongst the cadets who returned home there were many who could scarcely recall the time when England was at peace. Shortly after camp Lt.-Col. L. G. Anniss resigned his command owing to pressure of work and was succeeded by Lt.-Col. M. C. Clayton who had long associations with the Cambridgeshire Regiment and who had commanded 1st Isle of Ely Bn. Home Guard throughout its existence.

The end of 1945 and beginning of 1946, a transition period from war to peace, marked a decline in numbers. There was, however, a definite increase in purpose. By this time more huts were erected and with the assistance of the National Association of Boys' Clubs and the Army Cadet Force Association, a full-time Club Organiser for the County was appointed. At the beginning of July a parade was held in Cambridge attended by 600 cadets from all Cambridgeshire Battalions. Lord Bridgeman addressed the parade, the County Flag was handed over by the Archdeacon of Ely and the Mayor of Cambridge presented a Silver Bugle to the 5th Cadet Battalion in return for the services rendered by their Band on public occasions.

In 1946 a very successful Brigade camp was held at Firle Park in Sussex and was attended by 758 of all ranks, a detachment of the Girls' Training Corps from Cambridge attending for the third year in succession and giving assistance with Officers' Messes. This year saw the retirement of three Commanding Officers, Lt.-Col. Fendick Commanding 2nd Isle of Ely Cadet Bn., Lt.-Col. R. Brown Commanding 5th (Borough of Cambridge) Cadet Bn., and Lt.-Col. M. C. Burkitt Commanding 4th Cambs. Cadet Bn., their respective successors being Major A. H. Godfrey, Major R. C. Verrinder and Lt. K. H. Roscoe.

There were four Cadet Battalions in Suffolk whose war history proceeded on somewhat similar lines to the Cadet Battalions of Cambridgeshire and the Isle of Ely. The 1st Cadet Battalion The Suffolk Regiment under Lt.-Colonel E. R. Latham, M.C. had its Headquarters in Ipswich; and recruited in the area Ipswich, Hadleigh, Holbrook, East Bergholt and Chelmondiston. The 2nd Cadet Battalion came from Woodbridge, Stowmarket, Needham Market, Felixstowe, Framlingham and Wickham Market, with one Composite Company from Eye, Stradbroke and Hoxne. The 3rd Cadet Battalion under the command of Lieut. Col. F. H. Kelf drew its strength from Beccles, Bungay, Lowestoft, Southwold, Saxmundham and Leiston area. The 4th Cadet Battalion, Lt.-Colonel G. W. Hales, came from West Suffolk: Bury St. Edmunds, Sudbury, Haverhill. Many well known Suffolk Schools and Colleges such as Framlingham, Woodbridge, Ipswich, King Edward VI Grammar School furnished their quota.

The Suffolk Army Cadet Force camped in 1944 and 1945 at Shrubland Park, Claydon, near Ipswich, when all who visited the camp bore witness to the enthusiasm of the cadets, to their practical efficiency, thanks to the large staff of efficient regular army instructors.

Throughout the Country the Cadets of the Army, Navy and Air Force were uniformly good as was witnessed by an amusing description given over the wireless.

The speaker was given the job, as he put it, of running round the country to give instructions to various people, and he was laid on one evening to instruct a class of Cadets in a mining village in the Midlands. It was a wet night and he found about thirty boys in the corner of a large hall. Having been accustomed to adults, they looked to the speaker extraordinarily young and not outstandingly clever. He therefore thought he was in for an easy time, as he considered he knew his job pretty well. He went on to describe what he did and how he then invited the Cadets to ask questions. He said that the result was that for about an hour he was under a machine gun fire of questions, observations, arguments. They were not content to know the answers, they wanted to know why, and whenever he made a slip, as he did several times when the pace grew too hot, he was politely but very rapidly corrected by about five voices in unison. At the end of that hour he was literally sweating.

It is always invidious to single out the achievements of one unit when all have done well; but in the Army Cadet National Boxing Championships the contests at Cambridge for Eastern Command Championships led to the semi-final contests at Chelsea Barracks, London; in these the Eastern Command had nine of the sixteen finalists to go forward for the national championships held at the Albert Hall, London, on 19th April, 1945. Four of these nine came from Cadet Battalions of the Suffolk Regiment, one from the 1st Battalion Ipswich, and three from the 4th Battalion, No. 2 Company (Bury St. Edmunds).

The Regiment's representatives at the Albert Hall were Sgt. Mayes, 1st Battalion Ipswich, and Cadets Colson, Giles, and Boston, of No. 2 Company, 4th Battalion (Bury St. Edmunds). Mayes won his championship, but the unlucky failure of the others to bring off their bouts resulted in the Regiment losing the championship by one point. All the same, their efforts brought great credit to themselves and to the Regiment.

Major R. E. Partridge, the Secretary of the Suffolk Territorial Association, describes the object of Cadet training as follows:—

"In peace, as in war, the object of Cadet training is to give mental, moral and physical training to boys, and so form the character of each to enable him to make a good start in life, to develop in him the principles of patriotism and good citizenship, bringing out the qualities of self-confidence, self respect and ability to face and accept responsibility with the power to control himself and others. Thus a Cadet is fitted, in the event of a National Emergency, to take his place in the defence of his home and country.

The main object of any military training should be the development of soldierly qualities rather than the acquisition of military knowledge. The most important of these qualities are: Self reliance, alertness, pride and self-respect, a sense of discipline, loyalty.

A Cadet who, during his pre-service training, has developed these qualities, even to a limited extent, has already the making of a soldier; even if he never joins the Army, these are the factors which also lead to success in civil life."

The military standard aimed at was high. All Cadets were expected to pass Certificate 'A' Part I Exams and as many as possible Part II (Section Leaders). In addition they could take Certificate T (Technical Training). After obtaining Parts I and II of Certificate A the Cadets were used as Instructors and could be trained on a higher level by taking Post Certificate 'A' training. Two of the Cadet Battalions had a generous scale of Signalling Equipment which included wireless sets.

A Report by the Director of Military Training at the War Office in 1943 reads as follows:—

"From all reports which have reached the War Office it seems that the Army Cadet Force, of whom His Majesty is now Colonel-in-Chief, is beginning to reap the benefit of the scheme for training that was laid down when the expansion of the Force was approved.

This scheme, which is based on War Certificate 'A', has as its main object the production of leaders and technicians for the Army of the near future. The requirements of an army at war, or rather a nation striving for peace after victory, are insatiable, and we look to the Army Cadet Force to provide us with large numbers of those leaders and technicians that will be needed.

The training given to Army Cadets covered the basic subjects of soldiering which must be mastered by all soldiers before they can be efficient and certainly before they can aspire to leadership either as N.C.O.s or Officers."

The Cadets have come to stay; and their value to the Suffolk Regiment cannot be exaggerated. This cannot be better expressed than in the words of Field-Marshal Sir Harold Alexander in the message he sent in the beginning of 1944 from the 15th Army Group:—

"I am glad to have this opportunity of sending you a message from the battle front, and it is this: We in the Army look to the Army Cadet Force to provide us with the young leaders we need. A good army depends on its leaders whether they be section commanders or high ranking officers. The splendid organisation to which you belong trains you for those duties and it is up to you to take full advantage of your great opportunities. Our old Country has never lacked the spirit of leadership and as long as that spirit remains England will be England and all she stands for.

Good luck to you in your apprenticeship. A warm welcome awaits you when you join the Army."

THE 40TH SUFFOLK PLATOON

AUXILIARY TERRITORIAL SERVICE.

It was a war that spared none of either sex and the Suffolk women bore a noble part whether as housewives, members of the invaluable Women's Voluntary Services, or belonging to one of the many national services. Among these latter was the Auxiliary Territorial Service, known everywhere as the "A.T.S.'" One small unit of these wore the Regimental badge.

The 40th Suffolk Platoon A.T.S. came into being in September, 1939; but for most of the year previous its members had been doing individual training. They had started with 25 members in September, 1938, but quickly rose to 55, including 15 N.C.O.s. They were local girls, the majority in civilian employment; one afternoon a week they came to Gibraltar Barracks in mufti to learn what would be required of them on embodiment.

Miss Wentworth Reeve had been the first member and there could have been no happier choice of the first Company Commander than this lady. It was her keenness for the success of the Company—of which the 40th Platoon formed a part—that gave the organisation its great start. She proved herself a most inspiring leader and great was the regret when she died in the early days of the war.

But it was not until mobilization that the 40th Suffolk Platoon became a living organization. And mobilization came with dramatic suddenness to more than one member of this unit. Here is a letter from one:—

"At half past nine on the morning of the 2nd September, 1939, I yawned my way down to breakfast. On my plate, among two interesting-looking letters, was a small note marked "Urgent." To my horror it read: 'You will report for duty for the Auxiliary Territorial Service 8.30 a.m. on Saturday, September 2nd. Bring your lunch with you.' This was a pretty kettle of fish; here I was still in my dressing gown when I should have been a real soldier for at least an hour !

I tore upstairs to adorn myself in the decidedly uninviting-looking khaki uniform that I had shoved in my bottom drawer, thinking that I should never have to wear it except at meetings or in camp.

Trembling in my boots and my heart in my mouth, I eventually tracked my Company Commander to ground in her office, who, to my great relief, did not appear to mind in the least that I was two hours late.

'They're waiting for you in the cookhouse. Please go there at once,' were my orders. I felt odd enough clad in these extraordinary clothes in my bedroom; but now to have to walk the length of the barrack square in them, knowing that I was being laughed at from every angle, was still more blush-making. I reached the cookhouse as quickly as possible.

'Poof! The atmosphere!' So this was the cookhouse; in fact, my home for the war! It was more like an oven itself! The other three A.T.S. were covered from head to foot in flour, and so was I in less than no time, as meat pies were the order of the day. This was followed by the peeling and cutting up of onions, so we all four got down to them, only to get up again very soon with stinging, streaming eyes and cut fingers. However, that was nothing compared to the very uninviting-looking liver which appeared out of bloodsoaked wooden boxes for the A.T.S. to skin and cut up. 'Whose liver is this?' one A.T. asked. 'That's the Major's liver, I reckon.' Potatoes were the next item. Four cwt. to be done for to-morrow's lunch, which proved a slow business to begin with, but we soon got pretty snappy at it."

A note written at a later stage by another of the original members of the Platoon gives a good picture of Army life seen through A.T.S. eyes:

"We started our army career in a corner of the old barber's shop at Gibraltar Barracks, and even that we shared with the P.R.I. It was under his stern eye that we learnt our first Army lessons. We learnt how to do Part II Orders, which we typed with one finger; the much hated end-of-the-month-Part-II-Order took the best part of a week! We learnt that a 'casualty' was not necessarily an A.T.S. who had been run over; but above all, we learnt that if we wanted *any* information on *any* subject we went to 'H.Q.' Company.

Later we took up residence in the Museum. Here we nearly froze to death, and were not sorry when once again we moved, this time to a flat in the married quarters. After a brief stay there, we were moved to West Lines, to quarters which were beyond our wildest dreams of palatial comfort in a barracks. We felt that the Regimental red and yellow sign on our office door had done much to establish not only our identity but our position as people of importance."

In those early days they were maids of all work, but employed always in a subordinate capacity. They shared the work in the cookhouses under the Sgt. Cook who still kept a complement of his men. They served in the Officers' Mess under the indispensable Mr. Watts.

They not only worked in offices, stores and cookhouses, like the men in the ranks they were drilled and given physical training. I do not know what the general feeling was to this form of female soldiering; but as in everything else they did they went at it wholeheartedly. The A.T.S. on a big or little parade were well worth seeing. Not once but several times the Suffolk A.T.S. unit gave displays of drill and P.T. in Suffolk towns and gained great and deserved applause.

Bearing this in mind a letter signed Hypolita may be quoted: "My dear ———

Although it costs me 2½d. to write to you, I feel it will be worth it if only to put a stop to your wails of the burdens resting on the blue shoulders of an Auxiliary Firewoman. As far as I can see all you are responsible for is a length of hose and for a woman who has spent two years behind the stocking counter at....................

Change the F in A.F.S. to T and you would have cause to sigh. Frequently. However the worst is now over. Spring has entered the Barracks and with it the A.T.S. winter clothing. Enter our Barracks and you will fill our crates of..................

The peak event of the week is our drill parade, when the Barracks resounds to the stumbling feet of fifty women, all driven by one thought: 'Will she manage to stop us before we reach those lorries, that wheelbarrow and Sergeant Burrows ? As far as I know we have never descended to the depths of another Company in this locality. They were being drilled on the square by their officer, who was heard to say: 'Now, when I give a command, I don't want any arguments'.

And now rings out the practice Air Raid Call, so I must cease and go and sit upon a narrow bench under the water tank, while twelve miles off the Two Thousand Guineas is being won and lost.

Your inconsolable,

HYPOLITA."

From which letter it will be seen that not only were the A.T.S. a part and parcel of the Army, but that they brought with them a full measure of British humour.

But life was not all work and no play. There were constant records of dances, of hockey, of entertainments. Many references to the kindness of the neighbourhood in asking them out to dances and picnics. Though on one occasion they were rather taken aback on arriving for a picnic to find their hosts a unit of American coloured troops. The personnel of this unit however were most hospitable and entertained them royally.

But as the months passed the service that the A.T.S. were rendering to the Army became better appreciated and their individual responsibility increased. At the end of 1941 the numbers were increased so that the Platoon became a Company. The first intakes arrived in January, 1942, when the A.T.S. Officers had their first experience of "reinforcements." Although all preparations had been made for their arrival, affairs didn't quite go according to plan. In the first place there had been a very severe frost and no water was available; in the second place the party missed a connection and arrived after "Lights Out," having had nothing to eat or drink for some considerable time. After a frenzied sorting out of kits and A.T.S. in the pitch dark; a filling of kettles, cans, and all available receptacles from the only available water-tap across the road, a heavy meal was consumed about midnight, which, together with the extreme cold, probably accounted for the fact that there was very little sleep for anyone that night.

With the completion of reinforcements, the 40th Platoon ceased to be and the unit's Title became "C" Company Essex and Suffolk Area Group.

40TH (SUFFOLK) PLATOON, A.T.S., 1943. *Photo—H. I. Jarmin.*

Back row—Ptes. K. Burgin, Hazleton, Anderson, J. Winslow, K. Murray, R. Perkins, M. Martin, J. Wallace, D. Ratley, M. Altar.
Middle row—Ptes. O. Vanstone, J. Barber, M. Saunders, E. Sims, Smith, P. Sandford, J. Webb, Franks, B. Smith, L/Cpl. G. Ager, L/Cpl. B. Jenkins.
Front row—Pte. J. Brewster, L/Cpls. B. Eason, J. Washington, E. Cooper, Cpl. K. Lusher, C.S.M. M. Cook, Sub. P. Lanyon, Sgt. B. Ellis, Cpls. Y. Lusher, B. Fryer, L/Cpl. M. Smith, Ptes. Tricker, R. Shaw.

Goodbye was said to the very popular Platoon Commander, Subaltern The Lady Phyllis MacRae. Her stay had been a long and happy one. The new Commander was Junior Commander W. Backhouse.

The unit had gained Company status; but, while appreciating this importance, perhaps those who had known the "40th Suffolk Platoon" in the various stages of its career were tempted to regret the easy days when they were just a detachment.

The A.T.S. celebrated the fifth anniversary of their original foundation on September 9th, 1943. There was a special Church Service in St. Mary's on September 12th at which the lessons were read by Junior Commander Kinder and Subaltern Hill. After five years out of the original platoon only five members remained:—C.S.M. Cook, Corporals Fryer, Y. Lusher and K. Lusher, Lance Corporal Sandford. The original unit had lost its Suffolk title, but it still wore the Regimental Badge.

APPENDICES.

"A": Extract from "Citations"—"B": Honours and Awards—"C": H.Q. Company, Units, First Battalion—"D": The Daily Rations—"E": Copy of an Operation Order—"F": Third Division, Special Order of the Day—"G": "Canloan" Officers—"H": Letter From a Friend in Holland—"J": 2nd Suffolk and 1/17th Dogras "K": Jungle Patrols—"L": Succession List of Commanding Officers—"M": Employment of Regular Officers—"N": Some Abbreviations—"O": A Day's Action with a Tank—"P": Behind the Lines in Italy—"Q": The Japanese Attack on the Mound.

APPENDIX "A."

Extracts from "Citations." First Battalion.

Major Albert Henry Claxton (later killed in action) awarded M.C.

On September 21st, 1944, Major Claxton was commanding the leading Company of the First Battalion in an advance to contact the enemy. At 1700 hours the leading platoon of Major Claxton's Company was fired on from a railway embankment and from some farms along it on the near side.

The leading platoon was held up by automatic fire from about four enemy posts.

Major Claxton, after going forward to make a reconnaissance, launched an attack on two farms and the embankment between them with his two remaining platoons, supported by artillery and mortar fire.

When this attack was half-way to its objective the enemy opened accurate enfilade fire with a further two automatics.

After calling for smoke to blind the left of his objective, Major Claxton personally led the two platoons against the farm from which the nearest automatic fire was coming. Leaving these platoons in a ditch about 80 yards short of the objective, Major Claxton regardless of the enfilade fire went forward alone to within 30 yards of the enemy position and threw two grenades into the middle of the enemy. He then called up the platoons and led them into the enemy locality from which fire was still coming.

Despite a wound in his right hand he immediately organized the Company defensive position and returned to his fire platoon to deal with a threat on the right flank.

Throughout this operation Major Claxton showed the greatest coolness, determination and bravery. He only returned to the R.A.P. to have his wound dressed when ordered to do so an hour after the action was finished. This officer's example was an inspiration to all who saw it.

Major Claxton has consistently set a high standard of initiative and leadership and has at all times shown great bravery in the face of the enemy. The successes of his Company have to a great extent been due to his own personal example.

CORPORAL C. BLIGH-BINGHAM. Awarded M.M.

This N.C.O. was i/c Cable Party in the Signals Platoon. On 12th, 13th and 14th October, 1944, at OVERLOON, the whole First Battalion area was under heavy, sustained and very accurate shell fire.

Corporal Bligh-Bingham laid cable to all Companies in full view of the enemy and under constant fire of all kinds. During the following 72 hours the Battalion cables were cut at least fifty times. Battalion H.Q. itself received three direct hits and all cable routes to Companies were shelled without respite. No matter how heavy or accurate the enemy fire, this N.C.O. immediately and voluntarily left Battalion H.Q. with a tremendous grin on his face and calmly walked along the cable routes testing for faults until he had again re-established all communications. Shells constantly fell within a few yards and at times he was under direct small arms fire. He worked in the open quite imperturbably and unceasingly throughout the entire 72 hours in spite of all enemy attempts to prevent him doing so.

No praise is too high for his complete disregard of personal danger in the interests of duty. His cheerful exuberance, high morale and untiring efforts in the worst possible conditions were a shining example, which has the unstinted admiration of the entire Battalion.

PRIVATE S. CLARKE. Awarded M.M.

On 12th October, 1944, during the attack against OVERLOON, Private Clarke's company sustained heavy casualties and lost the company Commander, all its officers and every senior N.C.O. of the rank of Corporal and above. There were no communications either with Battalion H.Q. or the forward platoons except by runner.

The Company Sergeant Major assumed command of the company and after some hard fighting succeeded in getting the company on to its objective.

During the whole of this action Private Clarke as company runner was unceasingly employed in taking messages, under enemy fire of all kinds, backwards and forwards to the leading platoons, fetching and guiding stretcher-bearers, attending to wounded and generally acting as 'right hand man' to the Company Sergeant Major. He was quite oblivious to his personal danger and ran about in the open under heavy fire for about six hours.

Not once during the whole battle did he fail to deliver a message although in a moving battle of this kind it was always most difficult to locate the persons for whom messages were intended.

His cheering presence had an inspiring effect on all his comrades wherever he appeared. By his bravery and unselfish devotion to duty he contributed immeasurably to the success of his company attack on OVERLOON.

COMPANY SERGEANT MAJOR A. LEATHERLAND. Awarded D.C.M.

During the attack on OVERLOON on 12th October, 1944, "A" Company met very heavy opposition from the flanks. The company sustained many casualties from continuous shelling and from small arms fire. The company commander was killed. Both officer platoon commanders were wounded in trying to resume the advance. All the senior N.C.O.s were casualties.

Under heavy fire C.S.M. Leatherland went forward in the open to the leading troops, detailing three of the remaining Lance Corporals as acting platoon commanders and then personally led the company forward again towards the objective in the face of heavy fire from dug-in enemy positions. He overcame the enemy on the objective and consolidated it under continuous fire from M.Gs on the flanks and shell fire until the remainder of the Battalion later reached their objectives. C.S.M. Leatherland personally accounted for several of the enemy dead. The company captured some twenty prisoners in this action.

Throughout C.S.M. Leatherland was exposed to heavy fire of all kinds. Regardless of his own safety he coolly walked about in the open directing platoons during their advance and personally indicated to the supporting tanks the targets which were holding up the company. He displayed courage of the highest order and proved himself a first class leader under the most trying conditions.

His cool determination and inspiring example were entirely responsible for the success of the attack of this company.

PRIVATE R. K. LINGE. Awarded M.M.

On 18th October, 1944, Private Linge's company were engaged in clearing the woods to the West of VENRAY. The enemy, approximately 50 strong, were established round cross-tracks in the centre of a wood with M.Gs and 'Bazookas.' The tanks supporting the operation were moving up one of the approaches when suddenly a bazooka opened fire on one of the tanks. Its position was located by Private Linge who, regardless of the fact that he was in full view and under heavy fire from the enemy M.G.s, immediately ran out into the open and clambered on to the turret of the tank. From this position he directed the fire of the tank on to the bazooka which was destroyed. Enemy M.G. fire was being directed all the time at the tanks and at Private Linge himself.

His cool determination and courage undoubtedly prevented damage to the tank and his action was an inspiring example to all who saw it.

MAJOR JOHN STANLEY COPPOCK. Awarded M.C.

On 15th April, 1945, Major Coppock was commanding "D" Company, First Battalion, in the attack on the cross-roads south of BRINKUM. From the start of the operation the company was under sustained and accurate sniper fire and was constantly mortared and shelled. After some time the Company was held up having suffered several casualties, but Major Coppock retained full control of the situation, himself moving about between his platoons in all cases exposed to sniper fire.

Later, when it was dark, he led his Company towards the cross-roads and contacted "C" Company, where the situation was confused, as "C" Company Commander had been wounded and no officer had taken over. Major Coppock immediately set about restoring the situation and organised a force consisting of his own Company and a platoon of "C" Company supported by a troop of Crocodile flame throwers.

This force attacked the remainder of the objective, the assault being very skilfully thought out and controlled, lines of approach being difficult owing to burning houses. The attack was completely successful and the enemy either killed or captured. He then consolidated the position and sent out patrols.

By his initiative and drive Major Coppock turned a difficult situation into a decisive success and throughout the entire day showed great qualities of leadership, entirely disregarding his personal safety.

SERGEANT J. W. G. LANKESTER. Awarded:—Mention in despatches.

This N.C.O. has been continuously with the First Battalion since "D" Day, 6th June, 1944. Under all circumstances he has shown the greatest gallantry and qualities of leadership.

On "D" Day he was platoon sergeant of the leading platoon of "A" Company which assaulted the German Regimental Headquarters Strong-point Hillman near COLLEVILLE-SUR-ORNE.

His platoon commander was killed and Sergeant Lankester took over and led the platoon with great skill and bravery.

Since then he has on many occasions commanded a platoon and has always led them with complete confidence.

During the OVERLOON operation his company and platoon commanders became casualties and he led his platoon through to the objectives under the Company Sergeant Major.

Recently when on a night fighting patrol his platoon commander became a temporary casualty Sergeant Lankester organised the return of the patrol and himself carried a wounded man back to our lines—a distance of about a mile.

His personal disregard of danger has at all times been an inspiration to his men.

MAJOR H. K. MERRIAM. Awarded M.C.

On the night of 1st January, 1945, an attack by the enemy was made on the village of WANSSUM held by a company of 1st South Lancashire Regiment.

The situation became confused and it was suspected that some of the enemy had entered a small wood in front of the Battalion area.

An officers' patrol was sent out from Major Merriam's company to clear the wood. This patrol cleared the wood but on emerging from it was fired on by a strong party of enemy from the area of a house nearby and the officer was wounded.

It was obvious that a stronger party was required to clear up the situation and a platoon from a reserve company was sent up to Major Merriam's company.

Major Merriam decided to use this together with a carrier section which was under his command for the task.

He personally took command of this force and led it against the enemy. He cleared the house and decided to follow up and clear a wood near the river bank in which it was probable the enemy had collected. On approaching the wood the party was fired on heavily by what appeared to be Bren guns. Thinking this came from a cut-off party which he had sent out to intercept any enemy retreating, Major Merriam stood up and shouted for them to stop. This only produced heavier bursts of fire and a number of casualties were caused. It was later established that the enemy were using Bren guns.

It was now getting light and it was obvious that the enemy were holding this wood in strength and that the patrol would have to effect its return over flat country, entirely devoid of cover and under enemy observation both from the wood itself and from the East bank of the RIVER MAAS. By this time the enemy had started putting down his D.F. of both guns and Nebelwefers on to the area occupied by the patrol and over the ground through which it must return.

Major Merriam organised the return of his patrol most carefully and skilfully, slipping the party away in groups of twos and threes, including some wounded.

While this was going on the village of BLITTERSWICK, in which was Major Merriam's company, was subjected to two very heavy concentrations of shell and heavy Nebelwefer.

On return Major Merriam found that much damage had been done, a direct hit on his company H.Q. had injured his 2 I/c. and many houses had been knocked down, a number of men being buried. He immediately set about restoring the situation, visiting every section post while mortar bombs were still falling.

Throughout the whole operation Major Merriam showed complete disregard for his personal safety and his calmness and courage were an inspiration to those under him.

SERGEANT D. A. ELLIS. Awarded M.M.

Sergeant D. A. Ellis landed in Normandy with the First Battalion and served continuously with it throughout the campaign. At all times he showed the highest qualities of leadership and personal courage under battle conditions.

At BLITTERSWICK on the RIVER MAAS, Sergeant Ellis took charge of half the carrier platoon when his section commander had been wounded. He remained in this position for ten days under almost constant artillery and machine gun fire. During this period he was always cheerful and completely tireless in the performance of his duties. He led patrols each night and was instrumental in maintaining the high morale of the carrier platoon.

On the advance from BASSUM to BRINKUM on the 13th April, 1945, Sergeant Ellis's section was leading the advanced guard to the Battalion. He dealt firmly and skilfully with minor opposition met during the advance. When a company of S.S. troops was met his carrier section formed a firm base for the subsequent movement of a rifle company. Sergeant Ellis controlled the fire of his section with such great skill and coolness that the rifle company was able to advance considerably, until held up again by very heavy opposition.

The personality of this N.C.O., his powers as a leader on many successful patrols, and his care for the welfare of his men under trying conditions, won him the admiration, not only of the carrier platoon, but of every company to which his section was attached.

EXTRACTS FORM "CITATIONS." SECOND BATTALION.

LANCE CORPORAL ROBERT SHANKS. Awarded M.M.

On 7th June, 1944, L/Cpl. R. Shanks was in command of a section of 8 Platoon, "C" Company, Second Battalion, attacking the Japanese held position known as ISAAC.

His platoon was attacking the West side of ISAAC and on reaching the top, came under heavy L.M.G. fire from a bunker sited just over the crest. L/Cpl. Shanks got his section down and returned the fire, wounding six of the Japanese, who could be heard moaning.

During this time L/Cpl. Shanks took over command of the section on his left, as their section commander had been wounded. He remained in this position with his men under grenade and grenade discharger cup fire whilst efforts were made to bring the tanks forward to deal with the bunker. L/Cpl. Shanks ran forward alone and threw a grenade into the bunker and silenced it. This N.C.O. by his fine leadership and his complete disregard for his own safety was an example and encouragement to his men, who held their position under fire throughout the day.

LANCE CORPORAL JACK RICHMOND PECK. Awarded M.M.

OPERATIONS NEAR IMPHAL, MAY, 1944.

During the period 7/10th May, this N.C.O. took part in a raid on a Japanese occupied village. During the raid L/Cpl. Peck went forward with his Section to cover the L.M.G. group of the patrol. This L.M.G. group was attacked by the enemy. L/Cpl. Peck at once rushed forward with his Section and engaged the enemy who returned his fire with an M.M.G.; by accurate fire this enemy M.M.G. was silenced. L/Cpl. Peck then led his Section to collect identification from the casualties they had inflicted; but they were driven back by the fire from three enemy L.M.Gs. At the platoon rendezvous to which he withdrew he found that the patrol L.M.G. group was missing.

In spite of the fact that this N.C.O. had been on patrol for 48 hours over extremely heavy and difficult country, under the worst of weather conditions, he volunteered to return to locate the missing men who were believed to have become casualties. Whilst moving round the flank his party was approached by a Jap officer or W.O. and five other ranks. L/Cpl. Peck with the patrol 2 I/c., engaged the enemy with C.M.T. fire and grenades, killing or wounding all six at point blank range.

L/Cpl. Peck's enthusiasm, his able leading of his group and his outstanding offensive spirit against great odds, were not only an example to his men, but caused considerable casualties to the enemy.

SERGEANT J. BATES.

On 12th April, 1944, Sgt. Bates was in command of a platoon of "A" Company, Second Battalion, detached to assist "B" Company on a feature known as "MOUND."

His platoon was ordered to a forward position to cover the advance of "A" Company; but while taking post came under heavy and accurate enemy fire. Sgt. Bates directed his platoon's fire without regard to his personal safety and by his courage and leadership, although wounded, inspired his men. Sgt. Bates was carried back by the men of his platoon during their enforced retirement and died of his wounds.

APPENDIX "B."

Honours and Awards.

Among the Honours and Awards to Officers and Other Ranks of the Suffolk Regiment during the War 1939-45 were the following:—

K.C.B.

Colonel F. Garrett, C.B., C.B.E., T.D.
Hon. Colonel The 4th Battalion Suffolk Regiment.

C.B.

Major-General R. Gurney.

C.B.E.

Major-General H. P. Sparks, M.C.
Brigadier H. P. Gardham.
Brigadier H. C. N. Trollope, D.S.O., M.C.
Lt. Colonel R. H. Andrew, M.C.

O.B.E.

Colonel J. G. Frere, D.S.O., M.C.
Lt. Colonel W. A. Heal.
Lt. Colonel H. B. Monier-Williams, M.C.
Lt. Colonel I. R. B. Bond.
Lt. Colonel I. L. Wight.
Lt. Colonel A. A. Goodwin.
Lt. Colonel F. L. Tempest
Major H. R. Hopking, M.B.E.
Major A. C. French

M.B.E.

Major W. H. Payn; Major D. O. Roberts; Major E. C. V. Williams; Capt. T. V. Coate; Lieut. D. U. Fraser; W.O. (1) G. Sartain; W.O. (1) N. Davey; W.O. (1) D. F. Wakeling; The Rev. C. E. Alcock, C.F., Capt. F. E. de W. Cayley, R.A.M.C., and W.O. (1) J. Chalk, M.M.

B.E.M.

C.Q.M.S. A. P. Smith; Sgt. P. H. Shearman; Sgt. R. J. Catling; Sgt. G. A. Barclay; Cpl. D. H. Baker; Cpl. D. H. Hart; Pte. J. W. Darey; Pte. R. Bloom; Pte. C. Lomas; Pte. P. Constable and Sgt. Kathleen Lusher, A.T.S.

Croix de Guerre.

Capt. F. B. M. Russell; Sgt. J. W. G. Lankester.

Belgian Croix de Guerre.

C.S.M. D. Edis.

American Bronze Star Medal.

Lt. Colonel K. J. K. Pye.

Commander of The Order of Orange Nassau (Mil. Divn.).

Lt. Colonel F. A. Milnes.

D.S.O.

Lt. Colonel R. E. Goodwin; Lt. Colonel A. P. Johnson; Lt. Colonel F. Moysey; Lt. Colonel G. F. Foster, M.C., Lt. Colonel A. J. D. Turner, M.C.; Lt. Colonel G. G. Carpenter, D.S.O., (a bar); Major F. W. Roper; Major F. G. L. Lyne; Major R. C. Easton, M.B.E.

M.C.

Major A. T. V. Borrett, M.C. and bar; Major J. Austin; Major R. O. Prentice; Major H. K. Merriam; Major R. H. Willstrop; Major A. H. Claxton; Major A. J. D. Turner; Major J. C. Coppock; Major J. R. B. Prescott; Major G. V. Martin; Major G. R. Heyland; Major A. G. A. Jaques; Capt. P. B. Forrest, M.C. and bar; Capt. A. C. L. Sperling; Capt. R. S. Loveridge; Capt. L. J. Thomas; Capt. A. H. Dodson; Capt. L. Field; Lt. J. J. Powell; Lt. S. E. Sneezum; Lt. G. F. Foster; Lt. A. C. Woodward; Lt. R. J. Loewe; Lt. R. C. Rowe; 2nd Lt. A. F. Stubbs; 2nd Lt. G. F. Smedley; 2nd Lt. I. M. Stewart.

D.C.M.

C.S.M. G. Clarke; C.S.M. A. W. Leatherland; C.S.M. B. R. Bell; Staff Sgt. A. G. Campbell; Sgt. L. J. Gilbey; Pte. J. R. Hunter; Pte. Hunt.

M.M.

W.O.(ii) J. Wade; Staff Sgt. A. Lewty; S.S.M. A. McCleod; S.S.M. G. Lovett; C.S.M. F. Hawley; Sgt. R. J. Brown; Sgt. D. A. Ellis; Sgt. H. Foreman; Sgt. R. Beehag; Sgt. R. McGarrity; Sgt. G. A. V. Powell; Sgt. R. Scarlett; Cpl. C. C. Goldsmith; Cpl. C. Bligh-Bingham; Cpl. R. K. Linge; Cpl. E. Coneybeare; Cpl. A. O. Fordham; Cpl. G. A. Rivers; Lce. Cpl. F. G. Salter; Lce. Cpl. J. R. Peck; Lce. Cpl. R. L. Shanks; Cpl. A. Evans; Lce. Cpl. J. C. Offord; Lce. Cpl. F. Horwood; Lce. Cpl. R. H. Wise; Lce. Cpl. V. G. Edwards; Bandsman A. Filby; Pte. S. Clarke; Pte. L. A. Jaggard; Trooper A. Sayer; Trooper E. D. Smith.

Mentioned in Despatches.

Brigadier E. H. W. Backhouse; Brigadier H. P. Gardham (twice); Col. G. L. J. Tuck, C.M.G., D.S.O.; Lt. Colonel S. D. G. Robertson; Lt. Colonel R. H. Andrew, C.B.E., M.C.; Lt. Colonel I. L. Wight; Lt. Colonel A. S. Birkbeck; Lt. Colonel F. A. Milnes; Lt. Col. F. G. L. Lyne; Lt. Colonel L. J. Baker, M.C.; Lt. Colonel A. A. Johnson, M.C.; Lt. Col. H. B. Monier-Williams, M.C.; Lt. Colonel W. A. Rice; Major J. S. H. Smitherman; Major A. A. Goodwin; Major D. O. Roberts; Major J. D. E. Barnard; Capt. R. G. de Quincey; Major D. R. Gray; Major R. H. Willstrop; Major R. H. Maxwell; Major I. R. B. Bond; Major W. L. Wyatt; Major H. K. Merriam; Major R. A. B. Rogers; Major W. H. Payn; Major A. G. A. Jaques; Major E. C. V. Williams; Major A. Parkin (twice); Major C. J. V. Fisher Hoch (twice); Major K. E. J. Henderson; Major C. J. M. Watts; Capt. M. C. M. Arrindell; Capt. G. F. Foster; Capt. R. J. Garnham; Capt. S. Hemingway; Capt. R. S. Loveridge; Capt. P. D. A. Clarke; Capt. E. T. Sykes; Capt. J. G. Wilby; Capt. A. S. Chandler; Capt. B. Birchmore; Capt. K. R. Hopper; Capt. A. H. Dodson; Capt. A. H. J. Paddick; Capt. R. L. Leepèr; Capt. D. T. McLaren; Capt. W. Marriott; Capt. P. W. King; Capt. M. J. F. Shaw; Capt. F. G. Stoddart; Lt. R. C. del Valle; Lt. A. C. Murrills; Lt. R. A. Tomkinson; Lt. V. C. Amos; Lt. R. T. Barton; Lt. J. H. Dudin; Lt. J. R. Newberry; Lt. P. McCullock; Lt. T. E. Boycott; Lt. R. I. Brown; Lt. R. C. Carson; Lt. R. J. Paul; Lt. J. E. Forrest; Lt. P. T. Fry; Lt. B. N. Furness; Lt. E. W. R. Tebbell; 2/Lt. P. M. Gilbert; 2/Lt. F. A. V. Roberts; Lt. L. G. E. Pusey; Lt. D. A. Wise, Lt. D. R. Crellin; W.O. (i) R.S.M. H. R. Cotton; W.O.(ii)s:—A. G. Boast; F. A. Aldous; S. C. Kingston; G. A. Rivers; M.M.; C. Stiff; A.H. Newman; C.Hoddy; A.C. Langran. C.Q.M.S.s:—G. Paterson; A. C. Benham; W. A. Britchford. Sgts.:—J. W. Lankester; J. E. Bates; D. F. A. Steele; G. Bishop; R. F. H. Boyce; T. Batterham; A. Bush; R. Braunton; A. Evans; F. G. Doxey; D. C. Fuller; E. Martin; N. Underwood; A. L. Goodchild; S. C. Goodman; V. C. Bell; A. E. Brinkman; D. W. O. Paige. Cpls:—J. H. Day; R. J. Gardiner; C. A. Vallis; G. A. Andrews; C. Bligh-Bingham; H. A. Burton; E. J. Jones; R. E. Broom; A. Francis; J. I. Evans; P. R. Jackson. Lce. Cpls:—H. Stevens; R. E. Knight; C. W. West; C. J. Price; W. H. Dawkins. Privates:—G. A. Nicholls; J. W. Boyce; W. G. Taylor; H. B. How (bandsman); W. A. Constable; R. L. Flockton; E. M. Rivers; A. C. Andrews; F. Barrett; P. Constable; G. J. Lidbury; L. R. George; J. H. Kerridge; A. Smith; Trooper A. Hall; The Rev. J. N. Duckworth, Chaplain to the Forces.

APPENDIX "C."

First Battalion Signallers.

Team work was the prime asset in the 1939-45 War. Team work at every level. Team work is a peculiarly British quality; it was in this quality that the First Battalion excelled.

But while all must pull together in a Battalion for a full measure of victory, its connecting link in a Battalion is the Signal Platoon. The success of the operation, the lives of comrades, depend in no small degree on the individual courage and the efficiency of the men who maintain the signal communications within the Battalion. Lt. Colonel F. A. Milnes, Commanding the First Battalion during the retreat to Dunkirk, admitted afterwards that he would rather have jettisoned some of his arms than his signal equipment.

During the campaign that started on the coast of Normandy in June 1944 and ended the next year in Germany the First Battalion Signal Platoon carried out their work magnificently; but it was barely 50% of their numbers who landed on "D" Day who were serving with the Battalion on "V.E." Day.

A team depends in the greatest degree on its leader. Lt. A. C. L. Sperling (later Major Sperling, M.C.), a Cambridge man, served for five months in the ranks and a period at 163 O.C.T.U. before being commissioned in March, 1941, to the Suffolk Regiment. After a course at Catterick he became the First Battalion Signalling Officer in March, 1942, at a time when it was a surprise when the W/T worked. His personality and ability carried the section forward through the strenuous days of training before "D" Day, and it was his capable handling of the communications on the day of landing that maintained uninterrupted communications with all companies, and in no small degree contributed to the success of the assault.

He remained with the Signal Platoon until October, 1944, when he succeeded Capt. H. Merriam as Adjutant, an appointment he held until the end of the War. No officer in the Battalion had a longer record of unbroken service during the campaign.

It would be invidious to mention any name among his Signal Platoon other than the Platoon Commander, for although in the best sense a team, the work of all was individual.

When the Battalion was in action one Lance Corporal and two W/T Signallers were sent to each Rifle Company; one W/T Signaller to each carrier and Mortar Platoon, the remainder at Battalion H.Q. being divided into "Line," "Signal Office" and "Wireless" Sections, the size and distribution of these sections varying according to circumstances.

During the attack the Wireless Section worked with operators detached to the Companies; this was normally the busiest part of the Platoon, wireless being the best means of communication. When it failed, as occasionally it did, runners and despatch riders were substituted, a fruitful source of casualties. The wireless operators did fine work, transmitting their messages coolly and clearly under the most trying circumstances; for a man carrying a wireless set on his back is a conspicuous and particular target for an enemy sniper; he cannot easily take cover even from shell fire.

After the attack and consolidation the "Line" Section went into action, laying lines to the companies and the supporting arms; while the "Signal Office" Section organised its office; sometimes in a cellar, if they were lucky; sometimes in a dug-out.

Line-laying is an onerous task at the best of times; but it is worse under shell fire and at night. On many occasions a line party laid a line, only to find on their return to the Signal Office that it had been broken by shell fire. This happened in particular at OVERLOON and VENRAY in HOLLAND, where the battalion area was under particularly heavy fire and lines needed continual maintenance. It was here that Cpl. Bligh-Bingham, Commanding the Line Section, was awarded the M.M. for conspicuous bravery.

The "Signal Office" Section was kept busy for 24 hours a day in static positions; but all duties in the Signal Platoon were inter-changeable, and all took their share of Wireless, Line and Signal Office.

At all times, in or out of action, the D.Rs were in demand, and they carried out their unenviable tasks in all weathers, cheerfully and efficiently.

FIRST BATTALION SNIPERS.

The Sniper Section of the First Battalion that crossed with the First Battalion on "D" Day was a well trained unit consisting of Cpl. A. Newman and 7 men. On arrival in NORMANDY the unit was split up between the Companies, two going to each. At the CHATEAU DE LA LONDE Ptes. Freeman and Mortlock with "A" Company and Ptes. G. Lebbon and Watson used their skill and knowledge to good effect; but unfortunately Freeman was killed and Watson wounded.

After this fighting the Snipers were Brigaded under Lt. M. L. Drake, a Canadian officer, with Cpl. Newman as Second in Command. They were attached to No. 4 Commando, the Section at this time consisting of Cpl. A. Newman, Ptes. Mortlock, W. Chapman, G. Lebbon, J. Farmer, G. Weyman, G. Evans, Lce. Cpl. W. Glynn. Under No. 4 Commando they gained much experience. From No. 4 Commando they moved to the 6th Airborne Division, being constantly in action and losing Lebbon in the neighbourhood of VIRE cross-roads.

They had rejoined the 8th Brigade by the time the Battalion had reached BELGIUM and were daily in action, Brigaded either under the 8th or 9th Infantry Brigades. On the ESCAULT CANAL, Watson, who had already been wounded, was killed. Here they subsequently joined the "Recce" Corps and were employed far in advance of their own formations, being some 15 miles ahead of the Battalion when it reached WEERT. The snipers fought under Brigade orders at the battle of VENRAY-OVERLOON, rejoining the First Battalion in the MAAS Sector.

In the fighting towards BRINKUM the snipers were once again with the forward Companies of the Battalion, proving their worth. At the end of the war only Cpl. Newman, Ptes. Mortlock, Farmer, Lebbon (twice wounded), Chapman remained of the original section; but the casualties in killed that they had inflicted on the enemy far exceeded their own losses.

FIRST BATTALION INTELLIGENCE SECTION.

The Sniper Section was the aggressive unit, the Intelligence Section provided a front line passive comparison. It was this latter Section that selected and manned the Observation Posts, spending three weeks watching LA BIJUDE and EPRON from the shattered ruins of the CHATEAU DE LA LONDE, watching the enemy's withdrawal at the FALAISE GAP and gleaning all possible information before the attacks on OVERLOON and VENRAY. During the long winter months in HOLLAND on the RIVER MAAS, the Section O.P.s succeeded in pinpointing many of the enemy's camouflaged and cunningly concealed positions.

Back at the Section H.Q. Situation Maps, the Intelligence Diary, Mine Records and the Battalion War Diary were compiled.

The Section suffered heavy loss when Lt. P. Keville was killed shortly after landing in NORMANDY.

APPENDIX "D."

THE DAILY RATIONS.

The man in front is not concerned with the problems of the man behind. "It's stew again!" is his sarcastic comment when the rations arrive.

C.Q.M.S. L. W. Ablitt, one of the Company Quarter Master Sergeants, First Battalion, writes with knowledge of the men who ensured that the rations invariably arrived. "Yes, it's stew again; but don't forget the kaleideoscopic changes that are taking place every hour in the front line, the uncertainty of the number and the grouping of the men to be fed, the limited number of food containers, the choice of road to reach the Company

H.Q., the nature of the vehicle to suit the road." Thus it is that time after time the man behind decides that in this mathematical jigsaw the "Common denominator" is once again "Stew"—with tea as sweet as it can be managed on the sugar ration. It's not lack of imagination, it's just mathematics.

Sgt. Ablett then writes of a normal ration journey—with a "jeep" as the ration cart. The loading is not so simple as the vehicle suggests, fingers get jammed, while after a few bumps and falls into muddy pools, loads break loose. Then, when all is at last adjusted, a guide springs out from the side of the road to say that the route in front has recently been "stonked" and that the rations will finish their run on a 'Carrier.' More damaged fingers.

He writes:—"Off once more, head down, hoping vainly that the vehicle will not make itself heard in the enemy lines. Seemingly it does; for immediately after there is the whine of a "Moaning Minnie." A quick glance round, "Carry on, they're falling behind."

"Out of a doorway at Battalion H.Q. runs the Company guide. 'Jump in, let's get going!' At last the Company. The look of relief and then anxious enquiries as to whether there is any mail makes one realise that the discomfort, small danger, has been worth it all. Letters are collected, notes made to collect the Company Commander's boots, to scrounge some more cigarettes, bring some dry tea for a patrol who will be coming in late, and finally to see if the Q.M. has a spot of rum to spare!"

With the 'Thanks C/Sgt.!' from the Company Commander in our ears we go back a little lighter in heart to prepare for the next meal. That is often at a very early hour, and the cooks are already preparing the breakfast. Bread to be cut, 'jeep' to be loaded and it all starts again. Early morning, pitch dark, a light rain, with a longing for a bath and twenty-four hours' sleep, off we go. We know the way so its going to be better than last time we tell ourselves. Crash! That hole was not there before! No! The Hun has dropped a little hate on the road and as we struggle to get the jeep back on the road we wonder when the next load is due. We sweat and struggle and say things we never learned in Sunday School and off we go again . . . . ."

APPENDIX "E".

COPY OF AN OPERATION ORDER.

1 SUFFOLK O.O. No. 1.

S E C R E T
Copy No. 17.
10 Oct. 44.

Ref. Map: St. ANTHONIS (Eastern half) 19 N.W.

INFM.

1. **Enemy**

OVERLOON 7631 is held by 4 Coy Parachute Bn Paul. Wood 7632 NORTH of OVERLOON is held by 2 Coy Parachute Bn Paul.

It seems probable that the other two coys of the bn are in the area. It is also believed that the bn. has been strengthened by a proportion of SS Tps.

2. **Own Tps.**
   (a) 3 Div is to occupy OVERLOON and VENRAY.
   (b) 8 Br Inf Bde Gp is to capture OVERLOON 7631 with 1 SUFFOLK Right, 2 E YORKS left, and 1 S LAN R in reserve. For inter-bn bdy see att map marked 'A'.
   (c) In sp of 8 Br Inf Bde:—
   One Bn Coldstream Guards (Churchill Tks), incl one sqn Crocodiles.
   Nine Fd Regts R.A.
   Four Med Regts R.A.
   67 A Tk Bty R.A.
   246 Fd Coy R.E.
   2 Mx

INTENTION.

3. SUFFOLK will attack and hold SOUTH of OVERLOON from right, factory 758311 to left incl orchard 762315, see att map marked 'A.'

METHOD.

4. Bn will attack with two coys up:—

Right	'A' Coy.
Left ...	'B' Coy.
In sp ...	'C' Coy.
In reserve	'D' Coy.

5. Start line—From X tracks 745322 to cross tracks 753331.
   Leading tps cross Start Line at H plus 15.

6. Main Axis—Track 743330—OVERLOON.

7. Coy tasks:—
   (a) 'B' Coy will move astride main axis and clear houses from incl rd and track junc 155318 to incl rd and track junc. 759318. They will hold between those two areas.
   (b) 'A' Coy will capture and hold area of factory 758311. For axis see att. map.
   (c) 'C' Coy will move on 'A' Coy axis as far as track junc 754315, turn EAST and capture and hold area of two orchards 759314 and 761314.
   (d) 'D' Coy will be prepared to move behind 'C' Coy and destroy enemy in area shown on att map. They will then hold area of orchards 753313 and 755314.

8. **Mortars.**
   Mortar Pl will be situated in area 747327 and will engage opportunity targets as ordered.

9. **Carriers**
   Carrier Pl, less one sec, will est themselves in area 746318 NORTH of main rd and provide right flank protection to the bn.

10. A tk.
A Tk Pl will be initially under comd O.C. 67 A Tk Bty and will provide an A tk screen firstly in area of houses 751322 and secondly in area 'B' Coy from 756319.
When 'A' and 'C' Coys have reached their objectives, A tk pl will revert to bn cmd. On orders this H.Q. one sec will move to 'A' Coy area and one sec to 'C' Coy area. One sec will remain 'B' Coy area.

11. Pnr Pl.
One demol team in sp 'B' Coy. Remainder in res will move in rear of Bn H.Q.

12. Arty.
As per separate trace, to be issued later. 76 Fd Regt on call to engage opportunity targets.
FOO's with each 'A' and 'C' Coys.
Fwd coys will move behind a barrage which will stay on opening line from H to H plus 4 and will then lift 100x every 5 mins.

13. Tks.
Two tps in sp 'A' Coy.
Two tps in sp 'C' Coy.
Crocodiles in bde reserve—can be called upon to assist in village clearing.

14. MMG's.
See Arty Trace. Fire until H + 70.

15. F.U.P. as per separate sketch.

16. R.A.F.
Weather permitting RAF on OVERLOON and exits leading from it prior to H hr, with hy bombers and Typhoons.

17. R.E. One det in op each 'A' and 'C' Coys.
One mine clearing detachment moves behind 'B' Coy to clear axis of adv.

ADM.

17. Coys will arrange hot tea and haversack ration in F.U.P.

18. 'A' Ech Tot brigaded.

19. 'F' Ech Tpt:— (a) Sp Coy vehs and coy carriers rejoin bn in F.U.P. on orders this H.Q.
(b) Remainder move on orders this H.Q.

20. Med.
(a) One Lt Sec Fd Amb in sp.
R.A.P. will open on capture of 'B' Coy's objective 7483327, and will move on Bn axis.
(b) One Sec Carriers with R.A.P. for evacuation of casualties.

INTERCOMN.

21. Bn H.Q will adv along main axis. It will establish at 753323 thence moving provisionally to orchard 755318.

22. Wireless — Normal.

23. Success Signal for 'A', 'B' and 'C' Coys — Two reds.
24. Watches synchronised under Sig arrangements at 0600 hrs.
25. H Hr—1100 hrs—to be confirmed.
26. Final co-ord conf 741332 at 1015 hrs.

ACK.

F. M. B. RUSSELL
Captain,
Adjutant, 1st Bn. The Suffolk Regiment.

Method of issue. . . S.D.R.
Time of signature 1900.

DISTRIBUTION.

C.O.	2 IC	Adjt.	'A' Coy.
'B' Coy.	'C' Coy.	'D' Coy.	'H.Q' Coy.
'S' Coy.	I.O.	S.O.	Q.M.
Mortar Offr.	A Tk Offr.	454 Bty R.A.	Major Bridge.
War Diary (2).	File	Spares (2).	

APPENDIX "F".

3rd DIV.:—SPECIAL ORDER OF THE DAY.

Special Order of the Day issued by Major-General L. G. WHISTLER, C.B., D.S.O., Commander 3rd British Infantry Division:

"It is usual that units of the British Army put aside one day in the year on which to remember some great honour achieved in battle.

This day is observed with considerable ceremony. It becomes a part of the life of the Unit and through it the traditions of the past are brought home to the present.

It is not intended that the particular battle only should be remembered. It is the token of the fighting record of the Unit and it reminds those living of all the honours won in battle both ancient and recent.

This Third British Infantry Division, one of the oldest formations of the British Army, has earned much fame. In this war alone it has fought with distinction in two campaigns in N.W. Europe. It was for a long time in 1940 the only reserve in England and in fact the only Division properly equipped for battle.

It has, however, had one special honour, shared by only one English and one Canadian Division, that of the Assault on the beaches of Normandy on the real D Day of this present campaign.

First on the beaches of NORMANDY on June 6th, 1944.

Many now serving had not the honour to belong to the Division on that day. All that have served, for however short a period, must be proud to have had the honour to do so. All know and feel the spirit that goes with the D Day Division.

June 6th will therefore be considered the Divisional Day.

It is hoped that it will be possible to observe this day as a holiday throughout the Division each year."

APPENDIX "G".

CANLOAN OFFICERS.

During the Campaign in North Europe the First Battalion had on its strength at different times five Canadian Officers. All these came on the "CANLOAN" Scheme as volunteers from the Canadian Army for service with the British Army. In order of joining they were:—

Captain Ralph Brown, an outstandingly big man who joined in June, 1944. Posted to the H.Q. Company, in a short time he took over its Command, and became P.R.I. Much depends on the P.R.I. and he never failed the Battalion; whatever the N.A.A.F.I. produced Captain Brown took the Battalion's full share.

Lt. John Buchanan, a big hearted, brave fighter, who was badly wounded in the stomach at the VIRE-TINCHEBRAI Cross Roads.

Lt. John Midwinter, another gallant man who was wounded first at LE MESNIL Wood; returning in the shortest possible time he was again wounded and evacuated.

Lt. Jack Ayers who commanded 14 platoon 'C' Company for a longer time than any other platoon officer in the Battalion. He joined in Normandy in August 1944 and remained with his platoon until the last month of the war when he became Second-in-Command of 'C' Company. A courteous, gallant officer who lived most dangerously. He had the whole-hearted admiration of his platoon and company, and, indeed, of the whole Battalion.

Lt. Arthur Lawrence, an efficient officer who only came to the Battalion for the last months of the war.

The First Battalion will always remember with affection and gratitude the great qualities of five representatives of CANADA.

APPENDIX "H"

LETTER FROM A FRIEND IN HOLLAND.

The following is an extract from a letter from one of the many friends the 1st Battalion made in Holland. The Platoon in question was holding a position on the road OLDENZAAL—HENGELO.

"....In my eyes — Platoon will always be the model of soldiership conscious of fighting for the good sake of right and freedom. Afterwards I always missed in other Allied Forces, including in the Dutch, that simple and admirable soldiership. Your boys did not come to earn money (in the Black Market), to drink too much, nor 'buy' girls, nor make rows in the streets. Everybody in our neighbourhood remembers the Suffolks just as I remember — Platoon, and people often say 'Those were the good ones'.

"I don't like flattering, but you can tell those boys that they have made a deep impression on us. Now we know that the best soldiers are in the first lines..."

APPENDIX "J".

2ND SUFFOLK AND 1/17TH DOGRAS IN THE ARAKAN.

The scene is set in a narrow clearing surrounded by a wilderness of thick jungle and bamboo-clad slopes. In the background the hills of the MAYU RANGE roll away to the south. The afternoon is not an unpleasant one, the sun is low in the sky and a gentle breeze produces a quiet rustle in the surrounding undergrowth.

In the clearing is a gathering of soldiers, Second Suffolk, lean and tanned seated beside short, well-built little men of the 1/17th Dogras. In the centre of the group is a gramophone from which come strains, one minute an American string band, and the next, a song of ancient Indian rituals and customs. The men present are chatting and laughing, frequently clearing their throats with the contents of tin mugs. In another smaller group British officers and V.C.O.s of the Dogras are also inbibing refreshment from similar containers. To the casual observer the whole atmosphere is one of peaceful goodwill and friendship. He might even imagine that it is all in a quiet corner of a quiet cantonment somewhere in far away India; save for the distant thump of artillery, the high-pitched whine of shells passing overhead, the clouds of smoke and dust rising into the clear blue sky.

A brief interlude in war. A few hundred yards away sat little yellow men; which these British and Indian soldiers had only a short while back been fighting side by side to oust from their fox-holes in the surrounding hills. This gathering signified more than a short period of rest; it told a tale of comradeship, a mutual trust between men who in culture and manner were as far apart as the poles. That surely is what makes soldiering bearable even under the worst conditions.

In the tin mugs was rum and on the plates were heaped cakes which looked like mince pies, but were an ingenious concoction produced from ration biscuit and fruit and nuts! The British soldiers were men from the small villages and towns of SUFFOLK, NORFOLK and the surrounding counties; but here and there one detected the voice of the indomitable cockney, who is to be heard in every unit in the British Army. The Dogras, too, were soldiers of the land with an equally high reputation for doggedness. They had fought their way to DONBAIK in the first ARAKAN campaign, and were now fighting just as valiantly over country from which they had previously been forced to withdraw.

How well British and Indian soldiers converse. The Tommy using the few words he knows with an Anglicised pronunciation, the Sepoy mixing his small English with his native tongue. Between them they carry on a perfectly intelligible conversation. During this party, after some preliminary reserve, there was great hilarity.

Talking to Subedar Major Kanshi Ram, now in his eighteenth year of service with his Regiment, the writer of this note learnt that his father was an Hon. Lieut. of the Regiment and that in the last war he gained a decoration for successfully leading his Battalion at a time when all the officers had become casualties. Subedar Gian Singh, another warrior of fifteen years service, led his company in the last ARAKAN campaign, when his Company Commander was wounded. "Talking with such men made a subaltern, a veteran of four years' war service, realise that he is hardly past the recruit stage!"

Among those present, one sepoy, Kiroa Ram, in a recent action, was acting Company Commander's runner. He was sent with a message to the forward platoon; having delivered it he decided he might as well assist with the battle. A few minutes later a lone figure, minus shirt, pockets bulging with grenades, was seen climbing up a rock face, where he calmly lobbed them one by one into an enemy bunker that had been holding up the advance. Grenades exhausted, he donned his shirt and returned to his duties as Company runner!

When the party broke up, everyone was in high spirits. Pte. Smith was doing his best to perform a snake charmer's dance to an Indian tune, while Sepoy Bhim Singh was softly practising a Bing Crosby "Boo, Woo, Woo." "If only a Jap observer could have watched this party he would have gone away knowing that his painstaking broadcasts to front-line British and Indian troops telling one to split with the other, were nothing more than a waste of precious time and good gramophone needles! It will take far greater forces than Japanese bombast over the radio to break down the comradeship, based on mutual understanding and admiration, which exists between British and Indian troops in War!"

APPENDIX "K"

JUNGLE PATROLS.

1. **Strength.** Normally one Platoon or not less than two sections. The strength of a patrol will naturally vary according to its task; but a patrol of a platoon is strong enough to establish a firm base from which it can send forward small reconnaissance patrols, it can fight for and bring back the information wanted, it can evacuate its casualties.

2. **Dress.** Cap comforter, Green battle dress, blouse, and Trousers, Anklets and Boots. (A canvas rubber soled jungle boot was produced but was not a success.) Hands and face covered with green camouflage paint.

3. **Equipment.** Web braces and Belt, Pack and Utility pouches, Water bottle, Toggle Rope.

(Carried in pack and pouches). Rations, Socks, Cardigan, Gas Cape (as a water proof and for warmth), Canvas shoes, Towel and soap, Skat (Anti-Mosquito and Tide Typhus), Mapacrin, Sterilizing Tablets, Camouflage Paint, Foot powder, Mess Tin.

4. **Rations.** All Compo—The British Compo, the American K. or the Australian.

(a) British Compo—Sealed Tin containing: 2 blocks compressed oatmeal, 3 slabs chocolate, Tea Tablets and Tube of Milk, Salt and Vitamin Tablets, Packet Biscuits, Lemonade Tablets and Soup Powder, Lump Sugar, Boiled Sweets, Chewing Gum, Matches, 2 ozs. cheese. This was supplemented by one tin compressed liver and bacon and one tin compressed Ham and Beef.

(b) **American K.** Three sealed packets: Breakfast, Dinner-Supper, containing each: 1 tin ham and eggs or 1 tin cheese or 1 tin Meat Loaf, Biscuits, Coffee or Lemonade or Soup, Compressed Fruit Bar or Chocolate, Sugar, Chewing Gum, Cigarettes, Matches, Malt & Calcium Tablets.

(c) **The Australian.** Sealed Tin containing 2 highly compressed Meat Blocks, 1 do. Fruit Block, Tea, Sugar, Powdered Milk.

Of the three the British produced the best variety but was bulky and the tin required an opener. The American K. was slightly less bulky and very easy to handle. The container soaked in paraffin Wax was useful to cook on.

The Australian was small and easy to carry but not very palatable. Of the above three, Lt. Colonel S. H. Atkins, who has given these particulars, thinks the K. was the best. But he found that they "All tasted pretty awful" after a few days.

The number of days' compo rations carried depended on the time during which the patrol would operate. It could be as much as three days' rations with if necessary one blanket and one mosquito net for every two men.

5. **Arms.** All platoon weapons, Bren, Sten and 2 in. Mortar, plus a machete for cutting jungle, 50 rds S.A.A. per man and 2 or 4 grenades clipped on belt.

6. **Tasks.** The tasks normally given to such patrols were:

(a) To recce a track from A. to B.
(b) To watch a group of tracks.
(c) To report if enemy were in occupation of certain features or villages.

(b) METHOD. The first essential was the establishment of a firm base. To do this the platoon would move out to a concealed spot in the vicinity of its task and take up an all round defensive position. From this position small recce patrols of 2 or 3 men would be sent out to "make good" ground ahead and report if clear or otherwise. If clear the base would be moved forward.

Patrolling usually took place by day as night patrolling in jungle was noisy and reports were unreliable. The best method at night was to send out a recce patrol to lie up till dawn, then observe and return to report.

Small recce patrols were very lightly equipped. Probably only a rifle and 2 grenades, waterbottle and a few rations.

(c) FORMATIONS. The theoretical formation for a Platoon moving in jungle is Sub-Sections of three men. The distances between these Sub-Sections varying with the thickness of the jungle and the means of keeping touch. Maximum would be 3-5 yards between each man, 25 yards between Sections.

In thick jungle the above formation became impracticable as movement became very slow, touch was easily lost, and cutting made a lot of noise. In this case the platoon would move in single file along the track well spaced out.

In each Sub-Section one man looks right, one left and one at the trees.

7. **Action on Meeting Enemy.**

Leading Sub-Section group goes to ground and opens fire. Flanking Sub-Sections infiltrate forward right and left until held up.

Platoon Commander after summing up the situation carries out a right or left flanking movement with the remaining two Sections.

His object is to get behind the enemy and seizing the track with one Section sweep up towards his leading Section with the other.

Offensive action of this nature would of course depend on the original orders given to the patrol.

8. **Rendezvous.** Rendezvous were always chosen in the event of the patrol being ambushed and dispersed. These might be forward, back or to a flank. An easily recognisable nullah junction, track or feature was essential

if forward or flank Rendezvous were chosen. Small recce patrols always Rendezvous'ed back on the platoon base.

9. **Patrolling.** Two of the most important factors for successful patrolling were (a) selection of a good observation post (b) silence.

APPENDIX "L."

SUCCESSION LIST OF COMMANDING OFFICERS.

1929 — 1939.

FIRST SUFFOLK.

Lt. Colonel D. V. M. Balders, O.B.E., M.C.	1929—1933
Lt. Colonel A. M. Cutbill, M.C.	1933—1937
Lt. Colonel R. Gurney	1937—1938
Lt. Colonel E. H. W. Backhouse	1938—1939

SECOND SUFFOLK.

Lt. Colonel W. M. Campbell, D.S.O., M.C.	1928—1932
Lt. Colonel G. C. Stubbs, D.S.O.	1932—1935
Lt. Colonel H. R. Gadd, D.S.O., M.C.	1935—1938
Lt. Colonel D. R. A. Eley, D.S.O.	1938—1941

SUCCESSION LIST OF COMMANDING OFFICERS.

1939 — 1945.

FIRST SUFFOLK.

Lt. Colonel (Substantive)	E. G. Fraser. (Killed in Action.)
Lt. Colonel	F. A. Milnes.
Lt. Colonel	F. V. Oborne.
Lt. Colonel	R. E. Goodwin, D.S.O. (Severely wounded).
Lt. Colonel	J. G. M. Gough. The Lincolnshire Regt.
Lt. Colonel	R. W. Craddock, D.S.O., M.B.E., The Buffs. (Severely wounded).
Lt. Colonel	F. F. E. Allen, D.S.O. The Oxfordshire & Buckinghamshire L.I.
Lt. Colonel	R. E. Goodwin, D.S.O. (Brigadier).
Lt. Colonel (Substantive)	F. A. Milnes.

SECOND SUFFOLK.

Lt. Colonel	H. B. Monier-Williams, M.C.
Lt. Colonel	F. Ward.
Lt. Colonel	H. R. Hopking, O.B.E.
Lt. Colonel	K. C. Menneer. 4th Battalion Suffolk Regt.
Lt. Colonel	H. W. Dean.

FOURTH SUFFOLK.

Lt. Colonel (Substantive)	E. Cyril Rands., T.D.
Lt. Colonel	A. A. Johnson, M.C. (Wounded and P.o.W.)

FIFTH SUFFOLK.	
Lt. Colonel	J. F. Harter, D.S.O., M.C. (Major General). The Royal Fusiliers.
Lt. Colonel	L. J. Baker, M.C. (Prisoner of War).
SIXTH/30TH SUFFOLK.	
Colonel (Substantive)	H. R. Hooper, O.B.E., M.C., T.D.
Lt. Colonel	H. R. Hopking, O.B.E.
31ST SUFFOLK.	
Lt. Colonel	V. L. de Cordova, M.C. The King's Own Royal Regt.
Lt. Colonel	H. D. Wise, M.C.
Lt. Colonel	C. L. Wilson, M.C. The Essex Regt.
7TH BATTALION / 142ND R.A.C.	
Lt. Colonel	R. H. Maxwell (Brigadier). (Severely wounded).
Lt. Colonel	A. S. Birkbeck, R.A.C. (Killed in Action).
Lt. Colonel	S. D. G. Robertson. (Accidentally killed).
Lt. Colonel	F. A. Dow, R.A.C. (Severely wounded).
Lt. Colonel	P. W. C. Colan, M.C., R.A.C.
Lt. Colonel	G. A. E. Peyton, O.B.E. 15/19th King's Royal Hussars.
8TH SUFFOLK.	
Lt. Colonel	J. S. D. Lloyd.
Lt. Colonel	E. R. Daglish.
Lt. Colonel	J. R. Harper. The Hertfordshire Regt.
70TH SUFFOLK.	
Lt. Colonel	J. W. Josselyn.

APPENDIX "M."

Employment of Regular Officers at end of War, 1945:—

Temporary Major-General ...	Colonel H. P. Sparks, M.C.
Temporary Brigadiers ...	Colonel H. P. Gardham, C.B.E.
	Colonel V. C. Russell, D.S.O., M.C.
	Colonel E. M. Ransford.
	Lt. Colonel R. H. Maxwell.
	Major R. E. Goodwin, D.S.O.
Temporary Colonels ...	Lt. Colonel J. Yates, M.C.
	Major H. B. Monier-Williams, O.B.E., M.C.
	Major A. J. D. Turner, D.S.O., M.C.

The following Officers of the Regiment held acting or temporary appointments as Lt. Colonels:—

Majors:—J. S. D. Lloyd; I. G. Owen; A. A. Johnson, M.C.; H. C. Carrigan, O.B.E.; E. R. Daglish; O. A. Watts; H. R. Hopking, O.B.E.; H. W. Dean; S. H. Atkins; J. W. Josselyn; F. V. Oborne; B. W. J. Amphlett; A. A. Goodwin; G. H. M. Harper; I. L. Wight, O.B.E.; J. C. R. Eley; R. B. Freeland; Quartermaster J. Hill.

Captains:—P. A. Morcombe, O.B.E.; K. J. K. Pye; R. E. B. Moriarty; L. Field, M.C.; W. A. Heal, O.B.E.; J. W. Tyndale; K. W. J. Dewar.

Command and Staff:

Major-General J. A. Campbell, D.S.O.
(Temporary) Major-General R. Gurney, C.B., A.D.C.
Brigadier E. H. W. Backhouse.

APPENDIX "N."

ABBREVIATIONS.

LCA	Landing Craft Assault (35 men).
LCT	Landing Craft Tank (about 5 tanks).
LCT (R)	Landing Craft Tank (Rocket) (800 Rockets).
LCS	Landing Craft Support.
LCM	Landing Craft Mechanised (one large or two small vehicles).
LCI	Landing Craft Infantry (200 men).
LSI	Landing Ship Infantry (one Battalion approx.)
LST	Landing Ship Tanks.
ULO	Unit Landing Officer.
LOB	Left out of Battle.
DD's	DD Swimming Tanks (Valentines used on 'D' Day).
AVRE	Assault Vehicle Royal Engineers.
AGRA	Army Group Royal Artillery.
AGRE	Army Group Royal Engineers.
AFV	Armoured Fighting Vehicle.
WASP	Flamethrower.
KANGAROO	Troop Carrying Tanks.
T.C.V.	Troop Carrying Vehicles.
C.D.L.	Tanks with Searchlights for artificial moonlight.
F.U.P.	Forming up Place.
S.L.	Starting Line.
F.D.L.	Forward Defensive Locality.
O.P.	Observation Post.

APPENDIX "O."

A DAY'S ACTION WITH A TANK.

The following is taken from an account by Sergeant E. Martin, "A" Squadron, 142nd Regt., R.A.C.

"The tanks have returned to 'Forward Rally;' a sheltered piece of ground a few hundred yards behind the front line. Here the tank crews could refuel, replenish and overhaul. It had been an arduous day; the enemy had stubbornly contested every yard of ground; but at last they had been driven from their position and our infantry were consolidating.

It is night and in the dark each tank has to be guided to harbour by the waving of a lighted cigarette, the red glow showing the driver where to turn left or right and bringing him, after much manoeuvring, to the rest of his troop. Then the order 'switch off and dismount' is given, and with many grunts and groans the crew crawl out through the hatches.

The space in a tank is limited; all are cramped and stiff after sitting or standing in one position for many hours. The heat inside a tank is great; the faces of all are grimed with dirt and dust, almost closing eyes and noses. Some had not returned; but nothing was said. Words seem futile; they were good pals; talking would do no good, each kept his thoughts to himself.

There is no time to waste. The driver looks to his engine for leaks or faults, the gunners examine their guns, the wireless operator his radio. The tanks have got to be made fit for to-morrow's battle, and the fitters may have to work all night if necessary on a major fault. Maintenance is no light job when a heavy track has to be changed or adjusted. The full tally of fuel, oil, water, ammunition required is made out, to be supplied by "B" Echelon.

But all work with a will. There are moans, cheerful moans, the prerogative of British Tommies. Then comes food; and almost as quickly the Squadron Commander's orders for to-morrow to each tank commander, who has been summoned to him with maps, notebook and pencil. The guards are posted, for "Jerry" is within a few hundred yards and has a habit of pushing patrols out to cause trouble. Then sleep by about midnight.

But by 0300 the Squadron is roused; the day's fight is on. Breakfast, but with poor appetite. Outwardly cheerful, each has an apprehensive feeling of what may befall. Haversack rations are issued; for each tank has a small cooker on which tea can be brewed when occasion permits. Then, on a signal, engines are started, radios checked and once again, to the waving of a glimmering cigarette, line is formed.

Silence is impossible, and down come the demoralising 'stonk, stonk' of the enemy's mortars. It is still dark and the infantry are already in action, held up by machine gun fire, waiting for light and our help. Daylight comes at last and brings a more confident feeling to everyone. If the Boche has been shooting us up, now at last we can shoot back.

As soon as the battle starts the apprehensive feeling vanishes, every one is too busy, commanding, driving, shooting, and re-loading, attending to radio, to have any time to dwell on personal danger. The sight of a Hun running before a withering fire from a Besa gun. A jammed gun is followed by a curse; a sudden lurch over an unseen mound shakes everyone to the heels. But the almost continuous rain of enemy fire makes the crew want to give back all they can.

The position is captured, the infantry consolidate, the tanks take up a defensive position. Then come long hours of sitting, alert and ready; this is the most trying time of all for the enemy artillery have a shrewd suspicion of where we are. Tempers get frayed; but the good comradeship among a tank crew overcomes all difficulties and at last word comes to retire to the 'Forward Rally.' "

APPENDIX "P."

BEHIND THE LINES IN ITALY.

The following is taken from an account by Sergeant P. Addington, "A" Squadron, 142nd Regt., R.A.C.

We had some "Eyetie" prisoners attached to the Regiment whilst we were still stationed in Africa. Clean, decent fellows they were, amazingly hard working and surprisingly cheerful in their captivity. Doubtless they were glad that the war was over as far as they were concerned. They found an outlet for their spirits in their singing, which first amused us but later on became a nightly nuisance.

Perhaps Naples was a bad place for an introduction to Italy. However, that may be, our first impressions were of dirt and poverty, an impression which was to remain with us, if perhaps to a lesser degree, throughout our whole stay in the country. Not everybody was as dirty as it had at first seemed; but the majority with whom we came into contact were only too desperately poor.

But notwithstanding their poverty they made generous hosts whenever one of our number was fortunate enough to be taken into the bosom of a family, even if the home was but a one-roomed hovel with a few sticks of furniture, the most treasured possession a "Singer" sewing machine. The visitor was pressed to share the family's meal of a peculiar oily batter, spaghetti, or some other unusual dish, nor would they accept either refusal or payment, unless it was a piece of soap, a commodity non-existent to them at that time. Better still was the unconcealed joy and appreciation on a "bambino's" face at chocolate; a sight worth seeing. A luxury unknown in his young life.

A surprising number of Italians spoke quite good English, perhaps I should say American, for many had spent their lives in that country. One of our chief topics of conversation was Home. The Italian showed a great interest in England and was eager to learn more of it.

In our leisure moments there were many diversions to suit all tastes. Italy abounds in ancient ruins and monuments, is famous for its opera and its wine; very few of us failed to sample the native wines. Another pastime was shopping, to buy things which for a long time had been scarce at home, and to send these to our women folk.

These diversions were not complete without a visit to an Italian cinema. It was the audience who provided the main amusement. The Italian cinematograph operator appears to be a slap-dash incompetent fellow so that the film ran rarely more than five or ten minutes without a break. These breaks formed such a part and parcel of the show that there was scarcely a flicker of an eyelid between the breaking of the film and the switching on of the house-lights. This was the signal for pandemonium to break out amongst the audience, who would shout at each other and fight for better seats. Bedlam was let loose in the few minutes until the film was repaired and the performance continued.

Dancing too was a favourite pastime for soldiery, though here difficulties arose owing to the fair signorinas being strictly chaperoned, not merely by mother or an aged aunt, but by several generations of the family!

Compared with this, the different style of dancing presented little difficulty. The chief attraction at any dance organised by the military was the food. This was made only too plain, for no sooner had the buffet been opened than it was cleared, and no sooner cleared than the homeward trek began.

The British soldier has been praised as an ambassador, quick to acclimatise himself. In this respect the Suffolks were no exception and in their leisure hours did not fail to use their time in cementing a friendship and savouring to the full the many and varied pleasures which the country had to offer.

APPENDIX "Q."

THE JAPANESE NIGHT ATTACK ON THE "MOUND."

9th April.

The following is taken from an account by Major P. J. Hill who was commanding "B" Company, Second Suffolk, defending the "Mound," an important part of the defence perimeter of Imphal.

Just beyond the "Mound" lay the "Pimple," a small excrescence joined to the "Mound" by a saddle of about 50 yards. The Company was too weak in numbers to include this important sub-feature in the perimeter defences.

On this Easter Saturday preceding the attack patrols had been pushed forward, but brought back no information. No movement had been seen on the hills beyond the position; the countryside appeared completely deserted. In the plain below the villages lay quiet in the evening sun. It was hard to believe that the blue tinted hills hid a Japanese division poised for a decisive assault on Imphal.

The Company "stood to" at seven o'clock that evening, as usual. There was no wind and near-full moon was just rising above the dark line of hills. The bark of a distant pie-dog emphasized the almost unnatural silence as the men stood in their defences peering into the twilight.

Then the normal sentries, two or three to a Section, according to strength, were posted and the remainder of the Company lay down to sleep, dressed and with their weapons beside them.

About 8.30 a grenade booby trap on the "Pimple" went off with a startling roar—it might only be a jackal or it might be the Japs. Within ten seconds the Company was in position.

Then came the throb of the forward sections' L.M.G. Two more L.M.G.s opened up almost immediately after. At the same time the Japs appeared over and round the sides of the "Pimple," an officer in front, brandishing his sword; the latter was distinctly visible in the bright moonlight gesticulating and waving his men on.

The enemy attack was covered by fire from Jap grenade dischargers; but when our men started to throw grenades among the attacking line the enemy faded away, melting into the shadows.

Then quite suddenly, or so it seemed, there was silence and the night closed in again. But in the grass and on our wire there were bodies gleaming whitely.

After a little time the Japs could be heard digging on the reverse slope of the "Pimple"; but the Battalion's 3-in. Mortar bombs effectually found this range.

Next morning extensive patrolling found one dead Jap officer and six dead other ranks, while there were signs of many wounded having been moved. Later, during the fighting on and around the "Pimple," several more dead were found, the result of this night's action. How coarse and brutal their dead looked, scarcely human. The pile of captured equipment was an impressive sight.

There were further sleepless nights, but though the Japs fired into our lines they attempted no more attacks.

INDEX

C

G

T

U

V

W

APPENDIX.

Among the Warrant Officers and Sergeants on the strength of the Regiment in 1939, the following gained Commissions during the war, as shown:—

Bandmaster B. H. Gubbins ...	... Captain (Q.M.)
Bandmaster J. Longstaff ...	... Captain (Q.M.)
R.S.M. F. Nice	... Major
R.Q.M.S. F. W. Garrard ...	... Major (Q.M.)
R.Q.M.S. S. C. Balaam, D.C.M.	... Captain
R.Q.M.S. G. S. Parker ...	... Major
R.Q.M.S. H. R. Cotton ...	... Captain (Q.M.)
C.S.M. F. W. Phillips ...	... Captain (Q.M.)
C.S.M. S. D. Jackson ...	... Major
C.S.M. E. Spinks, M.M. ...	... Captain
C.S.M. J. Bendall ...	... Major
C.S.M. A. S. Chandler ...	... Captain (Q.M.)
C.S.M. P. W. Spurgin ...	... Major
C.S.M. J. R. Golding ...	... Lieutenant (Q.M.)
C.S.M. G. E. Weavers ...	... Captain
C.S.M. H. Tricker	... Major
C.S.M. A. Burgess	... Captain (Q.M.)
C.S.M. R. C. Attmore ...	... Captain
C.S.M. Hawkins	... Captain
C/Sgt. B. Durrant	... Captain (Q.M.)
C/Sgt. J. Barber	... Lieutenant (Q.M.)
C/Sgt. E. C. V. Williams ...	... Major, M.B.E.
C/Sgt. W. W. Gleeson ...	... Lieutenant
Sgt. V. Stammers	... Major
Sgt. C. Branch	... Major
Sgt. H. W. Bond	... Captain
Sgt. G. Ward	... Major
Sgt. G. Gilbert	... Major
Sgt. W. Stock	... Captain (Q.M.)
Sgt. R. R. Gooch	... Major
Sgt. F. Green	... Major
Sgt. A. Piper	... Major
Sgt. V. O. Aldred	... Major
Sgt. A. McCaffrey	... Major
Sgt. W. W. J. Rayner ...	... Major
Sgt. H. Case	... Captain
Sgt. C. Weston	... Lieutenant (Q.M.)
Sgt. A. Precious	... Lieutenant
Sgt. A. Jasper	... Lieutenant (Q.M.)
Sgt. F. Wyartt	... Lieutenant (Q.M.)
Sgt. E. Langran	... Lieutenant (Q.M.)
Sgt. E. Binks	... Captain (Q.M.)

Among Other Ranks on the strength of the Regiment, the following gained Commissions or were promoted to W.O. Class I.:—

C.S.M. H. R. Hopkins	R.S.M.
C.S.M. N. F. Davey	R.S.M., M.B.E.
C.S.M. F. Clarke	R.S.M.
C/Sgt. G. Clarke	R.Q.M.S., D.C.M.
C/Sgt. J. Kidd	R.S.M.
C/Sgt. J. Wade	R.Q.M.S., M.M.
C/Sgt. E. Pallant	R.S.M.
Sgt. J. Daley	R.S.M.
Sgt. J. Moore	W.O. Cl. I., A.C.C.
Sgt. E. Wragg	Bandmaster
Sgt. D. Matthews	R.S.M.
Sgt. G. Saunders	R.S.M.
Sgt. G. Squirrel	R.S.M.
Sgt. J. Tuck	R.S.M.
Sgt. F. Aldous	R.S.M.
Sgt. H. Mead	R.S.M.
Sgt. L. Kerry	R.S.M.
Sgt. W. Howard	W.O. Cl. I.
Sgt. H. Cox	R.S.M.
Sgt. J. Milsom	R.S.M.
Sgt. E. Isaacson	R.S.M.
Cpl. G. S. Jasper	R.S.M.
Cpl. A. Bell	R.S.M., D.C.M.
L/Cpl. R. C. Staff	W.O. Cl. I., A.C.C.
L/Cpl. A. S. Racher	R.S.M.
Cpl. G. W. Blake	R.S.M. (Devons)
L/Cpl. Ainger	W.O. Cl. I. (Airborne)
Pte. A. Fenwick (Hunt)	R.S.M.
Cpl. W. W. Cook	Captain.
Cpl. A. O. Greef	Major
Cpl. W. Castle (Sharman)	Captain

Printed in the United Kingdom
by Lightning Source UK Ltd.
117678UKS00001B/48

9 781847 341617